Modern Measurement

Theory, Principles, and Applications
of Mental Appraisal

STEVEN J. OSTERLIND

University of Missouri at Columbia

PEARSON

Merrill
Prentice Hall

Upper Saddle River, New Jersey
Columbus, Ohio

Library of Congress Cataloging-in-Publication Data

Osterlind, Steven J.
   Modern measurement : theory, principles, and applications of mental
appraisal / Steven J. Osterlind.
      p. cm.
   ISBN 0-13-025590-4
   1. Psychometrics.   I. Title.
   BF39.O82 2006
   150′.28′7—dc22

2005004717

Vice President and Executive Publisher: Jeffery W. Johnston
Publisher: Kevin M. Davis
Editorial Assistant: Sarah Kenoyer
Production Editor: Mary Harlan
Production Coordinator: Karen Ettinger, TechBooks/GTS York, PA Campus
Design Coordinator: Diane C. Lorenzo
Text Design and Illustrations: TechBooks/GTS York, PA Campus
Cover Design: Jason Moore
Cover Image: SuperStock
Production Manager: Laura Messerly
Director of Marketing: Ann Castel Davis
Marketing Manager: Autumn Purdy
Marketing Coordinator: Brian Mounts

This book was set in Garamond by TechBooks/GTS York, PA Campus. It was printed and
bound by R. R. Donnelley & Sons Company. The cover was printed by The Lehigh Press, Inc.

Pearson Education Ltd.
Pearson Education Singapore Pte. Ltd.
Pearson Education Canada, Ltd.
Pearson Education–Japan

Pearson Education Australia Pty. Limited
Pearson Education North Asia Ltd.
Pearson Educación de Mexico, S.A. de C.V.
Pearson Education Malaysia Pte. Ltd.

10 9 8 7 6 5 4 3 2 1
ISBN: 0-13-025590-4

I dedicate this book to those who fill my life—
my wife, Nancy, and our three children,
Alex, Janey, and Anna.

Preface

Modern Measurement: Theory, Principles, and Applications of Mental Appraisal presents a wide array of information on diverse but fundamental aspects of test theory and its application to practical problems in mental measurement for the advanced student and measurement professional. In general, these ideas can be classified under measurement science. The chapters build from foundations of mental assessment, beginning with a description of cognitive appraisal, moving through classical measurement theory, reliability, scaling, test and item construction, generalizability theory, item response theory (IRT), and on to item analysis, test equating and linking, and special issues of test administration, such as computer-assisted testing and computer-adaptive testing.

The content is decidedly directed toward modern notions of measurement, particularly in scaling (with IRT) and reliability (with generalizability theory), but also in many other areas. On any particular topic, I provide citations that direct the reader to a more in-depth treatment including (a) classical writings and research that provide ground-breaking work and (b) modern works that give up-to-date information. I also refer to many Internet sites where readers can locate even more information.

For technical focus, I attempt to draw a middle ground between needed mathematical and statistical description and a realization that many readers may not be mathematically trained. I let each topic be my guide—some are complex, requiring a lot of formulas and syntactic attention, whereas others are less so.

To profit from the information in *Modern Measurement,* readers will need preliminary background in tests and measurement, including some statistics and algebra. A graduate student with some background in educational psychology, a first course in tests and measurement, and a little work beyond elementary statistics should manage well. Although I discuss some topics from their beginning, this is not an introductory book.

The chapter topics are cumulative in that each builds on previous conclusions. Of course, there is much overlap among the ideas covered in the chapters, and readers should anticipate referring to various parts of the book. This links related ideas.

In particular, I want readers to find *Modern Measurement* especially readable, possibly even enjoying the language. Many technical books abound with good information but are nearly inaccessible due to poor composition. Regretfully, it seems pandemic in our field. However, quantitative professionals can write, too! Good writing is difficult, requiring deliberation on vocabulary, usage, and correct grammar. I hope that the time I spent attending to composition is noticeable, and that you read this book with both comprehension and interest.

The reader will also notice that I begin each chapter (excluding chapter 1) with a rather idiosyncratic opening paragraph. The opening paragraphs comprise stories that, for the most part, have nothing to do with psychometric methods; rather, they are about people, places, and things that interest me (e.g., baseball, mountain climbing, the space program, Edith Piaf). Call them an indulgence, an author's prerogative. I enjoyed writing them, and I want to share them with you. They do mean something, too. While teaching, I like to tell stories relating my personal interests and then transition (sometimes strained) into mental measurement. My students tell me they appreciate the stories, but you will need to ask them privately for their genuine opinion. Regardless, I hope that you enjoy reading each opening chapter story.

Most of all, however, I want you to find *Modern Measurement* useful in advancing your interest and work in measurement science.

Acknowledgments

Although my name appears singly on the title page, I could not have written this book without the help of many people. I cannot thank each of them enough as they provided valuable information and advice. Many of them patiently read drafts of chapters and proffered extended critiques and reviews. Some friends and colleagues, and many dutiful students, followed the chapters through various revisions. Others offered a quick comment here and there to a question I posed. I particularly thank those who reviewed the manuscript: Neil Abell, Florida State University; Patricia Busk, University of San Francisco; Timothy R. Konold, University of Virginia; Frederick Oswald, Michigan State University; Nancy Ryan-Wenger, Ohio State University; Michael Strube, Washington University; and J. Charles Zhao, Educational Testing Service. The book is much better because of their help. Although I did not keep a list of everyone who aided me, I wish I had to help my feeble memory now. Thank you—sincerely and heartily. Errors, misstatements, and omissions are my own.

EDUCATOR LEARNING CENTER: AN INVALUABLE ONLINE RESOURCE

Merrill Education and the Association for Supervision and Curriculum Development (ASCD) invite you to take advantage of a new online resource, one that provides access to the top research and proven strategies associated with ASCD and Merrill—the Educator Learning Center. At **www.educatorlearningcenter.com**, you will find resources that will enhance your students' understanding of course topics and of current educational issues, in addition to being invaluable for further research.

How the Educator Learning Center Will Help Your Students Become Better Teachers

With the combined resources of Merrill Education and ASCD, you and your students will find a wealth of tools and materials to better prepare them for the classroom.

Research
- More than 600 articles from the ASCD journal *Educational Leadership* discuss everyday issues faced by practicing teachers.
- A direct link on the site to Research Navigator™ gives students access to many of the leading education journals, as well as extensive content detailing the research process.
- Excerpts from Merrill Education texts give your students insights on important topics of instructional methods, diverse populations, assessment, classroom management, technology, and refining classroom practice.

Classroom Practice
- Hundreds of lesson plans and teaching strategies are categorized by content area and age range.
- Case studies and classroom video footage provide virtual field experience for student reflection.
- Computer simulations and other electronic tools keep your students abreast of today's classrooms and current technologies.

Look into the Value of Educator Learning Center Yourself

A four-month subscription to Educator Learning Center is $25 but is **FREE** when packaged with any Merrill Education text. In order for your students to have access to this site, you must use this special value-pack ISBN number **WHEN** placing your textbook order with the bookstore: 0-13-155315-1. Your students will then receive a copy of the text packaged with a free ASCD pincode. To preview the value of this website to you and your students, please go to **www.educatorlearningcenter.com** and click on "Demo."

Brief Contents

Contents

Part II   Classical Theory and Validity

PART III   Scaling Tests

Chapter 6   Dimensional Scaling and Norming   147

Chapter 7   The Normal Curve and Distributional Statistics   181

PART IV   Constructing Tests

Chapter 8   Constructing Items and Exercises for Tests   207

Chapter 9   Performance-Related Measures   233

PART V   Modern Approaches: IRT and Generalizability Theory

Chapter 10   Modern Scaling with Item Response Theory   261

Note: Every effort has been made to provide accurate and current Internet information in this book. However, the Internet and information posted on it are constantly changing, so it is inevitable that some of the Internet addresses listed in this textbook will change.

Chapter 1

Introduction to Psychological Measurement

Why Psychological Measurement?

The 18th-century poet and philosopher Samuel Johnson began his epic poem *The Vanity of Human Wishes* with these lines:

> Let observation with extensive view
> Survey mankind, from China to Peru.

Johnson goes on to cite manifold differences among lands, objects, and people across his contemporary world, pointing to physical and cultural variations, as well as to particular intellectual outlooks. Today, the vast differences in our world are no less distinct to us than the differences in his world were to Johnson. If we use the eyes and soul of a poet (like Johnson) to describe such differences, we know and appreciate them based on our use of potent and descriptive language. If, however, our perspective is that of a scientist, then we know and appreciate differences based on our use of precise language and quantification. Quantifying entities, whether physical or psychological, is the object of *measurement*. Like Johnson, we accomplish the action of measurement by means of observation, whether direct or filtered through instruments that extend our senses. This book is about making instruments that extend our sensory reach into psychological dimensions. That is, it is about mental measurements: educational and psychological tests.

As a text about making and using instruments, *Modern Measurements* is designed to be a student's or scholar's cathexis—an object of study to which one brings concentration, purpose, and energy. It offers readers theoretical and practical information about traditional and, especially, state-of-the-art psychometric methods. By learning about and properly employing traditional and modern psychometric methods, one can develop and use mental tests that yield sound, purposeful, and accurate appraisals of psychological constructs and educational domains. Such measurement can lead to more precise and fuller understanding, which in turn can increase the likelihood of better decisions. Unquestionably, the goal of this book is to assist persons involved in testing to make better decisions, the *raison d'être* for any assessment.

To comprehend what can be accomplished with well-grounded mental measurement, one must understand the process of making measurements, beginning with why we are interested in mental appraisal. One way to start answering this question is to examine how mental assessment differs from determining dimensions in the physical world. We realize, of course, that assessing psychological constructs and educational domains is fundamentally different from physical measurement. In the physical realm, quantification is mostly straightforward and accurate. In contrast with psychological phenomena, physical objects do not change much. For instance, a building's height, a rock's composition, or the proportion of hydrogen to oxygen in a water molecule is relatively invariant. Consequently, given this comparative stability, the instruments used for physical measurement have developed over time into gauges that are incredibly accurate and reliable. For instance, in Johnson's time, weights and measures were just crude balance scales with lumps of iron or metal used as rough standards. Today, some of the most sophisticated measuring devices of physical objects take into account even the atmosphere's magnetic interference and the gravitational pull of the Earth at different places and at varying times. Some physical objects are measured down to the level of the atom, and below.

Quantifying psychological constructs and educational domains, however, is altogether different. In the psychology and education realms, the entities to be measured are themselves only partly understood. How people effectually learn, remember, reason, adhere to beliefs, and exhibit their personalities are features of mental composition that we do not know much about. Over the years, many persons have theorized about these and many other aspects of our being. More recently, to gain clues into our psychology, scientists have begun exploring the chemical and neurological functioning of our physical body. Advances in understanding chemical brain activity (e.g., research made available by magnetic resonance imaging [MRI] and chronometric analyses) are simply fantastic. The Center for Brain Research at Yale University is leading some of these efforts. Individuals working at other institutions are also adding new information regularly. It seems that every day we discover more of who we are, both collectively and in our unique individuality. However, musings into our psychology, although reasonable and often sophisticated, are still mainly theoretical; they offer, for the most part, only rudimentary explanations. This makes measuring cognition a bit like shooting into a dimly lit fog: What is hit is not clearly illuminated.

Further, most aspects of our psychology are labile; that is, they continually undergo chemical, physical, or biological change. We process new sensory input by adding to and modifying existing knowledge, beliefs, and attitudes. Then, too, of course, we forget a lot of things, and that also leads to changes in cognition. Clearly, we are not today who we were yesterday, nor will we be the same tomorrow.

However, despite our limited understanding of cognition and its lability, we do realize that such features of our brain are how we bring consonance to our lives, whether acting alone or interacting with others. Such is the richness of our character— our humanity. Naturally, then, we are interested in learning more about ourselves. In doing so, we understand more of who we are and begin to appreciate why we act as we do. By such introspection, we are seeking to satisfy a fundamental, innate curiosity. Mental measures are our vehicle to gather information for this quest. Through educational and psychological testing, we satisfy, to some degree, our curiosity about ourselves in a quantitative fashion. The brilliant 19th century physicist and thinker Lord William Thompson Kelvin (1894/1991) expressed a fundamental point about measurement when he said,

> When you can measure what you are speaking about, and express it in numbers, you know something about it; but when you cannot measure it, when you cannot express it in numbers, your knowledge is of a meager and unsatisfactory kind; it may be the beginning of knowledge, but you have scarcely in your thoughts advanced to the state of Science, whatever the matter may be.

Perhaps for this reason, *Science* cited the mental test as 1 of 20 discoveries that have shaped our lives forever (Miller, 1984).

What Is Psychological Measurement?

Now, having established why we conduct educational and psychological measurement, the problem remains of describing what we measure, and ultimately, how we effect mental measurements. In the remainder of this chapter, as well as at various points in chapters 2 and 3, the aspect of what it is we are truly measuring is addressed. The "how we do it" part of assessment occupies chapters 4 through 16.

Measurement of Cognition

In the psychological realm, measurement is not of objects per se because, in the literal sense, psychological objects do not exist. There is no parallel in the mind to a rock or to water or to an atom, such as exists in the physical world. Although we can identify the physical part of the brain structure where some phenomenon, such as short-term memory, occurs, it is not the same as labeling that part of the brain an entity that can be called "short-term memory." Instead, we theorize that knowing something is actually a process involving neurological activity. We can detect and even quantify chemical and biological action in some part of the brain. We have come to label such mental activity as *information processing* or, more fundamentally, *cognition*. Cognition is a dynamic mental process through which one constructs an internal model to accommodate new information and map stimuli to similar, prior experiences in an ever-growing neurological network. Cognitive science advances the notion that knowledge is actually an internal dynamic: As stimuli are presented, neurological responses are activated. We label such activity *information processing*, and through processing information, we construct a concept, develop an attitude, or reinforce or abandon a belief. What we experience and learn adds to the tapestry of what we already know. Our life-cloth grows larger and more colorful with each new bit of information.

Mental measurement quantifies cognitive function. Snow and Lohman (1989) describe how this process applies to testing and measurement: "The evidence from cognitive psychology suggests that test performances are complex assemblies of component information-processing actions that are adapted to task requirement during performance" (p. 317).

In other words, in responding to test questions or exercises, examinees evidence deeply embedded mental processes (viz., information processing) by performing such tasks as reading with comprehension, accurately calculating sums, or exquisitely playing the piano. Performing these activities (and myriad others) is confirmation of a developed information processing system, or cognition. Hence, our measurement is of cognition.

This perspective on measurement shows how firmly grounded modern measurement is in the science of cognitive psychology. Such grounding for mental testing advances modern measurement from earlier ideas about testing that focused on gauging mastery of content per se, usually in a scholastic area. In earlier ideas of measurement, content domains such as reading, mathematics, or social studies were considered apart from the psychology of the individual, and a test strove to assess how much of that content an individual had mastered. By this earlier reasoning, mental assessment was based on developmental and behavioral psychological theories. As one advances in years and development, logically one can hold more knowledge and perform additional tasks. For instance, a 3- or 4-year-old child can likely count from 1 to 10, whereas a 4- or 5-year-old child can continue counting to 100 or more. A typical 6-year-old can add simple numbers, and an 8-year-old can subtract them and possibly even divide a few of them.

Today, measurement science is grounded in cognitive theories about knowing and learning, based on the belief that knowledge is not apart from one's psychological composition.

Introducing Latent Traits

Often, in modern psychometrics, particular cognitive processes are called *latent traits*. A latent trait is nothing more than a description to codify some aspect of cognition that manifests in task performance. Staying with the previous examples, some commonly cited latent traits are reading, calculating sums, and playing piano. Of course, the list of traits is as long as the number of possible abilities and proficiencies.

We measure latent traits by applying scientific methods as heuristic inquiry. That is, using the rules and systems of science (e.g., generalizability of results, replicability of methods), we probe and explore an individual's mind to gain clues about a particular latent trait. Our work is a process of discovery, and with each new assessment, we unearth more information about the latencies. The rules we use are assimilated to form the field of psychometrics.

It is useful to note that the term *latent trait* implies an underpinning of cognitive psychology, and psychometricians commonly refer to latent traits. In general psychology, a roughly parallel term—and one that carries implication for operational aspects of assessment—is *constructs*. It is to this new term that we next turn our attention.

Defining Constructs for Mental Appraisal

Constructs are "constructed" by social scientists to be meaningful descriptions of a particular psychological trait or latency. They set forth, in essence, a working definition of some aspect of cognition that can be theorized in research problems. For example, a researcher may want to compare two distinct methods for teaching reading to first graders. In doing so, the researcher imagines a reading construct as representative of cognitive functioning in that area. The investigator does not invent it or even suggest that reading is a "thing" in the brain. Instead, the researcher realizes that reading is a complex mental phenomenon—a complement of cognitive processes, if you will—that is known only indirectly to others through the actions exhibited by the examinee to particular stimuli (i.e., responding to questions about a reading passage). The theorized reading construct may be contrasted with other constructs such as intelligence or logical reasoning, but reading cannot be known as a reified entity unto itself.

At first blush, this explanation may appear to be merely a semantic manipulation and an example of seemingly ever-present psychological mumbo jumbo, but such a view would be a mistake and could leave the uninitiated reader with a distorted idea of what psychological measurement is and how it works. Although constructs are the bread and butter of measurement and should not be taken lightly, they are often misunderstood.

This point can be illustrated by a relevant quote familiar to many students and educated laypersons about the nature of intelligence tests. The quote originated at a 1921 symposium where 17 of the world's foremost psychologists, including Terman, Thorndike, Thurstone, and Yerkes (gifted individuals who were alive at the same time, worked simultaneously on expanding their understanding of the notion of intelligence and met to talk about their work), attempted to synthesize research about the question, "What is intelligence?" The debate was lengthy and grew contentious. By the end of the symposium, after bitter dispute, still no consensus had been reached on the question that centered their attention. Finally, one participant, the notable Edwin G. Boring (1923), ended the debate by declaring, "Intelligence is what the tests test" (p. 35).

Critics of psychological assessment, and others who are uninformed about how and why psychological measurement works, sometimes cite this quote to buttress a naive belief that even measurement experts do not know what they are measuring. In fact, Boring and the symposium participants were making a different point altogether—a profound point about mental constructs, with implications for our study of modern measurement.

First, they were identifying latent traits as those that typically occupy Euclidean space in the psychological domain, and second, they were saying that psychological and educational constructs are meaningful only to a given assessment, which of course varies from test to test. In other words, these psychologists reasoned that intelligence is a multidimensional, complex phenomenon and is not the result of a particular variable that can be reified. Further, it cannot be measured uniformly by all intelligence tests. One intelligence test may tap Construct A related to a general intelligence, whereas another test may assess Construct B, also related to a general intelligence but still independent from the first measure. Because consensus does not exist about the precise nature of intelligence (except that it comprises multiple constructs), each intelligence test measures a different facet of it, yielding various intelligence constructs, every one of which is independently valid.

Although this description illustrates the complexity of assessing intelligence, the ideas expressed in the sophistication of the symposium's perspective apply equally to other constructs. In other words, these notions about constructs are not limited to IQ but can also apply to self-efficacy, motivations, scholastic achievement, and so forth.

Psychometric Methods Defined

A Description Definition

What are psychometric methods? First, the word *psychometric* is the amalgamation of two foreign derivatives: probably the Greek nouns *psyche,* meaning breath or life, and *metron,* meaning to measure (or the Latin words *pushke* and *metiri*). Usually it takes the form of *psychometrics,* a singular noun (although ending in "s"), or as an adjective with a singular or plural noun, such as the phrase *psychometric analysis* or *psychometric methods.* Simply stated, psychometric methods are the mathematical, especially statistical, designs of psychological tests and measures. As such, psychometrics provides a means to address measurement questions of score interpretations. More generally, psychometrics embodies a unified, quantitative theory that describes how samples of cognitive processes or behavior react under various conditions. It is, thus, easy to appreciate the genesis of the term *psychometric methods* from *pushke* (the psychological part) and *metiri* (the statistical part).

Because psychometric methods always apply to measures of mental processes, they are inextricably linked with psychology. I explore the interdependence of psychometrics and psychology often in this text. For interesting reading about the history of measurement science from a philosophical perspective, see Michell's (1990, 1999) description of the notion of using numerical data to represent mental measurement and his accompanying conceit.

An important last note about our definition is to be aware that psychometrics is not synonymous with statistics. Each term identifies a distinct discipline. To be sure, criteria for quantifying a construct are statistical, but this fact shows only how heavily psychometric methods rely on statistics and not that they are the same discipline. Realizing the distinction between psychometrics and statistics is important for proper use of psychometric methods.

Conceptual Steps in Mental Appraisal

The cognitive processes or behaviors examined through psychometrically based instruments are first conceptualized as a construct. This step allows psychometricians and researchers to quantify them as a variable. Variables are usually expressed in tests as items or performance exercises, and they are considered a stimulus to which the examinee responds. The responses are then quantified in some fashion (e.g., scored as correct or incorrect, rated from low to high, or given some numerical score). From this information, inferences about an examinee's behavior to the construct—and ultimately to the cognitive functioning—can be drawn. This model of assessment is referred to as *representational*, and its logic is well established in the philosophy of science (Michell, 1990, 1999). (A more complete discussion of constructs, cognitive processes, behaviors, and traits is presented in chapter 2.)

It is the interpretation of inferences that gives life to the measurement process. Here is where we find our meaning in measurement, and it is the wellspring of assessment-based decision making. However, caution should be our watchword because interpretation of inferences is also our area of greatest challenge. This is where we can slip up most easily because an appropriate, meaningful, and useful interpretation of a test score is not easy. Psychometric methods are ultimately designed to make valid interpretations of test results more likely.

Limits of Mental Appraisal

Because, obviously, it is impossible to assess all the cognitive processes or behaviors of even a single construct (i.e., we cannot ask every conceivable question about "reading" that could be asked), *samples* of the construct must be taken and used for the analysis. Some degree of inaccuracy inevitably occurs in describing a cognitive process when examining only a sample of it. By chance, a given sample may include some extreme elements of the cognitive processes, or it may exclude some aspect that is important to the whole. However, within reasonable limits, we do know what processes we are appraising by using samples.

In addition, our appraisal is but a snapshot in time of the sampled behaviors. Recall, from the previous discussion, the lability, or changing nature, of cognition. Measurement professionals, and other persons who may use test-derived information for decision making, should keep this fact in the forefront of score interpretation.

Lest we go too far, however, in thinking that we need just to apply science to make elegant measurements, Walberg (1984) reminds us that "quantification hardly indexes scientific progress" (p. 369). That is, we definitely need science, but it must be cautiously applied. In educational and psychological measurement, the application of psychometrics methods is our science. We must use it not only proficiently, but also wisely.

Benefits and Danger of Measuring Mental Constructs

Contributions of Psychometrics to Science

In the broadest sense, psychometrics' greatest contribution as a science is to inform the grand question of all psychology: What is the nature of humankind? Employing psychometric methods to plan, develop, interpret, and use a mental measure takes advantage of the best science we have available. Through psychometrics, we can make meaningful, appropriate, and useful measurements of both simple and complex psychological phenomena. This is our route to exploring the grand question.

In less grandiose, but more practical terms, because of psychometric methods, schoolchildren, counseling subjects, psychologists, medical doctors, airline mechanics, engineers, architects, and people in virtually every field where a test is used have information produced about them that is better (i.e., with less error) than can generally be garnered through other means. For example, in education, the National Research Council's (NRC's) Board on Testing and Assessment (1999), part of the prestigious National Academies, in a report about high-stakes testing in schools, meticulously examines uses, abuses, and cautions of tests. The report forcefully articulates the viewpoint that employing test data to make policy decisions is logical and beneficial to students' welfare, to a degree far beyond any other means of making important, large-scale decisions.

This opinion is buttressed by another National Academy Press publication, *High Stakes: Testing for Tracking, Promotion, and Graduation* (Heubert, Hauser, & Committee on Appropriate Test Use, 1999), which maintains that tests are vital to educating students in schools. This statement is made about tests: "When tests are used in ways that meet relevant *psychometric* [italics added], legal, and educational standards, students' scores provide important information that, combined with information from other sources, can lead to decisions that promote student learning and equality of opportunity" (p. 4).

Contemporary political figures of both major political parties regularly tout the benefits of educational testing. In his call for a national crusade for education standards during his 1997 State of the Union address, former President Bill Clinton said, ". . . Good tests will show us who needs help, what changes in teaching to make, and which schools need to improve." On the other side of the political spectrum, President George W. Bush also proposed a system of national tests in his *No Child Left Behind* program, and has said, "Testing is an important tool for teachers, parents, and other school personnel to help children in the learning process." These citations demonstrate that the value of testing as an educational tool is recognized by public leaders, regardless of ideology.

Of course, testing-generated information is also important in other fields. Wood and Butterworth (1997) list advantages of psychometrics for guidance and counseling. For psychology, Brody (1985) offers a detailed study of IQ testing, concluding that intelligence is a concept worthy of serious study and that the tests used for its measurement can yield valid inferences about its constructs. These publications are representative of a rich and full literature on the benefits of using psychometrically sound tests to inform decisions in many fields.

Furthermore (and significant for present interest), despite public controversy about educational and psychological tests in general, the psychometric methods used to construct good mental tests are not generally disputed. Snyderman and Rothman (1987) surveyed specialists with expertise in areas related to testing and found near unanimity of positive opinion on the methods. In addition, their survey revealed ". . . that the experts held positive attitudes toward appropriately using intelligence and aptitude tests" (p. 137). Among measurement professionals, they report, little controversy generally exists about tests or measurement, especially about the psychometric methods used to develop them.

Cautions on Misuse of Test Scores

However, like Darth Vader in the *Star Wars* saga, psychometric methods can have a dark side. Undoubtedly, this blackness stems primarily from poorly developed tests or improper use of the information yielded by tests. Many tests lack psychometric rigor and should be labeled "poor." The late Oscar Buros (1972), while editing his famous catalog of tests, lamented the large number of poor quality tests extant, noting that "at least half of the tests currently produced should never have been published" (p. xxvii). Regrettably, Buros's commentary probably applies as well to today's crop of instruments. Poorly constructed tests are unable to yield good data, and sadly, when information from such tests is used in decision making, there is a regrettably high chance that inappropriate decisions will result.

The improper use of tests is an insidious problem for users of tests because it nearly always occurs through ignorance, rather than malice. The NRC's Board on Testing and Assessment (1999) grimly, but accurately, points out that "good tests could serve bad purposes" (p. 1). Measurement professionals must honestly recognize that the scenario in which even good tests are inappropriately used is all too common today. In schools, for example, teachers constitute a huge group of test users, yet many are uninformed about the proper interpretation of tests, much less the elementary principles of test construction (Frary, Cross, & Weber, 1993). Even psychologists, a group of highly educated professionals that rely heavily on tests and who should be well informed about them, are in many instances according to Fox (1994) deficient in actually possessing the information and skills necessary to properly interpret and use tests. Such poor testing practice need not be continued.

Certainly, promoting appropriate test use is an integral part of psychometric methods. It is not enough for psychometricians and measurement professionals to construct tests; they also must be bold and assertive when necessary, often taking the initiative in ensuring proper use of tests. They can instruct laypersons in how to properly use test information. The NRC reports cited previously are excellent sources for guidance on the proper use of tests.

Parents of school-age children have a stake in the outcome of assessment for their offspring. Popham (1999) encourages parents, along with all educators, to "become familiar with the innards" of standardized achievement tests, prodding their engagement by reminding them that "these tests are not sacrosanct instruments suitable to be scrutinized only by the psychometrically sanctified" (p. 32). Measurement professionals should encourage close scrutiny of their work, as well as help explain technical aspects of constructing tests and interpreting scores for interested laypersons. They should tell persons about the industry-standard guide *Standards for Educational and Psychological Testing* (American Educational Research Association, American Psychological Association, & National Council on Measurement in Education, 1999) and help them review it as appropriate.

Measurement professionals should also be sensitive to the fact that laypersons often distrust and are frightened by statistical process, psychometric or otherwise. Huff (1954) capitalizes on the fear of statistics in his infamous antimath book *How to Lie With Statistics.* However, Galton (1898), writing more than a century ago, saw the beauty in the mathematically elegant solutions of statistics. He said, "Some people hate the very name statistics, but I find them full of beauty and interest. Whenever they are not brutalized, but delicately handled by the higher methods, and are warily interpreted, their power of dealing with complicated phenomena is extraordinary" (p. 62).

Galton's comment is as apropos today as when he wrote it. For people not accustomed to mathematics, the arcane language and Greek symbols of the quantitative world of statistics and measurement can be intimidating. Many people fear being manipulated by numbers or being made fun of because they lack familiarity with numeric processes. For a wonderfully readable book filled with party anecdotes, see John Paulos' (2001) *Innumeracy: Mathematical Illiteracy and Its Consequences.* Psychometricians and others involved with testing should be perceptive to clues indicating a math fear and help people. Speaking in statistical argot and jargon does not dazzle parents, teachers, or students. It only alienates them. Such speech, and the accompanying attitude, should be assiduously avoided. Despite the intricacies of some statistical processes, any aspect of psychometric methods can be explained clearly, directly, and politely in a manner appropriate to the audience and circumstance.

Yet another dark aspect of testing affects the work of measurement specialists—the politics of public policy decisions associated with mental measurement, especially IQ testing and other forms of school testing, such as achievement and ability or aptitude testing. Measurement professionals should appreciate that the controversy over mental testing has existed since the pioneering days of psychological measurement. One early opponent of mental testing was Walter Lippman, the journalist who was notable for reporting the events of World War I to an anxious American public. His debates with Lewis Terman about testing, published as a series in the premiere liberal intellectual journal of the 1920s, *The New Republic,* are legendary (Lippman, 1922). The series makes for lively reading even today. Over the years, numerous others have also weighed in with their opinions about testing.

Lee J. Cronbach (1975) fairly chronicles the strife over testing in his classic article "Five decades of public controversy over mental testing," still as relevant today as when it was written. A more current recounting of the debate over assessment in America is found in Seligman (1992), and again in Herrnstein and Murray (1994) and Jensen (1980). Reading these books gives one insight into varying points of view and helps the measurement professional gain broader understanding of the public policy issues involved in assessment.

Regardless of one's feelings, the public controversy about mental tests—long standing and unabated—is firmly planted as a neon caution sign over persons working with psychometric methods. The sign reminds measurement professionals that the task of constructing and using mental tests is vastly more involved than the mere execution of statistical or psychometric processes in and of themselves. It is important to the lives of other humans. Measurement professionals should scrupulously adhere to high ethical standards, and must accurately and meticulously attend to even the smallest detail of their work. Professionals, in particular, should work with sensitivity to the individuals who may use the fruits of their labors.

Ethics and Conduct in Psychological Measurement

Several persons and organizations familiar with assessment have recognized the importance of setting high standards for measurement professionals. Many of them have put forth codes of conduct and other guides to address ethical issues and technical standards. These publications proffer direction and helpful information about proper conduct within the profession. At many points throughout this text, I refer to these publications as *guides*. Collectively, they can inform the work of measurement specialists and anchor it ethically in significant ways. The Suggested Readings for Selected Ethics Guides section at the end of this chapter comprises some of the better-known publications, although it is not comprehensive. Students and professionals should acquaint themselves with these rules, guides, and codes, and most significantly, should adhere to them.

Canons of ethics and other legal protections are necessary because mental testing is (as I discussed earlier) about discovering ourselves, a sensitive subject indeed! The educational philosopher Jerome Bruner (1956) reminds us of how central our view of ourselves is, when he says,

> . . . Man as individual has a deep and emotional investment in his image of himself. If we have learned anything in the last half-century of psychology, it is that man has powerful and exquisite capacities for defending himself against violations of his cherished self-image. (p. 26)

Acknowledging the truth of this statement constitutes a clarion call for psychometricians to follow to a high degree the precepts set forth in the codes of ethics and standards for assessment. Shoddy workmanship in psychometric methods cannot be accepted. The consequences are too important. Any party in an assessment—whether the test maker, the examinee, or a user of the scores yielded by an assessment—must exercise responsible assessment behavior. This dictum is absolute; no corners can be cut. Simply put, the ethics of proper conduct in psychological measurement are paramount.

Historical and Contemporary Context for Psychological Measurement

Roots of Psychological Measurement

Psychometric methods have no single historical progenitor but spring principally from a combination of pure mathematics and the statistics of varying disciplines, including economics, agronomy, biology, and chemistry. As an academic discipline, psychometrics arose primarily in the context of the developing science of psychology in the late 19th and early 20th centuries. The roots of psychometric measurement can be traced to both quantitative sciences and psychology. However, other influences have also pushed its evolution. Social trends, for example, have contributed to advancing measurement science. The intense attention in the last two decades to "test bias" and "item bias" (now more technically subsumed under the study of differential performance and discussed at many points throughout this text) is a direct result of societal concern for neglected attention to women and racial and ethnic minorities. New conceptions about validity are similarly implicated (see chapter 4). Our science is still an evolving discipline.

The history of scientific approaches to measuring mental abilities is not long, occurring mostly within the last hundred years or so, although the roots of measurement go back much farther, probably to the Hindu-Arabic numbering system of 700 or 800 years ago. The story is wrapped in the life events of a handful of remarkable people whose passion it was to advance the then infant science of psychology. The problem with which these individuals concerned themselves was one of the most interesting of all problems—how to consider the nature of humanity. Their approach to this problem (see the grand question discussed previously) was to employ the quantifying methods of probability and statistics, thus merging the rigor and objectivity of mathematics with the probing inquisitiveness of psychology. However, contemporary statistical techniques were elementary, crude, and inadequate for the complexities of the task. So, they invented new techniques (e.g., correlation and factor analysis), and in the process, created the field of psychometrics, making measurement a science.

Three men in particular contributed to the origins of psychometrics. They are Sir Francis Galton (1822–1911), Alfred Binet (1857–1911), and Charles Spearman (1863–1945), each a man of unimaginable high intellect. Their work had a massive cumulative impact on the field of measurement science and on education in general. Galton tested thousands of subjects in his Anthropometric Laboratory in the Natural Sciences Museum of South Kensington, England. His protégé, James Cattell, worked in tandem at the psychological laboratory at Columbia University in New York. Cattell is widely credited with first using the term *mental test*. Galton himself had a compulsion to measure. He was fond of saying, "Whatever you can, count!" He evidently practiced his pronouncement obsessively (Bernstein, 1998). He virtually founded measurement science by moving statistics from business interests (e.g., actuarial tables for insurance and risk management for stocks) to the serious study of human differences. A very useful Galton resource is at the Web site *http://galton.org,* a site that contains most of Galton's books, some of his papers, Karl Pearson's *Life of Galton,* and a photo gallery.

Binet's contributions to mental testing are also legendary. Working with Théophile Simon, Binet, one of the first psychiatrists, was commissioned by the Ministry of Education in France to devise a practical means of distinguishing normal children from those with "mental deficiencies," by his own terminology. Building on the work of Galton, Binet concentrated his efforts on finding a way to measure "higher mental processes," eschewing the Wundtian tradition of looking exclusively at sensory and motor functioning. He devised his series of "stunts" (as he called them), or exercises, appropriate to specific age groups. For example, a normal 4-year-old child could repeat three digits, whereas an 8-year-old child could note omissions from a picture of familiar objects. In one of the first efforts to fashion a scale of measurement, Binet devised a simple age scale to determine a child's level of mental functioning.

Lewis M. Terman, a psychologist at Stanford University, adapted and standardized Binet's work, molding it into a series of tests useful for large-scale assessment in the United States. This work set in motion a series of events leading to the famous Army Alpha and Army Beta tests used during World War I. Thereafter, and in large measure because of Terman's efforts, American public schools adopted standardized testing for widespread use, where it holds reign today. As is widely known, Terman (1916) wrote *The Measurement of Intelligence,* a profound work that has influenced thinking about educational and psychological appraisal since its publication.

It is difficult to exaggerate the extent of Spearman's contribution to measurement in general and psychometrics in particular. To think, just one individual fashioned so much of the basic theory and formulas of classical test theory! Of course, he had a great deal of help from his colleagues, especially E. L. Thorndike (who disputed Spearman's g and postulated an intelligence comprised of multiple neural bonds; this philosophy is now making a reappearance under the general guise of "multiple intelligences") and, later, L. L. Thurstone. Spearman's (1904a, 1904b, 1907, 1910, 1913) early papers, a delight to read today, show the breadth and depth of his contribution to this developing field. Among his many significant books, *The Abilities of Man* remains a genuine classic (Spearman, 1927). Spearman fashioned a two-factor theory of intelligence, concluding that there is a single, global mental ability, which he termed *general intelligence,* or *g,* and what remained of intelligence after the *g* portion was assigned to specific abilities. His theory is paramount in psychology and measurement, and despite repeated challenges to the concept (from Thorndike and some modern psychologists), Spearman's *g* still dominates psychological thinking and research.

Sources for More Information

This brief recounting of history barely scratches the surface of a rich and interesting story about psychology, testing, assessment, and psychometrics. To our good fortune, one need not stop learning the story here, as there are several good histories available. Thorndike and Lohman (1990) offer an outstanding history of a century of ability testing, and Fagan and VandenBos (1993) explore the field analytically by providing a critique of the history. Also, the respected journal *Educational Measurement: Issues and Practice* (1997) prepared a special issue on the history of modern psychometrics that includes several noted authors who discuss various aspects of the story. For a delightful read, see *Notes on Social Measurement: Historical and Critical* by Duncan (1984). Jensen (1981) also provides a no-nonsense recount of measurement's history in *Straight Talk About Mental Tests,* a clear, balanced appraisal for the nontechnical audience. Of course, many educational psychology textbooks also recount the history, although some remain spotty in doing so.

In addition, because psychometric methods are entwined with mathematics and statistics, readers can extend their knowledge by acquainting themselves with developments in those fields. Two excellent books trace the history of probability, measurement, risk, and statistics. The first is by the respected and excellent historian of statistics, Stephen M. Stigler (1986), and is titled *The History of Statistics: The Measurement of Uncertainty Before 1900*. The second is Peter L. Bernstein's (1998) *Against the Gods: The Remarkable Story of Risk*. Replete with fascinating information and anecdotes about the history of measurement science, Bernstein's book is interesting for both its readability as a story of adventurous men and women of profound intellect and its premise that probability theory is what distinguishes the thousands of years of ancient history from modern times. He says, "The revolutionary idea that defines the boundary between modern times and the past is the mastery of risk" (p. 1). Before humanity determined a methodology (probability theory) to reliably anticipate the future, people were at the whims of oracles and soothsayers to guess what might come next. Statistical reasoning, stemming from measurement, transformed progress from haphazard proceedings to predictable events.

Finally, as is often the case, referring to classic papers is productive for learning about current ideas. Several influential writings from throughout the history of measurement have already been cited. One comparatively current publication is a two-volume set that reprints many classic books and papers that define the field, *Educational Measurement: Origins, Theories, and Explications* (Ward, Stoker, & Murray-Ward, 1996). Although this edition lacks editing, it nonetheless contains wonderful writings by truly remarkable men and women. Readers will find the many classic articles and writings to be fascinating reading and wonderfully instructive.

Current State of Psychological Measurement

As quantification grows more pervasive in our daily lives, measurement science advances in pace. Changes are evident in theory, techniques, and practice. The progress is not limited to just one dimension of measurement or to one new psychometric technique; rather, the advances are broad in scope, contributing new ideas and methods to many areas of assessment. With each issue, the professional journals introduce and document many new ideas. I encourage students to read the contemporary journals and other publications to keep up in this fast-changing world. In addition, compendiums of significant measurement topics provide extensive discussion of advancements in the field. Two such books, both excellent resources for students and scholars, are *Educational Measurement* (Linn, 1989), which reports advancements in ideas up to about the mid-1980s, and *Handbook of Educational Psychology* (Berliner & Calfee, 1996), which extends the discussion of measurement to the mid-1990s. Both books are updated every few years.

Looking forward to tomorrow's assessment are two editions worthy of special notice. Lissitz and Schafer (2001), in *Assessments in Educational Reform: Both Means and Ends,* edited a collection of papers from well-known professionals who attempt to identify and even shape future directions through this work. Waltz and Bleuer (2001) offer an edition on new developments that attempts to appeal to a broad-based audience interested in assessment, including researchers, counselors, and even therapists.

In the following paragraphs, I highlight some of the major developments in measurement today. Of course, throughout this text, more detail on these trends is provided.

- Probably the most profound change affecting measurement science in contemporary times is the growth to dominance of the cognitive movement in education and psychology. A philosopher might summarize this change as an evolution in thought processes for measurement professionals wherein the world, previously viewed as external, is now conceived of as a much more complex interior phenomena. As described previously, education and psychology once operated generally from a behaviorist model in which content was learned, remembered, and eventually manifested in behaviors (e.g., reading, computing). Tests were viewed as assessing some particular inanimate content, such as reading, knowledge of history, or information related to professions such as electrical wiring or medicine. It was a staunchly behaviorist or trait model of assessment, and such thinking dominated measurement thinking for nearly 100 years.

  Cognitivists, however, believe that this approach to describing mental phenomena is simplistic and that, more likely, the mind is in a perpetual condition of cognitive activity, wherein new information is processed and assimilated into an ever-growing nomothetic framework. In this view, reading (and all other experiences) is not content independent of the receiver but is a web of mental activity constructed anew within each person. Hence, testing is not of content per se but is of cognitive processes that are shown indirectly as complex responses to the stimuli of a test item or test exercise. The measurement professional's job is to devise appropriate stimuli, and also to provide useful and meaningful interpretation of an examinee's response.

  This shift from a behaviorist and trait model to one of interpreting cognitive processes through tests has been gradual, but steady, for more than half a century. During the past two decades, the trend toward cognition has continually gained momentum, until now, as Mislevy (1996) declares, "the infusion of the cognitivist perspective into test theory is complete" (p. 379). As philosophical conceit, the cognitive movement in education suffuses nearly all other advances in measurement science. For a history of this measurement trend, consult Di Vesta (1987), who traces the cognitive movement within education generally.

  The cognitivist influence in mental appraisal can also be viewed from a broader perspective. It is part of a trend in modern measurement theory toward psychological interpretations that are grounded in philosophical, and often heuristic, argument. This advance is seen clearly in the work of the late, noted educational psychologist Sam Messick. In 1989, Messick identified and articulated five philosophical conceits about conceptions and practices of validity. Messick traces the movement wherein validity was a concern of instrument development and follows it to its role today as an interpretation of latent traits within a given context, a decidedly more psychological bent. Later, I explain more about Messick's approach to validity and its implications for psychometric methods.

Messick's push toward psychological interpretations for measurement theory is further reinforced by the modern description of validity as comprising inferences about scores. The guidebook of the test development industry, *Standards for Educational and Psychological Testing* (American Educational Research Association et al., 1999) unambiguously advances the psychological approach to measurement. It maintains that "it is the *interpretation* [italics added] of test scores required by proposed uses that are evaluated, not the test itself," elaborating that "the proposed interpretation refers to the construct or concepts that the test is intended to measure" (p. 9). Here, one clearly sees the dominance of the cognitivist point of view in tests and measurement. Psychometric methods operate in the context of this new philosophy about assessment, and indeed, this book reflects the changing environment.

- Following on the notion of mental measures as true indicators of cognitive processes is the fast-growing trend toward *multidimensional assessment,* which looks at the cognitive processes that are being assessed as having more than one dimension. The thought is that a multidimensional look into information processing is closer to what truly happens in neural activity than is an examination of just one aspect of cognition, often in isolation. One sees that increasingly more modern tests and assessment activities employ some form of multidimensional scaling or interpretation. These models have the disadvantage, however, of complexity in statistical processing, and even more important, in interpretation of results. When results from an assessment are overly complicated and require enormous sophistication to comprehend, they are usually less useful for widespread application. Regardless, we can look forward to seeing them in mental measures with growing frequency. van der Linden and Hambleton (1997) proffer an excellent edition of writings by many good thinkers and psychometricians about some of these multidimensional models, particularly as they incorporate item response theory (IRT).

    Multidimensional assessment usually requires a format for test items and exercises that is more flexible than binary formats like multiple-choice and true–false tests. Examples are writing samples, extended exercises, performances, rating scales, and interrelated tasks. Some new tasks allow responses to be developed and submitted by a team of examinees, rather than from just one person. The names used for these new formats vary widely, and include *constructed response, performance assessment, authentic assessment*, and *measurement with portfolio*, among other names. Osterlind and Merz (1994) developed a taxonomy for various formats of constructed response test items. In chapter 6, I address many of the issues involved with multidimensional forms, and chapter 9 is devoted to performance assessments specifically.

- Terms of measurement, expressing evolving vocabulary, are also part of the changing character of the field. Such terms as *trait level, differential item functioning, polytomous response models, generalizability, testlet,* and *multidimensional IRT models* are fast becoming common parlance in the field. Some of these terms are psychometric jargon, but more often they represent important advances in measurement or psychometric procedures. Throughout this text, literally dozens of these newer terms are described.

- There are still more trends in modern tests and measurement, two of which come about because of today's ubiquity of sophisticated computers. The mid-size desktop, and even many laptop computers, far outpace the mainframe monsters of just a few years ago. This technical universality has greatly increased our sophistication in many aspects of test development and use. The widespread use of IRT, which dominates many large-scale assessment programs, is but one example in which computers have brought technical sophistication to even modest assessment programs and isolated tests. This book explores aspects of IRT in detail, and I emphasize IRT approaches to psychometric methods whenever appropriate.

- The computer brings with it another movement in testing, this one in administration. *Computer-administered tests* and *computer-adaptive testing* are broad terms encompassing an array of methods of administering psychological assessments. We are just beginning to realize the potential of employing the computer in testing applications, and the effects are not yet well understood. We anticipate the phenomenon of examinees responding to test items and exercises on computer to grow, probably by leaps and bounds.

  Of course, it is easy to realize that in the future, the computer will be exploited much further for testing-related application, such as in scoring performance assessments. Credible computer programs already exist for automatic scoring of written essays, as well as for processing some exotic formats for test exercises in complex assessments.

- Also, although true score theory still predominates measurement science, there is an augmentation in reliability assessment that emphasizes a *universe score,* wherein an observed test score is held to be representative of any such score derived from a universe of appropriate measurements. This approach is perhaps best articulated in reliability assessment by *generalizability theory (G theory)*. As the name implies, this approach seeks to examine observed test scores for their veracity to generalize to universe scores. Methodologically, this is accomplished by decomposing the measurement error into identifiable facets. I devote an entire chapter to G theory, and I mention it at other points, too.

- As perspectives toward mental appraisal change, so too do the statistics and psychometric methods that support measurement science. Clearly there is a fresh look at significance testing generally, even beyond its application in examining test results. In one significant action, the Board of Scientific Affairs of the American Psychological Association (APA), in 1999, formed the Task Force on Statistical Interference whose charge was "to elucidate some of the controversial issues surrounding applications of statistics including significance testing and its alternatives; alternative underlying models and data transformation; and newer methods made possible by powerful computers" (Wilkinson & APA Task Force on Statistical Inference, 1999, p. 594). The task force made a number of recommendations about reporting statistics more meaningfully (e.g., emphasizing effect sizes over significant), many of which impact psychometrics and associated statistics directly. We look at some effects of these trends on test development and subsequent analysis at varying points in this text. Details on the trend are explored in Kline's (2004) *Beyond Significance Testing: Reforming Data Analysis Methods in Behavioral Research,* a book that follows up on the initial work of the task force.

● Another tentacle of the evolving vocabulary of assessment is the contemporary eschewal of the term *criterion referenced* as a model for assessment at all. In his brilliant essay, tellingly titled "The rise and fall of criterion-referenced measurement," Hambleton (1994) describes a contemporary context in which some educators' desires to not use multiple-choice items in an assessment stems from an outlook that multiple-choice, criterion-referenced tests are but a cliché for limited behavioral outcomes and narrowly focused instructional objectives. In this limited mindset, as cognitive philosophy and educational theory evolved, even good multiple-choice, criterion-referenced tests had to be abandoned to keep a constructivist philosophy in the fore. Hambleton laments, however, that the abandonment of criterion-referenced measurement is ill conceived and is a sad loss to measurement. He says,

> This is regrettable because the concept of criterion-referenced measurement when introduced by Glaser makes no reference to the nature of the skills being measured, their narrowness or breadth, or how they might be measured. On the contrary, the focus was on clearly describing the intended outcomes and then designing a valid assessment of those outcomes. (p. 22)

These advances, and many others like them, constitute modernity in psychological assessment—a milieu that pervades the information given in this book. Readers will find information about both traditional and state-of-the-art psychometric methods, with a decided emphasis on the latter. However, to keep our modernity in perspective, consider a true story about baseball frequently told by the feisty former owner of the Oakland Athletics, Charley Finley. He gave an enlightening viewpoint to our idea of modern times when he said, "The day Custer lost at Little Bighorn, the Chicago White Sox beat the Cincinnati Red Legs, 3-2" (quoted in Will, 1990, p. 293). Or, from the vantage point of measurement, the ball game and the battle took place at roughly the same time on the same day. Further perspective on modern time is achieved by realizing that Galton was formulating his seminal theories at this same time; only a few years earlier, Binet was developing his "stunts" and Spearman was devising methodological procedures for constructing reliable mental tests. "Modern," in terms of ideas about psychological measurement, has a short history, and distinctions between traditional and modern notions about psychometric methods are fairly artificial and unimportant. This book offers a thorough description of those mental measurement methods in current, popular use and those looming on the horizon.

Likely Future Directions

From past events, we see that some forecasts about measurement are likely to be accurate. It seems apparent that the trends discussed previously will continue and certainly advance in the next few years. There will be increasingly more emphasis on psychological interpretations of data, more use of sophisticated statistics for designing tests and analyzing data, and a greater presence of electronic test delivery systems, such as computers and Internet access.

In addition, we can anticipate that over the next few years, assessment will become even more integrated into curriculum and instruction. Thus, psychometric methods must not be thought of in the narrow sense of measurement after learning but in the broader context of supporting and facilitating active learning. Because of this trend, classroom teachers and professional psychologists will probably rely on measurement professionals even more in the future.

Another likely forecast concerns the format of multiple-choice test items themselves. Despite valid criticisms and some polemics, I believe the multiple-choice format for test items will remain the most popular genre for tests. Its characteristic advantages continue to keep the format in regular use. Accordingly, multiple-choice items present psychometricians with the challenge of understanding what information is garnered and how to improve them to reduce error. This challenge must be equally met for alternatively formatted test exercises and tasks.

Further, one can anticipate that other forms of technology will be invented that will affect assessment. Consider, for example, miniaturization and increasing speed of transmission in electronics, which allows all kinds of yet unforeseen devices. Beyond the border of one tenth of a micron (a micron is one millionth of a meter) begins the world of nanotechnology. Here, electronic components consist of a single device that is scarcely the size of DNA or hemoglobin molecules. Scientists at Rice University, Yale University, and elsewhere are working to develop such nanotechnology. What this miniaturization and increased speed in microprocessing means for measurement science is not significant for what it can do today but rather for what it signals: That is, that we should be ready to assimilate into many aspects of measurement—from psychometrically based test construction to the delivery of assessments—new ideas emanating from electronic inventions.

One final speculation about the future concerns how advances in the fields of medicine and psychology may affect psychometrics. Amazing discoveries are occurring in brain research. More recently, through next-generation MRIs and other sophisticated neurological measuring devices, neurologists and other medical doctors, psychologists, and even physiologists have meaningfully recorded brain activity during learning. This new kind of measurement adds to our understanding of what it means to know how people learn, from the neural processes to motivation to achieve. These investigations will doubtless lead to new hypotheses and theories of learning, which will in turn affect assessment, and then psychometric methods. Many advances in brain research, and how it may affect our view of learning, are expertly chronicled in the NRC's *How People Learn: Brain, Mind, Experience, and School* (Bransford et al., 1999). Measurement personnel should keep their antennae up for such advances in brain research, and then explore ways in which these changes may affect their own work.

From this discussion, it is easy to realize that where we are now is not where we are going to be. I am reminded of the refrain from a song in the musical *Oklahoma* that tells about how modern early 20th-century Kansas City had become, with its electric lights and other up-to-date inventions. The refrain hails:

They've gone about as fer as they kin go . . .
Yes sir, they've gone about as fer as they kin go.

The future of measurement science, indeed, of all psychology, is exciting. No, we have not gone "about as fer as we kin go." In fact, I anticipate prodigious advances in mental measurements and elsewhere in educational psychology, and we can look forward to participating in the advantages of such advances. Meanwhile, it is to traditional and modern psychometric methods useful for making mental measurement that we now turn our attention.

Note on Subsequent Chapter Organization

Before continuing our discussion of mental measurement in subsequent chapters, it is useful to describe how I organize the chapters. First, each chapter after chapter 1 begins with what may seem like an interesting but off-the-wall story (only a paragraph or two in length); that is, the opening remarks may appear to have nothing to do with psychometrics or even measurement generally. However, they are related. In the Preface, I explain why I wrote these beginning-of-chapter stories, and I hope you enjoy reading them. Organizationally, after each chapter introduction I provide a preview of that chapter's contents and end each chapter with a summary. In between, the chapter's contents are structured to build on precursory information and hence should be read from beginning to end. However, because the content of the field is not wholly linear, throughout the text I refer readers to related information in other chapters. This organization makes coherent threads for topics across several chapters.

Suggested Readings for Selected Ethics Guides

American Educational Research Association. (1992). *Ethical standards of the American Educational Research Association*. Washington, DC: Author.

American Educational Research Association, American Psychological Association, & National Council on Measurement in Education. (1999). *Standards for educational and psychological testing*. Washington, DC: American Educational Research Association.

American Federation of Teachers, National Council of Measurement in Education, & National Educational Association. (1990). *Standards for teacher competence in educational assessment*. Washington, DC: National Council on Measurement in Education.

American Psychological Association. (2002). Ethical principles of psychologists and code of conduct. *American Psychologist, 57*. Available from *http://www.apa.org/ethics/* Retrieved February 14, 2005.

Family Educational Rights and Privacy Act, 34 Fed. Reg. 103-182 (1994) (to be codified at 34 C.F.R. pt. 99).

International Test Commission. (2004). *ITC guide-lines on test use*. Available from *http://www.intestcom.org/itc_projects.htm* Retrieved February 15, 2005.

International Test Commission. (2004). *ITC international guidelines on computer-based and Internet-delivered testing*. Available from *http://www.intestcom.org/itc_projects.htm* Retrieved February 15, 2005.

Joint Committee on Standards for Educational Evaluation. (1996). *Standards for evaluation of educational programs, projects, and materials* (2nd ed.). Thousand Oaks, CA: Sage.

Joint Committee on Testing Practices. (1988). *Code of fair testing practices in education*. Washington, DC: American Psychological Association.

Joint Committee on Testing Practices. (2000). *Rights and responsibilities of test takers: Guidelines and expectations*. Washington, DC: American Psychological Association.

National Center for Education Statistics Data Confidentiality Task Force. (1996). *Guidelines for data confidentiality*. Washington, DC: U.S. Department of Education.

National Council of Measurement in Education. (1995). *Code of professional responsibilities in educational measurement*. Washington, DC: Author.

National Research Council, Board on Testing and Assessment. (1999). *Appropriate uses of educational tests*. Washington, DC: National Academy.

Chapter 2

Statistical Concepts, Probability, Expectations, and More

Introduction

The Real Work

In the game of baseball, the catcher is the workhorse for the team. This stalwart's involvement begins at the dawn of play and continues until the sunset of the ninth inning. Throughout the day of the game, there is scarcely a play in which the catcher does not touch the ball at least once. No other player can claim this, except the pitcher who initiates each play and thereafter is rarely involved. The catcher has the important role of guarding home—the place to where all enemy-offensive players aspire. He is the only player put at risk of physical harm at every pitch, by both the ball coming toward him at nearly 100 miles per hour and by the swing of the bat at just the level where he holds his head. Professional ball players know that catcher is the hardest position to play and few of them like to be catcher because of its toll on their knees and back. It is a workingman's place, not for sophisticated gentry. Great catchers such as Bill Dickey, Yogi Berra, and Johnny Bench were all men from a working class background. Yet, for all that the position is, catchers are possibly the least memorable of ball players. There are fewer statistics kept about catchers than there are for other positions, and it is rare for a catcher to make it into the National Baseball Hall of Fame. The position does not lend itself to show-offs or to spectacular, crowd-yelling plays, opportunities often afforded the third baseman or the shortstop. The catcher is there to get the job done, quietly and skillfully.

The statistics and measurement processes described in this chapter are like the catcher on a baseball team—they are the workhorses of many psychometric methods. Things cannot happen without them, but by themselves they do not appear glamorous.

Contents

Most of the items in this chapter are not independent procedures; rather, they infuse much of measurement (and particularly psychometrics), and they come from pure mathematics and related fields. The items include describing random numbers, elementary probability theory, statistical notation, and the central limit theorem. I also explain procedures commonly used by measurement professionals, such as the method of least squares and maximum likelihood estimation, although only cursorily. Topics covered in the first half of the chapter are primarily theoretical, whereas those touched on in the last half focus on terminology and some useful statistical knowledge. These are tools that measurement professionals need to conduct the methods of the discipline. Knowing about them provides context and understanding to the processes discussed in other parts of the book.

Readers who are already versed in prerequisite knowledge for our study of mental measures may skim this chapter to get right to the heart of measurement in chapter 3. For most, however, this chapter presents essential knowledge for understanding discussions in subsequent chapters.

Random Numbers

Random numbers seem simple enough. Many people know that random numbers form no discernable pattern, and selecting one is akin to picking a numbered slip of paper from a hat. Although this conception is essentially correct, it does not tell the whole story. There are features to explore and appreciate about random numbers that make scientific work, and psychometric methods in particular, possible.

What Are Random Numbers?

The condition of numbers being random is defined globally as extant when all values in a population are equally available for selection. In other words, any particular value has as equal a chance of selection as any other value. For example, the number 322 has the same chance of being selected as any other value, such as the number 2,400,017. Random numbers represent a continuum along $(-\infty, +\infty)$. In measurement methods, the notion that the numbers employed are random is generally presumed.

Random Numbers as Expected Value

When random numbers are used in mental measurement (and in many other practical contexts), they have an aspect termed *expectancy*. Expectancy, essentially, is the realization in practical events of real outcomes among random processes. That is, obtaining a particular value from among a set of numbers is a random process, but actually acquiring some number is an observed event that can be expected. Expectancy is denoted by E. I define E algebraically later in this chapter, after some background into "events" in probability theory. One point to note here, however, is that because of E, we have several phenomena that are themselves important to our study of problems in measurement. One of these is the *central limit theorem,* a concept of profound importance to measurement science, and indeed, to statistics in general. This theorem stipulates that as a sample approaches its population parameter in size, one can more closely anticipate a particular distribution among the random numbers. It, too, is studied later in this chapter.

Generating Random Numbers

Many statistical textbooks contain a table of randomly generated numbers, and virtually all major statistical computer programs have the capability of computing a set of randomly generated numbers from a given population size or from other defined characteristics. Not surprisingly, several Web sites offer random number generation (e.g., *www.random.org* and *www.randomizer.org/form.htm*). Researchers routinely use these tables and programs for selecting cases from a population of interest. In most measurement work—indeed, in nearly all statistics—these values are considered to be sufficiently precise for use in a given research inquiry or other project.

Often, persons are surprised to learn that the numbers printed in textbook tables and generated by computer programs are not truly random, rather they are *pseudorandom*. Because a computer is not a psychological being with infinite variety and capability, it must rely on coded instructions to make a list of "random" numbers. Actually, to generate true random numbers, there must be absolute reference to a source of entropy outside the computer—again, something a computer cannot do. Most computers employ calculations from the Lewis-Goodman-Miller formula, given in Equation 2.1, as a pseudorandom number generator:

$$Xn = 16,807 \times Xn - 1 \,(\text{mod } 231 - 1). \tag{2.1}$$

Beyond curiosity, it is not necessary for us to learn this formula. Nonetheless, it is interesting to note that even this pseudorandom number-generating formula shares something in common with nearly all other mathematical formulas: If the mathematics of it are replicated enough times with different numbers, the results will form a pattern. With today's powerful computers, and for someone with expertise and determination, it is possible to run the Lewis-Goodman-Miller formula a sufficient number of times to detect the pattern. Because random numbers are fundamental to computer security (e.g., from encrypting credit card numbers to personal passwords for gaining access to secure Internet sites), persons who trace the patterns can replicate a key for the seemingly random numbers and thereby gain access to confidential data. One can imagine that keeping the codes to nuclear secrets, for example, is vitally important.

To help solve this security problem with random numbers, some computer engineers are developing random number generators that harness thermal noise, one of the few known sources of truly random and indeterministic phenomena (i.e., entropy). Computer chips in the future may rely on such innovations to generate true random numbers. Fortunately for most researchers and measurement specialists the random numbers generated by today's computers are more than adequate for practical use in our testing problems.

Randomness Versus Sampling

It should be noted that the concept of random numbers and random variables (described in the Random Variables section) is distinct from sampling. Merely because the presumption is made that numbers in a population of values are random, one should not infer that any collection of values selected from a population is itself random. The sample (composed of random numbers) may or may not accurately represent the population. Ensuring it does is a concern of representative sampling, not randomness. In fact, randomness does not directly imply anything about representation. Conversely, however, most sampling strategies use random selections of numbers or values, usually following some criteria or rules.

Sampling is not addressed in this text, despite the fact that most psychometric procedures require samples that are appropriately representative of their population. Readers interested in sampling theory and techniques are referred to many specialized books, including the cleverly titled *A Sampler on Sampling* (Williams, 1978), and Yates' (1981) classic text (more complete but challenging), *Sampling Methods for Censuses and Surveys*.

Random Variables

In measurement, as well as throughout process research, variables are variously and often inconsistently labeled as *random, chance,* or in more statistical contexts, *stochastic.* The terms are practically synonymous, and seldom is a distinction made among them. Variables are defined precisely in chapter 3, and here I explain only what it means for a variable to be classified as "random." Variables we use in mental measurement are presumed to be random.

Random Variables as Part of a Class

At quintessence, a *random variable* is a random number. In psychometric work, where variables are most commonly scores from a test or assessment, random variables derive from any value that can comprise a "class." Here, a class is an event in reality. For example, an IQ test score is an event for the class of all IQ measurements, or a preference for pistachio ice cream is an event for all ice cream flavor preferences. The important point to realize about random variables is that any value defined within the class can be selected with equal probability to selecting any other value; hence, in the aggregate they constitute a random variable.

Figure 2.1 displays a very simple frequency function of scores (shown as a histogram) obtained from such a variable. Although this display is of only two classes, other random variables may or may not be so constrained.

Discrete Random Variables

Discrete random variables are generally a subset of random variables. They are usually distinguished by having only a limited range of eligible values, typically in mental measurement contexts ±3 or ±4 standard deviations of some mean score on a standard score scale. However, only values defined within the range are available for selection, and only one value can be expressed at a time. If, for example, a test is scaled from 40 to 160 points, and scored as 1 point for each correct answer, then

Figure 2.1
Values obtained from a
random variable.

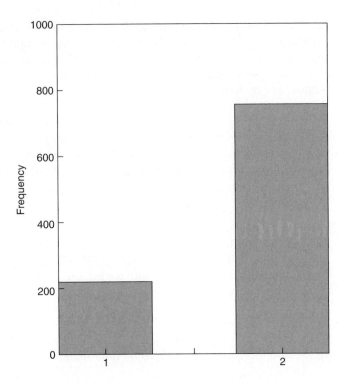

no one can obtain a score of 39 or 161. Because only whole numbers are used on this scale, no one can obtain a score of 4.6. In mental measurements, most scales are considered to be discrete random variables.

It is convenient to use the cumulative distribution function to express discrete random variables. One such discrete random variable is shown algebraically in Equation 2.2, which presumes the numbers to be random and thus in the range $(-\infty, +\infty)$:

$$F(x) = P(X \le x). \tag{2.2}$$

Figure 2.2 is a graph of the cumulative frequency function. The particular function displayed is *monotonic;* that is, it is always rising. This particular one is a step frequency function, but not all frequency functions are of this form.

A specialized but commonly used discrete random variable is the *Bernoulli random variable*. This variable is unique in that only two values are expressed: 0 and 1, as defined earlier in Figure 2.1. The probabilities for these values are often expressed as $1 - p$ and p, respectively. It can be used in many testing contexts, such as when test items are dichotomously scored.

Continuous Random Variables

Coextensive to discrete random variables are *continuous random variables*. Continuous random variables are values that can assume any and all points along a continuum, even when the continuum is delimited to a specific range, such as 0 to 100 along

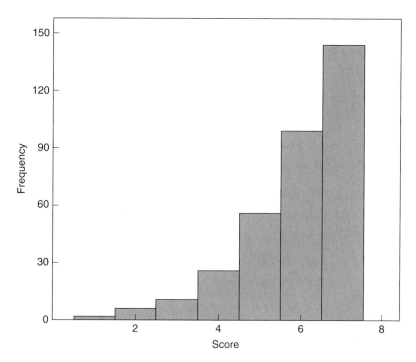

Figure 2.2
Monotonic (nondecreasing) cumulative distribution function.

some scale. In a truly continuous random variable, any value, not only whole numbers but also fractions (in any amount), may be obtained, and the scale ranges along the continuum $(-\infty, +\infty)$. The role of these kinds of variables is to express a frequency function, or more technically, in most measurement contexts, a density function, $f(x)$. In chapter 7, I explain much more about density functions and show how to calculate the probabilities that any particular value may fall within the interval (a, b).

Figure 2.3 displays a continuous trace line to portray the continuity of values possible for a continuous random variable. Contrast this graphic to the discrete random variable shown in Figure 2.1.

In measurement applications, however, continuous random variables nearly always delimit their scale to accommodate just ±3 or ±4 standard deviations of a mean score on a standard score scale.

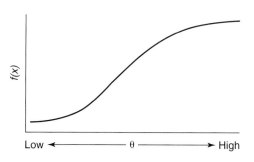

Figure 2.3
Trace line of continuous random variable.

Terms Associated with Measuring Variables

When data are employed in variables, further terminology is needed to complete their descriptions. Variables are always quantified into one of two classes: *ranked* or *scalar*. Ranked variables order persons or entities; that is, these variables represent ordinal measurement. Examples include saying where a runner placed in a race or which student attained the highest score on a test. Position among a group of examinees can be found in ranked variables.

Scalar variables, in contrast, describe an amount for the variable and typically represent an interval level of scale. Theoretically, scalar variables can be ratios, but these almost never appear in real world tests. As an example of a scalar variable, consider a music test with a range of scores from 1 to 100. Any given score along the test's range is a scalar (e.g., 23, 57, 99). Each is a score obtained on the test. Ordering scalar variables allows one to easily convert individual scores to ranked variables, a handy transformation.

Occasionally, researchers refer to variables as *exogenous* or *endogenous*. These terms refer to the source of variability for the object of measurement. For an *exogenous variable,* the originating cause for its variability (viz., measurement variance) is external to the variable itself or the model within which the variable is being considered. For example, often motivation is assumed to be caused by external stimuli. Or, when one loses weight, it is not done for the inherent value of pounds or kilos, but for some external reason, such as better health or a more attractive appearance. This is true even though the individual's desire for weight loss is considered an internal event. The measurement variance finds its source external to the variable or the causal model. These conditions distinguish that variable as exogenous. In some graphical displays of exogenous variables, such as in structural equation modeling (SEM), these variables have at least one relationship arrow pointing away from them to another variable in order to indicate the direction of association, and they do not receive any arrows.

Conversely, *endogenous variables* emanate from within a model. A popularly used school-based endogenous variable is academic achievement, which is caused in some measure by socioeconomic status, motivation, quality of the educational experiences, and other in-model influences. In SEM programs and other graphics-based models, endogenous variables receive arrowheads but do not send out any, indicating their own relationships.

Some Statistical Notation

In the days of the early popularity of snow skiing, equipment manufacturers deliberately made their skis, bindings, boots, and other interlocking equipment in idiosyncratic shapes, making it impossible for skiers to buy the pieces from different manufacturers. Of course, each firm intended this practice to increase sales of their brand. At some point, the manufacturers realized this practice was actually inhibiting the sales of ski equipment, and eventually they agreed on industry-wide standardization of shapes and mechanisms. Most companies voluntarily followed the prescriptions, and sales of ski equipment increased all around.

Although the situation for mathematical and statistical notation is not as disparate as the early days of ski equipment, there is a parallel in that statistical notation is only loosely standardized among authors. Regretfully, this absence of uniformity sometimes causes students to be confused when identical or similar concepts are presented with varying notation in different sources. I attempt to be consistent in my notation and generally employ the most commonly used notation, which is described in this section. A more complete listing of common statistical notation is given by Marriott (1991) in his useful compilation, *A Dictionary of Statistical Terms*.

Incidently, the Metamath Web site found at *http://metamath.flatline.de/symbols/symbols.html* lists thousands of mathematical letters and statistical symbols that are useful for a variety of purposes. They are formatted in transparent GIF (graphics interchange format), suitable for display on a web page, and PNG (portable network graphics). Be careful, however, to use a standard notation whenever possible and to employ consistent usage throughout a study or publication.

Notations for Common Variables

Capital letters are used to denote random variables (e.g., X, Y), and lowercase letters show sample observations or nonrandom variables (e.g., x, y). In measurement, data showing sample observations on variables (e.g., subjects' test scores) are typically displayed in a *matrix* with subjects in the rows and variables in the columns. A matrix is itself denoted by a bold capital letter. Several types of matrices are encountered in this text, including the data matrix ($\mathbf{X}$), the sums of squares and cross-products matrix ($\mathbf{S}$), the variance–covariance matrix ($\mathbf{\Sigma}$), and the familiar correlation matrix ($\mathbf{R}$). Table 2.1 is an example of an $\mathbf{X}$ matrix showing, first, particular

Table 2.1
Standard Notation for Data Matrix

Subject Number	X_1 (e.g., reading)	X_2 (e.g., IQ)	X_3 (e.g., gender)	. . .	X_j (any particular variable)	X_K (any random variable)
1	X_{11}	X_{12}	X_{13}	. . .	X_{1j}	X_{1K}
2	X_{21}	X_{22}	X_{23}	. . .	X_{2j}	X_{2K}
3	X_{31}	X_{32}	X_{33}	. . .	X_{3j}	X_{3K}
4	X_{41}	X_{42}	X_{43}	. . .	X_{4j}	X_{4K}
5	X_{51}	X_{52}	X_{53}	. . .	X_{5j}	X_{5K}
.	.	.	.	. . .	.	.
.	.	.	.	. . .	.	.
.	.	.	.	. . .	.	.
j	X_{i1}	X_{i2}	X_{i3}	. . .	X_{ij}	X_{iK}
n	X_{n1}	X_{n2}	X_{n3}	. . .	X_{nj}	X_{nK}

observations and then moving to the general case wherein subjects are identified by i (to indicate any particular subject) and by j and K to denote any given variable, whether nonrandom or random.

In Table 2.1, x_{11} identifies for the first subject (the first subscript 1: Subject No. 1) the observed score on the first variable (the second subscript 1: reading score). Likewise, x_{42} indicates the observed score for the fourth subject on the second variable (IQ). x_{1j} denotes for the first subject the score on any nonrandom variable, whereas X_{ij} indicates for any particular subject the observed score on any particular, nonrandom variable. This last notation (i.e., x_{ij}), especially, is commonplace in statistical notation.

One final aspect of this notation is to appreciate that the x_{ij} notation refers to any given variable *within a particular set of data*. The variable x_K indicates any random variable, without reference to a particular data set.

Summation of Variables

Usually, the observations within the cells of a data matrix need to be manipulated in some manner, like summing them or calculating a mean for all observations. The symbol Σ is used for summing events and numbers, or their representations (e.g., X, Y). This summation symbol is given more precision with additional annotations, as

$$\sum_{i=1}^{N} X_i.$$

Notation begins with the variable (here, X) and then moves to the operation (here, summation) and its particulars (from i to N). This complete notation provides that the is for each X are summed. Note that for this (and most) instance(s) the i equals 1 or the first case, meaning that the is to be summed begin with the first of them and thereafter incremented by one. The summation continues until the last (or n^{th}) i in the data set is reached (viz., the last number or case). Although seldom spoken aloud, if it were, this notation would read, "For variable X, sum the is, where i equals 1 to N." Because these specifications for summation are so commonly used in texts and elsewhere, variable summation of all cases is often abbreviated as follows:

$$\sum_i X_i \text{ or even, simply, } \sum X_i.$$

When one wants to identify the sum for a given variable for individuals from various groups, the following notation is used. As we have already seen, the (random) variable is identified by X, the i denotes the individual, and j signifies the group. Thus, in the following expression, the observations on the variable are summed, beginning with the first individual in the jth group (which could be any particular group) and continuing until the last individual's score on that particular variable (the x_{nj}) is reached:

$$\sum_{i=1}^{n} X_{ij} = (x_{1j} + \cdots + x_{nj}).$$

Sometimes, *double summation* is required to signify the sum of x_{nj} over all observations in all groups. This is symbolized in the following expression:

$$\sum_{j=1}^{J} \sum_{i=1}^{nj} X_{ij} = (x_{11} + x_{21} + \cdots + x_{nj-1,J} + x_{nj,J}).$$

Although formidable looking, this notation is straightforward. Begin with the variable j from the rightmost summation. Sum the scores on this variable (e.g., all n scores). Repeat this for each j group until all groups have been exhausted. Then, move to the left summation sign and sum these results over all groups (J groups). Because this process is used often, this particular double summation is frequently shortened to

$$\sum_{j} \sum_{i} X_{ij}.$$

This common notation scheme is logical; with a little study, one can appreciate how it accurately fits data by pinpointing exactly the desired case(s), cell(s), or group(s), as well as what arithmetic operation should be performed on them. As one might expect, there are additional summation rules, and advanced students may want to become acquainted with them. Many mathematical statistics books present these rules (e.g., Hays, 1988).

Alphabets to Denote Differences

One may recall from elementary statistics that when the letters are from the Greek alphabet, they show a *population,* whereas Roman (standard English) letters denote a *sample.* Caution is advised, however, because there are many exceptions to this generalization.

Of course, students recognize μ and σ as customary notation for the mean and standard deviation of a population (more completely, these are also written as μ_X and σ_X to show their associated variable). The corollaries for these population parameters are the sample statistics of $\overline{X}$ for μ_X, and sd for σ_X. In more statistical contexts (and for many formulas in this book), the standard deviation and variance for a sample are denoted as estimators of population parameters: $\hat{\sigma}_X$ and $\hat{\sigma}_X^2$. The "hat," or *caret,* above the sigma signifies that the statistic is an *estimate* of a population parameter (here, standard deviation and variance) because parameters are not fully known quantities. I do not use the caret symbol when it is presumed.

Notation for Functions

Throughout this text, we encounter functions. Customary notation for functions is $f(x)$ to denote a probability density function and $F(X)$ for a cumulative probability distribution function of any probability distribution. Common in measurement presentations, especially in IRT procedures, the variable of interest is generically designated as θ (theta) for trait, ability, or even proficiency; then, the function is expressed as $f(\theta)$.

Table 2.2

Various Sample and Population Statistics

Statistic	Parameter	Symbol	Formula
Mean	Population	μ	$E(Y)$
	Sample	$\overline{Y}$	$\sum_i Y_i/N$
Standard deviation	Population	σ	$\sqrt{\sigma^2}$
	Sample	$\hat{\sigma}$ or sd	$\sqrt{\hat{\sigma}^2}$, calculated by $\sqrt{SS/(n-1)}$
Variance	Population	σ^2	$E(Y-\mu)^2$
	Sample	$\hat{\sigma}^2$ or v or sd^2	$SS/(n-1)$
Covariance	Population	σ_{XY}	$E(X-\mu_X)(Y-\mu_Y)$
	Sample	$\hat{\sigma}_{XY}$ or cov	$SP/(n-1)$
Correlation coefficient	Population	P_{XY}	$P_{XY}/P_X P_Y$
	Sample	r_{XY} or r	$\hat{\sigma}_{XY}/\hat{\sigma}_X\hat{\sigma}_Y = SP/\sqrt{SS_X SS_Y}$
Sums of squares	Sample	SS	$\sum_i (Y_i - \overline{Y}_i)^2$, calculated by $\sum Y^2 - (\sum Y)^2/n$
Sums of products	Sample	SP	$\sum_i (Y_i - \overline{Y}.)(X_i - \overline{X}.)$ calculated by $\sum XY - (\sum X)(\sum Y)/n$

Some Important Formulas

From these ordinary notations flow a variety of other important formulas and expressions. Table 2.2 presents a few of the formulas and expressions commonly employed in psychometric methods, including variance, sums of squares, sums of products, covariance, and correlation coefficients.

Order of Operations

Mathematical operations must be performed in a specified order. To know the order, one will likely recall from early school days the handy mnemonic, "**P**lease **E**xcuse **M**y **D**ear **A**unt **S**ally." That is, solve first for quantities within the **P**arentheses (or other grouping symbols); next perform **E**xponents (powers or roots), **M**ultiply or **D**ivide (from left to right); and finally **A**dd or **S**ubtract (from left to right).

Elementary Probability Theory

Probability theory describes how variables are likely to behave. Not surprisingly, they follow a set of ordered rules that allow for the construction of models for measurement that are reliable. The rules are not too difficult and follow general lines of common sense. To start our brief look at some of them, it may be relaxing to appreciate the words of P. S. Laplace, who wrote in 1814 in "Essai Philosophique des Probabilitiés": "At the bottom of the theory of probabilities is only common-sense expressed numbers" (Dupont, 1977–1978, p. 127).

For persons interested in a more thorough study of probability models than is offered here, many sources are available, both in writing (e.g., Nutter, Kutner, Nachtsheim, & Wasserman, 1996) and on the Internet (e.g., *http://www.probabilitytheory.info, http://math.about.com/cs/probability/index.htm, http://www.cas.lancs.ac.uk/glossary_v1.1/prob.html#addrule, http://math.about.com/gi/,* and *http://davidmlane.com/hyperstat/probability.html*).

Probability and Events

In an idiomatic sense, probability is just the assignment of numbers to every event, or possibility, in a sample or population of events or possibilities. This may be expressed as a function: The occurrence of an event—such as event A—is a function of a certain probability; expressed as $p(A)$, and read as "the probability of event A." Readers may recognize that this is just a restatement of the first rule from the algebra of expectations now placed in the context of probability theory.

An *event* is anything that can happen within the limits of the given circumstance. For example, for a true–false test item on an assessment, only two outcomes are possible for the event: The subject responds with either a "true" or a "false." Thus, $p(A)$ is the probability of responding "true." Equivalently, $p(A)$ is also the probability of responding "false." Hence, probability is a function, in this case of being a "true" or a "false" event. If one were to guess blindly at the answer to such an item and event A is defined to be the "true" response, then $p(A) = .5$ because only two outcomes to the event are possible. Outside the arcane language of probability, we would typically say, "The odds of answering 'true' are fifty–fifty." However, realize, too, that probability and odds are not synonyms.

Conversely, if event A does not occur, there is its *complement,* called "the complement of A," or "not A." This may occur if an examinee skips a given test question. The complement of event A is written as $\overline{A}$. That is, for every circumstance we have an event and its complement. Further, events and their complements are considered to be *mutually exclusive*; that is, you cannot both respond and not respond to the test item.

In addition, for any class of events there is the corollary circumstance of being outside the class; or, more literally stated, not a possibility for a particular event. For example, endorsing "C" to the true–false test item is impossible given the class. In such a case, the event is said to be *null*. A null event is denoted with the symbol Ø.

Just for fun, in probability theory a number of interesting problems are often presented to illustrate association of events. One of them is the infamous birthday problem. Stated as a question, it asks, "How many people should be gathered in a room together before it is more likely than not that two of them share the same birthday?" The answer, it turns out, is 23 people. A description of how to arrive at this answer can be found at *http://www.probabilitytheory.info.*

Unions of Events and Other Associations

The possibilities for events are customarily expressed in set notation. Although the use of set notation is fading markedly in more recent times, one encounters it commonly enough in matrix algebra for this explanation to be beneficial for our use in addressing measurement problems. In this notation, $\cup$ signifies the *union* of event A with event B. That is, $\cup$ is read as "or" as in "event A or event B," and is typically written as $(A \cup B)$. $\cap$ signifies the *intersection* of events A and B. That is, $\cap$ reads as "and" as in "event A and event B." The intersection of two events is written as $(A \cap B)$. Mutual exclusivity of two events (viz., only one of them can occur, and without the other) is written as $A \cap B = \emptyset$.

Given these probability theory truths and notation, several statements about probabilities may be made. To start, consider Equation 2.3:

$$p(A_1 \cup A_2 \cup \ldots, \cup A_N) = p(A_1) + p(A_2) \ldots + p(A_N). \qquad \textbf{(2.3)}$$

The equation conveys information that the union of mutually exclusive events (labeled as A_1, A_2, and so forth to A_N) is the same as the sum of their individual probabilities. This is a concept central to probability theory. The logic expressed by the equation is important to measurement theory because it specifies relations among outcomes. Imagine these events as individual test scores, and it becomes readily apparent how the likelihood of a particular total score on the test is the sum of the likelihood of achieving the individual events, such as answering each item correctly.

By specifying the basic relations among events, a number of more detailed stipulations about the relationship among events naturally follow. These relationships are described as *rules of probability theory*. Significantly, the rules guide measurement theory, and indeed all statistics, in establishing logical relations among events. Some of the most significant rules are cited in Table 2.3. Of course, as one can imagine, these few rules are only some of the useful manipulations of probabilities that can be made. The logic of applying these rules to test scores parallels that given for the rule in Equation 2.3.

In the next section, I explain some aspects of these important rules of probability that are germane to measurement problems. We use these rules in developing scales and understanding distributions, features of chapters 6 and 7, and elsewhere.

Table 2.3
Some Elementary Rules of Probability Theory

Rule	Expression
Rule of complementary probability	$p(\overline{A}) = 1 - p(A)$
Rule of probability range	$0 \leq p(A) \leq 1$ for any event A
Rule of null event (impossibility)	$p(\emptyset) = 0$ for any $\oplus$
Rule of "or" probability	$p(A \cup B) = p(A) + p(B) - p(A \cap B)$

Events as Independent and Joint Probabilities

The *independence of events* is especially important to measurement theory. Logically, someone might believe independent events are simply probabilities that are wholly unrelated. Obtaining one particular score on a test is unrelated to obtaining any other given score, just as answering any given test item in one way (e.g., endorsing the C response on a multiple-choice item) is an event independent of answering the same item in another way (e.g., endorsing the D response). In a simple sense, this definition is not incorrect, but it is incomplete and does not follow probability rules. Statistical independence implies that knowing whether one event has occurred does not provide information for determining whether a second event has occurred. Two variables, A and B, are independent if their conditional probability is equal to their unconditional probability. In other words, A and B are independent if, and only if, the relations in Equations 2.4 and 2.5 are true:

$$p(A|B) = p(A) \qquad\qquad (2.4)$$

and

$$p(B|A) = p(B). \qquad\qquad (2.5)$$

Then, too, independent events can occur simultaneously, creating a *joint probability*. Joint probabilities express the likelihood that two or more events occur together. Consider the function $f(x, y \mid \theta)$, where f is the probability of x and y together as a pair, given the distribution parameters, θ. (This expression is a likelihood function, which I explain in chapter 7, presented here only to illustrate the notion of joint probabilities.) Often, events are not independent but occur simultaneously, and this circumstance can be expressed syntactically. As a relevant note, the correlation coefficient is interpreted to show interrelationship between variables or events but it does not describe joint probabilities because the events are not contemporaneously related.

In probability notation, the likelihood of a joint probability is shown in Equation 2.6:

$$p(A \cap B) = p(A)p(B). \qquad\qquad (2.6)$$

For illustration, suppose an examinee takes an achievement test and shortly thereafter completes an attitude survey about the subject content of the test. Further, suppose the individual is very able and has a 90% chance of answering all the achievement questions correctly, but may or may not have a positive attitude about the content, say it is just 50% positive. The joint probability of the examinee endorsing all correct answers and showing a positive attitude is just 45% (i.e., $0.9 \times 0.5 = 0.45$).

As one may surmise, statistical independence and joint probabilities do not describe all probabilities important to measurement. Another circumstance in probability theory relevant to psychometric work is where one event is contingent on another. This likelihood is called a *conditional probability*. Conditional probabilities play an especially important role in the statistics used in measurement.

Conditional probability is the basis for *statistical dependence* and *independence*. It means that the conditional probability of event B given event A is exactly the same as the probability of event B alone. Similarly, the corollary is also true: The conditional probability of event A given event B equals the probability of event A alone because A and B are independent events. However, to have these independent events occur conditionally is a new likelihood—namely, conditional probability.

Conditional probabilities have implications for all science for it provides a way to apply quantitative reasoning to the scientific method wherein two variables are simultaneously considered because of prior knowledge about each variable. As such, conditional probabilities routinely occur in many practical, statistical applications in a variety of fields, including psychometrics, engineering, agriculture, economics, and pure mathematics. In the general case, it is expressed as in Equation 2.7:

$$p(B|A) = \frac{p(A \cap B)}{p(A)}.$$ **(2.7)**

Some readers may recognize this as a probability notation for expression of Bayes' famous formula, which is developed into Bayes' theorem, presented in the following section. Because this conditional probability is vitally important to measurement, we study it in some detail.

Conditional Probabilities and Bayes' Theorem

As noted previously, many—perhaps even most—modern approaches to the scientific method depend on Bayes' theorem. Although some researchers may not realize it, we also routinely use it in measurement science. To understand Bayes' theorem, a little history will be instructive. An English clergyman named Thomas Bayes, working in the 18th century, suggested that previously known information be blended with new information to make better predictions. Bayes formulated a now classic problem in a 1763 paper entitled "An Essay Toward Solving a Problem in the Doctrine of Chances," which attracted little attention until more than 20 years after his death (Bayes, 1763). In fact, his paper was not even published until 2 years after he died, when Richard Price, a well-known member of the British Scientific Royal Society, used Bayes' work in his own economics treatise and subsequently sent Bayes' paper off for publication. If Price had not been of high ethical standards, he could easily have claimed the ideas for his own. Bayes' original paper can be accessed online at *http://www.stat.ucla.edu/history/essay.pdf*.

Bayes demonstrated his ideas in a pool hall. Considering that he was a minister by profession, his selection of such a site to conduct research is interesting! He first rolled a billiard ball across the table showing that it is free to stop anywhere on the plane. A second ball was rolled across the table, and a count was made of the frequency with which it stops to the right of the first ball. This count is considered the number of times an unknown event has happened. When the second ball rolled to the left of the first ball, it was counted as a failure because the event (ball rolling to

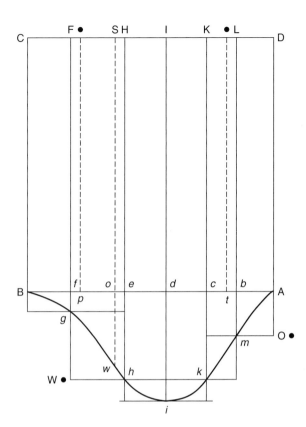

Figure 2.4
Reproduction of Bayes' drawing of billiard balls on a table.

the right) did not occur. Now, by Bayesian estimation, the probability of the first ball stopping at a particular location can be deduced by knowing the "successes" and "failures" of the second. In this way, Bayes showed how old information is used to predict new information. This point is key to understanding Bayes' theorem (see Figure 2.4).

Bayes' theorem provides a method that can be used to address a common research question: "Given that an event that may have been the result of any of two or more causes has occurred, what is the probability that the event was the result of a particular cause?" This situation is called an *inverse probability*, a special case of a *conditional probability*. Bayes (1763), using the fractured grammar of the day, enjoined the following scenario:

> *Given*: The number of times in which an unknown event has happened and failed.
>
> *Required*: The chance that the probability of its happening in a single trial lies somewhere between any two degrees of probability that can be named. (p. 273)

Bayes' problem is that for two events, A and B, where none of the probabilities is certain (i.e., the likelihood of event A, or event B, or the intersection of events A and B is neither 1 nor 0: 100% or 0%), then it must be true that the events, when presented together, are conditional. Equation 2.8 presents this idea in probability theory notation:

$$p(A|B) = \frac{p(B|A)p(A)}{p(B|A)p(A) + p(B|\overline{A})p(\overline{A})}.$$ (2.8)

In the formula, p is probability, and $\overline{A}$ is the complement of set A (i.e., the event "not A"). Bayes' theorem allows that the conditional probability of event A can be known given event B, as long as one knows a priori the probability of B given event A, the conditional probability of B given A, and finally, the conditional probability of B given $\overline{A}$. When $\overline{A}$ is known, its corollary $(1 - p(\overline{A}))$ is also automatically known.

Alternatively, and more commonly seen, Bayes' theorem may be written as follows in Equation 2.9. In later chapters, we modify this even further to capture its relation to a likelihood function:

$$p(B|A) = \frac{p(A|B)p(B)}{\sum_i p(A|B_i)p(B_i)}.$$ (2.9)

To calculate future probabilities, information is needed about the frequency of past events. In the language of statisticians, Bayes compared *posterior probabilities* with the *priors*. This terminology will already be familiar to readers with a working knowledge of regression and IRT. Bernoulli said Bayes' theorem was a posteriori to emphasize that the prediction only came after the evidence from a real experience had been identified and quantified. He maintained prediction could not be made a priori (as he called it), that is, without some prior evidence. However, probabilities could be calculated from even slight prior information, the "priors." He made only one assumption for this model: "We must assume that under similar conditions, the occurrence (or nonoccurrence) of an event in the future will follow the same pattern as was observed in the past" (Bernoulli, 1954/1738, p. 25).

Today, this assumption seems ordinary and even pedantic, but it had not yet been mathematically expressed until Bernoulli articulated the idea in probability theory terms. In fact, such reasoning was one of his major contributions to probability theory.

As an example of applying Bayes' theorem in a measurement setting, consider the circumstance in which a test is being scrutinized as a possible criterion for entry into a professional training program, such as for architects or engineers. Previously, although taking the test was a requirement, there was no "passing" score and all applicants were admitted into the program. Records indicate that in general only 60% of the admitted students passed the professional training program. Further, it is known that 80% of the successful students could pass the test at a specified level, whereas only 40% of those who failed the program could pass the test in the first place. The policy question for consideration is to determine whether to implement a passing score as criterion, and if so, what is the likelihood that a given student who is admitted on the basis of having scored higher than the cut score will be successful in the professional training program?

To answer this question, Bayes' theorem is put to work. Event A is defined as "success in the professional training program," and in this example, A is 60%: $p(A) = 60\%$.

Event B is defined as "can pass the test" and is 80%: $p(B) = 80\%$. The conditional probabilities are then defined as follows in Equations 2.10 and 2.11:

$$p(B|A) = .80, p(\overline{B}|A) = .20 \qquad\qquad \textbf{(2.10)}$$

and

$$p(B|\overline{A}) = .40, p(\overline{B}|\overline{A}) = .60. \qquad\qquad \textbf{(2.11)}$$

Remember that the policy question is to determine the conditional probability of event A given event B (viz., "What is the likelihood that a student can be successful in the program given that the student has passed the test?"). Following Bayes' theorem in Equation 2.8, the following computations are needed:

$$p(A|B) = \frac{(.80)(.60)}{(.80)(.60) + (.40)(.40)}$$
$$= \frac{.48}{.48 + .16} = .75.$$

Hence, .75 is the probability of success in the program given a passing score on the test. This level of success is greater than .60, the likelihood of successfully completing the program regardless of whether the test is passed. Hence, it seems like a good decision to implement the pass-the-test criterion to increase the likelihood of admitted students successfully completing the program. Bayes' theorem can be extended to incorporate other such decision-making scenarios, but this example shows the theorem itself.

Helpful (albeit advanced) information about Bayes' famous theorem can be accessed at *http://plato.stanford.edu/entries/bayes-theorem/*. Advanced students, in particular, are encouraged to learn more about Bayes' theorem and his related work.

Bayes' idea of using posterior and prior information to make likelihood judgments has developed into a field of statistics labeled *Bayesian statistics*. Many statistics associated with psychometric analysis (e.g., IRT) employ the Bayesian methods. In some contexts, Bayesian methods are contrasted with classical statistics that rely solely on the data extant for inference and do not refer to prior information.

Classical Versus Bayesian Statistics

It is important for persons working with conditional probabilities, and with Bayes' theorem in particular, to have a perspective on his approach to numbers and how they represent phenomenon. Statistical inference is often categorized as either *classical* (sometimes called *frequentist*) approaches or *Bayesian statistics,* which derives rules from Bayes' theorem more explicitly. There are important distinctions between these approaches. As a general rule—but one with many significant departures—classical statistics is well suited to hypothesis testing about real world (and often tangible) phenomenon, whereas Bayesian analysis is more appropriate for making estimates, especially about educational and psychological constructs. Because measurement science is aimed primarily toward latencies in cognition, most psychometric analyses employ Bayesian statistics.

We see this point in action many times throughout this text, but especially in IRT, which we study extensively in chapter 10. Bayesian analysis seeks to use prior information to estimate parameters of an underlying distribution, especially how the ratio of two normally distributed variables behaves. The prior information comes from observed data initially. Using this source, one then calculates the likelihood of the observed distribution as a function of parameter values. This likelihood is next multiplied by the prior distribution and normalized (i.e., transformed to standard units) to create a *posterior distribution.* The mode of the posterior distribution is the parameter estimate. Unfortunately, the validity of the posterior distribution cannot be statistically appraised, which adds much to the controversy about Bayesian approaches to statistical models. Nonetheless, in psychometric work, Bayesian approaches predominate.

Realize, however, the argument between these approaches is as much about the philosophy of science as about methods. There are many interesting sources to learn more about the debate, including Howson and Urbach's (1996) *Scientific Reasoning: The Bayesian Approach.* In addition, Woolley (2004) offers a short classroom exercise in his article, "Classical versus Bayesian inference: A classroom illustration" demonstrating the difference that students find engaging.

Laws of Distributions: Laws and Central Limit Theorem

Several notions about numbers apply more to distributions than do lexical statements about probabilities. They are implicit in statistical and measurement discussion, but they are seldom acknowledged. Some particularly important vertebra forming the statistical backbone of distributional psychometrics is the *central limit theorem,* the *law of large numbers,* and the *law of averages;* the first of these being the most potent for our study. (I discuss the central limit theorem last, however, because the other two laws build toward it.)

The Law of Large Numbers

The previous laws of distribution stem from the work of Jacob Bernoulli, another brilliant, 18th-century mathematician who contributed the notion that quantity matters. I introduce some of his ideas here and develop explanation of distribution more fully in chapter 7.

Bernoulli, like his contemporary Bayes, also showed how it is possible to infer previously unknown probabilities from known, empirical facts, even when such information is quite limited. He was interested in the idea of managing risk, an idea with direct applicability not only to making mental measurement and sampling techniques but also to such diverse activities as opinion polling, selecting stocks, testing medical procedures with new drugs, and even wine tasting. His ideas are best explained by example.

For learning about the law of large numbers, consider the following scene. Suppose you flip a coin many times, an exercise that is called *Bernoulli trials* in probability theory because there are exactly two possible outcomes (viz., "events"). While doing so, you realize, of course, that about half of the coin flips will result in heads and the remainder in tails. The law of large numbers tells us that by increasing the number of coin flips the ratio of heads to tails will vary from 50:50 by some stated amount, regardless of how small. This means that there is some error in the coin flip outcome ratio—the difference between the theoretically conceived ratio (50:50) and what is actually observed. Bernoulli asserted that by increasing the number of coin flips we can more accurately state this error and hence make prediction closer to reality. In other words, the law of large numbers tells us that the average of many coin flips is more likely than the average of a few coin flips to differ from the true average by some stated amount. As we see momentarily, this idea is different from the central limit theorem.

Imagine you flip your coin 99 times. If this exercise results in 50 heads and 49 tails, you may presume that the mathematical probability for the next coin flip in the sample of all coin flips would be 100% certain of coming up tails. However, in reality, we know this is not the case. Bernoulli quantifies what happens to the probability in such a circumstance. He devised a way to calculate the "next probability," and in doing so invented the law of large numbers. Knowing that the next probability can be calculated is an important concept because without the law of large numbers we would make many mistakes in sampling, measurement, and indeed statistics. To confirm his calculations, Bernoulli pulled white or black pebbles from a jar that contained 3,000 white pebbles and 2,000 black pebbles (rather than flip coins). He was able to demonstrate that with 25,550 selections of pebbles, his results deviated from the expected 3:2 (the ratio of white pebbles to black pebbles) by less than 2%. Interestingly, this is even more precise than the .05 level of precision we routinely use today in most educational and psychological research studies.

The law of large numbers relates to test data equally well. Suppose, for instance, that a single dichotomously scored test item is administered to 10 examinees and 5 of them endorse the correct response. Thus, the observed probability of passing the item by the group is 50% (5/10 = .5). Now, assume we know from an earlier administration of the same test (the earlier group is also from the same population) that 60% of examinees endorse the correct response. Hence, .6 is the previously known probability of passing the item for the population. This .6 is the same prior described by Bayes. From this information, we see that the difference in probability for passing the item with this sample is .1, or 10%, the difference between the previously known probability and the observed probability. By Bernoulli's law of large numbers this difference will decrease as the sample size increases. When the sample size is sufficiently large, the difference approaches but does not quite reach zero; or, in mathematical terms, it asymptotes, or when graphed, is tangent to a curve at infinity.

Data from a test, displayed in Table 2.4, bear out the theory in practice. Notice especially the rightmost column labeled *Difference in Proportions*. As the sample size increases (i.e., the *Sample N* column), the values in the *Difference in Proportions* column decrease, demonstrating the law of large numbers.

Table 2.4
Random Data Illustrating Law of Large Numbers

Observed N Passing	Sample N	Proportion Passing	Known prior for Population	Difference in Proportions
5	10	0.5	0.6	0.1
37	50	0.74	0.6	−0.14
140	250	0.56	0.6	0.04
571	1000	0.571	0.6	0.029
2950	5000	0.59	0.6	0.01

The Law of Averages

Bernoulli trials are also implicit in the law of averages. Readers should appreciate that the law of averages is different from the law of large numbers, although as close cousins it is understandable that one is often confused with the other. A contemporary of Bernoulli, Abraham de Moivre—another extraordinary man working in an age of enormous accomplishment in mathematics (we meet him again in a later chapter)—actually did most of the work on developing the law of averages. This law has two parts: (a) the ratio of two (or x number) certain events (e.g., a coin flip is either heads or not heads) is 50:50, and (b) the probability of an outcome for any event is independent of the probability for any other event. From the previous discussion, readers recognize this as statistical independence in probability theory. Gamblers routinely cite the "law of averages" as justification to continue a losing streak, hoping that "on the average" their luck will soon turn around. Regrettably, each losing (or winning) pull of the slot machine is independent of all other pulls, presuming, of course, that the machine operates only on an approximately random basis. Thus, whether the losing (or winning) streak continues or ends is a random event, but still one that can be mathematically anticipated by probabilities. The law of large numbers tells the gambler that having enough occurrences of slot machine pulls will make it more likely that the observed ratio of wins to losses will differ from the theoretical ratio (which may be known to the house but certainly not to the gambler) by some specified amount. To the gambler's disappointment, it does not inform us exactly when some winning or losing streak will turn around.

The information we garner from the law of averages has use in measurement problems, shown most directly through the central limit theorem.

The Central Limit Theorem

The law of large numbers and the law of averages are consistent with the central limit theorem, a parallel idea and more potent law. At its essence, the central limit theorem states that when a population has a mean (μ) and finite variance (σ^2), successively more samples of independent observations from the population will begin to approach normality, the condition presumed for most populations. The theorem further asserts that when the number of samples is very large, $\overline{X}$ (the mean of a sample) will approximate μ.

One way to grasp the concept of the central limit theorem is to imagine a scenario in which a sample of observations is drawn from a population. Regardless of whether the cases constituting the sample are selected at random, $\overline{X}$ will contain some amount of error and approximates the value of μ only generally. However, when another sample is selected from the same population and a new mean from both samples is calculated, it too will contain error and again only approximate μ, but the theorem specifies that the error will be less and $\overline{X}$ will more closely approximate μ. With each new sample, the error will decrease and the sample $\overline{X}$ will ever more closely approximate μ.

According to the theorem, the effect is derived due to the fact that $\overline{X}$ is calculated from a growing N. Actually, the central limit theorem is true solely because of the sample size and not because of the number of individual samples that can be created. If many small samples are drawn, the effect will not be as accurate as can be derived from fewer but larger samples. In simple terms, the central limit theorem tells us that, in measurement, quantity matters.

As can be imagined, if the sample size is increased sufficiently, the normal distribution is itself a reasonable approximation of the sample mean. This fact is especially significant because the theorem does not stipulate that the population distribution be normal in the first place. In fact, the central limit theorem sets no parameters on the population distribution at all. Its point is simple and elegant—the sample distribution of any number (N) will have a variance of

$$\sigma_x^2/N.$$

The central limit theorem is considered so robust to inspection of assumptions that some researchers consider a sample size of 30 as sufficiently large to estimate reasonably accurate parameters of an unknown population (Hays, 1988).

Proof for the theorem is beyond the scope of this book both in substance and in its technical intricacy. As a commentary on the difficulty of proving the central limit theorem, however, it is interesting to note that the proof was offered only many years after development of the theorem in 1810 by Laplace, and it came in bits and pieces from several mathematicians and statisticians, including Fredrick Gauss, whom we will meet in a later chapter.

Common Psychometric Mathematical Processes

Iteration

Iteration is a concept important to mathematical calculations in many statistical procedures, such as those used in *factor analysis* (FA), and *principal components analysis* (PCA). For psychometric applications, in IRT particularly, proportional fitting and Newton-Raphson calibrations rely on algorithms that use iteration to reach solution. The calculations for such iterative processes are typically complex and tedious and best performed by computers; however, knowing what happens in completing a solution is important to understanding many psychometric methods.

The definition for iteration is well known. It means to repeat, or when used as a noun, iteration is the act of repetition or redundancy. However, how its meaning translates into mathematical algorithms is less understood. Iteration is a circular reference in a formula or set of formulas. That is, information yielded by solving a formula is used as input to repeat the formula so a more accurate solution may be found. This new solution is, in like manner, input for solving the formula again, and so on. With each iteration, the solution grows more precise and stable. Eventually, the solution asymptotes, or approaches some limit that has been selected by the user so the solution is optimized. When this occurs, the problem is said to *resolve* and the iteration stops.

Table 2.5 shows an iterative process for the following two dependent formulas:

$$X = Q + P$$

and

$$Y = .5(X).$$

The problem is to find X such that Y equals exactly one half of X. First, 0 is presented as half of 1,000. Clearly this is not a satisfactory solution, but this information can be useful for recalculating, so it is fed back into the formulas. On the next iteration, 500 is found as the solution to one half of 1,500. This is still not satisfactory, but is a significantly better solution than the previous one. Again, this information is inserted into the formulas. The iterative solutions continue, each time gaining more

Table 2.5
Iterative Values Converging to a Solution

Iteration Number	X	Y	Iteration Number	X	Y
1	1000	0	11	1999.023	999.023
2	1500	500	12	1999.512	999.512
3	1750	750	13	1999.756	999.756
4	1875	875	14	1999.878	999.878
5	1937.5	937.5	15	1999.939	999.939
6	1968.75	968.75	16	1999.969	999.969
7	1984.375	984.375	17	1999.985	999.985
8	1992.188	992.188	18	1999.992	999.992
9	1996.094	996.094	19	1999.996	999.996
10	1998.047	998.047	20	1999.998	999.998
			21	1999.999	999.999

precision in becoming optimized. Finally, a satisfactory solution is reached through iterative cycles.

The values in columns X and Y change as the formulas recalculate in an effort to resolve the circular reference. Of particular importance, observe that the values change less with each iteration; eventually, after enough iteration (in this case, 21), the problem resolves. Here, 999.999 is almost exactly one half of 1999.999, the resolution value for the two equations presented in the previous problem. The exact value for Y to reach one half of X is not realized; however, because the difference between the obtained values from the 20th to the 21st trial is less than 0.001, the iteration is halted. This is as close to an absolute solution as can be attained and still be practicable. Such a resolution is typical in the iterative process.

Most statistical programs limit the number of cycles for the iterative process when it reaches some point of impracticability, such as when the iterative difference is less than 0.001, or when the number of iterations is unreasonable, such as 100. For FA and PCA, a problem typically resolves after about 10 or 15 iterations, with an upper limit usually of 25 iterations. (Programs such as SPSS, Systat, and SAS allow the user to set the maximum number of iterations.) Occasionally, a problem does not resolve even when the maximum limit for iterations is reached. In such cases, the procedure is terminated and the problem is left incomplete. No solution is reached. This can happen when variables are so disparate in their constructs that no common factors or components are extant, or in IRT, when an examinee responds to a set of items in vastly inconsistent ways.

Method of Least Squares

Many measurement specialists routinely employ the family of linear and logistic regressions to solve a variety of measurement problems. Of particular use are regressions, including, most generally, canonical correlations, and more narrowly, univariate and multivariate regression. Such regression procedures are common in studies that seek to establish evidence for validity evaluation.

Most regression procedures relevant to psychometric solutions are based on the *method of least squares*. Hays (1988) allows for the equivalent name *principle of minimum variance*. Regardless of the name used, implied in the nomenclature of the method is a procedure in which squared values from a predicted dependent variable are minimized.

Depicting the procedure graphically affords an easy way to realize the concept of minimum variance. Once comprehended, it is worthwhile to briefly explore how minimum variance works mathematically. Consider the regression problem presented in Figure 2.5. As is well-understood by many readers, the two axes represent scores for two continuous variables, each of which starts at the point of origin and extends the length of the respective scales. Every case in the data set has an observed score on both variables. The points in Figure 2.5 are the intersection, plotted, of each pair of scores for a subject. In nearly every data set there is variability (viz., variance) among the paired scores, and consequently, the plotted pairs of scores for the subjects form a constellation of points, as depicted in Figure 2.5. In statistical terms, the

Figure 2.5
Regression line showing
best-fitting regression line.

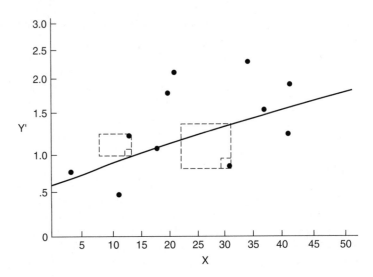

correlation between the variables is less than perfect (viz., $r_{xy} < 1$). (If no error variance existed within the paired scores [i.e., every score on the Y variable was perfectly predicted by its paired score on the X variable], the points would appear
exactly along a straight, 45-degree line, a rare circumstance in real world research.
Or, $r_{xy} = 1$.) The goal in the method of least squares is to draw a straight line that
comes as close to as many of the points in the constellation as possible.

A straight line that is the best regression fit of one variable (Y) on the other (X) is
the line of minimum variance. The regression line is straight because the relationship
between the two variables is presumed to be *linear* for the length of the respective
scales. Researchers verify linearity in their data prior to regression. Obviously, a straight
line cannot represent a curvilinear relationship.

Notice in Figure 2.5 that a vertical line can be drawn from each plotted point to
the regression line. Some of the vertical lines drop down to the regression line (for
the points above the line), whereas others reach up to it (for the points below the
line). If the data are distributed with perfectly symmetric linearity, those points above
the regression line will exactly equal those below the line, in mathematical balance.
Such symmetry is seldom observed in real world data. The distance between each
plotted point and the regression line can be measured. The values for points above
the line will be a positive value, and for those below, a negative value. Like all statistics of distribution about a mean, to avoid values of one sign canceling out those
of the other when they are summed, each of the distance measures is squared. They
are then summed to yield a total variance statistic. When the variance statistic is at a
minimum, the line is said to be the *line of best fit;* hence, it is the "least squares."

Mathematically, this distance is given in Equation 2.12:

$$D_i = Y_i - \hat{Y}_i. \tag{2.12}$$

Realize that two dimensions define the line: its slope and its intersection with
the Y axis (the point at which all X values are zero: the *intercept*). For contrast to

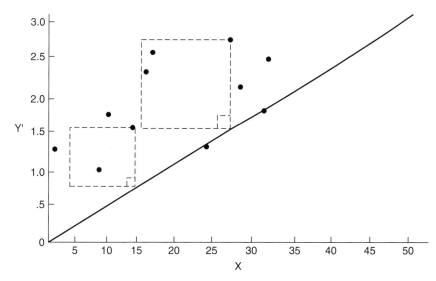

Figure 2.6
Improperly fitting regression line showing exaggerated least squares differences as residuals.

the best-fitting line in Figure 2.5, a misfitting line is depicted for the same data set in Figure 2.6. Observe in Figure 2.6 that the line has a slope and intercept vastly different from that in Figure 2.5. If one were to follow the method of imagining lines from the data points to the misfitting regression line, then measuring the distances and summing them, and finally finding a total, the result would be very different from the value arrived at with the best-fitting line. In the misfitting line of Figure 2.6, the total sums of squares would be higher than those yielded by the line of Figure 2.5, and consequently, the value would not be the minimum variance. The line would not be the best fit for the data, and regressed scores would be in error.

Calculating values for the distance statistic is easily done by extension of Equation 2.12, as exemplified in Equation 2.13:

$$D_i = Y_i - (B_0 + B_1 X_i), \tag{2.13}$$

where B_0 = intercept value,

$\quad\quad\; B_1$ = regression coefficient for the ith variable, and

$\quad\quad\; X_i$ = observed score for the ith case

From the equation, it follows that for a given set of data, the values would be defined as in Equation 2.14:

$$D_1 = Y_1 - (B_0 + B_1 X_1)$$
$$D_2 = Y_2 - (B_0 + B_1 X_2)$$
$$\vdots$$
$$D_n = Y_n - (B_0 + B_1 X_n). \tag{2.14}$$

Accordingly, the sum of the squared deviations is as follows:

$$\sum_{i=1}^{N} D_i^2 = \sum_{i=1}^{N} [Y_i - (B_0 + B_1 X_i)]^2. \tag{2.15}$$

With simple determinants in matrix algebra, the values for the slope and intercept may be calculated, but they are tedious to describe and outside the scope of this book. Such calculations and their proofs (including the relevant Cramer's rule) are given by Marascuillo and Levin (1983) and elsewhere in mathematical statistics texts. The point to understand here is how the values for the distances are calculated such that their sum minimizes variance.

Of course, many popular statistical programs (e.g., SPSS, Systat, SAS, MINITAB, BMDP) calculate the slope, intercept, and other relevant statistics and plot the best-fitting line for a particular data set. A wonderfully instructive program, called *The Geometer's Sketchpad*® (available online at *http://www.keypress.com/sketchpad/*), has a special JavaScript applet for demonstrating the method of least squares. This interactive program is excellent for showing the method in simulated hyperspace on a computer screen.

Maximum Likelihood Estimation

The methods of maximum likelihood estimation of parameters are built from the early work of the renown statistician Sir Ronald Fisher (1912, 1928). Along with the principle of least squares, *maximum likelihood estimation* is a "guessing" model in statistical decision theory. Importantly, it is educated guessing, not wild speculation; in measurement science, we rely on it often. The idea in maximum likelihood estimation is to maximize the chance that the parameters of a model are as close to the final solution as possible. The following example may show the point of maximum likelihood estimation. When a coin is tossed into the air, the likelihood that either side will show when it lands is 50%. After all, there are only two sides to a coin, so the likelihood of the coin landing heads is 50%, just as it is for tails. Already, although perhaps you have not recognized it yet, this simple explanation of a coin toss example shows two prominent features of maximum likelihood estimation. First, there is a known (or assumed) distribution (viz., side one and side two); and second, there are assumptions about the data (viz., if tossed, the coin will come down on just one side). Although these two points seem absurdly simple, they are prominent features in maximum likelihood estimation cases. Consider the next case to see how.

Imagine that the coin is flawed by a nick such that it is slightly heavier on the heads side, and the odds of it landing heavy-side down are 60%. There are now two circumstances: The first in which the freshly minted coin has a .5 probability of landing heads, and the second in which the flawed coin is at .6 probability for heads. The ratio of these two events is .6 to .5 or 12.5, which is called the *maximum likelihood ratio*. Syntactically, this ratio can be expressed as *joint density or frequency function*, as follows in Equation 2.16:

$$f(x_1, x_2, \ldots, x_n | \theta). \tag{2.16}$$

The maximum likelihood estimate is the value of θ that makes the observed data most likely, or most probable. The function is the likelihood of the first occurrence times the likelihood of the second occurrence, and iteratively for n times. Obviously, the occurrences can be more than simple coin tosses. In measurement, they are often item endorsement as correct or incorrect; or, just as commonly, a pattern of item endorsements on a test. In later chapters I show how to employ maximum likelihood estimation in solving measurement problems.

For further introduction to maximum likelihood estimation procedures, Alf and Graf (2002) offer a simple Excel workbook with worksheets for calculating maximum likelihood estimation in some circumstances. Many excellent books on mathematical statistics (Rice, 1995) provide more detailed discussion about this method of approximation.

Algebra of Expectations

The concept of expectancy was introduced earlier in this chapter, and it is easily imagined that the algebra of expectations of random variables plays a prominent place in theoretical statistics. It is closely related to probability theory, often being its operationalization. They are important to mental measurement because they provide a theory on which we can rest our use of random variables as descriptors of real events, like observed test scores. In addition, the algebra of expectations stipulates rules for how variables behave mathematically.

Algebraic Manipulations of Expectations

The manipulations of possible expectations are permitted by a series of algebraic rules, only a few of which are cited here. (For more complete information on the rules for algebraic expectations, see Hays, 1988.) One of the most basic of these rules provides that if a particular number is stipulated (viz., expected) for all observations (hence, it is a constant), then the mean of those expectations would be that number. Equation 2.17 gives this expectation rule:

$$E(a) = a, \qquad\qquad (2.17)$$

where a is some constant number.

Accordingly, if a is a constant real number from a random variable X that is an expected value $[E(X)]$, then Equation 2.18 follows:

$$E(aX) = aE(X). \qquad\qquad (2.18)$$

This equation defines a random variable as extant because each value of X is formed by multiplying it by the constant a. That is, the expectation of a random variable is simply a times the expectation of X. Thus, random variables can exist because we have defined certain stipulations for them (e.g., Equations 2.17 and 2.18, and others described as follows) that can be mathematically proven. The proof for Equation 2.18 is not provided here because it would digress from the point at hand: the introduction of logical and mathematically verifiable equations (see Equations 2.17 and 2.18), which suggest that random variables can be formed and that they have defined properties.

In addition, by the rules of expectation, if a is a constant real number and X is a random variable, then

$$E(X + a) = E(X) + a. \tag{2.19}$$

As before, if X is a random variable with $E(X)$ as expectation and if Y is a random variable with $E(Y)$ as expectation, it follows that an expectation of the sum of two random variables is the sum of their individual expectations, as in

$$E(X + Y) = E(X) + E(Y). \tag{2.20}$$

This rule allows the distribution of expectation over an expression that is itself a sum, a very useful principle. This rule may be extended to cover any number of variables, whether 2 or 2,000. In fact, this rule allows for calculation of the mean and variance of a sample. Now, we realize that values (and variables) are expected because of ordered rules.

Introduction to Algebraic Rules for Probability Density Functions

One of the most significant rules of expectations is the mathematical expectation of a discrete random variable. By convention, this is defined as in Equation 2.21, representing the probability density function. (I discuss these functions in chapters 6 and 7.) Such a function explains dimensional space for a construct:

$$E(X) = \sum_x xp(x), \tag{2.21}$$

where $\sum_x p(x) = 1.00$.

This equation informs us that the expected value (E) of a discrete random variable (X) is the sum of all the different individual values (x) that can be obtained [$p(x)$], assuming the probability for any and all particular values obtained is 1.0. In less technical language, the expression means that we can expect a random variable to be extant when we can sum the individual scores to form a scale. This is important because it renders a variable possible by defining it algebraically. For example, if the expectation is for the mean of a discrete random variable, then

$$\mu_X = E(\mu_X) = \sum_x xp(x_i). \tag{2.22}$$

Or, for the variance, the expression is

$$\sigma_X^2 = E(x - \mu_X)^2 = \sum_x (x_i - \mu_x)^2 p(x_i). \tag{2.23}$$

When the variable is continuous with the probability density function $f(x)$, then methods of calculus are used to evaluate the following integral:

$$E(X) = \int_{-\infty}^{\infty} xf(x)d(x), \tag{2.24}$$

where $\int_{-\infty}^{\infty} f(x)dx = 1$.

At this point, it is not necessary for us to integrate this function; instead, the formula is presented only to show that the probability density function is syntactically defined, yet by calculus.

Response Models Introduced

All displays of measurement theory, or *measurement models*, require an observed "response." The term *response* in this context does not necessarily mean that the examinee completed an answer to a question, prompt, or other stimuli; rather, it means that a class for a variable is defined and can be associated with each examinee. For example, when demographic information is associated with an examinee, such as gender, race, age, religious preference, or other, the data collected are usually nominal levels of measurement. Here, the measurement is identified as the *nominal response model* of measurement. Nominal response models also include assessments in which information is directly supplied by the examinee as long as it is in discrete classes.

In other instances, however, the examinee actually provides a response to the stimulus of the assessment and his or her information is scored according to the rules of the scaling approach used, which could be by classical or IRT measurement theory or other. This is called the *graded response model* of measurement. To qualify as a graded response model, a number of characteristics for the model are required. First, the assessment requires the examinee to offer some kind of self-initiated response to a stimulus, as in writing an essay in response to an essay prompt. Further, the examinee's response must be scored according to some rules, such as points for each graded category. Both nominal response and graded response models are used in modern assessment, and we encounter them at various places throughout this text, most prominently in chapter 10.

Summary

This chapter covers both theoretical and practical knowledge essential to understanding the remaining chapters. I discuss probability theory and laws of distributions. I also explain some common statistical notation, as used in this book and many others. A number of important laws are also described, including the law of large numbers, the law of averages, and most important, the central limit theorem. We move on to discuss the concept of iteration, and two algebraic procedures: least squares and maximum likelihood. These topics conclude with information on expectations. The chapter ends with a brief introduction to response models.

Chapter 3

Classical Test Theory

Introduction

A Real Problem

"Houston, we have a problem." Those words, spoken by Captain Jim Lovell of *Apollo 13* in April 1970, sent dozens of astronauts, engineers, and technicians in the National Aeronautics and Space Administration (NASA) space program on a quest to determine the source of the spacecraft's trouble. Although the problem's severity only became apparent slowly, they realized immediately that the astronauts' safe return to Earth was in jeopardy. An explosion on the outside of the spacecraft had disabled navigation and flight control instruments. Soon, oxygen was seeping through degraded hoses and power was nearly gone. Eventually, the spacecraft's electrical amperage had dropped to a level of power equivalent to that needed for a flashlight—vastly inadequate to guide a spacecraft. In most U.S. cities and across the globe, millions of people stopped their daily routines to listen on transistor radios to updates on the rescue mission. Everyone focused on the problem; nationally the space program was a bright spot in a nation divided over the war in Vietnam. The problem had to be solved—not only to save the lives of the three astronauts, but also to preserve national pride at a time when virtually everyone had genuine confidence in America's innate goodness. Three days later, despite incredible odds, the crew of Apollo splashed down safely in the Atlantic Ocean. At the good news, people literally cheered in the streets and hugged strangers.

Although it lacks the drama of *Apollo 13,* measurement theory also has a single focus for its mission—error-free measurement in appraising mental processes. Similar to NASA's Apollo problem, many of the best minds in the field are focused on the relevant issues. Of course, addressing error in mental measures is unlike the definable NASA problem of bringing astronauts safely back to Earth before their power and oxygen run out. Error in measurement is not a unitary problem that can be isolated and investigated. Rather, error in educational and psychological assessment is an expression about ambiguity and imprecision.

Contents

In this chapter, classical test theory (CTT) is introduced as both a theory in mental measurement and a focal point for psychometric methods. I begin by setting a context for it in both philosophy and psychology. I describe error and categorize its types into random and systematic. Then, I present relevant terms and additional important concepts. This information serves as a foundation on which a solid understanding of the mechanics of the theory can be built. The second half of the chapter is devoted to mathematical expressions of CTT, including its expectations in algebra and the various assumptions that undergird it. The expressions are presented in an order that builds to a complete description of the theory, culminating in its algebraic proof. The chapter contents are foundational to information presented in the remainder of the book and are especially related to information in chapter 5, where I discuss traditional reliability, a crucial aspect of CTT.

Philosophical and Psychological Groundings

Classical test theory is an illative argument in science that suggests a mental construct (viz., trait or proficiency) can be absolutely and perfectly known. Although in practice we never achieve this level of comprehension about a construct, we strive toward such knowledge as a goal. CTT provides a theory and associated psychometric methods to bring our measurement as close to the goal as possible. Further, and more abstractly but just as important, CTT is grounded in ontology, the branch of philosophy that delves into the fundamental nature of truth. First, I briefly examine the CTT argument, then I look at its ontology.

Basic Idea of True Score

The central tenet of CTT is the notion of *true score*. True score is the unbiased estimation of a construct. (I define "construct" momentarily.) Another way to state the same idea is that true score is educational or psychological measurement without error. Because true score is of a mental attribute, we cannot appraise it directly; rather, it must be inferred through examinee responses to appropriately presented stimuli. In the real world, the outcome of mental assessment is the *observed result,* usually expressed as a test score. This *observed score,* then, is the imperfect reflection of true score. With CTT, we seek to understand the discrepancy between the true score and observed score—a distance we call *measurement error*. Most of this chapter is devoted to explaining the meaning of measurement error.

By most methods of CTT, the discrepancy between true and observed score is inferred from repeated appraisals. The theory holds that consistency among a large number of identical testings is an indicator of precision, or *reliability*. Accordingly, CTT is also referred to as a *theory of reliability*. From this simple idea comes a number of important perspectives and varying syntactic expressions of CTT. We examine them throughout the chapter and commence by building the philosophical basis for the theory.

A Philosophical Foundation for Measurement Theory

When developing a theory, it is useful to ground it in philosophy. Measurement theory reflects an ontological philosophy; that is, it moderates an understanding of what is real. (Classical philosophy delineates four main ideas, including ontology. The remaining three ideas are epistemology [i.e., What is true?], axiology [i.e., What is good?], and aesthetics [i.e., What is beautiful?].) The ontological idea is reflected in Plato's allegory of the cave with his two worlds, through which he illustrates mankind's ability to differentiate reality from what is only imagined. So, too, in measurement theory, the quest is to differentiate between what is construed by evidence to be real and what is only conjecturally imagined. The question may be simplistically stated: Can we interpret test data so what we infer to be the status of a given cognitive process is really there?

For measurement, the implication of this particular philosophical question is profound. It means that in today's vision of mental appraisal we are not fundamentally focused on the instruments of appraisal (i.e., tests, performances); rather, attention is directed toward differentiating reality from illusion. Our measurement is of mental processes, and our quest is to discover whether the processes are real or illusory. Simply stated: Are we measuring some real process or trait (e.g., achievement, ability, skill), or is our measurement so illusory that the construct is not there at all, or not clearly focused in our measurement? The instruments come long after the philosophical—ontological—conceit is firmly made.

As one can see, answering this question is foundational to measurement theory because without a clear philosophical basis for mental appraisal, our efforts are worthless. For this reason, from the very beginning of psychology, measurement theory has been based on a firm rationale that has evolved today into mature philosophical conceit. Early on, measurement found its basis in behavioral, trait, and developmental theories, and continued its evolution even until today, when the more sophisticated cognitive psychology predominates. Momentarily, I discuss cognitive psychology, but for now it is important to realize that, as the basis for measurement theory, cognition addresses real—and not illusory—processes, making our theory well grounded. One noted authority put it plainly: "Just as the neural and mental levels of analysis are real, the cognitive level is real" (Best, 1999, p. 9). Test score interpretation makes distinguishable inferences about the reality of cognitive processes.

CTT's grounding in ontology is not simply pleonastic argument. It gives us a firm grounding. By operating from a defined philosophy, assessment can be consistent and uniform in designing, interpreting, and using test results. Measurement professionals can appreciate this foundation as they employ appropriate methods for particular results.

Definition and Concern of Cognitive Psychology

Clearly, mental measurement pertains to cognitive processes. Cognition is psychologists' abstraction of the events taking place at the neural level (Best, 1999). It is the common explanation of thought as having a material grounding in the brain and the nervous system. The classic definition of cognitive psychology is provided by Neisser (1967), who says, "Cognitive psychology refers to all processes by which the sensory input is transformed, reduced, elaborated, stored, recovered, and used" (p. 70).

Working through Neisser's list of (mostly action) verbs is a useful exercise to gain an understanding of the overall concept of cognitive processes. According to Neisser, information (i.e., sensory input) is first *transformed* or changed into a pattern of neurological events, or *neurological energy,* in Neisser's jargon. From there, it is *reduced* or distilled into its essence. In other words, what is vital to the neurological energy is kept, and what is not part of the transformation is forgotten or deleted from memory. Next, the neurological energy is *elaborated* on in an act of mental integration. In this act, the experience is placed into a context with other experiences and phenomena. Here, events are linked to other sources of neurological energy. The brain builds an ever-larger nomothetic net to construct what we know and experience. In doing so, we are creating a new "known." The process continues. The information is encoded in ways that can be *stored* (i.e., not immediately used) and later *recovered*. Recovery does not imply that the sensory experience is duplicated at some later time because by now the neurological energy has gone through transformation, reduction, and elaboration. It is something altogether unrecognizable from its original sensory input. It is part of a larger whole that is itself continually evolving as it creates new knowledge. The functions of storage and recovery are vital to cognition for the information to be real. If it was otherwise, the information could not be *used,* the final act in the cognitive play. The ability to use sensory input in new and novel ways is what comprises mental activity.

If the inference we draw from a test score is of the presence and extent of a particular cognitive process that is, in actuality, not present, we have made an error. This "error" is not a mistake in conventional use of the term, but it is a misapprehension. However, when we infer correctly the presence (and degree) of a cognitive process, then our measurement is meaningful, useful, and appropriate.

Evolution of Measurement Theory from Behavioral to Cognitive Psychology

Individuals familiar with psychological theories realize that cognitive psychology is different from behavioral or trait theory and that it is distinct from developmental theories. As noted in chapter 1, Mislevy (1996) traces this evolution within the measurement field and concludes that its infusion into measurement theory is currently in complete command of measurement thinking. Mislevy's pronouncement is significant, even profound, and we should understand the implication of what he deems factual about modern measurement. Clearly, he is more than merely identifying a trend, although that is also the case. As a leader in the field, Mislevy is placing modern measurement firmly within the cognitive school of thought. This means that interpretations of test scores are not merely a manifestation of behavioral artifacts but reflect innate mental processes—that is, cognitive processes. In other words, with psychological interpretations of mental tests, we acknowledge that we are not just gathering data about behavioral performance, but rather that we are truly looking into the mind of a human! From this perspective, our task is indeed important.

However, despite cognitive psychology's now-dominant position within measurement theory, one should not abandon wholesale other psychological theories that have served their purpose well, including behavioral, trait, and developmental theories. They still play a valuable role in aiding our understanding of psychometric measurement. They are to measurement what Morse code has been to maritime commerce: once preeminent, now secondary, but still useful. In like manner, a host of psychological theories, from past and present, can have an illuminating role in psychometric interpretations.

As is easily imagined, the link between cognitive psychology and measurement theory has a long and rich history. Early on, Spearman (1923) proposed three principles of cognition involved in the measurement of IQ. Later, in a classic article, Cronbach (1957) called for integrating cognitive psychology with psychometrics. We see then that Mislevy's important pronouncement completes a line of thought rather than initiates something new.

Recounting the history of this progression in thinking about mental appraisal would take us afield of our intent; still, it does offer fascinating reading, and there are several sources to which one can turn for information. Sternberg (1990) recounts completely the history of cognitive psychology and measurement theory in his delightfully readable book, *Metaphors of Mind: Conceptions of the Nature of Intelligence*. Another source is a collection of excellent essays, called *Testing and Cognition* (Wittrock & Baker, 1991), that presents a thoroughly modern exploration of the relationship of cognition and testing. More recently, Borsboom, Mellenbergh, and van Heerden (2003) provides an evolutionary tale of latent variable investigation. Many other books are also wonderfully instructive about the relationship of cognitive psychology and test theory.

Perspective on Classical Test Theory

It may also be useful to view CTT from the perspective of a history of the science of measurement. First, one should dispel the notion that classical theory is old or dated. As discussed in chapter 1, mental measurement as a distinct discipline of science is, after all, a comparatively young field of study, dating back to about the mid-19th century. Now, barely more than 150 years later, CTT is still the predominant theory of assessment. This foundational but current perspective is analogous to Shakespeare's writing: done a long time ago, yet contemporary in thought and impact. CTT is as useful to us today as it was in earlier times. The name, classical test theory, probably sticks not only because of past use, but also one hopes in part to show respect for early measurement theorists and practitioners, such as Galton, Binet, Pearson, and especially, Spearman, as well as E. L. Thorndike, Terman, Thurstone, and others.

An allied point—to dispel early on—is that CTT is outmoded by some modern theories of measurement, such as *generalizability theory* (which emphasizes a universe of possible scores) and IRT (which focuses on numeric calibration schemes suited to characterizing test stimuli and examinee responses). Although such modern ideas are decided advances in psychometric thinking and methods, one should realize that they are not in opposition to CTT, nor do they supersede CTT. In fact, their roots are firmly grounded in CTT. A more accurate view of modern theories is to hold that they extend CTT; they do not replace it.

Causes and Types of Error

Probable Causes of Measurement Error

CTT is a theory about error in mental measurement, and measurement error exists because of two conspicuously human characteristics: (a) Our cognitive functioning is labile, that is, readily and continually undergoing chemical, physical, or biological change; and (b) we have yet to produce a perfect (i.e., error-free) assessment device (Figure 3.1). Although these facts are obvious, their implications for CTT require explanation.

Cognition is characterized by a ready tendency toward change. We realize that the brain and neural system are continually in motion. As humans, we evolve, develop, and reshape our achievements, proficiencies, beliefs, attitudes, skills, and abilities. Often, we do this volitionally; after all, change and growth is what education is about. At other times, cognitive changes occur in ways we do not fully comprehend. In addition, altering cognition is idiosyncratic—each of us evolves his or her mental activity in different ways. We have individual responses to new information and fresh experiences. For instance, we do not learn or remember the same things, nor do we learn what we know in the same order or by the same means. In other words, our very lability is idiosyncratic. Although more than 6 billion people live on our planet today, no two possess identical cognition.

The assessment of a labile cognition is further complicated by measurement theory's assumption that examinees display their utmost or typical proficiency (or ability, aptitude, or competence) on every test question or assessment exercise. This notion is termed the *presumption of optimal performance*. We like to believe that

Figure 3.1

Possible factors contributing to error in measurement.

- Lability of cognition
  - Different for everyone
  - Change by differing amounts
  - Possibly implausible presumption of optimal performance
- Imperfect instruments
  - Imperfect representation of construct
  - Unintended and miscommunication in item or exercises
  - Only samples of behavior
  - Snapshot in time; not long-term, unwavering appraisal

people put their best foot forward in testing situations and that each examinee tries his or her hardest to show what they know or to reveal their honest attitudes or beliefs. However, as humans, examinees are not automatons that have a predetermined sequence of operations or that respond predictably to instructions. In fact, people respond to the stimulus of a test question or assessment exercise in a manner that may not support measurement theory's presumption. More accurately, scores on tests are a snapshot of a changing cognition that may or may not express the examinee's optimal performance. All we really know is that an examinee responded in a certain way at a particular time. Regardless, the assumption is made for veracity in the theory.

The second human characteristic that results in measurement error is our inability to produce a perfect appraisal, regardless of means. The instruments we employ for mental assessment are imperfect. We realize that a test's developer cannot interpret a construct with the absolute precision needed for unerring assessment because we do not know constructs with exactitude and because of the lability of the underlying cognitive process discussed previously. Also, an item writer may prepare test items and exercises that imperfectly represent intended constructs, due to problems such as ambiguous wording and unintended implication. (These features are explored more fully in chapters 8, 9, 12, and 13.) In short, our instruments are flawed.

An important, additional component in our less-than-perfect measuring instruments is that they only *sample* limited aspects of a construct. Obviously, it would be impossible to measure the entirety of a cognitive activity, even if we could accurately circumscribe it in a manifestly delimited construct. We cannot, for instance, measure the totality of anyone's reading or computational skills, or the full range of an attitude or sentiment. Our mental measurement instruments only assess a small part of such complex phenomena. Although domain sampling methods do provide a means to fairly represent a construct with just a small sample of test items or exercises, we must infer full meaning from just that limited sample.

Kinds of Measurement Error

It is useful to realize that there are many kinds of error, or stated more precisely, *sources of error*. Generally, sources of error are cataloged as either *random* or *systematic*. Random error is the difference between an individual's true score and observed score, whereas systematic error comprises consistent differences between groups that are unrelated to the construct or the proficiency being assessed. The differentiating aspect of these two kinds of measurement error is the target: Random error applies to an individual, whereas systematic error applies to group responses. Random error is believed to be much more common than systematic error, and its estimation is central to CTT. Systematic error is not considered directly in this theory, although it is in some other theories, generalizability theory in particular. Of course, systematic error can be studied in any measurement context, whether a test is constructed under the precepts of CTT, IRT, or by other means. I discuss random error first and then follow with an explanation of systematic error.

Characteristics of Random Error in Classical Measurement Theory

Classical measurement theory assumes random error exists in everyone's appraisal score. Random error is any event or circumstance that corrupts an examinee's *optimal performance*. The precise cause of random error in an individual's test score is unknown, but in a general sense, we imagine it to stem from environmental distractions, lack of trying (i.e., motivation), anxiety, and so forth. Presumably, this error is different for every individual, in both cause and amount. For some persons, the error may be large and influence their scores in significant ways, and for others, the error could be small and its effects minimal. The theory makes no distinction among individuals with regard to the cause or amount of random error present.

Another important aspect of random error in CTT is that it is considered only in the aggregate, although we realize that it is an individual phenomenon. Just one estimate applies to all examinees at one test, on one occasion. Usually, the error is indicated by the *standard error of measurement* (SEM). In CTT, the SEM is an average of the collective random error of all examinees. I discuss SEM later in the chapter and again in chapter 5.

Further, SEM applies to a specific testing context or test administration. Another group that took the same test—or the same group at another time—would have a different average of their aggregate amount of random error. Hence, this kind of error is expressed as a single index for a particular group on a specific test for a given administration time: SEM. This point has important implications for the way random error is estimated and interpreted. In practice, however, under some sampling conditions and usually for test-norming purposes, the error statistic can be generalized to other individuals in the same population.

Systematic Error in Measurement

Systematic error is altogether different from random error. It presents a special circumstance in which all members of a delineated sample are predisposed to respond to an assessment stimuli in a similar manner. In addition—and central to the notion of systematic error—is that this predisposition is *unrelated* to the construct being assessed. Nearly always, this kind of error is believed to affect scores to the detriment of the sample, although theoretically it could also affect scores positively.

It may be easiest to grasp the notion of systematic error by turning first to the world of hard science and physical measurement. Suppose a just-purchased bathroom scale was bumped on the way home from the store so it did not begin at zero weight, or a compass used on a polar expedition is unduly influenced by solar flares or Earth's magnetism so true north is not indicated, but magnetic north is shown. The bathroom scale and the compass would give inaccurate readings because of influences unrelated to their intended purpose (error), and they would give the inaccurate reading every time they are used (systematic). The consistency of the error is what makes it systematic. The same idea holds for systematic error in educational and psychological measures. Something unrelated to the intended purpose of the appraisal interferes with accuracy of measurement, but it is not random for an individual; rather, it is consistent for the group. These characteristics distinguish systematic error from random error.

A different illustration offers another way to grasp the notion of systematic error. Suppose a group of examinees comprised individuals from two different cultures. The groups are considered distinct subgroups of the examinee population. In this example, the cultural difference is reflected in the treatment of animals, especially dogs. One society considers dogs to be close family members. The dogs are allowed in the house, on the furniture, and often sleep at the foot of the bed (or even on the bed). The dogs are regularly groomed by their doting owners. In stark contrast, however, the other culture considers dogs as "nonfamily." By the mores of this second culture, dogs are meant for work, such as herding sheep or pulling a sled. They sleep outside, or possibly in a barn or doghouse. Although members of this society do not mistreat the animals, they think of them as dirty beasts, useful for work, but not for playing. In this culture, to learn that someone actually allows dogs on the bed where people sleep—well, that is disgusting, indeed! So, now we know how each culture regards dogs.

The examinees from both cultures are given the same reading achievement test. It turns out, in our example, that some of the test questions incidentally describe the treatment of dogs. Remember, this is a test of one's reading ability, not a test about dogs. However, each group's culture will influence the response of any particular individual to the dog-related reading items. Examinees of one culture will respond in one way, and those of the other culture will respond another way, regardless of reading ability. The cultural influence is consistent for all examinees in each group, and is therefore systematic. Because culture is not the construct being assessed by the reading items, the responses for each cultural group will have error. Hence, the error is systematic in this test.

Our dog example is, of course, a contrivance to describe systematic error. In real life, we usually do not know the specific cause (viz., source) of the error. We only have group differences in observed scores. To conjecture about reasons for error from this information alone can be dubious because discussion often reduces to mere guessing based on arbitrary, and even capricious, judgments. Reasons for group differences in performance, in many circumstances, lie in the eye of the beholder and no outside criterion exists to settle differences. With additional information, however, such as a familiarity with the testing context or expert knowledge about some aspect of the examinees, it is possible to make educated speculation about possible causes. However, usually, such discussion is outside measurement contexts. Our interest is in identifying whether a difference exists, judging its degree, and then finding ways to reduce its influence in test scores.

Test Bias and Differential Item Performance

Systematic error can lead to *differential item performance* (DIF), *differential test performance,* or *test bias* (not at all the same things). I begin this discussion by clarifying the terms. Wording and phraseology used in these considerations are sometimes difficult because technical definitions overlap, and they are often misunderstood and incorrectly used, regrettably even by measurement professionals. The meaning of DIF is probably the most tangible among them; hence, I start with it.

DIF is a technical term in measurement science. It describes the circumstance in which empirical evidence, derived using a methodologically based criterion, suggests that a test item or exercise is performing differently for two or more groups. All legitimate procedures for identifying DIF consider the varying ability of the groups (Osterlind, 1983). Also, DIF describes performance on individual items and is not associated with whole tests.

As psychometric argot, DIF is meant to steer attention away from emotionally and politically charged discussion about perceived test fairness (or lack thereof) or consequences of test use in decision making. Mostly, psychometricians that work on practical testing problems of DIF focus their efforts on accurately identifying the phenomenon. Unless the reasons for DIF are obvious, they are usually not explored; instead, when the phenomenon is noted, the items are then either repaired or eliminated. Sometimes, however, it is appropriate to leave DIF-exhibiting items on the test in their current state, depending on other overriding considerations.

As mentioned, an early step in most DIF procedures is an attempt to consider the abilities of individuals within each subgroup studied. That way, the item is examined under conditions similar for both groups. With CTT DIF studies, the subgroups are usually matched by stratifying samples or by some kind of regression. With IRT-based procedures, relevant characteristics can be expressed as common information functions. Only then—after this ability matching—are the subgroups contrasted. Most often, an individual's whole test score is taken as the proxy ability measure from which the matches can be made. Obviously, this is a convenience criterion; however, using it is usually also well justified. After all, it does represent a measure of trait level for the appraised construct. In chapter 12, during discussion of item analysis, I explain several methods useful to DIF investigation.

The next relevant term is *differential test functioning* (DTF), which is an aggregated DIF on a given test. When DTF is identified, there are implications for generalizability. As with DIF, DTF is a technical term used primarily by psychometricians, and imaginably it does not come into ordinary discussion, except rarely.

The final term in this lexicography is *test bias*. Test bias applies to a whole test and is concluded for an instrument only when two criteria are met. First, the conclusion must be based on empirical evidence of DTF (itself coming only from verifiable evidence through a DIF procedure); and, second, it requires an informed, reasoned judgment to explain some possible sources for the systematic error in a particular testing context. Both criteria are needed to make the conclusion. Appreciate, too, that merely noting a difference in test scores between groups is not *ipso facto* evidence of test bias, although a federal circuit court judge in California famously misinterpreted this as being so in a 1970s ruling on identifying special education children (see *Larry P. v. Riles* [1972]; and related issues in *Debra P. v. Turlington* [1981]). The judge's decision has had sweeping consequences that last to today.

Imaginably, then, determining test bias is difficult, and while often inexact it is decidedly not arbitrary. Thus, the careful measurement specialist will conclude bias for a test only when verifiable and empirical evidence supports it. The term is too important to cast about with only haphazard opinions, a reason why the term is fading from use among psychometricians.

Test bias is frequently heard in casual conversation among laypersons. In these nonacademic contexts, test bias seemingly has multiple definitions, most of which are saturated with emotion and have political overtones. Measurement professionals can do much to carefully, precisely, and patiently inform audiences about these terms so that rational discourse may thereby ensure.

For background into the study of test bias as a phenomenon, possibly one of the most quoted books is Jensen's (1980) *Bias in Mental Testing,* a work that is decidedly outdated in its explanations of psychometric methods but still filled with valuable information on test bias as a concept. In it, Jensen explores the notion in depth, from both a measurement and a sociological point of view. Beyond this single source is a library-sized literature on the topic that addresses it from nearly every imaginable point of view.

Essential Terminology: Constructs, Variables, and More

Before we tackle syntactic expressions of CTT, it is useful to have clear and precise understanding of important, relevant terms and ideas. This section describes several of them.

What Are Constructs?

In measurement (indeed, throughout all psychology), cognitive processes are particularized into *constructs*. A construct is a theoretical conception of a cognitive process. For example, if one theorizes neurological activity as directing one to make sense out of standardized markings on a page (i.e., reading letters and words in a book), the act is hypothesized as a *reading construct*. Likewise, a particular feeling about one's self can be hypothesized as a *self-image construct*. Often, in measurement, constructs are referred to as *traits*. Although some purists maintain these terms represent slightly different things, for practical discussion we may use them interchangeably.

Because there is no limit to cognitive processes, there is correspondingly no end to the number or variety of constructs. Nearly any hypothesized conception of a cognitive process can be construed as a construct, whether it is a proficiency, achievement, ability, aptitude, skill, belief, or attitude. No book contains a list of the constructs; instead, psychologists, researchers, and test makers devise constructs as necessary. That is, they formulate boundaries around particular, hypothesized cognitive processes. Once formulated, a cognitive process is put to use, such as in making a test or for other research. Although constructs are formulated by researchers and others on an "as needed" basis, they are not invented spuriously. Rather, they represent the particularization of cognition. It would be a mistake to believe that devising constructs is a capricious effort.

Latency

As we see, constructs are inherently psychological phenomena and hence subliminal. To acknowledge this fact, constructs are more completely described as being latent or embedded within the psyche; hence, we assess *latent constructs*. Measurement specialists often speak of "latent traits." Latency, in this use of the term, means that the constructs underlay the actual attribute to be measured. It does not imply that constructs are dormant or undeveloped, as the term may mean in some other contexts. In fact, we imagine just the opposite for latent constructs: They are both labile and malleable.

As a cognitive activity, assessing latent constructs requires that mental appraisal be linked to a theory (e.g., cognition, behavior, development, learning, memory). Such a relationship has been classically referred to by Cronbach and Meehl (1955) as a latent construct's *nomological net*. The term also implies the idea that linking a construct to a psychology is important for valid test inferences. Often, in empirical verification, this nomothetic link takes the form of a confirmatory model, such as structural equation modeling or other type of *confirmatory factor analysis* (CFA).

As caution, one should not go too far in hypothesizing constructs. They are not to be reified or regarded as an entity that has a life of its own. For instance, there is no IQ apart from theory. Some critics (e.g., Gould, 1981) accuse psychologists, test makers, psychometricians, and others of reifying constructs, the IQ construct in particular. These critics argue that IQ is too illusory to be treated as a nearly organic entity and suggest that users of the IQ concept inappropriately imbue it with properties that are either inflexibly inherited or can be manipulated at will. This criticism reflects a misunderstanding of the fullness and complexity of cognition in psychology (which makes no claim for reifying constructs at all), and it reveals an uninformed view of the basics of tests and measurement. For measurement science, the idea of measuring constructs is crucial to its very foundation. Furthermore, as we have already seen, the notion is solidly grounded in philosophical conceit and practical theory, and is backed by scientific verification.

Measurement of Attributes

We cannot appraise latent traits directly; instead, we assess their *attributes*. It follows from a precise understanding of latent constructs and their inherent dimensionality (see chapter 6) that, because they are not reified, their quantification is of attributes that are theoretically ascribed. As mentioned, there is no physical IQ or personality to which one may apply a measuring instrument. Rather, these aspects of cognition are conceived as theoretical constructs with attributes. Thus, IQ has the attribute of a "general disposition to reason" (or any other definition of IQ), and personality is a collection of relevant attributes, such as extroversion, self-awareness, and the like (or any other definition of personality). We cannot measure directly any construct (whether IQ or personality or whatever) that only exists in theory, but we can measure its attributes. For IQ, we measure a general reasoning attribute, and for personality, we assess the attributes of extroversion, self-awareness, and the like. From this measurement, we infer information about the construct and even the cognitive process.

Most attributes are envisioned as lying along a continuum from infinitely low (or absent) to infinitely high, or bipolar (e.g., from feminine to masculine). Of course, this is just a conception because we cannot measure things infinitely, regardless of

Figure 3.2
Illustrative continuum of an attribute or trait level.

which end of the scale is being addressed. As we know by now, in practice, measurement is along a comparatively small part of the infinite scale. Even within a limited portion of the possible infinite scale, we realize, too, that as measurement approaches the ends of the range being measured, the attribute attenuates. Figure 3.2 shows a representation of the attribute continuum. A hypothetical range of practical measurement within the continuum is also denoted.

Measurement of Variables

In test instruments or appraisal contexts, the attributes of a construct are measured as *variables*. Simply, a variable is the quantification of a given construct as measured by a particular instrument. It is just a descriptive term meaning that a numbering or naming schema (e.g., scale) has been attached to a construct. For instance, the life sciences construct is measured by a given test as a life sciences variable. If one were to discuss theoretically the cognition of life sciences, there is no quantification implied. However, when a particular instrument or measurement vehicle is employed for the purpose of gathering data about this cognitive process, a variable is used.

A variable is *scaled* along either a quantifiable continuum (e.g., from low to high or from preference to avoidance) or a qualitative description (e.g., males and females). It is common in research studies to identify the object of measurement as a construct and the scale used for quantifying the construct as a variable. Thus, a researcher may be inferentially measuring the *reading construct* but report it as the *reading variable*.

Measurement of Ability, Proficiency, or Trait Level

Commonly, measurement professionals and others refer to measuring abilities, implying cognition. Noted Cambridge geneticist J. Carroll exhaustively reviewed studies of cognitive abilities and developed a precise definition of the term. He said,

> Ability refers to the possible variations over individuals in the liminal level of task difficulty (or in derived measurements based on such levels) at which, on any given occasion in which all conditions appear favorable, individuals perform successfully on a defined class of tasks. (Carroll, 1993, p. 8)

Carroll's definition is useful to measurement professionals because it precisely defines the cognitive processes as employed in mental assessment. Included in the definition are many aspects of cognition, such as skills, aptitude, achievement, and proficiency. I use the term *ability* in Carroll's broad sense throughout this text.

However, in many measurement contexts there is a more recent trend to replace the term "ability," as well as many of the subordinate terms (e.g., aptitude, achievement), with *proficiency* or, in IRT contexts, with *trait level*. These alternatives seem a reasonable description for most measured constructs. Note that ability, despite Carroll's supple description of it, is sometimes interpreted as implying a fixed construct, which of course it is not. As is evident throughout the book, I use all these terms.

On occasion, some researchers make a distinction between ability or proficiency assessment and the appraisal of *personality,* maintaining that personality should be considered separately because it is more of a true psychological (and possibly even physiological) phenomenon than ability or proficiency. Although discussion of such distinctions is outside the scope of this text, the work does cover personality appraisal, and readers should be aware of the relevant issues.

Finally, it may be useful to clarify a common misnomer involving variables. Often, novice researchers mistakenly refer to a test instrument as the variable. Even more noticeably, authors of professional journal articles all too often write that a certain test is the (dependent) variable. As readers hopefully recognize, these assignments are incorrect. The object of investigation is the construct, the variable represents the scale along which the construct is assessed, and the test should be properly referred to as the *[dependent] variable measuring instrument.*

Sum for Logic of Constructs to Variables

For our discussion, then, the chain of psychology for psychometrics is thus complete: Neurological energy is conceived of as cognitive processes, which, when particularized in theory, are called constructs. Because constructs are made operational for measurement of their attributes, they assume the name "variable," a scalable entity. There are many terms associated with variables to show their various kinds and to identify pertinent characteristics. (The majority of chapter 7 is devoted to explaining some of these terms.) Last, a test instrument is the vehicle used to capture the data expressed as the variable. This chain for terminology applies to both classical and modern psychometric theory, and exact terms are employed throughout this book. Novice readers are advised to note the important distinctions.

As may be anticipated, there are many resources for learning more about variables. One excellent source of information is the *Journal of Applied Measurement,* a journal that describes its mission as publishing "scholarly work from all disciplines that relates to measurement theory and its application to developing variables" (see "Contributor Information").

Meaning of Parallel Test Terms

In CTT and its application through psychometric procedures, several terms important to the theory are used to describe relationships between tests, especially as applied to reliability appraisal. Almost always, the relationship of interest is stated as being between only two tests, but more than two tests is generally implied as each one leads to next. Some terms that fit here are *randomly parallel tests, τ-equivalent (tau) measures, essentially τ-equivalent measures,* and *congeneric tests.* In a gross conceptual sense, these terms are near synonyms expressing the idea given by CTT theorist Gulliksen (1950) that ". . . it makes no difference which test you use" (p. 11). However, the context for using each term differs and technical distinctions separate them.

Randomly parallel tests is an original idea in CTT, meaning that from among a large number of measures, any two (or more) of them chosen at random would have predictable, stipulated characteristics. First, they must appraise the same construct and assess it equally well in a given context. Second, they are independent measures, implying that the tests neither depend on one another nor would responses to any given stimuli (e.g., item, exercise) on one test in any way influence one's responses on the other test. This independence assumption applies not only across tests, but also within tests. In other words, an endorsement of a particular response to the third item is not contingent on a correct response to the second (or any other) item. Possibly the most restrictive stipulation for randomly parallel tests is that the means and error variances must be equal.

Imaginably, meeting technical requirements for randomly parallel tests is indeed challenging because it is difficult to know if they have been satisfied. A statistical test of parallelism was devised by Vatow (1948); however, the concept of a randomly parallel test is useful only for theory building in CTT.

The next term is *tau equivalent.* Tau- (τ)-equivalent measures meet all the considerations of randomly parallel tests, except that the error variance of the measures do not need to be identical (Lord & Novick, 1963). However, in CTT, because error is itself a random variable considered as an average over all persons taking the test, observed scores can fluctuate. Still, because such fluctuation is only random error and presumed to be symmetric for the population, the test means will not differ. This term is often employed during discussion of true score because it implies population parameters.

Following these measures is a closely related term for *essentially τ-equivalent measures.* Essentially τ-equivalent measures relax the stipulations still further, in that here the means can also vary. Still, such tests are characterized by a uniform linear relationship. In other words, for any examinee, regardless of position on the score scale, an equivalent score on the parallel test will differ only by a constant. If, for instance, the constant between tests is 3 points, any examinee's score on one test could be expressed on the essentially τ-equivalent measure by either adding or subtracting 3 points.

The final term in this list is *congeneric,* a term used frequently throughout this text. Readers may also encounter this term in other sources during discussion of test theory. The term was apparently first used by Jöreskog (1971), and its use in technical test literature is growing. It does not mean that independent tests are truly equal, nor is strict equivalence between them implied. Rather, for tests to be congeneric, two specific measurement conditions must exist. The first condition is that the scores between tests are characterized by a uniform linear relationship, as described for essentially τ-equivalent measures. The second condition was stipulated by Angoff (1971), who maintained that the error variances of each test must follow the precepts of CTT; that is, they are random and symmetric for the population.

Congenericity is the intersection of these two conditions. Only when both notions are satisfied are tests congeneric. Most authors (e.g., Feldt & Brennan, 1989) maintain that congeneric is the most open (least restrictive) of all these terms, while still preserving Gullicksen's original notion that it does not matter which test you use.

Test Components and Item Invariance

A few more pieces to our puzzle of CTT are tests as linear composites and item invariance.

Components of Composite Measurement

Probably the most recognizable syntactic characteristic of CTT is its reliance on linear combinations of scores. Practically, this means that items on a test can be combined, usually in additive fashion, to form an aggregate test score appraising a single construct. Further, following the rule of additivity, item responses need not just be summed; rather, various combinations are also allowed, as long as a positive relationship among all the items is consistent. Measures with such characteristics are referred to as *composite tests* or *composite measurements* or as measures that yield *composite scores*. Most often, the tests referred to in this text, as well as in other similar measurement books and articles, are composite measures. Some authors even prefer the term "composite measures" over the more generic "tests" because it directs attention to characteristics of individual items, the real heart of a measure.

Item Invariance

Also, as composite measures, CTT-based instruments are *item invariant*. This means that a given appraisal is built on specified characteristics for its items or exercises (e.g., their format or particular statistical properties, such as difficulty and discrimination). If the item characteristics change (e.g., the number of items on a test is changed or their difficulty is altered by modifying wording), the test is no longer the same instrument and the new appraisal will have its own characteristics. This is true even if two tests share large numbers of the items. For instance, two test forms (which may or may not share many items) are still two different tests, and their equivalence must be empirically established. Each test is item invariant, even those that are randomly parallel. Item invariance is a fundamental feature of tests built on CTT precepts.

Syntactic Explanation

Although the picture starting to form of CCT is gaining focus, it is not yet complete. A mathematical description is needed to put the ideas into use with practical testing problems.

Expectancy of True Score

In the classical theory of tests, true score is denoted syntactically with τ. For any particular examinee on a given variable, the true score is designed as τ_{ij}. I use τ several times in the ensuing discussion because it is essential to the theory, and I define it completely later in the chapter.

As readers undoubtedly realize by now, were we to know τ_{ij} mental measurement would be an exact science! Unfortunately, we do not know τ_{ij} so we must estimate it working from a theory and with data of an observed score, x_{ij}. Recall that in chapter 2 the notion of expectancy, E, was explained, and that information can be used here to assist with the problem of estimating τ_{ij}

By probability theory, we have x_{ij} as an expected score. That the expectation exists at all is an unproven assumption (Gulliksen, 1950), and therefore, is an inherently enervated basis for a theory involving both mathematical and psychological interpretations. Nonetheless, it provides important information to start building a mathematical model of true score.

True score can be syntactically defined as the expected value of the observed score for the variable X. Equation 3.1 shows this expectation for a given individual:

$$\tau_{ij} = EX_{ij}. \tag{3.1}$$

From Equation 3.1, it is clear that the true score and an expected observed score are without reference to error. However, by incorporating discussion from earlier sections of this chapter with some necessary assumptions presented in the following section, it will become apparent that error is present in all practical realizations of observed score. Therefore, the observed score may be expressed as the combination of true score and error. This relationship is stated in Equation 3.2 and its alternate, Equation 3.3:

$$X_{ij} = \tau_{ij} + \varepsilon, \tag{3.2}$$

where τ = true score,

$\quad\quad X$ = observed score, and

$\quad\quad \varepsilon$ = error.

Alternatively,

$$\varepsilon = X_{ij} - \tau_{ij}. \tag{3.3}$$

Equation 3.2 reads that for a given examinee the observed score on the random variable is the sum of an individual's true score plus random error. By rearrangement of terms, as in Equation 3.3, error is the difference between observed score and true score. Note that the subscripts are omitted from the error term because in classical theory the error term is universal (i.e., the same for all persons in a population irrespective of which variable is considered). Remember, τ is the expected value for X in the structural model, and hence, it is constant for the population at any given point. This equation is central to classical measurement theory.

One final point about Equation 3.3 is to be mindful of its notation. Here, and elsewhere in theoretical discussion of expectations, τ is used to represent true score.

Later, however, in practical application, *T* is employed to show true score. Both symbols represent true score. The different notation is accounted for as we move from the theoretical algebra of expectations given here to practical measurement problems discussed in subsequent chapters.

Practical Description of True Score

Because we cannot know anyone's true score, a practical explanation of the concept has come into common use. By this explanation, true score is defined as the average score an examinee would achieve in an infinite number of administrations of randomly parallel tests, given the presumptions described previously. The collection of scores is called one's *universe of scores*. In some modern assessment contexts, the true score is often referred to as a mean of the universe of all scores, or simply *universe score*. In CTT, however, it is most often still called "true score."

A scenario of the event of the true score is easy to imagine, although it could never happen in real life. Suppose a tolerant individual is willing to submit to take many administrations of the same test or of randomly parallel tests (assuming they exist). Moreover, imagine this person has the superhuman capacity to take each test without regard to any previous test administration (i.e., no effect from practice or fatigue, although random error still exists for any particular administration). Importantly, the examinee is unchanged by any trial so each appraisal is independent—an exact duplicate of the previous appraisals. The scores yielded by this exercise could form a distribution of scores with all the characteristics of any standard normal distribution. The mean of this universal distribution is considered the person's true score. Although this scenario may be humorous to visualize, it is important to the theory.

The notion of an estimable mean from a universe of scores can be conceptualized by imagining a distribution of the scores that our indulgent individual would have likely achieved over time, such as is presented in Figure 3.3. Note particularly that the distribution is normal in shape and that the middle value (mean) is also τ because it is hypothesized for the theory.

There is a special complication in this scenario that is germane to our discussion of estimating true score, called *the limit of an average*. This notion conveys the idea

Figure 3.3
Hypothetical distribution of scores for one individual after many administrations of congeneric tests.

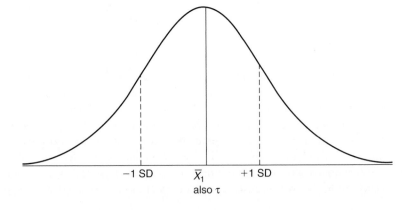

$-1\ \text{SD}$ $\overline{X}_1$ $+1\ \text{SD}$
also τ

that our repeated appraisal of the individual's construct is not as distinct as may have been originally imagined. Not one average applies to all circumstances. For true score estimation in CTT, we have defined the measures as randomly parallel, the numerous administrations as identical and independent, and the examinee as inhumanly stable. However, in real world assessment experiences, none of these conditions exist. So, one asks, what can be different between the appraisals? Are the tests different? the administration circumstances? the examinees? It is apparent that because conditions are allowed to vary (e.g., the tests are of slightly different difficulty, or the number of administrations varies between examinees, some have more or fewer occasions), the true score will have significant differences in perspective or definition. Accordingly, we move from randomly parallel tests to τ-equivalent measures and even to the more relaxed essentially τ-equivalent measures. The importance of this realization is that reliability as an indication of a measure's stability of measurement is not inflexible, but can vary, depending on the perspective on true score. Thus, many kinds of reliabilities are possible, one for each defined set of circumstances. Still, to have varying perspectives on true score is a strength to the theory because through it we can then estimate reliability in a manner appropriate to a particular set of conditions. We see this point directly when we contrast CTT with generalizability theory estimation for reliability in later chapters.

Assumptions

To grasp the full CTT, it is necessary to realize a number of assumptions that undergird it. These are discussed in the following sections.

The Logical Assumption of Error

CTT assumes that a true score exists, that it differs from the observed score, and that the difference between them is measurement error. Gulliksen (1950) explains this formulation as follows:

> The [classical, true-score theory] equation may be regarded as an *assumption* that states the relationship between true and error score; or it may be regarded as an equation defining what we are going to mean by error. In other words, once we accept the concept of a true score existing that differs from the observed score, we then say that the difference between these two scores is going to be called error. (p. 5)

Accepting this basic assumption is a rational or heuristic decision, not a statistical one. There is no mathematical proof for it, although many other stochastic processes involved in CTT do have proofs. Yet overall, the basic tenet of classical measurement theory, as articulated by Gulliksen, and many other theorists since his time, seems reasonable when gauged against a general theory of psychology or when viewed from the perspective of our real world observations of test results. We know that people cannot always exhibit maximal effort and that extraneous factors (e.g., practice, fatigue, distractions) do creep into examinee responses, resulting in depressed observed scores (error). In addition, the notion of expectancy, mentioned previously for true score and described more fully in algebraic terms in chapter 2, provides mortar for cementing the argument for measurement error. Once assent is given to this assumption, the theory can be extended both logically and syntactically.

Syntactic Rationale of the Assumption of Error

The first logical extension for CTT beyond allowing error extant is that the correlation between true score and error score is zero, shown as a zero correlation between the two variables in Equation 3.4. In other words, error is independent of true score, and vice versa:

$$\rho_{\tau\varepsilon} = 0. \tag{3.4}$$

This equation is an assumption, yet it is itself another definition of true score. It is especially important to the theory because it provides a basis for knowing that true score is without error. Hence, the notions correlate only randomly, that is, not at all in any systematic or predictable way.

The rationale for Equation 3.4 is shown in Equations 3.5 and 3.6. As may be anticipated, the logic again recalls expectancy theory. Two pieces of information are needed to fit together. First, it was shown that true score can be syntactically defined as the expected value of the observed score for the variable (see Equation 3.1) and is therefore a constant on the random variable X. Second, the expected error score is itself zero, as shown in Equation 3.5:

$$E\varepsilon = 0. \tag{3.5}$$

Because a constant on a variable correlates with zero randomly, the expected error reduces in true score to zero. This relation is shown in Equation 3.6. Note this equation carefully because it defines a basic rationale for the theory:

$$E\varepsilon = E(X_{ij} - \tau_{ij}) = \tau_{ij} - \tau_{ij} = 0. \tag{3.6}$$

Given that the assumption and definition of Equation 3.4 is correct (viz., true score and error are mathematically unrelated) and the expectation in Equation 3.6 is accurate, it follows that covariance between the variables of error score and true score is also zero, a point illustrated in Equation 3.7:

$$\sigma_{\tau\varepsilon} = 0. \tag{3.7}$$

This point is important to grasp because one would not normally expect a correlation (see Equation 3.4) and a covariance (see Equation 3.6) between random variables to be identical. However, because both are zero in CTT conception, they are identical. The outcome also leads us to the next assumption.

The Independence Assumption

Another important assumption in measurement theory springs from the relationship, or more technically, the absence of correlational relationship, between universe score and error seen in Equation 3.7—the *assumption of independence*. Because not only is error extant, but it also relates only randomly to τ. Hence, τ and error are truly independent. This independence assumption is also central to the structural model of CTT.

The Reliability Assumption

Because, as we see by now, universe score and random error are two separate variables, they can be employed in unique ways to make further calculations of interest. One of the most noteworthy ideas to come out of the relationship between true score and random error is reliability. Much of what is described in this section builds the foundation for establishing a *reliability index* (often expressed in practical testing contexts as a *reliability coefficient*), as well as another important indicator of reliability, SEM. For now, a useful definition of reliability is the *assessment of error in measurement*. Later in this chapter, the term is defined with greater precision and is accompanied by mathematical proof. And, we return to the SEM in chapter 5, as well as elsewhere. Chapter 5 is devoted to a thorough discussion of reliability in CTT, and chapter 11 to modern reliability analysis with generalizability theory.

Parallel Tests Assumption

One further assumption is specified. This assumption concerns *parallel tests,* as described previously. Such tests are of course also τ-equivalent, or in practice, *essentially τ-equivalent*. When congeneric criteria are completely satisfied, an examinee who takes parallel tests will have identical universe scores because no correlation exists between true score and error (see Equation 3.5), and the covariance for these variables is also zero (see Equation 3.7). Essentially τ-equivalent tests can exhibit slight variation in observed mean and variance scores, but not so much that practical effects result.

An alternate route to express equal reliabilities for genuinely randomly parallel (viz., τ-equivalent) tests states that they have equal means and absolute error variances. This being the case, then for $T_{i_1} = T_{i_2}$ to be true (in which T is the universe score derived from an observed score), it must also be true that $\sigma_{\varepsilon_1}^2 = \sigma_{\varepsilon_2}^2$. In fact, when this is the case, the expected values are the same, as shown in Equation 3.8:

$$E(X_j) = E(X_k). \tag{3.8}$$

Such separate and distinct measures are in fact *τ-equivalent,* a relationship shown in Equation 3.9:

$$\tau_{ij} = \tau_{ik}. \tag{3.9}$$

Based on this definition of parallel tests, it follows that for these tests the errors are uncorrelated (again, assuming perfect or absolutely equal reliability for each test). That is, the random error in the first test is independent of the random error for the second test. Equation 3.10 shows this relationship on parallel tests in correlational terms:

$$\rho_{\varepsilon_1\varepsilon_2} = 0. \tag{3.10}$$

Equation 3.10 plays an important part in CTT because when the errors for parallel tests are unrelated, a number of important calculations are permitted. In particular, this independence helps with estimating error for either test. Because of this, the idea in Equation 3.10 is employed in developing the reliability coefficient.

Assumption of Mean of Errors

Finally, a last assumption of CTT is that with a sufficiently large number of examinees, the mean error on a test will be zero because the errors are individually assumed to be random, that is, independent and symmetric. One way to realize this assumption is to visualize a regression line with errors on the positive side of a distribution of all errors canceling errors on the negative side, and vice versa. As a consequence, the mean of such errors is zero. The assumption then implies a least squares solution to proving errors. Such a regression is shown in Figure 3.4 for a

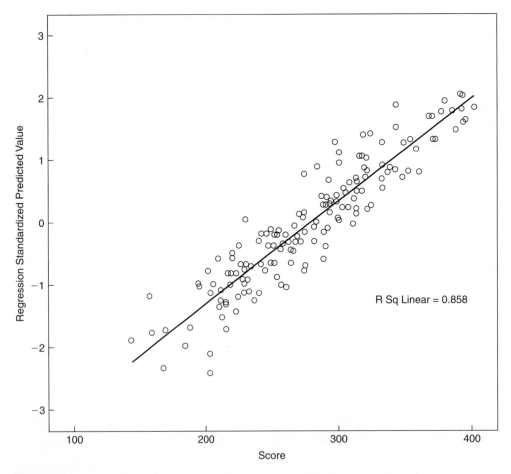

Figure 3.4
Scatter plot of scores showing randomness of errors.

large number of scores from an appraisal of English on a test that ranges from 100 to 500 points. In Figure 3.4, a scatter plot of scores has hypothesized true scores (labeled *Standardized Predicted Value*) regressed onto the observed scores. Notice in Figure 3.4 that the errors are randomly distributed about the regression line, and thus, are approximately linear throughout the range of the scale and heteroscedastic. By this assumption, the mean of these randomly distributed errors approaches in the limit, zero, a least squares solution. Do not forget that this description applies to theory, and any practical application will fall under conditions in the limit of the average described previously.

This final assumption may be written as in Equation 3.11:

$$\mu_{\varepsilon} = 0. \tag{3.11}$$

Notice in Equation 3.11 that because this is an assumption, the equal sign is employed to express the relationship rather than the limit approach equals symbol ($\cong$). This implies that for the assumption to be empirically verified, there is a sufficient number of scores available for the central limit theorem to effectively be zero, regardless of whether the scores result from repeated measures of the same individual or from distinct scores from a sufficiently large sample of examinees.

The assumption that the mean of all error is zero (or at least approaches zero in the limit) substantiates the true score formula of CTT (see Equation 3.2), because without this the expected value for an observed score could not be the universe score (see Equation 3.1), and the expected error term would not be zero (see Equation 3.5). Fortunately for the theory, they are as described.

Conclusions and Comments on Assumptions

From this point on, much of our development of CTT works with scores that are expressed as deviations from the mean. Thus, it is vital to have a clear understanding of the preceding assumptions. They are summarized in Figure 3.5.

As a last note to these assumptions, it may be useful to remind oneself that although the current discussion is focused on classical measurement theory, the assumptions also pertain to IRT and generalizability theory (G theory), both considered to be modern theories. The modern theories do adopt additional assumptions specific

---

1. The expected score is true score (τ), zero on a scale.
2. The correlation between true (universe) score and error score is zero on a scale.
3. The correlation between error score on one measure and true score on another parallel measure is zero on a scale.
4. The correlation between errors on distinct measures is zero on a scale.
5. The expected mean (average) error on a test is zero on a scale.

Figure 3.5
Essential assumptions of classical test theory.

to their purposes, and those particular assumptions are addressed during discussion of the modern measurement models.

With our understanding of these assumptions, both logical and statistical, firmly in place, we can now develop the basic equations of random error in classical measurement theory. It is to these basic equations of homogeneous tests of variable length that we now turn our attention.

Basic Equations

Syntactic Description of True Score Theory

From the assumptions for CTT described, several useful equations about random error can be derived. An especially important equation is used to determine the universe score for a group of examinees. We begin consideration of this critical equation by first remembering the fact that for a sample of examinees randomly drawn from a comparatively homogeneous population, any given individual may be selected. Thus, it is apparent that expressions apply not only to the population, but also to any individual (with appropriate changes in notation). This point is important because it reminds us that CTT applies to an individual as well as to aggregate scores from groups.

A linear model for the basic relationship between true score and error given in Equations 3.2 and 3.3 (given earlier in the algebra of universe scores in the structural model) may be expressed for observed scores as shown in Equation 3.12, read as "Observed score equals universe score plus error":

$$X_i = T_i + \varepsilon \tag{3.12}$$

and its alternate Equation 3.13:

$$T_i = X_i - \varepsilon. \tag{3.13}$$

In these equations, the τ used earlier to represent true score is replaced by T to signify that this score does not represent a population parameter but applies to individuals or to groups of particular persons. I talk more about this feature of the theory momentarily. First, however, a note about the importance of the idea expressed in Equations 3.12 and 3.13.

For mental measurement, whether girded by classical or modern test theory, it is difficult to overstate the importance of Equations 3.12 and 3.13. Quite simply, the formulas comprise the core of measurement theory, and the idea is foundational to all that flows from CTT. As Homer, Proust, and Joyce were each seminal to their respective eras of writing (the classical age, the romantic period, and 20th-century experimentalism), so, too, is the formula for true score decisive to the ages of measurement, regardless of whether classical or modern. Its simplicity and elegance both defines the theory and sets it on solid practical ground. Do not be deceived by its apparent simplicity. Such is its strength that, although direct and elegant, it allows development of a complex and complete theory of measurement, itself psychology's most important contribution to science (noted in chapter 1). Much of the remainder of this chapter is devoted to the explication of this basic relationship between error and true score, and I return to the basic formula often throughout the book.

Elaboration of the Classical True (Universe) Score Formula

Our attention is now turned to the error term in CTT, which is the focus of Equations 3.14 and 3.15. One thing to notice in these equations is that the error term (viz., ε) continues to be defined for the population because, in CTT, it is not sample specific. However, the other terms are sample specific. Accordingly, because the equations themselves are for a sample, observed scores can be summed for the random test variable. Summing scores for both sides of Equation 3.13 yields Equation 3.14:

$$\sum_{i=1}^{N} T_i = \sum_{i=1}^{N} (X_i - \varepsilon), \qquad (3.14)$$

which simplifies to Equation 3.15:

$$\sum T = \sum X - \sum \varepsilon. \qquad (3.15)$$

As a summed variable, it is useful to calculate the mean. Recall from the discussion of the expectation of random variables in chapter 2 that the mean can be calculated from summed expected values, the case that led us to Equation 3.15. To arrive at such a result, simply divide each term of Equation 3.15 by n, which produces the result shown in Equation 3.16. Observe, too, that the variables in the equation are for a sample, but the grand mean is for the population, indicating that this model holds for all samples from a (normally distributed) population:

$$\overline{X}_T = \overline{X}_X - \mu_\varepsilon. \qquad (3.16)$$

It was explained earlier that, by assumption in CTT, the mean of random error is zero (see Equation 3.11). Accordingly, the last term of Equation 3.16 drops off, producing the final remarkable statement, shown in Equation 3.17. The mean of true scores equals the mean of the observed scores:

$$\overline{X}_T = \overline{X}_X. \qquad (3.17)$$

This conclusion has profound implication for measurement theory. First, it allows us to interpret an individual's average score from many test occasions (each item can be considered a testing occasion) from just the single administration of a test. (Also, we can avoid the dreadful exercise of asking the examinee to take the test an infinite number of times to get the "truly" accurate score!) Second, the deduction can be extended to include the relationship between universe score variance and error variance. We explore this relationship next.

Before moving on, however, it is useful to note another point, one sometimes misunderstood by persons new to measurement science. This point is that it may appear to the novice that Equation 3.17 solves our dilemma of how to discover someone's universe score: Simply take the observed score as a proxy for universe score. Such an interpretation, however, is not correct. First, notice that the relationship in the formula is for test means of a sample from a population, not for individuals. This point is crucial, but even so, it does not explain fully why the interpretation cannot be applied to discovering any given individual's universe score. As a second point, realize that Equation 3.18 applies to tests of infinite length only. We saw earlier that the central limit theorem defines a relationship between samples and populations, and that the theorem applies to a population comprising groups of individuals and not any specific individual. Occasions of measurement will operate exactly the same. Hence, test length has a great deal to do with the veracity of applying Equation 3.17 to specific situations. I explore this feature for CTT in chapter 5 during discussion of reliability evaluation.

Determining the Relationship Between Universe Score Variance and Error

Now we are ready to explore the relationship between universe score variance and error score variance. Begin by considering the standard deviation of each term in the basic CTT equation (see Equations 3.2 and 3.12). Combining Equation 3.11, the classic universe score equation, and Equation 3.17 shows the new relationship, which may be written as shown in Equation 3.18:

$$X_i - \overline{X}_X = (T_i - \overline{X}_T) + (\varepsilon - \mu_\varepsilon). \qquad (3.18)$$

Recall from elementary statistics the computation for deviation scores $(X_i - \overline{X}_X)$, and notice in Equation 3.18 that the terms on each side of the equation represent just such deviation scores. This should not be surprising, given the earlier assumptions. For simplicity, Equation 3.18 is customarily rewritten using x to represent the observed score deviation (the left side of the equation) and t to represent universe score deviation, and then error deviation (the right side of the equation). Substituting these deviation terms into Equation 3.18 yields Equation 3.19:

$$x = t + \varepsilon. \qquad (3.19)$$

Once again, it is relevant that the mean of error scores is zero (see Equation 3.11) because it implies that, logically, error score deviation must equal e, as shown in Equation 3.20,

$$\varepsilon = e, \qquad (3.20)$$

so Equation 3.19 holds.

Continuing normal procedures toward the standard deviation and variance, the next step is to square and sum values for the terms, yielding Equation 3.21:

$$\sum x^2 = \sum (t + e)^2. \qquad (3.21)$$

Sensibly, expand the right term to produce a normal quadratic expression, as shown in Equation 3.22:

$$\sum x^2 = \sum t^2 + \sum e^2 + 2\sum te. \qquad (3.22)$$

Next, divide both sides of the equation by N of the data set to produce measures of variance for the terms, as shown in the calculations in Equation 3.23. (Note: df is not relevant here.) The calculations for this division are given first for the left side of the equation and then for the two terms on the right side:

$$\frac{\sum (X_i - \overline{X}_X)^2}{N} = \frac{\sum x^2}{N} = \hat{\sigma}_X^2$$

$$\frac{\sum (T_i - \overline{X}_T)^2}{N} = \frac{\sum t^2}{N} = \hat{\sigma}_T^2 \qquad \textbf{(3.23)}$$

$$\frac{\sum (\varepsilon - \mu_\varepsilon)^2}{N} = \frac{\sum e^2}{N} = \hat{\sigma}_\varepsilon^2.$$

The result of these calculations is shown in Equation 3.24:

$$\hat{\sigma}_X^2 = \hat{\sigma}_T^2 + \hat{\sigma}_\varepsilon^2 + \hat{\sigma}_T \hat{\sigma}_\varepsilon 2\rho_{T\varepsilon}. \qquad \textbf{(3.24)}$$

Notice that the last term is a correlation between true score and error score. Because we know by now that the correlation between universe score and error score is zero, this term drops off. Equation 3.25 shows the final relationship, expressed for the population:

$$\sigma_X^2 = \sigma_T^2 + \sigma_\varepsilon^2. \qquad \textbf{(3.25)}$$

Through this logic, it can be seen that the variance of observed scores is equal to the sum of the universe score variance and the error variance. Notice, too, that although the process requires several steps, the derivation of Equation 3.25 is from the basic classical measurement theory formula (see Equations 3.2 and 3.3) and the universe error correlation formula (see Equation 3.4).

The practical significance of this equation is that when error variance (the final term in Equation 3.25) is reduced, the observed score variance more closely approximates the universe score variance, thereby improving a measure. If the error variance could approach zero or be eliminated completely, our test would be nearly perfect, or even absolutely perfect, producing perfect reliability (1.00). In large part, the work of psychometric methods is to reduce the final term of Equation 3.25, random error variance, to nudge reliability as close to 1.00 as possible.

A Small-Sample Example

Because Equation 3.25 is true, it follows that its expression in standard deviation units is also true, as shown in Equation 3.26. This form allows one to construct a table of variance values for a small test (see Table 3.1) to illustrate the relationship between universe score variance and error variance. Because in practice this is applied to a given test, I use standard deviation units. (One may recall this equation from elementary geometry: It is the Pythagorean theorem, which was first introduced more than 2,000 years ago in the Tigris-Euphrates Valley. Indeed, the foundations of measurement theory are time tested!)

$$\sigma_X = \sqrt{\sigma_T^2 + \sigma_\varepsilon^2}. \qquad \textbf{(3.26)}$$

Table 3.1
Observed Score Variance for a Hypothetical Test

Error Variance Values	True Score Variance Values									
0	**1**	**2**	**3**	**4**	**5**	**6**	**7**	**8**	**9**	**10**
1	1.41									
2	2.24	2.83								
3	3.16	3.61	4.24							
4	4.12	4.47	5	5.66						
5	5.10	5.39	5.83	6.40	7.07					
6	6.08	6.32	6.71	7.21	7.81	8.49				
7	7.07	7.28	7.62	8.06	8.60	9.22	9.90			
8	8.06	8.25	8.54	8.94	9.43	10	10.63	11.31		
9	9.06	9.22	9.49	9.85	10.30	10.82	11.40	12.04	12.73	
10	10.05	10.20	10.44	10.77	11.18	11.66	12.21	12.81	13.45	14.14

For the small, 10-item test in Table 3.1, consider the instance in which the standard deviation (the columns on the horizontal axis) is 3 and the error standard deviation (the rows on the vertical axis) is 4. As is illustrated, the observed score standard deviation is 5. Notice, particularly, that the values increase as one moves in the table from upper left to lower right, which is consistent with the theory: As error variance increases, so too do universe score variances. Of course, the reverse holds true, too. Often, psychometricians want to investigate this relationship when constructing a test, as well as when evaluating validity in a particular testing context.

Relationship of Variances

One additional variance consideration is appropriate at this point. It is an extension of the expression of the relationship between error variance and universe variance given in Equation 3.25. By definition, the square of the correlation between observed scores and true scores equals the ratio of true score variance to observed score variance. Equation 3.27 gives this relation:

$$\rho^2_{XT} = \sigma^2_T / \sigma^2_X. \tag{3.27}$$

This relation is called the *coefficient of determination,* and it is an index of reliability, or measurement error. Notice that the index is a ratio. As such, it permits advanced exploration of correlational relationships by studying variance ratios, or more familiarly, analysis of variance. Further, this brings the regression of observed score on universe score squarely in line with explorations of the general linear model, especially as a least squares estimate of a population mean. Thus, the relationship is very useful in advanced explorations of measurement theory.

I discuss this important ratio in much greater detail in chapter 5, under the Reliability section.

Standard Error of Measurement

At this point in a presentation of CTT, it is necessary to discuss reliability assessment more directly, and to specifically delve further into the deep meaning of measurement error variance. Because CTT is fundamentally a theory of reliability, this information is basic. However, it is precursory to later and more advanced discussions of reliability in chapters 5 and 11.

In the previous equations, the variance due to error is identified from several perspectives as the *error variance term*. When the focus of attention is on this expression of error exclusively, another name—SEM—is more commonly employed to describe the phenomenon it represents. SEM is one of two principal components in reliability; the reliability index being the other. A basic equation of CTT is one that defines SEM. I begin discussion of SEM with some necessary background into its meaning. I then turn to the formula for calculation.

Logical and Graphical Description of Standard Error

Recall that true score is conceptualized in CTT as the mean score obtained from an infinite number of test administrations of randomly parallel tests and assuming identical administrations. Also, we considered the scores seeded by the infinite test administrations to represent an individual's universe of scores or all scorings that could likely be obtained. Such a theoretical universe of scores for three individuals is shown in Figure 3.6 as a distribution of scores for each individual. Figure 3.6 extends the idea presented in Figure 3.3 by adding two more persons to roughly represent some larger number of examinees. Notice that the first person exhibits low trait level (viz., ability); the second, middle trait level; and the third, high trait level. Note, too, that the three

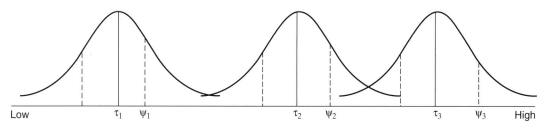

Figure 3.6
Hypothetical distributions of score variance for three individuals.

distributions are identical, each being normal in shape. This feature of the distributions is important because it reinforces that in CTT all universes of scores are (theoretically) normal, and hence, identical. We know that the mean of each distribution is an individual's conceptualized true score. The standard deviation of each distribution also has special interest: It is the range of average error of a given individual.

SEM is completely defined as *the standard deviation of a distribution of universe scores for all individuals*. Because the theory assumes equal and normal distributions for all examinees in the population, SEM may be viewed as the average of the standard deviations about (viz., above and below) the universe scores mean, despite heterogeneity in the population. Thus, it is *intrapersonal* variation.

SEM is useful in that it provides a gauge of the degree of accuracy for a given score in the distribution, namely, the mean. By both adding and subtracting a typical individual's SEM from the mean, for example, a rough and approximate confidence interval can be developed about the mean. (Note that this simple method becomes less precise as an individual's score deviates greater from the mean of all scores and as the reliability of the test is diminished. For more on this point, see the discussion of score bands in chapter 5.) The mean and the confidence interval tell us something about the dimension of the distribution of scores itself. When the confidence interval is small, the mean is a fairly accurate representation of the universe of scores. When the confidence interval is large, the mean is less helpful in conveying information about the distribution.

As a general rule, when SEM is more than half the value of the mean, the mean may not be a good indicator of scores in a distribution at all. For example, suppose a mean score of 66.4 is observed for some data set and the standard deviation is 45, a value greater than half the mean. This indicates that the value 66.4 is likely to be far from most of the scores, and hence, does not convey much useful information about how individuals scored. A variant on this precept is to prepare a ratio of SEM to the mean. The smaller the ratio, the greater confidence one may place in the mean as informative of a distribution. Regardless of the method used to evaluate the SEM-to-mean correspondence, SEM itself is a useful index of true score confidence.

Nonetheless, we seem to run into a hermeneutic problem at this point. Recall that CTT specifies the mean of all possible test administrations as an unbiased indicator of true score. How, then, can it be that SEM empirically denotes a level of error for the mean of a distribution if (in the theory) the mean is sans error by definition? We can properly say that SEM provides information about the accuracy of the mean as representative of the true score. In doing so, we realize that the mean is, in fact, an arbitrary (but statistical) indicator of error and thus can have error. This is an important point because it brings to the fore our realization that SEM is an indication of reliability—stability in measurement.

There is still more important information to garner from Figure 3.5. I have drawn attention already to the fact that the distribution for all examinees is identical, and therefore, all three individuals have the same standard deviation (i.e., SEM), regardless of whether each one's ability is low, middle, or high. This means that in CTT one SEM describes the error statistic for the population. Separate SEMs do not exist for each individual as long as they are drawn from the same population. Once we know SEM for a given score distribution, it remains constant on that measure for all individuals in the population, regardless of the group's heterogeneity. This property of the theory was realized almost from the beginning of measurement science (e.g., Kelley, 1921; Otis, 1922).

The fact that a single SEM on a given measure holds for the entire population is at once a distinguishing feature of the classical measurement model and its weakness. The weakness results from an obvious discrepancy between employing a single SEM to represent individual reliability for all examinees in a population and realizing that one SEM does not accurately convey the reliability for all score points (or trait levels) possible on a given scale. It is a prescient presumption that persons of varying ability or proficiency will have different amounts of error on a psychological assessment, even when they come from the same population. Random error is not static for a population. As we see in later chapters (especially in IRT and in generalizability theory), establishing different SEMs that more precisely reflect the error at a number of score points along the whole range of a distribution is a more accurate depiction of population parameters. For now, however, with our attention on classical methods, we hold to the notion that a single SEM is established for a population on an entire scale. Remember, however, that for individuals it is not truly accurate unless the test is highly reliable, the scores are normally distributed, and the individual under consideration obtained a score exactly at the mean value for the population. To the extent that any of these stipulations are violated, SEM is an increasingly inaccurate representation of error for that individual. It is important to grasp this point, which I discuss in more detail in chapter 5 during reliability estimation.

Syntactic Expression of SEM

SEM is commonly expressed simply as a single term, as shown in Equation 3.28:

$$\sigma_{T}. \qquad \textbf{(3.28)}$$

It is the standard deviation of a true score (viz., all error about the true score). By now, we realize that this term plays a central role in measurement theory. SEM, and its expression, follows us throughout the remaining chapters.

We have seen already that the correlation between parallel test forms is an indicator of reliability. We can use this information to build a formula for SEM.

Of course, when one test form is theoretically pure (i.e., a reflection of true score), a correlation between it and a given measure is also a gauge of reliability. Multiplying this reliability index by variance yields an expression of *true variance,* as shown in Equation 3.29:

$$\sigma_{T}^{2} = \sigma_{X}^{2}\, \rho_{XT_{i}}. \qquad \textbf{(3.29)}$$

From here it is an easy step to take the square root of both sides of the equation, thus producing the *true standard deviation* (see Equation 3.30):

$$\sigma_{T} = \sigma_{X}\, \sqrt{\rho_{XT}}. \qquad \textbf{(3.30)}$$

Error variance (i.e., SEM) may be obtained by substituting Equation 3.29 into Equation 3.30, to produce the variance expression in Equation 3.31:

$$\sigma_X^2 = \sigma_X^2 \rho_{XT} + \sigma_\varepsilon^2. \tag{3.31}$$

Solving this equation for the error variance produces the variance of the error of measurement, as given in Equation 3.32:

$$\sigma_\varepsilon^2 = \sigma_X^2 (1 - \rho_{XT}). \tag{3.32}$$

Taking the square root of the terms on both sides of this variance equation yields the square root of the error variance, SEM, shown in Equation 3.33. This equation is used to define SEM:

$$\sigma_\varepsilon = \sigma_X \sqrt{(1 - \rho_{XT})}. \tag{3.33}$$

SEM in Relation to Reliability Index

SEM is often understood by its analog, the *reliability index*. The reliability index is a measure indicating error deficit, the opposite of SEM. In the purest sense, the reliability index is defined as the simple correlation between parallel forms of a test. I discuss this important statistic in chapter 5.

Classical Works

Important Historical Writing on CTT

Classical measurement theory has been foundational to mental appraisal since the beginning of measurement science. Its roots are long and prestigious. In an early articulation, Thurstone (1931) explained the theory with vibrant writing that still instructs today. Later, more advanced presentations by Thorndike (1949) and Gulliksen (1950) provided additional authoritative coverage. The latter of these books, Gulliksen's *Theory of Mental Tests,* is still in print today because it clearly outlines many principle tenets of the theory; to some measurement professionals, it is the defining volume on the subject. In 1963, Lord and Novick published *Statistical Theories of Mental Test Scores,* a book that even today has profound influence on the field because it brought attention to latent variable assessment and reinforced emerging statistical concepts. (Regrettably, this book is out of print and can be difficult to locate; however, securing a copy through a rare book dealer or elsewhere is worth the effort.) At many points, I refer to these seminal works. For persons wanting to make psychometric assessment a regular part of their professional activity, I recommend adding them to one's library.

Of course, since the time of these classic works many authors have also proffered books about CTT. Some of these books are excellent and can also be recommended. Throughout this text, I cite numerous of them.

Summary

This chapter provides descriptions of CTT, both of the theory and of its expression in mathematical models. First, the underpinnings in philosophy and psychology are described. Then, I examine two types of error: random and systematic. Terms are also explained. A large portion of the chapter is devoted to presenting mathematical expressions of CTT—from assumptions to practical arrangements. It then builds toward reliability appraisal through the SEM. The chapter concludes with citations of some additional CTT resources.

Chapter 4

Validity

Introduction

Reasons of Science

Galileo Galilei, the great Italian scientist of the 17th century, is probably more responsible for the development of the scientific method than any other person. According to Aristotle, heavy objects fall faster than light ones, and ancient scholars accepted the Greek philosopher's teaching without question. However, Galileo, with healthy Italian skepticism, decided to test the theory. He discovered that, in reality, all objects fall at the same rate once the effect of air friction is taken into account. Air friction retards the rate of descent differently for an apple than it does for a feather—otherwise, they fall at the same rate. Galileo proved that the common perception was incorrect. (In modern times, astronauts, while on the moon and thus free from most air resistance, dropped a feather and rock together in a demonstration of Galileo's proof.) He took his observations further by developing a methodology for his experiments so other scientists could replicate his work, creating the scientific method in the process. Throughout his experiments, Galileo made extensive use of mathematical methods to prove his theory, another important feature of the scientific method.

Just as many persons in classical times misunderstood the important idea of gravity (like Aristotle, who was otherwise brilliant). Today many people misperceive a central concept of measurement: *validity*—the misunderstood validity! However, the concept is so central to measurement science that a clear understanding and right-sighted perspective on validity is an absolute necessity.

Contents

In this chapter, I present modern notions about validity, first describing its essence and then addressing a number of relevant considerations. In addition, given that the *Standards for Educational and Psychological Testing* (American Educational Research Association, American Psychological Association, & National Council on Measurement in Education, 1999) is widely accepted as a benchmark for validity's authoritative description, I recite and discuss pertinent aspects of this publication. Next, a bit of history about validity is provided to gain perspective on modern notions. Throughout, the chapter focuses on validity evaluation. The second half of the chapter describes and explains sources of validity evidence, such as those based on a test's content, its response processes, and its internal structure. Each procedure is useful to validity evaluation.

Validity at Its Essence

Essential Description of Validity

At essence, validity means that the information yielded by a test is appropriate, meaningful, and useful for decision making, which is itself the purpose of mental measurement. The *Standards* (American Educational Research Association et al., 1999) describes validity: "Validity refers to the degree to which evidence and theory support the interpretations of test scores entailed by proposed uses of tests" (p. 9). Hence, validity is about making use of a test's scores for decision making.

Although the basic notion of validity appears straightforward, it takes a bit of study—even heuristic inquiry—to understand and appreciate the sophistication and elegance of the validity concept. Through studying validity, however, we move metaphorically from the simple, flat world of Galileo, where explorers imagined they would fall off the edge, to a more complete and accurate view of reality, with all its richness and meaningful detail. This chapter provides a deep level of validity study.

Importance of Validity to Measurement

To fully appreciate validity as a scientific concept, one must first realize its centrality to measurement science. Plainly, validity is at the core of mental testing. Because measures of mental attributes can produce useful and meaningful information that supports appropriate decisions—that is, because of validity—measurement science exists. This point is widely recognized in the field. For instance, Robert Linn (1994), a celebrant in educational and psychological measurement, flatly states in a discussion of assessment: "The primacy of validity is not in dispute" (p. 4). As reinforcement, according to the *Standards* (American Educational Research Association et al., 1999), "Validity is . . . the most fundamental consideration in developing and evaluating tests" (p. 9).

In addition, given the role of validity in measurement, it is clear that, sans validity, psychometric analysis could not exist. There is no more direct purpose for psychometric methods than to enhance validity in measurement. William Angoff (1988), another important thinker in the field of test validity, anchors its place in psychometric methods by stating, "Validity has always been regarded as most fundamental and important in psychometrics" (p. 19).

Validity of Scores—Not of Instruments

Despite validity's central role in measurement science, it is commonly misunderstood and inaccurately described. One sees the misconstruing of validity most frequently expressed in a simple, but nescient, question asked by all sorts of people. From scientists to lawyers, from school personnel to journalists, this question is asked: "Is this test valid?" Albeit persons from these groups and others ask the question sincerely, it is a basic mistake to focus on the "validity" of a particular test instrument.

In fact, no given test instrument or appraisal activity can be validated in the sense implied by the nescient question, nor can a single question about a test's validity be answered with a concrete "yes" or "no." The reason—already becoming clear in our study—is that validity is not a concern of an instrument per se (regardless of content and whether delivered via paper and pencil, computer, performances, or other) but with decisions based on yielded scores of an appraisal activity.

As shown, a description of validity makes no reference to the instrument. Rather, in educational and psychological measurement, it refers to the degree to which interpreting and using test scores for a particular decision is supported by evidence and theory. In other words, using test-garnered information to make a particular decision because there is evidence or a supportable theory undergirding it is validity.

This depiction of validity presents us with a much more complicated notion than can be conveyed by a simple "yes" or "no" pronouncement about an instrument. Yet, this more complex view for validity is also a more accurate view of how we can use a test properly. Knowing the real meaning of validity enhances the likelihood that the information yielded by an appraisal can be properly employed in decision making—decisions about people in real-life situations. Hence, as we understand the meaning better, we are more likely to use the concept properly.

From this point of view, another important feature about validity (and one that harkens back to the previous nescient question) comes into focus; namely, the scores yielded from a test may be put to valid use for some decision but not for all decisions. For example, making decisions about predicting likely success in college from a test designed for that purpose may be supportable (valid), whereas using the same test for other kinds of decisions may not be justified. Throughout this chapter, I present many examples of proper and improperly supported decisions—hence, validity and invalidity in use.

Three Aspects of Validity

There are three elements to modern notions for validity; in this chapter, we study each of them. First, as we already see, validity refers to the interpretations of test scores in a particular assessment situation and not to features of a given instrument. Second, like Galileo bringing the scientific method to the description of falling objects, establishing validity invokes a formal, evaluative process. The majority of this chapter is devoted to providing information useful for validity evaluation. Third, consistent with the direction of measurement theory toward ever more sophisticated psychological interpretations, validity is also an exploration into psychology. As measurement science evokes more cognitive interpretations, establishing validity evidence is likewise more cognitively based. We see this point in many examples throughout this chapter and elsewhere.

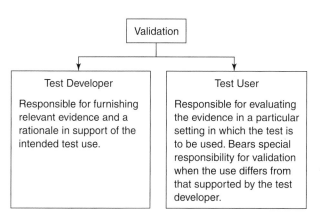

Figure 4.1
Relationship of validation to test developer and test user.

Establishing Validity Is a Shared Endeavor

We see that validity is about making supported decisions. Determining whether a decision is supportable from the information obtained through a mental appraisal is *validity evaluation*. Hence, validity is a process that demands some involvement in evidentiary support, a key feature of any scientific method. A relevant question then is "Who should carry out this activity, validity evaluation?"

Carrying out the activities involved in validity evaluation is a shared endeavor of both the test developer and the test user. The test developer must provide evidence and a rationale for the intended use of the test, whereas the test user is ultimately responsible for evaluating the evidence in a particular setting. Both parties contribute equally to the validation process. With emphatic deliberateness, the *Standards* (American Educational Research Association et al., 1999) describes this in clear, unambiguous language:

> Validation is the joint responsibility of the test developer and the test user. The test developer is responsible for furnishing relevant evidence and a rationale in support of the intended use. The test user is ultimately responsible for evaluating the evidence in the particular setting in which the test is to be used. (p. 11)

Understanding this shared responsibility is important for appropriate and meaningful test use. Figure 4.1 depicts this shared relationship.

Validity as Described by the AERA/NCME/APA Standards

The *Standards* (American Educational Research Association et al., 1999) is such a rich and authoritative source of information about validity that it is regarded as a benchmark for most conceptions of the term. The proffered description of validity is both philosophical conceit for common understanding and a kind of practical manual to be used in real world situations. Because of its importance to the topic, I quote the *Standards* more frequently and longer in this chapter that I do sources in other chapters.

The *Standards* begins description of validity by citing it as an action verb meaning "to validate." This grammatical choice is deliberate for it connotes active voice and participation. In addition, validation distinctly denotes a process:

> Validation can be viewed as developing a scientifically sound validity argument to support the intended interpretation of test scores and their relevance to the proposed use. The conceptual framework points to the kinds of evidence that might be collected to evaluate the proposed interpretation in light of the purposes of testing. As validation proceeds and new evidence about the meaning of a test's scores becomes available, revisions may be needed in the test, in the conceptual framework that shapes it, and even in the construct underlying the test. (American Educational Research Association et al., 1999, p. 9)

Further, when considering the validation process, it is important to also realize that validity is a unitary idea. In other words, there are not distinct kinds or types of validity, such as "content validity," "criterion validity," or "construct validity." There is only one validity. "Validity is a unitary concept. It is the degree to which all the accumulated evidence supports the intended interpretation of test scores for the proposed purpose" (American Educational Research Association et al., 1999, p. 11). I refer to the feature of validity as a unified concept at several places in this chapter and throughout the book.

One should not overlook or consider lightly the consequence of validity as a unitary concept. It means that evidence to support a decision must be related to that decision, not to various "kinds" of validity. This perspective places the focus for evidence where it should be—on the decision at hand. Of course, evidence for validity must come from sources that explain the content, construct, and likely external and internal criteria that may have a correlational relationship to the test's scores. However, these terms are only convenient labels for organizing a body of evidence during validity evaluation. They do not imply different kinds of validity.

In its opening chapter, the *Standards* articulates 24 individual standards for validity that highlight the importance of the topic to measurement. Each standard presents information about validity in a different context and for a specific purpose. Because these precepts are so widely accepted in test and measurement contexts as veritable truth, they are reprinted here in Figure 4.2.

Standard 1.1	A rationale should be presented for each recommended interpretation and use of test scores, together with a comprehensive summary of the evidence and theory bearing on the intended use or interpretation.
Standard 1.2	The test developer should set forth clearly how test scores are intended to be interpreted and used. The population(s) for which a test is appropriate should be clearly delimited, and the construct that the test is intended to assess should be clearly described.
Standard 1.3	If validity for some common or likely interpretation has not been investigated, or if the interpretation is inconsistent with available evidence, that fact should be made clear and potential users should be cautioned about making unsupported interpretations.
Standard 1.4	If a test is used in a way that has not been validated, it is incumbent on the user to justify the new use, collecting new evidence if necessary.

(continued)

Standard 1.5	The composition of any sample of examinees from which validity evidence is obtained should be described in as much detail as is practical, including major relevant sociodemographic and developmental characteristics.
Standard 1.6	When the validation rests in part on the appropriateness of test content, the procedures followed in specifying and generating test content should be described and justified in reference to the construct the test is intended to measure or the domain it is intended to represent. If the definition of the content sampled incorporates criteria such as importance, frequency, or criticality, these criteria should also be clearly explained and justified.
Standard 1.7	When a validation rests in part on the opinions or decisions of expert judges, observers, or raters, procedures for selecting such experts and for eliciting judgments or rating should be fully described. The qualifications, and experience, of the judges should be presented. The description of the procedures should include any training and instructions provided, should indicate whether participants reached their decisions independently, and should report the level of agreement reached. If participants interacted with one another or exchanged information, the procedures through which they may have influenced one another should be set forth.
Standard 1.8	If the rationale for a test use or score interpretation depends on premises about the psychological processes or cognitive operations used by examinees, then theoretical or empirical evidence in support of those premises should be provided. When statements about the processes employed by observers or scorers are a part of the argument for validity, similar information should be provided.
Standard 1.9	If a test is claimed to be essentially unaffected by practice and coaching, then the sensitivity of the test performance to change with these forms of instruction should be documented.
Standard 1.10	When interpretation of performance on specific items, or small subsets of items, is suggested, the rationale and relevant evidence in support of such interpretation should be provided. When interpretation of individual item responses is likely but is not recommended by the developer, the user should be warned against making such interpretations.
Standard 1.11	If the rationale for a test use or interpretation depends on premises about the relationships among parts of the test, evidence concerning the internal structure of the test should be provided.
Standard 1.12	When interpretation of subscores, score differences, or profiles is suggested, the rationale and relevant evidence in support of such interpretation should be provided. Where composite scores are developed, the basis and rationale for arriving at the composites should be given.
Standard 1.13	When validity evidence includes statistical analyses of test results, either alone or together with data on other variables, the conditions under which the data were collected should be described in enough detail that users can judge the relevance of the statistical findings to local conditions. Attention should be drawn to any features of a validation data collection that are likely to differ from typical operational testing conditions and that could plausibly influence test performance.
Standard 1.14	When validity evidence includes empirical analyses of test responses together with data on other variables, the rationale for selecting the additional variables should be provided. Where appropriate and feasible, evidence concerning the constructs represented by other variables, as well as their technical properties, should be presented or cited. Attention should be drawn to any likely sources of dependence (or lack of independence) among variables other than dependencies among the construct(s) they represent.

(continued)

Standard 1.15   When it is asserted that a certain level of test performance predicts adequate or inadequate criterion performance, information about the levels of criterion performance associated with given levels of test scores should be provided.

Standard 1.16   When validation relies on evidence that test scores are related to one or more criterion variables, information about suitability and technical quality of the criteria should be reported.

Standard 1.17   If test scores are used in conjunction with other quantifiable variables to predict some outcome or criterion, regression (or equivalent) analyses should include those additional relevant variables along with the test scores.

Standard 1.18   When statistical adjustments, such as those for restrictions of range or attenuation, are made, both adjusted and unadjusted coefficients, as well as the specific procedure used, and all statistics used in the adjustment, should be reported.

Standard 1.19   If a test is recommended for use in assigning persons to alternative treatments or is likely to be so used, and if outcomes from those treatments can reasonably be compared on a common criterion, then, whenever feasible, supporting evidence of differential outcomes should be provided.

Standard 1.20   When a mata-analysis is used as evidence of the strength of a test-criterion relationship, the test and the criterion variables in the local situation should be comparable with those in the studies summarized. If relevant research includes credible evidence that any other features of testing application may influence the strength of the test-criterion relationship, the correspondence between those features in the local situation and in the meta-analysis should be reported. Any significant disparities that might limit the applicability of the meta-analytical findings to the local situation should be noted explicitly.

Standard 1.21   Any meta-analytic evidence used to support an intended test use should be clearly described, including methodological choices in identifying and coding studies, correcting for artifacts, and examining potential moderator variables. Assumptions made in correcting for artifacts such as criterion unreliability and range restriction should be presented, and the consequences of these assumptions made clear.

Standard 1.22   When it is clearly stated or implied that a recommended test use will result in a specific outcome, the basis for expecting that outcome should be presented, together with relevant evidence.

Standard 1.23   When a test use or score interpretation is recommended on the grounds that testing or the testing program per se will reasult in some indirect benefit in addition to the utility of information from the test scores themselves, the rationale for anticipating the indirect benefit should be made explicit. Logical or theoretical arguments and empirical evidence for the indirect benefit should be provided. Due weight should be given to any contradictory findings in the scientific literature, including findings suggesting indirect outcomes other than those predicted.

Standard 1.24   When unintended consequences result from test use, an attempt should be made to investigate whether such consequences arise from the test's sensitivity to characteristics other than those it is intended to assess or to the test's failure fully to represent the intended construct.

Figure 4.2

APA/AERA/NCME *Standards for Educational and Psychological Testing* directly citing test validity.

Source: From *Standards for Educational and Psychological Testing* (pp. 17–24), by American Educational Research Association, American Psychological Association, & National Council on Measurement in Education, 1999, Washington, DC: American Educational Research Association. Copyright 1999 by American Educational Research Association.

Background of Validity

Not surprisingly, despite validity's preeminence among ideas in psychometric methods, it is not a static concept. In fact, its evolution has been pronounced. Tracking this evolution, even briefly, aids in understanding current conceptions. I briefly recount the relevant history.

Early Roots

From the earliest days of measurement until sometime in the mid-20th century, validity was usually explained in terms of a test's fidelity to its intent. Garrett (1937) articulates this with his famous phraseology: "The validity of a test is the extent to which it measures what it purports to measure" (p. 324). However, like Aristotle's primitive idea of differential gravity for objects of different weight (apples fall faster than feathers), Garrett's description of validity rested on faulty assumptions, and it neglected important psychological aspects of the term.

By Garrett's use of the term, validity was almost a truism in measurement, as long as a test's developer employed language consistent with whatever was the desired measurement objective. Sometimes this meant that when a test maker merely opined that the instrument under consideration was supposed to be "a measure of such and such," the conversation was over; the case having been made. Today, for such judgments, we demand more substantive evidence than someone's assertion, even when that someone is the test's developer.

During these early times, support for the argument to claim validity in an instrument was established primarily through correlations between the test's scores and some external criterion. It was believed that the more the correlational relationship between a test and a criterion was presumed to be relevant, the greater the validity of the test. This relatively simple notion for validity was accepted and used by prominent measurement experts of the day. For example, about half a century ago, the famous educational psychologist and psychometrician J. P. Guilford (1946) made the remarkable and unequivocal statement that, "In a very general sense, a test is valid for anything with which it correlates" (p. 429). Not long after Guilford's assertion, in the first edition of the *Educational Measurement,* Cureton (1950) defined validity as the correlational relationship between observed scores and a criterion's true scores, a definition closer to what we now use for reliability.

Throughout psychometric history, there are hundreds of examples of validation evidence based solely on correlational relationships. For example, Flanagan's (1948) Air Force Aviation Psychology Program continued the predictive notion for validity by correlating ASVAB (Armed Services Vocational Assessment Battery) scores with a pass versus fail criterion on bombardier training. In another quoted study, Brown and Ghiselli (1953) reported that among job applicants of various performance categories, the higher a worker's job performance rating, the greater the initial selection test's validity.

We have come to view the correlational relationship criterion for validity evidence as still important but not paramount. Instead, the psychological intent and practicality for decision making to which a test contributes is now emphasized. As such, no single source of evidence—whether correlations or something else—is sufficient. Validity must be evidenced by multiple sources.

Evolving to a Unitary Conception

As described, validity is a single, unified notion. This modern idea of a unitary validity is actually a return to its original conception, where it was also viewed as a single notion. In the intervening years, however, validity had been broken into different types, especially construct, content, and criterion related.

The evolutionary track for validity from a single notion, then to different kinds, and now its return to a single notion is clearly seen in the various editions of the *Standards*. In a 1954 set of testing standards by the American Psychological Association, validity was broken down into three types: predictive, concurrent, and content. The 1966 edition of the *Standards* changed the terms a bit by following ideas laid out in an important paper on validity by Cronbach and Meehl (1955). This edition added a new kind of validity, *construct validity,* and shuffled some of the other terms, combining predictive and concurrent validity into a criterion-related category. Additional changes, most emphasizing construct validity, were made in the 1974 edition.

However, the 1985 edition for the *Standards* eschewed these "types" of validity entirely, returning to its original unitary conception. The differences in types were seen as useful only for categorizing evidence. Validity evidence was believed to support construct, content, or criteria. *Differential prediction* was also added as another concern for validity in this edition.

The most recent *Standards* (American Educational Research Association et al., 1999) carries the trend still further. In this edition, the unitary focus for validity is even more impressed on the reader, and for emphasis, traditional nomenclature for kinds of validity evidence is abandoned altogether. Currently, there is no specific category of construct-, content-, or criterion-related evidence. Instead, many broad sources of validity evidence are named merely as a way to "illuminate different aspects of validity" (p. 11). Remember, in modern psychometrics, validity is "the degree to which all the accumulated evidence supports the intended interpretation of test scores for the proposed purpose" (p. 11). This is just a single validity, albeit supported from many lines of evidence. Validity is still just one notion.

Some modern researchers into validity (e.g., Netermeyer, Bearden, & Sharma, 2003) have adopted the notion that as a necessary condition for valid inferences the measured constructs should be tied to an underlying psychological theory. This line of validity evidence is called *nomological validity.* During empirical validation of a test, establishing nomological evidence may require some form of confirmatory FA, such as structural equation modeling or other look at a test's internal structure. I address the topic of structural examination in chapter 13.

Validity Advancing: Messick and Cronbach

To explore our contemporary conception of validity, it is helpful to know that its emphasis on score interpretation arises, in some part, from the work of Lee Cronbach and his protégé, Samuel Messick. These strikingly impressive thinkers brought to the term both a psychological perspective and a social awareness, elements critical to understanding today's view. I begin this discussion by examining Messick's contribution and then turn to Cronbach's work.

Messick's Imprimatur on Modern Validity

Samuel Messick was chair of the American Psychological Association's Committee for Standards for Educational and Psychological Testing in the 1970s. During his tenure, he developed a description for validity that serves as a significant marker. According to Messick (1989), "Validity is an integrated evaluative judgment of the degree to which empirical evidence and theoretical rationales support the adequacy and appropriateness of inferences and actions based on test scores or other modes of assessment" (p. 13).

This striking statement has influenced modern psychometrics enormously. First, note the inherent psychological aspect of Messick's definition. There are judgments made, the evidence is empirical, and the rationales are based on theory. The nouns Messick employs—*adequacy, appropriateness,* and *actions*—are assessments based on evaluative judgments, a cognition function. Most important, making inferences about score meaning requires both formal and informal logic, again features of cognition. By Messick's language, then, the definition of validity is firmly grounded in psychological interpretation.

Moving validity into psychological territory is consistent—indeed, even necessary—for validity to properly align with test theory. We should appreciate this direction toward psychology because it gives psychometric methods a more uniform outlook. With this emphasis, from theory to practical use, psychometrics has a consistent philosophical base, one firmly grounded in its parent psychology.

Finally, notice, in Messick's definition, that the objects of inferences are "test scores or other modes of assessment." The intent here is to describe tests in broad, generic terms so almost any mode of assessment is covered in the definition. Tests are not just paper-and-pencil instruments that may feature items in the multiple-choice or true–false formats; other methods of assessment are also included (e.g., performance assessments).

Developing Characteristics for the Validity Definition

As is clear by now, evidence is the *sine qua non* of validity and is indispensable to test interpretation. Thus, it is a matter not of primacy of evidence but of the adequacy of the presented evidence. A small amount of validity evidence may be useful in some contexts, whereas other situations require vast amounts of validity evidence. The amount of evidence necessary for confidence in score interpretation is dictated by particular circumstances and judged on a case-by-case basis. Indications that a child understands serration, for example, requires less rigid validity evidence than may be needed for a measure of reaction time of the skills required of test pilots or of self-efficacy among individuals with mild depression.

Further, because validation is a matter of degree, it is logical to understand that validity is a process of accumulating evidence, much like scientific inquiry into any given field. There is always more to be learned and more evidence to be presented. New contexts and better methods for exploration are continually employed in the search for validity evidence. Of course, like all scientific inquiry, findings are reported at appropriate times, but the search for more evidence is unending. This is why a test is never completely validated.

As in most scientific inquiry, evidence should not rely on only one source. Multiple lines of evidence should be explored. With validity, the sum is greater than the parts. The accumulation of many small bits of evidence from many different sources (some may be minor in and of themselves) pointing to proper inferences is validity evidence. This is referred to as *convergent validity*. The well-known southern American writer, Flannery O'Connor, titled a wonderful short story "All That Rises Must Converge." In a sense, O'Connor's title is an apt appraisal for validity assessment. Complementary facts coalesce and rise, converging to form a body of consistent evidence. Valid interpretations thus flow forth.

As a corollary, information that is divergent (i.e., leading away from specific inferences for test scores so unsupported inferences are not made) is also validity evidence. This is called *divergent validity*. Hence, there are both convergent and divergent sources for validity evidence. Messick (1989) supports the idea of having different (convergent and divergent) evidences for validity by explaining, "to validate an interpretive inference is to ascertain the degree to which multiple lines of evidence are consonant with the inference, while establishing that alternative inferences are less well supported" (p. 13).

As allegory, consider a lawyer who notes describing the numerous categories of corroborating evidence needed to convict a murderer, "One looks to eyewitness evidence, documentary evidence, corroborating evidence, rebuttal evidence, scientific evidence, psychological evidence, and circumstantial evidence." Whereas, obviously, we are most focused on evidence that satisfies criteria for scientific exploration (e.g., hypotheses, replication), the list for lawyers is parallel in spirit to the multiple lines of inquiry the measurement professional should pursue for validity evaluation.

Inevitably, too, validity is an evolving property of a mental measure. Its usefulness depends on the contemporary context. When circumstances change, the validity evidence must evolve to support the changes. Research can become dated, and evidence appropriate today may be deemed inadequate tomorrow. Validity interpretations are fragile, and their adequacy and appropriateness, and the actions based on them, must be continually monitored and updated.

Validity as Evaluative Argument

As we can see, validity is scientific inquiry. Messick (1989) said, "Inferences are hypotheses and the validation of inferences is hypotheses testing" (pp. 13–14.).

However, because validity evidence is contextual and is often a convergence or divergence of information, no single hypothesis will apply. Thus, according to Messick and others (e.g., Kane, 2001b), validity is an evaluation argument.

The validity as evaluative argument approach to validation was skillfully advanced by Lee Cronbach in a 1986 speech to invitees to a special conference entitled "Test Validity for the 1990s and Beyond" held at the Educational Testing Service in Princeton, New Jersey. Cronbach (1988)—drawing from the evaluation work of Ernest House (1980) and his "logic of the evaluation argument"—said, "I invite you to think of 'validity argument' rather than 'validity research'" (p. 4). With this single exhortation, Cronbach crystallized a slowly evolving notion for validity into a unified process of evaluation. By this evaluative standard, validity requires one to take a position and justify it—a position based on theory and empirical data, and arrived at by employing the methods of science.

Kane (2001b) specifies the evaluative argument as the "network of inferences leading from the scores to the conclusions and decision based on the scores, as well as the assumptions supporting these inferences" (p. 56). Of course, such an interpretive argument is not mere conceit. It must be based on evidence, as well as an initial clear statement of the argument itself. In short, the interpretive argument includes articulation, rationale, and supporting evidence for the argument and its underlying assumptions. The interpretive argument approach to validation presents measurement professionals with a particular path to validity evaluation.

Cronbach's Facets of Validity

Now, we specifically examine the work of Lee Cronbach because many persons consider his work to be the impetus for modern conceptions of validity. As already described, he emphasized the idea that validity is a single, unitary concept (Cronbach, 1988). A problem of logic with this conception arises, however, when one considers that two of the three formerly recognized categories (construct, content, and criterion) derive from the test scores themselves. One can only gather evidence about content or support for relation to criteria from the test itself, not from things external to it. This realization led to the conclusion that there can be just one category for validity: information about the construct. Cronbach seizes the former illogic to buttress his argument that all validity evidence is construct validation. He is careful, however, to remind us also that multiple lines of evidence are essential to arguments for validity.

From the unitary concept for validity, and with all evidence consolidated into just one category of construct evidence, Cronbach (1988) devised a summary framework for validity to reintroduce an organizational schema. He called validity's different aspects *facets*. One facet is the source of justification for the testing, which is the appraisal of either evidence or consequence. Another facet is the outcome, or reason, for testing. This facet is described as either information about test interpretation or test use. Figure 4.3 presents Cronbach's validity facets.

This cross-tabs view of the facets of validity is particularly helpful in examining how they interact. As is seen in Figure 4.3, from an evidential basis, test interpretation is Cronbach's construct validity. With the added information stemming from test use, this basis is strengthened by its relevance and usefulness to a given situation.

Figure 4.3

Representation of Messick's
Facets of Validity.

I. Justification source
   A. Evidential Basis
   B. Consequential Basis
II. Reasons for testing
   A. Test Interpretation
      1. Construct validity
      2. Validity implications
   B. Test Use
      1. Construct validity + relevance/utility evidential basis
      2. Social consequences

However, when test justification is one of consequence, very different ideas for test interpretation and test use emerge. In this view, value implications are central to test interpretation; for applied testing, social consequences are the foci.

The evidential basis for testing is well established in validity theory; however, the idea of a consequential justification for testing is not as widely accepted by measurement theorists. Some measurement professionals question whether test makers, examinees, and users of a test's scores should also include consideration of the social consequence of their actions as a part of the test validation process. Of course, responsible psychometricians and test developers are rightly sensitive to how a test is used. That is not in doubt. The core question is whether the consequences of using a test should be a part of the validation process. We explore the controversy surrounding this aspect of validity in a later section. At this point, it is useful to remember that validity is an evolving concept and Cronbach's validity facets are part of that evolution.

Sources of Validity Evidence

In this section, we examine various sources for validity evidence. As emphasized, in validity evaluation, the evidence should amass from multiple sources. Collectively, these sources present information about the confidence level for making score-based inferences in a specific situation. Among many other writers, Mislevy, Wilson, Erkican, and Chudowsky (2002) offer a framework for collecting evidence from multiple sources. In addition, some suggestions for common evidentiary support are given in the *Standards* and displayed in Figure 4.4. I elaborate on these categories one by one.

Validity Evidence Based on a Test's Content

Evaluating evidence for valid inferences of test scores nearly always includes some information about the content of the assessment, typically referring to the *content*

```
                                                          Figure 4.4
                 APA/AERA/NCME                            Possible sources for validity
   Standards for Educational and Psychological Testing    evidence.
             Evidentiary Suggestions
   • Evidence based on test content
   • Evidence based on response processes
   • Evidence based on internal structure
   • Evidence based on relations to other variables
   • Convergent and discriminant evidence
   • Test–criterion relationships
   • Validity generalization
   • Evidence based on consequences of testing
```

domain (in domain-based assessments) or the *construct* (in latent trait models). The assessment may be an academic content field (e.g., mathematics or English), a preference (e.g., when making choices among kinds of leisure activity), an opinion (e.g., reporting voting practices), or even supernatural beliefs (e.g., one's religious preference). Many other mental functions, such as IQ and other psychological processes, can also be construed as assessment constructs, traits, or domains.

Obviously, evaluating information about a trait or content domain for an assessment presumes that one has been articulated in the first place. Following precepts in the *Standards,* as well good common sense, test makers should initially develop a description of the intended construct or domain. Although this may sound obvious and simple enough, all too often one sees test development projects wherein the construct is not clearly or fully expressed and sometimes only given in perfunctory notes or comments. In test development work, where users must rely on information initially prepared by the test's developer, such presumption is not satisfactory.

In many instances, identifying and articulating a test's content domain is a comparatively straightforward job, although effort is still required. An illustration is a test of ninth-grade algebra or a simple test of preferences among various food flavors. Here, the content is readily identifiable and can be easily developed into test domains.

There are myriad sources to which one can turn for assistance in identifying and articulating content domains. With many school-based subjects, curriculum organization or professional associations have much relevant, and current, information. For instance, the National Council of Teachers of English, and its counterparts in mathematics, science, social studies, art, music, and physical education, have developed carefully crafted descriptions of their disciplines (see Kendall & Marzano, 1996). For additional information, one may refer to the Web sites for each discipline.

Similarly, when developing a test for licensing or certifying a profession or vocation, many professional associations and organizations offer a rich, primary source of information about their fields. For example, the American Association of

Labor Relations Negotiators, the American Association of Ophthalmic Administrators, The National Wood Flooring Association, The National Association of Professional Engineers, and literally hundreds of like-minded groups have developed precisely worded descriptions of their discipline. These content-based descriptions can be wonderfully helpful in initial considerations of test content.

However, when the appraised construct is psychological, and not easily covered by facile explanation, special problems for description arise. Often, no uniformly agreed-upon definition or description of many constructs exists. Many fields of counseling psychology and guidance, as examples, are not easily circumscribed by practical definition. Or consider IQ assessment. The field of human intelligence is replete with disparate thoughts and theories regarding what is included or excluded. In these cases, construct specification may require a different tack. Here, a description based on theoretical work in the field may be more appropriate than a dictionary-style definition. Of necessity, theoretical definitions are generally longer, and often they can be strengthened with documentation from citing primary sources.

Frequently, when building an instrument, test developers combine the description of the content and the type (and sometimes format) of response processes into a sort of cross-tabs outline of the test—the *test content specifications* (TCSs). Sometimes the TCSs are called a *test blueprint,* reminiscent of architects' blueprints used by contractors to build a house or other structure. TCS stipulate the test's architecture. They are addressed in chapter 8, but it is important to note here that when considering test content in validity evaluation, TCS can be an extremely useful document to test users. They inform users of the developer's intention, allowing more focus in validity evaluation.

As important as it is to offer a thorough, clearly stated content description, this does not exhaust considerations of a test's content in validity evaluation. A theoretical and practical rationale, as well as policies for administration of the instrument, can also be useful in garnering evidence of a test's content. It may be appropriate in relevant documents to specify intended assessment circumstances for the test and even suggest anticipated consequences of using the scores in particular situations. Further, such documents may offer information about subgroups (e.g., sex, gender, or racial) of examinees and how test interpretations could be related to them.

In addition, expert judgment, theory-based evidence, and other specifications can be rich sources for developing appropriate test content information. As an illustration of using experts, a simple methodology for them to rate the congruence of a test's items or exercises to a content domain can produce useful information. There are many schemes and worksheets for experts to match items to content description, and in chapter 8, I provide samples. Do not overlook the obvious value of involving persons with content expertise in any validity evaluation based on test content.

Validity Evidence Based on Response Processes

Examining the mental or cognitive process employed by an examinee to yield a response to assessment stimuli is another valuable source of evidence for validity. The

Standards almost stipulates this as a requirement for validity evaluation. It says, ". . . if a test is intended to assess mathematical reasoning, it becomes important to determine whether examinees are, in fact, reasoning about the materials given instead of following a standard algorithm" (American Educational Research Association et al., 1999, p. 12). As an illustration of where this can easily go awry in a test, suppose the test's developer intended for reasoning or a deductive path to be followed for success on a particular item, but the examinees were able to give a correct response by merely reproducing memorized information. Reporting on such response processes can provide powerful validity evidence.

Response processes are researchable phenomena through both simple and complex methods. Some methods based on latent variables and causal processes of the construct may include latent variable analyses, structural equation modeling (SEM), hierarchal linear modeling (HLM), conjectural analysis, path analysis, and even some types of meta-analyses. Although these methods can be daunting and may require specialized expertise in the particular method, they can also yield important information about examinee response processes. I present much information about these strategies in chapter 13 and elsewhere (see chapter 10 for latent trait analysis). In addition, many fine books and publications provide detailed information about one technique or another (e.g., Embretson & Reise, 2000; Longford, 1995; Maruyama, 1997).

Sometimes, taxonomies that categorize cognitive processes can also be useful. Bloom's (1956) well-known *Taxonomy of Education Objectives,* though quite old, is still somewhat useful, as is Hannah and Michaelis' (1977) *Comprehensive Framework for Instruction Objectives*. I discuss strategies for using these taxonomies in chapter 8. However, readers should exercise due caution with them, too, as they can be a convenient and inexact route to incorrectly identify an examinee's response processes.

Validity Evidence Based on an Internal Structure

In a general sense, examining the internal structure of a test encompasses the whole of validity's purpose. The internal structure of a test is concerned primarily with making appropriate and reliable inferences about the constructs being assessed. Many validity scholars consider the nature of all validity analysis to be construct-related—that is, concerned with internal structure (e.g., Angoff, 1988; Cronbach, 1988; Guion, 1977; Linn, 1980; Messick, 1975, 1980, 1989; Tenopyr, 1977).

Often, it is useful to begin consideration of a test's internal structure by examining its theoretical underpinnings. A carefully devised and well-researched theory can provide a better platform for the development of estimable constructs than can be done from weak or imprecise groundings. When the theory is clearly articulated, there is also a greater likelihood of devising appropriate items or assessment exercises. Further, when the undergirding theory is focused on a single dimension, specifying the construct for assessment can often be done with precision. However, if the theory and consequent domain for assessment is multidimensional, the situation is more complex to implement. In either case, psychometric methods are available to empirically investigate the internal structure. The questions, then, are which method to employ and when.

Obviously, no single methodology is considered universally "best." The appropriateness of the technique depends on the particular context in which a test is developed, along with careful consideration of how it is used and of the intended decisions it should inform. Strategies useful in one validity evaluation may be irrelevant in another. Nonetheless, the following list is illustrative of a number of strategies that are broadly relevant to studying a measure's internal structure:

- Factor analysis and related data reduction methods
- Cluster analysis, principal component analysis
- Confirmation of psychologically based theories: confirmatory FA (e.g., SEM, HLM)
- Multitrait-multimethod matrix (MTMM)
- Ability (proficiency) parameter estimation techniques, such as IRT
- Strategies involving generalizability theory or other reliability indices

Each cited technique, as well as others suitable to the task of examining the internal structure of a test, require a degree of specialized knowledge. In the following subsections, I describe a few concepts that reside in the heart of many of these procedures.

Common Factor Model

Most tests follow the common factor model alluded to in chapter 2, and most appraisals of a test's internal structure in some measure are directed toward it. Valid inferences often presume a common factor model. Here, I present a basic argument for introduction and its relevance to validity evaluation. In chapter 13, during analysis of whole tests, I discuss this route to structural examination in some detail.

The common factor model is the single factor of Charles Spearman's theory in which a test comprises items that both share commonalities and have unique influences. However, the commonality among items is not uniformly distributed. In other words, what is shared among them—the common factor—is not shared equally. Some items contribute more to the commonality and some less. The consequence of this common factor model is that an examinee's score on a given item is not only a function of the individual's knowledge of the construct, but also of the degree to which the item measures the construct. This may be expressed mathematically, as follows in Equation 4.1:

$$X_j = \lambda I + \varepsilon_j + \mu_j, \qquad (4.1)$$

where X_j = examinee's response in the jth item,

λI = commonality of item I to the common factor,

ε_j = uniqueness of item I, and

μ_j = difficulty value for the jth item.

According to the expression, an examinee responds to any particular item included in the assessment (X_j). The item (I) has an operational difficulty value (μ_j), but more important, it measures the examinee's knowledge of the construct only to the degree of its coefficient (λ). There is something insidious to the item that is also included in the examinee's response to it. This is the item's uniqueness, characterized as *error* (ε_j) because it detracts from the item being completely capitalized on the construct. Without the error, the λ would be 1 and the commonality of the item would be complete. The item's reliability would be correspondingly perfect.

The commonality, then, is a weight on the item, termed a *loading factor*. This loading factor represents the contribution of item variance to the construct. The higher the loading factor, the greater the amount an item's variance contributes to an overall test score. This is the loading coefficient seen in the preceding paragraph. To the extent that all the test's items share something in common, there is homogeneity in the construct. Accordingly, in the common factor model, the homogeneity for the test is the sum of these individual factor loadings. Equation 4.2 is the syntactic expression of this model. It shows the total commonality is the sum of the individual item-level communality:

$$\lambda_T = \sum_{I=1}^{n} \lambda_I. \qquad (4.2)$$

More usually, however, homogeneity is expressed in the more familiar variance terms. By this notation, the covariance between any two items is the product of their individual commonalities, shown in Equation 4.3:

$$\sigma_{jk} = \lambda_j \lambda_k. \qquad (4.3)$$

Finally, this logic leads to the score for an examinee on a given test, assuming a common factor. The score is the sum of the individual commonalities with their associated uniqueness and the difficulties. This conclusion is expressed in Equation 4.4:

$$X_T = \sum_{I=1}^{n} (\lambda I + \varepsilon_j + \mu_j). \qquad (4.4)$$

In practical testing situations for test validation, the common factor model is commonly assessed by either FA or PCA. The point of these procedures is to reduce the total variance among items of a covariance matrix to just the shared portion, so this amount may be estimated. In matrix algebra terms, the matrix of inter-item correlations is *diagonalized*. Considering all the items on a test, Equation 4.3 can build easily into a sum of squares and cross-products matrix (**S**), which, one will recall from statistics, is direct input to the correlation matrix. Then, reduction of an **R** matrix is the point of FA or PCA.

In FA (but not PCA), the amount of variation within individual variables that contributes to the commonality of all factors is examined. (In PCA, such commonality is defined to be 1.0, or 100%.) These amounts are the factor loadings described previously. When all (or nearly all) variables have high factor loadings on a given factor and very low factor loadings on all other factors, the test is said to be *factorally pure*. The closer a test is to a pure state, the more evidence is inferred for construct validity and unidimensionality.

Often, however, there is more than one factor or component retained in the model. When each retained factor or component explains a reasonable percentage of the overall variance in the set of variables, the test is *multidimensional*. Again, this finding can also be considered construct-related evidence for validity, although the interpretation is different from that for unidimensional tests. Frequently, in test development, multidimensional tests are divided into subtests composed of subscales along the dimensions of the factors or components. Such division of a test aids interpretation when each dimension is considered as a separate construct. Some major IQ tests, such as the Wechsler Intelligence Scales for Children, 3rd edition, Revised (WISC-IIIR), employ this methodology for construct validation of individual scales within the battery.

In many tests and measurement contexts, especially where the number of examinees is large, a useful validation strategy is to divide the population into groups and run analyses in each group employing identical methodologies. When the final, rotated component (or factor) matrices for the groups are compared and are found to be similar, the inference is justified that validity evidence for the consequent internal structure is strong. The division of groups, however, must be done by a criterion relevant to the task, usually by random assignment of cases to one or another group. Group membership based on sex, gender, race, ethnic-heritage, ability, location, or other such strata is not appropriate for this procedure because the assignment criterion may itself be an intervening variable, or may contain bias, thereby contaminating the results.

IRT Models for Examining Internal Structure

IRT models (discussed in detail in chapter 10) offer another route to examining the internal structure of a test. Hambleton and Murry (1983) offer a list of approaches for employing IRT in test development and for test validation investigations. (Although the authors produced this list more than a decade ago, it is not yet outdated.) They suggest looking at the unidimensionality assumption, checking for equal discrimination indices, investigating the guessing phenomena (for one- and two-parameter IRT models), and researching time analysis, such as comparing variance between scores on a test with set time limits versus one without such a limit. Much more on this important technique is discussed in a later section in this chapter. For extended discussion of IRT, one is referred to a more comprehensive treatment (e.g., Embretson & Reise, 2000).

Multitrait-Multimatrix Method

MTMM is conceptually similar to FA and PCA in that it, too, is a procedure to analyze relationships and determine patterns among data. It can, therefore, provide useful validity evidence when evaluating internal structure. As consistent patterns emerge from the data, construct-related inferences can be drawn. Caution is advised, however, to avoid the common mistake of confusing the information garnered through the MTMM with that yielded through FA and PCA. The techniques are different, and each offers a perspective on the structure of a test for validity evaluation that is different and largely discrete. Further, each approach rests on its own particular assumptions, and readers should be ever mindful of them when discussing results.

For MTMM, it is useful to remember that validity is a summative process in which a variety of information is evaluated. When appropriate information about test score use converges toward similar interpretations and dissimilar data yields divergent inferences, the cumulative evidence is interpreted as meaningful, useful, and indicative of appropriate use of the scores—hence, validity. This idea of looking for similarities and differences (viz., convergence and divergence) among data is the basis for the MTMM.

Although MTMM is useful in construct validation, in practice it is cumbersome to carry out and currently seems to be reported less frequently in the literature of test development, evaluation, validity, and psychometric methods than it had been in the 1990s. This probably suggests decreased use of the method. Still, psychometricians and others will find the technique useful and well worth the considerable effort.

Some proponents of MTMM (e.g., Campbell & Fisk, 1959; Lord & Novick, 1963) have suggested that one way to understand the method is to view reliability and validity as points at opposite ends of a continuum. At one end of the continuum lies reliability, which is, classically defined, the correlation between two perfectly identical measures (e.g., two strictly parallel tests). At the other end of the continuum is validity, which is described as the correlation between two completely dissimilar measures that assess the same construct (e.g., convergent evidence). Theoretically, at some point along the continuum is the correlation between maximally dissimilar constructs (e.g., discriminant validity). This point is identified through the MTMM. Figure 4.5 shows this conceptual continuum visually. In Figure 4.5, the shaded box represents a schema to organize the disparate information into an interpretable body of evidence.

Although the technique is not original to Campbell and Fisk (1959), these researchers did develop it into a useful tool for preparing validity evidence. They suggested the representation for data of the conceptual continuum that is displayed in Figure 4.5. They coined the term *multitrait-multimethod matrix (MTMM)*. Their idea was to prepare a matrix of intercorrelations among scores yielded by tests that assess various (and often overlapping) aspects of the construct under consideration.

It was proposed that three tests be used for the procedure, each employing a different method of assessment. For example, one test could comprise multiple-choice items, whereas a second could be a Likert-type scale, and the third might be an observer rating form. In addition, the measures should be conceptually different, although the constructs intended for assessment should be similar enough to have great overlap. For example, one construct may be a preference toward food, another could be a sentiment about food, and the third construct might be a desire about food. Constructs related to preferences, sentiments, and desires are similar, but not

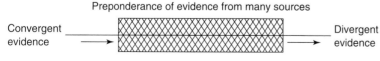

Figure 4.5
Conceptual continuum of multitrait-multimethod matrix showing relationship of convergent and divergent information.

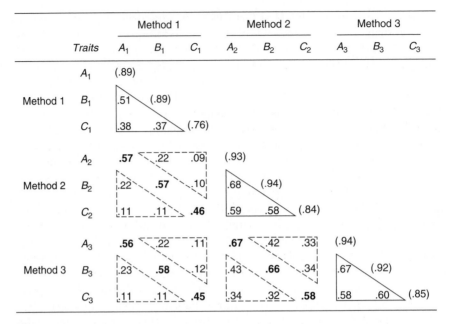

	Traits	Method 1			Method 2			Method 3		
		A_1	B_1	C_1	A_2	B_2	C_2	A_3	B_3	C_3
Method 1	A_1	(.89)								
	B_1	.51	(.89)							
	C_1	.38	.37	(.76)						
Method 2	A_2	**.57**	.22	.09	(.93)					
	B_2	.22	**.57**	.10	.68	(.94)				
	C_2	.11	.11	**.46**	.59	.58	(.84)			
Method 3	A_3	**.56**	.22	.11	**.67**	.42	.33	(.94)		
	B_3	.23	**.58**	.12	.43	**.66**	.34	.67	(.92)	
	C_3	.11	.11	**.45**	.34	.32	**.58**	.58	.60	(.85)

Figure 4.6
Hypothetical multitrait-multimethod matrix.

identical. Thus, a matrix of elements is generated: three constructs assessed by three methods. Figure 4.6 presents a MTMM.

The elements in the table in Figure 4.6 reveal the strategy of the MTMM procedure. Each off-diagonal element represents the correlation coefficients (usually Pearson r) of the combinations of the marginals: the set of trait-by-method levels. Of course, the diagonal elements are the correlation coefficient of each trait and method with itself.

In Figure 4.6, the patterns of the intercorrelations among elements reveal a variety of construct-related evidence. The correlation between the same method and the same trait is test reliability (r), whereas a correlation between two different methods that assess the same construct (viz., trait) is convergent validity evidence (cv). These evidentiary elements are the principle focus of the MTMM, and they are usually the main data reported in studies using the procedure.

Other important correlations signal divergent validity evidence useful for validity evaluation. Correlations between the methods measuring two different constructs (viz., traits) reveal all available aspects of divergent validity (dv1 and dv2). The two forms of this type of evidence are the correlations between the same method measuring two different constructs (dv1), and the correlations between two different methods measuring two different constructs (dv2).

Interpreting the data is usually not difficult, but several considerations should be kept in mind. First, according to Suen (1990), specific characteristics for the correlations are needed for the evidence to be considered meaningful for construct-related inferences. Second, and most evidentially, the reliability indicators (r) should be quite high. Here, values above 0.6 are meaningful. The cv values should be significantly different from random (cv = 0), at a minimum. Because these values are the main correlation of interest, the higher they are, the more they legitimately proffer evidence of convergent validity. At the very least, they should be greater than the dv2 values because failure of this condition would indicate a lack of strength for convergent validity. The same case can be made for cv1 and dv1 values. Third, the cv coefficients of correlation should be larger than both the dv1 and dv2 coefficients. Fourth and finally, there should be a similar pattern of dv1 and dv2 coefficients within each triangle.

Using Generalizability Theory for Examining Internal Structure

From the realization that the MTMM reveals direct information about test reliability, it is but a small conceptual extension to appreciate that generalizability theory (G theory)—with its focus on facets for reliability evidence—can contribute information useful to understanding constructs in assessment and to drawing conclusions in a given situation. Generalizability theory is an approach to measurement in which a particular test score can be thought of as a sample of many scores that could be obtained (viz., for most tests, the items selected are but a few of all those that could have been chosen). Also, validity inferences gathered from test scores from one circumstance are similar to inferences yielded by the same measure in other circumstances. Differences between inferences can be attributed only to error. By this reasoning, then, test scores can be considered to be samples of validity (Messick, 1989). In the MTMM, such sampling is analogous to examining the consistency of scores for all dissimilar tests (methods). I provide a more detailed look at G theory in chapter 11.

In parallel fashion, looking within a given method in the MTMM provides the opportunity to examine different scores for similar methods. This is parallel to consistency of scores for all similar tests (methods). In the theory, such differences are termed *score dependability*. In the matrix, score dependability is indicated by the differences in correlation coefficients between observed scores.

Both generalizability perspectives allow inferences for construct-related validity to be drawn. In one approach, scores are considered as facets, whereas in the other perspective, methods are facets. The first study investigates the extent to which scores are invariant across the methods of measurement. The second study investigates the degree of error in the several scores within a given method. For each study, variance is considered a validity coefficient.

In generalizability theory, a distinction is made between two types of studies: G study and D study. The goal of a G study is to anticipate the many uses for which a test score may be employed and to provide information about the sources of score variation. Shavelson and Webb (1991) state that the G study "should define the universe of admissible observations as broadly as possible" (p. 12). A D study, in contrast, makes use of information from a G study to design the optimal assessment for a particular purpose. In using generalizability theory for validity assessment in the terms described above, a D study would be conducted for each facet.

The two D studies of error variance would be parallel in approach, both being a one-facet crossed design. The variance components are given in Equation 4.5:

$$\sigma^2_{Abs} = \frac{\sigma^2_i}{n'_i} + \frac{\sigma^2_{pi,e}}{n'_i},$$

(4.5)

where σ^2_{Abs} = estimated absolute error variance,

σ^2_i and $\sigma^2_{pi,e}$ = variance components contributing to absolute error for a one-facet, crossed design, and

n'_i = number of items (e.g., methods, scores) in the design.

G theory can provide measures of reliability or error variance. When these sources for error (i.e., facets) are characteristics of the instrument or the trait, as in the MTMM process described, then they are also considered to be measures of validity. By extension, when the validity assessment is focused on overlapping traits and methods, they provide data useful for validity information concerning the internal structure of a test as a source for error.

Validity Coefficient and Coefficient of Determination
When the correlational relationship between a measure and a relevant external criterion is employed as criterion-related evidence in validity evaluation, it assumes the name of *validity*. This coefficient is not limited to expression only by Pearson *r*. Other types of correlation can also be employed for this purpose, such as the Spearman rho (expressed as r_s), the phi coefficient (ϕ), the tetrachoric correlation, or even the contingency coefficient (*C*), although use of the latter is rare. Generally, the biserial and point-biserial coefficients of correlation are reserved for item analysis during test construction and test review, and they are not often used in establishing criterion-related evidence. I describe some of these correlations in the next section.

Still, in correlational relationship terms, the absolute value of such a relationship is termed the *validity coefficient*. Equation 4.6 syntactically shows this relationship:

$$\rho_{XY} = \frac{\sigma_{XY}}{\sigma_X \sigma_Y}.$$

(4.6)

We return to this term in chapter 6 to study it more extensively in the context of reliability theory.

A squared validity coefficient is, not surprisingly, an indication of variance between the two measures. For example, suppose an individual's score on a reading test correlates 0.80 with standing in a spelling bee (the extreme criterion). In this case, about 64% of the variance in an individual's spelling bee standing is related to variance in the reading test score. As a measure of measurement error (and hence, reliability appraisal), the statistic is the *coefficient of determination*, which we discussed in chapter 3. Thus, one might predict an individual's spelling bee placement based on the scores of a reading test, although imperfectly.

Validity coefficients and the coefficient of determination are commonly reported in validity evaluations. Remember, however, that they are specific to a given testing situation, and values useful in one testing context may not be appropriate in another situation.

Finally, validity evidence based on response processes may call for investigation into differential performance on items between the two sexes (a biological description) or differences in gender influences (sociological conditioning). In like manner, exploring differential performance and bias between groups of different ethnic heritages can be revealing of response processes, when the study is so directed.

Standard Error of the Estimate

Because of the criterion problem and related statistical concerns, such as restriction of range or nonnormal distributions for variables, another statistic is sometimes reported along with validity coefficients: the *standard error of the estimate*. This statistic indicates the inaccuracy of predictions from the regression line. It is employed in regression descriptions of unexplained variance. Alternatively, it is a root-mean square error term, and is thus closely related to the SEM discussed in chapters 3 and 5. Syntactic expression of the SEM was presented in chapter 3 as Equation 3.33, repeated here for convenience:

$$\sigma_\varepsilon = \sigma_X \sqrt{(1 - \rho_{XT})}.$$

Recall that SEM is the standard deviation of a distribution of universe scores for an individual. Keeping this fact in mind, imagine a regression line that has a distribution of scores for each observed score value around a predicted score, as shown in Figure 4.7. (Readers should recognize that the figure is commonly used in considerations of homoscedasticity in a data set.) In other words, replace the intercept of a given observed score (the point at which the observed score falls on the regression line) with a normal-type distribution of scores about the point. This distribution represents the range of values for a given condition or observed score, hence its name, *conditional distribution*.

Note in the figure that although a few conditional distributions are displayed, there are, in actuality, many such distributions: in fact, one for each observed score, and in theory, one for each possible score. Because these are distributions of scores, it is easy to realize that each one has a unique mean and a standard deviation. However, as we discussed in chapter 2, because all conditional distributions are presumed to be normal, they all have the same standard deviation. This standard deviation value is the standard error of the estimate. Its computational formula is shown in Equation 4.7:

$$\sigma_{e \cdot e'} = \sigma_{e'} \sqrt{(1 - \rho_{e \cdot e'}^2)}. \tag{4.7}$$

One notices almost immediately that Equations 3.33 and 4.7 are nearly identical, but with modified notation—rightly so, because both estimate a conditional score for an observed response. However, with the SEM, the observed score is given, but for the standard error of the estimate, it is general for all observed scores in a prediction.

As a computational example of this useful statistic, return to the 0.80 correlation between scores on a spelling test and standing in a spelling bee, first presented in the discussion for the coefficient of determination. Now, take as a given that there are 100 participants in the spelling bee and that the standard deviation of the

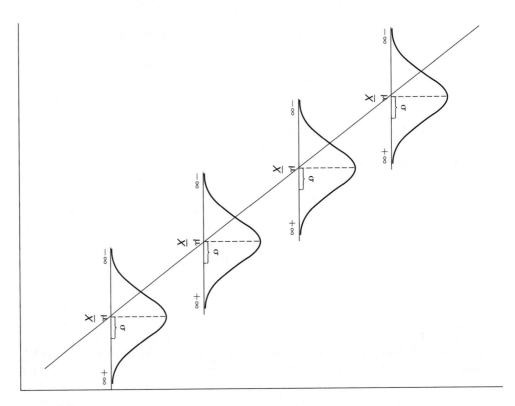

Figure 4.7
Conditional distributions of scores around regression line throughout scale range, showing homoscedasticity.

predicted scores (spelling bee standing) is 4.5. Using Equation 4.7, the standard error of the estimate is calculated as follows:

$$\sigma_{e \cdot e'} = 4.5\sqrt{(1 - .80^2)} = 3.9 \approx 4.$$

Thus, for a predicted spelling bee standing of 35th place, about 68% of the students or individuals tested at this point ($\pm 1\sigma_{e \cdot e'}$) will actually have achieved a standing somewhere between 31st and 39th place (35 ± 4).

Validity Evidence Based on Relations to Other Variables

It will come to most students as little surprise that although we no longer view the correlational relationship between a test and an appropriate criterion as the sole, implicit definition for validity, evidence based on relations between assessment variables is still enormously important. Hence, it is necessary to realize particular features about correlational relationships between tests.

The point in time at which the relationship between scores on a test and a criterion is examined is often identified by labeling the criterion evidence as *predictive-* or *concurrent-related evidence* for validity. Both types of evidence signal that a relation-ship is made between the test and an external criterion. The only difference is when the correlational relationship is appraised. As the name signals, *predictive* is an indi-cator between a test and some future, or posttest administration criterion. Examples of this temporal relationship may be between a Scholastic Aptitude Test (SAT) or an American College Testing (ACT) test score (often taken in high school or shortly there-after) and college freshman grade point average (GPA), or between a certification exam and some measure of subsequent success at the job. In both instances, the test is correlated with a criterion that occurs later than the test administration.

Concurrent, however, marks an index between a test and a contemporaneous criterion. Often, demographic or descriptive information, such as neighborhood average income or free and reduced lunch program participation, is used as the contemporaneous criterion for an achievement test. Theoretically, a parallel test, administered immediately before or after the target test, could also be the contem-poraneous criterion. Of course, when gathering such evidence, a rationale should be offered to explain the relatedness of the two measures.

Although current research substantively justifies employing criterion-related evi-dence as a data source for validity evaluation, a distinction between using predictive-or concurrent-related evidence for validity has not been established. Either or both types of evidence should be part of a measure of validity, and it is not necessarily stronger to have one or another or both types presented in evaluations. The merit of criterion-related evidence rests with the relationship, not with whether the crite-rion is concurrent or predictive. Regardless, the nature of the correlation should be stipulated in any validity evaluation.

The Criterion Problem

In real world validity evaluation, a problem arises when a correlational relationship is the sole or primary source for validity evidence. The difficulty stems from the fact that in CTT, true score is only theoretically conceived and cannot be known ab-solutely, despite our accommodations to make it apply to practical testing situations (hence, universe score discussed earlier). In practical work, it becomes apparent that the correlational reliability as criterion-related evidence for validity of a test is depressed by the degree of measurement error in the criterion. This circumstance is known as the *criterion problem,* and it comes into play in measurement science in many practical contexts.

The criterion problem, simply stated, is that the criterion's own reliability is de-pendent on the correlational relationship that it has with its external criterion, a flawed measure itself. The external criterion's validity is, in like manner, established with another flawed measure, and so on for each measure. The situation is a bit like trying to anchor one boat to another boat. The first boat is stabilized only insofar as the second boat is stable. However, that second boat is, in like manner to the first boat, stable only insofar as it is anchored to yet another boat. This situation sounds like we have an endless chain in which the stability of each link is hopelessly hooked to the stability of another link, and so on without end. Given this logic, one would imagine that stability (or reliability) in measures could never be achieved.

Fortunately, the criterion problem need not vex validity investigations too much. Just as the criterion problem arises only in real world investigations into validity (it does not exist in the theory), its solution is also grounded in reality. The situation can be addressed on two fronts. First, in measurement, we do not expect perfect reliability in any measure, nor are perfect correlations between a test and its criterion ever anticipated. We accept as useful data correlational coefficients that are less than 1; often 0.6 or 0.7 is all that is achieved, and useful test interpretation is made. Second, there are statistical corrections to this that are addressed later in the chapter and more extensively in chapter 5.

The Restriction of Range and Normalcy in Variables

A more mathematical, and less recognized, problem in establishing correlational relationships, however, is the sensitivity of the correlation coefficient to issues related to the range and normalcy (i.e., linearity, hetero/homoscedasticity) of the variables employed in making the correlation. Problems in range and normalcy can make interpretation of correlations spurious. Such problems may occur when the variables have restricted range or deviate from normality by a large amount.

An everyday example of a variable that is inherently restrictive is GPA. The measure is commonly employed as a criterion variable. This use of GPA is discouraged, however, because of its limited range in making continuous variable correlations. A common remedy by beginning researchers who recognize the problem is to simply add decimals to extend the scale, imagining that this adds needed variance. Unfortunately, this simple solution is unsatisfactory because it merely brings forth the question of the just noticeable difference (see chapter 2). After all, what teacher can reliably mark a 2.67 from a 2.68?

Restriction of range can also occur in the measurement of a variable, even when there is sufficient range in the scale to accommodate a population. Lord and Novick (1963) describe two circumstances in which this restriction of range can occur. The first situation is when a test's score is explicitly used as a condition for selection. An example is using Medical College Admission Test (MCAT) scores as a predictor of success in medical school. Here, there is exclusion of applicants who did not meet the criterion of a given relationship between the variables, and the range is restricted to just those who are previously successful on the predictor measure. This circumstance is labeled *explicit selection,* and it is particularly acute in affecting restriction of range.

In contrast to explicit selection is a second condition called *incidental selection.* Here, the scores from a related test or measure (as opposed to the test of primary interest) are used for selection, and the relationship masks the true range. An example of incidental selection is when the Graduate Records Exam (GRE) scores are used as a surrogate for MCAT prediction. The selection criterion of the GRE limits (hence, restricts) the possibility of the MCAT as a meaningful predictor criterion. Incidental selection is less influenced by the effects of restriction of range than is explicit selection. In either instance, however, less than accurate data are available for making reasoned, accurate data-based decisions.

Still another problem arises from restriction of range and lack of normalcy in variables. Restriction of range attenuates reliability estimates, and hence, arbitrarily depresses validity coefficients. Such restriction of range in criterion measures can be noted statistically by very large (either positive or negative) skewness and kurtosis indices. Typically, skewness or kurtosis values greater than ±3.0, and certainly, ±4.0, give one good cause to pay attention to this problem.

For this statistical problem, however, a remedy is available. Lord and Novick (1963) demonstrated that when two specific assumptions are made, a statistical attenuation correction to the criterion-related validity coefficient is available. The assumptions are (a) that a linear relationship exists between the test and its criterion measure, and (b) that there is homoscedasticity along the range of scores in the variables. This criterion-related validity coefficient, corrected for attenuation by restriction of range, is given in Equation 4.8:

$$\rho_{xc} = \sqrt{\dfrac{1}{1 + \dfrac{\sigma_{x^*}^2}{\sigma_x^2}\left(\dfrac{1}{\rho_{x^*c}^2} - 1\right)}}, \qquad (4.8)$$

where ρ_{xc} = corrected for attenuation validity coefficient,

   $\sigma_{x^*}^2$ = variance of scores for group with restricted range,

   σ_x^2 = variance of scores for group with unrestricted range, and

   $\rho_{x^*c}^2$ = correlation between the test score and the criterion measure within the restricted range.

Although this formula does offer correction for attenuation in these circumstances, it is not perfect. As Lord and Novick (1963) point out, the second assumption (i.e., homoscedasticity) is unavailable for testing by the very nature of the restricted range. Without a test of the assumption, the correction itself is suspect. It seems tautology is present in the problem and in its correction. In sum, then, it is best to avoid the problem in the first place rather than experience it and attempt a dubious fix. Hence, look for variables that have sufficient range in the scale.

There is yet another problem with small-range variables. As one may recall from early work in statistics, when correlations are calculated from continuous variables, they are especially sensitive to outlying values within those variables. This problem is acute when the number of cases included in the variable for a particular set of data is small. Here, only a few cases can throw the whole measurement out of whack.

One is cautioned, however, not to confuse every extreme value in a continuous variable with true outliers or to simply delete outliers as the best solution to advance normalcy in a data set (see Tabachnick & Fidell, 2000). Such linearity and normalcy issues should be carefully addressed in screening data and in examining other assumptions, prior to employing them as a source of evidence in validity evaluation.

Validity Evidence Based on the External Considerations

Face Validity as a Source of Evidence

Makers of canned, frozen concentrates, such as orange juice or lemonade, carefully attend to the notion that, when reconstituted with water, their drink has the look and feel of the real thing, something marketers call "mouth feel." The same idea holds with tests: They, too, should "look and feel" the way laypersons expect. For tests, such considerations popularly fall under the title *face validity*. This means that an examinee who sees a test instrument for the first time should not be confronted with a document that is surprisingly unfamiliar; often the result of unprofessional preparation.

Face validity cannot be examined by statistical methods. Such absence of statistical measurement for face validity, however, does not mean that professional test developers and psychometricians should underestimate its importance or simply dismiss it altogether. Test takers typically come to a test administration expecting to put forth their best effort, and they have a right to anticipate that the instrument is prepared with care and attention to detail. Indeed, offering examinees a test instrument that has a professional "look and feel" is a validity-related responsibility of a test maker. Osterlind (1998) offers some practical suggestions, with examples of style and appearance for professionally developed tests. This style manual may be useful to makers of tests.

Validity Generalization

The *Standards* defines *validity generalization* as a source for evidence that broadly encompasses issues relating to the "degree to which evidence of validity based on test-criterion relations can be generalized to a new situation without further study of validity in that new situation" (American Educational Research Association et al., 1999, p. 15). In other words, in validity evaluation, there are circumstances in which prior work done in other evaluations or research may be appropriately applied to the new situation. For example, often when relationships between one test and its criterion are contrasted to relations between another test and its own criterion, those differences are found to be the result of statistical artifacts, such as sample error and others. Formerly, any such differences were taken as a dictum for conducting a new test validation process for each new situation. However, more recently, meta-analytic studies have shown that in some domains, what is learned from the first validation process can be employed in another validity evaluation, thereby obviating the need for starting each new test validation from scratch. When such is the case, the researcher should document the primary sources and state explicitly that validity evidence is based on generalization and not on original work.

Consequential Validity Evidence

Measurement professionals generally believe that, just as with other social endeavors, a public responsibility arises for persons who develop, take, or use tests. There is fierce disagreement, however, about whether sensitivity to social issues is an integral part of validity. Two competing articles—juxtaposed in an issue of *Educational Measurement: Issues and Practices,* and whose titles capture the essence of each side's argument—are worth noting because they have garnered much public attention. The article espousing social consequence as integral to validity is entitled, "The Centrality of Test Use and Consequences for Test Validity" (Shepard, 1997), and its opposite has the title, "Consequential Validity: Right Concern—Wrong Concept" (Popham, 1997).

Lorrie Shepard argues that attention to social consequences of test-based decisions is part and parcel of what "true" validity has always been. She cites early definitions of validity by Cureton and Cronbach, as well as thoughts about test use by the classical psychometrician, Gulliksen, to buttress her point. According to Shepard, as soon as one conceives of validity as decisions based on test data (rather than as a characteristic of the test itself), one is immediately obliged to think about the effects or consequences of those decisions.

W. James Popham (1997), writing insightfully and with characteristic humor, has a different perspective on social consequences as part of validity. Emphasizing that although "every right-thinking measurement person ought to be concerned about the consequences ensuing from a test's use" (p. 9), he argues that there is illogic in the train of thought that test use consequences necessarily follow from validity inferences. Popham suggests that linking social consequences to validity arises from muddled thinking and is actually counterproductive because doing so adds obtuse logic and unnecessary complexity to validity concerns. When one is distracted from the serious attention that should be paid to making proper test-based inferences, validity is the causality. According to Popham, persons who espouse the validity as social consequence notion are, "unfortunately, headed in a dysfunctional direction" (p. 9). It is unrealistic and unfair, he maintains, to expect test makers and publishers to be responsible for misuses of scores by persons unknown, or known.

A present-day controversy illustrates the problem of considering test validity as social consequence. Currently, the U.S. Department of Education is drafting new guidelines for using standardized tests in making college admissions decisions. With more than 4,000 postsecondary institutions in the United States, it is easy to realize the widespread impact that dramatic changes in the guidelines would have. The SAT, published by the Educational Testing Service, and the ACT, published by the American College Testing Program, are administered collectively worldwide to more than 2 million persons annually and are used primarily for making college admission decisions. The proposed new guidelines do not suggest new criteria for test development or test characteristics, or even for test interpretation. Rather, they focus exclusively on the consequences of using standardized measures such as the SAT or ACT for making admission decisions, and specifically on the adverse impact they have on the number of persons whose heritage is an ethnic minority admitted (or not admitted) to colleges and universities. This is clearly a policy perspective and should be viewed separately from test development considerations.

Summary

This chapter covers validity, beginning with a clear description of its meaning and its importance to measurement science. Then, I examine the *Standards'* perspective on validity and move into some history of the concept. The largest part of the chapter discusses sources for validity evidence, including methods useful for building validity evaluation and argument.

Chapter 5

Traditional Reliability Strategies

Introduction

Knowing the "Why"

Knowing why something happens is often more complex than observing its occurrence. Conquering Mount Everest, the highest peak in the world, was a milestone not only in mountain climbing, but also in contemporary human achievement. Credit for this monumental accomplishment is usually given to Sir Edmund Hillary and his Sherpa colleague, Tenzing Norgay, who together reached the top on May 29, 1953. However, were they really the first to summit Everest? George Leigh Mallory and his climbing partner, Sandy Irvine, may have actually climbed to the top as early as June 1924, an even more astonishing feat given their primitive climbing ropes and limited bottled oxygen. The truth of which climbing party reached the summit first may never be known conclusively. Mallory fell during his climb and died on the peak—his body was finally found in 1999. (It is unclear what happened to Irvine, but apparently, he also died on the peak.) The quandary that haunts the climbing community is whether Mallory fell while ascending or descending—did he actually conquer the peak before dying? If the latter is true, then Mallory, and not Hillary, would be the first to have conquered Everest. The key to answering this question may lie in learning *why* he took the particularly precarious route he did. Most adventurers believe that if it can be determined why he took that route, the question of "Who was first?" will be solved.

Similarly, it is important to understand why measurement engages particular psychometric techniques and strategies. In a fundamental, technical sense, this chapter explains the "why" of psychometric methods by discussing *reliability* and explaining various means to estimate it. Reliability is the technical depiction of measurement error. Knowing about reliability, then, is a key to achieving a full understanding of mental measurements.

Contents

Given reliability's central position in measurement theory, one may readily surmise that the information presented here extends the discussion in chapter 3 of CTT and augments other theories of measurement presented in later chapters. Clearly, it does! Readers unfamiliar with the notions for measurement theory presented earlier are advised to have that background in place before attempting this chapter.

In this chapter, I explain many important aspects of reliability and present some methods of estimating it in varying measurement contexts. I begin by discussing the meaning of reliability and by providing a classic definition. Then, I introduce and develop a number of important considerations about reliability, necessary for its proper interpretation and use. This is followed by a thorough explanation of a theory of reliability and a description of how that manifests a reliability index. Thereafter, a number of methods for estimating reliability coefficients are described and I explain testing contexts where they may properly be used. Throughout the chapter, I emphasize that reliability estimation depends greatly on the context and meaning of a particular test, such as how the domain is defined (in the domain sampling model) or the latent variable conceived (in latent variable estimation). This approach is deliberate because it brings to the fore the perspective that for proper interpretation one must have a good grasp of the concept rather than merely knowing the mechanics of calculating a coefficient.

Generic Description of the Concept of Reliability

Meaning of Reliability

Reliability is a term with broad implications, but its meaning is specific. It refers to precision in mental appraisal. Precision is determined by the dependability or consistency across several appraisals of randomly parallel measures. The notion of reliability applies in two contexts. First, it reveals precision between or among mental measurement instruments (i.e., intertest), as given in a reliability index (often calculated as a reliability coefficient); and, second, it applies intraindividually for examinees, as specified in the standard error of measurement (SEM). Both the index and SEM are integral to reliability.

To state the idea more practically and from a thoroughly modern perspective, reliability labels the concept of estimating how well samples of appropriate assessment stimuli (i.e., the items or exercises on a test) represent the universe of possible stimuli (i.e., all eligible items or exercises) for a latent construct (or, indeed, cognitive processes) or a sampled domain of content. Over repeated trials, the more consistent a measure is in reproducing from the sample the universe of admissible observations, the greater its reliability. As is evident from this description, then, to the degree that reliability is present in measurement, error is absent. That is, the more reliable a measure, the less error in its yielded scores and the more confidence one may have in interpreting them.

A proximate depiction of "unreliability" is the saying that a person with one watch knows what time it is, whereas a person with two watches is never quite sure. This is, of course, because a single appraisal gives no information about consistency or dependability whereas the question of precision is always answered in the context of repeated measures—here, time is measured twice, once with each watch. If a number of identical watches were used to indicate time, however, the reliability of time telling by the watches could be known.

However, even from this beginning information, it is apparent that reliability depends in great measure on the context in which it is used. In other words, reliability is not a universal or absolute depiction of (the absence of) measurement error; rather, its meaning may only be properly interpreted in the framework of a particular assessment. This means that there are many accounts for reliability, depending on one's definition of "error" and how the latent construct or content domain is defined initially.

If, for instance, only the items employed as the sample representing a universe are considered as a cause of error, and the only source of variability is the interaction of differing responses by examinees to them, the meaning of reliability is constrained to just that concern. In many testing contexts, however, error is also considered for other facets of an assessment. Suppose, for example, the appraisal stipulates that the examinees produce a sample of writing and that sample is scored repeatedly by several judges (say, two or three). In such a situation, "raters" can also be included as a source of error variation for analysis. In like fashion, other appropriate sources for error may be considered, such as "occasion" when repeated assessments are used. Hence, in reliability estimation, error takes on varying perspectives, and the meaning of "reliability" will reflect that particular outlook.

As this chapter focuses on traditional reliability analyses, it should be noted that under CTT only one facet for error is considered: the residual of the interaction between items and examinee variability (viz., different responses to them). Under the theory, no other sources for error are included in analyses. Consequently, random error is uniform for the population. In some other measurement theories—most notably, generalizability theory (studied in chapter 11)—the error is considered multidimensionally, and estimating several facets simultaneously is the focus for attention. In traditional approaches to reliability, however, there is no such delineation of sources for error. From this CTT perspective, reliability can be considered a constrained case of reliability as a structural model, the generalizability case.

Then, too, just taking into account appropriate facets of an appraisal situation is not the end of error. Consider also the fact that there are many ways in which to define and sample a trait or content domain. This also influences reliability estimation. When a latent trait is defined broadly, as in the depiction of a whole field—say, biology, psychology, or other—there is greater likelihood that a sample does not hold enough breadth and depth to represent the field fully than when a trait is defined narrowly. In a narrow delineation—say, just simple division by fractions—the field may be more constricturally defined and likely more fully sampled. Hence, a test maker's depiction of the trait or domain for assessment itself will influence reliability.

Of course, because reliability addresses accuracy in measurement, it is an integral part of validity (as we learned in chapter 4). We can appreciate, then, that the two ideas are tightly bound together—that is, "inextricably interconnected"—according to Stephen Hawking's expression. Staying with an astrophysics metaphor, so tight is the bond between validity and reliability that they act like Heisenberg's Uncertainty Principle, which states that either the path of an electron moving through space is known or the electron itself is described, but both cannot be known simultaneously because any movement in one (e.g., measuring it) unavoidably disturbs the other. This also applies to validity and reliability.

In mental appraisal, reliability has a strict relationship to validity. Recall that this relationship was presented in chapter 4: *Reliability is a necessary but insufficient condition for validity*. This statement is logical because reliability is a measure of the absence of random error, and error is antithetical to valid inference. Reliability is an important part of validity evaluation but, by itself, is incomplete for validity inference.

However, to reinforce what was stated in the earlier chapter on validity, reliability does not constitute validity. The ideas are not wholly one in the same. Validity is a broader concept than reliability, addressing how faithfully the universe of admissible observations depicts the latent dimensions being considered in addition to the overlapping issue of precision in appraising that latency itself. Reliability is directed primarily toward the latter of validity's twin concerns.

Definition of Reliability in CTT

Notwithstanding the fact that the interpretation of reliability is contextual, the term has a fixed statistical definition. Lord and Novick (1968) offer a classic *definition of reliability;* namely, "the reliability of a test is defined as the squared correlation between observed score and true score" (p. 61). This definition is shown in the term in Expression 5.1. Implicit in this view of reliability is the notion of variance as an indicator of measurement error. Score variance is what we study in reliability theory.

$$\rho_{XT}^2. \qquad \textbf{(5.1)}$$

Reliability is evaluated by consistency of measurement when assessment is repeated for an individual or for groups of a population. Accordingly, the more constant measurement is over repeated administrations, the higher the reliability. When this is considered in theory it is a *reliability index,* given in Expression 5.2 as the correlation between an observed score variable and true score, reflecting the definition shown in Expression 5.1:

$$\rho_{XT}. \qquad \textbf{(5.2)}$$

This depiction, however, involves the correlation of an observed score variable with an unobserved variable, namely, true score, a theoretical variable. Although the theory gives us guidance, in real world estimation we have only observed scores to work with. True score only exists in theory. Fortunately, measurement theorists have given useful depictions of how reliability evaluation can work in practice. Gulliksen (1950), an early architect of reliability theory for psychometric application, famously said, "Reliability is the correlation between two parallel forms of a test" (p. 13). Hence, the notion in Expression 5.2 is given life in many formulas by a *reliability coefficient,* generically shown in Expression 5.3. In the coefficient, the correlation is between two observed scores or sets of scores. Importantly, however, realize that reliability coefficients are not ordinary correlations but a special type: The variables must be parallel, and the appraisals are necessarily independent.

These two stipulations also explain why reliability is not indicated for just any correlation:

$$\rho_{X_1 X_2}.$$

$$(5.3)$$

The three terms of reliability (see Expressions 5.1 to 5.3) are important to its understanding, and we explore them thoroughly in this chapter. Interestingly, note from these terms that both a correlation and a squared correlation describe reliability. Yet one term (Expression 5.1), although a variance expression, is not the variance of the other (Expression 5.2). We investigate this seeming inconsistency in a later section of the chapter because it has important implications in reliability evaluation.

Also, realize that the depiction of reliability thus far is delimited to show consistency among error-prone measures, that is, tests. A parallel idea of error in measurement is applicable to within-person inconsistency. This notion for reliability is revealed in the standard error of measurement (SEM), an idea introduced in chapter 3 during discussion of CTT. As we learned in that chapter, the SEM is the standard deviation of all errors about the true score for all individuals in a population or tested sample. We see later in this chapter that it is estimated by the observed standard deviation and the alternative forms reliability coefficient. In measurement generally, there are many circumstances in which the SEM is more satisfying to depict error than is a reliability coefficient by itself. In modern IRT, the SEM is given prominence, where it reveals the degree of internal inconsistency within each examinee's observed score pattern. In CTT, however, the SEM is usually relegated to a lesser role because in that theory it is only a gross indicator, showing average across-person error. Hence, under tenants of CTT, it may be an inaccurate depiction of error for a particular individual. The syntactic expression of the SEM was given in chapter 3 as Equation 3.30, repeated here for convenience:

$$\sigma_\varepsilon.$$

Because the SEM is essential to completeness in reliability appraisal, it too is explored in this chapter.

An Illustration

A simple example illustrates two basic notions of reliability: error in measurement and replication for its estimation. To keep things undemanding at the start, let us imagine reliability in physical measurement. Suppose we want to learn how far Tiger Woods typically drives a golf ball off the tee. This is a question of reliability. (We could use another subject as our example, such as the great Jean-Claude Killy's time for racing down a ski slope or, of course, that dreaded bathroom scale.) To help us out, Tiger agrees to demonstrate his skill at driving golf balls. He will drive a ball off the tee as far and as straight as he can. All the conditions are set: We chose a fairway without turns, and the wind is calm. His first drive goes long and straight, and is measured at 330 yards (a good drive, even for a professional). Is this really his "driving ability"? So far, there is no replication. The one attempt is just a single measure.

Neither do we know how far he can hit the ball (his maximum distance) nor may we surmise his typical distance. We only know how far he hit it on one occasion. In measurement, we are more interested in one's typical performance because this is presumed to represent true ability better than any single event. Remember, precision in measurement can only be estimated from repeated trials.

Now, Tiger hits a second tee shot (identical club, same effort, and so forth). This one goes a little to the left and is only 320 yards out. He hits two more drives: One goes an astounding 350 yards and the other lands short, only 290 yards long. The collection of Tiger's golf drives is referred to as his *observed scores*. Presuming he could make some infinite number of hits off the tee, we would have his *universe of scores*. So, now, our question for reliability is: Which shot actually shows Tiger's driving ability—the longest drive, the shortest one, or the one somewhere in between? Should we use the average of his shots, even though he did not take an infinite number of them?

The fact that Tiger does not hit the ball an equal distance every time means that there is some misrepresentation of "typical" in each of our observations—that is, we cannot know the precision from any single shot. The source of the variation in his shots is unknown and is considered random among all persons in a population (say, all golf professionals). The error could be something Tiger did differently each time, such as some slight variation in his swing. Or, it could come from the differing course conditions (e.g., wind variations). Just as likely, too, the error could emanate from an inaccuracy in the instrument used to determine distances (regardless of whether we are walking off the distance, are using yard markers on the course, or are employing a sophisticated light laser).

At this point (because we are using CTT), we are not interested in discerning precise sources of error. Even if they were known, it is unlikely we could control them all completely, anyway. Likewise, for reliability determination (under CTT), our interest is not in determining the *cause* for differences observed in Tiger's shots; rather, it is solely in expertly estimating the *magnitude* of error, regardless of its sources.

For the obvious reason that cognition is more abstruse than golf driving skill, one can easily imagine that assessing educational and psychological constructs is manifestly more complex than surveying driving distances off a golf tee. In the words of L. L. Thurstone (1931), "Measurement in psychology is usually made with the handicap of unknown and uncontrollable factors so that measurements are rather unstable" (p. 1). Still, we can make estimates of reliability that are extremely precise and useful in many measurement contexts.

Considerations for Reliability Assessment

With the previous background in place but before delving into the algebra of reliability theory, it is useful to know and appreciate a number of relevant considerations. I discuss these concerns here.

Reliability as Integral to Measurement Theory

For persons new to the study of reliability, an especially important point is to reiterate that it is indivisible from measurement theory. This is seen most obviously by the fact that when either the notion for true score or reliability is given algebraically, the same mathematical expression is used: $X_{ij} = \tau_{ij} + \varepsilon$. As mentioned in chapter 3, CTT is often referred to as a *theory of reliability*. Hence, to the extent that any discussion of measurement theory is advanced, reliability is addressed simultaneously. Simply, discussion of measurement theory—whether CTT, IRT, generalizability theory, or other—is to attend to reliability.

Reliability Is Not Defined as a Procedure

Readers should also appreciate from the outset that the concept of reliability is not defined by the procedures employed for its appraisal. That is, reliability is not "Cronbach's alpha" or "test–retest," or other statistic (we study both later in the chapter). Rather, it stands simply, but significantly, as an avowal of how precisely the universe of possible observations is sampled in the context of realizing what facets for error are being considered. The procedures are various methods available to estimate reliability, but their interpretation is only meaningful in light of knowing the overall concept. In other words, the coefficients are not *de facto* reliability. They merely give expression to the concept.

As evidence, consider this statement on interpreting and using *coefficient α,* probably the most popularly reported indicator of reliability, made by its developer, Lee J. Cronbach. He says that even this measure "is now seen to cover only a small perspective of the range of measurement uses for which reliability information is needed. The alpha coefficient is now seen to fit within a much larger system of reliability analysis" (Cronbach & Shavelson, 2004, p. 416). Thus, the methods employed for estimating reliability should reflect this perspective for proper interpretation.

The conditional existence of reliability on validity is given in hermeneutic argument by Li (2003). Li maintains that reliability has different uses, but not different meanings, and this paradox can lead to a misinterpretation of reliability. He reasons that "since random error cannot be useful for any inference or prediction, an instrument without reliability, because it is entirely random error, cannot have any validity" (p. 91). Hence, from reliability alone one cannot make complete validity inferences, but when making valid inferences, reliability is implicit.

Reliability of Scores—Not of Instruments

To elaborate the previous point, when interpreting evidence for reliability, we see a parallel to descriptions of validity in that it is inappropriate to label a particular test "reliable" or "not reliable," just as in an earlier chapter I explained that instruments are not in and of themselves "valid" or "not valid." Instead, when describing reliability in practical contexts, one should identify the occasion of measurement, the likely sources of error, and the decision-making context for the scores. Hence, reliability is of scores, not of instruments. A given test may yield scores that can be reliably used for some particular decision but not for others.

As a practical matter, however, if reliability is estimated in settings that generalize appropriately, then the statistics representing it in the first context (e.g., Cronbach's alpha, test–retest, SEM) may be meaningfully repeated in a new situation without recalculation. For example, if a school-based test of academic achievement is normed on sample populations of students from many schools across the state or nation that can generalize to a particular school district, then (in a structural sense) the reliability coefficient calculated from the norming sample may also be appropriately interpreted for the particular school sample.

Confusing Reliability with Validity

Although readers of this book are likely immersed sufficiently in measurement issues to not confuse reliability with validity, to some others confusing the two ideas is a common topsy-turvy of the terms. For example, medical procedures are often referred to as reliable when arguments for their efficaciousness (viz., issues of validity) are advanced. Hikers may say that their compass is reliable, some even calling theirs "ol' trusty," when what is more likely meant is that it points to (magnetic) north instead of somewhere else, again a concern of validity. A consistent inaccuracy is still inaccurate. As measurement professionals, we should realize the meaning of reliability in measurement science, where it has a specific meaning, with technical criteria for its estimation. In popular speech, where exactitude in language is not so important, the term is more liberally accepted to mean many things.

Reliability and Error as Used in Popular Speech

An additional point about proper use of the term "reliability" also comes from popular speech. In popular conversation, we speak of "error" routinely and the notion of error carries a connotation of an avoidable mistake. We hear such statements as, "I made an error in arithmetic" or "I made an error in judgment." However, to avoid such an error is not "reliability" and these uses of the term do no imply "measurement error." Reliability, in our context of mental appraisal, is a technical term—psychometrician's argot, if you will—that helps us to understand the precision of a particular measurement.

The AERA/APA/NCME Standards' Comments on Reliability

The *Standards for Educational and Psychological Testing* (American Educational Research Association, American Psychological Association, & National Council on Measurement in Education, 1999) emphasizes the importance of reliability by stipulating the reporting of reliability information as its first standard in the second section (viz., Standard 2.1). This standard reads as follows: "For each total score, subscore, or combination of scores that is to be interpreted, estimates of relevant reliabilities and standard errors of measurement or test information functions should be reported" (p. 31). The rationale given in the *Standards* is equally clear:

> The usefulness of behavioral measurement presupposes that individuals and groups exhibit some degree of stability in their behaviors. However, successive samples of behavior from the same person are rarely identical in all pertinent respects. An individual's performances, products, and responses to sets of test questions vary in their quality or character from one occasion to another. . . . This variation is reflected in the examinee's scores. The causes of this variability are generally unrelated to the purpose of measurement. (American Educational Research Association et al., 1999, p. 25)

Hence, by its prominent placement alone within such a seminal document, we realize the importance of reliability to the work of psychometricians and other measurement professionals.

The APA (Wilkinson & APA Task Force on Statistical Inference, 1999) is clear on when to report reliability information. Speaking of researchers who report research results in scholarly journals, they stipulate that "authors should provide reliability coefficients of the scores for the data being analyzed even when the focus of the research is not psychometric. Interpreting the size of observed effects requires an assessment of the reliability of the scores" (p. 597). Researchers particularly should heed this useful advice.

A Giant in the Field of Reliability Appraisal

Then, too, as an introduction to reliability, readers should appreciate that one name stands so tall in the field that it deserves special mention: the late Professor Lee J. Cronbach (1916–2001) of Stanford University. Much theoretical work in reliability assessment owes is origins and development to Cronbach. In chapter 11, when I discuss modern conceptions of reliability (as in generalizability theory), Cronbach again shows evidence of his great contributions. As just one example, he invented Cronbach's alpha, which remains today enormously important in test evaluation. A man of eclectic interests, Cronbach was famous for his charm, wit, and most especially, his brilliance. It is recounted that at age 4, he calculated the unit price of potatoes at a local grocery store, informing his mother that another store had a better deal. His mother was (obviously, more than a little) curious about her son's remarkable ability, and only a few years later she brought him to the famous IQ legend, Lewis Terman, who administered his early IQ battery to young Lee. The child's published score was an incredible 200, even an impossible score by many of today's IQ scalings (Shavelson & Eisner, 2002).

Theory of Reliability

Reliability is itself a theory of measurement, typically shown through CTT. However, the theory is not a simple pleonastic argument; it leads to equations useful to calculate an index for its expression or a coefficient that can be interpreted in real world testing contexts. We have already seen the outlines of this theory in Expressions 5.1 to 5.3 and the SEM. In this section, I present both the theory and its algebraic expressions. In a later section, I explain how to calculate several types of reliability coefficients, useful in practical testing situations.

Reliability as Error Variance

Following theory, reliability indicators are a specialized type of coefficient showing the correlational relationship of random variables for independent assessments of the same construct. The reliability index is a ratio of these assessments, making it technically a ratio of variances—specifically, true score variance over observed score variance. As mentioned previously, the variance can be considered unidimensionally (as in CTT) or multidimensionally (as in other modern theories like generalizability theory) to include several sources of error for simultaneous evaluation.

Although this idea is straightforward, it seemingly cannot be calculated in real world settings because we seldom have the repeated observations, and even less often do we have available even congeneric tests (less restrictive than the theory-required strictly parallel measures). Additionally, as we know, our consideration of error in CTT is constrained to just one facet: items and variability in endorsement by examinees.

At first blush, then, it may seem that real world circumstances have conspired to make reliability appraisal nearly impossible. However, and fortunately, this is not so. In fact, we can make precise reliability estimates with just the data available from one administration of a test. The key to our solution lies in the fact that probability theory allows a relationship between the two variables to be estimated even when one of them is only theoretically conceived. In chapter 2, I explain this concept and offer its proof (remember the idea of expectations and its relation to true score). In our case here, for reliability estimation we have an observed variable and an expected variable, the true score. With this, we can express reliability as a ratio of variances, shown in Equation 5.4:

$$\rho_{XT}^2 = \frac{\sigma_T^2}{\sigma_X^2}. \tag{5.4}$$

Our interest is in the error component of the reliability ratio because that is what we want to minimize. Of course, the error component in the ratio resides in the denominator of Equation 5.4. Recall that in CTT, observed score is actually a composite of two components: true score and error, as $X_{ij} = \tau_{ij} + \varepsilon$. With this information, we may rewrite the equation to more clearly show the error, as in Equation 5.5:

$$\rho_{XT}^2 = \frac{\sigma_T^2}{\sigma_X^2} = \frac{\sigma_T^2}{\sigma_T^2 + \sigma_\varepsilon^2}. \tag{5.5}$$

In the theory, this ratio is a basic assumption, and we use it to make estimates of both the reliability coefficient and the SEM. First, however, it is necessary to realize just how this index is developed.

Developing the Index

The reliability index may be developed from the variance equations given previously. By definition, variances and standard deviations of strictly parallel measures are absolute equalities, that is, $\sigma^2_{X_1} = \sigma^2_{X_2}$ and $\sigma_{X_1} = \sigma_{X_2}$. This allows that applying the equality to any set of parallel tests, all intercorrelations of the tests are likewise equal, except for error. For any two such parallel tests, then, the idea is expressed in Expression 5.6:

$$\rho_{x_1 x_2} = \rho_{x_1 x_3} = \rho_{x_2 x_3} \cdots = \rho_{x_g x_h}. \tag{5.6}$$

The conclusion that correlations among all parallel tests are equal is very important to measurement theory because it provides a proof necessary to establish that reliability is the correlation of one's observed score with a corresponding universe of scores on strictly parallel tests. Accordingly, the index of reliability may be written structurally as the term ρ_{XT}.

As with all indexes derived from ratios, the reliability index ranges (0, 1). Knowing this is useful to our purpose because it means that for Equations 5.4 and 5.5 to be true, at least one of the variances in the ratio must be greater than zero. Because true score is a structural component of observed score, by implication, then, the observed score variance is the quantity that must always be greater than zero. If no score is obtained on a test (hence, no observed score variance), then true score is obviated and reliability cannot be estimated.

Given the truism that observed score variance is extant, a number of deductions useful for estimating reliability can be made. First, consider the case in which reliability *approaches* zero, the lower bound. For the reliability index to be near zero, nearly all the observed score variance must be due to error, and the true scores of a group of examinees are virtually identical. In such a circumstance, there is little differentiation between examinees' abilities; hence, they lack much reliability at all and the ratio produces a nearly zero result. With such low reliability, there is little to help us *meaningfully* differentiate among individuals. The measure is said to have little *precision*.

Conversely, consider when reliability approaches the upper limit (i.e.,+1) and the observed score variance is almost entirely due to differences in true scores among the cases in the sample. Now, the error variance is itself almost nonexistent. In this case, reliability is very high and precision of measurement is correspondingly great. Palpably, then, it follows that reliability is an inverse measure of the error variance in relation to the observed score variance, a point emphasized throughout the theory.

Figure 5.1 depicts the relation between reliability and source for observed score variance, whether from mostly error or predominantly true score. Notice in Figure 5.1 that low reliability is associated with error as the primary source for error variance, whereas with high reliability the true score explains more of the observed score variance. See, too, that the curve does not ascend uniformly along the entire range of reliability. As true score is approached, reliability gains are greatly increased.

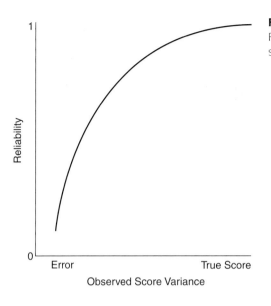

Figure 5.1
Relationship of observed
score variance and reliability.

The values used to produce Figure 5.1 are also revealing. They are displayed in Table 5.1 on page 129. Note in Table 5.1 that as observed score variance values increase, error also increases rendering less precision.

Index Versus Coefficient

Although reliability is generically expressed as a squared correlation between two random variables, no special characterization about the nature of the variables has yet been made. Such distinctions revolve around whether the variables employed for a correlation emanate from the theoretical true score or whether they represent observed data obtained from real test administrations. This peculiarity is important when discussing reliability theory because it means that there are significant departures from the theory in its application to practical testing problems. To see this point, it is necessary to understand the distinction between an *index* and a *coefficient*.

The index reflects theory manifestly and as such is an unbiased estimator. However, the *reliability coefficient* is a real world statistic, giving the correlation between the two sets of observed scores from standardized administrations of appropriately parallel measures. Because, in practice, we deal with live tests rather than theoretical ones, the index is popularly reported. In statistical terms, it is not unbiased.

There is more to appreciate about the difference between an index and a coefficient. In mental measurement, the coefficient is less precise than an index. The reason stems from the fact that measured, observed variables are not wholly representational of latent constructs themselves. There is some amount of error, as we know in our classic true score formula. A correlation between two real world and imperfect appraisals is systematically lower than the correlation between the latent constructs themselves.

Figure 5.2

Relationship between
reliability coefficient and
index of reliability.

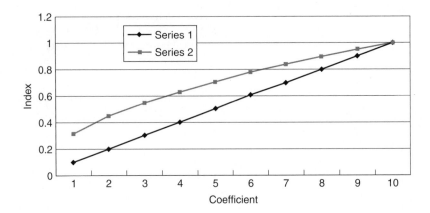

Hence, a reliability coefficient is shrunk by some amount from the true association between the constructs, a concept known as *attenuation*. Because it is attenuated, a reliability coefficient will always be less than the theoretical index of reliability. Figure 5.2 shows this systematic warp in the correlation.

In CTT, the index is the more interesting indicator of error because it involves true score, the test characteristic of greatest attention to the theory. However, the coefficient is routinely reported in test development work for reasons discussed in the next section.

Estimating True Score from Observed Score with Index and Coefficient

It is possible to estimate true score from observed score, although doing so requires some knowledge of issues that are discussed in chapters 6 and 15. Nonetheless, because the topic is germane to the present discussion, it is described here briefly to give a sense of what is involved. Realize, first, of course, this calculation is dependent on the reliability of a test. The more reliable the instrument, the more closely the observed score estimates the true score. Less reliable tests diminish confidence in observed scores as representations of true score so the estimated true score is closer to the mean. For tests with no reliability, observed scores are merely random estimates of true score. We can see this point by returning to Table 5.1. Table 5.1 illustrates this relationship for observed scores on an IQ test within a range of ±1 standard deviation, 85 to 115. Table 5.1 also displays values that, if graphed, would produce a function like that depicted in Figure 5.1.

Notice in Table 5.1 that at the mean score of 100, the estimated true score is the same as the observed score, regardless of reliability (read from observed score 100 down the column). However, as one moves the observed score away from the mean in either direction, the estimated true score deviates from the mean and closer to the observed score, until one reaches the point of perfect reliability ($\rho_{TX_i} = 1$), where the observed score and the estimated true score are identical. This shows that observed scores deviate from true score as a function of a test's reliability.

Table 5.1
Estimated True Scores at Various Reliabilities and Observed Scores

Reliability	Observed score						
	85	90	95	100	105	110	115
.00	100.0	100.0	100.0	100.0	100.0	100.0	100.0
.10	98.5	99.0	99.5	100.0	100.5	101.0	101.5
.20	97.0	98.0	99.0	100.0	101.0	102.0	103.0
.30	95.5	97.0	98.5	100.0	101.5	103.0	104.5
.40	94.0	96.0	98.0	100.0	102.0	104.0	106.0
.50	92.5	95.0	97.5	100.0	102.5	105.0	107.5
.60	91.0	94.0	97.0	100.0	103.0	106.0	109.0
.70	89.5	93.0	96.5	100.0	103.5	107.0	110.5
.80	88.0	92.0	96.0	100.0	104.0	108.0	112.0
.90	86.5	91.0	95.5	100.0	104.5	109.0	113.5
1.00	85.0	90.0	95.0	100.0	105.0	110.0	115.0

Problem of Parallel Measures

In as much as reliability and its index are functionally defined in the correlation coefficient, certain conditions must be present in order for the coefficient to be calculated in real-world testing scenarios. For starters, a cohort of examinees willing to participate in multiple, identical test administrations must be identified and secured. Because such cohort is not generally available, proximal means from a single group administration are used. However, possibly the greatest difficulty in real-world testing lies in another requirement—the availability of even reasonably congeneric (again, not to mention, randomly parallel) measures. It is to this concern that we now turn.

Identifying Parallel Measures

A primary difficulty with using parallel measures—regardless of whether they are strictly parallel, τ-equivalent, essentially τ-equivalent, or even congeneric—lies in recognizing them accurately. Recall that one criterion for determining whether measures are truly parallel is that they have equal reliabilities. However, a problem arises in determining whether the reliabilities are equal because the coefficient for each test is estimated by the correlation between these same tests. Hence, by definition, two such measures would necessarily have single joint reliabilities: The correlation of test 1 with test 2 is the same as that of test 2 with test 1. Because no outside criterion exists for unmixing the computations, it remains unknown whether equivalence exists for them or not. Gulliksen, Lord, and other psychometricians have noted this problem since the early days of reliability theory. Because of it, psychometricians have devised a number of means to treat measures as approximately parallel. Such procedures are essentially data collection schemes.

Test–Retest

One reasonable means to obtain parallel measures is to use the same test twice with repeat administrations. The test used twice would, by definition, meet the equal reliability criterion of parallel measures, presuming $\rho_{\tau\varepsilon} = 0$. When a Pearson r is calculated for such *repeat test administrations* (i.e., *test–retest*), it is called the *coefficient of stability*. This presumes that the same test form is administered to the same group of examinees on two occasions and all administration conditions are reasonably similar. Coombs (1953), however, criticizes this reliability statistic because only two administrations are involved, whereas CTT envisions many administrations. He suggests a better alternative is the *coefficient of precision,* a statistic representing a number of administrations of the same test to the same examinees. Of course, it too presumes that all learning and test administration conditions are held constant between testing sessions, an unlikely scenario.

However, even these arrangements with the same test do not ensure strictly parallel measures because, in real world circumstances, the examinees would likely have changed in some manner between the test sessions, and conditions of administration cannot be duplicated exactly. Nonetheless, for our daily reliability estimation, test–retest is considered reasonably proximate.

For reliability estimation, proximate measures may be appropriately substituted for true randomly parallel measures because that is a condition virtually unobtainable in real-world testing contexts. In science, reasonably proximate measures are used with regularity. For example, you may know that physics is made up of two disciplines: quantum mechanics (the very big: e.g., the distance between stars in our galaxy) and particle physics (the very small: e.g., looking inside atoms). Yet quantum mechanics and particle physics are governed by contradictory laws. Regardless, physics marches forward despite the discrepancy. Reasonable proximity exists between the inconsistencies. Fortunately for reliability appraisal in mental measures, proximal procedures are adequate. In fact, the proximal procedures we employ in reliability evaluation produce not just ballpark figures, but highly accurate estimates. As support for this statement, Raykov (2001) investigated the problem of nonparallel measures in the context of structural equation modeling and reported satisfying results. I now turn to describing some proximal means we may employ to substitute for strictly parallel measures.

Other Proximal Estimates

In most circumstances, of course, test–retest is not available; only a single test administration has been conducted. So, alternative methods for developing proximate data from one administration must be devised. One method is to use alternate forms of a test, presuming they have been developed for this purpose by using the same test content specifications and identical test construction procedures. A Pearson r between alternate test forms is called the *coefficient of equivalence,* or by some authors the *alternate (or parallel) forms reliability coefficient.* Generally, given the previous presumptions, these forms can be considered sufficiently parallel for practical reliability estimation.

We realize, however, that suitably alternate test forms are not often available. Therefore, we must be more creative and artificially devise alternate test forms. The most common means to develop approximately equivalent test forms is to split the test in half, accepting each half as an equivalent test administration. Such division is called *split halves.* Then, a single administration is presumed equivalent to multiple administrations. When a Pearson r is calculated between the test halves, it is called the *split-half reliability.*

The division of the test into halves can be done along any reasonable grounds, such as all odd-numbered items versus all even-numbered ones, or by random assignment into one half or the other, or by some other criterion. Most commonly, the odd versus even item split is used. Some tests, however, are built to specifications, that prescribe a particular order for the items, such as (roughly) from comparatively easy to more difficult, or so that items covering similar content appear together regardless of their difficulty. Thus, reliability researcher should consider the best splitting procedure to reflect nearly equivalent halves. Regardless, splitting the test by first half versus second half is not recommended because it is known that placement of particular items within a test (whether early or late appearing) influence endorsement.

When a test is narrowly focused and some number of its items are grouped together—say, into a *testlet* where a set of items are dependent on a reading passage, or all refer to the same graphic—arbitrarily splitting the items into halves is not recommended. Researchers (Sireci, Thissen, & Wainer, 1991) have demonstrated that if a testlet were split, error variance would not be distributed equally to both halves which would thereby spuriously deflate reliability estimates. Thus, considerable thought should be given to how best to split a test.

Depressed Calculations with Shortened Test Length

Readers should recognize, too, that an obvious limitation of using split halves as a means to obtain roughly parallel measures is that reliability is thereby computed from a greatly shortened measure, just half as long as the original. This is a serious limitation to accurately gauging a correlational relationship because the computed correlations tend to underestimate what would be more nearly true parallel forms. Reliability estimates are usually lower for shortened tests. (I explain the dependency of reliability appraisal on test length in a later section of this chapter.) In addition, reliability estimation based on split halves can be further underestimated because of the fact that the instability of examinees over a time interval is not considered, a point demonstrated by researchers Thorndike and Hagen (1969).

Realizing the problems with using split halves, psychometricians have set out to devise formulas that compensate for the shortened test length. It is to these remedies that we now turn.

Computing Reliability Coefficients

The Spearman-Brown Prophecy (or Correction) Formula

The *Spearman-Brown prophecy* (or *correction*) *formula* (ρ_{S-B}) compensates for using only half the test's length in reliability computation. In this procedure, it is hypothesized that a test split into halves is changed by some amount, K. The test's true (alternate or parallel forms) reliability can be considered as the ratio of its changed reliability over the event of such change, expressed in Equation 5.7:

$$\rho_{X_1X_2} = \frac{K(\rho_{X_1X_2})}{1 + (K - 1)\rho_{X_1X_2}}. \qquad (5.7)$$

Proof of this relation is available in more mathematical texts (e.g., Lord & Novick, 1968).

Then, by evaluating $K = 2$ in the formula to compensate for the fact that each K is one half of a test's actual length, we have the ρ_{S-B}, shown in Equation 5.8:

$$\rho_{X_1X_2} = \rho_{S-B} = \frac{2\rho_{Y_1Y_2}}{1 + \rho_{Y_1Y_2}}. \qquad (5.8)$$

For example, if the alternate forms reliability coefficient is 0.75, the corrected estimation for reliability is 0.86 following these computations:

$$\rho_{S-B} = \frac{2(.75)}{1 + (.75)} = \frac{1.5}{1.75} = .86.$$

This Spearman-Brown correction assumes a normally distributed data set from the same mental appraisal, randomly split in half, yields two equal and normal distributions with identical standard deviations. However, as discussed previously, such assumption is problematic for making calculations with real world tests.

The Kuder-Richardson Reliability Coefficients

Two mathematicians, Kuder and Richardson (1937), working in the early years of reliability estimation (the 1930s and 1940s), realized the problems of implementing the alternate (or parallel) forms reliability coefficient, and that such difficulties were amplified by their inability to meet the Spearman-Brown restrictions. They methodically set out to address the difficulties by devising a number of formulas. Their 20th and 21st formulas best addressed their concerns and remain today as standards for reliability estimation. These reliability formulas are likely recognized by their common names, KR-20 (ρ_{KR20}) and KR-21 (ρ_{KR21}). Both formulas use item intercorrelation variance as a measure of consistency rather than relying on splitting the test into two halves. Hence, they are referred to as reporting reliability via *internal consistency*.

The basic idea of internal consistency methods for estimating reliability involves a conceptual shift from the idea of using the whole test for reliability estimation to imagining that each item can have a reliability estimate. The idea, then, is to calculate the Pearson correlation between all possible pairs of items. The mean of the interitem correlations is a kind of item-level reliability, and then extending this by the Spearman-Brown formula one can estimate reliability for the entire test. The basic KR-20 formula is given in Equation 5.9:

$$\rho_{X_1X_2} = \rho_{KR20} = \frac{k}{k-1}\left(1 - \frac{\sum pq}{\sigma^2}\right). \tag{5.9}$$

where k = number of items in the test,

p = proportion of the population passing the item, and

q = proportion of the population not passing the item.

As an example, imagine the data derived from a set of scores on a short, four-item test that has a standard deviation of 1.3, and has passing proportions for each of the items of 0.92, 0.5, 0.73, and 0.88. Note particularly that this approach assumes items are dichotomous:

$$\rho_{KR20} = \frac{5}{5-1}\left(1 - \frac{\sum((.92*.08) + (.5*.5) + (.73*.27) + (.88*.12))}{1.3^2}\right)$$

$$= \frac{4}{3}\left(1 - \frac{.6263}{1.69}\right) = .84.$$

Although the calculations for the KR-20 are not difficult, in the precomputer days of Kuder and Richardson, they were still tedious because there are many interitem correlations, even in a relatively short test. For example, a 30-item test has 435 such correlations in its item matrix. Thus, the team sought to define an alternate formula that would approximate the results but be simpler to calculate. The result was KR-21. This formula requires only the test's mean, not the individual item passing proportions. Researchers have demonstrated that when tests are of sufficient length (e.g., 50 items or more, a common length in many tests), the two formulas produce coefficients that are nearly identical. KR-21 remains one of the most popular methods for calculating a reliability estimate. Its formula is given in Equation 5.10:

$$\rho_{X_1X_2} = \rho_{KR21} = \frac{k}{k-1}\left(1 - \frac{\overline{X}(k - \overline{X})}{k\sigma^2}\right). \tag{5.10}$$

A simple, numerical example illustrates this formula. Imagine a 100-item test has a scaled mean of 300 and a standard deviation of 65. Calculations are as follows:

$$\rho_{KR21} = \frac{100}{100-1}\left(1 - \frac{300(100 - 300)}{(100)(65)^2}\right) = 1.010\left(1 - \frac{60,000}{422,500}\right) = .87.$$

In contrast to KR-20, the KR-21 formula makes no differentiation among a test's items. Hence, it assumes equal difficulty among all items on the test. This feature of KR-21 is often criticized (Lord, 1959). For highly reliable tests, there is little difference between estimates calculated by the KR-20 and KR-21 formulas, but as a test's reliability decreases, the differences become ever greater. This is an artifact of the

KR-21 equal item difficulty assumption and the basis for the criticism. The degree of item difficulty in a test is proportionate to the amount of underestimate of KR-20 reliability by the KR-21 formula. Hence, the KR-21 is often considered a lower bound of KR-20 reliability estimation.

Coefficient Alpha

Cronbach developed a general model of KR-20 that derives entirely from the internal structure of the instrument. He realized that in a structural sense, the individual item pairs (i.e., interitem covariances) constitute whole test variance and that this score variance itself can be used to make the estimates more conveniently. Today, *coefficient α* (alternatively, *Cronbach's α*) is probably the most popular coefficient for reporting test reliability. Cortina (1993) credits it as "certainly one of the most important and pervasive statistics in research involving test construction and use" (p. 98). As evidence, his original description for his alpha procedure—published in a famous paper entitled "Coefficient Alpha and the Internal Structure of Tests" (Cronbach, 1951)—has been cited more than 6,000 times since its publication and is considered so significant that a *festschrift* honoring the achievement has been prepared (Cronbach & Shavelson, 2004; Shavelson, 2004).

Cronbach's famous formula is shown in Equation 5.11:

$$\rho_{X_1 X_2} = \rho_\alpha = \frac{k}{k-1}\left(1 - \frac{\sum \sigma_i^2}{\sigma^2}\right). \tag{5.11}$$

As is realized, the term $\sum \sigma_i^2$ specifies the summation of variance for all items. For illustration, suppose a five-item test ($\therefore k = 5$) has a standard deviation of 10.5 and individual item standard deviations of 3.1, 2.2, 1.9, 3.1, and 2.0. Then,

$$\rho_\alpha = \frac{5}{5-1}\left(1 - \frac{\sum\left((3.1)^2 + (2.2)^2 + (1.9)^2 + (3.1)^2 + (2.0)^2\right)}{10.5^2}\right) = .89.$$

The k refers to test parts, which typically are individual items, but such is not a restriction. The parts may also be subtests from a larger test. This point has implication for contemporary settings in which test parts could be testlets or specified subdivisions of a larger assessment program. When the elements are individual items, Cronbach's α yields the same estimate as KR-21; however, when the test is separated by split-halves, the estimate will be closer to KR-20 and exactly that of an estimate proposed by Falnangan (1937) and Rulon (1939), two early reliability researchers.

Another important characteristic of Cronbach's α is shown here. It is well known to researchers that individual item reliabilities are low, with small covariances. However, when they are aggregated into total score variance, as in the KR-21 and Cronbach's α formulas, the cumulative effect is greater reliability. In reliability assessment, it seems the sum is literally greater than its parts. Proving this aspect of coefficient alpha can become technical beyond our score, and Thompson (2003a) provides a thoughtful review.

	Scale mean if item deleted	Scale variance if item deleted	Corrected item-total correlation	Cronbach's alpha if item deleted
q71	19.19	25.720	.354	.484
q72	19.47	24.037	.432	.441
q73	20.38	26.363	.367	.485
q74	18.40	15.931	.407	.455
q75	20.06	26.574	.143	.593

Figure 5.3
Item-total statistics.

Coefficient Alpha in Testing Programs

In many testing programs, Cronbach's α is also employed in item-level appraisal. Often in test development work, the interest goes beyond just an assessment of an item's separable reliability to a more detailed look at the test's reliability when a given item is removed. In some tests, a particularly aberrant item may be sufficient to influence the entire test reliability. An example of this kind of analysis is displayed in Figure 5.3. In the figure, only a few items from the test are shown. Note the various statistics reported in the table, particularly the rightmost column: *Cronbach's Alpha If Item Deleted*. If the item labeled "q75" were deleted from the test, the test reliability (by Cronbach's α) would increase dramatically. Also, appreciate that the item-total correlation is very low ($r = 0.143$) for this item.

Special Problems in Reliability

Attenuation and Its Correction

When Galton, Spearman, Thurstone, and slightly later, Gulliksen were developing the fundamental precepts of reliability, they expressed concern about a limitation in estimation procedures. These pioneers hypothesized that if the true score of the measures could be estimated, then the correlation between such true scores would most accurately reflect the actual correlation between the latent constructs. The result would be a better gauge of reliability than when observed scores alone are used. The problem can be seen when test scores are mapped on a frequency function. In such depiction, the curves *attenuate,* or thin out, at the tails of a distribution, revealing regions of relatively greater error. In other words, reliability estimates (presuming CTT and for most tests where the developer hoped to achieve greatest differentiation among the largest number of examinees) would be most accurate for describing confidence in scores in the middle range and less so at the extremes. The aim of alleviating this circumstance is called a *correction for attenuation*. Recall that the idea was introduced in chapter 4.

For attenuation proof, draw on the earlier assumption (see chapter 3) that parallel measures exist, that is, $X_1 = X_2$ and $Y_1 = Y_2$. In addition, remember that a measure correlates at least as highly with its own true score as it does with the true score of a second measure, also as shown earlier. The importance of this proposition is that it allows the following concomitant statement: Any measure correlates with the true score on a second measure at least as highly as it does with the observed score on the second measure, a fact that also leads to the correlational relationship between any two observed measures. These relations are shown in Equation 5.12:

$$\rho_{X_T X_T} \geq \rho_{X Y_T} \geq \rho_{XY}. \tag{5.12}$$

Because the correlations in this expression are between various observed score and true score variables, several combinations may be devised, and hence, more than one correction formula results. To start, if we substitute the relations expressed previously into the original relations between true and observed scores (i.e., ρ_{TX_i}), the result is Equation 5.13:

$$\rho_{XY} = \rho_{XX_T} \rho_{X_T X_Y} \rho_{YY_T}. \tag{5.13}$$

This formula presents a correlation corrected for attenuation. The extremes variation is flattened. However, Equation 5.13 does not complete the attenuation picture. In fact, given the relation shown in the formula, the following interim relation toward full correction formulas, presented in Equation 5.14, is also true:

$$\rho_{X_T Y_T} = \frac{\rho_{X Y_T}}{\rho_{XX_T}}. \tag{5.14}$$

Equation 5.14 may be restated in Equation 5.15—another correction formula, but this time one that highlights the different measures:

$$\rho_{X_T Y_T} = \frac{\rho_{XY}}{\rho_{XT_X} \rho_{YT_Y}}. \tag{5.15}$$

Thus, from Equations 5.14 and 5.15, still another relation for attenuation (also in terms of true scores) is given in Equation 5.16:

$$\rho_{X_T Y_T} = \frac{\rho_{XY}}{\sqrt{\rho_{X_1 X_2} \rho_{Y_1 Y_2}}}. \tag{5.16}$$

Note in Equation 5.16 that the correlation between true scores is expressed in terms of the correlation of the observed scores of each measure and their reliabilities. This formula corrects for the degree to which the correlation between two variables is attenuated by their unreliability. Lord and Novick (1968) exactly described the meaning of this formula in the context of measurement theory when they said that the results of a coefficient derived from Equation 5.16 may be interpreted as the relation between the psychological constructs being studied (in terms of the observed correlation between the measures of these constructs) and reliabilities of these measures. This is at the very heart of attenuation corrections, reflecting the desire of early reliability theorists.

Finally, by viewing Equation 5.16 as a theoretical expression of a practical testing situation, a real world variable may be substituted in the place of X true score, as shown in Equation 5.17:

$$\rho_{XY_T} = \frac{\rho_{XY}}{\sqrt{\rho_{Y_1 Y_2}}}. \tag{5.17}$$

This correction formula is for the correlation between an observed score on variable X and the true score for a second variable (Y). Here, the relation exists as a result of the correlation between the observed measures and the reliability of the second measure.

As an example of the use of correction for attenuation formulas (see Equations 5.16 and 5.17), suppose that the reliability coefficient between two observed score measures is 0.72, and the correlation for the separate variables is 0.83 and 0.77, respectively. Using Equation 5.17, one can estimate the correlation between the true scores for the variables to be about 0.90; this is higher than any separate estimate:

$$\rho_{XY_T} = \frac{.72}{\sqrt{(.83)(.77)}} = .9.$$

A practical application of the correction for attention is commonly seen in testing programs where split halves are used for reliability estimation. The reliability of each half will be depressed by some amount of measurement error. However, by using Equation 5.17, the true score correlation may be estimated.

Effects of Test Length on Reliability Estimation

From the previous discussions, it is apparent that a whole test's reliability is dependent on the reliability of individual items. Not surprisingly, as more items contribute to variance expressions and interitem correlations, reliability also increases. In general, the more items, the higher the coefficient, and thus longer tests often manifest greater reliability. Two related reasons account for this, the first being conceptual and the second as an artifact of many statistical expressions for reliability.

Conceptually, because items are random samples of information about a construct from a universe of information defining that construct, it is logical that more samples of the information represent the universe more thoroughly. Likely, improved internal consistency is thereby achieved, and a higher reliability coefficient will result.

The statistical explanation for the effect of test length on reliability is a bit involved but still comprehensible. To begin, we need to review some earlier statistics and then apply this to the reliability formulas discussed previously. The mean in Equation 5.18 is the general (unweighted) sum of the variables, whether individual items or themselves sums of scores:

$$\overline{X}_{X_1 + X_2} = \frac{1}{N} \sum X_1 + X_2 = \overline{X}_{X_1} + \overline{X}_{X_2}. \tag{5.18}$$

For reliability assessment, the variables are parallel tests, hence only two are needed. Further, with only two variables, Equation 5.18 may be rewritten as Equation 5.19:

$$\overline{X}_{2X} = 2\overline{X}_x. \tag{5.19}$$

This expression can be extended to include many such parallel variables, as stated in Equation 5.20:

$$\overline{X}_{kX} = k\overline{X}_x. \tag{5.20}$$

The same logic and procedure also follow for the variance of variables, as seen in Equation 5.21:

$$\sigma^2_{X_1+X_2} = \frac{1}{N}\sum(x_1 + x_2)^2 = \sigma_{x_1} + \sigma_{x_2} + 2r_{12}\sigma_{x_1}\sigma_{x_2}. \tag{5.21}$$

The final term in Equation 5.21, by binomial expansion, is twice the covariance of each variable. This feature is important because the presumption is that the tests are equivalent and the effect of summing them is to double the test's length. Hence, this expression may be rewritten as Equation 5.22:

$$\sigma^2_{2X} = \sigma^2_X(2 + 2r_{xx'})^{1/2}. \tag{5.22}$$

A ramification is that when the test is increased by any specified length (k), the variance is correspondingly increased by $k + k(k - 1)r_{xx'}$, a variant of Equation 5.22. Now, suppose a case in reliability assessment in which true score on parallel tests is identical and therefore correlates at 1.0, and that errors (e) are random (i.e., $r = 0$). Then,

$$\sigma^2_{kT} = k^2\sigma^2_T, \sigma_{kT} = k\sigma^2_T \tag{5.23}$$

and

$$\sigma^2_{ke} = k^2\sigma^2_e, \sigma_{ke} = \sigma_e(k)^{1/2}. \tag{5.24}$$

Note in Equation 5.23 that the variance of the true score increases at a rate equal to the square of the change in the length of a test. However, in Equation 5.24, the error variance increases only linearly in relation to test length. Thus, as more items or exercises are added to a test, the relation of true score moves much faster than does that for error, yielding greater reliability. Hence, reliability computations with long tests yield a higher coefficient than do the same computations on shorter tests. This is an important concept for persons working in measurement to know.

Lord and Novick (1968) demonstrated the degree to which reliability (Spearman-Brown) is a function of test length by plotting a series of test curves and reporting the data in a table. Lord's data are reproduced here as Figure 5.4 and Table 5.2.

To read this information, first look at the base (abscissa) in Figure 5.4 for test length. Suppose each unit is adding one additional test item; hence, Figure 5.4 shows data for tests from 1 to 12 items long. (It can also be used for multiples.) The capital letters along the left side of the ordinate axis show various reliabilities for lengthening a test, whereas those on the right side of the chart show reliabilities for shortening the test. Exact values for the intersections are shown in the table, and intermediate

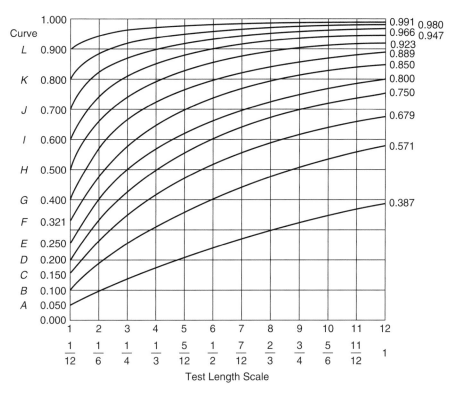

Figure 5.4
Reliability as a function of test length.
Source: From *Statistical Theories of Mental Test Scores* (p. 113), by F. M. Lord and M. R. Novick, 1968,
Reading, MA: Addison-Wesley. Copyright 1968 by Addison-Wesley. Reprinted with permission.

values can be estimated using Lord's reliability curves. For example, look at unit value
4 (e.g., a test that is four items long). Move vertically to the D curve and note that the
reliability value is 0.500 (from the left-side, vertical axis). Now, if the length of the test
is doubled to eight items, move in the right direction on the D curve to a test length
of eight. Read that the reliability is about 0.67 (actually 0.667). By tripling the numbers of items on the original test to 12, the reliability jumps to 0.750. Precise values
for the reliability curves shown in Figure 5.4 can be found in Table 5.2.

Lord's data are more than curiosity about proportional increases. The tables can
also be used to estimate the length of test required to achieve a specified level of reliability, a highly useful application. Although his data only go from 1 to 12, users
may multiply them to more realistic test lengths. Take curve *E*, for example, and note
that using either Figure 5.4 or Table 5.2, test length 2 has a reliability of 0.400. Move
along the curve or in the table to test length 12 and read that the reliability is 0.800.
Hence, a test with initial reliability of 0.04 must be increased six times in length to
obtain reliability of 0.800. A test of any length increased six times would evidence a
proportional increase in reliability.

Table 5.2
Reliability as a Function of Test Length—Test Length Scale

Curve	1 $\frac{1}{12}$	2 $\frac{1}{6}$	3 $\frac{1}{4}$	4 $\frac{1}{3}$	5 $\frac{5}{12}$	6 $\frac{1}{2}$	7 $\frac{7}{12}$	8 $\frac{2}{3}$	9 $\frac{3}{4}$	10 $\frac{5}{6}$	11 $\frac{11}{12}$	12 1
L	.900	.947	.964	.973	.978	.982	.984	.986	.988	.989	.990	.991
K	.800	.889	.923	.941	.952	.960	.966	.970	.973	.976	.978	.980
J	.700	.824	.875	.903	.921	.933	.942	.949	.955	.959	.962	.966
I	.600	.750	.818	.857	.882	.900	.913	.923	.931	.938	.943	.947
H	.500	.667	.750	.800	.833	.857	.875	.889	.900	.909	.917	.923
G	.400	.571	.667	.727	.769	.800	.824	.842	.857	.870	.880	.889
F	.321	.486	.586	.654	.702	.739	.768	.791	.810	.825	.839	.850
E	.250	.400	.500	.571	.625	.667	.700	.727	.750	.769	.786	.800
D	.200	.333	.429	.500	.556	.600	.636	.667	.692	.714	.733	.750
C	.150	.261	.346	.414	.469	.514	.553	.585	.614	.638	.660	.679
B	.100	.182	.250	.308	.357	.400	.438	.471	.500	.526	.550	.571
A	.050	.095	.136	.174	.208	.240	.269	.296	.321	.345	.367	.387

Source: From *Statistical Theories of Mental Test Scores* (p. 113), by F. M. Lord and M. R. Novick, 1968, Reading, MA: Addison-Wesley. Copyright 1968 by Addison-Wesley. Reprinted with permission.

Although there is nothing inherently wrong with increasing test length to improve reliability, one should realize that the increased consistency of measurement only applies to increased content sampling and does not also apply to temporal conditions of reliability (Curreton et al., 1973). In other words, the test-lengthening technique will show increased internal consistency among items because there are more of them, but it will not improve the test–retest reliability. This is an important consideration in many testing situations.

Group Heterogeneity and Reliability

We still have more concerns with reliability estimation. Another important consideration is the variability within a group. Groups' relative heterogeneity affects their relationships, thus impacting reliability. In essence, more heterogeneous groups typically evidence higher reliability than do homogeneous groups. Exploring precisely how group heterogeneity effects test reliability has been an object of interest since early measurement discussion. Such noted theorists as Kelley (1921), Otis (1922a, 1922b), and Thurstone (1931), among others, wrote about this phenomenon. In particular, Gulliksen (1950) investigated this aspect of test reliability extensively. He reasoned that by making some modest assumptions, it is possible to estimate the amount of change in reliability resulting from differences in groups' variability. We follow his reasoning here to develop several important reliability terms.

First, we build an expression that shows the amount of change in standard deviation in observed scores that is required to account for any given change in reliability, solely due to group differences in their true scores. Although stated differently from earlier, readers may recognize that this is the classic definition of SEM. The relevant equation was initially presented in chapter 3 (see Equation 3.33), and is repeated here for convenience:

$$\sigma_\varepsilon = \sigma_X \sqrt{(1 - \rho_{TX_i})}.$$

Applying this equation to particular sets of scores from each of two groups yields the following designations, given in Equations 5.25 and 5.26:
for group 1

$$\sigma_{\varepsilon_x} = \sigma_{X_1} \sqrt{(1 - \rho_{X_1 X_2})}, \tag{5.25}$$

and for group 2

$$\sigma_{\varepsilon_x} = \sigma_{X_2} \sqrt{(1 - \rho_{X_3 X_4})}. \tag{5.26}$$

The groups are identified as group 1 and group 2, and designated σ_{X_1} and σ_{X_2}, respectively.

Employing the assumption that measurement error is invariant to group heterogeneity allows for a check on the equivalence of Equations 5.25 and 5.26. Equation 5.27 can be used to test this between-groups relationship:

$$\sigma_{X_1} \sqrt{(1 - \rho_{X_1 X_2})} = \sigma_{X_2} \sqrt{(1 - \rho_{X_3 X_4})}. \tag{5.27}$$

Solving for either σ_{X_1} or σ_{X_2} yields an expression that reveals the amount of change in a standard deviation that would be required to account for change in test reliability, solely due to group heterogeneity in actual (error-free) variance. Accordingly, σ_{X_2} is given in Equation 5.28:

$$\sigma_{X_2} = \sigma_{X_1} \sqrt{\frac{(1 - \rho_{X_1 X_2})}{(1 - \rho_{X_3 X_4})}}. \tag{5.28}$$

If, in Equation 5.28, the *same* (or essentially τ-equivalent) test is administered in each of the two groups—that is, tests x_1 and x_3 are the same instrument, and likewise for tests x_2 and x_4—then σ_{X_1} or σ_{X_2} signify the reliability for the test for the respective groups. If any differences in reliability are attributable solely to a difference in the true variance of the two groups, then σ_{X_2} represents the observed standard deviation of group 2. This point is clearly seen if one only imagines perfect reliability and no error in either group mean or variance. Then, by equality, σ_{X_1} equals σ_{X_2}. The fact that they do not have equality shows that reliability is indeed influenced by the heterogeneity of a group.

Equation 5.27 is a famous formula, and it is often employed when equivalence between test forms is investigated. Equally famous is a variation of Equation 5.27, and the two formulas are often reported together. The associated equation—presented in Equation 5.29—is the square of each term in Equation 5.27 and shows the amount of change in reliability that can be expected from any given change in observed variance:

$$\rho_{X_1 X_2} = 1 - \frac{\sigma_{X_1}^2}{\sigma_{X_2}^2} (1 - \rho_{X_3 X_4}). \tag{5.29}$$

For Equations 5.26 and 5.28, Gulliksen's assumption is employed—that any change in reliability is due solely to differences in error-free variance (i.e., variance of the true score). Taken together, Equations 5.27 and 5.28 provide complete information on the effect of heterogeneity on test reliability.

To see the effects of these formulas in practice, multiple examples would need to be run as in a Monte Carlo study, with realistic reliabilities inserted. A more convenient way to observe the phenomenon, however, is obtainable by noting the values given in Figure 5.5.

The values in Figure 5.5 are derived from the combination of Equations 5.28 and 5.29, given here in Equation 5.30:

$$\frac{\sigma_{X_1}^2}{\sigma_{X_2}^2} = \frac{1 - \rho_{X_1 X_2}}{1 - \rho_{X_3 X_4}}. \tag{5.30}$$

Using specified values in Figure 5.5, one may take the reliabilities for two tests as, say, 0.64 and 0.91 (i.e., $\rho_{X_1 X_2} = .64$ and $\rho_{X_3 X_4} = .91$), and note that the intersection of the two reliabilities is on the diagonal line of 2.00. This is read that if a change in true variance resulted from a doubling (i.e., 2.00) of the standard deviation, a change in

Figure 5.5

Effect of group heterogeneity on reliability, axis of reliability index (Y), and standard error factor (X).

Source: From *Theory of Mental Tests* (p. 113) by H. Gulliksen, 1950, Hillsdale, NJ: Erlbaum. Copyright 1950 by Lawrence Erlbaum Associates, Inc. Reprinted with permission.

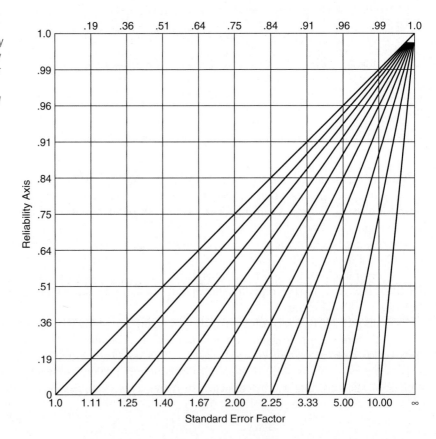

reliability from 0.64 to 0.91 would be observed. Other values can be read in the same manner, either from changes in reliability to differences in standard deviation, or the reverse. Similarly, if the standard deviation was changed by 25% (e.g., from 1.0 to 1.25), and that due entirely to enlarged true variance, the reliability would increase from 0.75 to 0.84.

Standard Error of Measurement

Introduction

The SEM was introduced during discussion of CTT in chapter 3, where it plays such an important role. We saw that SEM is an indicator of measurement error for individuals, and hence, a crucial indicator of within-person reliability. It is the discrepancy of an individual's observed score from a theoretical true score. Also, we saw earlier that SEM is often reported as a single term (repeated here—from Equation 3.28—for convenience):

$$\sigma_\varepsilon.$$

Now, we study how it is derived.

Because the SEM indicates discrepancies between observed scores and true scores, it is a good indicator of reliability. In fact, the SEM is a function of reliability (and vice versa) when the standard deviation of a test is known. In CTT, this relationship between SEM and reliability is readily seen, as we realize that the standard deviation remains constant across the range of scores for a test, as shown in Figure 5.6. In Figure 5.6, the standard deviation for the test is arbitrarily 15, chosen for this illustration because it represents the widely know standard deviation of most IQ tests. A constant standard deviation is also the case when scores are expressed as standard scores, that is, in standard deviation units.

The abscissa in Figure 5.6 represents the range of reliability expressed as an index, and the ordinate is the SEM. As illustrated, when reliability is completely absent from a test ($\rho_{TX_i} = 0$), the SEM is the same as the standard deviation (i.e., SEM = 15), indicating randomness in scores from this test to a parallel one. Conversely, when reliability is perfect ($\rho_{TX_i} = 1$), the opposite circumstance prevails: No error at all (SEM = 0) exists between a test and its parallel form. From any particular value, then, it is apparent that the SEM is completely determined by the reliability index and vice versa. The relationship between them is symmetric. Once one term is known, the other can be easily calculated. Likewise, if one term is disturbed, the other is altered, commensurately.

Making Error Bands with SEM

Often persons working with test scores employ the SEM as a convenient means to calculate score intervals or *error bands*. Certainly, it is convenient to simply add and subtract the SEM from a given individual's score and interpret the range as a reasonable reflection of likely true scores. Presuming the distribution of all scores is normally distributed, then ±1 SEM would give one the impression that there is roughly a two out

Figure 5.6

Plot showing relationship of reliability index and SEM for a test with 15 as its standard deviation.

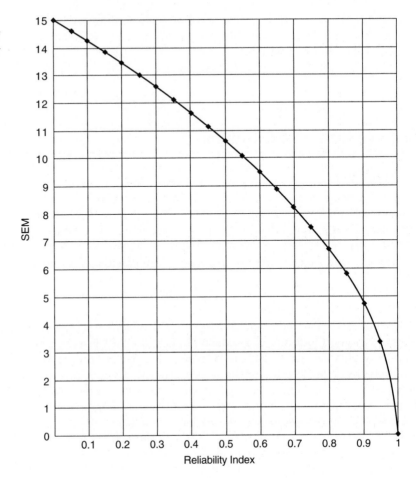

of three ($\approx 67\%$) chance of an individual's true score being in the range or even a $\approx 98\%$ for the range (x, ± 2 SEM). However, test users should exercise extreme caution to not overinterpret such a finding. Remember, under stipulations of CTT, the SEM is merely the average of across-person error, and unless the individual's observed score fell exactly at the mean of all scores, the characterization of an error band by SEM would be inexact. In fact, the further one's observed score was from the mean of all observed scores, the more imprecise would be the SEM for characterizing an error band. At the extremes, even the approximation would likely be grossly incorrect. Thus, using SEM for calculating error band for deriving confidence bands for individual scores is not recommended. Such a procedure is useful however for gauging group measurements.

SEM as Coefficient of Alienation

An interesting revelation is evident from the SEM, and some readers may have recognized it much earlier, during the derivation of the formula for SEM. The realization is that the SEM is actually a specialized regression formula, a means to argue one case from a general situation. Consider what happens when SEM terms are rearranged, as in Equation 5.31:

$$\frac{\sigma_\varepsilon}{\sigma_X} = \sqrt{(1 - \rho_{XT})}. \tag{5.31}$$

It is apparent that this formula yields a more general expression of error. It makes the problem of predicting scores of test 2 based on those known scores of test 1 an ordinary linear regression. This general expression of the SEM is called the *coefficient of alienation.*

More on Reliability in Other Disciplines

Sources for More About Reliability

In this brief chapter, I present a lot of information about reliability, but I do not explore the topic to its more complex end. For that, one should consult any of several fine sources, particularly an exciting (but technically demanding) edition by Thissen and Wainer (2001) titled *Test Scoring.* For other useful works on reliability, see offerings by Kane and Mitchell (1996), Thorndike and Thorndike (1994), and Traub (1994). In addition, readers may profit from several classic reliability-related publications. Three of them are Gulliksen's (1950) *Theory of Mental Tests,* Lord and Novick's (1968) *Statistical Theories of Mental Test Scores,* and Cronbach, Gleser, Nanda, and Rajaratnam's (1972) *The Dependability of Behavioral Measurement.* These works, despite their older publication dates, are must-haves for measurement professionals. A more recent and approachable edition of essays that explores contemporary perspectives on reliability issues is also offered by Thompson (2003b).

Exploring the history of the topic is also interesting. Among many histories available, Brennan (2001b) offers an informative and valuable essay, placing reliability's history in the context of anticipating its future.

Reliability in Other Contexts

Last, when learning about reliability, one should also realize that its use extends beyond educational and psychological measurement to many other disciplines. For instance, measurements in agronomy, economics, anthropology, and other fields of study also have issues of reliability integral to them. When the term reliability is used in some hard sciences, such as engineering, computing science, systems analysis, and pure mathematics, it is conceived of as a process by which one develops *models of reliability,* which can be subsequently assessed for their viability to a particular purpose. For more details on reliability modeling in these contexts, consult Wolstenholme (1999).

Summary

In this chapter, I discuss reliability and some of its forms and procedures for estimation. I emphasize understanding the concept and only then describe several common procedures for calculating reliability coefficients. The chapter also touches on a number of cautions in estimating and interpreting the reliability coefficient or index. The SEM is discussed, extending the comments about it provided in chapter 3. The chapter concludes by citing many sources that are useful for a more detailed discussion of the concept of reliability.

Chapter 6

Dimensional Scaling and Norming

Introduction

Another Dimension

The average theater admission cost in 1940 was 23¢, and most children were admitted for a dime. It was whole family entertainment, and Saturday afternoon was a favorite time for a trip to the movies. Cartoons such as Mickey Mouse and Betty Boop preceded the double feature, at least one of which was almost certain to be a western. Favorite stars included John Wayne, Gary Cooper, Lauren Bacall, and Fred Astaire. Most films of the time were predictable, but one that opened at the Broadway Theater in New York City on November 13, 1940 surprised the world. It was Walt Disney's *Fantasia,* and although the event took place more than two generations ago, the film retains its reputation among an army of movie buffs as the most profound celluloid achievement of all time. Not even the debut of *Star Wars* in 1977—although quite a happening itself—matched the public's reaction to Disney's masterpiece. *Fantasia* is a movie without words; it relies solely on music and visual effects. In the film, the renowned Russian composer Leopold Stokowski is shown in shadows, directing his orchestra to play Bach's "Toccata and Fugue in D Minor", "The Sorcerer's Apprentice" from a Goethe ballad, a tone poem called "Night on Bald Mountain", and Franz Schubert's "Ave Maria". Its cartoon characters—Mickey Mouse, dancing tulips, nude centaurs, and hippos in pink tutus—dance and move to the classical melodies in extraordinary ways. The movie played, nonstop, at some theater or another for almost 25 years, when it was pulled by Disney executives for fear of overexposure. When released again in the 1990s, it was once more acclaimed by critics, although this time it was lost in a sea of competing films and largely skipped by an audience more accustomed to violence and spectacular effects. As for "special effects," however, *Fantasia* was the copula of film industry's best technical expertise and its finest artistic creativity. It remains an unmatched experience for the imagination.

Just as *Fantasia* requires energy and imagination to understand and appreciate, so too does scaling in test items. However, scaling is essential to meaning in measurement, providing a way to interpret the responses given by examinees to assessment stimuli.

Contents

This chapter addresses issues in scaling as applied most commonly in educational and psychological tests. First, I introduce the concept of scaling and articulating its place in mental measurement. Then, I explain issues about interpreting scales, including its meaning in deep psychology. Next, deterministic and probabilistic scales are discussed. Background into early scaling models is provided, along with an explanation of dimensionality in scaling, both unidimensional and multidimensional. In the chapter, I also describe types of scales, identify some common ones used in measurement, and explain scale levels. Two essential sections in this chapter are presented deep in the chapter because their meaning is only comprehensible with the earlier-presented knowledge firmly in place. These sections describe derived scales (detailing scales made by a linear and nonlinear transformations) and norming. Significantly, this chapter and chapter 7 are close cousins in topic and presentation. They should be considered together.

Defining Scaling and Establishing Its Need

Introduction to Score Scales

Let us begin this exposition on dimensional scaling and norming by defining a *score scale*. I explain scales with technical accuracy in a moment, but for now—and very simply—a score scale is the point system used for reporting test results. There are many types of score scales for tests; however, most commonly, a reported score corresponds directly to the number of questions answered correctly. When 1 point is given for each correct answer, the scale is called a *raw score scale*. Hence, on a 50-item test, with 1 point awarded for each correct response, the test's score scale holds the range (0, 50).

Of course, a raw score scale is only one type of scale, and an elementary scale at that—and, significantly, one with a number of technical deficiencies, which we study in a later section in this chapter. Other systems can also prescribe a score scale. For instance, almost everyone reading this text is familiar with the Scholastic Aptitude Test, or SAT[1] (College Board, 2005). This test reports scores on a 200 to 800 score scale. The more achievement or ability one demonstrates on the test, the higher one's score. Even so, 200 does not mean that no questions were correctly answered, nor does an 800 score mean that all questions were correctly endorsed. We explore reasons why this is so in a later section of this chapter. For now, the illustration highlights the fact that there is an assortment of score scales and that each kind of scale has particular features.

From this precursory information, readers will readily realize that the score scale employed in a test is enormously important to how the yielded results of an

---

[1]The SAT is changing dramatically—beginning with the student high school class of 2006 (first administered in Spring 2005)—to be more aligned with current curriculum and institutional practices. A new section on writing has been added, the Verbal test has been reworked and is now called Critical Reading, and the math content has been expanded. Details can be accessed at *http://www.collegeboard.com/student/testing/newsat/about.html*. Retrieved February 10, 2005.

assessment are interpreted and to what kinds of decisions they may properly support. Further, the score scale has implications germane to a great variety of testing-related problems. For instance, when equating and linking tests, the score scale can allow or limit particular methodologies.

Determining what score scale to employ for a given mental measurement is the responsibility of the test developer. The developer's most important criterion for deciding which one to use is that the score scale is useful in making valid score inferences for that appraisal instrument in a well-defined assessment setting.

Then, too, scaling in mental appraisal is *dimensional*. In earlier chapters, I mentioned the concept of dimensionality and we explore it much further here, after a bit more introduction to the initial notion of putting points to a test. Later, we merge the two ideas into a unified concept of dimensional scaling.

Norming a test is an idea closely associated with score scales; in fact, norming derives from a particular score scale applied in an assessment context. It labels a process in which the score scale can be interpreted in relation to a peer (or other appropriate) group. Let us turn first to the concept of scaling, and then to its application in developing and using test norms.

Scaling Defined

Scaling is a method used in mental appraisal for numerically ordering or qualitatively listing objects of an assessment, or, more precisely, attributes of the objects. In educational and psychological measurement, the objects of assessment are generally latent traits or proficiencies. The attributes are one's ability to demonstrate particular manifestations of the trait or proficiency, such as reading with understanding or making correct computations. Scales are generally limited in range (e.g., from 0 to 100, although the construct being appraised actually comprises the gamut, with range $[-\infty, +\infty]$). Scales are usually numerical, but names can also be used to represent the qualitative properties of an object, as long as they have meaning that is inherently transparent (e.g., males and females; high, medium, and low income).

Scaling in measurement is a departure from scaling people as is done with common statistical classifying procedures, such as factor analysis, cluster analysis, or profile and discriminant analyses. In the psychometric application, scaling simply—but significantly—orders the variable. Nearly always, the order reflects some hierarchy, such as from low to high.

It may be easiest to grasp the concept of a scale by looking at instances of scales. To begin, consider that male and female is a simple scale. It has only two divisions and is, accordingly, a two-value scale. (This scale is so simple that it carries the very unusual property of not being hierarchal, but nearly all other types of scales are.) In another simple example, high-, medium-, or low-proficiency is also a type of scale. In these cases, *nominal* names suffice for the scale. Such jejune scales, however, are only the starting point of the concept. Within the definition, too, are scales that present more information, such as when objects are serially or sequentially ordered. For example, in a foot race, contestants are ordered as first, second, or third. Here, the object's "attributes" (their finish position) are expressed *ordinally,* and hence more information is provided than in the nominal labeling. In like manner, a scale can express intervals, such as IQ scores derived from some intelligence measure that ranges from, say, 40 to 160 points, or a test of earth sciences that is scaled from 0 to 100, or a single Likert-type item that ranges from 1 to 7 (e.g., strongly disagree to strongly agree). Most score scales in mental measurement are *interval* or considered as interval. As a final instance, scales can be *ratio* equivalents, like the ratio for length to width of rectangles of 1.61803 (the so-called Golden Ratio). In each instance, objects (viz., attributes) are ordered numerically or qualitatively and hence can constitute a scale. (I provide more information about characteristics of each scale type in the Types of Scales section.)

A real-life example of an early scale in mental measurement—surprising, too, for its sophistication—is Binet's "absolute" (his words) determination of IQ in 3½-year-old children, shown in Figure 6.1. Although we may remark on his absolutist interpretation, the scale is illustrative. Note the scale units, and note that the measured attribute (viz., IQ) of examinees is marked according to a numbering schema derived from responses to his "stunts" (again, his term for examinee responses), such as when a young child names the days of the week. Also, realize that the scale is of interval measurement.

Famous Examples of Scales

It may be useful to begin a technical look at scaling by seeing it from a familiar frame of reference, namely, a widely recognized graphical depiction of the normal curve

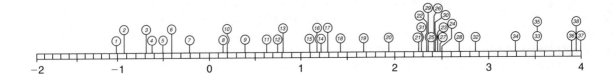

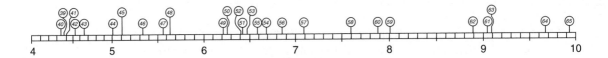

An Absolute Scale of Binet Test Questions
Linear Unit: Standard deviation of Binet Test intelligence of 3½-year-old children
Origin: The mean of Binet Test intelligence of 3½-year-old children

Figure 6.1
Binet's absolute scale questions.
Source: From "A Method of Scaling Psychological and Educational Tests," by L. L. Thurstone, 1925, *Journal of Educational Psychology, 16,* p. 449. Copyright 1925 by American Psychological Association. Reprinted with permission.

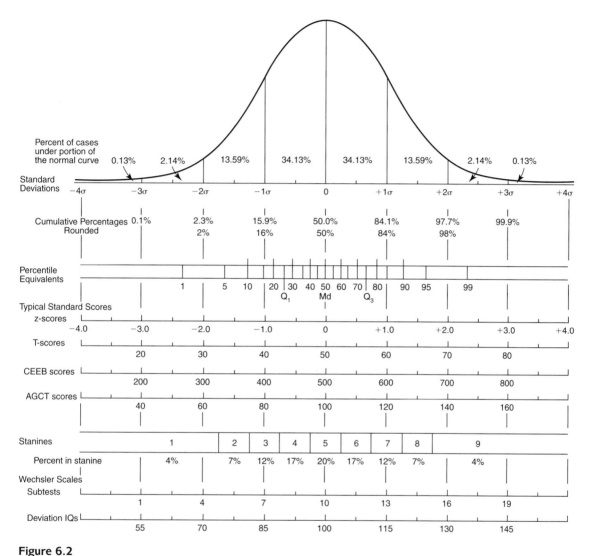

Figure 6.2
Normal distribution with various reporting scales.
Source: From The Psychological Corporation, (1955). *Test Service Bulletin,* January 1977, with permission.

that shows many ways in which scale values can be expressed on it as test score scales. The famous graphic is reproduced in Figure 6.2 and shown early in this discussion to help one realize the basic concept of dimensional scaling.

Figure 6.2 is from *Test Service Bulletin #48* (The Psychological Corporation, 1977). At the time, educational information bulletins were fairly common and often widely disseminated to parents and school personnel. The famous *Test Service*

Bulletin #48 was meant to educate audiences about proper test interpretation. Today, the information is just as pertinent to our understanding of test scales.

Notice particularly in Figure 6.2 that the most direct scale is the one expressing the mean and standard deviation, cited as 0 and 1, respectively. The other scales are derived from this moment-based metric.

Employing the Proper Scale

The concern for scaling in educational and psychological measurement is more than just to devise a scale arbitrarily; rather, it is to apply a scale to the traits for appraisal that is appropriate for a particular purpose or decision. For instance, if the purpose of a test is the assessment of attitudes toward a given political figure, it may be useful to have just a few categories constitute the scale, such as favorable, neutral, or unfavorable. However, when the scale is of the IQ construct, a long, continuous scale (e.g., from 40 to 160) is more likely appropriate. Hence, characteristics of the scale are meaningful only in a particular assessment context and useful only for relevant decision making. What is an appropriate scale in one setting may not be similarly used in another testing situation; one with a different decision context.

Then, too, the audience for the reported scores needs to be considered when devising a scale. If, for example, an appraisal is of personality and the intent is to diagnose individual deficiencies for use by a counseling professional, then a particular score scheme suited to that purpose may be devised, probably one that allows relatively fine discriminations in a number of subtle and related subareas. Contrast this scenario to one in which the test is used to protect public safety or instill public confidence, the goal of many professional licensing and certification programs. A difference score scale altogether—one that allows for reliable discrimination between masters' and nonmasters' in a prescribed body of skills or knowledge—is more suited. Here, individual diagnosis is not the intent, and there is little reason to differentiate among individuals at the ends of the knowledge range (say, between merely skilled persons and genuine experts); rather, the need is to make reliable distinction at some prescribed point along the scale so the individual may be deemed "certified" or "not certified." Hence, the task of establishing a suitable score scale should consider the appraisal's purpose, as well as the likely audience who will use the scores. Again, in scaling, context matters.

Indifference in the Scale

It is important to appreciate that a scale must be indifferent to the object being measured. In other words, the scale used to represent progress on a test of academic achievement, for example, must not be influenced by who takes the test (presuming the appraised population is appropriate, of course). If, for example, a weight was considered "heavy" solely because a certain very strong man could lift it, the scale would be tied to that man's weight-lifting capacity. The scale would not be indifferent to all people who lifted weights, and such a person-dependent interpretation of the scale would be useless. Of course, one individual may lift more weight than another, but they are both being measured in pounds or kilos (or whatever metric) on a scale that is independent of them. As another illustration closer to our study of educational and psychological measurement, consider that if a scale rendered academic achievement differently for boys than it did for girls, then no meaningful comparisons between the sexes (or genders) could be made. The differences could be attributed spuriously to the examinees' gender. There would be some gender-related bias or manifestation in the scale, rather than true differences in achievement. This point was articulated early in the history of measurement by L. L. Thurstone (1928) when he said,

> A measuring instrument must not be seriously affected in its measuring function by the object of measurement. To the extent that its measuring function is so affected, the validity of the instrument is impaired or limited. If a yardstick measured differently because of the fact that it was a rug, a picture, or a piece of paper that was being measured, then to that extent the trustworthiness of that yardstick as a measuring devise would be impaired. Within the range of objects for which the measuring instrument is intended, its function must be independent of the object of measurement. (p. 547)

This is what is meant by having a scale that is indifferent to the object of assessment.

The Need for Scaling

The need for standardizing data in mental measurement probably has the same logical basis as it does in the realm of physical measurement. Since early in the sixteenth century, and likely even before, people recognized that standardizing physical measurement along a common scale was beneficial to interpretation. As one of the first scales, the English set out to codify their units in the Magna Carta, wherein King John of England decreed a standard unit for measuring:

> There shall be one measure of wine throughout Our kingdom, and one of ale, and one measure of corn, to wit, the London quarter, and one breadth of cloth, . . . to wit, two ells within the selvages. As with measures so shall it be with weights. (quoted in Wright, 1997, p. 34)

The French, despite recognizing the necessity of having a uniform scale for weights and measures, were much slower to adopt a coherent system countrywide. In fact, some historians contend that the lack of standard units of measurement contributed to prolonging the French Revolution. The reason for this was that each city, hamlet, and township resisted uniformity in scales for fear that such a system would disadvantage their own metric. History tells us that between courts, shouting matches often ruled which metric was adopted. Moving goods among the populace in France must have been a hassle, indeed, as each day a different unit of measurement could be used.

Although mental measurement cannot be codified into a single score scale, we learn that there are characteristics of meritorious score scales that contribute to making them interpretable, and thus useful. Therefore, the convention of scaling described here is a necessary part of mental appraisal. Lacking such standardization, we, too would be as the French of long ago, simply yelling out idiosyncratic rules without hope of making them comprehensible.

Reliably Making Judgments

Because scales order attributes of an object, it is clear that they rest on our ability to make reliable distinctions between the attributes. In this section, I explain how this is done, both theoretically and mathematically.

The Just Noticeable Difference

A concept foundational to experimental psychology (and indeed, dimensional scaling) is the notion of specifying our ability to reliably discriminate along a continuous scale. This means that you and I can tell differences: We make distinctions. Do not laugh just yet because expressing this idea mathematically—so it can be implemented in tests and other measures—is a profound human accomplishment. Indeed, it is one of psychology's remarkable contributions to science. The following illustration shows the importance of making distinctions. Suppose you and I see two people, one smiling and the other frowning, and we decide to measure them along a "happiness" continuum. We can both tell the difference in outlook between the two people, and we easily agree on which person is happy and which is dour. If we see the people again some time later but they have reversed their expressions (the smiling person is now frowning and the previously frowning person is now smiling), we can just as accurately report our new finding. In other words, we are able to discern differences along the happiness continuum, and we can do so reliably.

Now, consider the next logical step in the scenario—to identify the exact point at which we, as observers, see a difference between the smile and the frown in our subjects. At this point, the scene is exponentially more complex. We can still discriminate along our scale, but we may not agree on the point at which the smile and the frown are different. If our subjects have very little expression, would each subject's countenance be closer to a smile or to a frown? We can say, "Well, it's in the middle." However, significantly, that is the problem because we may have different ideas of where to place the middle. Still, there is somewhere along the continuum where we can agree on a point of reliable discrimination. This point is called the *threshold*.

The threshold represents a concept called a *just noticeable difference,* articulated first by Thorndike (1904) in one of the earliest books on psychometrics. The just noticeable difference is a scientific acknowledgment that we can identify at some point along a continuous variable where we agree that a change has occurred. It means there is a threshold on all score scales, regardless of whether the measurement is of physical characteristics (e.g., a smile vs. a frown) or degrees of an attitude, sentiment, belief, proficiency, trait, or ability. The notion of score scales having a threshold is what makes them useful to mental appraisal. When we study particular item characteristics in chapter 10, we see the threshold directly mapped on a curve representing a likelihood function. In IRT, the threshold is optimally held to be 0.5, indicating that an examinee of precisely average ability on the trait has a 50–50 chance of responding correctly to the item or exercise (presuming binary scoring).

Thurstone (1927) explored the idea more fully and used it to develop his *discriminant model*, which we use today in many statistical applications (e.g., in discriminant function analysis and even in structural equation modeling). Thurstone noted the *law of comparative judgment*, which today is the basis of all discriminant function analyses and firmly grounds the just noticeable difference in psychometric theory.

Subtle yet important differences exist between the just noticeable difference and the law of comparative judgment—and its close cousin, the *law of categorical judgment*. They are best seen though as mathematical models, to which we now turn.

Fechner's Law

Mathematically, the just noticeable difference is expressed by Fechner's (1966) law shown in Equation 6.1 as originally written. The Φ (phi) is the term to attend to here because it signifies a dichotomy and is employed notationally to be consistent with the phi coefficient of binary correlational relationships. A particular point at magnitude Φ is the just noticeable difference (threshold), where a distinction is made:

$$\psi = b \ \log(\Phi) + a, \tag{6.1}$$

where ψ = a scalar variable,

Φ = magnitude, and

b, a = scaling constants.

The ψ (psi) in Equation 6.1 can be any variable when expressed as a scalar. In measurement it may be a proficiency, achievement, ability, attitude, belief, or other like variable. The logarithmic function (i.e., log[Φ]) is typically adopted in depictions of latent scales because it yields equal ratios, making it easier to portray the notion that thresholds can be adopted at any point along the scale's range. It is also used because likelihood functions often calculate to a very small number and a log can portray a very small number more realistically. (Scaling constants in the equation are not relevant to this discussion, but for interest, represent the transformation part of the equation.)

For our interpretation of psychological constructs, it means our capacity to determine the just noticeable difference exists equally along the full range of the scale. More simply stated, we can distinguish among magnitudes of a construct regardless of where we are on a scale. We can reliably differentiate between two hues of light greens just as well as we can tell the difference between two hues of dark greens.

Figure 6.3
Logarithmic function
portraying Fechner's law.

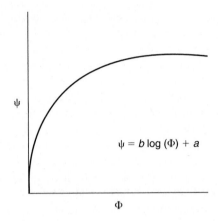

$\psi = b \log (\Phi) + a$

ψ

Φ

Figure 6.3 presents Fechner's law graphically in the form of a (semi)logarithmic cumulative function for a scale such as may be used in mental measurement. In the graphic, it is apparent that theta is associated with increased trait proficiency. Higher ability or proficiency is expressed as more theta. Also, note that the relation is not strictly linear, although it is *monotonic* (always rising). There are important mathematical implications of this type of scaling beyond the points I have made here, and for a discussion of some of them in statistical decision theory, see *Foundations of Measurement, Volume III* (Luce, Krantz, Suppes, & Tversky, 1990). Our interest is merely in establishing the notion that the just noticeable difference is a convincing concept in psychology, and one that can be expressed mathematically.

Early Scaling Models to Today

Deterministic and Probabilistic Scaling Models

From the previous discussion and from that of probability theory in chapter 2, readers realize that in educational and psychological testing an "event" can be the occurrence of a particular score, representing a certain level of latent trait or proficiency. In scaling, such an event either can be wholly determined or may be likely. To reflect these conditions, scales are often classified as *deterministic* or *probabilistic*. In deterministic scaling, an event can be accurately predicted by a given circumstance. For instance, when coal is placed under a specified pressure for a known and very long time period, it gets harder and harder until a diamond results. A scale of pressure and time for coal transformation could be easily developed because it is a completely predictable phenomenon. The resulting scale would be deterministic. Deterministic models are common in the physical and natural sciences, such as chemistry and physics.

For our study of scales, however, beyond historical roots in Guttman's early work (see Guttman's Early Work on Scaling Models section), strictly deterministic models are not considered further in this book because they play no appreciable role in modern psychometric methods.

Probabilistic models, however, estimate the *likelihood* of an event, such as the chances of observing a certain test score given a particular set of conditions (e.g., item difficulty, trait level of the examinee). An illustration is the relationship between practice in reading and an outcome of reading comprehension. The more one practices reading for comprehension (the condition), the greater the likelihood of a higher score on a relevant test. However, as a probabilistic relation, it is far from certain that a higher score will automatically result with increased practice. Higher reading scores may or may not be seen from more practice reading. Instead, it is a "likelihood" or probability. Virtually all (I cannot think of exceptions, but one never knows) educational and psychological tests in use today are designed as probabilistic models.

Guttman's Early Work on Scaling Models

Early attempts at applying scaling models to measurement are an idea for which the French coined the perfect expression—*une fausse idée claire*—a terrific idea that does not work. I explain two of these early scale response models: one developed by Guttman and the other by Lazarsfeld and Henry. Each is a terrific idea, but neither is sufficient for modern mental measurement. Regardless, they form a backbone to the probabilistic models that we do use today.

Guttman (1941) developed a step function to show probabilities of correct and incorrect responses. He labeled his method *scalogram analysis;* it is sometimes referred to as a *perfect-scale model*. Guttman's model is shown in Figure 6.4. In the model, a response to an item is simply determined to be correct or incorrect at one particular ability (or proficiency) value. The scale is represented in standard score metric, making it

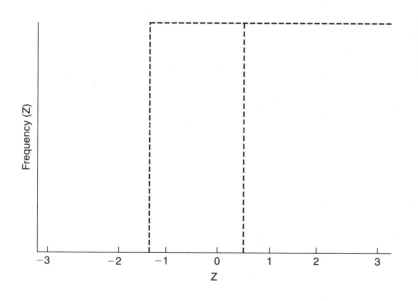

Figure 6.4
Step frequency function of Guttman's scalogram (perfect-scale model).

available to a wide variety of tests. In this model, only one discrimination point is possible for all ability values—at the threshold and nowhere else. All abilities below the given value have no chance of a correct response, and conversely, values above the threshold have a certainty of correct response. Because of these characteristics, this is not a probabilistic model, but a *deterministic model*. Here, one's score is absolutely determined by the ability or proficiency at the threshold. If mental constructs are neither malleable nor labile, Guttman's model suffices to describe mental measures.

The importance of Guttman's work lies in the fact that scalogram analysis sets the stage for probabilistic models. Today, our most widely recognized probabilistic models are the item characteristic curves (ICCs) of IRT-based scales. (I address the ICC in detail in chapter 10). These IRT probability function scales stem directly from Guttman's early efforts.

Before Guttman's perfect-scale model, deterministic models had not been articulated clearly, although psychometricians had worked with crude versions of them. With Guttman's perspective displayed plainly, it was plain to see the shortcomings of the deterministic model, making it possible to move to an evidentiary-defined probabilistic model. Thus, Guttman was at the fore of modern scale development.

Building to More Advanced Scaling Models

Lazarsfeld and Henry (1968), working from Guttman's machinations, developed a more detailed description of a latent, probabilistic model, albeit still crude. This model is depicted in Figure 6.5. The abscissa (x-axis) in this graphic of the model, ability, is also considered in a z-score metric. This is a tremendous advance from Guttman's model. Notice in Figure 6.5 that the probability of a correct response increases as ability values increase. This is logical and should be expected: More able examinees have a higher probability of getting an item correct than do less able examinees. It is a rudimentary probabilistic model.

Unfortunately, like Guttman's scalogram approach, a problem arises in applying real-world data to the Lazarsfeld and Henry model. The difficulty is that the model is strictly linear, and as such, except for in the middle portion of the ability range, the slope can easily rise too steeply to be of practical value. Nonetheless, the model does

Figure 6.5
Linear frequency function of
Lazarsfeld and Henry.

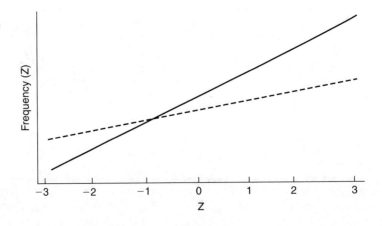

show further evolution of the basic notion of probabilistic models: Probabilities rise as a function of ability values, making the scale monotonic. This idea holds for modern scaling models that assume discrimination is constant for all abilities.

To view probabilistic scaling models that are useful for our work in measurement, it is necessary to define scales as reflecting a functional relation.

Functions in Scaling

Scaling models are built from mathematical functions. We have seen this already in several places, including in Fechner's expression of the just noticeable difference. As a frequency function, the score increases on the abscissa as the function specifies a higher frequency or greater probability on the ordinate axis. Such functions can readily be expressed mathematically in a structural, or general, form, as shown in Equation 6.2:

$$x = \varphi(\theta), \tag{6.2}$$

where $x =$ observed value,

$\theta =$ a scalar of any independent variable (whether observed or unobserved), and

$\varphi =$ any function.

As is evident, Equation 6.2 clearly invokes Fechner's law. When θ (ability on the latent trait) is known, the x value is likewise specified. This is true for all variables, regardless of type or level of measurement; hence, it fits the general case for variables and can be applied universally. In educational and psychological contexts, the functional relationship is more commonly written as $f(\theta)$. Equation 6.3 expresses the general form (i.e., structural model) of the probabilistic model as used in scale development in mental testing:

$$x = f(\theta) + e. \tag{6.3}$$

The terms here are as expressed in Equation 6.2, and e represents error of measurement. This new term makes a huge difference. The error in the equation is the composite effect of the associated variance unaccounted for in the true score and is used to represent in the model our imprecision in measuring a phenomenon, in our case, a trait or proficiency.

Dimensional Scaling

Dimensionality Explained

Scales for mental measurement have a psychological inherency in that they quantify some particular aspect of cognition. In other words, scales of mental appraisal do not reflect random events in the brain; rather, they numerically delineate a deliberate response from a particular locus for neural activity. The stimulus for the response, of course, is a set of decently targeted items or exercises. Also, there is the presumption that the examinee is motivated, the "maximal effort" or presumption of optimal performance discussed in chapter 3. This aspect of scales is expressed in a test's *dimensionality*. The concept of dimensionality of a trait is of all mental appraisals, regardless of whether the measure is of achievement, proficiency, ability, attitude, or belief.

To grasp the concept of dimensionality, imagine that there is a "space" in neural activity that is occupied by a particular cognitive process, such as the reading construct or some attitude. This space is the locus of neural activity and is focused on just the particular aspect of cognition under consideration; therefore, it is identified with the performance of that activity. Of course, the "space" is not a wholly identifiable, physical locale in the brain at all, but it exists as neural activity nonetheless. Dimensionality is a description of this latent space.

In many contexts, and especially in theoretical mathematics and geometry, this kind of dimensionality is termed *Euclidean space,* after Euclid's famous theorem and associated axioms. Students in advanced courses in mathematics and statistics routinely study their characteristics and implications, including the general Euclidean model and its many variants. Often, when a function is represented graphically, a line is fitted to it—called a *vector*—and is used to represent the manifestation of Euclidean space as a test response. Detailed discussion of Euclidean vectors is beyond the scope of this text (see Logan's [1996] popular text *Applied Mathematics*), except that the idea of typifying neural activity in geometric space is important to representing constructs with scales.

For our level of use, tests are considered to be either *unidimensional,* when a singular locus for neural activity is tapped, or *multidimensional,* when more than one trait dimension is included in the appraisal. In the ensuing discussion, we examine the dimensionality concept more thoroughly, and then look at unidimensional assessments and multidimensional appraisals.

Most tests (especially those invoking proficiency in a content discipline) are unidimensional in their focus. In these cases, the numeric manifestation of unidimensionality as a quantitative or qualitative scale can only have a single interpretation, namely, that which is specified by validity evidence as the focus for appraisal. This means that an examinee's score on a test of language expression can only be interpreted in terms of the examinee's ability or proficiency in language expression and not in terms of other constructs (e.g., reading).

Lord and Novick (1963) stated this idea more practically using the terminology of latent traits:

> We might give one possible interpretation to this term [viz., latent trait] by saying that an individual's performance depends on a single underlying trait if, given his value on that trait, nothing further can be learned from him that can contribute to the explanation of his performance. (p. 538)

Hambleton, Swaminathan, and Rogers (1991) reinforce this by specifying that the Euclidian space is fully explained in unidimensional tests. They state, "When the assumption of unidimensionality holds, the complete latent space [of measurement] consists of only one ability" (p. 11). Clearly, the unidimensionality concept has profound significance for test interpretation.

Dimensionality in tests is not a new notion. It was held as early as the 1940s (e.g., McNemar, 1946). Today, it remains paramount in our conception of how mental appraisals operate (e.g., Embretson & Reise, 2000; Stout, 1990; Thissen, Wainer, & Wang, 1994).

Unidimensional Scaling

Procedurally, unidimensionality is generally held when the factor structure of a test is unitary; that is, the unique variance of all stimuli can be located within a given factor, which for now may be alternatively labeled as a factor, dimension, component, or even cluster. This means that a test is appraising one, and only one, construct or trait. Interpretation is straightforward. Responses by examinees to the test's items or exercises reflect progress along the trait or proficiency scale. From more correct endorsements by examinees, test users may infer higher proficiency. Thus, the instrument's scale is a proxy way to express the latent trait. Because only one latency is being investigated, the test is scaled unidimensionality.

Factoring observed data from a test is one route to investigate its unidimensionality. Eigenvalues revealing the percent of variance in the model explained by its factors are often calculated to evaluate the factor structure. A single strong first factor, followed by a large gap in percent of variance explained by the second factor and thereafter progressively weaker factors, is given this data pattern. Figure 6.6 shows such eigenvalues.

The eigenvalues may be plotted in a scree plot to give visual rendering of the relative strength of the factors to complete variance in the model. Figure 6.7 is a scree plot for the values in Figure 6.6. When such factors are plotted in factor (Euclidian) space, the notion of unidimensionality is clearly seen, as in Figure 6.8.

However, caution is advised to not interpret the data at this point. Although Figures 6.6 to 6.8 convey a sense of unidimensionality through factors, they merely

	Component	Initial Eigenvalues		
		Total	Percent of Variance	Cumulative Percent
Raw	1	2.703	50.134	50.134
	2	.596	11.058	61.192
	3	.501	9.294	70.486
	4	.410	7.600	78.085
	5	.275	5.107	83.192
	6	.261	4.837	88.030
	7	.223	4.144	92.174
	8	.187	3.469	95.643
	9	.151	2.800	98.443
	10	.084	1.557	100.000

Figure 6.6
Eigenvalues revealing a strong first factor followed by dramatically weaker factors.

Figure 6.7
Scree plot of components
indicating unidimensionality.

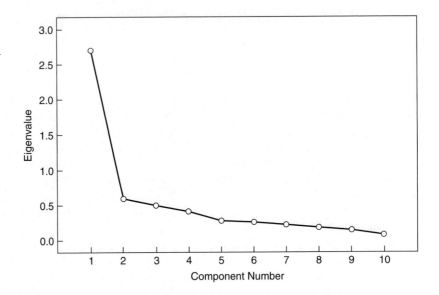

suggest unidimensionality and do not provide conclusive evidence. Actually appraising the dimensionality of a test is more difficult. Both psychometric expertise
in relevant methodologies and a familiarity with the construct under consideration
(probably garnered from content knowledge and field experience) are needed. In
chapter 13, I explain more about appraising unidimensionality and describe many
methods useful to its determination, each appropriate for a different circumstance.

Figure 6.8
Plot showing clustering of
questions.

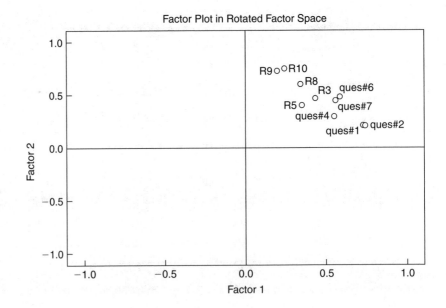

Most educational and psychological tests strive for unidimensional assessment. School- and college-level tests—such as the Iowa Test of Basic Skills (ITBS; Hoover, 2004), Stanford Achievement Test (The Psychological Corporation, 2003), and College Basic Academic Subjects Examination (CBASE; Osterlind, 2004)—are generally directed at a single construct, even when a battery of such tests is administered during a testing period. Tests with unidimensional scales are also common in other contexts, especially with tests used for licensing and certification. An interesting example of a unidimensional scale is the Test of Infant Motor Performance (Campbell, Wright, & Linacre, 2002), an assessment of posture and other selected movements needed by infants for normal function in daily life (e.g., head turn, hip-knee flexion).

Before we discuss multidimensional scales, persons working in measurement should realize that what applies to whole tests does not necessarily pertain to the separate items that compose it. Tests can be either unidimensional or multidimensional in their appraisal of mental functions; however, individual items or exercises on a test *must* be unidimensional. The reason for this dictum is that test items that lack unidimensionality are impossible to interpret accurately. A simple example shows what happens when dimensionality is not preserved for an item. Suppose a dichotomously scored, multiple-choice test item is intended to assess a mathematics computation construct, but the item is lengthy and requires the examinee to read a difficult passage. If an examinee responds incorrectly to the item, should test users interpret the incorrect response as a lack of mathematics knowledge or that the examinee is deficient in reading proficiency? When the dimensionality for the item is inexact, there is no way to distinguish. Hence, binary test items are considered reliable proxies for a construct only when they are unidimensional.

Multidimensional Scaling

Assessment can also be *multidimensional,* meaning that several latencies are being assessed simultaneously, a difference in response magnitude to a single trait. Many psychological inventories and personality appraisals are multidimensional in their focus. This aspect for tests can generally be recognized through *multidimensional scaling* (MDS).

Multidimensionality as a conceptual notion is easy to grasp by extending our knowledge of unidimensionality. Usually, a multidimensional appraisal is a test composed of two or more unidimensional constructs. The items and exercises are individually unidimensional: some being focused on one trait, whereas others target another. This circumstance of a multidimensional appraisal is easy to imagine in practice. For instance, extroversion and self-efficacy are distinct phenomena, and each can be hypothesized as a latent construct. When considered concurrently, however, their individual variances overlap, meaning that their latencies have an oblique relationship. When appraised simultaneously, the assessment is multidimensional.

In psychology and education there are many examples of multidimensional tests, including the Wechsler Intelligence Scale for Children, Third Edition–Revised (WISC-IIIR; Wechsler, 1991), the Woodcock-Johnson Psycho-Educational Battery, Revised (WJ-R; Woodcock & Johnson, 1989), the Wechsler Adult Intelligence Scale (WAIS-R;

Wechsler, 1981). Many other measures of personality or perceptions about complex topics (e.g., religious and supernatural beliefs) are also multidimensional in nature. Often tests with multidimensional scales are used in counseling and other settings where it is appropriate to consider many dimensions of an individual's mental makeup simultaneously.

One supposes, a multidimensional test could include any number of dimensions, but deriving a separate interpretation for each of them could be complex and probably specious if there were very many of them. Hence, most multidimensional tests appraise only two or three meaningful divisions. Usually, multidimensional tests have items grouped into sections, or at least similarly focused items are placed together.

Technically, multidimensional models appraise *distances* between traits and the specified dimensions. When the traits have a lot in common, the distance to a dimension is slight, but it becomes greater as the traits are increasingly unique. MDS locates the distance of each item relative to the dimensions. Torgerson (1958) proposed the first, well-known MDS model that fits the Euclidean space. His idea was to use vectors to represent a trait's existence in Euclidean space. A measure may have several such vectors. The distance between any two of them could be measured by mathematical equations. The results would indicate whether the scaling was unidimensional or multidimensional.

In MDS, the space between computed vectors need not necessarily represent different constructs or traits. In fact, in measurement, "dimensions" often does not mean different traits. In educational and psychological testing, the space is just as likely to represent differences in response magnitude to the same trait. For instance, suppose an attitude measure is made up of 5-point Likert items, from *Agree* to *Disagree*. The distance in attitude between the 5 points is measured multidimensionally. If two vectors are found by regression in a multidimensional model to occupy the same space, then no difference in attitude on the construct is measured. However, when the distance is great, a large difference is recorded. In either case, the trait of attitude is not different; rather, it is the same trait, and MDS reveals differences in responses to it along the dimension.

To see MDS in statistical output, consider both a numerical and a graphical representation, as in Table 6.1 and Figure 6.9, representations of distances of Likert-type items to an attitude measure's hypothesized dimensions. Note the distance of each item to the two dimensions, each having a reference axis of 0. Some items are clearly more associated with one dimension than another. In this illustration, more of them are associated with the second dimension than are with the first. Other items have a less distinct interpretation. Note, too, that there are only two dimensions in this example, making interpretation relatively straightforward. A more precise distance measure is given by the stimulus coordinates shown in Table 6.1. In addition, a regression-type expression showing Euclidean distances can also be fit to the data. An example of this is shown in Figure 6.10.

MDS also allows three-dimensional solutions with graphical representations. Usually, however, as the number of dimensions increases, the interpretation is more difficult. Often many distances represent orders of magnitude about a single trait rather than separate traits. Some statistical and graphics computer programs allow the users to manipulate such graphics by rotating axes, thereby facilitating interpretation. The same attitude measure used as illustration in Figure 6.8 is analyzed in three dimensions in Figure 6.11.

Table 6.1

Stimulus Coordinates of Multidimensional Assessment

		Dimensions	
Stimulus	Stimulus name	1	2
1	E18	1.8738	0.153
2	E19	−0.9615	−0.2559
3	E20	1.1335	−0.2859
4	E21	−0.7253	0.8142
5	E22	1.2946	−0.9785
6	E23	−1.4297	0.2691
7	E24	1.3577	0.5067
.	.	.	.
32	E13	−0.861	0.1578
33	E14	1.5894	−0.6271
34	E15	−1.6139	−0.2363
35	E16	−0.146	−0.5503
36	E17	−1.0161	0.1504

As we see from the preceding data displays, MDS is well suited to graphical representation. This is in fact considered one of its more appealing features in data analysis. MDS fits the old adage, "a picture is worth a thousand words."

Further, as can be seen in the graphics, and especially with the coordinates table, MDS is a factoring procedure, and it shares much in common with conventional FA

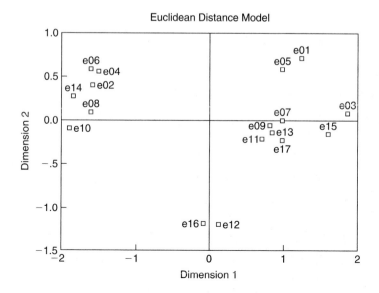

Figure 6.9

Plot of multidimensional appraisal.

Figure 6.10

Scatter plot of Euclidean distances for all observations in a multidimensional assessment.

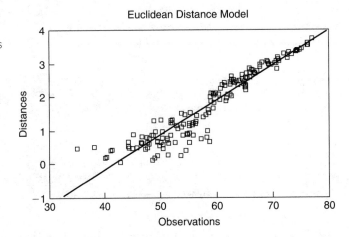

and PCA. Both methods seek to reduce data to some smaller amount: in factoring by identifying common factors and in MDS by associating stimuli with dimensions. However, there is a major difference between conventional FA and MDS in that FA can only work with matrices of correlations or covariances, whereas MDS can analyze any kind of matrix of similarity or dissimilarity. Hence, MDS can be used to represent constructs in a large variety of tests, whether the data are binary or polytomous.

This also suggests that MDS is a flexible procedure with broad application for exploring data and confirming hypotheses. Indeed, MDS is used in many fields and not just as in psychometrics. Demographers, cartographers, astronomers, medical researchers, and engineers in many disciplines employ MDS as a model of similarity. For instance, sociologists employ MDS when determining whether language and regional dialects represent distinct cultures. An interesting application of MDS is used by FedEx (and likely other delivery companies, too) in determining efficient delivery routes where "distances" are literally distances!

The procedures and theory of MDS are vastly more detailed and interesting than are described here. Readers are encouraged to seek more information from any

Figure 6.11

Graphical representation of three-dimensional Euclidean distance model.

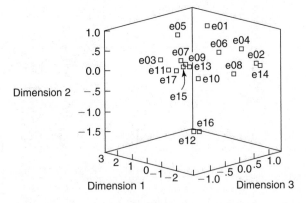

number of excellent sources. One especially fine resource is Borg and Groenen's (1997) *Modern Multidimensional Scaling,* which presents information in an introductory fashion and builds to complex mathematical models. Young and Hamer (1987) also have a fine, technical offering. An excellent Web site to learn more about dimensionality in tests can be accessed at *http://www.statsoftinc.com/textbook/stmulsca. html.*

Types of Scales

General Conditions for Ordered Scales

Quotidian use of numerical scales for mental measurement has made it necessary to devise organizational schemes. Stevens (1946) put forth one of the most useful taxonomies of this type in a classic article titled "On the Theory of Scales of Measurement." He proposed that scales of measurement be classified by the kind of transformation each allows without fundamentally changing its meaning. He identified a number of general conditions for scales based on this idea. Lower-ordered scales, with fewer restrictions, permit more kinds of transformations than do higher-ordered scales. Stevens identified four "boundaries for scales" that categorized them into four types: *nominal, ordinal, interval,* and *ratio.* Today, Stevens' boundaries are referred to as *levels of measurement,* to reflect the major mathematical characteristics of each one. Soon after Stevens' original work, his categorization schema was extended and refined by Coombs (1953) and then again by Stevens (1951) himself.

The scales are hierarchically ordered by applicable characteristics. The order, from lowest to highest is thus: nominal, ordinal, interval, and finally, ratio. Scales classified as a particular type cannot be transformed into the next higher level without changing the meaning of the scale. That is to say, a nominal scale cannot assume the characteristics of any of the other scales because the other scales are higher classifications. An ordinal scale can assume nominal characteristics, plus features of ordinality. In like fashion, an interval scale has characteristics of the two lower levels, as well as its own attributes, but it cannot be transformed into ratio measurement. The highest scale classification, ratio scale, can have features of all the other scale types, in addition to its own unique properties.

I discuss each scale type below, and readers who want more information are directed to Stevens' (1951) and Torgerson's (1958) original, book length works.

Nominal-Type Scales

The nominal level is where all scaling begins, with the simplest characteristics of representation. Scales in this category can assume only assignment of a particular feature. That is, a given scale merely names the characteristic for a variable. For example, labeling subjects *boys* or *girls,* or assigning companies on a stock exchange to equity-averaging indexes, such as the Dow Jones Average or the New York Stock Exchange are examples of this kind of labeling. There is virtually no limit to such labels. Labels could be left-handed persons versus right-handed persons, or categories of clinical diagnosis for behavioral disorders, such as paranoid, schizophrenic, or delusional. Furthermore, the labels can be attitudes and preferences that may change or fluctuate depending on myriad considerations, such as voting habits or a favorite type of coffee bean. Arbitrary symbols may even be used to separate categories, such as the alpha group and the beta group. All types of transformations are possible with scales at this level.

Although the nominal scale category may appear lowly and obvious, the important role a nominal scale plays in our daily lives should not be underestimated. Pedhazur and Schmelkin (1991) cite a biblical example as illustrative. Quoting from the book of Judges, they cite the rule that the Lord gave Gideon for classifying men—by the way they drank water! In the biblical context, kneeling to drink was not insignificant because it could indicate idol worshiping:

> But the Lord said to Gideon, "There are still too many men. Take them down to the water, and I will sift them for you there. . . . So, Gideon took the men down to the water. There the Lord told him, "Separate those who lap the water with their tongues like a dog from those who kneel down to drink." Three hundred men lapped with their hands to their mouths. . . . The Lord said to Gideon, "With the three hundred men that lapped I will save you and give the Midianites into your hands. Let all the other men go, each to his own place. (Judges, 7:4–7)

The story also shows that context is important for determining what label is employed. In fact, whether the categories employed for classification in nominal measurement are meaningful or pedantic depends entirely on context. Within the psychometric domain, typically such decisions rest on what research questions are being addressed. Essentially, whatever category is appropriate to a given research question is the determining factor. As long as the category is a quantitative property, it can be used.

Ordinal-Type Scales

The next higher type of measurement is the *ordinal scale*. By definition, ordinality reflects an order or ranking of the elements within a category. Examples of ranking are seen in the questions: Who or which is first? Last? Higher? Longer? Better? Any time the elements within a category (or, in research, a variable) can be ranked along a dimensional scale, they are ordinally measured. Every day, sports teams are ordinally ranked in newspapers by number of games won. To say, "I came in fifth," is ordinal classification.

Ordinality is a higher classification of measurement scale than nominal measurement. It is common for mothers and fathers of toddlers to see the difference between nominal and ordinal numbering when observing their child grow and develop. At first, they typically see their beginning speaker label things nominally: "Mommy," "spoon," "kitty." However, soon, toddlers understand ordinality, often as early as age 2 or 3. Every toddler has the experience of placing blocks or balls in order by shape or size. Such a game is done on an ordinal type of scale.

Another point to appreciate about ordinal scales is that, although variables along these scales are ordered, they are not necessarily equally ranked. In other words, the distance between two rankings is unrecognized in the ordinal scales. In technical terms, ordinal-type scales may be either equal interval or nonequal interval, but this information is not known directly from ordinality.

Interval-Type Scales

Magnitude of difference between units on a scale (viz., equal interval vs. non-equal interval) is, however, reflected in the next higher level of measurement, *interval scaling*. Meaning can be inferred from the differences between units of measurement along an interval scale. A frequently cited example of interval scaling is the measurement of temperature. Suppose it is 90°F today versus 80°F yesterday or 72°F today versus 62°F yesterday, the differences between the temperatures being compared is the same, 10°F. Thus, there is a meaningful interpretation of the distance between two points along the scale, even though the points for comparing the range difference were selected for their very difference. This is a central characteristic of interval levels of scaling.

Although the differences in magnitude are constant with interval scales, such scales themselves are not equal because each one has an arbitrary metric with a different starting place. This means that ratios (not a characteristic of interval measurement) between the scales are not equal. Consider the case in which 80°F is twice the number of degrees as 40°F (although technically it is not twice as hot). However, when these Fahrenheit units are converted to Celsius values (27°C, 4°C), the Celsius degrees do not present the same difference—27°C is not twice as much as 4°C! It is considerably more than twice; and, the difference in actual temperature on this scale is a lot hotter! Novelist Lewis Carroll demonstrates this point comically in *Alice in Wonderland* when Alice ponders such a circumstance with the Red Queen.

> "Are five nights warmer than one night, then?" Alice ventured to ask.
> "Five times as warm, of course."
> "But they should be five times as *cold,* by the same rule—"
> "Just so!" cried the Red Queen, "Five times as warm *and* five times as cold—just as I'm five times as rich as you are, *and* five times as clever!"

Interval scaling implies that a linear function for X may be multiplied by a factor and have a constant added to it without fundamentally changing the meaning of the scale. This can be expressed with the familiar linear transformation (Equation 6.4):

$$X' = a + bX. \qquad \textbf{(6.4)}$$

Usually, but not always, mental measurement instruments for which the range of scores is continuous and large are considered to have interval levels of scale. Psychometricians frequently employ the *assumption* of interval level of measurement when analyzing tests and test scores. This is an important fact because there is technical merit in arguing against such an assumption. Unfortunately, for test scales that are inherently ordinal measurement, there are few useful procedures for analyzing the instruments and the scores resulting from their administration. Thus, the assumption of interval scaling is often made.

Some time ago, Coombs (1950) was troubled by the common proposition that continuous test scales are interval level, and he suggested an alternative to the pseudoassumption. He posited a sort of quasicategory between ordinal and interval levels of measurement. This additional category, which he did not name, would be a mathematical holding place for scales used on many conventional tests. Coombs' idea, however, has not been widely accepted, and today the practice of using tests *as if* the scales are interval is common practice in psychometrics. Nonetheless, psychometricians should be attentive to the technical characteristics of the measurement scale used so the interpretation is uncompromised.

Ratio-Type Scales

The ratio of magnitudes between objects is the central characteristic of the *ratio*-level scale. This is the highest level of scale type, according to Stevens' taxonomy. Ratio-level scales have all the characteristics of nominal, ordinal, and interval scales, plus this unique one—differences between units are expressed as ratios. This also dictates that ratio-level scales have only a single transformation possible; namely, multiplication of the scale values by a positive constant. A ratio scale can be changed only by the unit of the measurement originally used.

In other words, in ratio scales, the numerical measurements are *ipso facto* ratios of magnitudes between objects, as in the expression of Equation 6.5. This expression suggests all the preceding rules plus its own, showing the ratio aspect of the scale:

$$\frac{b(X_i)}{b(X_j)} = \frac{c(X_i)}{c(X_j)}. \tag{6.5}$$

Another important property of ratio-level scales is that an absolute zero point exists for them. This is because the quantity of zero ratio exists absolutely. For example, there is point of zero temperature (at least in theory), regardless of whether temperature is noted on a Fahrenheit or Celsius scale. This point also brings to light the important relationship between interval and ratio levels of measurement. When relationships are expressed on interval-level scales, the differences between units on that scale are measured on a ratio scale. An example of a ratio scale is sometimes used in IRT work when the odds scale is expressed as the antilog of the logit scale (described in chapter 10).

Probability Theory and Scale Types

The rules for probability theory presented earlier in Table 2.3 (see chapter 2) are especially helpful in realizing distinctions among levels of measurement for test scales. Recall the four rules: (a) rule of complementary probability, (b) rule of probability range, (c) rule of null event (impossibility), and (d) rule of "or" probability. The first statement applies to the nominal level. The next two statements apply to the nominal and ordinal level. Statements 1, 2, and 3 define the interval level. Finally, all four statements describe the ratio level of measurement.

Intervals for Scales

Beyond the type of scale, an especially important property of a scale, regardless of its range or metric, is the interval between its eligible units. Units on a scale are either equidistance from one another or they are not. In the language of scaling, this characteristic for scales is referred to as either *equal interval* or *nonequal interval*. Understanding whether the units of a particular scale are or are not equidistant has enormous implication for interpreting scores yielded by a measure.

Equal and Nonequal Interval Scales

Equality of units for a scale is readily understood by examining the following question: "Does the distance between any two nearby units on a scale—say, between 2 and 3 points—represent the same growth, change, or distance as between any other two points on the same scale—say, between 50 and 51?" In other words, are all units equal in distance, and hence, are they identically interpreted? If the units are equidistant through the entire range of the measurement, the scale is said to be *equal interval*.

Often, but not always, when achievement test scores are expressed in standard score units, the scale is considered to be equal interval. Hence, the distance between points along the scale can be meaningfully contrasted. If, for instance, two examinees are five units apart, there is approximately an equal difference in their achievement or proficiency on the test regardless of each one's overall score. Another example of an equal interval scale is seen in the rankings of hardness gradation on the Selzer scale for judging rocks. In this scale, equal values of increasing density (i.e., hardness) in the rock's composition are what separate the gradations on the scale. A rock classed as a 4 is exactly twice as dense as one that is a 2, just as a rock classified as a 6 is three times as dense as another rock classed as a 2. The units on the scale are equally far apart all along the scale's range. There are many scales in which the units are interpreted as equally spaced.

The analog of an equal interval scale is the *nonequal interval scale*. On scales with nonequal intervals, units are not equidistant throughout the range of the scale. Further, the differences may or may not be proportionally different. The familiar percentile scale is composed of nonequal interval units. The difference between scores at the 50th to 51st percentile ranking represents a vastly different gap than does the difference between scores at the 98th and 99th percentile.

Figure 6.12

Comparison of percentile, nonequal interval to standardized equal interval scales.

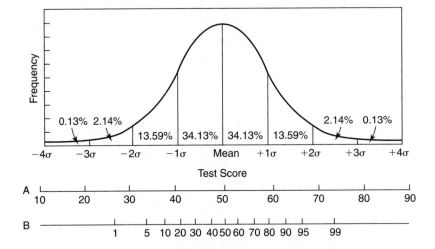

To illustrate this point, imagine that three sprinters finish a race. Suppose the first two runners are very close to each other—only a small fraction of a second separates the winner from the next finisher. However, imagine that the third-place finisher is very far behind the first finishers. In ordinal scale, the sprinters are ranked first, second, and third—no information is contained in the classification to indicate the distance between the racers. Yet, in reality, the distance between the runners is of nonequal intervals. In this example, the race reporting is a nonequal interval.

Figure 6.12 presents a graphical display of two scales, one of equal intervals (Scale A) and another of nonequal intervals (Scale B). This graphic allows the comparison of different intervals on two scales. Although equal interval scales seemingly allow a more straightforward interpretation, they do not convey as much information about the distribution as does the nonequal interval scale.

Types of Measurement

It is often useful to categorize scales on the basis of how resulting scores may be used or interpreted. Some useful types of measurement are given in the following sections.

Ipsative Versus Normative Measurement

Score scales that have preferences, or measures that may be hierarchically ordered, necessitate particular kinds of interpretations. One special scale of this type is *ipsative measures,* a term introduced by Cattell (1944) during his consideration of ordinal scales. Ipsative measures have a raw score that sums to a constant for a given examinee. In the format, an examinee has a forced choice and must rank order response options within an item. By this prescription, ipsative measures order preferences *within* an individual, yielding *intraindividual* differences. Thus, an ipsative measure produces scores that represent the *relative* strength of the construct compared with other constructs for that individual, rather than the *absolute* score. An example would be comparing a person's moral relativism with that same individual's position on a particular religious issue. Personnel selection profiles, such as commonly used in business for screening applicants to a position where the candidate must select either true/false or yes/no, are ipsative measures.

Generally, ipsative measures are obtained from items in forced-choice formats, where examinees order sets of items associated with different scales, but they can also be generated mathematically from Likert-type items by removing the variance due to total score so the deviation scores sum to zero. In either case, dependence is introduced between the different scale scores by constraining the overall sum of scores. As such, they are ordinal levels of measurement, a feature that is viewed as a weakness for many educational and psychological tests that require interval level of scaling.

An especially interesting example of an ipsative measure is the scale used by judges of a dog show (although this is scarcely mental measurement). In Best of Breed dog shows, it is usual for many dogs from various breeds to be shown and judged simultaneously. However, the rating is not between the dogs as no two of them are contrasted directly. Instead, each dog is ranked *intraindividually,* from 0 to 100. The top of the scale represents the perfect dog for a given breed: ideal color, conformation, gait, temperament, and other characteristics. The winner is the dog that comes closest to the breed's ideal—a perfect ipsative measure.

Ipsative measures are contrasted with *normative measures,* which are measures that may be interpreted *interindividually.* Examples of normative measures are scores on an essay assigned by various judges or rankings for professional athletes when sportswriters select players for a "dream team." In these measures, subjects are directly compared. Percentile ranking is a well-recognized example of normative measures. Momentarily, I discuss derived scales and norms; which are classically normative measures. But, first, let us continue discussion of other types of measures.

Isomorphic Measurement

Measurement is said to be *isomorphic* when a direct, one-to-one relationship exists between the entities used for measurement and the object that each represents. An example of isomorphic measurement is when the Red Cross uses a giant, plywood thermometer in a town square to represent pints of blood given by the townspeople during a blood drive. Each time the Red Cross paints another unit of red on the giant thermometer, it represents so many more pints of blood given by the townspeople. Another instance consists of the widely seen pictographs printed in newspapers and magazines in which the bars in a chart are replaced by multiple copies of a pictograph, as for example, when one picture of a cow represents quarts of milk consumed.

For researchers, most nominal-level measurements are isomorphic. Labeling various ethnic or racial groups as "1" for White, "2" for African American, "3" for Asian, "4" for Hispanic, and so forth, is isomorphic measurement. In isomorphic measurement, changing the assigned numbers does not change the meaning of the measured variables. Such measurement is still isomorphic.

When the values for the numbers are changed, it is called an *isomorphic transformation*. This kind of transformation occurs in testing studies that examine bias and differential performance. Frequently, samples divided into racial or ethnic groups are not evenly split; often there are many Whites and only a few African Americans, Hispanics, Native Americans, and so forth. To more closely match the sample sizes, researchers recode the groups into "1" for White and "0" for all non-White, a step labeled *dummy coding*. Such isomorphic transformation does not change the data, although it may change the interpretation of findings because, as in this example, no single other racial group is compared with Whites.

Ideographic Versus Nomothetic Measurement

When a construct is defined in terms of a primary trait or behavior, then the measurement is said to be *ideographic*. In contrast, when the construct is viewed in relationship to other constructs, the measurement is *nomothetic*. For example, an individual may demonstrate superior mathematics skills, but another study may show that individuals with superior mathematics skills tend to score well on tests that assess the ability to detect logical fallacies. In the first instance, the measurement is ideographic, whereas in the second it is nomothetic. Sometimes, psychologists call a person's collectively related mental constructs a *nomothetic net*.

Derived Scales

Understanding Derived Scores

Derived scales, as the name implies, are scaling units resulting from a common source, nearly always raw scores. Commonly, raw scores are converted to a standard score and then further derived scales are calculated. There is a great variety of derived scales, including

- Standard score (e.g., z, t, T)
- Percentiles
- Scaled scores
- Normal curve equivalents
- Grade-level scores
- Stanines

Publishers of school-based tests typically present a menu of derived scores to teachers, parents, and other school officials to select for their reporting. Many such derived scales are famously depicted on the normal curve equivalents graphic shown in Figure 6.2.

The *z-score* is, perhaps, the most commonly used derived scale. Readers of this text probably already know that in the elementary version, z-score units are *located* at 0 with a *scale* of 1. Here, in fashion typical for scaling discussion, the terminology of "location" and "scale" is used, instead of the more common labels of "mean" and "standard deviation", to more aptly describe the function of the numbers.

Score scales are derived by transforming them from original raw scores to a metric more meaningful for a given context. The transformation may be either linear or nonlinear. Linear transformations have the structural model of Equation 6.4, our familiar expression for the general linear model.

Most researchers (e.g., Petersen, Kolen, & Hoover, 1989) prefer using some kind of derived score scale over the raw score for many educational and psychological tests. Generally, a scaled score provides more practical information for decision making than does the raw score. A raw score can be misleading in a number of contexts, as for instance when two tests are equated but the identical raw score is interpreted as indicating different levels of achievement on the two different tests.

Basic Transformations in Scale Scores

Now we examine transformations of scale scores. The location and scale of scale scores can be computed with Equation 6.6, where the A and B represent the slope and intercept of a line representing some function. To produce the numbers with Equation 6.6, a value on the raw score scale is related to another value on the scaled score. For instance, a score of 1 on the raw score scale may be designated as a 10 scaled score. This is done twice to establish reference points (e.g., 1 raw score is designated as 10 scaled, and 10 is newly designated as 100). The values chosen are arbitrary and established by the test's developer, but selected values should follow the seven characteristics of good scale alignment provided under the "Characteristics of Score Scales" section, later in the chapter. Following these stipulations is important as it will make a scale more interpretable:

$$A = \frac{(s_2 - s_1)}{(x_2 - x_1)} = \frac{(s_1 - s_2)}{(x_1 - x_2)}$$

$$B = s_2 - Ax_2 = s_1 - Ax_1.$$

(6.6)

A set of values available for transformation, chosen arbitrarily, are given in Table 6.2 to illustrate score scale transformations. As shown in Table 6.2, some values are inherently more comprehensible than others, even in this contrived set. For instance, the value selected for test A is not especially useful for most interpreting contexts because it will have extreme slope relative to the scale, and hence, raw score amounts will change dramatically when transformed. This could lead to confusion when examinees with close raw scores but vastly disparate scale scores are contrasted. Tests B, C, and D seem to be more reasonable transformations. Other selected values also produce clearly unacceptable results, such as in tests F and G, and most exaggeratedly of all, in test H. Hence, choosing values—even with guidance from the list of seven characteristics—should be done carefully.

Table 6.2
Slope and Intercept Values for Several Hypothetical Raw and Scale Valves

Test	Raw 1st X_1	Raw 2nd X_2	Scale 1st S_1	Scale 2nd S_2	Slope A $(S_2 - S_1)/(X_2 - X_1)$	Intercept B $S_2 - AX_2$
A	1	10	10	100	10	0
B	10	20	50	75	3	25
C	25	30	75	90	3	0
D	50	75	75	90	1	45
E	75	50	200	150	2	50
F	90	60	500	300	7	-100
G	99	70	750	250	17	-957
H	100	80	1000	500	25	-1500

An alternative to Equation 6.6 is given in Equation 6.7. This manipulation uses variance to specify equivalence between scores. When the distribution is normal, identical values for slope and intercept should result from either formula:

$$A = \frac{\sigma_S}{\sigma_X}$$

$$B = s_1 - Ax_1.$$

(6.7)

Such transformation of scales is not limited to just raw scores. Percentiles or population means can also be used. Petersen et al. (1989) also described methods in which test content and characteristics of score distributions can be incorporated into transformational decisions.

Nonlinear Transformations

Nonlinear transformations from original scale scores to derived scales are also permissible. Nonlinear transformations are more flexible and may accommodate particular circumstances, such as when the initial distributions are especially skewed but a researcher has reason to believe that the population in which the test scores will be used is not similarly skewed. This may be the case when percentiles (discussed in more detail in chapter 7) are used as the original score scale. Or, when test content has changed between alternate test forms, a changed distribution may facilitate test interpretation. In these instances, it may be desirable to change the shape of the distribution, something not possible with linear transformations. With linear transformation, the distribution of scale scores will follow nearly the identical shape as the raw score distributions.

A common nonlinear transformation in school achievement testing is one in which the raw scores are first transformed into percentile ranks; then, employing the inverse normal transformation, the percentile ranks are themselves transformed into normally distributed scores. Normalized T-scores, a very common scale for expressing many school achievement tests, is calculated in this manner.

Stanines and normal curve equivalents (NCEs) are two other examples of non-linearly transformed, normalized scores. However, these score scales are vastly different from percentiles. Stanines—which represent the full range of scores in nine standardized categories—are good for representing large differences, and diminishing small and sometimes insignificant differences. Sometimes this is a desirable feature when only gross indicators are needed. Also, they can be expressed as a single digit, another convenience (mostly during the time of their invention when computers read nine-digit columns on computer punch cards). NCEs are much better suited to showing small differences for most portions of the achievement range. Unfortunately, they do not differentiate well among the low (or higher) achievers, the group for whom the scale was initially developed.

When transforming score scales, it may be useful to consider scale reliability because it is an indicator of precision in measurement. Precision transformations take into account errors of measurement. Kolen (1988) offers details on how this is put into effect, although it can become technically complicated.

Transforming IRT-based scales is a further elaboration of a nonlinear transformation that takes score precision into account. In this method, standard errors at each score point are considered. However, when making these transformations, one must be watchful of the extremes of the distributions because stable IRT ability estimates presume sufficient samples at every score point, not the case in some data sets. Even with adequate samples, often IRT distributions have acceptably low errors for scores in the middle of a distribution but large errors at the extremes. Fortunately, with IRT scaling, this is readily detected as information about where the error in a range is large and small is shown in the test information function (studied in chapter 10).

Transformations for Developmental Scales

Score scales can further be transformed to a variety of *developmental scales,* such as *age-equivalent* or *grade-equivalent* scores. For some clinical and diagnostic situations, such as in personality assessment, age-related scales are needed. The concern for developing age-related scales is that groups used for developing samples are of appropriate ages. Although feasible, it is difficult to gather and assess enough persons in the required age categories. Hence, users of age scales should pay special heed to information about sampling characteristics when using and interpreting age-related scales so they understand who is included and what inferences about group comparisons are justified. When the groups are available, however, the development of age scales can be straightforward and the interpretation valid. Of course, to have this information available is important, and a test's developer should clearly specify such information in a technical manual or other public document.

Grade-equivalent scales, however, are an especially troublesome kind of derived, developmental scale because they can appear easily interpretable to lay audiences, whereas they are actually relatively complex to develop and require a high level of measurement expertise to properly interpret. Commonly, parents and many school personnel do not possess such expertise, and consequently they can interpret grade-equivalent scales erroneously. For example, it would seem that an obtained reading score of 6.3 grade-level equivalent indicates that a student's reading level is about at the third month of the sixth grade, almost regardless of the student's attended grade. Uninformed audiences may think that if it is November (assuming the school year began in September), a sixth grader with this score would be reading "at grade level." However, only in one atypical circumstance is this interpretation correct—namely, the event when the student (presumably, a sixth grader) takes the test in the third month of the sixth grade and achieves a score precisely coincidental to the mean of the norming population. This is a highly unlikely result for all but a slight few examinees.

For students who received other scores (likely, nearly all of a tested group), the grade equivalent does not accurately convey this meaning. To see why this is so, consider this scenario. Suppose a youngster is assessed not in November but in May (frequent spring testing time), is enrolled in the seventh grade, and received the 6.3 grade-level score. Here, it is incorrect to interpret the score to mean that the child is reading 1 year or so behind grade level. First, as described, the test was not normed with seventh graders. Second, the content is circumscribed to reflect things a sixth grader should know and be able to do. A more closely accurate interpretation—if indeed one can be made—is that a student enrolled in the eighth month of the seventh grade took the sixth-grade test, then he or she answered as many questions correctly as did the exact average sixth grader on the sixth-grade test. To complicate the matter, the seventh grader in all likelihood took not the sixth-grade test but instead took a seventh-grade test, which was then interpreted into year-below norms. Now the interpretation is even more convoluted, making it confusing beyond meaning or usefulness. One is left wondering, "Huh?"

Of course, full grade-level norms can be developed, but only when an appropriate sample of students from all grades takes the complete battery of tests (one designed appropriately for each grade level). Even then, it is problematic to suggest that a ninth grader could reliably take a sixth-grade reading test. Too many life experiences, apart from reading achievement, will likely influence the score a ninth grader can obtain on a test designed for sixth graders. Hence, it is manifestly difficult to make authentic grade-level–derived score scales.

Regardless, some accommodations to developmental grade-level scores can be made so the idea is carried forward. After all, grade-level scores are popular with parents, legislators, and others, and one is loath to lose a willing audience. One good example of a reasonable accommodation in making grade equivalent scores is seen in the ITBS (Hoover, 2004), a battery of grade-level achievement tests. For this test, the developers employ a unique procedure to develop grade-equivalent score scales that are plausibly meaningful. It is a multistep process. First, each test is constructed so one third of the items appear on each adjacent grade-level test. That is, on the sixth-grade test, one third of the items are shared with the fifth-grade test, one third is unique, and the remaining third are shared with the seventh-grade test. The items in each group are carefully selected for content and other considerations. Then, when norms are prepared, students from the fifth, sixth, and seventh grades take the test as a combined norming sample. Finally, from this information separate grade-level norms are constructed for each grade level of the test. Obviously, this process is a lot of work but is probably worth the effort for accurate norms, and is recommended for widely used programs that have grade level derived scores.

Characteristics of Score Scales

With the preceeding background in place, we are now prepared to cite characteristics of score scales. In practice, when developing a score scale—regardless of whether originally or when transforming the primary scale to a derived one—it is essential to consider characteristics of meritorious score scales. Dorans (2002) developed a useful and practical list of characteristics:

1. The scores of the reference group used to define the scale should be centered near the midpoint of the scale. The average score (mean or median) in the reference group should be on or near the midpoint of the scale.
2. The distribution of aligned scores for the scale-defining reference group should be unimodal, and that mode should be near the midpoint of the scale.
3. The distribution should be nearly symmetric about the average score.
4. The shape of the distribution should follow a commonly recognized form, such as the bell-shaped normal curve.
5. The working range of the scale should extend enough beyond the reported range of score to permit shifts in population away from the scale midpoint without stressing the endpoints of the scale.
6. The number of scale units should not exceed the number of raw score points, which is usually a simple function of the number of items. Otherwise, unjustified differentiation of examinees may occur.
7. A score scale should be viewed as infrastructure that is likely to require repair. Corrective action should be taken whenever the average score distribution of current populations move sufficiently far away from the midpoint, or when distributions move far enough away from an endpoint to jeopardize the integrity of the scale at that endpoint, or when reference groups lose their relevance.

This list is valuable from both an introductory point of view—to learn about score scales preliminarily—and as a guideline in scale development.

Norms

I have already mentioned norms in the context of specialized scales (e.g., age, grade, and developmental scales). The idea of *norms* is simple; namely, a test is administered to a group of persons broadly appropriate to the test and who are like most future examinees. From their results, distributional characteristics of score attainments are developed. Scores achieved by subsequent examinees can then be compared with any of the developed score scales (i.e., norms). The group is called the *norming group*. Although stretching probability theory a bit, the group may reasonably be labeled a *norming population* because later tested groups are generally considered samples and the original group is presumably much larger and more representative of the test developers' intention.

Of course, if any meaning is to be garnered from the norming exercise, selecting persons for the norming population must be based on carefully developed criteria. Most primary score scales are based on norming populations; then, derived score scales emanate from this information.

In norming, it is important that a prescribed, appropriate, and specified sample plan be developed, articulated, and followed. It is advised that if expertise in sampling is not at hand, a technical specialist or other resource should be consulted. It is too easy to merely administer a test to a convenient group or to administer a test haphazardly and imagine that a sample has been appropriately done. In my opinion, the lack of devising an appropriate sample—and of communicating the needed information to test users—is one of the most flagrant weaknesses in many tests today. Regretfully, this indictment is made not just against some casual tests but is evidently true in some large-scale, national tests.

Finally, to ensure proper interpretation, the test developer is responsible for providing detailed information about the sampling procedures employed in norming. Just as important, this information should be readily available to intended test users. Remember that validity is a shared responsibility of both the test maker and the test user. Providing the information can only come from the developer; it is the job of the test user to determine whether the information is appropriate for a given testing situation.

Summary

This chapter discusses an essential characteristic of mental measures, namely, their scales. Both a simple and a technical description of scaling in measurement are provided. We study its meaning in deep psychology, including the just noticeable difference and Fechner's law. A number of scaling models are introduced and explained, particularly deterministic and probabilistic scales. The important concept of dimensionality in scaling is explained and extended to two types: unidimensional and multidimensional scales. Common scale types and various levels of measurement are described. This is followed by a recitation of some types of measurement, both common and specialized. Then, information particular to derived scales and to norming a test is given. The information presented in chapter 7 builds on the foundation provided in this chapter.

Chapter 7

The Normal Curve and Distributional Statistics

Introduction

Simply Great Ideas

The term *horsepower* seems almost self-explanatory. Even if we do not know its exact definition, we imagine it is somehow equivalent to the power a horse can generate—say, how much weight a typical horse can pull a specified distance. This image is an easy one because most of us have been close enough to a horse at least once in our lives to view its impressive muscular structure. Indeed, when British engineer James Watt first coined the term in 1809, he defined it as the amount of power a pony exhibits when hauling a bucket of coal up from a mine shaft to ground level. Since the time of Watt's crude designation, horsepower has been adopted worldwide as a standard unit of power. A more modern definition specifies horsepower as the work required to raise 770 pounds a distance of 1 foot in 1 second. This definition allows that the power could be from a horse, or just as easily and more likely today, a motor. Surprisingly (and charmingly), despite our modern and more precise definition, the old term continues. It is fun to play games with this metric, such as guessing how much horsepower a human can generate while skiing or hiking or cycling. Biomechanists have determined that elite sprinters typically generate just over 1 horsepower when accelerating off the blocks. The world's strongest man at the time of this writing, Russian Andrei Chemerkin, generated about 7.84 horsepower when clean-and-jerking 776.7 pounds! The human heart—undoubtedly our most invaluable power-generating muscle—typically produces a paltry 0.008 horsepower. The human brain, site of millions of electrochemical explosions per second, is only slightly more potent, at 0.02 horsepower—about the same as a low-wattage light bulb!

Although we do not typically express test scores in terms of horsepower (let me know if you find an example of such), understanding how measurement data can be displayed and used is profoundly important to our understanding of the science. It is to an understanding of our most common strategy—using the normal curve to convey meaning—that we now turn.

Contents

This chapter builds on information presented in chapter 6 on dimensional scaling, and together the two chapters present a complete topic. Here, I explain distributional statistics—particularly, the normal distribution, and more specifically, the standard normal distribution. First, I introduce the normal distribution and spend some time describing its significance to measurement, and even more important, to our lives generally. The chapter moves from this description to various forms of distribution for expressing variables. Then, we move on to cumulative probability functions, including how they are derived and computed. I also provide rationale and proof for the standard z-scores on a standardized normal distribution. Finally, the chapter concludes with a discussion of percentiles and percentile ranks, of course, a very common mode for displaying test information in a standard normal distribution.

Description and Characteristics

Background

Although people have long recognized that most physical and psychological phenomena (e.g., people's height or weight, achievement, or attitude) tend to have few values at the extremes and more values in the middle, the important idea of representing it as a distributional curve arose in 1730 when Abraham de Moivre suggested the structure of the *normal distribution*. His idea for a normal distribution ranks as one of the greatest mathematical advances of all time. By this conception of data, he gave statisticians, economists, agronomists, social planners, and others a method to statistically quantify both physical and psychological phenomena. Today, we characterize de Moivre's work syntactically by the *frequency distribution function,* which is most often shown by one of its many forms as a *standard normal distribution.* The standard normal distribution is what we commonly and imprecisely call the *bell curve.* The distinctive bell shape of de Moivre's distribution is recognized around the world by both scientists and laypersons. After an introduction to the normal distribution, I explain how and why this remarkable idea is so important not only to measurement science, but also to our daily lives. (A note to persons who may mistakenly believe that the renowned mathematician Fredrick Gauss invented the normal curve: Do not worry! I describe his enormous contributions to the field later in this chapter.)

The significance of the normal distribution to science arises from its clever and original perspective on data. Prior to de Moivre's work, researchers viewed all objects of measurement as having zero for a starting point and then graduating to higher amounts. First there is nothing—zero; then there is quantity. A jar is first empty and as it fills the quantity rises. In this view, physical things are either absent or present in some amount. Measuring physical quantities follows this structural logic.

However, human traits, characteristics, and other psychological phenomena are torpid to the form of zero and higher because in cognition there is no absolute anything—no "zero mental ability," "zero IQ," "zero personality," or complete lack of knowledge or opinion. de Moivre reasoned that these phenomena cannot start at zero and measure quantity greater than nothing. Instead, he conceived the notion that psychological traits are more accurately viewed as relative quantities, and measurement of them can be made more meaningful by starting from the middle and extending outward in both directions. For a population, there is a central opinion, or mean IQ, or middle sentiment or emotion. Quantities of apt phenomena are viewed as being either above or below the center as reference point. Quite literally—and profoundly—psychological quantities are *distributional.*

Features of the Normal Curve

A distribution of values is most often characterized by its middle value, the median. Then, distances away from the middle are measured in a symmetric amount, usually expressed by the standard deviation. Mathematically, in normal distributions, these amounts can be expressed as real variables of the function $f(x)$. Sequences of this function ($n = 1, 2, 3,...$) form regular *moments* of the probability distribution. When such sequences are numbers in standard form, the middle point is the first moment, the *mean* or *median*. The second central moment is the variance. These distributions have the range $(-\infty, \infty)$. The first moment is our referent and is called the *location*. Standard deviations are described as the *scale* because they define the distribution's length. A standard T-scale distribution, for instance, has a location of 50 and a scale of 10. (We see these terms in use in chapter 6.)

Two views of the normal curve of distribution are displayed in Figures 7.1 and 7.2. Each curve is distinct and perspicuous. Note that neither the curve nor the plot begins at a zero point; rather, both have a center and all values are viewed as deviating from it.

Further, normal distributions are probabilistic functions. That is, there exists a *probability* for an observed score to be at any given point, depending on the variable under consideration—in this case, the $f(\theta)$ we studied in chapter 6. In addition, from the center to that point, the curve has area, or *density*. In other words, it can "fill up" as one moves to cover greater area. This is, in concept, the notion for dimensionality for psychological constructs we studied in the earlier chapter. Here,

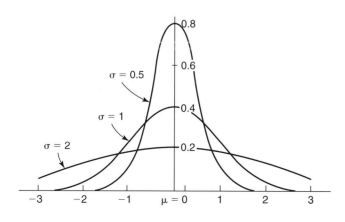

Figure 7.1
Normal curve of distribution at varying standard deviations.

Figure 7.2
Mesh plot of hypothesized trivariate view (multivariate case) of Gaussian distribution.

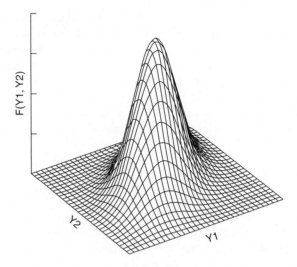

it applies mathematically to represent a proportion of the function contained within specified limits. We can see this in Figure 7.3, which shows density in two amounts. Hence, the distinguishing feature of distributional curves is that they each represent a *probabilistic density function*. Another way to view the same idea is that the normal distribution describes deviations from the mean of repeated measurements. Importantly, positive and negative deviations from the median are equally likely.

Although this chapter focuses on the standard normal curve of distribution because it is most pertinent to our study of mental measurement, there are also many other kinds of probability distributions. An illustrative list is provided in Figure 7.4. However, even this list of distributions is far from exhaustive. A useful compendium of many more kinds of density distributions can be accessed at *http://www. causascientia.org/math_stat/Dists/Compendium.pdf*. Retrieved February 20, 2005.

Figure 7.3
Normal distribution showing density in different amounts.

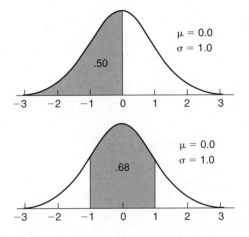

Bernoulli	Laplace
Beta	Log normal
Binomial	Logistic
Cauchy	Normal
Chi square	Pareto
Exponential	Poisson
Extreme value	Rayleigh
F	Rectangular
Gamma	Student *t*-test
Geometric	Weibull
Gompertz	

Figure 7.4
Illustrative mathematically representable distributions.

Historical Prescience of the Discovery

Abraham de Moivre came to his remarkable discovery while trying to resolve a probability problem first posed by the mathematician Jacob Bernoulli. Recall from chapter 2, when discussing the law of large numbers, Bernoulli reasoned that the probability of drawing samples of black- and white-colored pebbles from a jar would be very close to the exact proportion of each color of pebble in the jar originally. De Moivre knew that there were 3,000 white and 2,000 black pebbles in the jar—a proportion of 3:2. To start, he randomly took pebbles from the jar and, indeed, as he drew more and more pebbles, he saw the proportion of black to white pebbles grow closer to the predicted 3:2 ratio. In other words, he repeated his simple experiment and gradually realized that the result was more accurately revealed on each subsequent occasion.

Fortunately for us, de Moivre grew very interested in Bernoulli's probability problem and in probability theory in general, at the time an infant offshoot of mathematics. Perhaps his interest in probability theory stemmed from the fact that he supplemented his meager income as a mathematics tutor by calculating odds for gamblers in local pubs. Applying calculus to the underlying principle of Pascal's triangle (the binomial theorem), de Moivre succeeded in demonstrating mathematically how samples of random drawings would distribute themselves around the average value. In mathematical terms, he described how moments in a distribution behave: predictably, uniformly, and symmetrically, although it remained until Fredrick Gauss for actual proof of the normal curve. Significantly, de Moivre's syntactic description of his pebbles was also generic to all such distributions; that is, it did not matter what object was being sampled: hands in a card game, political attitude, eye color, reading ability, IQ, or whatever. The distribution of values for any appropriate phenomena can be characterized by the symmetry he observed. This point is fundamental to understanding the normal curve of distribution because it means we can apply it structurally, that is, to many circumstances that meet underlying assumptions and a few calculus stipulations.

Origins of the Standard Deviation and More History

de Moivre extended his work to calculate another statistical measure, this one of dispersion "*about*" (viz., above and below) the mean. Today, we call his measure the *standard deviation,* and it is the most common method of reporting error in the mean of a distribution. In a syntactical sense, it is the "average" error, or in gross terms, the average amount by which the mean will describe a distribution. By giving us the standard deviation, de Moivre provided a mathematical rational to explain the fact that in a normal distribution approximately 68% of the observations fall within one standard deviation of the mean of all the observations. By extrapolation, more than 97% of observations fall within two standard deviations, or similarly, any other derivative along the distribution. Because this measure is about the mean, it is evenly distributed on either side of the central statistic. It is a method of mathematical moments. Gauss formalized this movement of data precisely by integration.

Reflecting the philosophical milieu of his time, de Moivre saw a grand design in this symmetry, which he attributed to God. Using the stilted composition of the day, he explained his ideas by saying, "tho Chance produces irregularities, still the Odds will be infinitely great, that in the process of Time, those irregularities will bear no proportion to recurrency of that Order which results from ORIGINAL DESIGN" (Stigler, 1986, p. 234).

More Relevant History

Two other figures from history also helped set the stage for today's preeminence in measurement science of the normal distribution. One of them was the genius mathematician and astronomer, Karl Fredrick Gauss, whom we have already met. Gauss became interested in probability while trying to calculate the orbit of various planets. As part of his calculations, he decided to carry forward the work of Bernoulli, de Moivre, and Bayes. While making geodesic measurements of the curvature of the earth at locales around his Bavarian home, he realized he could not make enough such measurements to complete his calculations. He knew he must have some means to interpolate probabilities of an occurrence between his measurements. Then, too, he realized he must also calculate the frequency of error for his measurements. Sometime during his work, he reasoned that his error calculations were entirely symmetric. This being the case, he could apply calculus to figure out the probabilities of observing any intervening point. Unwittingly, Gauss had mathematically described the normal curve of distribution by integration! Gauss's initial description of the normal curve as a logarithmic integral is shown in Figure 7.5.

Although de Moivre brought the mean and standard deviation into play as ways to characterize a sample or population, Gauss provided the mathematics of determining the value of any point along the function, and correspondingly the density. Today, we almost take his seminal work for granted. In mathematical statistics particularly, the normal curve is commonly referred to as a "Gaussian distribution" to honor the great German.

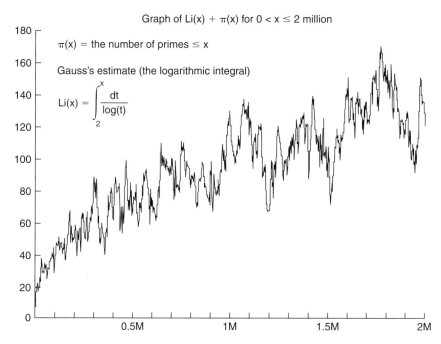

Figure 7.5
Gauss's initial description of the normal curve as a logarithmic integral.
Source: Retrieved from http://www-gap.dcs.st-and.ac.uk/~history/Curves/Curves.html (October 15, 2004.)

It is gratifying to say that Gauss's accomplishments were recognized even during his lifetime (1777–1855). He was indeed a remarkable man. Beyond integrating the normal distribution for the first time, he made similarly important contributions to astronomy, physics, and particularly differential geometry. Apparently, he was also a kind and gentlemanly person. Two of his last graduate students wrote of him:

> Usually he sat in a comfortable attitude, looking down, slightly stooped, with hands folded above his lap. He spoke quite freely, very clearly, simply and plainly: but when he wanted to emphasise [sic] a new viewpoint . . . then he lifted his head, turned to one of those sitting next to him, and gazed at him with his beautiful, penetrating blue eyes during the emphatic speech. . . . If he proceeded from an explanation of principles to the development of mathematical formulas, then he got up, and in a stately very upright posture he wrote on a blackboard beside him in his peculiarly beautiful handwriting: he always succeeded through economy and deliberate arrangement in making do with a rather small space. For numerical examples, on whose careful completion he placed special value, he brought along the requisite data on little slips of paper. (O'Connor & Robertson, 1996)

In measurement science, we are indeed indebted to Gauss.

The other person important to completing this picture for the normal curve of distribution is Lambert Adolphe Jacques Quetelet, a contemporary of Gauss and inspirer of Galton. Quetelet propounded the notion of the confluence of the natural measures to an average. He liked to find averages, something not previously done in a disciplined way. Using the population statistics of 19th-century France and working principally from de Moivre's formulations, Quetelet set out to find averages in nearly every category he could think of. He found averages for drunkenness, for suicides, for insanity, and for crime. He prepared tables of averages for birth and death by temperature and by time of day, by season, by locale, whether working or in prison, and so on. Employing all population statistics that were available to him, Quetelet continually calculated. In short, he seemed to love averages and other central tendencies. He published his findings in *A Treatise on Man and the Development of His Faculties* (Quetelet, 1835/1969), a work that was original in design and scope and so influential that today it is routinely followed by virtually every government statistics office on the planet. Historian Bernstein (1998) characterized Quetelet's life by declaring that he gave statistics a hero: *l'homme moyen,* the average man. For his prodigious work, many people today consider Quetelet the father of social sciences. Irrefutably, by applying statistical principles to contemporary problems, he laid the groundwork for modern-day statistics. The bell curve is popular, in significant measure, due to Quetelet.

Significance to Our Lives

Profound Significance to Us

It is important for us to have a genuine appreciation of the normal distribution because the idea behind it profoundly affects our view of the world and our place in it—our *weltanschauung*. Of course, the fact that it provides a method for quantifying social science phenomena is important to us, but even more so it allows us to create order in our lives by anticipating events and thereby facilitating adaptation to our environment. It does this by presenting us with a method to make reasonable estimation of future events (e.g., likely rainfall, expected birth and death rates, credible crop yields, probable stock market fluctuations in the coming quarter), as well as to describe present circumstances (e.g., estimating heights for men and women, gauging developmental rates for infants). Such quantification is vastly more important to us than mere assimilation of data. The normal distribution provides a way for us to move beyond operating our lives as though events occur randomly, or at the whim of the gods, without our foreknowledge. With the normal curve as a tool, we can reasonably anticipate many phenomena in our lives and act accordingly.

This is not to suggest that the normal curve permits prophecy. It is not magic and does not allow us to precisely foretell particular events. Instead, it is merely, but significantly, a beautiful scheme for organizing phenomena, one that affords us a way to anticipate likely events in an aggregate. There is soothing consonance to having such order brought to our lives. Thus, in a very real sense, the normal curve calms the storms of uncertainty—in earlier times, named Fate—in our lives and gives us assurance that we will prevail.

Francis Galton, whom we met in chapter 1, spoke almost adoringly about the normal curve. In the mid-19th century, he said,

> [T]he "Law of Frequency of Error" . . . reigns with serenity and in complete self-effacement amidst the wildest confusion. The higher the mob . . . the more perfect is its way. It is the supreme law of Unreason. Whenever a large sample of chaotic elements are taken into hand . . . an unsuspected and most beautiful form of regularity proves to have been latent all along. (Bernstein, 1998, p. 141)

Furthermore, the normal curve gives attention to the average of a phenomenon. There is something recondite and innately attractive to humans about the "average." Physically, it defines something known to artists and mathematicians as far back as ancient Greece that has come to be call the *Golden Mean*. The Golden Mean is a proportion for shapes that demonstrates a length-to-side ratio of 61.8%. For some unknown (and possibly unknowable) reason, shapes that use this proportion harmonize with our sensibilities. It is no accident that this proportion is evident in structures as diverse as the Parthenon, playing cards, credit cards, in the General Assembly Building of the United Nations, and even the horizontal-to-vertical members of the Christian cross.

The Golden Mean appears both in manmade objects and throughout nature: in flower patterns, in the leaves of an artichoke, and on the fronds of the palm tree. Even the length of each successive bone in our fingers approximately bears this ratio! The proportion of the Golden Mean can be calculated into a number sequence that has amazing characteristics. Mathematicians call this sequence of numbers *Fibonacci's sequence* or *Fibonacci's proportion*, after the brilliant 11th-century mathematician Leonard Pisano, who used the pseudonym Fibonacci when writing. Figure 7.6 shows Fibonacci's proportions used in the construction of an equiangular spiral. So, the mean,

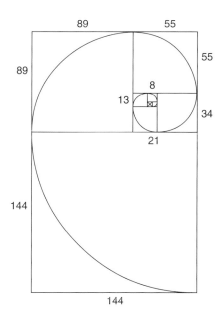

Figure 7.6

Construction of an equiangular spiral using Fibonacci proportions.

as a figment in shapes and proportions, as well as a mathematical representation of psychological phenomena, plays a role in our everyday lives of enormous significance.

Caution Against Overinterpretation

A final point about perspective on the normal distribution curve is a caution against overinterpreting the information it conveys. There are, of course, quantifiable phenomena in both the physical and social science worlds that do not map to the normal curve. For instance, many of the constants in quantum mechanics (e.g., gravity) or rules in particle physics (e.g., differently charged electrons in the atom repelling each other) do not fit the normal curve structure. Similarly, the product of writers, musicians, and artists who explore the human condition in novels, essays, painting, and music, and through other fine arts genre portray phenomena that are not amenable to mapping as a normal distribution.

Our world is gloriously complex, and it cannot be neatly depicted by one tidy normal curve of distribution. To employ a Latin phrase, the normal curve does not cover our world *ab ovo usque ad mala,* from soup to nuts (literally, "from the egg to the apples"). Useful and important as it is, the normal curve cannot serve all descriptive purposes, even in mental measurement.

Forms for Expressing Data in Variables

Considering how data are mapped on the normal curve of distribution (as a frequency function), however, yields three ways in which data may be cited, including

- In discrete classes
- As a graphic
- By stating a rule

Let us examine each of these means for expressing the occurrence of data.

Frequency Data in Discrete Classes

In the most elementary instance for expressing data as a frequency function, classes and their frequency are merely listed. For example, suppose the variable of interest is geography, with some attribute distributed as in Table 7.1. The number in each category is cited to complete this basic frequency distribution. A simple table is all that is needed here.

Using Graphics to Display Frequency Distribution Data

A second method for citing frequency distributions is to display the information in a graphic form. Of course, there are numerous ways to express the frequency of data graphically, including the step frequency function, the histogram, the stem-and-leaf display, the bar chart, the line chart, the area graph, the box plot, and more, in addition

Table 7.1
Numbers for Geographic Regions

Geographic region	Count
North America	91
South America	181
Europe	108
Africa	266
Asia	303
Australia	12

to various combinations of these kinds of graphics. Figures 7.7 and 7.8 are illustrative. In publication and dissemination of research, there is growing use of graphics to communicate quantitative information.

As a relevant aside, with graphical displays (and their easy production by graphic programs), it is tempting to get "too cute by half" and produce graphics that are clever but only minimally revealing. One should eschew what Edward Tufte (1983) terms "chart junk" in his informative, opinionated, and humorous book *The Visual Display of Quantitative Data*. For further information on displaying data graphically, there are any number of books describing rules and suggestions, including Kosslyn's (1994) *The Elements of Graphing Data*, Charland's (1995) *Sigma Plot for Scientists*, SPSS's (2002) *Sigma Plot 2002 for Windows*, and the widely disseminated *Publication*

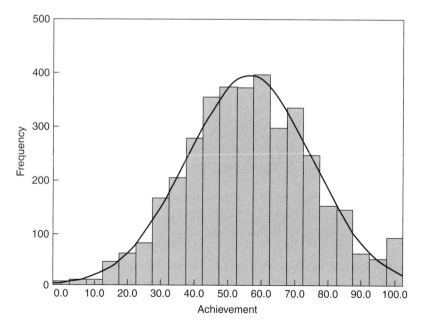

Figure 7.7
Step frequency distribution with normal curve overlay.

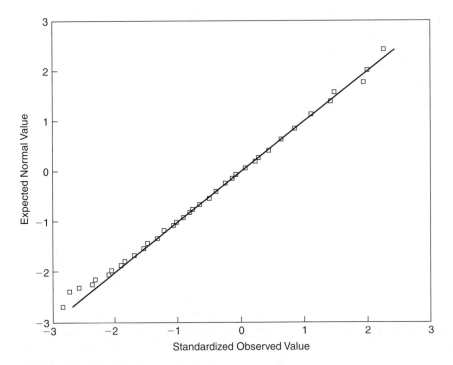

Figure 7.8
Normal probability plot with values standardized.

Manual of the American Psychological Association, Fifth Edition (American Psychological Association, 2001), which contains apt, but limited, information on this topic.

Using Rules to Describe Frequency Distribution Data

The third method to display frequency of data is by a mathematical rule. Most rules related to displaying data of mental measurement are in the form of a function, $f(x)$, and even more completely, of a density function showing the distribution. Representations of data by such functions are distinct from the preceding methods of giving only frequency counts because they prescribe trace lines for data and fit a more general case. In other words, the data need not be limited to test scores (or other educational or psychological variable) but can be of any type, whether coins for a currency or stars for constellations. The rules for our functions explain the binomial and move beyond it to cover a host of sampling distributions, both normal and otherwise (see the compendium cited in the previous section), making these rules structural. Such adaptability shows the power of de Moivre's work in defining the normal distribution and Gauss's development of an algebraic proof. It is to this more technical depiction of the normal distribution that we now turn.

Technical Depiction of the Normal Distribution

Characteristics of the Normal Distribution

The normal distribution curve follows the description of frequency data by a rule. This rule sets forth a probabilistic function. As always in displaying probabilistic functions, for the normal curve there are two axes—one horizontal (*abscissa*) and another vertical (*ordinate*). The horizontal axis represents the random variable X and the vertical axis is the frequency of occurrence for cases on the variable by the rule, $f(x)$. Although this information is, by itself, elementary and obvious, it does remind us, too, that a function prescribes how the data mapping is done by giving class boundaries. The curve that defines the function itself is a trace line of cumulative, or relative, frequency. The curve is technically termed an *ogive*. Theoretically, the ogive can assume any value of x in the range $(-\infty, \infty)$ and is absolutely symmetric about the center. It is, therefore, *unimodal*—having an identical value for the mean, median, and mode. As expected, this is rarely the case with real-world data, but nonetheless, it is a defining characteristic.

Another rule defining our cumulative function is that the curve's density equals one, by definition. In more common language, the area under the normal curve all equals one. This characteristic makes calculating areas under the curve a lot easier than would be otherwise, as we see in a later section of this chapter.

Still another rule to define the normal distribution is that, because the normal curve is a probabilistic function, there is always some chance that any particular value can be obtained, regardless of how infinitesimally small. The odds for observing specified scores at the extremes become increasingly small; in fact, they approach infinity. This rule is shown as the ogive *asymptotes;* that is, it approaches but never fully reaches the limit of zero or infinity at either extreme. The trace line for the function is highest in the middle and symmetrically descends away from the center until it almost touches the horizontal axis at either end of a truncated line. Figure 7.9 shows these basic characteristics for the normal curve.

To present the characteristics of the normal distribution graphically, it is necessary to reveal pertinent statistical properties. These may appear obvious, but nonetheless are needed. It presumes, for instance, that X is any variable from among $X_1, X_2, \ldots X_n$,

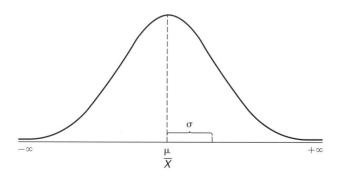

Figure 7.9
Normal distribution showing asymptote at upper and lower extremes.

which are independent, random, and normally distributed. Each is represented by μ_X and σ_X^2 for its mean and variance, respectively. With these presumptions, Equation 7.1 is true for any linear combination of Xs plotted in the normal distribution:

$$Y = a_1X_1 + a_2X_2 + \cdots + a_nX_n. \tag{7.1}$$

Given that the Y variable is normally distributed with a mean of $\mu = \sum_{i=1}^{n} a_i\mu_i$ and variance of $\sigma_X^2 = \sum_{i=1}^{n} a_i\sigma_i$.

These terms and expressions are straightforward, although it may take a bit of slow reading to work through the notation. The ideas they represent are important but not complex; in fact, they are common and sensical. They make the normal distribution structurally complete.

With these characteristics and properties in place, we can now turn to defining normal distribution density functions, the famous *Gaussian distribution*. These functions are expressed by the rule given in Equation 7.2, a famous formula and one that may be recognized by some advanced students. (We see it in simplified form—more often presented—momentarily.)

$$f(x) = \frac{1}{\sigma\sqrt{2\pi}}e^{-\frac{1}{2}\left(\frac{x-\mu}{\sigma}\right)^2}. \tag{7.2}$$

This formula produces functions such as those shown in Figures 7.1 and 7.6, as well as many others throughout this chapter and text. Because it is central to our discussion, we work through it in simplified form. First, however, recall that there are many forms to Gauss's distribution, making it useful in almost any context where data are cumulative. Accordingly, Equation 7.2 actually defines a *family of distributions*. Some of the more recognizable ones in statistics are given as the chi-square distribution, the student t distribution, and the F distribution. The chi square is shown in Equation 7.3 and shown in Figure 7.10:

$$f(x) = \frac{1}{2^{v/2}\,\Gamma(v/2)}\,x^{v/2-1}e^{-\frac{x}{2}}, \tag{7.3}$$

Figure 7.10
Chi-square distribution with probability density function.

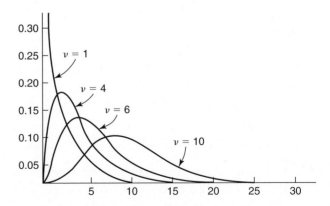

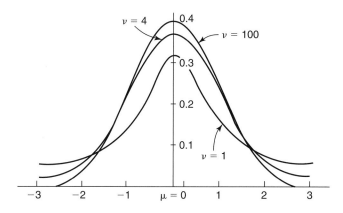

Figure 7.11
Student t distribution of a
standard normal random
variable.

where $\mu = v,$
          $\sigma^2 = 2v,$ and
          $v = n - 1\,df.$

The student t distribution is given in Equation 7.4 and shown in Figure 7.11:

$$t = \frac{\overline{X} - \mu}{s/\sqrt{n,}} \qquad (7.4)$$

where $v = n - 1\,df.$

The F distribution is derived as a ratio of two independent chi-square variables, as shown in Equation 7.5:

$$F = \frac{\sigma_2^2 \sigma_1^2}{\sigma_1^2 \sigma_2^2}. \qquad (7.5)$$

Each distribution is pertinent to psychometric work, and it is likely that readers have encountered them previously.

Standardizing the Normal Curve

z-Score Solution to Too Many Distributions

As we have seen, the number of distributions for expressing "normal" distributions is inexhaustible. This fact presents psychometricians with a problem when comparing various curves or when relating data from different variables. If each variable yields a unique normal frequency distribution, it seems that generalization would be impossible and research would be tedious at best. A common standard for expressing the normal curve of distribution is thus needed; however, because each curve is

developed independently from all others, discovering or developing such commonality would seem complex.

Fortunately, simple, practical solutions to complex problems can sometimes be
found, and psychometricians have devised a simple solution to the "too many normal curves" problem. Because all normal curves begin at the mean and move symmetrically away from it in moment units (expressed simply as standard deviations),
it is logical to simply express any score, regardless of its original metric, in standard
deviation units. These standard deviation units have become a *standard* unto themselves, and they are common to all the curves. Thus, merely transforming particular
test scores to *standardized scores* (*z*-scores) is a convenient way to reduce the family of curves to a single, generalizable case. A seemingly complex problem is thus
resolved with a simple, practical solution. (Although I present proof for the calculation of *z*-scores later in this chapter, it is now more pertinent to stay with solving our
normal distribution.)

Given this logical argument, the Gaussian distribution of Equation 7.2 simplifies
to just a single case, the standard normal distribution with a defined mean of 0 and
standard deviation of 1 ($\mu_X = 0$, $\sigma_X = 1$). Our more convenient form is expressed
in Equation 7.6. In psychometric work, this standard normal form is usually cited and
used for calculation:

$$f(x) = \frac{1}{\sqrt{2\pi}} e^{-\frac{1}{2}X^2}. \tag{7.6}$$

Solution of Normal Curve Density Function

Solving the standardized normal distribution function of Equation 7.6 will aid enormously in understanding density functions generally and the normal curve of distribution particularly. Although this task may look formidable, the solution is
straightforward, and we already know how the function looks when its values are
plotted: bell shaped. I explain Equation 7.6 step by step, but first, take a breath to
relax and ponder this quote from Samuel Johnson: "Many things difficult to design
prove easy to perform." From this perspective, Equation 7.6 can be calmly approached.

First, look at the left term in the equation, something readily recognized by most
readers. It specifies a function for any distribution of *x* values that has a particular
mean (μ) and variance (σ^2). Now, begin solving the right-hand term by identifying
the mathematical constants in Equation 7.6. They are π and e. Each value is a positive integer, so using them in equations is not difficult. The value for π is well known
(i.e., 3.14159 . . .), and it is even a programmed function key on most sophisticated
handheld calculators. The letter *e* is the base of the natural logarithm, $e \approx 2.718281828$,
also common on advanced calculators. The base *e* value relates natural numbers to the
log scale, thereby obviating integration and making calculations simpler. For this reason, it is commonly used as a constant in mathematical expressions generally, particularly in psychometric work. Because these values account for nearly all the equation,
there is little left unknown in Equation 7.6.

In the expression, only the exponent of the e remains to be explained before we begin calculating: $-\frac{1}{2}X^2$. Even here, relative simplicity reigns: The x represents, of course, any given observed score. It is easy to calculate this exponent, leaving it as a negative for now. Remember from algebra that a value raised to a negative exponent is solved by making it a fraction with 1 as the numerator, and for the denominator, change the sign of the exponent (here, from negative to positive) and raise the subject value to that power. With this in mind, we can work Equation 7.6 to solution.

For instance, suppose the problem was to find the function value for $x = 2$, given $\mu_X = 0$ and $\sigma_X = 1$. Following the order of operations, begin by solving for the e exponent, temporarily leaving the sign as negative, and then bring it to solution:

$$e^{-\frac{1}{2}X^2} = e^{-2} = \frac{1}{e^2} = .13533528.$$

Then, solve the fraction,

$$\frac{1}{\sqrt{2\pi}} = \frac{1}{2.506628} = .39894228,$$

and product

$$(.13533528)(.39894228) = .0539909.$$

Thus, for our parameters, $f(2) \approx .054$. If we were to calculate many of these values and develop an ogive, it would be bell shaped.

As can be seen, then, once the x, mean, and standard deviation are specified—as in the standard normal distribution—solving the expression for a particular case of the normal curve is straightforward. Of course, there are also numerous programmed computer algorithms to perform the operations we just did by hand. In practice, they would be used, but our manual solution serves present didactics.

Rationale, Computation, and Proof for z-Scores

Likely, readers are long familiar with standard scores and appreciate that our previous solution relied on such z-scores. These are an interesting lot in themselves. An explanation for their derivation and use is given here. Because z-scores define $\mu_X = 0$ and $\sigma_X = 1$ for all populations, only the particular value for x remains to be known for any given distribution to transform it to the z-score metric. Transforming values from a population with a given mean and standard deviation to a standardized distribution with $\mu_X = 0$ and $\sigma_X = 1$ is simply done, as illustrated in Equation 7.7:

$$z = \frac{x - \overline{X}}{sd}. \qquad\qquad (7.7)$$

Notice that in the transformation only values for a currently considered sample are used ($\overline{X}$, sd, x). The formula relates these sample values to the standardized normal distribution with population parameters $\mu = 0$ and $\sigma = 1$. Also, note that because the standard deviation is the denominator in the expression, z-scores are given in standard deviation units.

Proof that the mean of a distribution of z-scores is 0 and that the standard deviation is 1 is readily shown. Equations 7.8 and 7.9 provide the needed expressions:

$$\bar{z} = \sum_i \frac{z_i}{N} = \sum_i \frac{(x_i - \bar{x})}{NS}. \tag{7.8}$$

In Equation 7.8, N and S are constant over the summation. Accordingly, Equation 7.8 simplifies to the expression shown in Equation 7.9:

$$\bar{z} = \frac{1}{NS} \sum_i (x_i - \bar{x}) = 0. \tag{7.9}$$

Once the mean is set at 0, it is a small step to see that the variance of z-scores is 1, as shown in Equation 7.10:

$$S_z^2 = \sum_i \frac{z_i^2}{N} = \sum_i \frac{(x_i - \bar{x})^2}{NS} = 1. \tag{7.10}$$

From here, of course, the standard deviation, as the square root of the variance, is also 1, presented in Equation 7.11:

$$\frac{S^2}{S^2} = 1 \quad alternatively$$

$$S_z = \sqrt{S_z^2} = 1. \tag{7.11}$$

It is important to realize that the normal curve expressed in standardized scores is not the normal curve expressed in the metric of a particular measure. Remember, each normal curve is uniquely fixed to its population. Seemingly, then, one might reason, they could have different distributions. Fortunately, this is not the case because standardized scores have the identical format in cumulative probability functions to those in frequency distributions, and the form of the probability distribution is not affected by the transformation to z-scores. Thus, it is possible to use the standardized normal distribution as an accurate representation of any given distribution curve.

Normalized Standard Scores

When standard scores are placed in a ranking that corresponds to the percentile rank of the raw scores of a particular set of data, the scale is said to be *normalized*. Computing such normalized scores is accomplished by simply locating the standard normal distribution score that corresponds to the raw score when expressed as a percentile. By the normalizing, the distances between scores are changed allowing for intrapersonal comparisons. It also means that the relationship between the scales is nonlinear.

Cumulative Probabilities

Considering cumulative probabilities and areas under the normal curve requires the background provided in chapter 2 in the algebra of expectations. Recall from the earlier discussion that one of the most significant rules of expectations is that of a discrete random variable X. This rule for the probability distribution function was stated in chapter 2 in theoretical form (Equation 2.2), but is given here in Equation 7.12 with a slightly modified notation, as is more often seen in psychometric discussion:

$$F(x) = P(X \leq x). \tag{7.12}$$

This function expresses the area under the normal curve in an area bounded by $-\infty$ and the value x. Because this is the general case, the probability for any value can be found by it. Figure 7.12 depicts this function for one value, x.

Notice in Figure 7.12 that the shaded portion is the area under the normal curve up to and including the value for x and is the probability density function, or in this case, the cumulative probability. Because the probability density function is bounded by 1, the remaining, unshaded portion of the normal distribution is the corollary to the cumulative probability, or 1 minus the function up to the value for x.

By this logic, the cumulative probability of any interval, with limits of a and b, can also be found. In this instance, Equation 7.13 defines the rule:

$$P(a \leq X \leq b) = F(b) - F(a). \tag{7.13}$$

For example, suppose the value for x lies between 10 and 60, given that μ and σ are known (viz., $\overline{X}$ and sd). Then, by substitution,

$$p(10 \leq X \leq 60) = F(60) - F(10).$$

When standardized values are employed, the formula for each side of the distribution (the area covered by the function and the remaining area) is as follows in Equation 7.14:

$$F(2) = P(z \leq 2) \quad \textit{alternatively}$$
$$F(-1) = P(z \leq -1). \tag{7.14}$$

In statistical textbooks, tables of areas under the normal curve of distribution are developed using Formula 7.14.

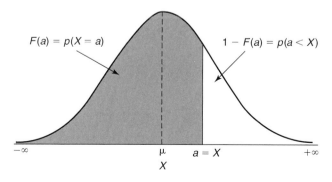

Figure 7.12
A cumulative probability.

Example: Area Under the Normal Curve

Take as a given that the cumulative probability is positive. Also, suppose this distribution is normal in shape and has a mean of 500 with standard deviation of 100, and we want to know the cumulative probability for the score of 680. In this positive case, the value for the associated cumulative probability can be read directly from the table of values for area under the normal curve, available in most statistical texts. First, because the table is for z-scores, the value must be transformed into the standard deviation units of the z scale. We know this calculation from Equation 7.7:

$$z = \frac{680 - 500}{100} = 1.8.$$

From the table of normal deviates in a statistics book, the associated cumulative probability for 1.8 $F(z)$ is 0.964. This value is the likelihood of observing a z-score value less than or equal to 1.8 in a standardized normal distribution with a mean of 500 and standard deviation of 100. In other words, the probability of observing a score less than or equal to this one is 96.4%. It is also the cumulative density function to this point. The interval for this value is shown in Figure 7.13.

Of course, z-scores can assume a negative value when they are less than 0, the mean of the hypothetical, standardized distribution. (In a normal distribution of values, half of them will be negative, by definition.) This circumstance necessitates a corresponding adjustment in the procedure to determine the cumulative probability, when such values are determined by way of a table. This adjustment to the procedure is, simply, 1 minus the cumulative probability for the z-scale value with a positive sign. This expression is written as presented in Equation 7.15:

$$F(-z) = 1 - F(z). \tag{7.15}$$

Suppose, for example, a population has a mean of 18.5 and a standard deviation of 3.5, and we want to determine the cumulative probability of 17. Procedurally, the first step is to transform the x-value to a standardized score:

$$z = \frac{17 - 18.5}{3.5} = -.428.$$

Figure 7.13
Probability of an interval in a normal distribution.

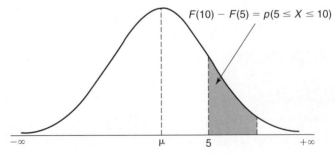

$F(10) - F(5) = p(5 \leq X \leq 10)$

$-\infty$ μ 5 $+\infty$

Now, momentarily for the procedure, ignore the minus sign and look up the value for 0.428 in any table of standard normal deviates. It is 0.666. Next, apply Equation 7.15 to this value to produce a result:

$$F(-.428) = 1 - .666 = .334.$$

Thus, the cumulative probability associated with an observed score of 17 for a population with 18.5 and 3.5 as the mean and standard deviation is 0.334. Also, this means that about 34% of the cases in this population fall below or equal to 17.

Understanding the Logic Behind the Computations

Although the computation of this adjustment is simple, understanding what transpires is more complex. Figure 7.14 aids in this comprehension. In Figure 7.14, first examine the shaded portion of the function that is on the left side of the middle point. This is the cumulative probability for a value $z = -a$. However, one quickly realizes the numbers in the table only provide values for the area below (or equal to) the point $z = a$. We can address this feature in the reported values by looking to the corresponding area in the other side of the symmetric distribution, $1 - F(a)$; that is, the right-hand shaded portion. As can be seen in Figure 7.14, the two shaded areas $[1 - F(a)$ and $F(-a)]$ are identical in area. Hence, we may take the right-hand portion as the value needed, and then merely accommodate this to the left-hand shaded area by subtracting it from the total area, 1, as expressed in Equation 7.15.

As we have seen, in like manner, one may determine the x value for a given probability by simply reversing the procedure. This calculation is often useful in real world testing situations. For example, consider the true scenario in which a multiple-choice exam is used by NASA to determine eligibility for a certain category of advanced training for test pilots. The high scorers constitute a very select group of test pilots. From this group, NASA selects the astronauts to participate in the space program. The training program and facilities can accommodate 15 trainees at a time. The exam, which has psychometric merit, is given across the country at various sites and at different times to an aggregated total of 467 hopeful pilots. The groups' mean and standard deviation are 153.4 and 17.6, respectively. For one particular administration, there are 79 examinees. They all know that only 15 of the group (about 19% of the 79 examinees) will be

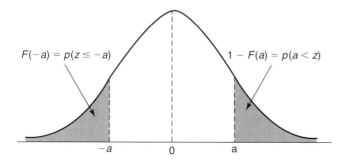

$F(-a) = p(z \le -a)$

$1 - F(a) = p(a < z)$

$-a$ 0 a

Figure 7.14
Probabilities on the extreme tails of a normal distribution.

able to attend the advanced test-pilot training school. Pretend you are NASA's project psychometrician and the research question asked of you is, "What score will one need to obtain to be among the top 19 percent in the group?"

The research question can be addressed by determining the area under the normal curve for this test population for the corollary of 19%, or 81% of the area. From the table of areas under the normal curve used earlier, you see that $z = 0.88$. Next, transform this z-score into the metric of the exam. (This calculation is simply the reverse of arriving at the z-score originally.) You report that in order to be selected, candidates must achieve a score greater than 169. Calculations are shown as follows:

$$x = 17.6(.88) + 153.4 = 168.88, \ or \approx 169.$$

In addition to determining cumulative probabilities for particular areas of the normal curve, various intervals may be calculated. Here again, the table of standardized values is useful. For example, a common concern is determining the proportion of cases in a normal distribution that lie within one standard deviation. Because standardized scores are defined to be $\mu = 0$ and $\sigma = 1$, the interval is expressed as follows:

$$-1 \leq z \leq 1.$$

The procedure now is to determine the area (and hence, the number of cases) between the -1 and the mean and between the mean and 1. From a table of values under the normal curve, the value for $F(1) = .841$ is given (see Equation 7.12). This is the value from the mean to 1. The corresponding value for the area from the mean to -1 (see Equation 7.15) is as follows:

$$F(-1) = 1 - .841 = .159.$$

With these values derived, then, we can now calculate the full cumulative probability for the interval $-1 \leq z \leq 1$ (see Equation 7.4). This probability is as follows:

$$P(-1 \leq z \leq 1) = F(1) - F(-1) = .841 - .159 = .682.$$

Thus, 68.2% of the cases lie within the interval described. Similarly, when one needs to find the proportion of cases for intervals in the normal distribution $\pm 2\sigma$ or ± 3 standard deviation from the mean, the calculations are, respectively:

$$P(-2 \leq z \leq 2) = .977 - .023 = .954$$

and

$$P(-3 \leq z \leq 3) = .999 - .001 = .998.$$

These results are well known to persons working in the field of tests and measurement, and many psychometricians use them so often that the values are memorized. Table 7.2 presents some of these values. One may compare them to those given in the normal curve displayed earlier in chapter 6 in Figure 6.2. The differences are due to gross rounding by the authors of Figure 6.2. Now that we have calculated these areas precisely, we have truer estimations of the areas involved.

Table 7.2
Number of Cases Under the Normal Curve for Specified Intervals

Interval	Approximate percentage of cases
$\pm 1\sigma$	68.2
$\pm 2\sigma$	95.4
$\pm 3\sigma$	99.8

There is yet another wrinkle when the interval needed to define the cases is not adjacent to the mean, either plus or minus. This is the circumstance when one needs to determine the proportion of cases between some other interval, such as between 1 and 2 standard deviations above the mean. By the symmetry of the distribution, this interval is expressed as follows:

$$P(1 \leq z \leq 2).$$

Earlier, it was mentioned that the values for each of the areas under the normal curve is 0.841 and 0.977, respectively. By simple application of Equation 7.4, we see the result as follows:

$$P(1 \leq z \leq 2) = .977 - .841 = .136.$$

Thus, 13.6% of the cases in the normal distribution fall in the interval between 1 and 2 standard deviations above the mean.

Common Measurement Indices Used with the Normal Curve of Distribution

Readers of this text are unquestionably thoroughly familiar with common measurement indices used with the normal curve of distribution, including those for centrality (e.g., mean, mode, standard error of the mean), dispersion (e.g., standard deviation, variance, range), and distribution (e.g., skewness and kurtosis). Other common statistics are briefly discussed in this section. These statistics build on the information provided in chapter 6 on scales and norming and on the information provided here because they occur in distributions of the normal curve.

Percentiles and Percentile Ranks

Explanation of Percentiles

Percentiles are a special type of derived score, a topic discussed in chapter 6. It goes without saying that percentiles and percentile ranks are terms and figures common in discussion of testing and measurement issues. They are used by persons in virtually every scientific field, as well as by school teachers, parents, and psychologists—and most of the time one presumes that they are properly interpreted. A *percentile* is simply a value indicating the percent of cases out of the total number that fall at or below the given value. In other words, say a percentile rank for the value x is 72. Most knowledgeable persons recognize immediately that 72% of the cases are at or below the x value. The x is said to fall at the 72nd percentile. In a probability distribution, this is stated as follows in Equation 7.16:

$$percentile\ rank = 100F(x), \qquad\qquad (7.16)$$

meaning that the percentile is 100 times the cumulative probability associated with $X = x$. It is also widely recognized that because of this definition the percentile rank for the median must be 70 because 70% of the cases in any distribution fall at or below the median, or

$$F(X = Md) = .50.$$

Percentile ranks apply to persons in a standardization sample. Like percentiles, a percentile rank is the percentage of cases less than or equal to a given score. The key to understanding percentiles and percentile ranks lies in the realization that two continuous scales are mapped to one another in some fashion, usually by linear interpolation. One scale is, say, the range of raw scores possible on a given test and the other is the range of percents from 0 to 100.

Percentile ranks can be accurately calculated, even when a particular score is absent from a distribution. Because two continuous scales are mapped to one another, it is not necessary that scores be observed at every value on the test scale in order to determine the associated percentile ranking. The correspondence is between the continuous scale distributions, not individual observed scores. By interpolation, then, it is justified to determine a percentile equivalent as if that score had been observed in the sample of scores.

In most testing contexts, percentiles are calculated from grouped data. There are both theoretical and practical reasons for this approach. From a theoretical perspective, this method more easily displays the continuous nature of a test's scale. (Recall from chapter 2 that test scales are infinitely continuous in theory, although in practice they only display certain values within a range.) From a practical point of view, grouped scores are usually more convenient for calculation. To facilitate this discussion, achievement test data are given in Table 7.3. The table displays individual scores and cumulative frequency counts on a 10-item test for 100 examinees. Also shown is the corresponding percentile value, for which calculations are discussed momentarily.

The fact that the scores are grouped is purposeful. By so doing, the cumulative frequency for particular scores is more easily seen as a score interval, a necessary condition for calculating percentiles. In psychometrics, the score 9 (using the scores given in Table 7.3) actually represents a portion of a larger continuum. This portion extends from interval 8.7 to 9.7. The larger continuum, of course, is the full range of scores possible on the test, from 0 to 10. The scores at each interval represent the entire range of the interval. In other words, say there are three persons who obtain

Table 7.3

Grouped Raw Scores With Percentiles

x	f(x)	cf	Percentile
10	2	100	99%
9	3	98	97%
8	5	95	93%
7	16	90	82%
6	24	74	62%
5	18	50	41%
4	12	32	26%
3	9	20	16%
2	6	11	8%
1	4	5	3%
0	1	1	0%

the same observed score. One score among the three is treated as being above the midpoint for that score interval, one score is dead on the midpoint, and the remaining score is below the midpoint. Further, even when there is only one score for a particular interval, that single score is treated as though half the score is above the midpoint for the interval and the other half of the score is below the midpoint. In this way, the scores represent the range of the interval. This treatment preserves the true continuum for the scale, thereby allowing another continuum—that of the percentiles—to be properly mapped to it.

Cautions, Strengths, and Weaknesses of Percentiles

The immense popularity of using percentiles to express and interpret test scores is *prima facie* evidence of their usefulness. They give a relative ranking of one individual against the population and allow some limited comparison between and among particular examinees. Also, they are widely recognized and thus require little initial explanation, although psychometricians should be ever mindful of their role to assist users in proper test score interpretation. As a handy method of expressing test scores and data garnered from other variables, their place is well established.

However, percentiles are not without shortcomings. One problem of usually minor consequence is that due to the ordinal nature of the percentile scale, few statistical manipulations are possible. This can cause difficulty in research contexts where test scores or other data are reported in percentile units, but related statistical manipulations are performed on the same variable and expressed in a different metric. Usually, however, a clear explanation of what is being done minimizes any confusion.

An especially pernicious problem with percentiles, however, is the distortion in scale when percentiles are calculated for tests used with small groups of examinees, or when the test scale is limited in its range. Both circumstances can corrupt the mapping process and lead users to misconstrue the results. Although theoretically two continuous scales are uniformly mapped to one another, in practice, if only a few examinees comprise the data for the test score scale, then interpolation is needed between very large gaps in the scale and only gross approximation of actual points is possible.

When the small distribution is skewed, this problem is exaggerated, causing yet further distortion in the mapping process. For these reasons, calculating percentile ranks is not recommended when sample size is less than 70, when the sample distribution is highly skewed, or when a large number of the possible score values are not observed. Conversely, when the sample used for percentile calculation is more than 70, and the score distribution has skew and kurtosis indices of less than ±3, percentile ranks may be accurately calculated.

Percentile Ranks as Nonequal Interval Scale

Even with unbiased percentiles, another problem can arise when they are misconstrued. This problem stems from the fact that the percentile scale is not of equal intervals. In other words, the distance between points on the percentile scale is not uniform through its range. On an achievement test, for example, scholastic attainment is not equal between examinees at the 50th and 51st percentiles as contrasted with achievement differences between examinees at the 97th and 98th percentiles. The differences are more modest toward the middle of the scale and much greater at the ends, both high and low. Unmistakably, this has enormous implications for interpretation. It is also a reason that percentile ranks should not be used for expressing change (e.g., post minus pre) scores. Visually, an example of this was given during an earlier discussion and shown in Figure 6.12. Thus, percentile ranks are expressed in *nonequal interval* units.

Summary

This chapter elaborates on the information about distribution provided in chapter 6. Here, because of its importance to measurement of educational and psychological variables, I focus on the normal distribution, with primary attention on the standard normal curve as commonly seen in measurement problems. Attention is paid to understanding the significance of the normal curve, not only to psychometric procedures, but also even more important, to our daily lives. I show how the normal curve is derived and how areas under it may be calculated. I also explain z-scores and some derived scores, such as percentiles and percentile ranks.

Chapter 8

Constructing Items and Exercises for Tests

Introduction

The Heart of It All: Items and Exercises

Aside from music aficionados, few people today know the French chanteuse Edith Piaf, her fame and life given no special due. However, for more than 50 years—from the generation-long depression in Europe, through World War I and the Occupation, to the end of World War II when Americans liberated the countries of Western Europe—Edith Piaf was a hero and a comforter to hundreds of millions of people throughout the world.

The years during which Edith Piaf had fame were hard times for many people, especially in Europe and Eurasia. War seemed both interminable and everywhere. Even getting basic food supplies was difficult, and disease was common. Opportunity lacked on almost every level, but Edith Piaf sang to these hurting people as no one else had. Her songs, such as "L'Hymne a l'Amour" and "Je t'ai dans la Peau", and her signature "La Vie en Rose", touched the lives of common folks. She became an outlet for their life-filling emotions. People believed that *La Mome Piaf* ("The Little Sparrow") understood their immense problems, and especially, communicated the true pathos of deep and unsatisfied love. Everyone knew, almost instinctively, that she was one of them.

Edith Piaf was abandoned by her (probably prostitute) mother at birth and then given by her traveling-showman father to the madam of a cheap Normandy brothel for her care and her rearing. As an adult, she lived a sad life, bouncing from one disastrous affair to another, even witnessing the tragic death of her own children. However, she could sing with an emotion previously unheard in other singers. Her voice was clear and tonal, but it was not exceptional. What was exceptional was Edith herself. She was a beacon of understanding in an unforgiving world. If one were asked why they loved her so, the reply was usually something about how she *knew* their life. Standard bearers in the popular culture of the past half-century, such as Elvis, the Beatles, Frank Sinatra, and the Rolling Stones, and even today's rappers, are known for their influence on music and sometimes even on culture, but not especially for who they are. Edith Piaf is not celebrated because of her influence. Instead, she is loved for something much more—her understanding of the human condition in a way that goes deeper than words, her connection to the hurting people. In the manner of a morality play, at her soul, Edith Piaf is Everyman.

Just as Edith Piaf expressed the heart and soul of her time and place, a test item or assessment exercise is likewise the heart and soul of valid assessment. Such stimuli are, after all, the *stuff* of measurement—the figurative "body" of tests.

Contents

Chapter 8 discusses issues with constructing test items and exercises, along with some item writing strategies. In addition, a theory of test item development is presented. All topics emphasize learning characteristics of meritorious test items. In describing the important issues, I focus on a few common formats, including multiple-choice and true–false, Likert, and Likert-type items. Constructed response formats are covered in chapter 9. Although I give solid direction useful to preparing meritorious items, this chapter is not strictly a "how-to" guide; however, books and publications that offer such direction are cited. I eschew lists of dos and don'ts for item writing, although I do offer a number of practical techniques, culminating in a detailed list of suggested item specifications. The chapter concludes by introducing the reader to schemes for automatic generation of test items. Throughout, I stress the paramount importance of good writing to meritorious test items.

Importance of Test Items and Exercises to Measurement

Role of Items in Tests

In mental measures, the items (or exercises in some performance tests) are magisterial, representing the hypothesized constructs and proficiencies. Except in direct assessment of performance skills, the role of test items is to stimulate an underlying trait that can evoke a volitional reaction. An examinee's response to such directed prompting is sum and substance for estimable data, which, ultimately, is interpreted into meaningful information. No appraisal of an educational or psychological trait or proficiency is possible without items playing their vital functionary role. Perhaps someday—possibly even in some not-too-distant future—we may be able to identify, understand, and interpret cognitive functions by other means, such as brain scans that reveal chemical reactions (a means that can already reliably detect differences in various emotional experiences, different colors, even Coke vs. Pepsi). For now, we employ items and exercises as the sole source to excite mental processes that evoke a measured response—the raw information we evaluate.

It is vital that a test's items and exercises be developed with skill and care so they possess meritorious characteristics, thereby making accurate interpretation more likely. This is an important point for measurement professionals to keep in mind when developing or revising a test, so due care is taken during this crucial step—it is a task that cannot be taken lightly or with velleity. Merely dashing off some multiple-choice questions or Likert-type statements or an interesting pseudoperformance exercise is a fast track to invalid appraisal of complex mental functions. It is a disservice to all persons—especially examinees—to develop test items from a "hurry up and just get it done" point of view.

Regrettably, sometimes persons involved with measurement become so engrossed in interesting, mathematically intensive treatments of data that they lose sight of the fundamental reality that no amount of item analysis, statistical manipulation, or psychometric procedure can improve the interpretation of cognition beyond the intrinsic characteristics of the item or exercise.

If tests were comprised of only well-crafted and meritorious items, it is possible that there would be less of a mélange of charges swirling around tests and a wider audience would be open to embracing the useful results of measurement science. As it is, consider the unfortunate advice given some years ago by W. H. Auden (1966) to Harvard students in his poem in "Under Which Lyre":

> Thou shalt not answer questionnaires
>
> Or quizzes upon World-Affairs,
>
> Nor with compliance
>
> take any test. Thou shalt not sit
>
> With statisticians nor commit
>
> A social science. (p. 225)

By using our best efforts to produce meritorious items for comprising valid assessments, we hope to change such opinions.

Difficulty in Producing Meritorious Items and Exercises

Preparing meritorious test items and exercises is difficult and intense work, as we see in this chapter and elsewhere. In fact, producing meritorious items or test exercises commonly requires a lot more blood, sweat, tears—and especially time—than is planned. In many test construction projects, preparing the items is the hardest step. It takes a carefully devised plan, technical expertise, and commitment to see the job through. Test item development often requires many revisions and iteration of analyses using multiple criteria. Developing a test's items is as difficult as engineering a bridge over a treacherous gorge, as hard as designing a microchip that can steady a heart's rhythm, or as complicated as making a usable system of flight patterns that direct hundreds of planes each day into an international airport. The expertise and effort of professionals needed for these accomplishments are no more than measurement professionals should expend on the important task of item development.

Measurement professionals should appreciate *why* the task is so difficult. Understanding this will help one attend to pertinent features when involved in item development or revision. Probably the most obvious reason for the difficulty involved in making meritorious test items is that psychology is scarcely an exact science; thus, to some degree, we are working in a "glass darkly", to borrow a Biblical phrase (1 Corinthians, 13:12). That is, there is much about the field we do not understand,

and some other parts are only dimly comprehended. We do realize, however, that the content of educational and psychological measurement is vague in many of its aspects and that cognition is labile. Hence, aiming items at such an indistinct target as we have is a complex enterprise, indeed.

Another reason for the difficulty experienced in preparing high-quality test items is that the job is largely an exercise in good writing, a difficult undertaking in and of itself. Here, I explain some relevant aspects of good writing in test items:

> The intended meaning [in test items and in exercises] must be clear. Additionally, grammar, spelling, punctuation, and syntax must be correct and exact. Since many test items are no more than a single sentence, there is often little opportunity to garner meaning from context. Because good writing is difficult, it is distressingly easy for a test-item writer to inadvertently convey hints, prejudices, opinions, or confusing information. (Osterlind, 1998, p. 2)

Regardless of the difficulty of composing words well, writing is a craft that can be learned by most people. Writer John Gregory Dunne (October, 1986), who was known for colorful descriptions of writing and the creative process, in an *Esquire* article, called writing a "manual labor of the mind: a job, like laying pipe." Dunne's proclamation communicates two essential (and often unrealized) points about writing. First, that it is hard work, like manual labor, and second, that it can be learned, like one learns any other job, such as that of laying pipe. As with many jobs, learning to write well takes dedication, attention to conventions, much practice—and then more practice.

Perhaps the first step in learning to write well is to be aware of what constitutes good writing. For example turn to the scribner who many view as the greatest writer of all time—William Shakespeare. His writing has been described as remarkably beautiful, interpretive, and well executed. Reading and appreciating Shakespeare is a pleasure for people studying writing as craftsmanship. Studying many other authors who are also good craftspersons (e.g., Laurens van der Post, Loren Eisley, Ernest Hemingway) can bring the same illumination. I recommend that measurement professionals be attentive to good writing as they read for enjoyment, when they read professional journals (notorious for bad writing), and most particularly, when they read their own writing. Such determined attention heightens one's awareness of good writing and helps bring it to mind when preparing test items.

Knowing the fundamentals of composition will also help inform one about the technical aspects of the craft. There are numerous excellent sources to learn about writing. One fine resource for technical aspects of the craft is *The Elements of Style,* the classic book by Strunk and White (2000), originally written more than 50 years ago. No writer should be without this brief, exceptional reference book.

Of course, writing also involves creativity. Thinking and acting as an artist is part of the effort needed to write well. This is fun stuff, however. It is where one can stretch the mind and work in ways that are given opportunity only occasionally. Creative writing can be an expression of the self. Even technical writing (which includes test item writing), with its stipulations and ground rules, has room for personal expression. Often, authors enjoy this aspect of writing most of all.

Kingsley Amis (1986), praising the compositional craftsmanship of gifted Christian author G. K. Chesterton's *The Man Who Was Thursday*, said of good writing, " . . . one needs a capacity for suggesting fine shades and picking perfect words" (p. 6). Amis describes the level of writing expertise needed and conveys the subtlety of skill required for the good writing that Chesterton displayed. Preparers of test items need that skill set.

Finally, writers in the assessment field should recognize that preparing test items and other assessment exercises is a specialized kind of technical writing. There are conventions and rules to follow. I describe many of them in this chapter and make reference to sources where more can be found. Item writers should heed these conventions.

Raw Materials Needed for Writing Good Test Items

Professionals know that when developing a test's items, the writing can be informed by test-related information. For instance, stipulations of *item specifications* can be vital to good item preparation. Item specifications are, as the name implies, a list or description of criteria or elements intended for a particular set of items. Later in this chapter, I describe item specifications and provide several examples (see Figure 8.14).

Also helpful to success is the information garnered from item analysis. From this rich source of information, the item writer can revise the wording and improve item quality. Chapters 12 and 13 address appropriate item analyses in detail, and there I offer many examples and suggestions for application.

Current Sources for Item Preparation

Two current books provide helpful advice on constructing items by traditional means, used in the vast majority of test development projects today. The first of the two applied books is titled *Constructing Test Items: Multiple-Choice, Constructed-Response, Performance, and Other Formats* (Osterlind, 1998). This book presents practical information for item writers, and includes strategies for making good stems and credible distractors. It also enumerates steps for ensuring congruence between an item and the intended construct or proficiency. Finally, it gives information to test developers about directions and even standardized page layout. Particularly, the book emphasizes the importance of good writing. The second helpful book is *Developing and Validating Multiple-Choice Test Items* (Haladyna, 1999). This book also offers many helpful hints to item writers and test constructors. Additionally, Haladyna and Downing (1988a, 1988b) contribute valuable work when cataloging some common item writing rules.

Yet another book for item writers and test developers is *Item Generation for Test Development* (Irvine & Kyllonen, 2002), an edited volume describing specialized approaches to item generation via computer-driven algorithms. I discuss computer generation schemes later in this chapter.

Theory of Test Item Development

Imaginably, imbuing meritorious characteristics to items and exercises requires a deliberate plan of action. The work begins with articulating a coherent *theory for item development* or generation. Such a theory offers a conceptual framework to the task by giving it structure, organization, and fluency. Rules, expressions, terminology, and many other aspects of item development can be consistently expressed when a theory is followed. Most important, however, such a theory commands and directs the item development activities so the constructs intended for appraisal are more likely to be accurately, fully, and appropriately addressed in the item.

Item development theories have long been part of the test development scene. The earliest theory of item development may have been put forth by Guttman (1941) in his scalogram analyses, described in chapter 6. For Guttman, in rudimentary fashion, an item either absolutely contained or did not contain particular elements of an intended aspect of mental functioning. Also, in his scheme there was a sort of elementary difficulty level—hard or easy. These item characteristics persist today but in much more sophisticated forms.

In the first (and classic) edition of the industry-acclaimed *Educational Measurement,* Ebel (1951) wrote a seminal chapter on preparing test items. In that chapter, he identified many item formats that are still commonly used. Although not strictly a coherent theory of item writing, Ebel's offering did help standardize many important aspects of the task.

Some years later, Bormuth (1970) sought to advance item development theory from the crude beginnings of Guttman's model. He called item development (up to that point) a "dark art" that could no longer rely on "homey recipes." Writing with awkward syntax in his treatise *On the Theory of Achievement Test Items,* he warned his colleagues that "education has become too vital to human welfare, and achievement testing too central to the improvement of education, to permit achievement test writing to rest on anything but the soundest basis scientific methods can achieve" (p. 2).

Bormuth (1970) set out to develop a set of operations and instructions for item writing, and his methods included both objective-based and linguistic approaches. Item writing today still follows many of his precepts and guidelines.

In the 1970s, James Popham contributed mightily to item theory development. He advanced the notion that preparing highly detailed specifications for instructional objectives was a useful activity because they could provide a set of concrete directives for writing items. Item development by these rules was dogmatically prescriptive. Popham himself and others in the measurement community eventually abandoned the movement, due, in part, to the weight of effort involved in defining nearly every imaginable aspect of each objective. He did, however, markedly advance the idea of a theory-driven approach to item development, and the field is indebted to him for his work.

Currently, there is an exciting effort to develop a theory of item generation using computers to perform writing tasks by algorithms and other modern strategies. Loosely labeled *item generation,* this is a specialized approach to item construction that seeks to capture the logic of compositional syntax in computer code so a near infinite number of items can be generated from a list for grammatical or syntactical prescriptions. This approach is stimulating for what it may portend in next-generation item developments, although in its current form it is not fully developed. I describe some promising item generation models later in the chapter.

Despite these advances in item writing theory and item development technology, there remains a deficiency in today's practice of item development. As noted in previous chapters, educational and psychological measurement today is undergirded largely by cognitive theory, but theories for item development have not similarly evolved or developed. In fact, much item development work today loosely rests on the outdated behaviorism of Ebel and later writers. Reflecting this, and regrettably, many test developers still seek simple rules of item writing and lists of dos and don'ts as their guide. Clearly, there is a need to modernize item writing theory and present a mature, cognitive-based approach to the task. This is a call for research in this area.

Practicalities: Item Types and Their Classification

Popular Formats

Items and exercises are generally categorized by their format or layout, such as multiple-choice, true–false, completion, Likert-type statements, essay, various performances, and so forth. To orient the ensuing discussion, Figures 8.1, 8.2, and 8.3

Use the sketches below to answer the question that follows.

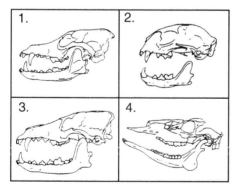

Skull 4 probably came from which type of animal?

    A. parasite
    B. carnivore
• C. herbivore
    D. saprophyte

Figure 8.1
Illustrative exercise of complex appraisal in multiple-choice format.

Figure 8.2

Illustrative exercise of sophisticated appraisal in matching format.

Match the category from the left column with the corresponding characteristic in the right column.

1. SENSATION	a. condolence
2. AFFECTION	b. rocks
3. SPACE	c. incombustibility
4. PHYSICS	d. hearing
5. MATTER	e. interval

present three examples of items, each in a different format: a multiple-choice item, a very simple matching exercise, and a Likert-type statement. As noted, this chapter mostly focuses on multiple-choice items, Likert-type statements, and other traditional formats, whereas chapter 9 is devoted to developing and interpreting performance assessments. Many examples of performance assessment are given there.

When classifying item types, formats for items are often assimilated into one of two broad categories: *selected response* and *constructed response*. These terms describe as genre the activity that denotes an examinee's required action. In the selected response, the examinee chooses an answer from among the alternatives provided, and if a scannable answer sheet is used, the examinee typically fills a corresponding circle by "bubbling" it. Selected response is often associated with multiple-choice and Likert-type items, but it is not necessarily limited to these two formats.

In constructed response formats, as the name implies, the examinee must supply an original response and usually does so by writing the reply on paper or on a more generic answer sheet. Most performance assessments specify some kind of constructed response for their exercises.

The main point to realize here is that each item format presents a different kind of activity to an examinee, and thereby stimulates a different aspect of mental functioning or cognition. This is itself an important point to bear in mind when preparing items for it directs the available interpretations.

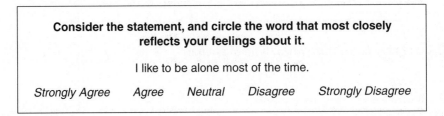

Consider the statement, and circle the word that most closely reflects your feelings about it.

I like to be alone most of the time.

Strongly Agree   Agree   Neutral   Disagree   Strongly Disagree

Figure 8.3

Illustrative exercise of appraisal in Likert-type format.

Definition of Test Items and Exercises

Surprisingly, although mental tests have been commonplace in psychological enterprises for more than 100 years, no lexical description of items and exercises—beyond merely calling them "scorable units"—was available before 1990, when the following definition was proffered:

> A test item in an examination of mental attributes is a unit of measurement with a stimulus and a prescriptive form for answering; and, it is intended to yield a response from an examinee from which performance in some psychological construct (such as ability, predisposition, or trait) may be inferred. (Osterlind, 1990, p. 3)

This definition sets the genre as etiology for measurement itself, causing a reaction by the object of assessment—an examinee. In addition, the definition allows standardization and agreement, which leads to criteria for evaluating the quality of items. Criteria, in turn, can be codified and improved, making the whole task of item development much more organized. This definition, then, sets a foundation for building better test items.

Anatomy of an Item

Figure 8.4 details the anatomy of an item in the multiple-choice format. It presents an item that has been exploded to reveal information useful for developing each part of it. Although the parts are self-evident, it is useful to study them with some deliberation before actually writing items.

Test Item Nomenclature

Readers have undoubtedly noticed that throughout this text I refer to test stimuli as either *items* or *exercises,* and that I mentioned earlier that no clear distinction is made between them in the field. In a loose sense, however, *item* refers to test stimuli that are in a selected response format, whereas *exercise* applies to constructed response activities. For most test-related discussions, either term communicates clearly. Still, it is worthwhile to be aware of the differences because it is important to distinguish between them in some contexts. I recommend that measurement professionals and item writers avoid calling test stimuli *questions* because this implies an interrogative statement, and of course, many items and exercises are not worded as interrogatives.

The nomenclature for items is fairly simple. Figure 8.5 provides a graphic that illustrates many common terms. Most likely, this is run-of-the-mill material to readers of this text but still useful for our purposes. I follow these terms throughout the text.

Testlets as Item Format

In more recent years, a manipulation of some common item formats has been revived from earlier times but with more scrutiny and increased sophistication. This item scheme is called the *testlet*. A testlet is not a distinct format. Rather, it is a kind

Read the passage and use the illustration to answer the question.

In the nineteenth century, Louis Pasteur performed an experiment in which he bent the necks of flasks into "S" shapes, leaving their ends opened. Then he boiled broth in the flasks to force air out and kill any microbes inside. After the flasks cooled, he left some of them upright for observation. Before setting aside others to observe, he tilted them so that the broth moved up into the bent necks and then back into the flasks. After the flasks had been prepared, he watched them for signs of microbial growth.

broth pasteurized

some containers upright for observation

other containers tilted... then observed upright

Which hypothesis was Pasteur testing in this experiment?

A. Flasks with bent necks would cause microbes to grow in the broth.

B. Cooling broth in the flasks would cause microbes to grow in the broth.

C. Heating broth in the flasks and then cooling it would cause microbes to grow in the broth.

D. Contact of the broth with something in the necks of the flasks would cause microbes to grow in the broth.

Clear directions guide examinee.

Wording is precise and succinct. Grammar is correct, following rules of composition.

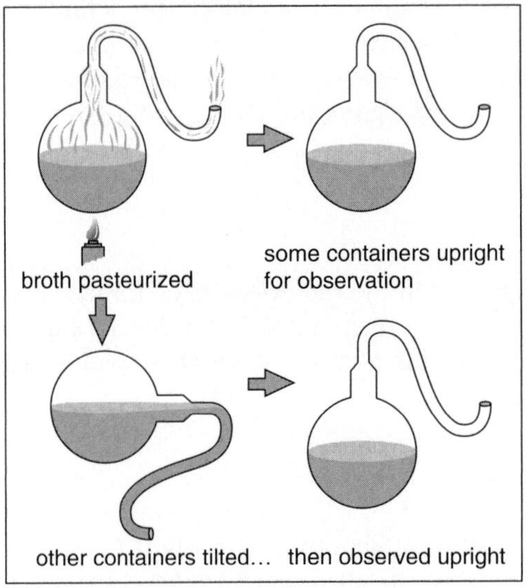

Appropriate graphic supports item without giving undue clues.

Item stem asks reasoning type question (not just recall of facts).

Distractors are plausible; none can be rejected out-of-hand. A single, clearly correct response.

Figure 8.4
Anatomy of a test item in multiple-choice format.

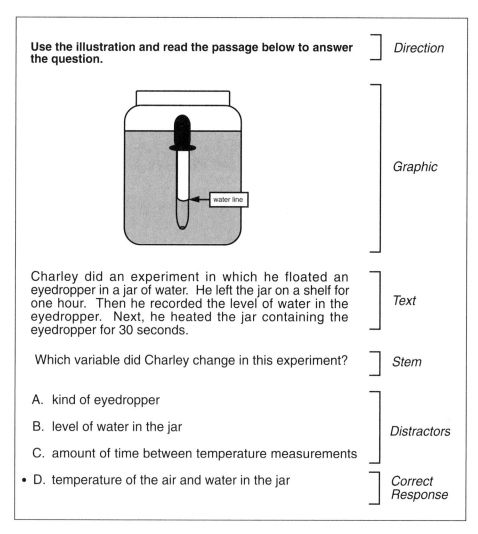

Figure 8.5
Test item nomenclature.

of hybrid design for items or test exercises, wherein several of them share common information. Most often, a testlet is composed of three or four items in the multiple-choice format that all derive needed information from a common paragraph. Directions for a testlet may be as follows: "Read the following paragraph and use its information to answer questions 19 to 23." However, testlets are not restricted to this format. In 2003, Microsoft introduced a variety of testlets in some of its Microsoft Certified Professional exams. The questions are sort of a branching tree that the examinee must construct. It was believed that these question types present a more realistic visual representation of the tasks a computer technician might perform on the job.

(More information on these testlets can be accessed at *http://www.microsoft.com/ learning/mcpexams/policies/innovations.asp.* Retrieved February 20, 2005.)

Testlets are not stand-alone minitests; in fact, they are generally insufficient for a reliable assessment of a given construct because they contain too few items for this purpose. Instead, they can provide useful starter information as part of a longer assessment. Testlets are parallel to a screening test of, say, beginning reading used with kindergartners. The screening test is not a full appraisal of a child's reading proficiency but is a useful, early divider that can point to a targeted and more thorough diagnosis. Testlets are used in many large-scale testing programs, such as the GRE or the MCAT. In addition, testlets have implication for psychometric analyses, some of which are discussed in other chapters.

In IRT applications, particularly with computer-adaptive tests, testlets can provide useful information for preliminary evaluation of an examinee's ability or proficiency and in determining particular items to present to the individual. Currently, their use is primarily in computer-assisted and computer-adaptive testing, and is accompanied by a considerable body of research (e.g., Sireci, Thissen, & Wainer, 1991; Wainer & Lewis, 1990). Testlets are also employed in special applications, such as in some studies of differential item performance.

Multiple-Choice Items and Sophisticated Thinking Skills

Now, we examine the degree of confidence that can be placed in the information garnered from using test items as proxies for cognitive processes. It is often said that test items are too simple for a meaningful assessment of complex cognitive functions because, as this logic maintains, "items tap only an examinee's memory of trivial facts." This accusation is usually made with reference to multiple-choice items but is also levied against appraisal activities in other formats. Sadly, more than a few classroom teachers and public officials repeat the criticism. It must be conceded, of course, that some tests (perhaps too many) contain weak items or point to trivial or inconsequential information. Still, a shoddily developed test is not grounds to denounce an entire science. Obviously, sloppy or incompetent work will lessen a test's value. Therefore, when a measurement professional spots a test with ill-conceived or poorly prepared items, the professional has an ethical obligation to point it out and discourage use of that instrument.

However, the good news is that teachers, public officials, parents, and other audiences can—by and large—have confidence in the information yielded by a test because of the items. To be clear, well-designed and carefully constructed tests of mental processes, when linked with appropriate and substantiated interpretations, offer the most objective, reliable, and fair means to obtain information about an examinee's mental traits and proficiencies. For our present concern, good tests are meritorious, in large measure, because of the quality of the items. In fact, the reason that tests with multiple-choice items have thrived over the years is precisely because educators and others have found the information they provide useful. If this was not

The graph below shows the relationship of temperature and time as constant heat is applied to an ice cube.

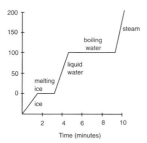

Which statement is consistent with the graph?

   A.   The rate of boiling equals the rate of ice melting.
   B.   More heat is required to melt ice than is required to boil water.
   C.   The same amount of heat is required to melt ice as to boil water.
 • D.   The temperature of melting ice remains constant until all of the ice is melted.

Figure 8.6
Illustrative item 1: multiple-choice formatted test item evoking deep cognition in science domain.

so, then the instruments would have decreased in importance long ago. Instead, their use—worldwide—is greater than ever before.

Moving to the specific charge about items tapping only memorized, trivial facts, we counter with the following: Measurement professionals realize that test items can tap complex constructs and engage an examinee's deep cognition. Looking at just a few well-done items is ample proof. Three illustrative items are given in Figures 8.6, 8.7, and 8.8. Other items in this chapter are still more examples. Each item is in multiple-choice format and represents a different aspect of cognition.

The item depicted in Figure 8.6 is intended for 10th graders in basic science. It allows for examinee flexibility in the thinking process but has a single correct answer. Whatever thinking strategy an examinee may employ, the deduction reaches a logical conclusion. Clearly this item is well crafted and sophisticated.

The next item for consideration, Figure 8.7, taps basic writing skills that may be taught in the fourth, fifth, or sixth grade. It, too, requires higher-order thinking for a proper endorsement. It is another good test item. The item also demonstrates that a variety of important writing aspects may be addressed through the multiple-choice format.

The last example, Figure 8.8, addresses elementary science content. Here again, but in a completely different reasoning context, the examinee must employ sophisticated thinking to arrive at the correct answer. The examinee must realize the characteristics

It was my first camping experience and I wanted to prove that I could do my share. The leader assigned each of us to a group. My group first unpacked the tents and camping equipment. Next, we put up the tents and set out the necessary equipment for preparing dinner.

What characteristic is **not** evident in this paragraph?

    A. logical sequence
    B. effective sentence
 • C. concluding sentence
    D. related supporting details

Figure 8.7
Illustrative item 2: multiple-choice formatted test item evoking deep cognition in compositional skill.

Figure 8.8
Illustrative item 3: elementary-grade, multiple-choice formatted test item evoking deep cognition in scientific understanding.

What is an example of a chemical change?

    A. rainbow
    B. lightning
    C. burning tree
    D. melting snow

of a chemical change and apply them to all four circumstances, eliminating three as not exhibiting them.

The main point of these examples is that items do tap complex, sophisticated reasoning skills and can be carefully and well crafted. These example items are representative of many others from thousands of well-developed tests.

Characteristics of Meritorious Test Items and Exercises

Because items and exercises are a form of technical writing, it is possible to specify criteria for them. One list of criteria stipulates that meritorious items should do the following:

1. Be congruent with key objectives (or psychological constructs).
2. Have clearly defined key objectives (or psychological constructs).
3. Contribute minimally to error in measurement.
4. Be presented in a format that is suitable to the test's goals.
5. Meet specified technical assumptions.

6. Be well written and follow prescribed editorial standards.
7. Satisfy ethical and legal concerns.

These criteria are useful from both theoretical and practical perspectives. They provide a reasonable set of conditions for developing test items, and as criteria, can be applied in most test development contexts to gauge the quality of particular items. From a purely pragmatic point of view, they can be readily employed when a measurement professional is developing a test in an item development workshop. If a team of item writers is assigned the task of preparing a set of test questions, these conditions can form the nucleus of discussion as the writers address their task.

Also notice that the criteria in the list are not limited in their applicability to a single format; rather, they represent a broad set of conditions appropriate to many formats. They set an appropriate register for evaluating already developed items or for refining an existing set of items.

Techniques for Item Writing

Beyond the criteria cited previously, there are many practical considerations to writing meritorious test items. A few practical elements of the task are described here, but for more information readers are referred to either Osterlind (1998) or Haladyna (1999).

Considerations in Item Development

Some particularly important considerations in developing test items and exercises are to ensure they do the following:

- Emanate from a coherent test item writing theory or an overall test development plan.
- Are congruent with the item specification.
- Contain accurate content.
- Avoid bias or stereotyping language.
- Contain clear, specific wording at an appropriate reading level.
- Conform to an editorial style.
- Conform to developed criteria.
- Exhibit overall quality.

The following sections discuss important parts of this list of considerations. Of course, there are many other issues involved in item preparation to which the careful item writer must attend, such as examinees' degree of "test-wiseness" (Rogers & Bateson, 1991), reducing test anxiety for those who may be so predisposed (Messick, 1989), and English language acquisition for non-native speakers. There is also a concomitant of practical concerns, such as when to use the option "none of the above" in multiple-choice items (which Frary [1991] recommended as "compatible with good classroom measurement" [p. 115]). It is to some of these concerns that we now turn.

A Consolidated Approach to Test Development

It should be manifestly clear to readers that developing items is not an isolated event in test construction. Rather, it must be integrated with all aspects of an overall test development plan. Ideally, there should be steps described and criteria set forth so the test developer can objectively determine when a particular action is complete. The plan should also include steps needed to review items, thereby helping to ensure their quality. One logical starting point is to specify information about the items, a point discussed next.

Test Content Specifications

Following the criteria for meritorious test items listed previously, the first and probably foremost consideration in item preparation is to work from a clear and well-prepared *TCS* (test content specification) or *test blueprint*.

The TCS identifies the skills, proficiencies, or abilities that are placed on the test. Most commonly, this list is in outline format, with varying levels of detail. Usually, the TSC stipulates the number of items or exercises matched to particular skills. It is also desirable for the TCS to note the level of intention for examinee response, whether high level or recall of important facts. Test constructors often address this aspect for the TCS by specifying that items should reflect a particular level of a taxonomy of cognitive functions, such as Bloom's (1956) famous one or Hannah and Michaelis's (1977) comprehensive framework for objectives. Some test constructors may devise their own, suited to a given purpose, as with CBASE (Osterlind, 2004). This exam has four hierarchical levels for its items, including (a) factual recall, (b) interpretative reasoning, (c) strategic reasoning, and (d) adaptive reasoning. Such taxonomies can be helpful in focusing attention on the complexity of cognitive activity required for endorsement of a given response by an examinee. A simple TCS is displayed in Figure 8.9.

Still, I recommend that any particular taxonomy not be taken too prescriptively for item development work because they can direct item writers only in an approximate manner. As any experienced item writer knows, directing items at a given cognitive level is dicey work. Using all six levels of Bloom's taxonomy is probably not too helpful because reliable distinctions between some of the levels simply cannot be made in items. Instead, it is probably more useful to target items at one of two gross categories of reasoning, like recall of important facts and global deduction or induction. The examples of items already cited in this chapter provide adequate illustration. The rule here is to use commonsense.

Specifying details about items is also important. Caution is advised, however, to not get so detailed as to make the item writer's task overly prescriptive. An example of item specification is shown in Figure 8.10.

Finally, providing overall guidelines to item writers is worthwhile, particularly to address modern concerns. These guidelines may include various kinds of relevant information, such as included in a "General Logistics" list of one testing program,

Skill: Read critically by asking questions about a text, recognizing assumptions, and evaluating ideas.

Major Content Areas	Intellectual Process*		
	Interpretive Reasoning	Strategic Reasoning	Adaptive Reasoning
Identify the literal meaning of a text and recall its details.	4	3	
Identify the main idea of a text and differentiate it from subordinate ideas.	2	4	
Summarize the rhetorical development or narrative sequence within a text.	4	4	1
Recognize the implicit assumptions and values that inform a text.	3		2
Assess the logical validity of the rhetorical development within a text.	3		1
Evaluate ideas in a text by their implications and relationships to ideas outside the text.	1	2	

* Number of items.

Figure 8.9
Sample table of content specifications.

shown in Figure 8.11. This information is exceedingly valuable to writers, and programs are encouraged to devise such lists appropriate for their own use.

In summary, then, good TCSs are an extremely important part of test development. They lay a foundation for the items and provide focus to eventual valid interpretations of yielded data.

Congruence of the Item or Exercise to the Specification

Making an item or test exercise consistent with its specification is termed *item objective congruence* or *item specification congruence*. Determining congruence for items

Subject Area: Social Studies

Cluster: History

Skill: Recognize the chronology and significance of major events and movements in United States history.

Enabling Subskills:

A. Identify and compare key institutions and participants[1] in major events and movements of United States history.

B. Identify the sequence of major events and movements[2] in United States history.

C. Describe the significance of major events and movements in United States history, including their causes and effects as well as their relationships to broader historical trends.

D. Identify technological developments and environmental changes[3] in United States history and relate them to historical events and movements.

E. Describe the principles and development of American Constitutional democracy and the significance of major Supreme Court decisions.

F. Describe the interaction among peoples of different national origins, races, and cultures and how such interaction has shaped American history.

1 For example, public schools, daycare industry, New York Stock Exchange, Chicago Commodities Exchange, Congress; Thomas Jefferson, Susan B. Anthony, Carrie Nation, Franklin Roosevelt, Martin Luther King, Jr.

2 For example, Revolutionary War, Louisiana Purchase, Lincoln-Douglas debates, Civil War, populist movement, woman suffrage, Prohibition, Great Depression, civil rights movement, first moon landing.

3 For example, telephone, automobile, airplane, satellite communications, genetic engineering, acid rain, depletion of the ozone layer, deforestation of rain forests.

Figure 8.10
Content description for a social studies skill.

is a matter of judgment by experts who employ a criterion. There are many methods for objectifying these judgments. A common means to check for congruence is to use a simple item specification matching form, such as shown in Figure 8.12. This one was suggested by Hambleton some time ago, in 1984, but because it is simple and clear, it is still useful today.

Another more sophisticated congruence scheme is to develop a congruence index and then set a criterion that the index must meet before the item is accepted. One credible congruence scheme was developed by Rovinelli and Hambleton (1977). In this procedure, a congruence index is calculated with a given limit for acceptance. The congruence index must equal or exceed the established limit as a condition for accepting the item onto the test.

To use the procedure, a panel of judges is established. The number of judges may vary but is usually between four and nine. Each judge should have appropriate content expertise. After carefully reading and reviewing the item or exercise, the

College BASE
Guidelines for Item Writers: General Logistics
Introduction

The Assessment Resource Center (ARC) at the University of Missouri developed *College BASE* as an instrument for assessing the general education achievements of students and as a screening device for entry into teacher education programs in Missouri colleges and universities. Each item on *College BASE*, a criterion-referenced exam, links to a specific learning objective defined in the test content specifications. Questions assess knowledge and skills usually acquired by the end of the college-level sophomore year and include material covered in the general education coursework.

General Logistics

No "best" formula exists for writing good test items. However, all questions on *College BASE* are 4-response, multiple-choice items, and constructing good multiple-choice tests requires creativity and careful attention to detail. Observing certain conventions and guidelines in writing test items will assist the process. Also remember that all prospective test items go through extensive review of content and bias and are field-tested before inclusion on a published exam.

1. Purpose: *College BASE* assesses not only the examinees' basic factual knowledge, but also the examinees' ability to reason and apply knowledge (reasoning competencies). About ¾ of *College BASE* items test reasoning competencies rather than recall of simple facts. These reasoning competency items frequently accompany passages or graphics that require interpretation and analysis. Additional information is contained in the document *College BASE Item Writing Guidelines: Reasoning Competencies*.

2. Difficulty: Item writers often overestimate the ability of examinees. Generally, the most effective items in terms of discriminating between students of differing abilities are those which around 60% of the examinees answer correctly. Items which are easy for poor examinees (e.g., 90% answer correctly) or which are difficult for good examinees (e.g., 20% answer correctly) serve no purpose on a criterion-referenced exam.

3. Diversity: Items should be unique, varied, and significant, testing a wide range of important knowledge and cognitive skills. Items should cover contemporary information as well as classical concepts. Science items, for example, should include space biology, genetic engineering, and quantum physics, as well as thermodynamics, Mendelian genetics, and Darwinian evolution. Passages and items for English and Social Studies should span a wide variety of styles and periods. Math items should cover all topics expected in a college-level, general education curriculum.

4. Fairness: All items used on *College BASE* go through extensive content, congruence, and bias reviews to ensure that items are appropriate for all ethnicities, regional backgrounds, and genders, and that special advanced training or coursework provides no particular advantage. In writing items, avoid the use of offensive and stereotypical language or situations as well as items that require knowledge that would be gained in a specific advanced course. This does not necessarily mean that controversial subjects or items requiring advanced knowledge should be avoided. Controversial subjects can be addressed in a manner free from personal prejudices. One way to test higher order thinking skills is to provide some specific advanced information in the passage or stem to an item that an examinee can apply in responding to the stem.

Figure 8.11
Illustrative guidelines for item writers.

5. Use a separate Item Writing Form for each item. (The Item Writing Forms are in Microsoft Word format and may be copied as many times as necessary.) Item Writing Forms are provided for each of the skills for which items are needed. The forms also indicate which reasoning competencies are needed and list the subskills for that skill. Complete each Item Writing Form as follows:

   - indicate the reasoning competency tested by your item
   - indicate the subskill tested by your item
   - indicate the source of any passage or graphic used; if the source is a published work, provide a photocopy of the material, and include the author, title, copyright date, and publisher
   - indicate your name and the date the item was written
   - indicate the correct answer to the item

   If two or more items share a passage or graphic, that passage or graphic must be repeated on each Item Writing Form.

6. Write stems in interrogative format. An imperative format may be used **only** for certain math items that require calculation (e.g, **Solve for x.**)

7. Frequently, stems require a brief, introductory "given" statement in order to supply necessary information or establish a logical sequence of thought. This part of the stem should be no more than 50 words long and the final sentence should still be interrogative.

8. Avoid generating clones of items. Clones will be considered (and paid for) as a single item. Clones include: rearranging response options without changing the stem. Please contact ARC with any questions regarding what constitutes a clone.

9. Generally avoid negative stems such as "Which country does **not** have nuclear weapons?".

10. Stems should ask direct and complete questions. The examinee should not have to read the response options in order to understand the point of the question. Ideally, an examinee should be able to read the question, formulate an answer, and then match that answer with one of the response options.

11. Stems should be written in third person and active voice.

12. Do not repeat information in the response options that appears in the stem. For example, if the stem asks "How many years did the Hundred Years War last?", it is not necessary to include "years" in each response option.

13. Make all four options roughly the same length, or make two long and two short options. Options should be parallel in construction and grammatical form. Distracters should be reasonable (i.e., common errors in logic, arithmetic manipulation, or information), and the correct response should not stand out by being longer, shorter, different format, more technical, or by having a special link with the stem.

14. Options generally appear in a random order. However, order numerical options in a logical fashion (e.g., sequentially in ascending order in math, chronologically in history, etc.) unless that would give away the answer.

15. "All of the above" and "None of the above" are **not** acceptable as response options.

16. Indicate the correct option with an asterisk.

Figure 8.11
(*continued*)

Item/Objective Matching Task

Reviewer   _____

Content Area   _____

DIRECTIONS:

First, read carefully through the lists of domain specification and test items. Your task is to indicate whether or not you feel each test item is a measure of one of the domain specifications. It is if you feel examinee performance on the test item would provide an indication of an examinee's level of performance in a pool of test items measuring the domain specification. Beside each objective, write in the test item numbers corresponding to the test items that you feel measure the objective. In some instances, you may feel that items do not measure any of the available domain specifications. Write these item numbers in the space provided at the bottom of the rating form.

Objective	Matching Test Items
1	
2	
3	
4	
etc.	
No Matches	

Figure 8.12
Example of form for recording judges' matching of items to test objectives.

judge assigns one of three numerical ratings to the item, indicating the congruence. The ratings are as follows:

- 1—if there is a strong match
- 0—if the match is moderate or unclear
- −1—if the match is weak or nonexistent

Judges also may make comments about the items. A form that can be used for this method is shown in Figure 8.13.

These ratings are collected and a congruence formula is applied to the data to create the *Rovinelli-Hambleton Index,* a congruence index. The Rovinelli-Hambleton Index formula is given in Equation 8.1:

$$I_{ik} = \frac{(N - 1)\sum_{j=1}^{n} X_{ijk} + N\sum_{j=1}^{n} X_{ijk} - \sum_{j=1}^{n} X_{ijk}}{2(N - 1)n}. \tag{8.1}$$

This index ranges $(-1, 1)$. Of course, the closer the index is to 1, the higher the congruence between item and specification by these judges. To use the index,

---

Item/Objective Congruence Rating Form

Name _____

Instructions: Read Objective #1 below. Next, read the first item in the test booklet. Consider carefully the degree to which the item is congruent with the skill. Rate the congruence according to this scheme:

> H = high degree of congruence
>
> M = medium degree of congruence
>
> L = low degree of congruence or uncertainty

If you have comments about the congruence of this item, record them in the space provided. After you have finished with this item, proceed to the second item, and thereafter all subsequent items, rating each in the same manner

Objective #1: Use mathematical techniques to solve real-life problems.

	RATING	COMMENT
Item #1	_____	_____
Item #2	_____	_____
Item #3	_____	_____
Item #4	_____	_____

Objective #2: Use the properties of two- and three-dimensional figures to perform geometrical calculations.

	RATING	COMMENT
Item #1	_____	_____
Item #2	_____	_____
Item #3	_____	_____
Item #4	_____	_____

Figure 8.13
Example of form for recording judges' congruence ratings and comments.

the judges must also set a floor level below which no item would be eligible for placement on the test. The criterion might be that at least seven of nine judges (presuming a nine-judge panel) would rate the item as strongly congruent, and hence, a standard of 0.78 would be established.

There are also other item-to-specification quantification schemes (Klein & Kosecof, 1975; Polin & Baker, 1979), and item developers are advised to select one appropriate to their goals.

More Considerations for Items

It goes without saying that when developing test items, having a single correct answer or best alternative is paramount. This statement may appear self-evident, but in fact it illustrates the subtlety and complexity of preparing good items. Sometimes the correct answer is not easily known. A famous case occurred in 1981 when the ETS offered the "rolling circle problem" (illustrated in Figure 8.14) as an item on the SAT (Wainer, Wadkins, & Rogers, 1983).

The correct answer was inadvertently left out of the response alternatives, although the item had been reviewed numerous times by ETS employees. The item appeared on several forms of the test and had been administered to more than 100,000 examinees before the mistake was discovered by an (evidently) exceptionally bright examinee. Much publicity ensued and articles about the mistake appeared in more than 600 newspapers. Certainly a costly error, both in bad publicity and in dollars spent trying to correct it.

Another aspect of having a correct possibility is when a selected response item appears to have several correct options and the examinee is directed to select the "best" among them. These items are called *best answer type,* and they can

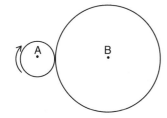

In the figure above, the radius of circle A is 1/3 the radius of circle B. Starting from position shown in the figure, circle A rolls along the circumference of circle B. After how many revolutions will the center of circle A first reach its starting point?

A.   3/4
B.   3
C.   6
D.   9/2
E.   9

Figure 8.14
The "rolling circle" problem.
Source: From *Was there one distractor too many?* (Research Report RR-83-34), by H. Wainer, J. R. Wadkins, and A. Rogers (1983) Princeton, NJ: Educational Testing Service. Retrieved December 23, 2004, from http://www.ets.org/research/researcher/r933557.htm. Copyright 1983 by the Educational Testing Service. Reprinted with permission.

often make useful discriminations between examinees. Here, too, it is sometimes difficult to determine a single correct response. I recommend that the criterion be a consensus of expert opinion, using at least three individuals with relevant content expertise.

The Case Against Lists of "Dos and Don'ts"

Still around in test development literature and back drawers, but thankfully declining in popularity, are lists of "dos and don'ts" when writing items. Such lists make the task seem automatic and mechanical, and do not address the very essence of good items, namely, their ability to stimulate deep cognition. Nor do these lists convey the necessary sense of skill involved in technical writing or meet considerations for technical merit. Although a few such rules can be helpful, an entire list is rarely so. I do not recommend using such simple lists of dos and don'ts when writing items; if you must, refer to them with caution. Knowing about characteristics of meritorious items—the subject of this chapter—is a route that will more likely conclude in well-crafted test items.

Automatic Generation of Test Items and Exercises

What Is Item Generation?

Along with increased use of the two primary forms of computerized testing—*computer-administered testing* and *computer-adaptive testing* (terms discussed in chapter 16)—there is revived interest in automatic generation of test items. *Item generation* is loosely understood as employing technology to create original test items and exercises. The technology implied in automatic item generation is computer science wedded to a linguistic theory. A question seems to convey the meaning of item generation: "Can we write a mathematical algorithm (and the computer code needed for its execution) that implements linguistic theory sufficiently to create sensible and original multiple-choice test items?" To date, the answer is not clear. Although progress is being made, much more remains before this is an alternative available to implement in a variety of tests.

The reason for this renewed interest is twofold. First, individuals and organizations who construct tests are faced with the enormously high cost of producing items by traditional means (having highly trained experts write them one at a time). Second, computerized testing can implement assessment plans that require large numbers of items, creating a need for many more of them.

Linguistic Roots for Item Generation

Item generation has its roots in linguistic theory. Noam Chomsky (1957) developed a linguistic theory, put forth in his book *Syntactic Structures*. Chomsky outlines a methodology for describing the relationships between sentences expressing similar concepts to underlying "deep structures" by means of various transformational rules. His theory came to be known as *transformational grammar*. (Information about transformational grammar can be accessed at *http://people.umass.edu/kbj/homepage/ Content/601_lectures.pdf*. Retrieved February 20, 2005.) Initially, it was hoped that transformational grammar could make cross-language translation automatic because the linguistic rules were about deep structures of meaning that may be expressed in any language of conventional form. Unfortunately, such thinking could never be satisfactorily implemented in a practical manner, and today authentic translation is still performed painstakingly by people who speak both languages, or less satisfactorily by simple look-up matching word programs. However, the idea of using deep structure to express language still holds.

Some item writers and test developers of the days when transformational grammar was popularly used as a means to study language tried to adapt the deep structure approach to the craft of item writing. These efforts were without initial success, and such direct application methods are no longer used in item development work. However, the idea of employing linguistic approaches to item development persisted, and some improvements in linguistic methods were obtained (Bormuth, 1970). Others continue to research the ideas of automatic item generation (Bejar, 1986).

Another earlier effort, popular throughout the 1960s and 1970s, was the idea of formulaic item development with highly specified instructional objectives. Here, long and tediously detailed descriptions of school-based curriculum concepts were developed and employed as a basis for formulaic item generation. For a time, this approach to item development seemed to hold some promise, and its most renowned advocate, James Popham at IOX (Instructional Objectives Exchange) and of University of California, Los Angeles, had many assessment programs trying it out. However, the initial enthusiasm eventually faded, and these item generation schemes with their highly prescribed rules and devices were viewed as authoritarian, cumbersome, and nonfunctional. Popham (2001), a valued national resource on testing, works to find ways of making tests more instructionally useful. (Popham was interviewed in 2001 for *Frontline,* a PBS TV special on testing in our schools, and it is instructive for measurement professionals to read Popham's insights; for more information, go to *http://www.pbs.org/wgbh/pages/frontline/shows/schools/inteviews/popham.html.*)

Hopeful Attention and More Research

Still, some measurement theorists such as Samuel Messick and Lee J. Cronbach have maintained hope that practical item generation could become a reality, and limited research continues (Bejar & Yocom, 1991). Before his untimely death in 1998, Messick organized an invitational seminar on item generation at ETS. This seminar produced a plethora of new thinking on item generation and has spurred promise for advancement. The seminar proceedings are published in a useful book edited by Sidney Irvine and Patrick Kyllonen (2002).

Item generation continues as an area ripe for continued attention and research. As the need for the promised results grows, it is hoped that the incentive will provide impetus for greatly expanded attention and research. ETS has taken the lead in asking some thinkers to produce a novel computer program that can produce "reasoning" test items of known difficulty for the GRE (Newstead, Bradon, Handley, Evans, & Dennis, 2002).

Summary

This chapter focuses on the technical task of writing test items and exercises that contain characteristics of merit, which are themselves explained. A theory for item writing is described, and a number of common item formats are analyzed. Throughout the chapter, I emphasize the importance of good writing. Then, too, a number of techniques for producing items are presented and the automatic generation of items is explained.

Chapter 9

Performance-Related Measures

Introduction

A Plethora of Changes

In 1968, athlete Dick Fosbury won the high jump event at the Summer Olympic Games in Mexico City. Before Fosbury, the high jump was considered about as exciting to watch as a late-night TV infomercial. Gangly athletes ran toward the high jump stanchion, lifting a foreleg as high as possible in a scissors kick over the bar, typically at heights of around 6 feet. During his Olympic event that memorable year, Fosbury ran mightily toward the bar, threw his body into a sort of inverted U and sailed to a new world's record of more than 7 feet with his "Fosbury Flop," a position for the jump that had never been seen before. The crowd was literally hushed in amazement until they realized fully what had happened—then, they cheered wildly. It soon became apparent that Fosbury had transformed not only high jumping, but the entire Olympic Games, into a frenzy of change and experimentation. Novel sports techniques, innovative equipment, and original coaching methods became the order of the day. New events, previously unimagined, began making their way into the games. Sports such as skateboarding, surfing, and ballroom dancing are now invited to the Summer Games. The Winter Games have added ski ballet, snowboarding, and trick skiing to the traditional slalom and downhill racing. Although some may argue that the original intent of holding a series of classic track and field events to honor the Olympus-to-Carthage runner is being diminished, others approve of the game's new direction, claiming that it celebrates ingenuity, creativity, and novelty.

Like the Olympics after Fosbury, assessment practices also experienced a renaissance, beginning a decade or more ago. No longer was a standardized test with its rigid, multiple-choice–formatted items the only measure considered true and good. Nontraditional assessments were suddenly eligible for serious attention, too. Performances, demonstrations, logic problems, and even group-produced products began to appear in tests, many in state-mandated programs. Appraising a student's writing proficiency by judging a sample composition is now commonplace. Here, we explore these formats from a psychometrician's perspective. As is obvious, there is much more to performance models for assessment than merely the verity that this item format is "other than multiple choice."

Contents

Chapter 9 focuses on assessment exercises and performance activities that are of a constructed response format, that is, a format other than selected response. I begin with the foundation of identifying what constitutes performance assessment (PA), stipulating a number of essential criteria. I provide examples of PAs and also cite several of their specialized types. After this preliminary information, two primary questions guide the discussion: (a) What do PAs measure? and (b) can they be reliably scored and meaningfully interpreted? From this perspective, I discuss validity issues and describe numerous strategies for setting passing scores. Essays, as a prominent part of PAs, are treated extensively. The chapter concludes with a short history of this approach and some cautions about using PAs. Throughout, I cite many sources devoted to developing PAs. Like the companion chapter 8, which covers items in selected-response formats, this chapter is not a "how to" set of instructions; rather, the chapters focus on characteristics and features of PAs.

A Psychometric Perspective on Performance Assessments

Terminology of Performance Assessment

Many writers loosely use the term *performance assessments* to label appraisal tasks and activities that are formatted in a way other than strictly selected response. Occasionally, PAs are called *PBAs* for performance-based assessments. Although acknowledging a certain technical inexactitude of PA (or PBA) as a title, it is a reasonably accurate term to describe the lexis of "constructed response," "novel formats," and other commonly used descriptors, such as "direct," "authentic," or "alternative." Using PA is also deliberate because some experts (e.g., Baker, O'Neil, & Linn, 1993) view the term PA as "neutral . . . and more descriptive" (p. 1210) than other expressions or names. Following these authorities, I use the term PA throughout this text. There are times, however, when it is appropriate to specify a particular word or jargon to identify a type of PA, such as authentic assessment, and I note these as well.

Defining Performance Assessment

For practical work with PAs, most measurement professionals find it more useful to describe characteristics of a PA and provide examples, rather than to merely recite a dictionary-style definition. I also follow this convention, and accordingly, the focus of this chapter is on the characteristics of PAs. Some of these important characteristics are listed in the next section, and thereafter, attention centers on them. Readers of PA literature will undoubtedly encounter traditional definitions of such assessments, and there are times where a succinct description can be useful. One oft-cited definition is put forth by the U.S. Congress, Office of Technology Assessment (1992), which describes PAs as "testing methods that require students to create an answer or a product that demonstrates their [students'] knowledge and skills . . . and performance assessment can take many forms including conducting experiments, writing extended essays, doing mathematical computations" (p. 1).

Other professionals in the field provide similar definitions (e.g., Elliott, 1995; Murray-Ward, 1999). However, my focus throughout the chapter is on elucidating characteristics for PAs, rather than on constrictive definitions.

Separating the Wheat from the Chaff

Clearly, the surfeit of PA forms can be overwhelming. Articles about the new forms for assessment pervade both academic journals and popular magazines. In the words of a prominent measurement authority, "one of the most striking features of the measurement literature in the last decade has been the attention given to performance assessment" (Brennan, 2001b, p. 307). It is no wonder, because so many assessments can be configured as a PA. As illustration of the point, Figure 9.1 provides a listing of some items, tasks, and activities that could be used as PAs. From the list it would seem that almost any thought or idea can—sometimes by rewording alone—be articulated into a kind of task or activity to become a PA.

Indeed, the variety of PAs is so great that one is left wondering whether some avant-garde tasks presented as PAs are really assessments. Superficially, it would seem that as long as an appraisal instrument is not comprised of multiple-choice items, anything goes. This reminds me of the story from 1961, when Henri Matisse's *Le Bateau* was inadvertently hung upside down in New York City's Museum of Modern Art. Despite thousands of visitors, it was 47 days before someone realized the mistake! The reason it took so long to discover the blunder was, of course, that viewers could not make heads or tails of Matisse's creation. In PA, too, one must distinguish between what is worthwhile appraisal of important mental activity and what is merely upside-down nonsense. We should realize that any PA (or appraisal with exercises formatted in some way aside from multiple choice) is not

Demonstrations	Performances
Essays	Portfolios
Exhibitions	Projects
Experiments	Research papers
Fill-in-the-blank	Recitals
Formal discussions	Reviews
Grid-in response	Self-/peer evaluations
Interactive video	Short answers
Observations	Structured interview
Oral reports	Writing samples

Figure 9.1
Examples of performance assessments.

ipso facto a good PA, namely, one with worthy characteristics for appraisal of a mental construct.

That chaff aside, there is a lot of useful, creative expression in some PAs. For instance, airline pilots take a job-related PA in a flight simulator. The simulation activity is marked according to criteria. It is an expertly conceived PA, albeit a bit expensive. Another example of a well-done PA is that used in the national licensing exam for professional architects. This test is presented to examinees on a computer. Then, candidates are instructed to design a structure (e.g., house, office building, bridge), while considering its appearance, functionality, environmental concerns, and a host of engineering stipulations, such as structural fatigue and local availability of raw materials. Examinees work with customized computer-aided design (CAD) software, similar to procedures performed in a real-life setting by practicing architects. The computer program reacts with likely response scenarios to the examinees' CAD drawings. This is a sophisticated PA. Both appraisals (pilots and architects) are examples of novel and purposeful PAs.

In educational and psychological settings, there are also numerous useful and well-crafted PAs. Figures 9.2, 9.3, and 9.4 are additional examples of credible PAs. Note the vast differences among them as illustration of the variety in these specialized kinds of assessment. Obviously, these few illustrations are insufficient to represent the full range of PA, and readers are undoubtedly aware of many other examples.

Sheer Volume of Performance Assessments

Aside from the variety of PA activities, the sheer volume of PAs and information about them is overwhelming. Imaginably, little more than a simple keyword search in a social sciences–related database (e.g., ERIC, PsycINFO) or an Internet search, unearths

---

Directions for this mathematics problem: You are to find as many correct results from the data in the table as you can. You can use addition, subtraction, multiplication, and division, and you can use each more than once. Here's how to do it. First, select a number from column I. Next, choose an operation from column II. Then find a number in column III that will give you a correct result from the choices in column IV. Find as many answers as you can.

I	II	III		IV
2	+	1	=	1
3	–	2	=	3
4	*	3	=	5
6	/	4	=	6

Figure 9.2
Example of a performance assessment illustrating mathematical reasoning.

Game of Checkers

Marc, Anna, Julia, and Daniel decided to have a checkers tournament at school. They want to be sure they get a chance to play each of the others one time. They ask you to make a schedule for the tournament. Here is the information you need to make a plan that works:

- They want to finish the tournament in 1 week. They can play from Monday through Friday.
- They will play only at lunchtime. There is enough time during lunch period to play one game of checkers.
- The students have two checker sets, so two games can occur at once.
- Marc can't play checkers on the days he is a lunch helper (Mondays and Wednesdays).
- Each player must play every other player once.

DIRECTIONS:

Make a schedule for the tournament using both written and graphic form. It should be creative. Your schedule should make it easy for everyone to see who plays whom each day. Then prepare a series of charts, one for each day of the tournament, showing who won the matches for that day, as well as the odds of the forthcoming matches. Finally, devise a set of handicapping rules that give the losing players more chances to win against the winning players.

Figure 9.3
Example of a performance assessment requiring complex and extended reasoning skills.

an ocean of references about PAs, in fact, thousands of them. Payne (2002) informs us that most of the current writings describe how particular PAs are employed in educational settings, or more generally, their role in education reform policies and their place in curricular improvement.

Again, however, the reader is cautioned to view PA information and illustration with healthy skepticism. When working from a psychometrician's perspective, the two guiding questions of this chapter may be applied to review specific illustrations and information (e.g., what do PAs measure? can they be reliably scored and meaningfully interpreted?). One useful resource to begin addressing these questions, especially when working with PAs in large-scale contexts such as state-level assessment programs, is the Council on Chief State School Officers. This organization has established a technical task force to examine particular issues related to developing and using PAs in state-mandated programs (go to *http://www.ccsso.org*. Retrieved February 28, 2005.).

Portfolio Assessment

Another term often heard in PA discussions is *portfolio assessment*. As the term is most commonly used, portfolio assessment is not an assessment at all but is merely a

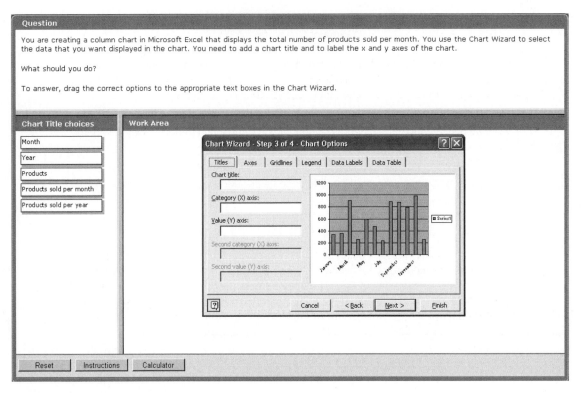

Figure 9.4
Example of a performance assessment from a Microsoft Certified Technician Practice Session.
This exam must be administered interactively on a computer.

convenient label for a collection of a student's work. Included in portfolio assessment can be any and all manner of student work, depending on context. The inclusions can be representative of all past assignments, tests, performance records, and previous ratings by teachers, peers, and others, or they can show capabilities by including only the best of a student's efforts. The portfolio itself is similar to a painter or writer collecting various works into a portable case to be reviewed for exhibition or publication.

Obviously, however, items included in a portfolio of academic accomplishment should represent progress toward some specified end. As a teaching and learning aid, the portfolio can be valuable to both teachers and students. Reviewing past work systematically is one way to evaluate what has taken place, whether scholastically, developmentally, or otherwise. Portfolios as collective review of a student's work are outside the scope of our psychometric study, however, and, aside from this mention for the sake of clarity, I do not discuss them further. For more information about portfolio assessments, consulting a subject area curriculum organization (e.g., Association for Supervision and Curriculum Development) is often helpful.

Characteristics of Performance Assessments

Three Common Characteristics

Generally, PAs feature three characteristics, each of which distinguishes them from selected response test items. The first characteristic of PAs is that they require an examinee to respond to the stimulus in a manner other than selecting one choice from the presented alternatives. In other words, examinees must produce something or perform in some manner. "Perform" is used in a broad sense, as shown in the previous examples.

The second distinguishing characteristic of PAs is that they nearly always intend to gauge sophisticated thinking skills. Baker and colleagues (1993), prominent researchers in this area, state flatly that "virtually all proponents of performance-based assessment *intend* [italics added] it to measure aspects of higher order thinking processes" (p. 1211). Other experts agree (e.g., Resnick & Resnick, 1992; Wiggins, 1990). Emphasizing this point, some preparers of PAs seek to deliberately exclude rote recall as a direct measure of achievement or aptitude, although of course, knowing facts and other information is implicit in all responses.

The characteristic that PAs gauge higher-order thinking skills is probably cited most often as their perceived advantage over selected response formats. Yeh (2001), in an especially insightful piece on PA, even argues that state-mandated PAs *must* emphasize critical thinking in order to be effective.

The third characteristic of most PAs is that to score them, someone (presumably not the examinee) must inspect the response and apply evaluative judgment. A human-devised scoring scheme comes first. Still, remarkable progress is being made with adapting computers to simulate human judgments. But, even sophisticated computer scoring schemes make no independent judgment; rather, they merely apply decision rules programmed into their machine logic. As of now, there is no algorithm or mechanism of artificial intelligence that suffices for reliable scoring of PAs generally. In chapter 16, I discuss some computer-administered tests and electronic scoring systems that can be applied to PAs.

We can use the three characteristics of PA as a list of criterion for judging the merit of particular ones.

Although the three characteristics are useful for circumscribing PAs, readers should realize that they do not present a universally accepted list. Other authors provide different characteristics or aspects for PA. For example, Ashbacker (1991) offers a list that includes these key features:

- Students perform, create, or do something that requires higher-level thinking or problem-solving skills (not just one right answer).
- Assessment tasks are also meaningful, challenging, engaging, and instructional activities.
- Tasks are set in a real world context or a close simulation.
- Process and cognitive behaviors are often associated with the product.
- The criteria and standards for performance are public and known in advance.

Regardless of the particular list cited, the idea of determining characteristics for PAs is useful. It provides information for test developers and is particularly applicable to validity evaluation of PAs.

Organizing Performance Assessments

Two Rough Categories of Performance Assessments

Often, it is useful to categorize PAs. One categorization effort comes from a 1991 study of PAs conducted by the U.S. Department of Education's Office of Educational Research and Improvement (OERI) entitled *Principles and Practices of Performance Assessment* (Khattri, Reeve, & Kane, 1998). In this scheme, PA appraisals are divided into two broad categories: *task centered* and *construct centered* (p. 44). Task-centered PAs are activities primarily aimed at specific skills and competencies, whereas construct-centered PAs sample from a specific domain of skills and competencies, presumably to make inferences about a broader domain.

Task-centered measures allow the respondents little variation in task performance and employ highly prescriptive scoring rubrics. As focused tasks, they may be useful as pedagogical activities and for heuristic inquiry, but they typically do not allow inferences about principles underlying the tasks. Often, one sees these kinds of assessments integrated into instruction, where the performance activity is used not only as a student evaluation, but also as an instructional tool. Also, and likely due to their specificity, reliable scoring schemes for task-centered PAs can be easily devised, even when they involve multiple raters.

In rough contrast, construct-centered activities allow a great deal of student variety in the required performance and usually have broad categories for scoring. They also have the advantage of providing information that applies more generally to learning. An example of construct-centered PA in action, cited by the authors of the OREI study, is that of Harrison, Colorado, School District 2, where teachers first prepare the students for the assessment by explaining the goals of the appraisal and the scoring scheme. It is an extended PA, lasting several weeks and involving numerous activities and exercises. The assessments are integrated into daily classroom activities. Teachers make notes about students' in-class speaking, reading, and listening behaviors. It also includes self-scored exercises and peer-reviewed tasks. As is easily imagined, for these involved PAs to succeed in providing useful appraisals of student proficiencies and abilities, there must be a nearly all-embracing commitment of time and energy by teachers, administrators, and sometimes even parents, in addition to, of course, the examinees themselves.

The PA categories of task centered and construct centered can be represented along a continuum from tightly prescribed to loosely arranged, with many activities falling in-between. Figure 9.5 displays this level-of-prescription continuum, along with relevant descriptors.

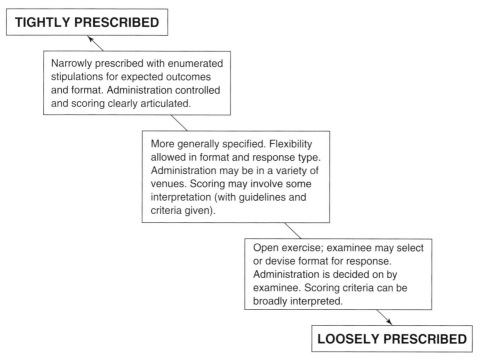

Figure 9.5
Degree of prescription for performance assessments.

This categorization scheme is especially useful for constructing PAs initially and for evaluating them. It offers the test developer or test evaluator a framework within which to gauge a PA.

A PA Taxonomy

A taxonomy of PA characteristics is also useful for designing a classifying scheme. One such taxonomy has been developed by Osterlind and Merz (1994). It is built around three distinct dimensions, including the following:

1. Type of reasoning competency employed
2. Nature of cognitive continuum employed
3. Kind of response yielded

The first two dimensions of the taxonomy identify a particular kind of cognitive activity that an examinee may employ when responding to the PA stimuli. The third dimension relates to the kind of response yielded by a particular format for a given PA and has much to do with how a given response is scaled for scoring. Figure 9.6 is a visual representation of the taxonomy.

Figure 9.6

Graphic representation of three dimensions of the performance assessment taxonomy.

Source: From "Building a Taxonomy for Constructed Response Test Items," by S. J. Osterlind and W. M. Merz, 1994, *Educational Assessment,* 2(2), p. 140. Copyright 1994 by Lawrence Erlbaum Associates, Inc. Reprinted with permission.

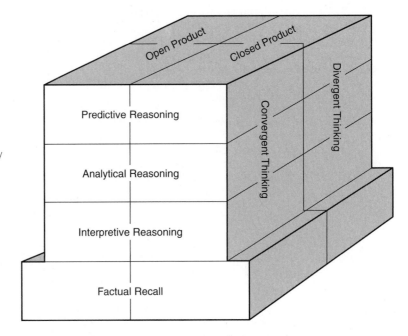

Notice on the face of the cube-like figure that four reasoning competencies are involved. The first, and lowest-order competency, is at the base—factual recall. This is the keystone for all other kinds of reasoning, akin to the lowest level of classification in Bloom's (1956) classic, *Taxonomy of the Educational Objectives,* but still useful in this context. From this level, complex reasoning begins, building into three increasingly more developed reasoning competencies, including interpretive reasoning, analytical reasoning, and adaptive reasoning. *Interpretive reasoning* is a cognitive process by which we understand information that has been remembered or observed. *Analytical reasoning* is the process employed to interpret information, such as logically deducing implications from known events. The highest level of reasoning in this schema is *predictive reasoning,* whereby one extends, or predicts, what is known and analyzed to new contexts. This level is brought into play when one synthesizes disparate information into a new idea or when one uses evaluative judgment to determine the value of an abstract idea. For a number of practical purposes, PAs can be meaningfully placed into one of these levels.

Moving to the side of Figure 9.6, the taxonomy presents the next dimension—the kind of thinking. Like the reasoning competencies, the kind of thinking is also psychological in nature. It depicts PAs as eliciting either divergent or convergent thinking from examinees when they respond to an item. Of course, classifying which kind of thinking an examinee brings to bear on a given problem is speculative and even arbitrary, but it is clearly not capricious. The taxonomy's authors describe the difficulty as follows:

Clearly, it is difficult (and possibly neigh impossible) to precisely identify the processes an examinee may use to respond to a particular stimulus, even when employing the specialized vocabulary of cognitive psychology. But divergent and convergent thinking appear to describe the continuum on which meaningful separation of intellectual processes can be defined because they relate clearly to the sought objective. (Osterlind & Merz, 1994, p. 138)

Convergent thinking requires a kind of sorting, or narrowing, process. New information is compared and contrasted with what is already known. Similarities are identified and the focus is sharpened. Synthesis is the result. An example is interpreting various historical events into a unified *Weltanschauung,* or philosophical worldview. Divergent thinking is not the opposite of convergent thinking but is its analog. In divergent thinking, one begins with a premise and seeks to explore new contexts into which the idea may appropriately fit. It is suspected that Thomas Edison was thinking divergently when he took disparate facts about physics and mechanical engineering and applied then in entirely different ways to build something unknown until that time—the electric light bulb.

The third dimension of the taxonomy for PA is represented by the top plane of Figure 9.6. This is the simplest aspect of the taxonomy. It merely classifies whether the product of the PA is *open* or *closed.* Open product responses are virtually infinite, but closed product responses are restricted to a lesser number of possibilities. Writing a creative essay or giving a recital of original music is an example of an open product response. The illustrative PAs shown in Figures 9.2 and 9.4 are examples of closed product responses, whereas that in Figure 9.3 is open product. This dimension grossly parallels the notion of PAs being either task- or construct-centered activities, as described by OERI.

Special Types of Performance Assessments

Authentic Assessment as Performance Assessment

One PA variant has special properties all its own: *authentic assessment.* This kind of appraisal is of a task or exercise that is useful to do in and of itself, apart from any purpose as a measurement device. For instance, playing a musical instrument in a recital, a thespian performance, driving a car, and flying an airplane are worthwhile activities in and of themselves, regardless of their use for appraisal. Some forms of writing can be considered as authentic assessment.

The rationale for authentic assessment as a genre is captured by this common-sense question: "If we want to assess one's ability or proficiency in some particular area, why not just ask the examinee to perform the activity?" The requisite proficiency can thereby be demonstrated directly, a clear advantage over using a proxy format. In many assessment contexts, the task makes perfect sense and the authentic activity can be implemented as an assessment. It is logical, for instance, to demonstrate driving skill by sitting behind the wheel and driving a car. Likewise, to earn the demanding national ski instructor certification, one must actually get out onto the snow and ski, as well as demonstrate aptitude and patience in teaching skiing to others, especially beginners. These appraisals are manifestly obvious, although criteria must be established for their scoring. (Scoring criteria and appropriate organizational schemes are discussed in a later section of this chapter.)

However, not every activity can be captured into an authentic format for appraisal. Authentic assessments are restricted to observable events (consider the examples provided), rather than to psychological processes of deep cognition, such as attitudes and beliefs. An authentic skill is specific to the observable action. For this reason, assessments do not generalize to skills or abilities beyond the particular performance, and inferences derived from a specific performance to other skills, knowledge, or activity are dubious. Obviously, driving a car well does not imply skill in flying a plane, for example, or even something as closely related as driving a large truck or bus. One imagines most sports performances also fall into this category. Remember when Michael Jordan—arguably the greatest basketball player of all time—was demoted from major league baseball to a minor league club. Evidently, despite his great athleticism and hoop-shoot proficiency, this did not transfer to the three acts required for baseball: hitting, fielding, and throwing.

This lack of transference—the ability to generalize results to other related contexts—is a shortcoming of authentic assessment and one that stands in contrast to items in the multiple-choice format. The utility of the multiple-choice format for items lies in the fact that they are proximal activities of broad cognitive functions from which findings can be reliably generalized. Multiple-choice test items are useful correlates of valued things (e.g., knowledge of American history, rules of composition and grammar, algebraic computation), but they are not valued tasks in themselves, as are authentic assessments. This is the difference between the two kinds of assessment activities.

It is arguable whether writing samples are truly considered to be a form of authentic assessment because there are many kinds of writing. Skill in one type of writing may or may not imply skill in another. For instance, writing a strong personal narrative does not imply the author can also craft a cogent argument. In addition, it says nothing about whether one could artfully write poetry. Still, some writing genres do seem related. Many skilled playwrights, for example, also compose superb poetry (Shakespeare, for one).

Some disciples of PA enthusiastically endorse authentic assessments beyond its merit, even suggesting that all assessment should be authentic (e.g., Stiggins, 1994; Wiggins, 1990). This is a position that is not easy to defend because many—possibly even most—PAs are not performances of an observable activity. Nonetheless, authentic assessments often have advantages over using selected response format items as proxies for cognitive activities. Hence, when circumstances exist for its appropriate use, it is desired.

Complex Performance Assessments

A current trend in PAs is toward developing complicated formats, often involving multiple tasks and requiring a variety of responses. Sometimes, these assessments can involve branching instructions wherein the examinee is directed to a particular subsequent task, depending on level or kind of response given to a prior task. Such activities are referred to as *complex performance assessments*. Generally, simulations of real-life circumstances (e.g., in pilots' training with a cockpit simulator), demonstrations (e.g., science experiments), musical recitals, and intricate problem-solving scenarios are complex PAs. Complex PAs are not different in type from other PAs, but their very involvedness makes them harder to construct, more difficult to administer, and for psychometric analysis, more tenuous to interpret. Linn (1994) provides a useful and extended discussion of these issues.

Figure 9.7 presents an example of a complex PA in biology developed for the New York Regents Examination (Kreisman, Knoll, & Melchoir, 1995). Here, students are instructed to perform a complex but imaginary task, namely, invent an organism. In accomplishing the task, they must keep a notebook and have it reviewed by other students. The scoring criteria for complex PAs is involved, and can be difficult and unsubstantiated. It often requires much time and energy to score just one criterion. Psychometrically, too, garnering validity evidence to support interpretation of complex PAs is exceedingly difficult. An example of such a scoring scheme is given in Figure 9.8. Because of these conditions, complex PAs are generally ill suited to large-scale assessment programs. Still, when employed on a much smaller scale, such as with a single teacher who has only a few students, such an approach may be exceedingly useful for individual diagnosis.

Task: Invent an Organism

You have the distinct pleasure of being a genetic engineer. You have been given the task of looking at a selection of organisms, taking the best of the life functions from the amoeba, paramecium, hydra, earthworm, and grasshopper and creating a brand new organism for any place on Earth.

You may decide to create this organism in any way that you like. You may place it in any environment as long as you can convince me and your critics that your organism can survive where you have placed it. You may present this to me in any way. It can be: (1) a written report, (2) an audiocassette, (3) a videotape, (4) a drawing, (5) a model, or (6) any other way that you first clear with me.

As a part of your work, you must keep a research notebook with all pertinent information about the five organisms and your organism as it develops (for example, questions, ideas, thoughts, sketches as you begin to create).

Also, as part of this creation process you will have the chance to be reviewed by your peers and to become a peer critic. This is very important to you because it gives you the chance to rethink your ideas before your work gets turned in. Plus, being a critic lets you help your classmates and helps you really see how much you are learning.

Figure 9.7

Example of a complex performance assessment.

Source: From *Assessment in the Learning Organization: Shifting the Paradigm* (p. 128), by A. A. Costa and B. Kallick, 1995, Alexandria, VA: Association for Supervision and Curriculum Development. Copyright 1995. Reprinted with permission.

INVENT AN ORGANISM
Critique By: _____
For: _____

1. They have chosen _____ as the environment for their organism.
2. Some special considerations for life functions in that environment are:
    a.
    b.
3. The _____ type of _____ has been chosen.
4. Can explain the process of _____ .
       NO   SOME   YES
5. Can explain the _____ 's type of _____ .
       NO   SOME   YES
6. Can convince you why this type of _____ will work for their organism in the environment.
       NO   SOME   YES
7. Anything else that could help them think more about their organism?

Critic's Rating Sheet

Critic's Name: _____
Rater's Name: _____

1. Critic made me explain my choices.
              NO   SOME   FULLY
2. Critic asked me questions other than those on the critique sheet.
              NO   ONE   SOME
3. Critic asked me questions that made me think more about or change my ideas.
              NO   ONE   SOME
4. Critic thought only his/her ideas were correct.
              NO   ONE   SOME
5. Anything else about this critic that made him/her especially good/bad?
6. Would you choose this person as a critic again?
        YES   NO
                              If NO, why? _____
                              If YES, why? _____

Figure 9.8
Scoring criteria use in complex performance assessment.
Source: From *Assessment in the Learning Organization: Shifting the Paradigm* (p. 131), by A. A. Costa and B. Kallick, 1995, Alexandria, VA: Association for Supervision and Curriculum Development. Reprinted with permission.

Validity Issues

Importance and Difficulty in Amassing Validity Evidence for PAs

In validity evaluation of PAs, many professionals would agree that this work has a Jeffersonian purpose (high rhetoric) but requires Madisonian determination (willing to toil to complete the work) to actually garner the evidence. More succinctly, validity evaluation is necessary but difficult. Still, such work is necessary if the genre is to be used for effective and meaningful appraisal of mental abilities.

The first and most obvious reason for difficulty is because these assessments intentionally strive to measure deep levels of cognition. This pushes interpretation toward multidimensional aspects of cognition, something manifestly more complicated and involved to interpret than appraisal directed at a single, latent construct. This presumes one is sure what aspect of cognition is the intended target of the appraisal. Alas, sometimes with PAs it is difficult to identify what latencies are intended for appraisal, even in a general sense.

A second reason for the difficulty of understanding mental appraisal by PA is that PAs are often idiosyncratic and unique, sometimes being employed for only a single administration. Even PAs that are used more than once are rarely standardized in form or administration. More typically, they evolve from one version to the next so each constitutes a separate appraisal. Khattri et al. (1998) note this difficulty: "The assessment tasks and scoring methods that comprise a performance assessment system are continually changing. Consequently, it is difficult to comment on whether or not a system is valid and reliable" (p. 53).

Compounding this is the circumstance that PAs are frequently administered only to small numbers of examinees; thus, large data sets for PA responses (which may be checked for normality, linearity, and the like) are often not available.

This leads to yet a third reason that makes working with PAs challenging. This reason is that evidence for validity for PAs is often not garnered from traditional test-related statistics, such as item p-values, point–biserial relationship indices, and methods of FA and component analysis.

As a consequence of these circumstances, sources appropriate to validity evaluation of a PA are indirect and the evidence is often ephemeral. Still, strategies for garnering evidence for valid score interpretation of a PA are available, and it is to some of these concepts we now turn.

PA Validity Evaluation as Interpretive Argument

Kane (2002) suggests that validity evaluation for a given PA may be stated in terms of an interpretative argument:

> Interpretative arguments generally contain a number of inferences and assumptions, and the validation effort should focus on studies that are most relevant to the inferences and assumptions in the interpretation argument, preferably paying particular attention to the weakest link in the argument. (p. 31)

It would seem, then, that this interpretive argument approach offers a reasonable route down the difficult highway of establishing evidence in PA for valid score interpretation.

Messick (1996) offers a list of criteria for validity evaluation that some researchers (Miller & Linn, 2000) maintain can be useful when making Kane's validity conceit. I cite Messick's (1996) list in his own words (with some fractured grammar) to ensure fidelity to his original intent:

- The content aspect of construct validity includes evidence of content relevance, representativeness, and technical quality.
- The substantive aspect refers to theoretical rationales for the observed consistencies in test responses, including process models of task performance, along with empirical evidence that the theoretical processes are actually engaged by respondents in the assessment tasks.
- The structural aspect appraises the fidelity of the scoring structure to the structure of the construct domain at issue.
- The generalizability aspect examines the extent to which score properties and interpretations generalize to and across populations, groups, settings, and tasks.
- The external aspect includes convergent and discriminant evidence from multitrait-multimethod comparisons, as well as evidence of criterion relevance and applied utility.
- The consequential aspect appraises the value implications of score interpretations as a basis for action as well as the actual and potential consequences of test use, especially in regard to sources of invalidity related to issues of bias, fairness, and distributive justice. (pp. 12–13)

Messick's list is primarily useful as a guide to follow for the validity evaluator because the points cannot be easily checked off one by one. Regardless, as a guide, it is very useful. I recommend that test constructors and test users adopt these items as criteria for valid PA assessment. When incorporated in an interpretative argument, useful validity evaluation can be accomplished. Especially because construct evidence is foundational to validity evaluation, it is a good starting point.

Construct Evidence for PAs

For PAs to be effective (viz., produce information that can be meaningfully, appropriately, and usefully interpreted), both the test developer and the test user should have a reasonably clear notion of the intent of the assessment. When the target for appraisal is complex and involves multiple dimensions of cognitive activity (the usual case of PAs), this requirement is even more important. For best information, the description should not only be sensibly articulated, but it should more properly link the assessment's tasks and activities to a grounding theory. Only with such information available can the results of a PA be interpreted at some reasonable level of comprehension.

Especially, developers and users of PAs should be especially attentive to a purposeful and lucid description of a PA's intent. Regrettably, it seems that far too many developers and users of PAs ignore the important (and commonsense) stipulation—given by APA *Standards* and elsewhere—that, in addition to the PA activity itself, the content to be assessed should be thoughtfully and thoroughly described. As evidence of this failing, I cite the following anecdote. When reviewing relevant literature and examples of PA for writing this chapter, I examined hundreds of PAs and dozens of assessment programs that employ them as their principal means for gathering data. Only a scant few had even a rudimentary description of what the authors themselves believed was being assessed, and from among those few the descriptions were often blithe generalities such as "This test is of higher order thinking skills" or "Reasoning skills are measured." (Both quotes are from PA descriptions used by large-scale, statewide programs.) For serious purposes of validity evaluation, such phraseology is empty because it scarcely articulates the latencies being assessed by the PA. That, after all, is the purpose for the appraisal in the first place.

Setting Standards and Establishing Cut Scores

Setting standards and establishing cut scores for use with PAs is an issue of validity of score use. It is critically important to PAs, and extensive discussion is required to address the issues and to present some commonly used methods of establishing standards. Despite its criticality to PAs, I do not discuss standard setting here. Instead, Chapter 14 is devoted entirely to establishing standards, where a more thorough treatment is presented.

Essays as Performance Assessments

Some Technical Issues and Practical Considerations

Because essay writing is frequently employed as a task in PAs, it is worthwhile to explore characteristics and implications of this particular genre. We are all familiar with the assignment of submitting a writing sample to a teacher or other professional for review. Usually, the sample is judged and scored not only to appraise our success in writing the particular essay, but also to infer our writing ability generally, within the domain. However, to obtain generalizable interpretations from a single writing sample is problematic, at best. Merely asking an examinee to produce a sample of writing and then grading it as one would any class assignment—something commonly done, regrettably—is insufficient for making valid generalizations to a variety of writing types and for different purposes.

Proper interpretation of writing samples demands consideration of both technical issues and practical considerations. These concerns begin with developing the writing prompt initially, and then assume an even heightened importance for scoring and interpreting it. The following list presents some important considerations in developing, scoring, and interpreting writing:

- Developing the writing assignment or prompt (from substantive theory to specifications to selection of language used for the prompt itself)
- Instructing the examinee on how to appropriately complete the task, as well as information on time limits and other logistical details

- Establishing criteria for scoring the essay and articulating these into rubrics or other meaningful schemes
- Training and rehearsing scorers (in addition to establishing qualifications for becoming a scorer in the first place)
- Setting performance standards to allow for meaningful interpretations of the scores
- Determining reliability in scoring
- Understanding validity inferences of the scores for decision making (with reference back to the first issues in this list)
- Communicating decisions to the examinee and other audiences (i.e., parents)
- Understanding the educational, social, and political implications of the decisions, especially because these may involve fairness and nondiscrimination

Even this list is not a complete explication because the considerations run deep and wide. I discuss some of them in the next section, but an extended discussion of them would take us afield of our psychometric perspective on PA. Fortunately, there are a number of good sources on developing and using writing assessment in PAs. One especially informative book was edited by Cizek (2001) and is titled *Setting Performance Standards: Concepts, Methods, and Perspectives*. The volume comprises 19 chapters, each detailing a different aspect of PAs, most of which are relevant to writing samples. Persons actually working with essay tasks in PAs are encouraged to review particular chapters in Cizek's excellent book. In addition, the electronic journal *Practical Assessment: Research and Evaluation* (accessed at *http://pareonline.net/ Home.htm*. Retrieved February 28, 2005.) provides extensive resources for persons interested in writing assessment, as well as other aspects of PA.

Kinds of Writing Tasks: Prompts

As widely known in school settings and in some psychological contexts, with essay PAs, the stimulus for the writing task is called a *prompt*. The prompt is the direction given for the assignment. It includes the topic for exposition, as well as practical information, such as stipulating the kind of writing expected (e.g., argumentative, personal narrative) and explaining administrative details (e.g., length of response). Illustrative prompts—all from actual writing assessments—include the following:

- Tell about an incident from your childhood that significantly shaped your character.
- Write an anecdote whose point supports the following statement: Two wrongs do not make a right.
- Describe the most famous person you have ever met.
- Consider the past election of the mayor in your town. Did you participate in this election, either by voting or campaigning? Did you not vote? Write an essay about your participation (or lack thereof) and justify it.

Sample Question

Imagine that you are attending a college that is contemplating a change in its curriculum. The current curriculum is called a "core curriculum." All students who attend the school are required to take the same set of courses during the freshman and sophomore years. This requirement, supporters argue, ensures students have many experiences in common, and it gives them the information they need to select a major during their junior year. The proposed curriculum, called an "open curriculum," would not go into effect for at least 3 years and thus would not affect you. It would, though, completely do away with requirements for all students entering after it is adopted. Supporters of the open curriculum argue that it will encourage students to make their own choices and thus better prepare them for life after college.

The College Policy Committee, composed of faculty members and administrators, has asked students to submit statements expressing their attitudes toward the current and proposed curricula, and you have decided to submit such a statement.

In an organized, coherent, and supported essay directed to the committee, explain what you believe the committee should do and why it should do so, as well as your general attitudes toward the priorities your school must set.

Figure 9.9
Sample writing prompt from a performance assessment.

A more complete prompt, including supporting information, is shown in Figure 9.9.

Topics for prompts in PA vary widely because most topics are acceptable as long as the subject is appropriate for the audience. However, the wording of a prompt usually specifies (whether the prompt's developer intended to or not) that the response be one of three major essay types: *descriptive essay, narrative essay,* or *argumentative essay.* We briefly examine each type.

A *descriptive essay* is typically more informal than the other two types and is often personal. The first topic in the previous list of sample prompts falls into this category.

A *narrative essay* is more formal than descriptive writing and may include anecdotes, biographies, and histories. Often, holding the reader's interest is a primary consideration of narratives; hence, many pop-culture magazines are filled with narratives. Education and information are often less central in narrative essays.

An *argumentative essay* is the third major type of writing style. The primary aim of argumentative writing is to convince and persuade. Most academic and professional writing we read is argument type. As a writing style, argumentation is much broader than mere debate between two individuals or between competing points of view. It includes speeches, sermons, and editorials, as well as research papers, with their attention toward cause and effect. The writing prompt given in Figure 9.9 demands an argumentative response.

I realize that the decision about whether to retain the core curriculum or to adopt an open curriculum is very difficult. Nonetheless, I urge the Committee to adopt the open curriculum because this enables students to make their own choices as to what curriculum they want to follow.

Many Freshmen and Sophomores are undecided about what area to follow because they haven't experienced a varied high school curriculum. A big part of figuring out what interests one is by taking a lot of different courses which are varied. But some students have a general idea about their interests. Thus it would be a waste to take Art classes if one was interested in the sciences.

Generally every major requires classes that pertain to different subject matters. This will certainly guarantee the student a well rounded education. But with a declared major students are also able to concentrate on their area of interests. With the closed core system many students are stuck in classes with which they have no interest. But an open system would allow thesm to take their preferred classes along with the required classes.

Forcing students to stick to a closed core system may also be detrimental to the students study habits as well as grades. If students are forced to take classes they don't like then they are less likely to work for the top grade. When students are forced into a curriculum a negative feedback is likely to occur. But if students are able to chose their own set of classes then they obviously know what is required. When entering a class that's interesting to a student, he/she is much more likely to put time and energy into it.

A closed core curriculum also puts limits on the students variety of friends. If Freshmen and Sophomores are all thrown into the curriculum then obviously these will be the majority of the people they meet. It is important to become acquainted with students the same age, older, and younger. Older students have gone through a lot and have much good advice to offer younger students. It would be unfortunate to put limits on the age of ones friends.

I've argued strongly against the closed core curriculum mainly because I enjoy the freedom of choosing my own classes. I would strongly oppose being forced into certain classes with which I have no interest. True the closed curriculum exposes a student to a variety of subjects. But I feel that the requirements of one's major does a good enough job of giving a student a well rounded education.

Figure 9.10
Response to writing prompt from a performance assessment.

A live response from an examinee to the prompt of Figure 9.9 is shown in Figure 9.10. With the exception of being typed, the essay is reproduced exactly as it was written.

Writing can be fun, and a prompt can elicit fun writing. A wonderfully whimsical, narrative essay contest administered by the English department at California State University, San Jose, is the Bulwer-Lytton Fiction Contest (for more information refer to *http://www.bulwer-lytton.com*. Retrieved February 2, 2005.), inspired by Edwin Bulwer-Lytton, whose opening line "It was a dark and stormy night . . ." was made famous by the cartoon beagle, Snoopy. Edwin Bulwer-Lytton was a minor Victorian novelist who, it is generally acknowledged, wrote in a long-winded and uninspiring style. In fact, his seriousness and verbosity was such that his work was read as comedy. The point of the contest is to top Bulwer-Lytton's horrific first

line by writing one that is even more wordy and meaningless. Each year, one winner is chosen from thousands of entries.[1]

Persons preparing writing prompts should be cognizant of what kind of writing
the examinee is asked to produce.

Developing Writing Tasks: Rubrics

Whereas the prompt elicits the examinee to respond in a specified manner, the scoring should be formalized and standardized across similar administrations. *Scoring
rubrics* provide this vehicle. These are the standardized rules and prescription-
describing characteristics of an expected response. Typically, rubrics are organized
into categories of compositional characteristics—the more categories obtained, the
more proficient the writing. The first rubric category may describe only elementary
or basic writing characteristics. The next category contains other, more sophisticated,
compositional features. The list of writing characteristics becomes increasingly complex as the number of rubric categories increases. It is common for sophisticated
writing PAs to have six or more rubric categories. An example of scoring rubrics is
given in Figure 9.11.

Developing rubric categories is more difficult than is sometimes imagined. It requires expert knowledge of composition and heuristic inquiry. Moskal and Leydens
(2000) suggest three questions that guide the development of scoring rubrics:

1. Are the scoring categories well defined?
2. Are the differences between the score categories clear?
3. Would two independent raters arrive at the same score for a given response
   based on the scoring rubric?

Figure 9.12 shows a content specification and accompanying discussion of the
characteristics that may suitably comprise a prompt. This kind of written statement
is particularly helpful for developing a writing-based PA.

Developing rubrics is sometimes done *post hoc,* or after the assessment, as in the
case of the NAEP program (Burstein et al., 1996). This approach has the advantage
of examining actual writing samples for evident characteristics, thereby making the
rubrics manifestly relevant to the examinee population. However, this approach may
be criticized as too sample dependent, and thus yield a score that only has meaning
within that group. Such *post hoc* development is therefore recommended only for
large-scale assessment programs, where sufficient numbers of essays for generalization are available.

Although, as noted, the task of rubric and prompt development is difficult, help
is available. In fact, this field is overflowing with resources to which one can turn

---

[1]Just for fun, the opening sentence reads as follows: "It was a dark and stormy night; the rain fell in
torrents—except at occasional intervals, when it was checked by a violent gust of wind which swept
up the streets (for it is in London that our scene lies), rattling along the housetops, and fiercely agitating
the scanty flame of the lamps that struggled against the darkness" (Bulwer-Lytton, 1830).

Scoring Procedures

Your essay will be read by at least two professional evaluators familiar with college-level writing. *College BASE* essay readers are trained to evaluate your work as a whole. While the mechanics of composition (e.g., punctuation, spelling, grammar) certainly affect their reading, they understand the time constraints you are under. They will score your essay based on its overall success in satisfying the demands of the question and in meeting the standards described below. Your essay is evaluated on the following 6-point scale, with 6 being the highest score possible.

Score of 6: Essays assigned a "6" will be excellent in nearly all respects, although the circumstances under which the essays were written allow for some imperfections. The "6" essay should employ a sound organizational strategy with clearly developed paragraphs proceeding from a sharply focused and clearly identifiable main idea or thesis. Assertions should be sufficiently developed and directed to engage the specified audience and should be supported through appropriate examples, details, and/or other fully integrated rhetorical techniques (e.g., analogy, narration). Again, considering the writing situation, there should be few, if any, distracting grammatical and mechanical errors.

Score of 5: Essays assigned a "5" will be good, but not excellent, in almost all respects. Specifically, look for a thesis or main idea that is clearly discernible and for sophisticated reasoning and/or support, going well beyond the information provided by the prompt. The writer will engage the opposition, beyond a passing reference, and may even redefine the problem while not evading it. A "5" may be marred by some stylistic and/or organizational problems, or it may be well-organized and fairly sophisticated at the sentence level but fail to use or fully integrate a variety of rhetorical devices. There should be few distracting grammatical and mechanical errors.

Score of 4: Essays assigned a "4" will present a competent thesis and adequate organization and will acknowledge the opposition, even if that acknowledgement takes the form of an indictment. A "4" may rely heavily on the prompt for ideas but supply sophisticated examples, or it may present ideas beyond the prompt but offer scant or predictable support. An essay which shows some insights but fails to unite them may also receive a "4." Generally, a "4" may contain a few distracting grammatical and mechanical errors, although essays appreciably damaged by major errors should not receive a "4."

Score of 3: Essays assigned a "3" will contain some virtues, although they may contain an unengaging or poorly focused main idea or thesis or be marred by inadequate development. A "3" might, for example, express some ideas that reflect a thoughtful consideration of the problem, but at the same time be obscured by unclear or "incorrect" writing. On the other hand, it might represent clear and competent writing but convey superficial ideas, or ideas which fail to account for information provided in the prompt. A "3" may be primarily a list of responses to the prompt, but with some development of the listed ideas, or it may show an organizational strategy which goes beyond listing, but offers support only in list form. As an argumentative essay, it may exhibit specious or circular reasoning or lack the coherence necessary to foster a complete understanding of the writer's meaning. A number of major and distracting grammatical and mechanical errors may place an otherwise thoughtful and well-written essay in this category.

Score of 2: Essays assigned a "2" are weak because they are poorly written throughout (with consistent errors in grammar or mechanics), or because they fail to support major points, or because they are exceedingly superficial. A "2" may be flawed by a lack of unity or discernible organizational pattern, or it may rely on a clearly organized list with little or no development or simple development which presents personal examples as proof.

Score of 1: Essays assigned a "1" will be clearly unacceptable as college-level writing or will demonstrate an only momentary engagement with the topic, concentrating instead on some tangential concern(s). A "1" will be riddled with major grammatical and mechanical errors and/or will consist of a collection of random thoughts or undeveloped ideas. In short, essays that appear to have been written in careless haste or without effort should receive a "1."

Score of 0: Essays that for any reason cannot be read should be assigned this score.

Score of NT: Essays assigned this score are designated as "not taken."

Figure 9.11
Scoring procedures and rubrics to a writing prompt from a performance assessment.

English subject

Skill: Write an organized, coherent, and effective essay.

Enabling Subskills

- Formulate a central idea suitable to the occasion for writing, focusing it as required by the work's format and the expectations of the audience.

- Select a rhetorical strategy and pattern of development that effectively organize ideas.

- Develop ideas logically and coherently with adequate supporting detail.

- Employ unified paragraphs, varied syntax, and precise diction to present ideas clearly and efficiently.

- Create a voice and tone appropriate to the audience and purpose.

- Observe the conventions of standard written English.

This is the only skill in *College BASE* that is not evaluated through multiple-choice questions. Instead, you will be asked to write an essay in response to a specific prompt. You will only be required to write one essay during any given administration of *College BASE*. There is no choice among prompts. *College BASE* essay prompts focus on issues and concerns common to college campuses rather than on course-specific knowledge or current events. The prompt will provide you with a specific situation and an equally specific audience to which you should direct your response.

In order to demonstrate mastery of this skill, you must analyze a specific situation and compose a thoughtful, well-supported essay directed to the particular audience specified in the prompt. You will have 40 minutes in which to compose your essay. You are encouraged to use a portion of that time to make notes or to do any other pre-writing activities that you find helpful. However, you should not plan to revise extensively or to recopy your essay.

The sample writing prompt below is typical of the kind of question you may encounter in the essay portion of *College BASE*. Following the sample question, you will find a competently written student essay. With the exception of being typed, the essay is reproduced just as the student wrote it. Beginning on page 10 you will find a description of the scoring procedure used to evaluate the *College BASE* writing exercise, detailed commentary on this particular essay, and the score it received. Reading the sample essay and the scoring criteria will help you appreciate what is expected of your own essay.

Figure 9.12
Supporting skill and discussion for examinee of writing prompt.

for assistance. In addition to academic journal articles (e.g., Moskal, 2000), there are many Web sites devoted to the topic, and there are helpful persons at state departments of education, testing companies, and local school districts.

In addition, developing scoring rubrics should not be done apart from prompt development. As with all test development activities, the job begins with establishing a rationale for the assessment. Guiding questions might be as follows: Why do this assessment? What decisions will be based on it? What are the anticipated logistics? Are we complying with codes of ethics, as well as other relevant policies and conventions? Following closely on the heels of this discussion is a consideration of the skills and objectives that are to be measured. Also playing an important role in development is whether the decision to be made from the scores concerns writing diagnosis or establishing different levels of writing proficiency (Brookhart, 1999).

Scoring Writing Tasks: Rubrics

Most commonly, scaling rubric categories is simply done with 1 point assigned for each score category. Because the categories are hierarchical, higher scores result from essays that exhibit compositional characteristics described in the later categories. An essay that meets only criteria in the first category is given a 1, whereas a composition that satisfies the first and second rubric categories is given a 2.

Scaling rubric categories do not need to be limited to this simple scheme. Sometimes the score points are transformed into other, more sophisticated scales, even employing IRT and MDS. BILOG-MG IRT and other programs allow such a *graded response model* (discussed in chapter 10).

More often, rubrics result from a scoring program that either evaluates particular features of an essay or gives an overall impression of the degree to which the rubrics are evidenced in the essay. The first approach is called *analytic scoring*, and the second perspective is *holistic scoring*. Analytic scoring defines evaluative criteria such as spelling, punctuation, usage, organization, and other similar characteristics of composition. Points can be assigned based on the degree to which these features of writing are present (or absent) in the essay, as judged by the reader. The scoring rubric given in Figure 9.11 is analytic. (In some discussions, this example may be considered to have characteristics of both analytic and holistic scoring, but the point being made holds.)

Holistic scoring takes a broader perspective toward essay scoring and attempts to gauge the merits of a piece as a complete work. With holistic scoring, the sum is greater than the individual parts. The scorer gains an overall impression of the essay and then determines the degree to which the totality of the essay exhibits the characteristics cited in the holistic rubric.

Finally, among judges it is especially useful to discuss the PA responses to writing prompts so they work from a common perspective. Users of writing samples are encouraged to adopt this practice because it will enhance interpretability and help build validity evidence. An example of this is shown in Figure 9.13.

Perspective on Performance Assessment

History of Performance Assessment in Perspective

It is worthwhile to appreciate that, although there is much excitement about performance-based assessment models, few are wholly new ideas. In fact, although often labeled in PAs as "a novel approach," many mimic exercises from tests developed prior to the early 20th-century growth of multiple-choice testing. For example,

---

Discussion of Sample Essay

The preceding sample essay opens with a clearly stated thesis, and the writer acknowledges, although sparingly, that the opposing view has its merits. In addition, the writer provides basic support for the thesis with ideas and examples. Some of the examples tend toward generalities rather than specifics, however, and their relevance is not always readily apparent. In fact, without a great deal more support, an overtly opinionated generalization—such as the statement that concludes the second paragraph—could easily alienate a reader. Aside from the fact that many scientists deeply appreciate the arts, members of the committee debating the curriculum probably include faculty from the arts and humanities—faculty who may be so put off by the comment as to dismiss the writer's arguments altogether. Nevertheless, the writer generally demonstrates basic competence in organization and development as well as grammar and mechanics. While the essay has a few errors in grammar and mechanics, none is so distracting or confusing as to prevent the reader from understanding the writer's intended meaning. Taking all aspects of the discussion into consideration, readers determined that the essay should receive a score of "4," in accordance with the scoring criteria.

Figure 9.13
Illustrative discussion of a writing prompt from a performance assessment.

consider Binet's early "stunts"—which is what he called his test exercises, such as asking a young child to touch his hands behind his back as a marker for certain kinds of development—as decidedly PAs. A short and informative history that gives valuable perspective is provided by Madaus and O'Dwyer (1989). A more detailed history of PAs, one from the point of view of school-based reform, is offered by Khattri and colleagues (1998). The history of PA is interesting and well worth the time spent reading it.

Performance Assessment and Public Policy

Commonly, new assessment paradigms are discussed in the context of educational reform and other policy considerations (e.g., Kane & Mitchell, 1996; Khattri et al., 1998). Apparently, many policy makers and other discussants have hope that PAs will play a leading role in educational program reform. Says one expert, "Proponents of assessment-centered reforms expect great things to be accomplished for education through the use of performance-based assessment systems" (Linn, 1994, p. 4). Crocker (2002) discusses issues related to stakeholders in the discussion. Readers can acquaint themselves with the relevant topics by reading a special issue of *Phi Delta Kappan* (1999), which was devoted to a social and political discussion of PA. Review of the article by Elliot Eisner (1999a), guest editor of the special issue, is especially helpful in seeing PA in a broad educational and social context. Obviously, the political context for discussion of assessment can have profound implications for the technical issues involved. Measurement professionals working with PAs should participate in this debate, both to learn and to contribute.

Performance Assessment and Instruction

PAs are valued by some persons because of their perceived closeness to instruction. To some, merely the fact that the assessments look akin to a curriculum activity, coupled with the fact that they are quite unlike tests with multiple-choice–formatted items, makes them "instructionally relevant" (see Stiggins, 1994; Wiggins, 1998). In one approach—labeled *dynamic assessment*—the examiner is even part of the assessment process, interacting with an examinee by providing continuous feedback (see Swanson & Lussier, 2001). Classroom assessment is aimed at helping teachers make better decisions and is less directed toward policy makers or other audiences (Anderson, 2003; Arter & McTighe, 2000). Of course, examinees learn while taking a test (just as one also learns while reading or studying in other settings), and the two cannot be separated. However, one should not be confused that they are the same. Validity is empirically established for a PA in a given context, one assessment at a time.

Still, well-designed, psychometrically sound assessments are invaluable to good instruction. To illustrate, a helpful approach to PA is offered by the Commission on Instructionally Supportive Assessment. This group, chaired initially by the renowned teacher-advocate for assessment, James W. Popham, was convened in 2001 by five prominent national associations of educators. The commission, which focused on state accountability assessment, identified a number of requirements for tests to be instructionally supportive. Although their work—published in two reports titled *Illustrative Language for an RFP to Build Tests to Support Instruction and Accountability* (Commission on Instructionally Supportive Assessment, 2001b) and *Building Tests to Support Instruction and Accountability: A Guide for Policymakers* (Commission on Instructionally Supportive Assessment, 2001a)—was aimed primarily at state-level policy makers and not measurement professionals, they do provide a valuable, professional perspective.

Caution Against Too Much Enthusiasm

Now, I provide a word of caution about PA: regrettably, PA is often practiced as a puerile approach to measurement, where ardor replaces reasoned judgment. To some, the new assessment models are instantly accepted as progress, sometimes without requisite analysis. It seems that these advocates merely follow the *zeitgeist* of anything but multiple choice in a sort of oniomania—get on board before it is gone. During a recent conference of prominent thinkers in the area, Linn, Baker, and Dunbar (n.d.) observed with understatement that, "Many issues concerning the evaluation of the new forms of assessment being developed have not been sufficiently addressed" (p. 5). They further expanded their comments with the following observation:

> Relatively few of the proponents of alternative approaches to assessment have addressed the question of criteria for evaluating the measures. Simply because the measures are derived from actual performance or relatively high fidelity simulations of performance, it is too often assumed that they are more valid than multiple-choice tests. (p. 5)

An uncritical approach to mental measures is lamentable from two points of view. First, although improvement in assessment is a laudable goal, without evaluative judgment of psychometric characteristics, the goal remains unfulfilled. Second, such uninformed acceptance diminishes the benefits that PA can contribute to meaningful advances in measurement science. Unfortunately, some persons working with PAs are prone to attach a spurious novelty to ideas of the moment simply because they seem to be new.

The scientist must rise above simple excitement and be guided by methods. Our role as measurement professionals demands it, and through it we will contribute to sustained advances in cognitive measurement. We must apply Aristotle's sense of logic and Galileo's exactitude for scientific methods to our work. Progress in technical psychometrics is tough, and it cannot come about without deliberative thought and extensive investigation. Caution is advised against letting eagerness itself become titular advancement.

Recall from chapter 4 during the discussion of validity, that validity generalization is the empirical justification for using scores from one assessment to make inferences to another circumstance. In 2002, the Council of Chief State School Officers commissioned a study to examine the generalizability of performance-based assessments for state-mandated assessment programs. The study investigated a broad range of content areas, including mathematics, reading, writing, social studies, literature, and interdisciplinary studies, to determine whether some state-mandated PAs provide useful information for making generalizations about statewide performance. It was concluded that "the level of generalizability is not as high as that found for more traditional forms of assessment. Thus, other advantages of PAs—such as their consequences for instruction—are necessary to justify their use" (Miller, 2002, p. 5). Persons working with PAs should be mindful to empirically verify using PA results in validity generalization.

Summary

Readers learn here that PA is an important genre for making mental appraisals but only when particular assessments are developed with criteria for merit. This chapter specifically examines the significance of PAs in mental measurement and discusses ways to address validity evaluation to allow for particular score interpretations.

Along the way, I offer examples and practical suggestions. The chapter closes with a word of caution about substituting enthusiasm for rigor when adopting the novel format. Still, PA makes a valuable contribution to measurement science. Our job is to use it to our advantage in understanding constructs.

Chapter 10

Modern Scaling with Item Response Theory

Introduction

The Great Revolution

The Cultural Revolution swept through China for 10 years, beginning in 1966. Revolutionaries led by Mao Tse-tung and other mostly young, radical communists violently thrust a massive shift in public policy and social planning on the most populated country in the world, envisioning an idealized proletariat. Chairman Mao was elevated to the level of a god and worshiped for his beliefs. Except for a few national leaders, no one was to be above anyone else, whether financially, educationally, intellectually, or vocationally. According to Mao, "sameness" was the only route to progress and happiness; utopia would thereby be achieved. The Red Guard (the student army of the communists) slaughtered anyone and destroyed anything that did not fit Mao's ideal. Millions of people were killed or imprisoned, often when merely suspected of being unsympathetic to Mao's vision. Books were burned, and schools (which, it was believed, fostered an intellectual class) were closed. The government looted the bank accounts of millions of ordinary persons. Many more millions of workers were displaced. In sum, forward progress for Chinese society stopped, to be replaced by destitution and starvation. The horror finally began to end when President Nixon visited China in 1973 and made credible his belief that the United States and the West were not a threat, and that China could be welcomed into the family of nations. With this impetus, the Red Guard's reign of terror at last ended, and the Gang of Four (the top-level communist leadership that took power after Mao's death) was arrested. Today, although communists still control China, they are more moderate than the Red Guard. Since 1979, China has adopted an open-door policy and is making remarkable progress in improving the lives of her people.

Like China, measurement has also opened up in the past few decades, with widespread use of the scaling techniques of IRT. To psychometrics, introducing IRT is like overthrowing the old guard and bringing renewed vigor to applied measurement. Many advances in measurement science are a direct result of IRT, such as new techniques for improving the development of tests, more precise estimates of examinee ability, methods for adaptive testing, and progress in specialized areas, such as equating test forms and investigating test bias and differential performance on items.

Contents

In this chapter, I describe IRT and explore its uses for solving practical measurement problems. First, we look at IRT as a theory of mental appraisal with a preliminary description of IRT procedures. Next, we explore some contrasts between IRT and CTT. Thereafter, attention is devoted to discussion of relevant IRT assumptions and explanation of various IRT models, including Rasch-based approaches. Then, there is a description of estimating item and ability parameters, exploring both a purpose and how it is done. Some IRT computer programs, useful for making parameter estimates, are also described. Finally, I offer a brief history of the development of IRT. Because this chapter is introductory, I cite numerous sources where interested readers can turn for more information.

Introductory Description of IRT

What Is IRT?

In the most general sense, IRT is a psychologically based theory of mental measurement that specifies information about latent traits and characteristics of stimuli (e.g., test items and other appraisal exercises) used to represent them. IRT theory maintains that there is an estimable latency for an examinee to any particular trait or proficiency that covers the range $(-\infty, \infty)$ and that its estimation does not depend on particular items or assessment exercises. The concepts of IRT are more determinedly rooted in cognitive science than are the ideas of CTT.

IRT methods address two basic aspects of cognitive appraisal: (a) estimation of characteristics of measurement stimuli (e.g., their difficulty, their power for discrimination), and (b) illation of examinees' latent abilities or proficiencies. In practice, it is necessary to determine with reasonable accuracy relevant features for test items (e.g., difficulty, discrimination), as well as ability or proficiency for some examinees. Significantly, such estimates are made independent of any given item or particular examinee. Further, and just as important, both item characteristics and examinee ability estimates are expressed on the same scale. Thus, building mental appraisal instruments (i.e., tests) is merely—but critically important—a matter of attaching items to a scale representing the latency continuum, irrespective of examinees' ability. In parallel fashion, estimation of a given examinee's ability or trait (i.e., latency) is done on the same scale, regardless of the particular test items employed for that estimate. Another way to express this idea is to realize that it is the relation of an individual examinee to the latency continuum, and not the particular items used for appraisal, that is important; just as the relation of item characteristics to the scale is important regardless of to whom it has been administered.

Obviously, to make the mutualistic estimates, the trait must be expected as extant for the examinees and the items must be suitably targeted. For example, scale estimates for neither items nor examinees can be properly made if calculus items are administered to primary school-age youngsters who, having learned little more than basic addition and subtraction, would not have developed any latency for higher math. Nor can assessment activities geared toward, say, geography be employed in personality appraisal.

Because item and person estimates for IRT are independent of particular items or persons, it is sometimes referred to as *item-free/person-free* measurement or *item invariant/person invariant* measurement. Other names are also used, such as *sample-free* or *person-free item parameter estimates* and *group-independent statistics*, along with *item-free ability estimates*. Any of these names are acceptable. Still, a note of caution on IRT terminology is advised. Occasionally, IRT is classified with a family of statistics called *distribution-free statistics;* IRT statistics are decidedly not nonparametric (with some exceptions noted later); hence, this label is a misnomer and should be eschewed. As we study the methods in this chapter, these names will probably take on more meaning than may be realized at this early introductory stage.

Relation of IRT to CTT

As another point of introduction to IRT—and building on the notion that it is a measurement theory—one should also realize that it is decidedly not a measurement theory that contradicts or competes in idea or direction with CTT. It neither obviates CTT nor necessitates a different way of thinking about mental measurement. Indeed, a clear grasp of CTT is a prerequisite to understanding IRT. In significant and even profound ways, IRT builds on traditional approaches to measurement. Many features of IRT have a corollary in CTT. As one example among many possible cases in point, consider the following extension of CTT: With CTT, a single standard error is used to describe measurement precision for all persons in the population. With IRT, however, many errors, one for each level of ability appraised, can be calculated. One way to gain a conceptual context for IRT is to simply realize that it strengthens CTT by emphasizing the cognitive science in mental measurement and provides a set of powerful mathematics useful to implementing this measurement theory. Because IRT rests on assumptions that are stronger than those associated with CTT, it is sometimes referred to as *strong true score theory*.

A Cautionary Note on Studying IRT

Persons studying measurement science should appreciate that IRT is, first and foremost, a psychologically based theory about mental measurements. However, implementing the theory involves powerful mathematics, including some fascinating aspects of Bayesian statistics. Sometimes persons studying IRT become so immersed in the interesting mathematics that they lose sight of it as a broad theory, focusing only on various, relevant procedures. Clearly, the mathematics available to the theory are interesting and offer advantages over methods of CTT for many practical testing problems, but that fact does not reduce IRT to a mere set of algorithms. Remember, conceptually, it is a theory about latencies and how they may be estimated.

Uses of IRT

IRT is attractive principally because of its applicability to practical testing problems. The following list is illustrative of some measurement circumstances where IRT can be gainfully applied:

- Test and item scaling
- Estimating examinee ability
- Generalizability of test results
- Various item analyses
- Examining test bias and differential item functioning
- Equating test forms
- Vertical equating between test levels
- Estimating construct parameters
- Domain scoring
- Adaptive testing

Clearly, then, IRT can be employed in addressing an array of measurement problems and in widely varied assessment contexts.

IRT and Invariant Measurement for Items and Persons

Not surprisingly, because IRT can be thought of as extending CTT, it addresses shortcomings inherent in traditional approaches. Some of these problems are described in this section.

The Problem of the Lack of an Independent Scale in CTT

As readers of this text realize by now, measurement under precepts of CTT does not have a common perspective that can be uniformly applied across test scales. In other words, we only know the attributes of particular items (e.g., their difficulty or their discrimination) by the performance of a given group of examinees. Likewise, nothing can be known about examinees' ability except how well they performed on the set of items administered. Each important piece of information (whether about items or examinees) is known only relative to the other piece. Thus, substitute different items for those originally used and the measurement of ability or trait is incomparably different. Or, administer the test to a different group of examinees and the characteristics of the items are altogether different. (Again, we see the Heisenberg principle at play: Alter one facet—even by its measurement—and you inescapably change the other.)

In CTT, each instrument comprises a separate measurement of a construct; and, as we learned in chapters 6 and 7, each test has its own scale. The place at which the scale begins (the *zero point*) is arbitrary and unique to a given instrument. However, this system does not adequately describe measurement of latent traits. Recall from the earlier discussion of Thurstonian scaling (see chapter 7) that psychological constructs occupy a latent space that can be quantified along a hypothesized infinity continuum, ranging from $(-\infty, \infty)$. The portion of this continuum that is included in any particular assessment is selected and defined by the test's maker and comprises the appraisal completely but not the construct itself. Easy tests may occupy only a portion along the lower end, and broadly based tests may cover a long range of it. But such is idiosyncratic to a given test. Thus, any two tests—even when aimed at the same construct—probably still do not measure the identical abilities or proficiencies because they are likely measuring different portions of that construct's hypothesized continuum. This means that what is considered "low self-esteem" on, say, a hypothetical My Self-Esteem Instrument A is likely to be different from what is interpreted as "low self-esteem" on My Self-Esteem Instrument B, even if both claim to assess a self-esteem construct and each is associated with evidence that allows valid inferences of its resultant scores. The primary reason is that they do not share a common starting (zero) point. Significantly, it is not possible to view a score on one test as reflective of a score on the other test. Self-esteem (or nearly any other construct) measured at different levels of proficiency is the result, simply and decidedly, of two distinct tests.

Persons new to the concept of no common zero point for mental measures may suggest that this problem can be addressed by simply converting particular test scores into standard score units (viz., z-score). Then, everything can be compared on this moment-common scale, as discussed in chapter 7. However, converting various mental measures to z-score units does not address the problem of no common starting (zero) point; rather, it merely allows for certain linear transformations in scales so the compared instruments have scores expressed in the same metric. Similarly, equating procedures, even when properly employed, will not obviate the circumstance. It still does not establish a common point along the construct. Returning to our example of two instruments appraising self-esteem, if Instrument A and Instrument B have scores that can each be expressed as -1 SD, this does not mean that -1 SD below the mean can be interpreted as the same degree of low self-esteem on both instruments. Each interpretation is relative to what is measured by that test and no other. The suggestion of z-scores is, therefore, an unsatisfactory solution.

Group-Dependent Items and Item-Dependent Groups

Without an identifiable starting point for mental measures—in some sense parallel to those that exist for physical measures (e.g., no height, absence of temperature)—assessment of cognitive processes is left with *relative* comparisons, even between instruments that target the same construct. Such relative interpretation is particularly acute in instruments scaled with CTT. A vivid example of this can be seen in a typical four-response, multiple-choice test item (Figure 10.1).

From even a quick scan of the item, it can be easily realized that students in different classes would probably obtain very different scores on the item. High school students in an 11th-grade American history class might easily achieve class-average correct scores at a rate of more than 80% ($p \geq .80$); whereas 8th graders who have not had such a class might achieve class-average scores at a rate as low as

Figure 10.1

Dichotomously scored, multiple-choice items eligible for item response theory scaling. (*Note:* Correct answer indicated with an asterisk.)

What is the correct date order for these wars in American history—from earliest to most recent?

1. Civil War
2. World War II
3. Gulf War ("Desert Storm")
4. Revolutionary War
5. Korean conflict
6. Vietnam

A. 1,2,3,4,5,6
B. 2,4,5,1,6,3
C. 4,1,2,3,6,5
• D. 4,1,2,5,6,3

25% ($p \approx .25$). Given this reality, two practical measurement problems arise: one about characteristics of the item and the other about trait-level scores for examinees. Let us look at these problems closely because we soon examine how IRT offers a means to satisfactorily address them.

First, consider characteristics of the test item itself. Which p value represents the best estimate of difficulty for the item $p \geq .80$ or $p \approx .25$? "Well," one may say, "it all depends on which group you're referring to—those who have taken the course in American history or those who did not." The answer, of course, is that we do not know which p value best describes the item unequivocally. Because there is no zero point for this construct and every scale's floor is arbitrarily selected by the test's developer, no absolute value of item difficulty is known. The only thing that can accurately be said about item difficulty then is, "It depends on the group being tested!" For the 11th graders, it may be an "easy" item, whereas the 8th graders may find it "difficult." In CTT, then, the difficulty value for the item—usually expressed as the proportion passing—is *group dependent*. CTT does not provide a means to address the fundamental question of absolute values for items that refer to psychological constructs. A test item or exercise can only be defined in terms of a reference group.

Other characteristics, such as an item's discriminating power among examinees of differing abilities, are similarly tied to a particular group of examinees. In CTT, all item characteristics are group dependent. This is an important statement about CTT.

Move your attention now from the test item to a consideration of the examinees. We see here the second problem of CTT—estimating examinees' ability (or proficiency or trait level). Referring to Figure 10.1 again, one imagines that, if a given individual correctly endorsed the item and is enrolled in the American history class, the individual's achievement might be considered typical or average because most people in the class also got it right. However, if the same examinee were in the eighth grade and had not taken such a class, the student's endorsement would be considered atypical. In this example, the eighth grader would be seen as brighter than average—after all, only about one fourth of the class got the item right. So, we are now left with a question about this examinee's ability: Is it typical, or is it high? Again, we do not know for sure. With CTT methods, we only gain information about ability (or proficiency or trait level) by also knowing which group the examinee is in. That is, in CTT, measuring examinee ability is item dependent. This is another important statement about CTT.

So, here we have our two problems in CTT. First, the difficulty value and other characteristics for the item are *group dependent*. Second, estimating examinee ability is *item dependent*. Understanding these dependencies is crucial to learning about IRT.

It is difficult to overstate the degree to which these two practical testing problems—(a) appraising absolute item difficulty and (b) assessing one's ability apart from the context of the particular items used for its measurement—vex classical measurement theorists. If we had an absolute zero point for measuring constructs (or a common scale), all tests could be anchored to it and our twin problems would evaporate. Alas, we have no such starting place for assessment. With CTT alone, we cannot know the characteristics of test items (e.g., difficulty, discriminating power, likelihood of guessing) without tying such knowledge to a particular group of examinees, and we cannot estimate an examinee's ability without referencing it to a given set of items. Clearly, it would be advantageous to identify characteristics of items and exercises independently of any specific group of examinees, just as we would want to ascertain ability without necessarily linking it to particular test items and exercises. IRT gives us a theory and a set of procedures useful to a practical resolution of these two dilemmas.

IRT as Item and Person Invariant Measurement

Methods of IRT allow for calculating characteristics of test items and exercises that are not group dependent. With IRT, item characteristics are said to be *calibrated* to a fixed scale by estimating values for them. Although this does not specifically give all employed test items a common zero point, it does allow different values for item characteristics to be placed logically along a hypothesized common continuum of ability for a given construct. For instance, items can be arranged in order of difficulty or discrimination, or by both characteristics, as well as others. Such serial arrangement of items is not possible under CTT. Understand, however, that even with IRT, there is not one scale for all measurement, rather, just one continuum for a given construct as appraised by a particular measure. IRT does not give us a universal scale.

Further, IRT algorithms are useful for estimating an examinee's ability or proficiency on the same scale used for item placement. Thus, a given individual's ability or proficiency can be stated in terms that do not reference the trait level of others. Although oversimplifying a bit, for purposes of introduction, one may think of IRT as allowing for group-independent item calibration and item-independent ability estimation.

The Notion of Invariant Measurement

Often, students new to IRT find the concept of invariant statistics for item characteristics and ability estimates illogical, and admittedly, at first blush it may seem impossible to fulfill the claims. The very idea may even appear counterintuitive.
However, a familiarity with probability theory and the family of transformations and
regressions that are part of the general linear model illustrates that invariance is an
estimable concept, one that is not new or unique to IRT methods. For example, consider ordinary least squares regression. Here, sample data are used to estimate an
equation that defines a relationship between one or more independent variables
(IVs) and a dependent variable (DV). Once that relationship is specified, it is considered invariant. With appropriate assumptions, the solution fits for all data samples
of the population. When new data are known, they are simply fit to the model equation by applying the constant and coefficients. The relationship between the IVs and
the DV is invariant for that population. In IRT, too, once a relationship is specified,
it holds for all new data from the same population and with appropriate assumptions. (A note of clarification on this description of invariance may be in order, lest
there be misunderstanding: Although the statement about invariance is descriptive
of how the feature can work in IRT, it does not mean that invariance is a statistical
property of linear models generally. It is only used to make the point that once a relationship is mathematically specified, it holds for all data in that population, a characteristic of IRT models.)

The logic for IRT invariance of estimates for item features and ability (or proficiency or trait level) is the same as in regression. Item characteristics and examinee
ability estimates are defined, and new data do not alter those characteristics and estimates as long as the data are from the same population of examinees and assumptions are considered. New test items and additional examinees may enter into the
model, but the relations specified within the model need not be redefined each time.
Instead, additional data augment what is already known about the relationships.

Introduction to IRT Models

Some Commonly Used IRT Models

Thirty-two sonatas constitute the great composer Beethoven's piano repertory, and
there are many more, smaller pieces that are variously classified by musicologists as
additional sonatas or other kinds of works. Similarly, there are many variations of
IRT, called IRT *models*. For purists, not all IRT variants are clearly IRT "models." A
model refers to the mathematical specification of item characteristics and examinee
ability estimates and how they relate to the probability of a particular response that
may be correct, incorrect, or otherwise graded. Some variations of IRT do not meet
this condition. However, such IRT variants are not considered in this chapter. Readers who want to pursue the study of other IRT forms (as well as several advanced
models) may consult van der Linden and Hambleton (1977).

Models are usually identified by the number of characteristics they estimate about the test's stimuli. The *one-parameter model* mathematically defines just a single characteristic for a test item or exercise, a *two-parameter model* defines two item characteristics, and so forth for other models. Some research-based IRT models specify many item parameters. One model identifies 24 parameters, including a variety of them for the whole item, as well as for each response alternative.

Even labeling models is sometimes a bit tricky. Not all IRT models are named for the number of item specifications they mathematically define. Some other models are called by terms that describe their function, such as the *nominal response model,* the *graded response model,* and the *item option characteristic curve model.* Thissen and Steinberg (1986) offer an instructive taxonomy of many IRT models with various characteristics identified, although more models have come into consideration since their schemata were developed.

The three most popular IRT models in use today are the *one-, two-,* and *three-parameter IRT models.* As argot, these models are often abbreviated as 1PL, 2PL, and 3PL. The "PL" stands for parameter estimates of a logistic function. Only an item-difficulty parameter is estimated in the 1PL, and although item discrimination is considered in this model, it is fixed as a constant (and hence, equal) for all items. The 2PL estimates separate difficulty and discrimination parameters for each item, allowing for a more thorough description of an item. The examinee's probability of guessing or *pseudochance* is given attention in the 3PL. After some necessary background, I describe characteristics of the models thoroughly.

As one can easily imagine, each model has particular features, including different advantages and disadvantages. Persons working with IRT should not imagine that estimating more parameters for test stimuli or for examinees is better than estimating fewer of them. Instead, one should decide which model to employ in a given testing context based on information drawn from an array of sources. A logical place to begin gathering the information necessary to make an informed judgment of which model would be best is to consider IRT assumptions.

Assumptions

The Centrality of Assumptions to IRT

Although important assumptions are made for measurement models based on CTT, they do not play as central a role in conceptual understanding of the theory as assumptions do for IRT. In classical theory, the assumptions are tautological and generally cannot be verified. Hence, in validity evaluations of measurement based on CTT, little attention is paid to assumptions. With IRT-based measurement programs, however, exacting attention is directed to providing evidence for the veracity of main assumptions. This is because IRT describes relationships mathematically, and the algorithms are wholly reliant on assumptions.

Specifically, there are four basic assumptions for IRT. Psychometricians use these assumptions to determine whether a given set of data or a particular group of examinees fits an IRT model. Implicit, then, in using IRT is a concomitant responsibility by a test developer to examine the veracity of the assumptions in a particular measurement context.

Unfortunately, proper consideration of IRT assumptions is not easy. They can be theoretically complex and difficult to understand, and it is often complicated to verify them in a particular assessment situation. To make matters worse, for the most part, their viability cannot be determined directly. Still, one can collect indirect information about IRT assumptions and assess them obliquely, so there is the potential for empirical verification.

IRT Assumption: Unidimensionality for Items and Tests

First among the IRT assumptions is *unidimensionality for items and tests*. Whereas unidimensionality has been mentioned several times in earlier chapters, it is discussed here for its relevance to IRT. This assumption implies that within IRT estimation, a given test item or exercise is directly targeted at a single cognitive process, and in theory, it fills that latent space completely. The latent space of a construct can be defined mathematically by calculus integration as a density function. Because a density function is singular (viz., only one can be accommodated at a time), if the mathematical depiction of the construct is reached to solution, it is by definition *unidimensional*.

Albeit the unidimensionality assumption may seem obtuse, students may be happy to learn that unidimensionality density functions are not actually calculated in practical testing situations. Instead, IRT estimates values for this function in terms of item parameters and ability estimates, and from them infers unidimensionality. Still, this is not the end of checking the assumption because a host of exploratory and confirmatory methods exist, including FA, PCA, full information FA (and bifactor FA), structural equation modeling, hierarchal linear modeling, some forms of path analysis, and other multivariate techniques (e.g., canonical analysis).

Of course, the unidimensionality assumption applies only to unidimensional IRT models, including (as most commonly practiced) the Rasch, 1PL, 2PL, and 3PL. The more complex *multidimensional IRT models* do not adopt it. They have different issues of structural integrity, and I explain them later in this chapter.

IRT Assumption: Local Independence

Another IRT assumption closely related to unidimensionality is *local independence*. This assumption means that an examinee's response to a given, specific measure (whether a whole test or just one test item) reflects an independent and autonomous reference to a latent trait in cognition. In other words, a cognitive process that inflects the reading construct is tapped autonomously during an examinee's endorsement of a reading-specific item. Other aspects of cognition (e.g., motivation, inattention) are presumed to be unused by the examinee during such item endorsement. Of course, psychologists correctly inform us that the human mind is actually more complex than this undemanding model, but the simpler view informs our measurement theory, so we adopt the proposition and use it as best as we can.

To understand this assumption, one should focus on a key word in the definition—*independent*. In practical testing situations, *independence* means that when an examinee responds to the stimulus of a test item or exercise, he or she approaches the stimulus without also thinking about other items or exercises. In the ideal situation, for example, when answering question 20, the examinee did not gain clues to a correct response from the information provided in an earlier question. Regrettably, in poorly constructed tests, this assumption is violated all too often.

The rationale for local independence is straightforward. When an examinee uses information from the first-appearing item, there is a degree of learning (regardless of whether what is learned is correct or incorrect), and thus examinee ability or proficiency is altered by the time the second-appearing item is reached. In technical language, the latent space of the construct measured by the second item is interfered with by the latent space of the first item. In theory, at least, each response to test stimuli should be independent of other latent spaces. To accommodate this problem in theory, we do not use latent space to specify responses for individual items; rather, latent space defines the ability or proficiency needed to answer all the items collectively.

Mathematically, the proposition of local independence may be represented as shown in Equation 10.1:

$$\text{Prob}(U_1, U_2, \ldots, U_n | \theta) = P(U_1 | \theta) \, P(U_2 | \theta) \ldots P(U_n | \theta)$$

$$= \prod_{i=1}^{n} P(U_i | \theta), \tag{10.1}$$

where $1, 2, 3 \ldots n =$ items (exercises) and

$P(U_i | \theta) =$ probability of a correct response on an item for any
particular examinee of ability θ.

The key to understanding Equation 10.1—and the local independence assumption—lies in knowing the $P(U_i | \theta)$ expression. The term P expresses probability, and as cited earlier, theta (θ) represents examinee trait level or ability. Thus, the probability of responding correctly to each item on the test is conditional on trait level or ability, presumed by the assumption to be just from the tapped aspect of cognition and no other cognitive processes. By the rule of additivity, then, the property of local independence exists as the product of the probabilities of responses on a set of independent items for a given examinee of ability theta (θ).

This equation is central to our work because it holds a foundational precept of IRT—that the response to a test item (expressed as a probability of endorsing a correct answer on individual items) is based wholly and completely on the examinee's ability (i.e., it is locally independent). In the aggregate sense of a whole test score, it is no more than the product of the individual item probabilities.

There is a direct relationship between the assumptions of local independence and unidimensionality. Local independence exists when the latent space for a mental measure is completely specified, which is also a condition for unidimensionality.

Lord (1980) demonstrated in his classic text on measurement that when the unidimensionality assumption is met, so too is the local independence assumption. Hence, local independence is itself a condition of unidimensionality. By this logic, some persons hold that local independence is actually subsumed under the unidimensionality assumption. However, the reverse is not necessarily true. Unidimensionality carries conditions beyond just local independence. By itself, the local independence assumption does not satisfy unidimensionality completely. It is said, therefore, that local independence is a necessary but insufficient condition for unidimensionality.

The assumption of local independence is even more acute in the case of *not-reached items* and *omitted items*. In IRT estimation of item parameters, not-reached items are generally excluded from consideration (except in the case of speeded or tightly timed tests), whereas data from omitted items are used in gathering item information for overall ability estimation.

IRT Assumption: Item Characteristic Curve

The third major IRT assumption is the *item characteristic curve assumption*. This assumption holds that defined characteristics of test stimuli (whether items, exercises, or some other) are reliably estimable functions. In most contexts with IRT, there are three such characteristics, including item difficulty, item discrimination, and pseudochance. Each is estimated as a probability function, and because the functions are integral to the structural model of IRT, they are estimated for the population. Hence, the item characteristics are known by their *parameter estimates*. A parameter, of course, is a mathematical limit, and generally inferred from a sample to a population, such as $\overline{X}$ to μ or SD to σ. From this logic, then, stems the 1PL, 2PL, and 3PL models, respectively, estimating one, two, or three parameters of item characteristics.

Logically, then, too, the examinee's trait level is also an estimable function, and again as a probability of response. Hence, with IRT, estimates are of both item parameters and a single person parameter, namely, ability.

The graphical depictions of these characteristics are central to IRT, and we explore them thoroughly, after noting a final IRT assumption.

IRT Assumption: Certainty of Response

Some researchers specify a fourth IRT assumption, although others consider it implicit within the unidimensionality assumption, that is, the *presumption of optimal performance*. This assumption is not often cited; I mention it only briefly here because it was discussed in chapter 3 during consideration of CTT. The assumption holds that if an examinee possesses the latent ability to respond to a stimulus, then he or she will do so to the best of his or her ability. On first blush, the assumption may appear self-evident, but closer examination shows that the assumption presents a reasonable proposition. Consider the circumstance when an examinee responds incorrectly to an item. Here, by the assumption, the examinee's trait level in the measured construct was insufficiently developed to evidence a correct choice or proper endorsement of a given response. However, significantly, the opposite is not true. If the examinee's response to the item is correct, it does not necessarily mean that the response was solely due to sufficient ability or proficiency. After all, the correct response may have been a lucky guess, or perhaps partial knowledge was employed. If the item had been correctly endorsed by a factor unrelated to ability (e.g., lucky guess), test interpretation would be impossible, hence, the assumption.

We presume a correct response was certainly caused by the examinee's maximum effort, regardless of whether the item was easy or difficult. Such reasoning is vital to IRT because, in the theory, the probability of a correct response is a direct function of one's ability. Measurement theory does not account for less than maximal effort unless such behavior is treated as a distinct factor in a research context.

Understanding these four major assumptions of IRT is necessary to comprehend the mathematics of the IRT models, as well as the richness of IRT as a measurement theory.

ICCs and IRCs

In practice, the estimable functions of IRT (for both an item and an examinee) are usually displayed graphically as an item trace line that is placed along the ability and probability continuums. These are called *item characteristic curves (ICCs)*. By some authorities, the ICC should be referred to as the *IRC* for *item response curve,* because it originates from examinee-observed responses.

Most often, the ICC represents parameters of the 1PL, 2PL, or 3PL model, but the ICC can also represent other characteristics implicit in more advanced models. Our discussion, however, is limited to estimates of just three item parameters. Then, too, it is worthwhile to appreciate that empirical ICCs can display item descriptions under CTT, but they are seldom prepared. In fact, the estimation of item parameters, as well as the construction and interpretation of ICCs in graphical form, is highlighted as an area that shows stark contrast between the approaches of IRT and CTT. This difference is easily appreciated when one realizes that CTT is focused mostly on the entire test, whereas IRT gives more attention to the individual test stimuli.

Specifying ICCs Generally

Probably the simplest way to explain ICCs is to present a graphical depiction, as is done in Figure 10.2, and describe its parts. Notice the two axes, the abscissa labeled *ability* (θ), and the ordinate identified as *probability*, $P(\theta)$, as shorthand for *probability of theta*. Most often, the x-axis is labeled *ability* despite our realizing this term's limiting implication. In some nonachievement contexts, such as with personality appraisal, the term *trait level* is more accurate and may be more generic regardless. The plotted values are shown as the smoothed *item response function*, technically an *ogive*. It looks like a cumulative distribution function, and in fact, it is one; it is for item characteristics, however, and not for population values, as one may be more used to seeing.

Figure 10.2

Ogive representing one item.

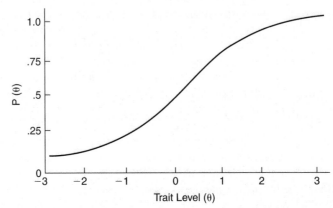

The abscissa (horizontal axis) represents ability as a progression from low to high, left to right. In IRT work, this ability scale is normalized, placing zero in the center and symmetrically counting moments away from there. As with any normal frequency, the scale actually can represent a continuum along $(-\infty, \infty)$, but such long range is not practical and usually four *moments* (showing the range ±3 SD units) are sufficient to describe the ability range for nearly all populations.

The ordinate (vertical axis) displays probability of theta from 0 to 1, bottom to top. This scale is self-evident, showing probability, logically, from none to absolute along the range (0, 1). Together, the scales allow a trace line to describe a functional relationship between characteristics of an item and the trait level of the examinee. This is consistent with what we learned about the local independence assumption, namely, that probability of a correct response is conditioned on just one aspect of cognition—trait level.

It is common for the ogive of ICCs to plot to a sort of lazy S shape, but they may assume other forms to convey the information provided by the function. In all cases, however, ogives rise *monotonically*—that is, their slope is always progressive. In the lazy S design, it begins low, rises, and then tapers off as it reaches its upper limit, but the line never actually touches either the lower or upper limit. It *asymptotes*, a term we learned in chapter 7.

Now, notice the ICCs presented in Figure 10.3. This graphic shows item response functions for three items simultaneously, so we can see differences among them. Note that the lower asymptote varies among the items. For item 1, it is about .1; for item 2, it is slightly above .25; and for item 3, it is near .5. This lower asymptote has important implications for lower-ability examinees as it indicates the "starting" probability for the item trace line. No measurement is inferred below this starting point.

An interpretation of the different starting points for the various ogives is that item 1 appears more difficult for low-ability examinees (about 10% probability of responding correctly to the item). In contrast, item 3 affords nearly 50% probability of an examinee of the same ability obtaining a correct response. For examinees of low ability, these items clearly present varying levels of difficulty. Because examinees at this end of the scale have such a low probability of correct endorsement, this beginning point

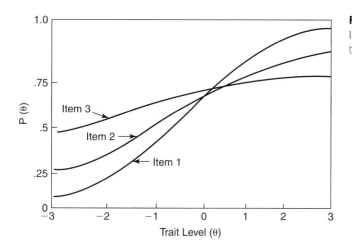

Figure 10.3
Item characteristic curves for three items (1, 2, 3).

is referred to as a guessing, or more currently, a *pseudochance* value. Looking at the other asymptote, one sees that for examinees of high ability (above 2 on the θ scale), there is a parallel interpretation at the upper end of the scale. It is readily apparent which item is easier (i.e., has a high probability of success) for this group.

The Inflection Point

One aspect of ICCs that is especially important to IRT is the point that is half the distance between the upper and lower asymptotes, where the slope is maximal. This place is called the *inflection point,* and on perfectly suited items, it represents the point at which the probability of a correct response is .5, when the c parameter (explained in the next paragraph) is 0. In other words, the inflection point is where the odds of an examinee responding correctly to an item change from less than 50% to greater than 50%.

When the $c > 0$, however, the inflection point is technically where the probability is $(1 + c)/2$. Below the inflection point $P(\theta) < .5$, whereas the opposite is true above the inflection point. For an easy item, the odds may change at some low point along the theta scale; conversely, for a difficult item, the odds may not change until very high along the ability continuum. When an examinee's ability on the theta scale is also at the item's inflection point, the item is said to be perfectly matched in difficulty to that individual. The goal of many testing programs is to present to examinees items that match their ability at .5. Of course, this is easier said than done because any group of examinees does not have a single ability, but a distribution of them.

Figure 10.4 shows the same three ICCs that appear in Figure 10.3, but with their inflection points noted on the theta scale. Here, item 1 has an inflection point at $-.5$. For items 2 and 3, the inflections points are at 0 and $+1$, respectively.

Studying this threshold point is important to work in IRT for a number of reasons. First, it shows the ability level at which the item is maximally discriminating (viz., the

Figure 10.4
Item characteristic curves for three items (1, 2, 3) with inflection points identified.

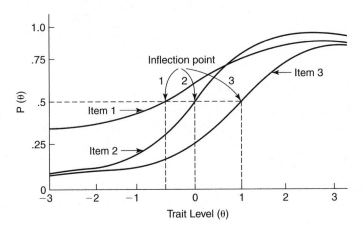

slope of the curve is zero). An item that has discriminating odds different from .5 yields less information about ability because the examinee may find the item either too easy or too difficult for meaningful measurement. Given this information, then, we can determine the suitability of presenting a particular item to a given examinee.

By the same reasoning, threshold is also important as an indicator of the item's difficulty level, as denoted along the theta scale.

IRT Models

Introduction to the Models

We have learned by now that there are many IRT models, typically named for the number of test stimuli characteristics they estimate. However, IRT also estimates an ability parameter for each examinee. If, for instance, a three-parameter model is employed in a given testing context, there are four parameters to be determined: one for each item characteristic of interest and one for the ability of an examinee.

I discuss the common IRT models first; then, I briefly mention more complex models. The 1PL concentrates on item difficulty almost exclusively, whereas the 2PL brings attention to item discrimination and item difficulty. The 3PL attends to both item difficulty and item discrimination, and it adds the consideration of a pseudochance probability of getting the item right. Actually, in technical estimation, no parameter is ignored; rather, its value is fixed as a constant for all examinees in the population. That is, when using the 1PL, the second and third item characteristics are set at constant values.

There are important distinctions between the 1PL and other models. The two- and three-parameter models follow the mathematical form of the IRT formula directly. The one-parameter model is a variant of the three-parameter model and was developed independently of other item response models. I describe the one-parameter model, but its meaning is more apparent after first gaining a familiarity with the basics of the two- and three-parameter models.

The Likelihood Function

In the simplest IRT form, a probability function is specified. That is, an examinee of a particular ability level (i.e., theta) has a certain probability of getting an item correct. This form was specified in Equation 10.1 in the discussion of the local independence assumption, and is also seen in Figures 10.2 and 10.3. As should be clear by now, this is a *probabilistic function*.

It was shown in Equation 10.1 that the expression $P(U_i|\theta)$ is the probability of a correct response on an item for any particular examinee of ability θ. The analog is the probability of an incorrect response on the item, expressed as Q in Equation 10.2:

$$Q_i = 1 - P(U_i|\theta). \tag{10.2}$$

However, when the probabilistic function is actually put into practice with observed data, the name is no longer appropriate because the IRT model actually specifies the sum of many probabilities, one for each test item, as discussed in the previous local independence and unidimensionality assumption. This being the case, the expression for the joint probability is termed the *likelihood function*. The likelihood function is the joint probability of getting several items correct or incorrect, using observed data, and is shown in Equation 10.3:

$$L(u_1, u_2, \ldots u_n|\theta) = \prod_{i=1}^{n} P_i^{u_i} Q_i^{1-u_i}. \tag{10.3}$$

This expression is the likelihood of a correct or incorrect response to the first item times the likelihood of a correct or incorrect response to the second item times the likelihood of a correct or incorrect response to the last item. It is the "joint likelihood." For instance, suppose the following response pattern on a five-item test is observed for an examinee where 1 is correct and 0 is incorrect: $u_1 = 1$, $u_2 = 1$, $u_3 = 1$, $u_4 = 0$, $u_5 = 0$. The first three items are endorsed correctly, but the last two are not. Hence, the likelihood function is as follows:

$$L(u_1, u_2, u_3, u_4, u_5|\theta) = (P_1^1 Q_1^0)(P_2^1 Q_2^0)(P_3^1 Q_3^0)(P_4^0 Q_4^1)(P_5^0 Q_5^1).$$

Or, it is more simply stated as

$$= P_1 P_2 P_3 Q_4 Q_5.$$

When this function is expressed along the θ scale, there is, of course, a range of values. The θ value that is at maximum for an examinee is the *maximum likelihood estimate* for that person. This is the reported θ score, considered his or her ability or proficiency on the latent trait.

Also, as a practical matter, because each probability is limited to the range (0, 1), calculation of the joint probabilities (i.e., their product) will become a very small number as the test length increases. For long tests, it will even approach zero. To make the estimation more comprehensible, then, the likelihood values are transformed to a log scale, providing more range for interpretation and a different specification for scale intervals. As is seen shortly, expressing values on the log scale is almost the same as expressing them in a normal number metric, although a small transformation

Figure 10.5

Log likelihood function for two examinees, with Maximum likelihood estimate shown.

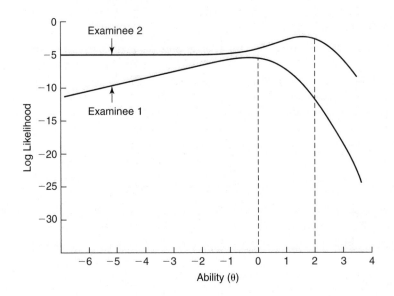

constant is needed to maintain the ratio between scales. In addition, it is much simpler to manipulate values on a log scale than to do so with numbers in a normal metric. For these reasons, a final theta estimate is expressed in log units, along a standardized *logit scale*. This scale is the log expression of the joint likelihood function and values are referred to as the *log likelihood*.

The log likelihood estimates for two examinees are illustrated in Figure 10.5. Note particularly the *maximum likelihood estimate* for each examinee. For the first examinee, this value appears at about 0, whereas it is considerably higher (approximately 2) for the second person, indicating much higher ability or proficiency in the trait. The maximum likelihood estimates are the most common form for calculating values that represent IRT parameters, although there are also other methods.

More on Working with the Log Scale

The transformation from real numbers to log scale is accomplished by incorporating e, the base of the natural logarithms: $e \approx 2.718281828$. As IRT calibrations are often purposed to achieve distribution functions, it is necessary to add a constant to the log scale to allow its frequency function to closely approximate a normal frequency function. The constant is 1.702, although it is usually rounded to 1.7 and, in equations, it is denoted by D. This value is used because it equates to an upper limit of the interval for the logistic frequency function, ranging (0, 1.702).

A necessary and fortunate artifact of this transformation is that there is little loss of information. When the transformation is supplemented with a constant to keep the adjustment uniform across the range of the scale, the frequency function for the normal curve and the logistic curve are approximately equal, a point shown graphically in Figure 10.6. With standardized values, the difference between the curves is less than 0.01 units at its widest point (Birnbaum, 1968).

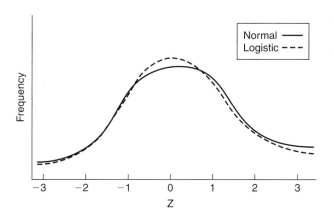

Figure 10.6
Frequency functions for normal and logistic curves.

Much of the literature uses a standardized notation of *phi* (Φ) to represent the normal ogive and *psi* (Ψ) for the logistic ogive. As a side note, there are some IRT software programs that incorporate algorithms that do use the normal ogive and evaluate it using approximations that are slightly more accurate than the logistic ogive. However, they are not widely used, in large part because of the intractable math.

The Two-Parameter Model

In the 1950s and again later, Birnbaum (1958, 1968), suggested a nonlinear, logistic model to describe two distinct parameters for items. The two parameters he described are discrimination and difficulty. Of course, these features for items are classic, but in IRT their description is manifestly syntactic. To understand these characteristics for items, first look at the parameters graphically, which will aid in understanding the mathematical definition. Figure 10.7 displays an ICC with these two characteristics for each of two items labeled items 1 and 2.

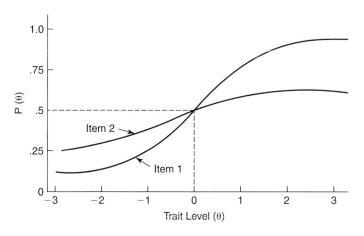

Figure 10.7
Item characteristic curves with identical inflection points but different slopes.

Notice that the ICCs are not identical. They have different slopes, although both curves inflect at theta zero and $P = .5$. Again, as theta increases, the likelihood of a correct response also increases. It is evident in Figure 10.7 that the slope reflects this feature for items. The differences in slopes for the two items reveal an inequality in *discrimination* for examinees of varying ability. For item 1, discrimination is gradual for persons with low ability, then, at about the value of −1 theta, the discriminating characteristics rise more steeply, until at about +1 theta the discrimination fades for higher-ability examinees.

Contrast this slope to the discrimination shown for item 2. For this item, all along the theta scale, the discrimination is much less pronounced, despite the fact that it follows the general form of item 1's slope. This characteristic is called the *discrimination parameter* or the *a parameter*. When the slope of an item is especially steep at one point along the theta scale, the resultant ICC will assume the form of a Guttman scale. Observing the discriminating properties of items through ICCs is a fundamental task of examining items with IRT.

Two more items with yet different characteristics are shown in Figure 10.8. Here, they are labeled items 3 and 4. Significantly, realize that the slopes of items 3 and 4 are virtually identical in the middle but that the inflection points (and hence, the thresholds) are far apart on the theta scale. In other words, the left-to-right shift of the ICCs is what differentiates items 3 and 4, not their slopes. Clearly, then, for equally able examinees, item 4 is more difficult because it is located higher along the theta scale, despite the fact that the discrimination is fairly similar. This difference in position along the theta scale for the ICC shows a divergence in difficulty; hence, this parameter is called the *difficulty parameter* or the *b parameter*.

In probabilistic models, the theta value that represents a 50:50 chance for an examinee to respond correctly or incorrectly to the item is believed to be the optimal place for an index of item difficulty, as noted previously. If the odds are greater than 50:50 for a correct or incorrect choice, the item is considered relatively easy for an examinee. Conversely, when the odds are less than 50% for a correct response, the item is difficult, relative to ability. This optimal place on the theta scale is *b*, our difficulty parameter.

Figure 10.8

Item characteristic curves with same slopes but different inflection points.

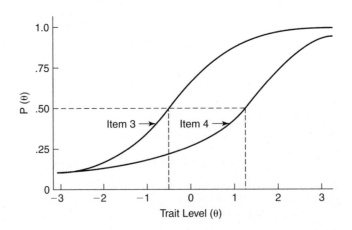

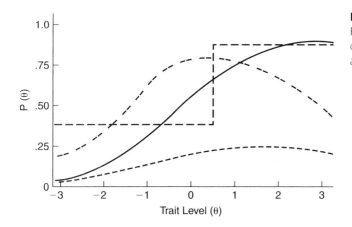

Figure 10.9
Four item characteristic curves with different slopes and inflection points.

Sometimes, in IRT, an item difficulty value is referred to as a *location parameter* because it locates the theta value at which the probability function is $.5[P_i(\theta) = .5]$. Another name for this parameter is the *item threshold*. In fact, even some computer programs (e.g., BILOG-MG) refer to this parameter by the name *threshold*.

So, in brief, Birnbaum defined two parameters for items along a nonlinear, prob- abilistic function called an ICC. The parameters he specified are the *a* parameter re- vealing discrimination (shown in the item's slope) and the *b* parameter reflecting relative difficulty (shown by the placement of the threshold along the theta scale, the left-to-right shift).

Because these two characteristics for items—discrimination and difficulty—are so commonly cited in IRT work, it is worthwhile to study them with some additional examples. Four ICCs are presented in Figure 10.9. For each item note and interpret the discrimination (*a*) and difficulty (*b*) parameters.

Syntactic Description of the *a* and *b* Parameters

With the background in ICC interpretation in place, we are now ready to describe the discrimination and difficulty parameters syntactically, that is, by their mathemat- ical definition. I begin by assimilating several pieces of information we have already learned. First, we know that we are describing characteristics for dichotomously scored test items. Second, we presume that for most present-day IRT work, there are just three characteristics to be considered: discrimination, difficulty, and a lower as- ymptote, which for the moment is presumed to be 0 (remember the upper asymp- tote is ignored for practical discussion). Further, each item characteristic is a mathematical parameter to be estimated as a logistic distribution. Last, to give these parameter estimations a context, we consider them in the ICC, which itself displays the probability of getting a correct response to the items as a function of an exami- nee's ability and other item characteristics.

This is a lot of information to be cobbled together into a single equation. How- ever, it can be done rather efficiently, as shown in Equation 10.4. Although initially this equation may appear formidable, it is straightforward, and given the information already discussed, we can begin to approach it meaningfully. Appreciate, too, the centrality of this expression to IRT. For this reason, I describe it in detail:

$$P_i(\theta) = \frac{e^{Da_i(\theta - b_i)}}{1 + e^{Da_i(\theta - b_i)}}(i = 1, 2, \ldots, n), \tag{10.4}$$

where i = indexes of any particular item or exercise,

b_i = item difficulty parameter,

a_i = item discrimination parameter,

$P_i(\theta)$ = probability of correct response on item i for a given examinee of ability θ, and

D = 1.7, the scaling constant.

Note in Equation 10.4 that the left side is just our familiar function, namely, the probability of success on item i is a function of one's ability, expressed as a theta value.

For the right side of Equation 10.4, begin by focusing attention on the numerator. Recall from earlier discussion that the e is the base of the natural logarithms. By algebra, the exponent of e indicates transformation to the log scale. Next, following the order of operations, move to clear the parentheses in the exponent. To do this, one simply subtracts from theta the value of b for a given item. Remember, the b represents a particular point along the theta scale, the difficulty parameter. To make things a bit easier, we can anticipate b will have a value in the range ±3 because we learned earlier that whereas, theoretically, ability may range $(-\infty, \infty)$, the log scale is standardized and hence any b value rarely reaches more than ±3 units, just like z-scaled range. We now have our difference value from the parenthetical calculation.

Next, consider the term of the exponent Da_i. This is the point where the a parameter enters the logistic function. The D is the constant (viz., ≈ 1.7) employed in logistic calculations to force the logistic frequency function to closely approximate the normal frequency function. The term is the product of the constant and the value for the a parameter. This value is then multiplied by the earlier-obtained parentheses value to yield a grand product. We now have a single value for our exponent. Obviously, this exponent applies to e, the base of the natural log scale.

Having arrived at a value for the numerator, we can now solve the denominator in Equation 10.4. This is, as the saying goes, "a piece o' cake!" Note that nearly all the terms in the denominator are the same as in the numerator; hence, their description is as I have already stated. A "1" is added to the denominator to complete calculation of the probability function.

The final part of the expression (viz., $[i = 1, 2, \ldots n]$) is readily recognized by persons with even rudimentary algebra knowledge. It merely specifies that the functional expression applies to all items in the set. The significance of this subscript is that because it applies to every term, one can see that all ICCs share the same functional form, differing only in their parameters.

Finally, it is worthwhile to note an alternate to Equation 10.4, shown in some texts. The alternate formula—an even more compact expression—is given in Equation 10.5. Equations 10.4 and 10.5 are functionally equivalent:

$$P_i(\theta) = [1 + e^{-Da_i(\theta - b_i)}]^{-1}. \qquad (10.5)$$

The Three-Parameter Model

The three-parameter logistic model is employed in assessment programs less often than the one- or two-parameter models, but understanding the third characteristic for parameter estimation is important to grasping a more complete picture of ICCs. This third characteristic adds to the two-parameter model and the accompanying ICC a consideration of guessing by examinees of comparatively low ability. To understand how the phenomenon of examinees guessing at a response is treated in IRT, it may be useful to realize a misconception about it that is often seen in traditional assessment.

Popular belief (especially among laypersons) holds that examinees of low ability have a chance of guessing correctly on test items in direct proportion to the number of response alternatives. By this well-liked reasoning, on four-response, multiple-choice items, the chance of correctly guessing on an item is one in four, or 25%. There are some scoring algorithms in computer scoring programs that attempt to "correct for guessing" by employing this logic. Unfortunately, this reasoning is faulty most of the time. In fact, it holds true in only one particular circumstance—when the examinee has no idea about the item or anything in any of the responses and simply selects one of the response alternatives blindly. Even in IRT work, when no information is known about the examinee's responses to other items, a guess is presumed to be 1 divided by the number of response alternatives.

Researchers have long realized that random guessing, even by low-ability examinees, occurs in testing situations only occasionally. More often, examinees do not wildly guess at test items, but employ some strategy for selecting a response, even when they are unsure of the correct choice. Hughes and Trimble (1965) identified six combinations of information that might influence an examinee's response to an item, including partial information that is correct, partial information that is incorrect, and complete information that is incorrect. Lord (1974) speculated that well-crafted items have incorrect response alternatives that draw low-ability examinees to them as positive evidence for item discrimination. Interestingly, according to Lord, because low-ability examinees are drawn to incorrect responses by their faulty knowledge or incorrect deduction, the probability value for such guessing is typically lower than one would expect for guessing; thus, examinees may actually achieve a lower score than would be attained by random guessing.

In any event, in IRT, the third parameter of the ICC attempts to account for a response selection strategy used by very low-ability examinees. This parameter is the c parameter in IRT models. As we saw earlier, in technical discussion, it is referred to as the *pseudochance level*, but often it is simply called the "guessing parameter." In the ICC for a three-parameter IRT model, the c parameter is the lower asymptote, the bound of the curve as it approaches zero. Technically, c is the value the probability

Figure 10.10

Item characteristic curve with parameters labeled.

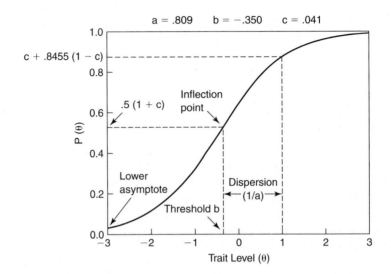

takes at the lowest numerical value of theta. Graphically, it is the point at which the ogive begins, and it appears on the left side of the ICC (see Figure 10.2, 10.3, or 10.4).

Formulaically, the pseudochance level adds a *c* to the mathematical form of the two-parameter model. The full three-parameter logistic model is shown in Equation 10.6. All terms of the equation are as defined for Equation 10.4, with the addition of *c*. This important formula should be carefully studied because it represents the fullest expression of IRT as most commonly practiced in testing today:

$$P_i(\theta) = c_i + (1 - c_i)\frac{e^{Da_i(\theta - b_i)}}{1 + e^{Da_i(\theta - b_i)}} \quad (i = 1, 2, \dots, n). \qquad (10.6)$$

A graphical representation of the full three-parameter logistic model, with item characteristics identified, is given in Figure 10.10. Studying the parts of Figure 10.10 will aid in understanding.

Considerations of the Three-Parameter Model

When considering the number of parameters to use in a particular assessment context, one should follow procedures for empirical assessment of the fit of data to a given IRT model. A number of authors (e.g., Embretson & Reise, 2000; Hambleton, Swaminathan, & Rogers, 1991; van der Linden & Hambleton, 1997) provide technical guidance.

To untrained persons, it would seem that the choice is easy—the 3PL because it is based on the most information. Yet, be cautious in this consideration because 3PL is known to have serious limitations. First, there is a sort of illogic to the 3PL notion in that it regards guessing as integral to ability or proficiency. This seems nonsensical on the face of it. Also, algebraically, calculations involved in parameter estimates with 3PL can easily degrade proper estimation of the *a* and *b* parameters when there are out-of-normal examinee response patterns, such as all correct, all incorrect, or anomalous patterns. Finally, in practical application, estimates of ability and estimates of slope are highly correlated anyway so that often a lot of mathematics is employed for little practical gain. Still, there are occasions when 3PL is appropriate—again, use model fit indices as your guide.

Sample Calculations for Conditional Probability in the Three-Parameter Model

With explanation of the ICC of the three-parameter logistic model in hand, it will be useful to work through a few examples of calculating the probability of a correct response $[P_i(\theta)]$ for a given set of parameters.

To begin, take any parameter values within range: say, $a = .9$, $b = -.4$, and $c = .2$. Now, using a handheld calculator with exponent and reciprocal key functions, one may calculate the conditional probability of a correct response using Equation 10.6. In this example, the conditional probability equals .916.

Because knowing these calculations is critical to understanding IRT, I demonstrate the steps. Keeping with our example (i.e., $a = .9$, $b = -.4$, and $c = .2$) as given parameters and theta as 1 for a starting point, begin the solution by first reducing the fraction portion of Equation 10.6 to a more convenient form, as in Equation 10.7. This equation results from division of both the numerator and denominator by $e^{Da_i(\theta - b_i)}$; it is equivalent to Equation 10.5:

$$P_i(\theta) = c_i + (1 - c_i)\frac{1}{1 + e^{-Da_i(\theta - b_i)}}. \tag{10.7}$$

Clearing the initial parentheses, $(1 - c_i)$, further simplifies the equation to the form expressed in Equation 10.8:

$$P_i(\theta) = c_i + \frac{1 - c_i}{1 + e^{-Da_i(\theta - b_i)}}. \tag{10.8}$$

Now solve for terms with the simplified Equation 10.8. (Note: Watch for positive and negative values and decimal points.) Follow these steps:

STEP 1: Calculate the numerator, which is simply 1 minus c: $1 - .2 = .8$.
STEP 2: Solve the exponent in the denominator, starting within the parentheses, for theta minus the b value: $1 - (-.4) = 1.4$.
STEP 3: Multiply this times both the a value (.9) and the scaling constant (-1.7): $1.4 \times .9 \times -1.7 = -2.142$.
STEP 4: Take the exponential value. (Recall that e^x is a number applied as an exponent to the base of the natural logarithm, or $e \approx 2.718281828$.) Fortunately, this calculation can be conveniently done with the e^x key on a handheld calculator: .117419768.
STEP 5: Add 1 as the constant: $1 + .117419768 = 1.117419768$. This completes calculation of the denominator.

STEP 6:   With values for both the numerator and the denominator ready, convert the fraction to its decimal equivalent by simply dividing .8 by 1.117419768 to get .71593507. (Alternatively, use the reciprocal key for the denominator [$1/x$ = .894918837] and multiply the result by the numerator [.8: .894918837 × .8 = .71593507].)

STEP 7:   Add the c value (.2) to this decimal equivalent: .71593507 + .2 = .91593507, or .916, for the conditional probability of this item.

For practice, one could calculate the respective conditional probabilities for the parameter values given previously at various points along the theta scale, using the following values: 3, 2.5, 2, 1.5, 1, .5, 0, −.5, −1, −1.5, −2, −2.5, and −3. Then, plot the values on a grid. The ICC should assume a familiar ogive shape. In fact, it will be just like that shown in Figure 10.10. One can set this up as a simple Microsoft Excel macro, and by doing so, any number of probabilities can be calculated quickly for given theta values and item parameters. The resultant curves can also be plotted as ICC using the Excel Graph Wizard or (and likely more technically accurate) through a plotting program such as Sigma Plot. Of course, a macro can also be written in SAS or SPSS to map these functions graphically.

The One-Parameter IRT Model and Rasch

As mentioned previously, the 1PL is a peculiar model that does not follow all stipulations of the traditional two- and three-parameter models. To some—especially proponents of Rasch IRT modeling—it is a separate IRT model altogether, whereas for others, it is a special case of the three-parameter IRT model. Both arguments are discussed in this section.

The Rasch Model

The Rasch IRT model is a specialized single-parameter IRT-based approach to measurement that was developed separately by Georg Rasch (1960, 1966), a Danish mathematician working from antecedents dating back to Thurstone's (1925) scaling explorations in the 1920s. At the heart of the Rasch model is a philosophical conceit. Rasch proponents believe that a mental measure is the ratiocination of a discovery process. The test developer first identifies a particular construct for appraisal and then prepares stimuli that require just the relevant aspects of cognition. In other words, the assessment model is first selected and then test items or exercises are prepared by criteria so they fit into the Rasch model. The only psychometric consideration lies in determining the difficulty that the stimuli present to an examinee for endorsement. When the examinee responds to a set of items conceived in this way, trait level is directly manifest. A correct response to difficult items means more trait is shown; incorrect responses mean less trait.

The approach has theoretical appeal but is demanding to put into practice in pure form. It presumes that stimuli are unambiguously focused on just the construct of interest and that examinees employ only relevant cognitive processes. Test stimuli cannot be misconstrued and examinees must put forth maximal effort during response. In other words, in the Rasch approach to IRT, unidimensionality, local independence, and maximal effort are not casual assumptions. They are the bedrock of the approach. In contrast, with more traditional IRT, which acknowledges imperfection in instruments and some flexibility on the part of examinees (e.g., discrimination and pseudochance), a set of data is tried out with varying IRT models to determine which is most robust. To proponents of Rasch methods, traditionalists seem to put the cart before the horse.

In the Rasch model, an examinee's odds of success on any given test item are solely the product of that person's ability and the difficulty of the item. Hence, the presumption in Rasch measurement—contrary to complete IRT models—is that b values for item difficulty are group dependent, if the scale is ability centered. By this logic, then, the validity of considering discrimination and even pseudochance as not dependent on characteristics of a particular group is denigrated. In the model, the scale is $(-\infty, \infty)$, and the odds for a correct response by an examinee on item i are given in Expression 10.9:

$$\frac{\theta_a^*}{b_i^*}. \tag{10.9}$$

The asterisk used for the Rasch model indicates that with this approach ability is not independent of item difficulty. In addition, the odds for an event occurring are defined as $P/(1 - P)$, per usual. On a test, the chances for a correct response are expressed as the ratio of the probability of a correct response to the probability of an incorrect response. Thus, the equivalence of the ability odds with the chances of correct response odds is stated in Equation 10.10:

$$\frac{\theta_a^*}{b_i^*} = \frac{P_i(\theta_a)}{1 - P_i(\theta_a)}. \tag{10.10}$$

The expression can be simplified to Equation 10.11:

$$P_i(\theta_a) = \frac{\theta_a^*}{\theta_a^* + b_i^*}. \tag{10.11}$$

When this equation is solved, it also means that the thresholds are scaled to be a mean of 1, and hence, the slope parameters (i.e., discrimination) are equal for all items. Obviously, this is a significant departure in logic, presumption, and rationale from that of IRT models that are broader in orientation or scope. In fact, fixing item difficulty at 1 is a distinguishing feature of Rasch-based IRT. In 1PL without Rasch presumptions, the difficulty parameter is fixed at some value defined by the user, which may be 1 or another value. When fixed at 1, a Rasch model has been defined.

Conforming the Rasch Model to Traditional IRT Models

By making two critical assumptions about the one-parameter model, Rasch may also be expressed in terms similar to the traditional two- and three-parameter models.

This is why the Rasch model is sometimes considered a special case of the 3PL model. These assumptions are (a) that all items discriminate equally and (b) that the pseudochance parameter is defined as zero. Then, by setting values for the ability value and the difficulty value, as in Equations 10.12 and 10.13, the Rasch model assumes the form of Equation 10.14. Also implied is the fact that persons with the same number of items correct will have the same theta value, regardless of various items having been answered differently:

$$\theta_a^* = e^{D\bar{a}\theta_a} \tag{10.12}$$

$$b_i^* = e^{D\bar{a}b_i} \tag{10.13}$$

$$P_i(\theta_a) = \frac{e^{D\bar{a}\theta_a}}{e^{D\bar{a}\theta_a} + e^{D\bar{a}b_i}}. \tag{10.14}$$

It is significant to note that, by reduction, Equation 10.14 is equivalent to the traditional IRT model expressed in Equation 10.4. Thus, with the added assumptions about the Rasch model, it can also be considered within the family of traditional IRT models.

There is a special caution, however, to observe when including the Rasch model with other traditional IRT models, which relates to the dubiousness of adopting the additional Rasch-dependent assumptions. Some experts are harsh in their criticism of the assumptions (e.g., Divgi, 1986; Hambleton & Murry, 1983). Canadian researcher Traub (1983) sums up many criticisms bluntly by stating that "these assumptions about items fly in the face of commonsense and a wealth of empirical evidence accumulated over the last 80 years" (p. 64). To confuse the matter, however, some of these same researchers suggest that under certain conditions, violating the assumptions to some degree probably does not diminish the item parameter or ability estimates to such an extent as to render the Rasch model unserviceable (see Hambleton, 1989).

Some Rasch History and Sources

Rasch (1960) set out his ideas in *Probabilistic Models for Some Intelligence and Attainment Tests,* a work that one proponent, Benjamin Wright (1968), zealously describes as "the most important work on psychometrics since Thurstone's articles of 1925–29 and the 1929 monograph by Thurstone and Chave" (p. ix). Rasch models of item parameter estimation were popularized in the United States by Wright (1968; formerly of the University of Chicago) after his landmark presentation titled "Sample-Free Test Calibration and Person Measurement" given at an ETS conference on testing problems.

Today, there are many proponents of Rasch scaling. Some "Raschites" maintain a lively discussion through an active Internet listserv that is open to new subscribers (send an e-mail to *IRT@Listserve.vt.edu*). The Institute for Objective Measurement, Inc. (see *http://www.rasch.org/*. Retrieved February 22, 2005.) provides information on many Rasch conferences, videotapes, books, and so on. The American Educational

Research Association has a Rasch Measurement Special Interest Group. Not surprisingly, the Rasch measurement model is adopted in many assessment programs. Interestingly, it seems that the Rasch IRT is overwhelmingly popular in assessment programs throughout Australia. In that country, for example, the *Graduate Australian Medical School Admissions Test,* the *Undergraduate Medicine and Health Sciences Admission Test,* and most public school testing employ Rasch scaling. Details can be found at the site for the Australian Council for Educational Research (see *http://www.acer.edu.au/.* Retrieved December 5, 2004).

Many authors offer a more thorough explanation of Rasch-based IRT than space here allows (e.g., Andrich, 1988; Bond & Fox, 2001; Fischer & Molenaar, 2002). Wright's later book on this approach (Wright & Stone, 1979), although decidedly dated, is still wonderfully instructive to the novice. The *Journal of Applied Measurement* regularly publishes authoritative Rasch-oriented articles, as do other professional journals. In addition, there are several computer programs that implement Rasch scaling; I cite some of them in a later section on IRT computer programs.

Other IRT Models

As emphasized, IRT—both in theory and in mathematical application—is available for many approaches to measurement problems beyond the models discussed, which are primarily constrained to binary test items. Some of these models actually predate the models already described, but they are only now coming into prominence. Hence, they are often referred to as "new" or "modern" IRT. These new models include IRT approaches that cover test stimuli with polytomous response formats, models for response time or multiple attempts on items, models for multiple abilities or cognitive components, nonparametric models, models for monotonic items, and models with special assumptions about the response process. In a very real sense, these approaches can be viewed as the wave of the future in IRT models.

Nominal and Graded Response Models for Polytomous Items

One such IRT approach is called the *IRT nominal response model* and was developed by Bock (1972). This model advances a characteristic curve for each response alternative for an item, even for omitted items. The approach assigns weights to responses reflecting their degree of correctness, rather than to the whole item as correct or incorrect. It is suited to test development only after appropriate field-testing of items with the weighting scheme. A parallel, non-IRT and nonparametric approach to examining items is offered by Ramsay (1998) as a computer program and is discussed in chapter 12, analyzing individual items.

Samejima (1969) also proffers an *IRT graded response model* that works like the nominal response model but for Likert-scaled items or other multiple category responses. The ICC for a graded response model is shown in Figure 10.11. Note that there are multiple curves, one for each response alternative, as would be appropriate

Figure 10.11

Example of response curves from three-option graded response model.

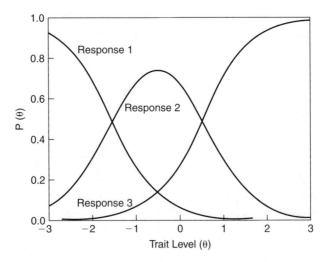

in Likert-type items. Their interpretation is essentially the same as for the single trace line ICC, except that each response alternative can be interpreted. Follow each curve to determine the probability of response relative to ability. For the first curve (labeled 1), there is a high probability of selecting the response for persons of low trait level, there is middle probability to select the second response for persons of middle trait level, and finally, there is high probability for high trait recognition and selecting the third response for persons of high trait probability. The overlapping portion of the curves conveys information about trait level that is common to more than one response. The small portion covered by all three responses means that only for a few persons in the middle of the trait distribution is there even a small probability of selecting any of the three responses. This model is gaining increasing popularity in psychological and other personality-type assessments. Samejima's approach is available in the PARSCALE computer program.

Richly Cognitive Models

Some psychometricians have attempted to incorporate cognitive parameters into IRT models in an effort to more fully understand the cognitive process that underlies examinees' responses and how it influences item parameters. Two such models are the *linear logistic latent trait model* (Fischer & Formann, 1982) and the *multicomponent latent trait model* (Embretson, 1984). Because these models are complex, their explanations can be quite technical. Hambleton (1989) reports on these models and others lucidly. A special issue of *Applied Psychological Measurement* (Weiss, 1996) is devoted to such multidimensional models.

Understanding and using many of the newer, complex IRT models requires technical sophistication beyond the scope of this book. Despite the difficulty in understanding these IRT approaches, however, they are quite useful in interpreting assessment that incorporates many dimensions of cognition. One particularly informative source about these extensive models is van der Linden and Hambleton's (1997) book, with each chapter describing a single, new IRT model. Technically savvy readers will discover a wealth of information about complex IRT models in this valuable volume.

Estimating Item and Ability Parameters

Iterative Estimation Procedures

In real world testing contexts, the particular technique used to estimate parameters for items and examinees is of great importance. There are several methods available to make the estimates, each emphasizing a different aspect of the model and yielding slightly different results. Basically, however, the estimation procedures use iterative processes, wherein ability-parameter estimates provide information to calculate item parameters, and item-parameter estimates give the values needed to make ability estimates. The developed values are successively used to calculate ever more precise estimates of the parameters. When a criterion of precision is reached, the iterative process stops and the final values are considered as solutions. (Recall that iteration is described in chapter 2.)

Developing Priors

The primary mathematical problem with the iterative approach to developing parameter estimates is in determining what values to use as a starting point. The starting values are called *priors,* for their being prior known quantities. The use of priors in estimation procedures is what classifies the whole approach as *Bayesian statistics.* Readers remember the notion of Bayesian statistics introduced in chapter 2, and those interested in learning more are referred to an excellent treatment of the topic in *Bayes and Empirical Bayes Methods for Data Analysis* by Carlin and Louis (1996). The priors typically come from the raw scores of a relatively large group of examinees. From these scores, various points along the distribution are selected as the priors to represent the entire distribution. Usually about 10 data points are chosen, but this number can vary greatly depending on circumstance. Often, a researcher will vary the number of priors to determine different levels of efficiency and precision in estimating the parameters. A statistical procedure to select the points and weight them for their relative dependency along the distribution is usually done. A commonly used procedure is called Newton-Raphson. At these prior points—called *quadratures* in most computer algorithms—the log of the ratio of number right to number wrong responses for examinees is taken as the value for that prior in maximum likelihood procedures.

As one can imagine, then, it is important that the scores used in developing prior values come from a population with normally distributed characteristics and that there be sufficient data to judge homoscedasticity at the extremes. When insufficient information is known about the population from the priors, the estimates may be less precise.

PARAMETER	MEAN	STN DEV
SLOPE	0.627	0.280
LOG(SLOPE)	−0.580	0.515
THRESHOLD	0.184	1.495

QUADRATURE POINTS AND POSTERIOR WEIGHTS:

	1	2	3	4	5
POINT	−0.3611E+01	−0.2812E+01	−0.2014E+01	−0.1216E+01	−0.4183E+00
WEIGHT	0.1998E−02	0.5949E−02	0.2530E−01	0.1399E+00	0.3594E+00

	6	7	8	9	10
POINT	0.3798E+00	0.1178E+01	0.1976E+01	0.2774E+01	0.3572E+01
WEIGHT	0.2858E+00	0.1170E+00	0.4554E−01	0.1382E−01	0.5244E−02

Figure 10.12
Summary information about quadrature estimates and posterior weights.

Checking the accuracy of the quadrature points is important in determining whether the model estimated the parameters with acceptable accuracy. The check is accomplished by recalculating the values at the quadrature points with the known distribution of parameters. At this stage, the recalculated values assume the name *posterior weights* because they are calculated after the fact. The posterior values are then compared with the priors to determine whether the original starting values have been recovered accurately. If they have been, the model is believed to be a good fit to the data. Figure 10.12 shows quadrature points and posterior weights for one achievement test.

The Test Information Function

In IRT, a *test information function* (TIF) is developed to show the degree of precision in parameter estimation at various points along the distribution. This is an index of the measure's reliability that is unavailable in CTT. It is an average of item information at each trait level. Significantly, these values are independent of the particular group of examinees. TIFs can also show an analog of standard errors.

In IRT work, examining the TIF is important to understanding the degree of confidence one has in interpreting score value based on estimates of parameters. A sample TIF with its analogous measurement error curve is shown in Figure 10.13. As plotted in BILOG and many other programs, the TIF is shown along with the standard errors at the various points. The table shows the two curves, each interpreted with a scale on opposite sides of the graph. The scale on the left shows values for the TIF, whereas the scale on the right side shows values for standard errors. As is typical, more information is available in the middle to make accurate parameter estimates than is available at the low and high ends of the distribution. The standard errors are correspondingly lowest in the middle, where more information about parameters is known.

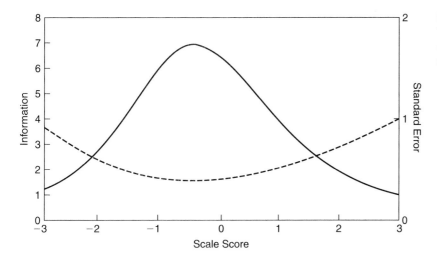

Figure 10.13
Test information function and standard errors across scale range.

The TIF is an important piece of IRT information about the accuracy of scores and how to interpret them. The TIF is available only because an error can be calculated at each ability level, in contrast to reliability in CTT, which can only estimate a single average error (i.e., SEM) for the entire distribution.

Some Estimation Procedures

There remains a mathematical problem with using dichotomous data as priors. Often in tests there are some items that all examinees responded to correctly or that all missed. Analogously, in polytomous items, there are occasions in which all persons selected the same response. In Likert items, for instance, suppose everyone marked the highest (or lowest) alternative. In this circumstance, when an item correlation matrix is prepared, the intersection of all correct or all incorrect items will produce a coefficient or index of 1 or 0, making estimation implausible. Under such a circumstance, calculating parameters for ability would reach indeterminacy and no estimates could be made.

There are numerous methods available to accommodate these rather routine circumstances in tests: *conditional maximum likelihood, joint maximum likelihood, marginal maximum likelihood, Bayesian,* and *heuristic*. In addition, promising newer models involve *Markov Chain Monte Carlo* methods, especially for more complicated IRT models. Each method has its proponents, but one of the most popular is marginal maximum likelihood (MML). MML is implemented in many computer programs, and some programs allow the user to determine which estimation method is to be used. Measurement professionals preparing test documentation should indicate which estimation method has been employed in a given testing context.

Computer Programs Available for Parameter Estimation

There are a number of useful computer programs available to estimate item and ability parameters along with other relevant information. As one can imagine with computer programs, some grow dated as new ones come along, so readers planning to use one should investigate which of the ones cited here have been superseded by newer versions or are no longer available.

Presently, BILOG-MG (Zimowski, Muraki, Mislevy, & Bock, 2002) is probably the most widely used program for calculating IRT parameter estimates in educational and psychological settings. BILOG-MG is a flexible program allowing estimates of one-, two- and three-parameter models, as well as choices among a host of relevant options. With it, one can perform several kinds of bias and DIF analysis, linking and equating, some computer-adaptive testing, model fit estimation, and some test development. It also includes a special Rasch option that rescales parameter estimates according to Rasch model conventions. However, BILOG-MG is limited to analysis of binary data. It is accompanied by an extensive manual that includes a wealth of information about the program, including useful data about the algorithms used in various computations. The current version of BILOG-MG provides a Windows-like interface in which the user enters values for commands. It is available from the publisher, Scientific Software International (SSI; *http://www.ssicentral.com*. Retrieved February 20, 2005.), as part of a suite of programs that handle a variety of measurement problems.

Packaged with BILOG-MG is another IRT calibration program, MULTILOG (Thissen, Chen, & Bock, 2002). This program permits analysis of multidimensional data that is useful for performance assessments with their multiple categories and for Likert-scaled items with many categories. Also in this bundle is a third IRT program, PARSCALE (Muraki & Bock, 2002). It is useful for analyzing and scoring rating scale data. These programs are especially helpful for exploring polytomous data and other advanced models. They can be used in a myriad of research contexts, despite their rather steep learning curve.

Additional calibration programs focus on Rasch modeling, including WINSTEPS (see *http://www.winsteps.com/*. Retrieved February 20, 2005.) and a companion, BIG-STEPS. RASCAL and RESGEN (Muraki, 1992) also estimate IRT data for the Rasch model. The latter program also generates item response data for a wide range of non-traditional IRT models. The RUMM2020 (accessed at *http://www.rummlab.com.au*. Retrieved February 20, 2005.) program offers rich exploration in Rasch modeling and a variety of associated statistics, including DIF, facet analysis, and more. A student version (minus some features and with size limitations) is also available. There are dozens of other programs to calculate Rasch estimates. They can even be calculated in SAS and SPSS by invoking various syntax commands.

These IRT programs are not designed for the casual user. For effective application, nearly all demand that users have a solid grasp of measurement theory, and obviously, IRT. Individuals must be willing to invest a significant amount of time to learn a given program's individual features and peculiarities. Nonetheless, most of the programs are remarkable. They are typically flexible, and with patience and diligence, a variety of IRT-related information can be developed. We are grateful for the expertise and hard work of the programs' developers because their expertise makes practical applications of IRT available to students, researchers, and psychometricians. Without the programmers, IRT would remain a theory, remarkable in promise but unavailable for practical application by most users.

Exploring Output from One Program: BILOG-MG

Examining the computer output from the programs can be beneficial to gain familiarity with IRT in general, and with its implementation by a given model and options in particular. I described some features for BILOG-MG because it is popular, flexible, and current. The program includes a plethora of commands, which are used in the syntax statements to produce varying outputs for different kinds of item information useful to different purposes. A sample command file for BILOG-MG is shown in Figure 10.14.

```
>COMMENT  Sample run with ASA data (Int'l test).  PLOT=1 specification
(on the SCORE command) is used to plot all the item response functions.
The scoring phase includes an information analysis (INFO=2) with
expected information indices for a normal population (POP). Rescaling of
the scores and item parameters to mean 0 and standard deviation 1 in the
estimated latent distribution has been requested (RSC=4).  Several files
with individual stats (for items and examinees) have been saved,
including parameters, scores, IRT statistics, and traditional with
reliabilities.

>GLOBAL DFName = 'INTLDATA.dat',
        NPArm = 2,
        SAVe;
>SAVE PARm  = 'ASA01.PAR', SCOre = 'ASA01.SCO', TSTat = 'ASA01.TST',
      ISTat = 'ASA01.IST';
>LENGTH NITems = (188);
>INPUT NTOtal = 188, NALt = 5, NIDchar = 4,
       KFName = 'INTLKEY.key', OFName = 'INTLOMIT.OMT';
>ITEMS INAmes = (ITEM001(1)ITEM100, ITEM0101(1)ITEM0188);
>TEST1 TNAme = 'ASAtest',
       INUmber = (1(1)188);
(4A1, 188A1)
>CALIB CYCles = 50, NEWton = 25, CRIt = 0.1000,
       PLOt = 1.0000, ACCel = 0.0000;
>SCORE METhod = 3, RSCtype = 4,
       INFo = 2, POP;
```

Figure 10.14
Sample command file for BILOG-MG.

Because IRT can yield a surfeit of information about items, tests, and examinees' traits, it is recommended that users focus on just what is important to item analysis within a particular context. For instance, in test construction, it is instructive to examine information about the likelihood function of an item and its maximum effectiveness, whereas for item bias or DIF studies it may be more valuable to compare parameter estimates of the focal and reference groups. Another use may be to detect and correct for *item parameter drift* because item parameters may change over time with multiple administrations and equating.

Figures 10.15 and 10.16 provide selected output and explanation from BILOG-MG (Zimowski et al., 2002). This output is but a small portion of the information that this program (or others) can generate. Figure 10.15 is BILOG-MG output for information about test items. Each statistic is accompanied by its standard error (labeled *S.E.* in the output and denoted with an asterisk). Statistics for the intercept ($-a_ib_i$) and slope (*a* parameter) are given first. Next is the threshold, which is the difficulty

ITEM	INTERCEPT S.E.	SLOPE S.E.	THRESHOLD S.E.	DISPERSN S.E.	ASYMPTOTE S.E.	CHISQ (PROB)	DF
I26	0.473	0.287	−1.650	3.486	0.000	8.5	9.0
	0.052*	0.062*	0.364*	0.750*	0.000*	(0.4855)	
I27	0.127	0.834	−0.152	1.199	0.000	9.5	7.0
	0.056*	0.097*	0.065*	0.139*	0.000*	(0.2195)	
I28	−0.279	0.607	0.460	1.646	0.000	17.5	9.0
	0.053*	0.073*	0.096*	0.198*	0.000*	(0.0407)	
I29	0.939	1.170	−0.802	0.855	0.000	6.8	6.0
	0.096*	0.149*	0.070*	0.109*	0.000*	(0.3384)	
I31	−1.109	0.275	4.027	3.631	0.000	10.1	9.0
	0.071*	0.074*	1.028*	0.978*	0.000*	(0.3402)	
I33	0.022	0.529	−0.042	1.892	0.000	5.5	9.0
	0.050*	0.069*	0.095*	0.245*	0.000*	(0.7905)	
I34	0.081	0.807	−0.101	1.239	0.000	14.2	8.0
	0.054*	0.090*	0.067*	0.138*	0.000*	(0.0774)	
I35	−1.151	0.388	2.969	2.580	0.000	8.2	9.0
	0.078*	0.083*	0.566*	0.552*	0.000*	(0.5151)	
I36	0.372	0.413	−0.902	2.423	0.000	10.1	9.0
	0.052*	0.067*	0.170*	0.394*	0.000*	(0.3399)	
I38	0.552	0.371	−1.487	2.694	0.000	15.9	9.0
	0.054*	0.067*	0.273*	0.489*	0.000*	(0.0681)	
I39	0.820	1.196	−0.686	0.836	0.000	10.2	6.0
	0.083*	0.136*	0.063*	0.095*	0.000*	(0.1138)	

Figure 10.15
Output from BILOG-MG showing foundational item response theory item statistics.

GROUP WEIGHT	SUBJECT TEST	IDENTIFICATION TRIED	RIGHT	PERCENT	ABILITY	S.E.
1	4					
1.00	CB_LP	41	23	56.10	257.3604	26.9994
1	6					
1.00	CB_LP	41	23	56.10	258.1218	27.0236
1	7					
1.00	CB_LP	41	21	51.22	239.2328	26.5854
1	9					
1.00	CB_LP	41	37	90.24	448.5562	49.1936
1	10					
1.00	CB_LP	41	33	80.49	380.1861	37.2035
1	11					
1.00	CB_LP	41	36	87.80	430.5871	45.5065
1	12					
1.00	CB_LP	41	13	31.71	160.6420	28.9973
1	13					
1.00	CB_LP	41	34	82.93	388.3141	38.3532
1	14					
1.00	CB_LP	41	35	85.37	424.2879	44.3092
1	15					
1.00	CB_LP	41	36	87.80	421.4551	43.7864
1	18					
1.00	CB_LP	41	28	68.29	312.6899	30.0427
1	19					
1.00	CB_LP	41	34	82.93	395.6766	39.4558

Figure 10.16
Examinee statistics by item response theory calibration of 2PL model.

(*b*) parameter. The dispersion estimate is the reciprocal of the slope, which as we saw earlier is used in calculating theta. Because this example employs the two-parameter model, statistics are not computed for the lower asymptote (the *c* parameter); hence, it is set to zero. The chi-square statistic is offered as a measure of fit for each item to the model and is useful for validity evaluation. I discuss these statistics further in chapter 12 during the presentation of item analysis.

As computed, these statistics employ the original metric for computations, but they can be easily rescaled by a linear transformation to scores with location and scale of the test developer's choosing. The new values are centered relative to the overall distribution of scores. For example, the CBASE uses a location of 300 and a scale of 65, whereas the SAT uses a location of 500 and a scale of 100. The particular location and scale values chosen are arbitrary.

There are several important examinee statistics presented in Figure 10.16. Most of the variables reported are apparent. It is of enormous value, still, to inspect the column labels and identify them as a simple exercise. In Figure 10.16, subjects are identified by numbers and the test is given a weight of 1.00. (BILOG-MG allows subtests to be differentially weighted.) These numbers are followed by several traditional item statistics, including the number of items tried, the number correct, and the percentage correct, raw score. The output then gives the IRT rescaled ability estimates. Usually, this is the score reported to the examinee. The standard error for each examinee is also provided. High standard errors indicate less relevance ("fit") of the model to the response pattern for a particular examinee. (Technically, a particular standard error is not tied to a given examinee but to a response vector.) This individual-response-vector-standard error statistic is an IRT measure for which there is no corollary in traditional item statistics. It allows for analysis of error at every score point along the scale.

In Figure 10.16, one can also observe that response vectors are analyzed by IRT methods rather than by just number of items correct, demonstrating that two examinees who obtained the same observed score attained different ability estimates. As we know by now, this occurs because of their different response patterns. For example, examinees 4 and 6 (cf column labeled "subject identification") both achieved a raw score of 23, but they have different ability parameters, 257 and 258, respectively, albeit slight in this instance. The same situation is more dramatically illustrated for examinees 11 and 15. Here, both examinees achieved a raw score of 36, but have different estimates of their ability.

Brief History and Major Contributors to IRT

Within the realm of psychology, IRT has a comparatively long history that is only highlighted here, to give perspective and context. An exceptionally well done but brief history of IRT is given by Bock (1997a), and a detailed history is offered by Hambleton et al. (1991) and many others.

Although some trace IRT's history back to Thurstone's work on scaling in the 1920s, it probably came more into focus somewhat later. G. A. Ferguson (1942) first explored the idea of item invariance from a statistical perspective, as *terra incognita,* pointing out that group dependence for item difficulty estimates may be obviated by employing sophisticated sample-free distribution statistics. At about the same time, Lawley (1943) reiterated Ferguson's point with his independent work. Contemporaneous progress on IRT was made by several psychometricians and measurement specialists, such as Brogden (1946), Tucker (1946), Carroll (1950), and Cronbach and Warrington (1952). Much of this early work in item invariant statistics for tests was published in *Psychometrika,* a still flourishing and highly respected journal.

Early IRT papers did not attract much attention, even within the measurement community, probably due to the highly technical nature of their descriptions and the fact that traditional measurement science was gaining popular acceptance. Recall also from the history of education that at about the time of World War II there was a tremendous surge of popularity for installing achievement and ability tests in elementary and secondary school assessment and evaluation programs. One can only guess that IRT was ignored partly because the sophisticated statistical procedures must have seemed unnecessary, not to mention the toilsome difficulty of computing IRT statistics manually in precomputer days.

At first, during this period of early development in IRT, the advances were mostly limited to explorations of item invariance and did not have a unifying core or theory. The terminology "item response theory" was not even used. The work was kept in the world of arcane statistics. Then, Fredrick Lord (1952), a brilliant graduate student working on his dissertation, developed IRT as a full-fledged measurement theory, elucidating assumptions and describing models for the approach. His dissertation stands today as a remarkable tour de force of theoretical brilliance and practical elegance. Lord is credited with naming the approach, previously referred to as ICC, for its focus on item statistics, even though he may not have been the first person to use the term (Atkinson, Krantz, Luce, & Suppes, 1996). He called it IRT, reflecting the fullness of the approach to measurement science.

Lord continued to make substantive contributions to IRT throughout his illustrious career at ETS, finally being named a Distinguished Research Scientist. Lord is referenced often in this chapter and throughout the IRT literature, an indication of his contribution to this psychometric theory. Sadly, he died in February 2000, but leaving behind a record of remarkable achievement.

Particularly since about the mid-1960s, much work has been done to advance IRT, both technically and through significant publications. For example, Lord and Novick (1968) published a psychometrics textbook that is still considered invaluable reading for students and scholars of psychometrics, entitled *Statistical Theories of Mental Test Scores*. Readers have doubtlessly recognized that I cite this book frequently because it is so complete and authoritative.

Lord and Novick's (1968) book contains four chapters contributed by Allan Birnbaum. These four chapters, presented under the section heading, "Some Latent Trait Models and Their Use in Inferring an Examinee's Ability," were devoted to IRT, a first for such texts. The Birnbaum chapters not only described IRT, but also articulated the mathematics for two new IRT models, the *soi-disant* two- and three-parameter models. They provided a basis for many scholars to begin exploring IRT on their own, and the chapters quickly became required reading for psychometricians. Today, scarcely 30 years after it first appeared, Lord and Novick's work is classic text. Birnbaum's contribution to IRT has been munificent and the field of assessment owes much to this scholar, as it also does to the work of both Lord and Novick. Soon after Birnbaum's chapter in Lord and Novick's book appeared, Vern Urry, a personnel research psychologist with the U.S. Civil Service Commission, offered a cogent comparison of the two- and three-parameter models in his own remarkable doctoral dissertation.

The 1960s saw a stirring of interest in IRT. The impetus came in large measure from the Danish mathematician, Georg Rasch (1960, 1966), when he published his sample-free IRT model and through which he popularized the term *one parameter*. Rasch's work attracted considerable attention, especially in the United States. No one was more enthusiastic about the one-parameter model than Benjamin Wright, a psychoanalyst at the University of Chicago. For many years, Wright was a one-man traveling show, promoting the Rasch model, which he so named after his hero. Throughout the 1970s and into the 1990s, Wright lectured, conducted workshops, and consulted across the country, promoting IRT in general and the one-parameter

Rasch approach in particular. In the mid-1970s, he even persuaded Portland (Oregon) Public Schools to implement a large-scale, systemwide test that was scaled and scored with the Rasch model. This test and evaluation program was probably the first large-scale implementation of an IRT-based assessment program, and it was manifestly ahead of its time. In the 1980s, many other state-testing agencies and school districts followed Portland's lead.

In 1979, Wright, along with his protégé Mark Stone, published his most popular work, *Best Test Design* (Wright & Stone, 1979), which articulates the Rasch model in simple terms. Today, this work stands as an exemplar of lucid description of technical information. *Best Test Design* caught the attention of measurement specialists across the United States and, for a number of years, was virtually required reading in advanced measurement courses. With its publication and use, IRT rapidly gained acceptance. Since the mid-1990s, with the ready availability of some excellent computer programs to handle the computations, there has been a further explosion of interest in IRT. An easy prediction is that the trend will grow and develop even further.

Sources for More IRT Information

There are oodles of first-rate sources and resources available for learning more about IRT. In *Item Response Theory for Psychologists,* Embretson and Reise (2000) present a solid work for educators and other social scientists interested in IRT in those settings. Hambleton offers two readable, book-length introductions to the topic: *Item Response Theory: Principles and Applications* (Hambleton & Swaminathan, 1985), and a monograph entitled *Fundamentals of Item Response Theory* (Hambleton, Swaminathan, & Rogers, 1991). Although Hambleton's publications are relatively old, they are decidedly not out of date and still offer excellent introductions. Lord (1980), gives us an excellent, but technically demanding, treatment in *Applications of Item Response Theory to Practical Testing Problems.* McDonald (1999), in his book on test theory, provides several chapters of valuable information. Another excellent and advanced book is one that focuses on extensions of IRT to polytomous models: *Handbook of Modern Item Response Theory,* edited by van der Linden and Hambleton (1997). I have already cited Birnbaum's several chapters on IRT in *Statistical Theories of Mental Test Scores,* an influential textbook authored by Lord and Novick (1963). Another informative source about IRT is the thorough manual accompanying a popular IRT computer program offered by SSI: *IRT from SSI: BILOG-MG, MULTILOG, PARSCALE, TESTFACT* (du Toit, 2003). There are also many excellent for-profit companies (e.g., SSI [*http://www.ssicentral.com.* Retrieved February 28, 2005.], Assessment Systems Corporation [*http://www.assess.com/.* Retrieved February 28, 2005.]) that offer books, training courses, and other resources for learning about IRT.

Of course, a literature search through a relevant database (e.g., ERIC, PsychInfo) will return thousands of journal entries, although many deal with specialized topics within the field. For instance, go to volumes of the respected journal *Applied Psychological Measurement,* wherein one will find a treasure trove of IRT-related research and scholarship. Measurement professionals may want to add some of these books and articles to their personal library for continued reference.

There are also many Web-based resources. For instance, the University of Illinois has established an online, elementary tutorial (found at *http://work.psych.uiuc.edu/irt/tutorial.asp*. Retrieved February 28, 2005.) that can be useful to newcomers. Also online is an ERIC reissue of a book that Baker (2001) wrote on the topic. His original work (written in 1985) attained popularity in the measurement community, although it has idiosyncrasies with portions now dated. Baker's 2001 update, complete with original software, is available at *http://edres.org/irt/baker/*. (Retrieved February 28, 2005.)

Summary

In this chapter, we explore IRT, explaining what it is and how it can be applied to many practical testing situations. Deliberately, I keep the mathematical manipulations of IRT that allow for its application to a minimum, although some essential features oblige a numeric or algebraic explanation. The focus is on a basic understanding of the theory and how it may be used to advantage in various measurement contexts. Particularly relevant is discussion of IRT assumptions and estimation procedures.

Chapter 11

Modern Reliability Analysis: Generalizability Theory

Introduction

A Gem Reclaimed

Probably the most famous painting in the world is Leonardo da Vinci's *Mona Lisa*. For more than six centuries, her venerated smile has seared the lady to our soul. Yet, few people realize that on August 21, 1911 the *Mona Lisa* was stolen right off the wall of the Louvre Museum in Paris. It was such an inconceivable event that she was not even noticed missing until the following day. When the crime was realized, the astonished museum director, Théophile Homolle, exclaimed, "[you] might as well pretend that one could steal the towers of the cathedral of Notre Dame" (quoted in McMullen, 1975). The Louvre was closed for a week; and, when reopened, people came to stare at the blank space on the wall where she once hung, temporarily replaced by a bouquet of flowers. Incredibly, the famous lady was missing for more than 2 years. Most of that time the painting lay under the bed of the thief, who was too afraid to attempt to sell, trade, or exhibit it. In the crime story, the thief was an Italian painter of modest repute named Vincenzo Peruggia. He had simply taken it off the wall when the viewing room was empty at the end of the day, put it under his coat, and walked off! He said later that he wanted to return it to Italy, the home of da Vinci, but was too afraid to do so for fear of getting caught. At some point he did try to sell it, and indeed, he got caught. The news of finding the *Mona Lisa* made headlines across the globe. Parisians cheered in the streets, saying they got their hearts back. The news was so welcome throughout the continent that the painting toured Italy before it was returned to France in 1914, where it remains today, viewed by more than 1 million people annually. It is now heavily guarded.

In a (very) rough and persiflage parallel, generalizability theory is like the *Mona Lisa:* enigmatic and often missing from its expected location. Yet it has a beauty and elegance that can aid test development and analysis enormously. Students and professionals who know the concepts and put the procedures to use often find it invaluable to their work in reliability assessment. However, because generalizability theory is complex and broad in scope, it is necessary to acquire a level of understanding beyond superficial awareness in order to appreciate its elegance and its contributions to psychometrics. In this chapter, we attempt such gain.

For convenience, the appellation *G theory* is used interchangeably with the complete name *generalizability theory;* both are used in the literature.

Contents

This chapter covers G theory, beginning with a description of what it is. Necessarily much of this description makes a contrast with reliability estimation by assumptions of CTT. I then explain the benefits of this modern approach to reliability and spend some time discussing common misconceptions about it. After that, I explain the two types of common studies in this context: G studies and D studies. Then, the chapter moves to the mathematics used in G theory, including a small, sample example. I also describe how to calculate G theory reliability coefficients. Two primary G theory decisions (relative and absolute) are discussed. The chapter concludes by citing a few computer programs that can be employed in G studies and D studies.

What Is Generalizability Theory?

Identifying the Theory

Generalizability theory is a conceptual approach to mental measurement that provides information useful for understanding how well-selected conditions of a particular facet of the assessment represent their domain. More completely, G theory maintains that for each facet of an appraisal (e.g., items, occasions, raters) the facet conditions actually employed are but a sample of possible ones that compose a universe. Then, variance statistics—applied with architectonic intricacy so as to be an important part of the theory in itself—provide a method to estimate a variance error for each facet considered.

In practice, G theory is implemented by decomposing the error term of CTT into identifiable facets through multivariate analyses. Noted G theory authority Robert Brennan (2001c) describes it thus: "Generalizability theory liberalizes classical theory by employing ANOVA methods that allow an investigator to untangle multiple sources of error that contribute to the undifferentiated E in classical theory" (p. 3).

For instance, it may be hypothesized that the test's items, the appraisal occasion, and the scorers (in the case of, say, multiple raters of a writing sample) are crucial facets of an assessment. The idea is to understand how well each one represents a relevant universe of admissible observations. Accordingly, G theory is a multivariate approach to reliability appraisal. Reflecting this perspective on measurement precision, G theory is sometimes called *modern reliability analysis* or even *dependability of measurement.*

The idea of a "universe of admissible observations" is central to G theory. Because in nearly all circumstances the items used for a particular appraisal are arbitrarily selected from a much larger pool (which may or may not have been developed), attention is directed toward appreciating the generalizability of the sample to the population. For one facet of assessment—in this example, test items—the idea is shown in Figure 11.1.

Of course, only facets specified by the researcher are accounted for in analysis. For example, items are commonly considered to be facets for the reason just given.

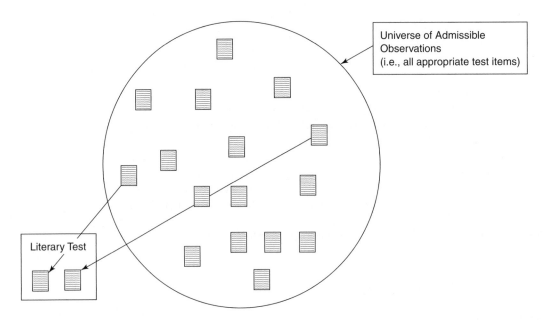

Figure 11.1
Representation of universe of possible test items, only a few of which appear on the test.

Scoring, however, would only be considered when appraisal items or exercises are scored by multiple raters (as in many writing assessments), but not for binary scoring (the case with most selected response formats) when the mechanics of marking is done by a machine. Obviously, no rater variance is extant for machine scoring.

G Theory in Relation to Other Measurement Theories

The G theory approach to reliability develops a more complex view of error than does CTT, involving both psychology (even psychophysics) and statistics. Whereas CTT is focused on identifying a *true score*, defined as the mean of a large number of administrations of randomly parallel measures, G theory is not similarly riveted. With this theory, the inherent error of mental appraisal is separated into distinct parts that can be attributed to observed sources and whose variance can be individually estimated.

Be aware, however, that G theory—despite its more complete view of error—still is a random effects approach to measurement in that the error term (as well the observed score) is a random variable. This is in contrast to IRT, which does not presume random variables.

The Facets of G Theory

Logically, assessment comprises *factors* that influence how an examinee may respond on any given assessment occasion. The factors contribute to measurement error and aggregate to compose a random error for measurement. Although CTT makes no attempt to identify such sources of error or make distinctions among them, G theory does. In G theory, these features are termed *facets*. A facet is a set of conditions of measurement that are similar to one another in some reasonable regard. As mentioned, items are commonly considered to be test design facets, with each being an *occasion* of measurement.

However, items are not the only facet of measurement that can have implication for generalizability. Any number of facets can be examined for their relative variance. The gender of the examinee may be a facet for study of error variance. Or, there may be administrator effects, such as when a gruff-speaking iconoclast barks out test directions as opposed to the soft-spoken comforter who slowly reads them aloud and then just as deliberately rereads them, checking to ensure each examinee is following along properly. (The point here is not that one administrator is better than the other, but rather to illustrate that an administrator can—however inadvertently—influence how an examinee responds to a set of test exercises, producing administrator effect as a facet for possible study.)

Other factors can also be similarly influential. For instance, in direct writing assessment it is common to employ multiple raters for scoring a single appraisal. Here, the raters themselves by their uniformity of scoring (or lack of) can have an effect on reported scores. In many contexts, studying the interrater consistency as a variance component is worthwhile. A similar case exists for other assessments that are scored in multiple categories, such as in personality appraisal or many PAs.

Of course, the selection of which facets to study, although arbitrary, is not capricious. The careful researcher selects facets appropriate to a given assessment context, after careful deliberation and by developing a just rationale.

G Theory's Multifaceted Approach

CTT considers error to be a single random variable. This conception of error presumes no differentiation among its possible sources, an untenable position by mere *prima facie* evidence. Many aspects of a measurement occasion—some internal to the measuring instrument (e.g., confusingly worded items), some within the examinee but apart from the construct being assessed (e.g., anxiety, motivation), and some due to external conditions (e.g., physical arrangements, scorers for some PAs)—can contribute to error. Cronbach, Gleser, Nanda, and Rajaratnam (1972) realized this problem with CTT and began to wonder whether the CTT notion of identifying a true score from a single observed score (itself a random variable) was really an accurate conception of how measurement works. More reasonable, they opined, is the consideration of how precisely the observed scores and other aspects of a particular measurement occasion represent an individual's ability or proficiency in a defined construct in general. In other words, restated as a question, "can the information obtained from a set of observed scores be generalized to represent all possible scores within a defined domain?"

Cronbach's approach to answering this question was to view error as multifaceted, with different parts of the error being identified and quantified. He attempted to estimate variance of distinct facets of measurement. This information, he believed, would allow one to generalize from the observed data to a universe of observations, giving a more accurate picture of assessment. He called G theory "a multifaceted concept of observational procedures," describing his musing as follows:

> Reliability theory and generalizability theory have hitherto looked at the accuracy of one score at a time. That is, they have been univariate in conception. Even for examining profiles of scores, the only special procedure invoked was the calculations of various difference scores, for each of which a univariate reliability study was made. In 1966 we stumbled into the realization that all the data in a profile may help one to estimate the universe score any one of the variables. (Cronbach et al., 1972, p. 13)

Through this historical note, Cronbach introduced a multivariate conception of measurement error, and subsequently, G theory. In practical application, a multivariate approach to analysis suggests that the covariance matrix and an analysis of variance (ANOVA) be analyzed as in a random effects variance model. Quoting Brennan (2001c) again, "G theory is best viewed as a multivariate theory in which there is a random effects model associated with each condition of every fixed facet and the linking of the fixed conditions is statistically indicated by covariance components" (p. 5).

Such simultaneous analysis of more than one source for error is a principle feature of G theory. Hence, analysis of error by G theory versus methods of CTT is analogous to the difference between an ANOVA model with random effects versus one that examines fixed effects.

Recognizing an Important Contribution to G Theory

To offer some G theory history, Cronbach—considered by many to be the inventor of G theory—evolved a methodology to explore the multifaceted error by employing the statistical work of R. A. Fisher's ANOVA. He documented his work in a delightful and readable (albeit technical) treatise titled, *The Dependability of Behavioral Measurements: Theory of Generalizability of Scores and Profiles* (Cronbach et al., 1972). This book is widely recognized as a progenitor of G theory. The book also makes contributions to other aspects of measurement theory, and for this it stands tall on the shelves of many practitioners of G theory.

Benefits of G Theory

The most cogent benefit of G theory is also its most fecund, giving significance to all other advantages. It is that G theory focuses like a laser on the construct or intent of measurement and less on the instrument per se. In other words, the concern of G theory is not solely reliability of a particular instrument used on a given occasion (the concern of CTT); rather, it is on what we can learn about the cognitive process under consideration, regardless of instrument, occasion for measurement, or other source of variability. In short, G theory helps us maintain a proper perspective—namely, on the construct of interest, realizing that the test instrument, the occasion of measurement, and other facets of appraisal are only vehicles for understanding constructs.

To implement this perspective in practical testing contexts, G theory considers error in terms of variance, both explained and unexplained. The explained portion is identified thorough the studied facets. Of course, not everything is explained or known, so some amount of error is still unknown.

Further, because in G theory at least two error variances are simultaneously considered, their interaction can be studied, which is another advantage of this approach. Thompson (2003c) contends that this feature of G theory is especially important because many people working with traditional reliability approaches tend to not even realize that error sources can interact:

> Too many classicists would tend to assume that these 10 persons [from a study in an article] are the same and also tend to not realize that in addition to being unique and cumulative, the sources may also interact to define disastrously large interaction sources of measurement error not considered in classical theory. The effects of these assumptions are all the more pernicious because of their unconscious character. (p. 49)

Another benefit of G theory is that its processes can include variance components from both quantitative and qualitative variables. Thus, the procedures can be applied for study in a wide variety of contexts. Indeed, G theory has been successfully employed in education, agriculture, medicine, business, and many other areas. G theory truly does extend measurement theory.

Half-Truths and Misconceptions

Because G theory is complex, both theoretically and procedurally, persons new to its study or only superficially informed often develop misunderstandings about it. Brennan (2001a) identified three instances where misconceptions about G theory can appear, including its relationship to CTT, its role in validity evaluation, and its reliance on the ANOVA statistic. He maintains that the following misstatements about generalizability theory characterize common misunderstandings:

- G theory is another theory of testing, one that contrasts with CTT.
- G theory is a validity procedure, exclusively.
- G theory is the application of ANOVA to test scores.

Like a rumor that contains a half-truth, these statements contain partially correct information, but as characterizations of G theory they lead practitioners away from important understandings. Let us examine them briefly, one by one, to see their insufficiencies, and thereby highlight what to need.

G Theory's Relationship with CTT

Perhaps, by merely labeling G theory as a "theory," one could infer that it contradicts important aspects of CTT; however, such is not implied. G theory is not a theory of measurement wholly distinct from CTT. It neither rejects the classical assumptions nor does it dispute CTT attestations. It relies on them as much as CTT itself does! In comparison to CTT, G theory's multifaceted approach considers variance in test scores more completely than can be done with CTT alone. Therefore, G theory simply—but significantly—augments the CTT.

Notwithstanding its close reliance on CTT, there are features of G theory that express ideas differently. For example, G theory does not conceptualize a true score as the mean of some infinite number of randomly parallel measurements. In fact, G theory does not focus on a true score at all. Instead, by the theory, there is a universe of measurements. A researcher's task is to explain the variance of obtained scores representing this universe as fully and accurately as possible. As we see, this is done by isolating and labeling sources of error variance, rather than just treating all error variance as unexplained.

G Theory Validation Procedure

The second area of possible misconception of G theory concerns its role in validity evaluation. The misconception is to believe that its only role is to provide validity-type information. Of course, in a broad sense, anything learned about how a mental appraisal operates in a given context can contribute information that is useful in decision making and hence validity evaluation. However, having validity evaluation as its sole purpose limits potential. G theory is enormously useful for making decisions in its own right. G theory is a substantive means to unearth particular information about identified sources of error variance in test scores. As such, the procedure is useful in making many testing decisions, as we will see momentarily.

G Theory Difference from ANOVA

The third area of possible misconception of G theory lies in its reliance on the ANOVA statistic. Imagining that G theory is just the application of ANOVA to test scores is perhaps the most difficult of all misconceptions about the theory to dispel. Sometimes, people first learning about it point to its close association with ANOVA and are tempted to suggest that G theory is only the application of ANOVA to variance in test scores. This conclusion is partially correct but vastly inadequate to accurately characterize the procedure. Let us examine some important distinctions.

First, G theory does not define universe score variance as the combination of variance components, a central notion in ANOVA. In G theory, universe score is defined and then its variance is extracted. Also, the F ratio plays a different role: For ANOVA, it is critical for interpreting experimental effects, but in G theory the F ratio plays only a minor part in identifying and naming error variance. Further, notions such as planned contrasts and *post hoc* analyses, also integral to ANOVA, are not used in G studies. (In a later section, I describe both G studies and D studies.) Finally, when working with G theory, realize that it is a multivariate approach to data using random effects, and although ANOVA can accommodate random effects under controlled conditions, it is more often used to characterize fixed ones.

To keep them straight, remember that G theory is a perspective on test scores, whereas ANOVA is primarily a procedure used for investigating research hypotheses, between or within groups. They each have an important role to play in research, but they are distinct ideas.

Formulation and Estimation of Variance Components

Calculating variance components in G theory is analogous to variance in ANOVA, but as we know by now the focus of attention is different. Instead of attending to the F ratio and evaluating its location in the F distribution, the concern is with the variance estimates themselves, particularly as they reveal information about differences in conditions in facets. These are described for G theory first, followed by a small example.

Conception of Variance Components

To begin, let us examine the components of variance for a simple case. The components are hypothesized as variance from an observed score. Imagine we have a population of persons, labeled p, and facet i, with facet conditions A, B, C, . . . n. Further, in this example, for each person a score is observed for every facet condition. This is syntactically represented in Equation 11.1:

$$X_{pi} = (X_{pA}, X_{pB}, X_{pC}). \qquad (11.1)$$

(It is logical to presume that facet conditions for this example can be *occasions of measurement* or test items.)

The research question investigates the extent to which the observed scores can generalize to all facet conditions. Or, to state this question simply, "what is the universe score of p to μ_p?" We know from the algebra of expectations (see chapter 2) that this is an expected value, which for the present example can be written as an equation, here in Equation 11.2:

$$\mu_p = EX_{pi}. \qquad (11.2)$$

This leads to the simple identity expressed in Equation 11.3, covering all conditions of measurement within this design:

$$
\begin{aligned}
X_{pi} &= \mu & \text{(mean)} \\
&= \mu_p - \mu & \text{(person effect)} \\
&= \mu_i - \mu & \text{(occasion effect)} \\
&= X_{pi} - \mu_p - \mu + \mu & \text{(residual).}
\end{aligned}
\qquad (11.3)
$$

As we are dealing with a universe for occasions, there exists an infinitely large number of possible observations of p for any one of them (e.g., A, B, C . . . n). This implies a *random effects model* for G studies, and the estimation of random effects variance components. Such a model is characteristic of G theory.

However, other unconsidered facets with unique facet conditions may also exist. Hence, there is a residual in the model, which is resolved to the expected e_{pi}. Leaving Equation 11.3, stated summarily as Equation 11.4:

$$(\mu_{pi} - \mu_p - \mu_i + \mu)e_{pi}. \qquad (11.4)$$

Also, and for the same reasons, it will be realized that each score component is actually a distribution of observed scores for that facet. Following usual variance procedures, for the distribution of $\mu_i - \mu$, the mean is 0. Finally, μ is not included in these component estimates because it is constant for the population. The variance of these values is the *variance component*. Realize, particularly, that there is a variance component for each facet and population, as expressed in Equation 11.5:

$$\sigma^2(X_{pi}) = \sigma^2(p) \qquad \text{(person component)}$$
$$+ \sigma^2(i) \qquad \text{(occasion component)} \qquad \textbf{(11.5)}$$
$$+ \sigma^2(pi, e) \qquad \text{(residual).}$$

Collectively, the formulations in Equation 11.5 are the variance of the obtained scores. The term $\sigma^2(p)$ represents the true score variance of CTT, and $\sigma^2(i)$ shows the variance of constant errors for all facet conditions. The residual component $[\sigma^2(pi, e)]$ equals the interaction of persons with occasions. Because this example is for a single fact, it cannot be decomposed, or *unmixed*.

Generally, both G studies and D studies include at least two facets, creating seven variance components. These are shown in Figure 11.2. Examination of Figure 11.2 reveals that there is a person and two-facet conditions, plus interaction. This is a random effects model with a nearly infinite number of observations for both persons and occasions.

		Estimators of Variance Components	Expected Mean Square
	X_{pij}	$= \mu$	$\sigma^2(X_{pij})$
Persons	p	$+ \mu_p - \mu \;\; \sigma^2(p)$	$+ \sigma^2(p)$
Condition-1	i	$+ \mu_i - \mu \;\; \sigma^2(i)$	$+ \sigma^2(i)$
Condition-2	j	$+ \mu_j - \mu \;\; \sigma^2(j)$	$+ \sigma^2(j)$
Interactions	pi	$+ \mu_{pi} - \mu_p - \mu_i + \mu$	$+ \sigma^2(pi)$
	pj	$+ \mu_{pj} - \mu_p - \mu_j + \mu$	$+ \sigma^2(pj)$
	ij	$+ \mu_{ij} - \mu_i - \mu_j + \mu$	$+ \sigma^2(ij)$
Residual	pij,e	$+ \mu_{pij} - \mu_{pi} - \mu_{pj} - \mu_{ij}$ $+ \mu_p + \mu_i + \mu_j - \mu$	$+ \sigma^2(pj)$

Figure 11.2
Facets of variance components.

Generalizability Coefficients

Generalizability theory incorporates two types of reliability coefficients: the *generalizability coefficient* and *an index of dependability*. These indices range (0, 1) and are interpreted similar to internal consistency reliability coefficients of CTT (e.g., Cronbach's alpha). However, they are not the same index as a classical reliability coefficient. They are calculated differently and used in different contexts from CTT.

Both the generalizability coefficient and the index of dependability are symbolized by single terms. For the generalizability coefficient, it is as follows in Expression 11.6:

$$E\rho^2, \qquad\qquad (11.6)$$

whereas the index of dependability is denoted by a single phi, shown in Expression 11.7:

$$\Phi. \qquad\qquad (11.7)$$

The $E\rho^2$ is used in both G studies and D studies (described momentarily), especially with relative decisions. The Φ is used in D studies when absolute decisions are sought, most particularly in criterion-referenced and some contexts of domain-referenced contexts.

To present these terms syntactically, it is first necessary to clearly and precisely understand the meaning of another previously used term—universe score. Brennan (2001c) describes universe score with an example from a fictitious reliability investigator named Mary Smith. He says, "In principle, for any person, Smith can conceive of obtaining the person's mean score for every instance of the measurement procedure in her universe of generalization. For any such person, the expected value of these mean scores is the person's *universe score*" (p. 9).

In many ways, this is parallel to the operational definition of the true score, but remember that a basic difference between classical true score theory and generalizability theory is that classical theory conceives of a score that exists without error, the true score. G theory maintains that observed measurements are only representative of a universe of admissible observations, implying variance. Thus, each person has a universe score; for all persons, there is score variance over all persons in the population, or a *universe score variance*.

Without having labeled it as such, we have already seen universe score variance in earlier reliability discussion. It is repeated in Expression 11.8:

$$\sigma^2(p). \qquad\qquad (11.8)$$

When applied to absolute decisions in D studies, an absolute determiner (Δ) is applied to the universe score variance term, as shown in Expression 11.9. It represents random error:

$$\sigma^2(\Delta). \qquad\qquad (11.9)$$

Returning now to the generalizability coefficient and the index of dependability, we see that the generalizability coefficient (see Expression 11.8) can be expressed syntactically as in Equation 11.10:

$$E\rho^2 = \frac{\rho^2(\tau)}{\rho^2(\tau) + \sigma^2(\delta)}. \qquad\qquad (11.10)$$

where the population values are used: τ represents the generic case for persons. Equation 11.10 shows us that the expected value of universe score variance is, technically, the ratio of *universe score variance* to itself, plus error variance.

Not surprisingly, then, the index of dependability is also a ratio but for the population and *absolute* error variance. It is shown in Equation 11.11:

$$\hat{\Phi} = \frac{\sigma^2(\tau)}{\sigma^2(\tau) + \sigma^2(\Delta)}. \tag{11.11}$$

We use these equations to calculate a generalizability coefficient and an index of dependability later in the chapter, after discussion of research design and formulation and estimation of variance components.

More on Facets

We already know that to decompose error, G theory considers facets of an appraisal. Procedurally, the facets have more than one category, analogous to levels of a factor in an independent variable of an experiment. These *facet conditions* (or just *conditions,* for short) may be either qualitative attributes or quantitative amounts but are more usually the former. It is useful to know what facets and conditions are commonly employed in G studies of educational and psychological tests.

Three Facets Commonly Used in Studies

Content, occasion, and *rating* are three facets of reliability commonly used in generalizability studies. Content is, logically, the description of the construct intended for assessment. In reliability evaluation, the primary consideration of a test's content is its breadth of coverage of the domain being assessed. For some tests content is defined broadly, whereas for others the content is stated more narrowly. For example, if a test were about the language arts, the scope of coverage would be quite broad; however, if only word usage of synonyms, antonyms, and homonyms were included on the test, the scope of content would be narrower.

The same holds true for the *occasion* for assessment, another commonly employed facet of assessment, and a concomitant variable. Occasion is another way to state the number of times the content is assessed. For example, in writing assessment, it is a popular technique to collect more than one writing sample from an examinee. If a writing appraisal requires three samples, then there are three occasions for assessment. Occasion can also be considered a multiple-choice test item or a single test exercise. In practice, this is generally considered the number of items or exercises on the test. That is, a test with 75 multiple-choice items presents 75 occasions for assessment. When there is only one item or exercise, there is no opportunity for variation in response, and occasion could be considered a constant, a variable without variance. Of course, most tests contain many items or exercises; hence, estimating the error involved in having assessment over a number of occasions is an important consideration. In modern theories of measurement, the occasions (viz., the test items or exercises) on a test are but a sample from a nearly inexhaustible pool of possible occasions.

Likewise, the principle holds with *raters,* or persons scoring the assessment. In this context, "raters" is itself a facet to be estimated in reliability assessment. When a test is scored only once, as when done by machine (whether optical scanning or otherwise), then there is only a single scoring and no variance exists in this facet, so it is not an estimable variable by G theory. However, often modern assessment programs involve several scorings done by different raters. Essays are often graded by more than one rater, and PAs can involve more than one source (e.g., teacher rating, self-assessment, peer editing, psychologist evaluation), and in this instance, "rater" is a facet with variance. It is, then, part of reliability assessment.

G Studies and D Studies

Two Types of Studies

Generalizability theory provides for two kinds of test examination, called *G studies* (*generalizability studies*) and *D studies* (*decision studies*). G studies seek to identify error sources and then quantify them into variance components. D studies use the variance estimates of test components in a utilitarian design to make practical testing decisions. Although there are important differences between these kinds of studies, there is also considerable overlap in approach and methods; therefore, making the distinction between them is sometimes fuzzy. According to Cronbach et al. (1972), "The distinction between G and D studies is no more than a recognition that certain studies are carried out during the development of a measuring procedure, and then the procedure is put to use in other studies" (p. 19).

Often, studies of both types are conducted simultaneously. Ideally, for more robust findings, researchers should use different samples with separate data for each kind of study, but often that is impractical. It is common, therefore, in real world settings, to use the available data set for both types of study.

G Studies

Typically, G studies are research that is theoretical in nature and yield information for building structural equations of interest. As theory, G studies examine error as a psychometric phenomenon. The intent is to benefit the entire realm of measurement science. Almost always, work involving generalizability theory begins with a G study because G studies are the heart of G theory. Much of the methodology and estimation formulas discussed in this chapter are primarily geared toward G studies.

G studies depart from reliability investigation that uses traditional indices in two important ways. First, G studies focus on differentiating sources for error variance, making them a distinctly different kind of research effort from that done with CTT, wherein a single source of error is reflected by a given reliability coefficient. Obviously, this means that G studies must involve at least two sources of error for simultaneous evaluation.

The second dissimilarity in the different reliability studies is that the G studies follow an ANOVA design and thus give attention to reporting variance of main and interaction effects. CTT only provides a means to compute one reliability coefficient at a time. This feature has profound implications for test interpretation.

D Studies

G studies often lead to D studies, which focus on practical aspects of decision making. It is not absolutely necessary for every G theory investigation to include a D study because sometimes just a G study yields the desired information. However, more often than not, researchers, test developers, and others also have practical test questions in mind. Such questions in G theory often concentrate on a specific instrument used in a particular assessment context, or they seek information about the sample population, hence, the D study. The primary feature of the D study is that it is utilitarian, providing valuable information about practical testing problems. Illustrative D study scenarios are as follows:

- The board of directors of a school district has mandated a high school exit exam and requires each student to meet or exceed a certain cut score before receiving a certificate. The history of this exam is that about two thirds of the students pass on their first trial, but the remaining students often take the exam more than twice, some of them taking it three, four, and even five times. The same exam is used on all testing occasions. The district's director of research wonders whether exam reliability is reduced for students taking the test repeatedly.

- A certification program has a two-step certifying process in which candidates must pass a 40-item regional exam, and then, if successful, go on to a 60-item national exam. The logistics and expense of two test administrations are considerable, and officials at the certifying organization want to learn whether a single 80-item exam, containing both regional and national content, would provide equally reliable assessment. If so, then obviously a single test administration would have the added benefit of less cost to the organization and the candidates.

- A medical researcher wants to perform clinical trials of several treatment methods for the same disease symptoms. The disease symptoms occur only in combination with other, preexisting medical conditions. The researcher develops several crossed and nested designs for the study and wants to know which design will yield the most reliable results.

- A human resource officer is faced with hiring 50 persons from an applicant pool of 312. The open positions require skill in organizing materials, writing reports, and interacting with people from many of the company's diverse departments. The officer requires the job applicants to take a lengthy battery of tests, followed by two thorough interviews, each with a different interviewer. Obviously, this hiring process is both expensive and time consuming, so the officer wants to explore whether hiring decisions could be just as reliably made by using a short writing sample and one brief interview.

Absolute and Relative Decisions

Absolute versus relative decisions are also an important distinction with G theory. D studies are conducted to provide information for decision making, but not all decisions based on a test score are parallel in form or substance. For some decisions, the absolute score is the critical element in making the judgment. This is the case when a cut score is employed, as in a licensure or certifying decision. When the candidate achieves the given score, the decision is automatically triggered. In these contexts, reliability is concerned with consistency at a given score point. The principle issue here is to avoid committing false-positive or false-negative evaluations. Decisions of this type are called *absolute decisions,* and they require one type of coefficient. From among the previous illustrative D study scenarios, the first (high school exit exam) and second (certification decision) are decisions of this type.

In other contexts, however, the absolute score is not as important as is standing within a group, and the decision is *relative*. Hiring and admissions decisions are examples of relative decisions. Suppose, for example, a college admissions officer has 600 available places and must select those most likely to succeed in the program from among 2,100 applicants. Here, a slightly different variance estimate is used.

The distinction between absolute and relative decisions has been important in test analysis and validity evaluation for a long time. It is shown by difference coefficients, such as when one contrasts the reliability coefficient with an index of agreement. A practical illustration of this difference, in the context of interrater reliability for assessment of writing samples, is given by Tinsley and Weiss (1975). Harris (1997) also offers a helpful discussion on using reliability coefficients and indexes in decision making, the topic to which we now turn.

Univariate and Multivariate Research Designs

Because G theory relies on variance procedures for estimating error effects, a design tailored to a specific research investigation is needed. In a very general sense, the design possibilities parallel those in ANOVA or multivariate analysis of variance (MANOVA), including full factorial and many varieties of custom ones; but, there are also some restrictions. Remember, G studies and D studies examine component variance rather than attending to significance tests, so the F distribution is not especially important here.

As can be anticipated, the research designs may be organized into the two traditional general linear model (GLM) categories—univariate and multivariate—depending on the arrangement of factors, or facets. Multivariate designs are more flexible than univariate designs in that a greater number of facets with more complex arrangements are considered. Also consistent with the GLM, univariate designs are regarded as a special case of multivariate designs. This is parallel in logic to ANOVA designs being treated as a special application of multivariate regression designs. Regardless, due to the complexity of multivariate designs, most G studies and D studies are univariate. Figure 11.3 shows typical one-facet designs as used in G theory.

Figure 11.3

Possible one-facet designs.

Source: From *The Dependability of Behavioral Measurement: Theory of Generalizability for Scores and Profiles* (p. 35), by L. J. Cronbach, G. C. Gleser, et al., 1972, Hillsdale, NJ: Lawrence Erlbaum Associates. Copyright 1972 by Lawrence Erlbaum Associates. Adapted with permission.

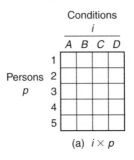

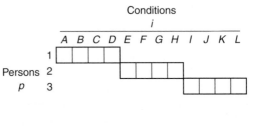

Our focus here is on univariate designs because most multivariate generalizability designs are beyond the scope of this text. Brennan (2001c) offers a thorough treatment of multivariate design in G theory, as does Cronbach et al. (1972), whose discussion, although dated, is still excellent.

G theory studies can also accommodate more complex designs, including both *crossed* and *nested* research designs, which are generally necessary for studies that include two or more facets. When two variables or more are considered together and every subject is tested on every condition, yielding full interaction, the design is said to be crossed. For example, if i and p are crossed, every p has a score for each level (or facet condition) of i. The design is $p \times i$. Here, we can say, "Persons is crossed with items." Simply put, every person has a score for each item. When additional conditions are present—for example, there are n occasions of j—the crossed design appears as $i \times j \times p$, meaning that for p (persons) a score is present for each pairing of ij. Figure 11.4 shows some two-facet designs.

In such research efforts, three facets of reliability commonly used are (a) the *content* for assessment, (b) the *occasion* for assessment, and (c) the *rating* of the assessment. Also, "persons" is not generally considered a facet. Using these facets in a crossed design is common in G studies and D studies. Let i be the occasion, j the content, and p the persons, or population. This crossed design can be expressed as shown previously (viz., $i \times j \times p$). However, to convey the notion of population as separate from facets, it is more commonly expressed as $p \times (i \times j)$. In this instance, it means that every person in the population has a score for all occasions and all levels of content. This is a popular design to evaluate reliability with G theory.

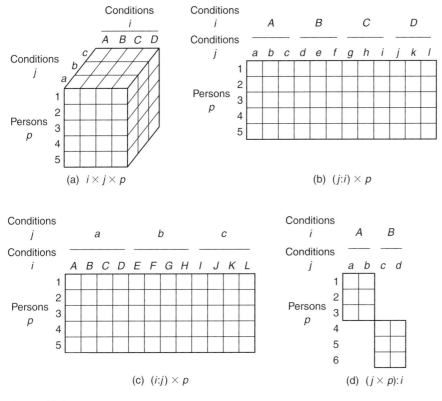

(a) $i \times j \times p$

(b) $(j{:}i) \times p$

(c) $(i{:}j) \times p$

(d) $(j \times p){:}i$

Figure 11.4
Possible two-facet designs.

Source: From The Dependability of Behavioral Measurement: Theory of Generalizability for Scores and Profiles (p. 36), by L. J. Cronbach, G. C. Gleser, et al., 1972, Hillsdale, NJ: Lawrence Erlbaum Associates. Copyright 1972 by Lawrence Erlbaum Associates. Adapted with permission.

A Small-Sample Example of Component Estimation

An example of calculating variance components is useful to illustrate how G theory is practiced. The data for this illustration are invented scores for 10 examinees on a hypothetical writing appraisal. For the pretend assessment, examinees were given five writing prompts and were directed to write five short, coherent, and responsive paragraphs. The writing samples were scored three times each by independent raters, who employed an agreed-upon scoring rubric that followed a 0- to 9-point scoring system.

Arranging these assessment features into a research design yields possible variables of persons ($n = 10$), items ($n = 5$), and raters ($n = 3$). Logically, in such a design, the dependent variable is the score received. Each rater's scores are considered a testing occasion. Also, typically, "persons" is considered to be the population and is excluded as a facet, leaving items, occasion, and score as final facets for analysis.

Table 11.1
Hypothetical Data for G Theory Variance Illustration

Examinee	Rater #1					Rater #2					Rater #3				
	I1	I2	I3	I4	I5	I1	I2	I3	I4	I5	I1	I2	I3	I4	I5
1	6	6	5	0	5	5	5	3	5	7	5	7	4	4	4
2	7	2	5	9	8	5	6	8	8	9	6	9	3	5	9
3	8	3	5	3	9	6	7	7	4	8	4	4	2	5	6
4	6	5	6	7	5	6	5	5	5	7	6	9	8	8	8
5	1	1	1	1	1	1	1	3	2	1	3	1	5	2	1
6	2	7	3	2	8	2	5	3	1	9	2	9	3	3	6
7	2	8	1	6	4	7	7	7	7	7	5	2	8	0	4
8	3	3	0	5	4	5	4	6	8	4	7	6	6	4	8
9	9	2	8	5	5	5	2	8	3	4	9	6	4	5	2
10	9	9	5	6	7	5	7	8	9	4	6	4	7	6	9

Table 11.2
Correlations Matrix for Scoring Occasions

| Source | α | Occasion | | |
		Rater A	Rater B	Rater C
Rater A	0.66	1		
Rater B	0.78	0.72 (51.75%)	1	
Rater C	0.63	0.65 (42.84%)	0.53 (27.63%)	1

In an ANOVA between-subjects design, for each of the five items, there are 30 observations involved in the analysis (three raters for 10 examinees); for each of the three raters, there are 50 observations (five items for 10 examinees); and finally, for each of the 9 score points, there are a possible 150 nonoverlapping observations. The raw score data for each facet is given in Table 11.1.

A variety of traditional reliability indices for these data are presented in Table 11.2. First, Cronbach's alpha is given. For this example, all indices are within a typical range, if slightly at the low end of what is acceptable, depending on assessment context. Also shown are test–retest correlations and associated variance statistics (expressed as percentages). These statistics are often also used as a gauge of inter-rater reliability.

For analysis, the data must be organized in a manner that allows for independent treatment of all 150 observations. For most statistical packages (e.g., SPSS, SAS, Systat, Statistica), the data will be arranged as in Table 11.3.

The SPSS syntax for the ANOVA, as well as for computing variance components (explained momentarily), is shown in Figure 11.5. These can be run as a single analysis. Within SPSS syntax, the VARCOMP procedure estimates variance components for mixed models, following the GLM approach. It estimates the contribution of each random effect to the variance of the dependent variable, in this case, "score." VARCOMP is available in the SPSS Advanced Models option.

The variable list specifies the dependent variable and the factors in the model. The RANDOM subcommand allows one to specify random factors. The METHOD subcommand offers four different methods for estimating the variances of the random effects. By default in SPSS, MINQUE(n)—*minimum norm quadratic unbiased estimator*—is the method used. The INTERCEPT subcommand controls whether an intercept term is included in the model. For the ANOVA and MINQUE methods, negative variance component estimates may occur when either the specified model is not the correct model or the true value of the variance equals zero. When it happens, they can be ignored.

With the previous information, a factorial ANOVA can be performed on the data file. The resultant ANOVA source table is shown in Table 11.4.

Table 11.3
Arrangement of Data in Statistical Package Data Matrix

	Person	Item	Rater	Score
1	1	1	1	6
2	2	1	1	7
3	3	1	1	8
4	4	1	1	6
5	5	1	1	1
6	6	1	1	2
7	7	1	1	2
8	8	1	1	3
9	9	1	1	9
10	10	1	1	9
11	1	1	2	5
12	2	1	2	5
13	3	1	2	6
.	.	.	.	.
.	.	.	.	.
.	.	.	.	.
148	8	5	3	8
149	9	5	3	2
150	10	5	3	9

Note particularly in the table that no values are reported for columns tradition-ally containing the *F* values and significance levels. Because in G theory the focus is on the sums of squares rather than the *F* ratio per se, it is standard practice that those columns are not reported. Realize, too, that the effects are random, not fixed, a cus-tomary presumption in G theory. Such a presumption is logical because each ob-servation in a facet is only a sample for any possible observation.

Regardless, some fixed effects and mixed effects models are available in G theory, but these approaches are beyond the current discussion. For these models, readers are referred to Frederick (1999) or Shavelson and Webb (1991).

Next, using the mean square values in the ANOVA source table, the separate variance components can be computed. Variance estimates for each facet and their interactions are provided in Table 11.5. These values are central to G theory, show-ing the amount of variation attributable to each facet.

Before discussing these values, however, it will be instructive to learn how they are computed because the process reveals much about the resultant numbers. The

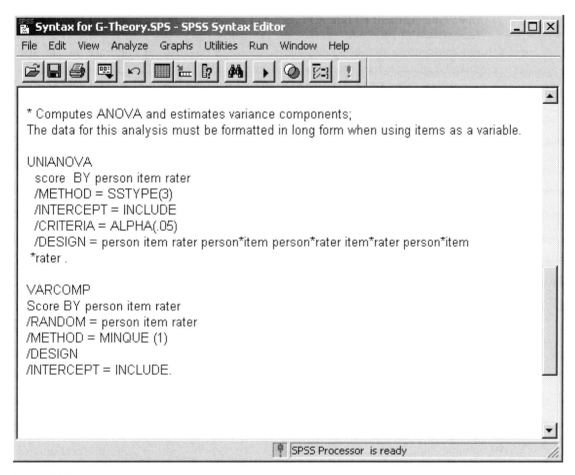

Figure 11.5
SPSS syntax for computing G theory variance components.

computation is not difficult, although it involves some related steps, beginning with the mean square of the ANOVA.

As a first step, mean squares for each facet are combined in the manner shown in Table 11.6. This is the application of the identity of the conditions of measurement included in the design, as originally given in Expression 11.8. The rightmost column in Table 11.6 displays the sum, our statistic of interest.

The next step is shown in Table 11.7. Here, the sum of squares for facets is divided by the total number of elements included in a given facet: 15 for persons, 50 for items, 30 for raters, and so forth for the interactions. The result of these manipulations is the variance estimation given in the right-hand column. These estimates match those in Table 11.5. It is interesting to note that some values are computed to be negative variance, an illogical source. These are considered as zero variance because

Table 11.4
Tests of Between-Subjects Effects

Dependent Variable: SCORE

Source	Type III sum of squares	df	Mean square	F	Sig.
Corrected Model	905.873[a]	149	6.080	.	.
Intercept	3881.127	1	3881.127	.	.
PERSON	289.073	9	32.119	.	.
ITEM	22.040	4	5.510	.	.
RATER	8.493	2	4.247	.	.
PERSON * ITEM	199.427	36	5.540	.	.
PERSON * RATER	93.107	18	5.173	.	.
ITEM * RATER	25.040	8	3.130	.	.
PERSON * ITEM * RATER	268.693	72	3.732	.	.
Error	.000	0	.		
Total	4787.000	150			
Corrected Total	905.873	149			

[a] R Squared = 1.000 (Adjusted R Squared = .)

variance is expressed in squared scores. Some explanations for this circumstance are that the model does not describe the data to a satisfactory degree or, of course, that the true variance is zero. In either case, the result is for no variance to be considered.

Finally, we get to the heart of the matter, computing the mean variance components and transforming each to a component percentage. These calculations are shown in Table 11.8. Immediately, one is likely struck by the large percentage for "persons," especially as a first-order variable and, to a lesser degree, in the interactions. This is

Table 11.5
Variance Estimates

Component	Estimate
Var(PERSON)	1.676
Var(ITEM)	.019
Var(RATER)	−.006[a]
Var(PERSON * ITEM)	.603
Var(PERSON * RATER)	.288
Var(ITEM * RATER)	−.060[a]
Var(PERSON * ITEM * RATER)	3.732
Var(Error)	.000[b]

Table 11.6
Related Interactions of Variance Components

Effect	MS$_{Effect}$	Related interactions				Sum
		−MS	−MS	+Mspri, ej		
Person	32.12	−5.54	−5.17	3.73	=	25.14
Item	5.51	−5.54	−3.13	3.73	=	0.57
Rater	4.25	−5.17	−3.13	3.73	=	−0.32
Person * Item	5.54	−3.73			=	1.81
Person * Rater	5.17	−3.73			=	1.44
Item * Rater	3.13	−3.73			=	−0.60
Person * Item * Rater	3.73				=	3.73

Table 11.7
Computation of Variance Components

	Sum	Persons	Rater	Item	Total		Variance component
Person	25.14		3	5	15	=	1.68
Item	0.57	10		5	50	=	0.01
Rater	−0.32	10	3	5	30	=	−0.01
Person * Item	1.81		3		3	=	0.60
Person * Rater	1.44			5	5	=	0.29
Item * Rater	−0.60	10			10	=	−0.06
Person * Item * Rater	3.73					=	3.73

Table 11.8
Component Statistics

	Variance component	Frequency	Mean	Percentage (%)
Person	1.68	10	0.17	27
Item	0.01	5	0.00	0
Rater	0.00	3	0.00	0
Person * Item	0.60	5	0.12	19
Person * Rater	0.29	3	0.10	15
Item * Rater	−0.06	15	0.00	−1
Person * Item * Rater	3.73	15	0.25	39
Total			0.63	100

not surprising given the fact that our premise for the analysis is that "persons" differ. In fact, the remainder of the analysis concentrates on how and why they differ. If they were not different, they would not be the focus for the research.

All other nonzero interactions also include "person" as a component.

Calculating G Theory Reliability Coefficients

Recall from the previous discussion that G studies can be informed by two reliability indices, depending on whether the consequent decision is relative or absolute. Relative decisions are usually set in the context of a specific group, whereas absolute decisions are often meant to last for some time and apply to many groups. In either case, the calculations needed for determining the reliability coefficients rely on error variances. The error variances, however, are employed in slightly different manners to yield the two coefficients.

Mathematically, we realize that because variances are used for G theory reliability coefficients, they are always expressed in a squared metric. Confusion can arise regarding this point, however, because G theory employs the traditional notation for measurement of phi coefficient and reliability coefficient (i.e., ρ_ϕ, $\rho_{X_1X_2}$), which does not explicitly show the square superscript. Knowing that the metric is squared, however, makes the calculations more meaningful and simpler.

Reliability for Relative Decisions

When the intent is to make a relative decision, it is necessary to consider only the error variances that influence ordinality of scores. This means that only first-order sums of squares (those related to main effects) plus the confounded second-order interaction effect need to be considered. In the small-sample example, this is the person × item, person × rater, and the final person × item × rater variances. Here, other variances do not play a role. Table 11.9 shows these error variances in a manner that easily presents them for both types of reliability coefficients.

In Table 11.9, the data for relative error variances sum to 4.62. Total error variance for the relative decision is the sum of the systematic error variance (1.68) and the relative error (4.62) for a total observed error of 6.30. Then, a ratio of the systematic score variance to the total score variance is a reliability estimate, or in this context, a generalizability coefficient. As a ratio of these error variances (i.e., relative to total), the following calculation results:

$$\frac{1.68}{6.30} = .267.$$

In this example, the small coefficient results from the few observations (10 persons on five items) and the ensuing large measurement error. Of course, such low reliability in most real-life testing contexts would be unacceptable for decision making. Nonetheless, it illustrates the procedure.

Table 11.9
Component Statistics

| | Variance component | Systematic variance | Measurement error | |
			Relative error variance	Absolute error variance
Person	1.68	1.68		
Item	0.01			0.01
Rater	0.00			0.00
Person * Item	0.60		0.60	0.60
Person * Rater	0.29		0.29	0.29
Item * Rater	−0.06			−0.06
Person * Item * Rater	3.73		3.73	3.73
Total		1.68	4.62	4.57

Reliability for Absolute Decisions

When the decision to be rendered is absolute (e.g., as against a cut score for passing a hurdles exam), the variances measured are those relating to a criterion. In our small-sample example, it is the items and all interactions; in other words, the sum of variance from all sources. In Table 11.9, these values are shown in the right-hand column, and the total is 4.57. The total observed variance is 6.25 (viz., 1.68 + 4.57). In a manner parallel to calculating the relative G theory reliability coefficient, the absolute coefficient is still the ratio of variances, only this time the ratio is of the total absolute error variance to the systematic error. Hence, the following calculations result:

$$\frac{1.68}{6.25} = .269.$$

In this example, the absolute value reliability coefficient is a tiny amount higher than the value obtained for relative decisions (again, due to the small number of observations); however, it is consistent with the expectation that in G theory, reliability estimates for absolute decision are usually higher than are parallel estimates for relative decisions.

G Theory Reliability Coefficients and the Phi Coefficient of Correlation

Some astute readers may quickly realize a commonality between G theory reliability values and the specialized phi coefficient of correlation (ϕ), used when two variables are true dichotomies and often employed in analysis of multiple-choice test items (see chapter 12). The phi coefficient of correlation is also a ratio of variances, this one of systematic variance and total score variance.

In our small example of G theory, the ratio is what was just shown for absolute decisions.

Under certain conditions, the G theory absolute reliability coefficient and the phi correlation coefficient will be identical. This can occur when all measurement variances associated with G theory absolute decisions are zero. Obviously, this circumstance will never truly occur in real-life decision making, although it is presumed in CTT. This fact is, not surprisingly, a rationale for using the G theory reliability coefficient when making absolute decisions.

G Theory Computer Programs

As is apparent to readers, the procedures for research and other psychometric applications of G theory are complex, and it is desirable to have a programmed algorithm available for calculating estimates of variance components and the appropriate reliability coefficients. Brennan (2001) wrote three such programs for varying the application of G theory and generously offers them to interested persons in both PC and Mac versions. They can be accessed the Iowa Testing Programs Web site at *http://www.education.uiowa.edu/casma/computer_programs.htm* (Retrieved March 9, 2005). The first program is called GENOVA for GENeralized analysis Of VAriance. It is appropriate for complete balanced designs with as many as six effects (e.g., five facets and an object of measurement). The second program in the suite is urGENOVA which is appropriate for unbalanced designs, and the final one is mGENOVA which is used with multivariate G theory designs.

The programs are written in FORTRAN and require a certain level of expertise to run. A mini-manual is available as an appendix in Brennan's (2001c) *Generalizability Theory,* and a complete manual can be obtained the web site.

Summary

Modern reliability analysis is the focus of this chapter. Specifically, we look at G theory, first explaining what it is and then dispelling common misconceptions. We also look at both G studies and D studies, understanding the differences between them and when each is used in measurement. We calculate G theory coefficients and work through a relatively simple example. In addition, we examine the kinds of decisions (relative and absolute) that can result from such studies. The chapter concludes by noting a few computer programs that are useful to G theory program implementation.

Chapter 12

Examining Individual
Test Items and Exercises

Introduction

Endurance and Quality

In 1914, Sir Ernest Shackleton set out from England on a daring expedition. His goal—to make the first crossing of the Antarctic continent, from the Weddell Sea to the Ross Sea. Among adventurers this was a prize to visit unclaimed territory where no human had ever stood. However, in a place where weather is hostile to humans at any time, the storms of that year were especially fierce. For awhile, his ship, the *Endurance,* gamely broke the ice with her wooden hull, but eventually the frozen pack became too thick and *Endurance* stuck fast. Virtually overnight, it became bound to the ice. Shackleton and his crew had no alternative but to wait until the spring thaw, about 6 months away.

At first, this did not seem to be difficult because they had food to eat and whale oil for lamps. They lived in the ship, singing songs, reciting poems, and performing ad hoc plays. Soon, however, their situation worsened. They discovered that the supplies were not as extensive as first thought. The ice shifted and *Endurance* listed precariously. They had to abandon her and move to the open ice. There they made flimsy tents from blankets and sheets. The ice shifted again, this time literally crushing *Endurance* until she was nothing but a pile of wood.

Their boat gone, the crew was forced to move among ice floes and eventually to a small, rocky island. They ate seal and were constantly cold, taking turns wrapping themselves in the available blankets. Their grueling saga continued for nearly 2 years, with the slow realization that rescue would never come. At the end of their collective rope, Shackleton made a momentous decision. He would sail a tiny lifeboat to the whaling stations of South Georgia, more than 800 miles away across the most dangerous ocean on the planet. He and five sailors experienced storms and unrelenting rain for nearly 3 weeks in their slim craft, but, almost unbelievably, they made it to the island.

Once there, they found that they had landed on the uninhabited, cliff-lined side of it. Barely alive, Shackleton climbed the cliffs in darkness and walked 3 days across the island to the settlement. He was alive, but he cared not about himself; he did not even wait for his health to improve to commence a rescue of his crew still on

Elephant Island. It took four sailing attempts to reach his men, but he finally did rescue them all, most barely surviving. The saga of their survival is filled with greatness: their ingenuity at making things work, their despair and loneliness in a remote, icy land, and especially Shackleton's almost mythic heroism. It is a true story of heroism, grace, and will.

Shackleton's devotion to duty, his leadership, and his unwavering demand for quality kept him and his men alive. Adherence to similar characteristics will aid the measurement professional in examining test items because this task is both technically challenging and obliging of a commitment to quality workmanship. In a rough sense, we strive to become the Shackletons of measurement, finding inventive ways to accomplish a goal despite disappointment. In the end, our measurement is the better for our efforts.

Contents

This chapter addresses issues in examining individual test items and exercises, and looks at methods of analysis in particular. It focuses on the item (exercise, PA), a single unit for measurement, and therefore, serves as one half of the topic of understanding test functioning. When items and exercises are considered in the aggregate, they constitute a whole exam. Whole test analysis is the subject of chapter 13, which serves as the companion to this chapter. In this chapter, I discuss the purpose of this singular kind of analysis and explain various strategies and methods. I describe techniques based on CTT and IRT. An especially important part of the discussion is an explanation of procedures useful for examining DIF, or item bias. For convenience, I call our subject *item* analysis (as is popularly done), although I mean the term to apply to nearly all test stimuli, regardless of format (e.g., multiple choice, Likert-type, PA).

Initial Considerations in Analyzing Items

Purpose of Item Analysis

An examination of test stimuli (i.e., items, exercises) is done for two reasons: (1) to understand how they contribute to the assessment phenomenon so valid interpretations of the constructs they represent may be inferred, and (2) to identify aspects that can be improved for subsequent administration. Most procedures used for analyzing items and exercises supply information constructive to both purposes.

Significantly, both reasons for examining items and exercises contribute to validity in measurement at its most fundamental level. In chapter 8, I described items and exercises as "the stuff" of measurement. Indeed, in their analysis we see the truth of this statement more than anywhere else. No statistical number crunching or psychometric procedure can make a test better than the inherent quality of items and exercises administered to the examinee—its initial "stuff."

Types: Traditional Versus Modern

Like measurement theories themselves, the varying processes employed for analyzing items are often classified as *traditional* or *modern*. Traditional item analysis is associated with statistics calculated under CTT conventions, and modern approaches generally refer to an IRT-based analysis. We learned earlier that traditional measurement theory provides information that is dependent on the data given by a particular group of examinees, whereas IRT-based measurement theory relies on a psychological perspective of latent traits and is not similarly group dependent.

Item analysis classed as traditional is limited in interpretation to the single group from whom the data for analysis was obtained, or at most, to a population that can be appropriately inferred. IRT-based, modern item analysis, however, is not similarly constrained. Because item information from this source is grounded by assumption in the underlying construct itself, the information applies to any examinee (regardless of group characteristics) who is suitably appraisable by the item or exercise on that construct. Another way to think of the distinction is to imagine that item analysis by traditional methods is targeted toward group characteristics; in contrast, such information garnered by modern means is more focused on how well the item or exercise reveals the underlying construct, regardless of particular examinee characteristics.

Focus for Attention During Item Analysis

Item analysis typically focuses on two characteristics: (a) *item difficulty*, and (b) *item discrimination*. As is well known among measurement professionals, the *p* value—an index indicating the percentage of examinees in a group who endorsed a particular response (usually noted as the correct response)—is the most common measure of item difficulty. Often, test constructors working with multiple-choice test items seek to develop questions that eventuate in a *p* value in the range of .6 to .8, meaning that somewhere between 60% and 80% of examinees typically endorse the correct response. The use of this guideline is limited to items measuring achievement and general ability or for other measures where a spread of scores is sought. It may not be appropriate for items on other tests, such as a proficiency test (as may be used for licensing and certification), or for diagnostic assessments like personality appraisal.

For group analysis, the obtained range for the difficulty index is important because little information is garnered when the stimuli is outside the limit of most examinees. Consider the case when all (or nearly all) examinees endorse the correct response, or conversely when none (or few) of them do. Items with *p* values of 0 or 1.0 convey little group information and usually need revision. This circumstance is mostly limited to analysis by traditional means.

With modern, IRT-based analyses, item difficulty is more directed at the latent trait under consideration and not just to the observed performance of the particular group from which statistics were gathered. In IRT-based item analyses, difficulty is individualized and considered optimal when the examinee is presented with an item that is located at the place on the ability scale where a .5 probability of correct response is observed. We have learned already that this value is estimated as a parameter location, namely, the *b* parameter.

The item discrimination index carries more subtle information than the difficulty indicator. This statistic is meant to show performance on an item relative to overall ability or proficiency, itself usually expressed by total test score. It provides information useful for test users so they may meaningfully interpret distinctions between those who exhibit the characteristics (e.g., amount or degree) of the construct being assessed and those who do not. For test constructors, discrimination is especially helpful in identifying aberrant items. For instance, an item with limited discrimination may indicate that the test stimulus makes no distinction between overall high test achievers and overall low test achievers. It may also reveal information useful for items revision, such as when unearthing a poorly worded item that contains a confusing distracter that is inadvertently interpreted as correct by overall high test achievers.

An item discrimination index may be calculated by any of varying ways, but often it is taken as the difference in *p* value between two particular groups of examinees: those in the top and bottom 27% of scores on the entire exam. When item discrimination is considered by this calculation, the index is sometimes interpreted as a rough gauge of reliability. Another common method of indicating item discrimination is to use the *point biserial coefficient of correlation* (r_{pbis}). This coefficient can be calculated for either just the correct response or for all response alternatives. Examples of both discrimination indices are indicated in the next section.

Discrimination in IRT-based programs is also an estimated parameter, but one that is indicated by the slope of the item characteristic curve (the *a* parameter). This statistic was discussed in chapter 11 and is put to use later in this chapter.

Organizing Item Data for Analysis

A useful way to view item analyses is by the unit for disposition of item responses or scores. It could be the raw responses, such as A, B, C, and D; it could represent the responses as correct and incorrect in binary items, using 1 and 0; or it could be the score on graded stimuli, such as 0 to 8 on an essay score. Each scheme for organizing test data presents different possibilities for analyses. Figures 12.1, 12.2, and 12.3 show these three common data organization schemes.

Figure 12.1 is called by various names, such as *data matrix,* but terming it a simple *response matrix* may be the most accurate. It displays the responses selected by each examinee (before scoring); in this example, the data are from multiple-choice formatted items. Figure 12.2 shows the items scored in a *right/wrong matrix*. This is used with binary items, dichotomously scored. In this illustration the total score is also displayed, but to do so is not mandatory in a right/wrong matrix. Figure 12.3 shows a *graded response matrix* for graded items, such as an essay or other PA. In this example, there are only three items, reflecting the obvious fact that most PAs have fewer items (exercises) than tests composed of selected response formatted items. The fractional points in the matrix appear because, in the illustration, a given score is the result of averaging the ratings of two judges.

	subno	q1	q2	q3	q4	q5	q6	q7
1	11	D	B	B	A	B	A	A
2	21	B	B	B	A	B	A	C
3	31	D	B	B	C	B	A	A
4	41	B	B	B	A	B	A	C
5	51	B	B	B	A	B	A	A
6	61	A	B	B	A	B	A	C
7	71	B	B	C	A	B	C	B
8	81	B	B	B	C	B	A	C
9	91	B	D	B	A	B	A	D
10	101	B	B	B	A	B	A	C
11	111	D	B	B	A	B	A	C
12	121	B	B	B	A	B	A	C
13	131	B	B	B	A	B	A	C
14	141	B	B	B	D	B	A	C
15	151	B	B	C	A	B	D	A
16	161	B	D	B	A	B	A	C

Figure 12.1
Item response matrix.

Sub #	Q1	Q2	Q3	Q4	Q5	Q6	Score
11	0	1	1	1	1	1	5
21	1	1	1	0	1	1	5
31	0	1	1	1	1	1	5
41	0	1	1	1	1	1	5
51	0	1	1	1	1	1	5
61	0	1	0	1	1	0	3
71	0	1	1	0	1	1	4
81	0	0	1	1	1	1	4
91	0	1	1	1	1	1	5
101	1	1	1	1	1	1	6
111	0	1	1	1	1	1	5
121	0	1	1	1	1	1	5
131	0	1	1	0	1	1	4
141	0	1	0	1	1	0	3
151	0	0	1	1	1	1	4
161	0	1	1	1	1	1	5

Figure 12.2
Right/wrong matrix with total score.

Figure 12.3
Graded response matrix for
graded items (e.g., essay).

Sub #	Q1	Q2	Q3
11	8	4	4
21	5.5	6	6
31	6	0	4.5
41	8	4.5	4.5
51	5	5	7
61	8	7	8
71	5	5	8
81	6.5	4.5	6
91	7	4	7
101	8	0	7
111	5.5	0	6
121	4.5	5	6.5
131	5	6	6
141	6	5.5	6
151	7	6	6
161	6.5	6	6

In each matrix, no scale or derived score information is provided. At this point, it is just the basic information from the test or appraisal scenario.

Item Analysis Based on CTT

Of course, calculating the statistics employed in analyzing individual test items and exercises is typically done via computer. There are seemingly dozens of computer programs that one can employ to this end. Three programs that generate information based on CTT assumptions are illustrated in this section. Beyond the three programs described, another, simpler CTT item analysis package is Lertap Item and Test Analysis Program, version 5 (*www.lertap.curtin.edu.au.* Retrieved February 20, 2005.). This program offers limited traditional item analysis and some interesting graphics. Its strength is that it is easy to configure data for analysis because it operates within Microsoft Excel.

MERMAC Item Analysis with SAS

The first set of statistics—displayed in Figure 12.4—is shown in the output from a custom computer program, written in SAS syntax (SAS Institute, Inc., 2002) and modeled after a MERMAC program. The statistics derive from a certification test administered to 1,059 candidates.

Matrix of Responses by Fifths for Question 14

A Is Correct Response   Percent of Correct Response by Fifths for Question 14

	(A)	B	C	D	E	OMIT	
5th	201	0	0	3	0	0	5th +
4th	190	2	12	11	0	0	4th +
3rd	182	1	19	25	0	0	3rd +
2nd	133	1	27	37	0	1	2nd +
1st	104	2	54	54	0	0	1st +

```
5th +                                                      *
4th +                                               *
3rd +                                         *
2nd +                                *
1st +                        *
     +----+----+----+----+----+----+----+----+----+----+
     0   10   20   30   40   50   60   70   80   90  100
```

DIFF	(0.76)	0.01	0.11	0.12	0.00	0.00
RPBI	(0.42)	−0.02	−0.30	−0.25	0.00	−0.02

Figure 12.4
Item analysis fractile table and display showing classical item statistics for a reasonably well-performing item.

Notice in Figure 12.4 that two displays of item statistics are provided for this analysis, one a table and the other a graphic. Also, in both displays, the group of examinees is divided into quintiles of approximately equal number, about 200 or so each in this example. The quintiles represent approximate fifths of the distribution when considered as percentiles of overall test achievement. Persons in the fifth group obtained the highest total test score, those in the fourth group got the next highest total test score, and so forth down the levels of achievement, to the first level—examinees who performed poorly on this test relative to the other test takers.

Tables such as these are termed *fractile tables* and they may be produced with different fractiles, depending on the distribution or intended use. If the overall distribution were perfectly normal in shape, there would be exactly equal numbers in each fractile. As a distribution becomes more skewed, the number in each group will vary. Skew and kurtosis statistics indicate the shape of the distribution; and the semi-interquartile range and modal score can be used to determine the score ranges for the fractiles.

In Figure 12.4, view the two summary rows below the matrix, labeled "DIFF" and "RPBI." These are abbreviations for *item difficulty* and the *point-biserial coefficient of correlation* (r_{pbis}). Also, easily realized in this figure, the correct answer is enclosed in parentheses (here, the A response). In this program, the *p* value is given for the correct response and for each distracter. In the data, 76% of examinees endorsed the correct response, whereas 1%, 11%, and 12% chose the B, C, and D incorrect responses, respectively. This test has only four options, so the E column is ignored. Seeing here that all distracters are endorsed is useful information because it reveals that each one apparently had some plausibility for at least a few examinees. If no one had selected a particular distracter, the test developer may be guided to improve it.

Now look downward in a given response column, say, at the column for response A. Notice that fewer examinees in each quintile (ability) grouping endorsed this response. This indicates good discrimination for the item by ability, usually a desirable feature for items. Conversely, more persons in the lower quintile groupings selected an incorrect response.

The *point-biserial correlation coefficient* (r_{pbis}) is a numerical indicator of this selection phenomenon. This index is a specialized correlation, wherein the response scale is dichotomized as right or wrong. When this dichotomy is matched against the score that an examinee received on the overall test, a coefficient may be calculated. In a good item, the r_{pbis} will be positive for the correct response and negative for each incorrect alternative. Again, this indicates positive discrimination. As a coefficient, the r_{pbis} may range ± 1, but in item analysis work, the r_{pbis} typically is closer to range 0.2 to 0.5 for the correct alternative and even lower for incorrect alternatives.

Many computer programs can calculate r_{pbis}; however, because this statistic is commonly used in item analysis and is not typically reported in many general statistics or measurement texts, I present the formula in Equation 12.1:

$$r_{pbis} = \frac{\overline{Y}_1 - \overline{Y}_0}{\sigma_y} \sqrt{\frac{N_1 N_0}{N - (N - 1)}}, \tag{12.1}$$

where $\overline{Y}_1$ = mean of the persons of the continuous variable in dichotomous category "1",

$\overline{Y}_0$ = mean of the persons of the continuous variable in dichotomous category "0",

N_1 = N in dichotomous category "1",

N_0 = N in dichotomous category "0", and

σ_y = population σ for continuous variable.

(Note that the term under the radical is a probability, which may also be written as $\sqrt{\dfrac{p}{1 - p}}$.)

The significance of r_{pbis} (i.e., H_0: $r_{pbis} = 0$) can be tested by the t test, with $N - 2$ degrees of freedom, but that may be overkill for this purpose.

Now, return attention to Figure 12.4, this time looking at the graphic. This is a handy, but very approximate, guide to several functions for the item. Each asterisk is horizontally aligned with a quintile (or ability) group; thus, the topmost asterisk represents the highest-achieving group and so on. They are placed on the graphic at the percentile of that group who correctly endorsed the item (see bottom scale). As can be seen, nearly 100% of the highest quintile group responded correctly to the item, but only about 49% of the lowest-ability group did so. As expected in a normally discriminating item, the asterisks flow from right to left in a lazy curve, as each lower quintile exhibits a smaller percentage endorsing the item correctly.

Matrix of Responses by Fifths for Question 53

	(A)	B	C	D	E	OMIT		Percent of Correct Response by Fifths for Question 53
	A Is Correct Response							
5th	65	121	8	10	0	0	5th +	*
4th	66	108	16	25	0	0	4th +	*
3rd	80	93	20	34	0	0	3rd +	*
2nd	84	70	18	26	0	1	2nd +	*
1st	91	57	38	28	0	0	1st +	*

```
                                          +----+----+----+----+----+----+----+----+----+----+
DIFF   (0.36)  0.42   0.09   0.12  0.00   0.00      0   10  20  30  40  50  60  70  80  90  100
RPBI   (-0.11) 0.23  -0.13  -0.07  0.00  -0.02
```

Figure 12.5
Item analysis fractile table and display showing classical item statistics for a poorly performing item.

In the main, the item illustrated in Figure 12.4 is performing well for most achievement or ability tests. In contrast, examine the information presented for a poorly performing item, such as given in Figure 12.5. Obviously, distracter B (and to a lesser extent C) is causing confusion among examinees of all abilities but especially for those of relatively higher abilities.

Item Analysis with TESTFACT

Among the item-analyzing computer programs discussed in this chapter, the one with the most complete information is *TESTFACT: Test Scoring, Item Statistics, and Item FA* (Wood et al., 2002). Version 4.0, released in 2003, is replete with item statistics, both conventional and IRT based, and the program incorporates the IRT-based "full-information FA (factor analysis)" (discussed in chapter 13). Here, I explain only the program output related to classical item analysis. For complete information, refer to the extensive manual (du Toit, 2003). The program is flexible and can produce a variety of statistics, but it is difficult to use (requiring the user to build syntax statements with FORTRAN command lines). Hence, it is not recommended for the casual user. For a trained psychometrician, however, it is an extremely valuable tool to produce assorted measurement-related information.

The first step in using TESTFACT is to format the data in a manner accessible to the program. Figure 12.6 displays a portion of a window showing the data file. For TESTFACT, this must be a flat file in fixed format, also called text and formerly labeled ASCII.

At the basic level, TESTFACT produces eight item statistics in phase 2 of its operation. The output for the first 12 items in a set of scores from a test of scholastic achievement is given in Figure 12.7. The information begins with identifying the item

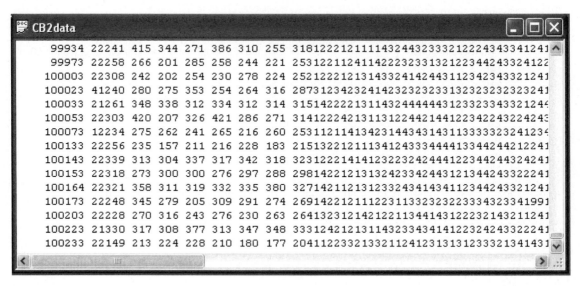

Figure 12.6
Typical fixed-column formatted data file (*.txt or ASCII [dated]), appropriate for many item analysis programs.

PHASE 2: ITEM STATISTICS
CB (LP)_TESTFACT– ITEMS FROM COLLEGE BASE, FORM LP CLASSICAL ITEM STATISTICS

MAIN TEST ITEM STATISTICS

ITEM	NUMBER	MEAN	S.D.	RMEAN	FACILITY	DIFF	BIS	P.BIS
1 Q1	1999	28.60	7.02	30.23	0.676	11.17	0.437	0.336
2 Q2	1996	28.58	7.01	29.93	0.680	11.13	0.367	0.281
3 Q3	2000	28.59	7.02	29.40	0.832	9.15	0.382	0.256
4 Q4	2000	28.59	7.02	29.26	0.885	8.20	0.436	0.265
5 Q5	1997	28.60	7.02	29.50	0.854	8.79	0.481	0.312
6 Q6	1999	28.60	7.02	30.52	0.756	10.22	0.662	0.483
7 Q7	1996	28.62	7.01	30.26	0.635	11.62	0.397	0.310
8 Q8	1998	28.60	7.02	29.46	0.840	9.02	0.425	0.282
9 Q9	1995	28.60	7.02	31.17	0.534	12.66	0.492	0.392
10 Q10	1999	28.59	7.02	31.69	0.507	12.93	0.560	0.447
11 Q11	1999	28.60	7.02	31.11	0.358	14.46	0.343	0.267
12 Q12	1999	28.60	7.02	29.62	0.789	9.79	0.397	0.281

Figure 12.7
Classical item statistics as produced in TESTFACT output (phase 2).

by number and name (e.g., 1, Q1). Next, Figure 12.7 shows the number of respondents to the specific item. This sample comprises 2,000 examinees, but only 1,996 responded to Q2, for instance, whereas all of them responded to Q3 and Q4.

This number is followed by the mean and standard deviation of total score achieved by examinees for each item. To calculate this number, the program counts only valid cases by omitting examinees who did not respond to the item. The next statistic is the RMEAN, which is the mean score of only those examinees who correctly endorsed a given item. The RMEAN can be compared with the MEAN and its SD. This can be considered a rough gauge of item discrimination. If the RMEAN is higher than the MEAN, a positive correlational relationship between the item responses and the total test score would be indicated.

In TESTFACT, item FACILITY is the item's p value, using only valid numbers. For the displayed items, the highest is .885 for Q4 and the lowest is .358 for Q11. The term *facility* as a descriptor of an item's difficulty is more suited to IRT interpretation, and, as I explain it here, during discussion of IRT-based item statistics.

In the program, DIFF for *difficulty* is given as the delta statistic (Δ), which is calculated as shown in Equation 12.2. The delta statistic is also employed in DIF studies:

$$\Delta = -4\Phi^{-1}(p) + 13, \qquad \textbf{(12.2)}$$

where p = item facility, and

Φ^{-1} = inverse normal transformation, which has an effective range (1, 25), with a mean of 13 and SD of 4.

The last two statistics are coefficients of the biserial (r_{bis}) and point-biserial (r_{pbis}) correlation. Some psychometricians prefer the biserial, holding that it more accurately reflects the fact that a dichotomized item is only artificially derived, an assumption for the biserial but not for the point-biserial. However, the biserial coefficient can exceed 1 in some situations, making interpretation spurious. The point-biserial, however, assumes the dichotomy to be true, and as calculated, will always be a much lower number.

In phase 3 of the program, an "item difficulty by item discrimination" plot is produced, like the one shown in Figure 12.8. To interpret the plot, notice the scales for abscissa and ordinate axes. When the point-biserial statistic for an item is properly functioning relative to its facility, a 1 is indicated. Poorly functioning items are given a 2 in the plot. The program uses facility as a default criterion against which to judge the point-biserial, but allows the user to set another external criterion if desired.

Conventional Item Analysis with ITEMAN

ITEMAN (Assessment Systems Corporation, 1995) is another program that displays classical item statistics but in a simpler manner than the MERMAC. The output from this program for two items is shown in Figure 12.9. It provides statistics similar to those already discussed; however, there is one particular common item analysis number given here that is not also shown in the SAS program. This number is the *discrimination index,* described previously. This discrimination index is calculated as the difference

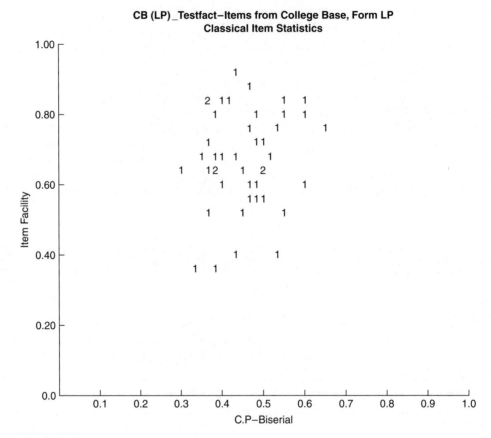

Figure 12.8
Plot of item difficulty (e.g., facility) by discrimination index (point-biserial) as produced in TESTFACT output (phase 3).

between the *p* values of two groups of examinees—the highest and lowest 27% on total test score. When the index is relatively high, as in the first item shown in Figure 12.9 (Seq. No. 8), the interpretation for the item is that it shows positive and desirable discrimination between examinees of differing ability. When the index is negative—the case with the second item in the figure (Seq. No. 9)—the opposite interpretation holds.

Modern IRT-Based Item Analysis

IRT-based methods for analyzing items can produce copious information about items useful for analyses. Like methods based on CTT, the IRT procedures also focus on item difficulty and discrimination, but conceptually they convey different

Seq. No.	Scale −Item	Item Statistics				Alternative Statistics				
		Prop. Correct	Disc. Index	Point Biser.	Alt.	Prop. Total	Endorsing Low	Endorsing High	Point Biser.	Key
8	0–8	.57	.45	.36	1	.21	.00	.00	.02	
					2	.00	.00	.00		
					3	.18	.43	.13	−.17	
					4	.57	.43	.88	.36	*
					Other	.04	.00	.00	−.87	
9	0–9	.29	−.05	.16	1	.25	.14	.38	.12	
					2	.39	.14	.25	.12	
					3	.29	.43	.38	.16	*
					4	.04	.14	.00	−.09	
					Other	.04	.00	.00	−.87	

Figure 12.9
Item analysis of some classical item statistics for two items.

kinds of information and they are procedurally distinct from the methods of CTT. Understanding latent trait interpretations (including relevant assumptions) is necessary for conducting item analysis with IRT-based methods. When studying IRT-based methods of item analyses, recall from earlier IRT discussion (see chapter 10) how parameter estimates for items, as well as for examinees, are calculated and interpreted. Because calculating IRT statistics is more difficult than computing item values in CTT, computer programs are nearly always employed for the task.

Programs and Perspectives on Item Analysis

Seemingly, there are just as many computer programs that can calculate IRT-based indicators for items as programs that produce classical item statistics. I cited many IRT programs in chapter 10. Some are general in their capabilities, but others are specialized and directed toward a particular purpose. Among the general IRT programs especially useful to item analysis, probably the most popular is BILOG-MG (Zimowski, Muraki, Mislevy, & Bock, 2002). Although powerful and abounding in options for varying analyses, BILOG-MG only accommodates binary data (viz., items scored as right or wrong).

However, several other computer programs can produce IRT-based statistics for multiple-response items (e.g., Likert items, graded responses, other formats with multiple responses). Some examples are PARSCALE (Muraki & Bock, 2002) and MULTILOG (Thissen, Chen, & Bock., 2002). These programs employ different algorithms, so varying parameter estimates would result if the curious investigator wants to compare outputs. Before using any program, be sure to learn how it estimates parameters from the raw data (e.g., marginal maximum likelihood). This information is usually given in the manual, but sometimes, for obscure programs, the investigator may need to contact the program's author. Two popular programs for Rasch unidimensional model estimates are TestGraf98 (Ramsay, 1998) and RUMM2010 (Sheridan, 2000). The latter program abounds in interesting graphics, and an entire manual is devoted to describing them.

Item Information Functioning

To begin item analysis with IRT, look at statistics that reveal the maximum information about an item. Maximum information is the place along the characteristic continuum where the item produces information best suited to a given examinee. When this spot is properly matched to the ability of an examinee, the item is said to operate maximally for that individual, hence the name *maximum information*. For instance, when the *b* parameter estimate is at the median of the theta scale, and the slope (*a* parameter) is at .5, the item is perfectly suited to an examinee of median ability. Logically, information about such functioning is called the *item information function*. Some numbers indicating item information functions, produced by BILOG-MG, are shown in Figure 12.10.

The numbers include the point and value of maximum information, and the point of maximum effectiveness. Associated standard errors are also indicated. These statistics provide valuable information about the precision of measurement at different ability levels. They are useful in determining whether an item is suited to the ability of an examinee or groups of examinees. For items to be nicely suited to a group of examinees, one would look for the point of maximum information to cluster around 0 for a set of items in an achievement or ability test. For a test of skill proficiency, such as those used in many licensing programs, it may be lower at, say, −.1. In Figure 12.10, most of the items operate at a lower range, indicating that this is a relatively easy test or at least one on which many examinees perform well. For ITEM04, observe that the point of maximum information is less than −3. In item analysis, a decision rule is commonly employed to not include items that are outside the range (3, −3). Hence, ITEM04 would likely be rejected from this test. However, the other items shown in the figure do fall within the ±3 decision rule. Also revealed is that easier items appear early in the test, whereas more difficult ones appear later.

In analyzing the items with IRT, it is especially important to consider the particular IRT model employed for parameter estimation. (The 2PL model is used for estimates given in Figure 12.10.) Different models yield estimates that vary markedly. The formulas for the three most common IRT models (i.e., one-, two-, and three-parameter) are identified in the BILOG manual (du Toit, 2003), following advice provided by Hambleton and Swaminathan (1985). For the one-parameter model, the item information function is specified in Expression 12.3. The maximum value here is at the b_i value and is constant, as this model only considers the one (difficulty)

ITEM INFORMATION STATISTICS FOR TEST CB_LP   FORM 1
FOR A NORMAL POPULATION WITH MEAN = 0.000   AND   S. D. = 1.000

ITEM	MAXIMUM INFORMATION STANDARD ERROR*	POINT OF MAX INFORMATION STANDARD ERROR*	MAXIMUM EFFECTIVENESS POINT OF MAX EFFECTIVENESS*	AVERAGE INFORMATION INDEX OF RELIABILITY*
ITEM01	0.1042	−1.1947	0.0363	0.0849
	0.0126*	0.0771*	−0.0499*	0.0783*
ITEM02	0.0866	−1.5863	0.0283	0.0675
	0.0111*	0.1037*	−0.0511*	0.0632*
ITEM03	0.1049	−2.6763	0.0219	0.0553
	0.0155*	0.1787*	−0.0585*	0.0524*
ITEM04	0.1106	−3.3331	0.0160	0.0426
	0.0177*	0.2410*	−0.0482*	0.0408*
ITEM05	0.1689	−2.4860	0.0285	0.0749
	0.0219*	0.1393*	−0.0661*	0.0696*
ITEM06	0.4151	−1.1490	0.1093	0.2408
	0.0358*	0.0418*	−0.1240*	0.1941*
. . .	. . . . .	. . . .	. . . .	. . . . .
ITEM36	0.1026	1.1498	0.0362	0.0845
	0.0116*	0.0753*	0.0480*	0.0779*
ITEM37	0.1211	0.8888	0.0443	0.1016
	0.0130*	0.0605*	0.0456*	0.0922*

Figure 12.10
Item response theory likelihood functions for items, including standard errors and reliability.

parameter. This formula may appear formidable on first glance, but actually, it is quite similar to RIT formulas we studied in chapter 11. Also, its variants (given in Expressions 12.4 and 12.5) are simple modifications:

$$D^2\{1 + \exp[-D(\theta - b_i)]\}^{-1}\{1-(1 + \exp[-D(\theta - b_i)])^{-1}\}. \qquad \textbf{(12.3)}$$

When two parameters are involved, the equation is extended with an *a* estimate, as shown in Expression 12.4. Here the maximum value is proportional to the square of the item discrimination parameter (a). The larger the a_i value, the more information that is implied. Still, maximum information is obtained at b_i:

$$D^2 a_i^2\{1 + \exp[-D(\theta - b_i)]\}^{-1}\{1 - (1 + \exp[-D(\theta - b_i)])^{-1}\}. \qquad \textbf{(12.4)}$$

The expression grows still more complete when three parameters are included for consideration. This equation is given in Expression 12.5:

$$\frac{D^2 a_i^2 \{1 + \exp[-D(\theta - b_i)]\}^{-1} \{1 - (1 + \exp[-D(\theta - b_i)])^{-1}\}}{\{1 - c_i\}^2}. \tag{12.5}$$

In this case, maximum information is obtained at the point given in Expression 12.6:

$$b_i + \frac{1}{Da_i} \ln\{1/2 + 1/2\sqrt{1 + 8c_i}\}. \tag{12.6}$$

In addition, in this same display of item statistics (see Figure 12.10), there is an IRT-based reliability index cited in the rightmost column (e.g., for ITEM01, it is 0.0783.). IRT offers users both a theoretical and an empirical reliability computation. For item information statistics in BILOG-MG, this is calculated as a theoretical reliability, meaning that it is estimated by maximum likelihood methods and depends not only on the examinees' observed scores, but also on the associated function. Such Bayesian assumption makes this statistic particularly useful to item analysis in terms of increased generalizability. A normal distribution is assumed, and from this assumption one can evaluate the reliability of a particular item. However, as is widely recognized (and discussed in chapter 6), reliabilities for individual items are notoriously low, so do not confuse the value given for an individual item with what would be expected for whole test reliability. The program's authors (Zimowski et al., 2002) provide a detailed explanation of how this value is calculated, including algorithms (see du Toit, 2003, p. 33ff).

Because IRT information for items is calculated from a function, the function's allowed range can readily be mapped on a graphic, revealing the continuum of relationships. In IRT, the relationships, of course, are between the particular item characteristic and the probability of a given examinee's success on the item. Such graphics are useful to explore, and we examine some of them in the next section.

In addition, item information can be averaged over many items on a test to produce a *test information function*. I discuss the test information functions in the next chapter, as they relate to whole tests.

Item Characteristic Curves

Item characteristics represent the calibrated values for various IRT parameter estimates, and as such, they are enormously valuable in analysis. An illustration of ICCs is presented in Figure 12.11. Associated statistics are given in Figure 12.12. Recall that similar information was presented in chapter 10 (see Figure 10.13), where ICCs are discussed briefly. Here, I present information in greater detail, mainly as it may be used in analyzing items.

In Figures 12.11 and 12.12, the slope and intercept can be viewed. For this illustration parameter, estimates are done by the marginal maximum likelihood method. Again, it is important that users be aware of which estimating method a

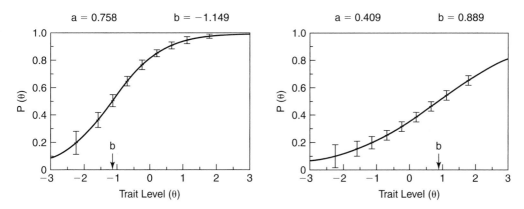

Figure 12.11
Item characteristic curve for two items, including error bands at selected ability levels.

ITEM	INTERCEPT S. E.	SLOPE S. E.	THRESHOLD S. E.	LOADING S. E.	ASYMPTOTE S. E.	CHISQ (PROB)	DF
ITEM01	0.454	0.380	−1.195	0.355	0.000	13.0	9.0
	0.019*	0.023*	0.077*	0.022*	0.000*	(0.1633)	
ITEM02	0.549	0.346	−1.586	0.327	0.000	12.5	9.0
	0.020*	0.022*	0.104*	0.021*	0.000*	(0.1865)	
ITEM03	1.020	0.381	−2.676	0.356	0.000	11.1	9.0
	0.026*	0.028*	0.179*	0.026*	0.000*	(0.2702)	
ITEM04	1.304	0.391	−3.333	0.364	0.000	9.8	9.0
	0.031*	0.031*	0.241*	0.029*	0.000*	(0.3679)	
ITEM05	1.202	0.484	−2.486	0.435	0.000	14.0	9.0
	0.030*	0.031*	0.139*	0.028*	0.000*	(0.1214)	
ITEM06	0.871	0.758	−1.149	0.604	0.000	42.6	9.0
	0.027*	0.033*	0.042*	0.026*	0.000*	(0.0000)	
. . .	. . .	. .	. .	. . .	. . .	. .	. .
ITEM36	−0.433	0.377	1.150	0.353	0.000	17.4	9.0
	0.019*	0.021*	0.075*	0.020*	0.000*	(0.0432)	
ITEM37	−0.364	0.409	0.889	0.379	0.000	13.6	9.0
	0.019*	0.022*	0.060*	0.020*	0.000*	(0.1357)	

Figure 12.12
Item parameter estimates for selected items in 2PL model.

given IRT computer program employs (or what method is selected, if given a choice), so the data may be appropriately interpreted. The intercept is calculated as shown in Equation 12.7. (The unusual use of italics is consistent with BILOG syntax notation, the program employed for these estimates.)

$$int\ ercept\ =\ -(slope * threshold).\tag{12.7}$$

The slope is shown next. It is the discriminating parameter (a_i). When just one parameter is considered, all slopes are equal. The threshold is the *location* parameter, taken as the mean in calculations. As we saw in chapter 10, this parameter represents the value of a difficulty parameter, indicated by b_i. It is the only parameter considered by all IRT models.

Next is a loading value. It represents item dispersion. It is a one-factor item loading and may be interpreted similarly to loadings in principal axis factoring. The expression given in Equation 12.8 shows its calculation:

$$Loadings\ =\ Slope/\sqrt{1\ +\ Slope^2}.\tag{12.8}$$

The asymptote is the lower bound of estimation for difficulty, as may be used when gauging performances of very low-ability examinees. When used, it is the pseudochance (i.e., guessing) parameter, shown as c_i. It is only employed in the three-parameter model and in some specialized models, where it is estimated separately for each item. For one- and two-parameter models it is not considered, and all lower asymptotes are equal at zero.

Finally, an item fit statistic is provided in the form of a number that can be evaluated on the chi-square distribution. The degrees of freedom (DF) are also given.

Examining the ICC in relation to the item information function provides a more complete picture than does the ICC alone. Figures 12.13 and 12.14 present

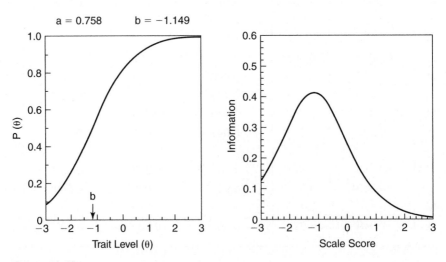

Figure 12.13
Item characteristic curve and information function for item 6.

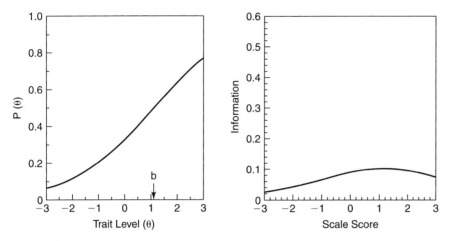

Figure 12.14
Item characteristic curve and information function for item 36.

these two graphics, each for two items conveying vastly different information. Associated statistics for both items are given in Figure 12.12. Notice in the ICC the location parameter (b) for each item. They are at markedly different points along the ability continuum, suggesting that the items may not be appropriate for the same examinee, depending on the purposes of the assessment. When each item is viewed in terms of its total information (the Item Information Function), it is easy to see how the item operates for the different examinees. In Figure 12.13, for instance, the item discriminates among examinees along the entire range, but especially for examinees with less than average ability in this construct. Contrast this information with what is given for the next item in Figure 12.14. Here, the item is much more difficult, but provides little information regardless of an examinee's ability.

Item Characteristic Curves for Variant Items

Sometimes, in longer tests especially, it is useful to explore characteristics of particular items, allowing for a more focused review of just the suspicious items. BILOG-MG includes the commands needed to write syntax for variant item analysis. By the procedure, the items not considered variant are calibrated as normally done, whereas the parameter estimates for the variant items are computed with respect to the latent dimension by the main items. That is, the suspicious items are calibrated separately, but on the same scale as the main items, thereby providing a means to contrast the two sets directly. The output is the same as given for item information functions and for item characteristics, except of course the items are grouped as described.

Specialized Models for Items

IRT methods of item analysis can also provide parameter estimates in a number of specialized approaches unavailable by classical statistics. These specialized models include full information of the nominal model, graded response models, rating scale models, multiple response models, and partial credit models. Thissen and Steinberg (1986) organized these advanced approaches in a useful taxonomy. They are mostly used in research contexts by academics or specialists and a few testing programs that have the assistance of highly skilled psychometricians. However, such sophisticated strategies are gaining advocates as more people become trained in how to use them and in how to interpret the findings. The methods are also receiving more attention in the testing literature. Likely, this trend will continue, and their use will grow.

In this section, I describe some of these special approaches and models, but only briefly—just enough to give one a flavor for them because much about them is beyond the scope of this text. Individuals who want to explore them more thoroughly, or even to consider employing one of them in research or in some live assessment context, should consult primary sources. One excellent source is the *Handbook of Modern Item Response Theory* (van der Linden & Hambleton, 1997), an advanced text edited by two persons of remarkable intellect and talent in the field. Other valuable resources are by Bock (1997b; Bock et al., 2002) and Thissen and Steinberg (1997).

Nominal Response Functions

One of the special IRT models is called the *nominal response model*. There are manifold item statistics associated with this model, and they can be used to advantage in test construction and test interpretation. The basic idea of nominal response models is to provide information about multiple-choice, Likert-type, and other nominal response formats beyond just the dichotomized responses. Here, response functions for all alternatives to an item are produced and analyzed. In other words, for a four-choice, multiple-choice item, four ICCs are produced. The various ICCs can be separately analyzed, or they may be contrasted.

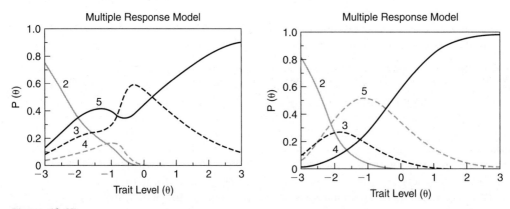

Figure 12.15
Item response trace lines in a multiple-response model for two items.

Item response trace lines of the multiple response model for two items are shown in Figure 12.15 and are produced by MULTILOG (Bock et al., 2002). The information they provide is useful for both item interpretation and test development. These plots are interpreted in the manner of any ICC, except that a separate trace line is produced for each response alternative or possible graded score. Notice in Figure 12.15 that there are four response choices to this item. One can study how the separate response functions operate. For illustration, see the fluctuating probabilities for the alternatives of the item in the left panel (#1), whereas the functions are more stable and closer to expectation of normality for the item in the right panel (#3).

The statistics associated with one of the items (3, in the right panel of Figure 12.15) are given in Figure 12.16. The statistics include numbers in each category, contrast coefficients, and ability or proficiency information, expressed in the output as a

```
ITEM    3:            5 NOMINAL  CATEGORIES,   4 HIGH
CATEGORY (K):   1        2       3       4       5
   A(K)        −0.06   −2.19   −0.17    1.84    0.58
   C(K)        −0.80   −3.81    0.12    2.50    1.98
   D(K)                 0.15    0.27    0.46    0.12

                  CONTRAST-COEFFICIENTS (STANDARD ERRORS)
FOR:                   A                      C                      D
CONTRAST  P(#)   COEFF. [DEV.]   P(#)   COEFF. [DEV.]   P(#)   COEFF. [DEV.]
   1       21   −2.13  (1.20)     25   −3.01  (2.52)    18    0.58  (0.33)
   2       22   −0.11  (1.02)     26    0.92  (1.53)    19    1.12  (0.32)
   3       23    1.90  (0.99)     27    3.30  (1.39)    20   −0.21  (0.46)
   4       24    0.64  (0.95)     28    2.78  (1.37)

@THETA:          INFORMATION:    (Theta values increase in steps of 0.2)
−3.0  −  −1.6   0.826   1.101   1.354   1.510   1.511   1.366   1.142   0.917
−1.4  −   0.0   0.741   0.627   0.566   0.539   0.528   0.518   0.500   0.470
 0.2  −   1.6   0.430   0.382   0.331   0.280   0.232   0.190   0.153   0.122
 1.8  −   3.0   0.097   0.076   0.060   0.047   0.037   0.029   0.022

OBSERVED AND EXPECTED COUNTS/PROPORTIONS IN
CATEGORY (K):            1           2           3           4           5
OBS. FREQ.               0          29          84         550         313
OBS. PROP.          0.0000      0.0297      0.0861      0.5635      0.3207
EXP. PROP.          0.0285      0.0293      0.0854      0.5654      0.3198
```

Figure 12.16
Statistics for one polytomous item (item 3) of the nominal response model.

theta value. The final section to the output is the observed and expected proportions for each response. Notice how the data of Figure 12.16 are consistent with its display in Figure 12.15. Together, they provide the user with much useful information.

Graded Response Functions

Analyzing all response alternatives is an important part of many advanced IRT models. Fukimo Samejima (1969), working at the ETS and later at the L. L. Thurstone Psychometric Laboratory at the University of North Carolina, conducted inventive and pioneering work with graded response models. The graded response models deal with ordered, polytomous categories, and can be applied to Likert preference scales, attitude surveys, and various performance or even personality inventories. They are most commonly employed, however, in writing assessments.

Samejima (1997) describes the graded response model as follows:

> Suppose, for example, that a cognitive process, like problem solving, contains a finite number of steps. The graded item score u_i should be assigned to the examinees who successfully complete up to step u_i but fail to complete the next step $(u_i + 1)$. Let $M_{u_i}(\theta)$ be the *processing* function of the graded item score u_i, which is the probability with which the examinee completes the step u_i successfully, under the joint conditions that (a) the examinee's ability level is θ and (b) the steps up to $(u_i - 1)$ be the next graded score above m_i. (p. 86)

In other words, a graded response is one that has an ordinal scale where lower achievement or proficiency is assigned fewer points than higher proficiency. As an example, imagine an assessment that includes an essay that is graded by a conventional rubric. Points are assigned to each essay based on the degree to which it manifests attributes of good writing, according to the rubric. A higher number of points is interpreted as better writing because the essay contains elements that indicate higher compositional skill. The response is graded. Samejima's graded response model examines each score point.

The graded response model allows graphic display of the response functions similar to those of the nominal response, and graded response functions for one item are given in Figure 12.17 in the left panel. Also displayed in the adjacent panel is the item information function. Notice the distribution of the various responses relative to the ability scale.

Partial Credit Model

The partial credit model is a variation of the graded response model. It can find application in a variety of assessment contexts, most particularly in writing assessments, but also in other PA forms. The response function for one item under this model is shown in Figure 12.18. These functions are interpreted similarly to the graded response model, except that information for each response function is viewed in proportion to its relative weight.

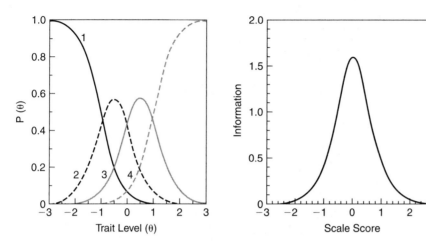

Figure 12.17
Item characteristic curve and item information function for graded response model.

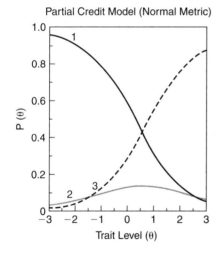

Figure 12.18
Partial credit model for one
item.

Differential Item Functioning

Preliminary Cautions

Differential item functioning (DIF) is an important concept in measurement, even beyond its bearing to item analysis. Having a clear understanding of what DIF and test bias mean in psychometric contexts is essential for proper interpretation of the statistics obtained through item analysis. Before beginning a study of DIF, it may be worthwhile to review the basic notion of test bias and DIF explained in chapter 3 and elsewhere.

Item bias has long been a concern of test developers, but serious study of the phenomenon did not begin until about the 1960s. Today, it is an integral part of nearly every professional test development enterprise. As is widely understood in the measurement community, simple comparison of mean test scores between groups is not an indication of bias or DIF. Appropriate investigation of DIF and test bias must consider the varying ability or proficiency level of individuals within each group. Nearly always, then, DIF studies employ some scheme wherein examinees are matched by ability before a difference on a particular item is investigated. DIF study is generally between two groups, although some techniques can be applied to simultaneous study of more than two groups (see Kim, 1995).

There are many procedures available to study DIF. When conducting a DIF study, the measurement professional must bear in mind the purpose for such an undertaking. Sometimes, a simple method is adequate to the purpose. At other times, more in-depth analysis, requiring a sophisticated procedure, is required. Complicated approaches to DIF are not necessarily better than simple ones. With DIF investigation, the method should be matched to the circumstances.

There are many good sources available to explain DIF procedures in more detail than I offer here, and readers are encouraged to investigate some of them. Holland and Wainer (1993) edited a useful volume that reviews DIF and bias methods in standardized tests. In fact, their book may be the most thorough coverage of DIF currently available. Hambleton and Rodgers (1995) offer some practical advice for conducting an item bias review. Many more sources are also valuable (e.g., Embretson & Reise, 2000; Hambleton & Zaal, 1991; Holland & Thayer, 1988; Lord, 1980; Osterlind, 1983; van der Linden & Hambleton, 1997; Wainer, 1993).

Groups Used for Comparison

In DIF investigation, groups are referred to as the *focal group* and the *reference group*, primarily just to keep the groups straight. There is no methodological advantage to either group and it matters very little which group is called "focal" and which "reference." The focal group comprises the individuals who the researcher hypothesizes to be different from the reference group. For instance, if one wants to investigate differences between Caucasian examinees and non-Caucasian examinees and presumes that the difference on item responses is for the non-Caucasians, then Caucasians would constitute the reference groups and non-Caucasians would be the focal group.

Procedurally, however, the focal and reference group scores are not treated the same. In an IRT DIF study, for instance, the reference group's responses are calibrated to final estimates. The focal group's calibrated estimates are first independently made and then *recentered* (viz., adjusted) to appear on the same scale as the reference group.

An early procedural step in a DIF study is to explore the distribution of scores in the tested construct for each group, usually by measures of central tendency (e.g., mean, median) and dispersion (e.g., variance, range). This information helps a researcher understand any overall discrepancy in proficiency or ability between the groups. When a group's score distributions are not the same (or reasonably similar) in the appraised area, a scheme to ensure such differences are properly considered should be devised. This scheme may include omitting true outlier scores or even transforming the distributions to another scale by a log transformation or a square root transformation.

Overall ability or proficiency is usually assumed to be as evidenced on the whole test. This is done for more than mere convenience; studies have shown that if the item selected for DIF investigation is well suited to the whole test, then the whole test score is likely the most appropriate indicator. Then, too, often it is the only measure of overall ability available.

Group Size and Variances

Another consideration in setting up a DIF study is the size of the focal and reference groups, or more exactly, their relative sizes. The groups should be roughly equal, especially when ability strata are considered. Often, however, one finds that the number of subjects in arbitrary groups in a sample vary widely. When this is the case, the researcher may modify the investigation by randomly selecting some percentage from the larger group so it more nearly matches the size of the smaller one. Also, when contrasting several groups, as with many ethnic and racial studies, categories with small numbers may be combined (if logical) into a single "combined minority" or "non-White" group. Alternatively, the researcher may employ statistical methods, such as sampling by *bootstrap* or other procedure, to produce groups of comparable size. Sometimes, to get a proper view of a test, it could even be necessary to abandon live data in favor of a *Monte Carlo study* using simulated data.

As important as the relative size of groups is their heterogeneity of variance. Even when groups are subdivided into ability strata, it is necessary to investigate their relative variance. Many statistics are available for this purpose. One common statistic is Levene's test. Another is the less precise Brown-Forsyth procedure. As a simple gauge, one may divide the variance of the largest group by that of the smallest group to produce an F_{max} statistic. This ratio should be less than 9 for appropriate contrasting of groups.

DIF Methods Based on Classical Test Theory

Many classical methods of item analysis can also be applied to DIF study, as long as the ability of each group is correctly considered. For instance, the fractile tables of MERMAC analysis—shown in Figures 12.4 and 12.5—can be properly used in DIF investigation, although only as a rough guide. To do so, one would produce the fractile tables for each group. The rows on each group fractile table indicating the r_{pbis} (shown as RPBI in Figures 12.4 and 12.5) for the response alternatives can be contrasted. Caution is advised when using the r_{pbis} because this statistic is very sensitive to item difficulty, and thus may distort cross-group discrimination findings. Its sensitivity means that the r_{pbis} will be large for items of middle difficulty (relative to all

Table 12.1
Rank Order of Item Difficulties for Two Groups

	Group I		Group II	
Item	Rank	*p* value	Rank	*p* value
1	3rd	.62	2nd	.64
2	1st	.93	1st	.81
3	4th	.55	3rd	.51
4	2nd	.71	5th	.19
5	5th	.28	4th	.38

others) and when groups are far apart in mean value on the overall test. The associated graphics, too, may be a rough gauge for DIF between groups, albeit they are only a gross indicator. Realize, too, that in the MERMAC graphics, the rows for *p* value cannot be similarly compared because they do not consider ability.

Another simple method to screen early indications of DIF is to compare ordinal rankings of items between groups, as shown in Table 12.1. Simply, prepare a table with the ordinal ranking for items for each group, placing the groups side by side for easy comparison. The suspicion of DIF is raised for an item when its ordinal placement deviates sharply from the general trend revealed in all ordinal rankings. For example, note that item 2 is the easiest for both groups, regardless of the vastly different *p* values. However, the pattern is not continued for item 4. This item is ranked second for group I but lowest of all (and hence, more responded incorrectly) for group II. This should not be taken as an indication of DIF because the method is very inexact, but it does give one an early indication of suspect items. Confirmation would require more exact procedures. Such ranking procedure can be called a "quick but incomplete method."

Transformed Item Difficulty or Delta Plot

As mentioned, from the earliest test item bias studies in the 1960s, psychometricians realized that simple comparison of *p* values between groups was insufficient for proper interpretation of the phenomenon and that examinee ability was too pertinent a factor to be ignored. An early method that addressed this concern was developed by Angoff (1972, 1982). Because his route to DIF uses a delta plot for transformed item difficulties, it is called the *delta plot* or *transformed item difficulties* method. This procedure has serious shortcomings and is not recommended for use today; nonetheless, I describe it for reasons more important than mere historical interest. Through this procedure, one can readily grasp a clear understanding of the basic idea of differential item performance relative to group ability, a concern germane to virtually all methods now in use.

Conceptually, the approach is similar to a factorial ANOVA in that a group $\times$ items interaction is investigated. It is presumed that such interaction exists and that when its relative difference between groups is great, item *bias* (as Angoff used the term in the 1970s) is inferred. It is important to know that in Angoff's approach, the phenomenon of bias is considered always present and its relative amount is the focus of attention.

The logic of the procedure is that when test items interact in the same way with different groups of a population, the item's variations of difficulty are approximately the same among equally able individuals, regardless of their particular group membership and irrespective of group mean scores. When this is not the case, it is inferred that the item manifests different kinds of responses from the groups. As is true in ANOVA, the assumption of unidimensionality is made.

Procedurally, a hypothesis is established as follows:

$$H_0: \Delta_{i1} - \Delta_{i2} = 0$$
$$H_A: \Delta_{i1} - \Delta_{i2} \neq 0, \qquad \textbf{(12.9)}$$

where Δ = index of item difficulty.

The Δ is called *transformed* because it is the item's p value converted to a normal SD, expressed on a scale with a mean of 13 and SD of 4 (i.e., $\Delta_{ij} = 4z_{ij} + 13$). Figure 12.19 shows a bivariate distribution of Δs for two groups.

As seen in Figure 12.19, as the ability of the groups differ, different regression lines will be fitted. The perpendicular difference of any particular item plot from the major axis line is considered a function of the interaction of groups $\times$ items. This distance is given as in Equation 12.10, and details are provided by Osterlind (1983):

$$D_i = \frac{bX_i + a - Y}{\sqrt{b^2 + 1}}. \qquad \textbf{(12.10)}$$

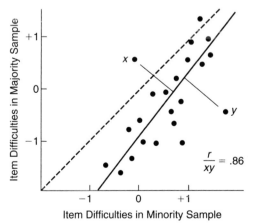

Figure 12.19
Transformed item difficulties for two groups.

$\frac{r}{xy} = .86$

Item Difficulties in Majority Sample

Item Difficulties in Minority Sample

Again, this method is not recommended for DIF studies involving live data but is shown to illustrate the conceptual value of considering relative group ability in item comparisons, itself an idea that pervades DIF analyses.

The Mantel-Haenszel Procedure

Over the years, the shortcomings of delta transformation, simple chi-square approaches, and similar methods have led researchers to explore other strategies for detecting DIF. One approach that gained popularity during the 1960s and 1970s was advanced by Holland and Thayer (1988). This is the *Mantel-Haenszel procedure,* a DIF investigation strategy actually developed by Mantel and Haenszel (1959) in a retrospective study of diseases that is widely used today. The Mantel-Haenszel procedure, although based on a chi-square distribution, takes a slightly different tact. It employs a variant of a usual chi square (with a contingency table) called the *full chi square.* The test known as the *Mantel-Haenszel chi-square test* is even a slight variation on the full chi square.

The full chi square takes a page from the early recognized strategy of stratifying the population by ability groupings, again based on total test score as the criterion. Typically, four or five groups are used because this is believed to represent levels of the population's ability with reasonable accuracy. For each ability level, a 2 × 2 chi-square contingency table is prepared, one of which is shown in Figure 12.20.

The table in Figure 12.20 is straightforward: Frequency counts for correct and incorrect are cited in the columns, and the reference and focal groups compose the rows. (Note that this statistic should not be used for nominal data.) From the data in each table, a Mantel-Haenszel index is calculated. The Mantel-Haenszel index begins as an α statistic that is computed to represent the ratio of the odds (expressed as p/q, for correct and incorrect) that the reference group examinees answered the item correctly to the odds on the same criterion for the focal group. The α statistic is called an *odds ratio.* It is a measure of linear association between the row and column variables in a cross-tabulation. The formula for calculating the odds ratio is given in

Figure 12.20
Chi-square contingency table citing cell contents and marginals for Mantel-Haenszel procedure.

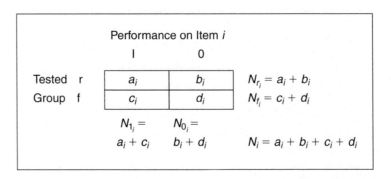

many forms by different authors, but working from a contingency table it may be calculated as in Equation 12.11. Many computer programs (e.g., SPSS) can calculate the odds ratio, as well as associated *M-H* statistics:

$$\alpha_i = \frac{p_{r_i}}{q_{r_i}} \bigg/ \frac{p_{f_i}}{q_{f_i}} = \frac{\dfrac{a_i}{a_i + b_i}}{\dfrac{b_i}{a_i + b_i}} \bigg/ \frac{\dfrac{c_i}{c_i + d_i}}{\dfrac{d_i}{c_i + d_i}} = \frac{a_i}{b_i} \bigg/ \frac{c_i}{d_i} = \frac{a_i d_i}{b_i c_i}, \tag{12.11}$$

where p_{r_i} = proportion of the reference group (*r*) in the score interval *i* who answered correctly;

q_{r_i} = proportion of the reference group (*r*) in the score interval *i* who answered incorrectly (i.e., $q_{r_i} = 1 - p_{r_i}$), and similarly for the focal group (i.e., p_{f_i} and q_{f_i}).

If there is no difference between groups, then the *odds ratio* is at equilibrium (i.e., $\alpha_i = 1$). When the reference group performs better on the item than the focal group, then $\alpha_i > 1$. When $\alpha_i < 1$, the focal group has performed better. For general purposes, this is a significance value, which is essentially a *t* test distributed on *x* DF and is more important than the actual value of the statistic. The common criterion of $p < .05$ is adopted for significance testing.

The α statistic is estimated across the match groups in all strata, according to Equation 12.12:

$$\hat{\alpha}_{MH} = \frac{\sum_i p_{r_i} q_{f_i} N_{r_i} {}^{N_{f_i}}\!/N_i}{\sum_i q_{r_i} p_{r_i} N_{r_i} {}^{N_{f_i}}\!/N_i} = \frac{\sum_i a_i d_i \!/ N_i}{\sum_i b_i c_i \!/ N_i}. \tag{12.12}$$

As can be seen in the formula, $\hat{\alpha}_{MH}$ is an estimated index of the weighted average factor in which the odds that a person in the reference group endorses the correct choice for the item exceeds the parallel odds for an individual in focal group. In practice, however, the $\hat{\alpha}_{MH}$ is an awkward number to interpret; it is therefore transformed to the more convenient log scale by Equation 12.13. The resultant index is called *MH D-DIF*:

$$\text{MH D-DIF} = -2.35 \ln(\hat{\alpha}_{MH}). \tag{12.13}$$

This new scale references the center of the index around zero, so MH D-DIF = 0 is interpreted as the absence of any DIF. Also, the minus sign reverses the interpretation so when MH D-DIF is positive, the item favors the focal group, and when MH D-DIF is negative, the item favors the reference group.

As a variance statistic, MH D-DIF is also a measure of effect size. This feature can be used to advantage in interpreting the index. When large samples are used in a *t* or chi-square distribution, it is well known that statistical significance nearly

Crosstab-Question #1				Crosstab-Question #3			
Count				Count			

		Sex		Total			Sex		Total
		MALE	FEMALE				MALE	FEMALE	
Q1R	0	138	156	294	Q3R	0	85	121	206
	1	162	144	306		1	215	179	394
Total		300	300	600	Total		300	300	600

Mantel-Haenszel Common Odds Ratio Estimate:				Q #1	Q #3
Estimate				.786	.585
ln(Estimate)				−.240	−.536
Standard Error of ln(Estimate)				.164	.174
Asymptote Significance (2-sided)				.142	.002
Asymptote 95% Confidence Interval	Common Odds Ratio	Lower Bound		.571	.416
		Upper Bound		1.084	.822
	ln(Common Odds Ratio)	Lower Bound		−.561	−.877
		Upper Bound		.080	−.195

The Mantel-Haenszel common odds ratio estimate is asymptotically normally distributed under the common odds ratio of 1.000 assumption. So is the natural log of the estimate.

Figure 12.21
SPSS output for Mantel-Haenszel procedure for two test items.

always results. This is also the case when using large samples to test $\hat{\alpha}_{MH}$. The MH D-DIF variance value adds perspective for interpreting practical significance beyond calculated statistical significance.

To see the process as commonly practiced, data for investigating DIF at one ability level are given for two items in Figure 12.21 (using output from SPSS). In Figure 12.21, estimates for both the real number value and transformed log of $\hat{\alpha}_{MH}$ (see Equation 12.13) are given. Also note that the statistic confirms an advantage in the ratio favoring the focal group (males), but significance of the difference (from a hypothesized zero difference) is only exhibited for the second item, labeled Question #3. Thus, DIF is indicated for Question #3, but not for Question #1.

DIF Methods Based on IRT-Calibrated Parameter Differences

Both theoretically and procedurally, the IRT DIF methods provide an opportunity for a more comprehensive examination of the underlying, psychological phenomenon than can be done by methods based on CTT. To readers of this text, the reasons are quickly grasped. At its core, IRT theorizes latent constructs on a continuum of ability or proficiency. Although any item that appears on a test is independent of an examinee's ability to evidence proficiency in the latent construct itself, the item's characteristics are scaled to be expressed on the same continuum as the examinee's ability. This feature allows the psychometrician to examine the DIF phenomenon for a particular test item relative to the test taker's ability on the same scale, a decided advance over what is possible with CTT DIF investigation through CTT methods, where the ability is taken from the sum of the items.

Of course, DIF is not extant for just an individual; rather, it is a group characteristic. Hence, it is a group's distribution of the trait (rather than in individual's ability or proficiency) that is considered in relation to the item's functioning. Figure 12.22 presents this idea graphically; trace lines for two items are shown. These are based on 1PL estimates, as only difficulty is considered in IRT DIF investigation. A hypothetical distribution for two distinct groups is given along the ability or proficiency (θ) scale. By noting the difference in the group mean values, it is apparent that the probabilities for success are disparate, evidencing DIF of both items, but much larger in item 1 than in item 2. Then, too, mere differences are not axiomatically significant. A criterion must be applied to the difference for that determination.

The purpose of using IRT in DIF investigation is to determine whether an item appraises the ability or proficiency similarly for all the groups taking the exam in the portion of the continuum that the item covers. Accordingly, only item difficulty (i.e., the b parameter) relative to each group is of research interest. It makes little difference where on the continuum the comparison of difficulty is made; so, the item's discrimination (i.e., the a parameter) among ability levels per se is not of direct concern in DIF. Also, the pseudochance parameter is not of interest in DIF studies because it is mostly a measure of error at a low-defined proficiency

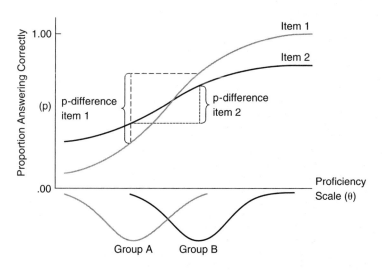

Figure 12.22
Item characteristic curves for two items shown in relation to ability distributions for two groups.

```
College BASE data- Form LP
>COMMENT
Sample run with CB data, form LP for DIF.  Two groups are used: Male & Female
The needed files (beyond this *.blm file are labeled:
          the data file              CB2data.dat
          the answer key             CB2KEY.key
          the omit file (coded as 9)  CB2omit.omt
Scoring phase is not invoked as it is invalid for DIF analysis; but PLOT
  command is used.
After the data is run, use Run-->Plot to activate the graphics module.

>GLOBAL DFName = 'C:\Program Files\bilogmg\Examples\CB2data.dat',
        NPArm = 1;
>LENGTH NITems = (41);
>INPUT NTOtal = 41, NALt = 5,NIDchar = 8, NGRoup = 2,
       KFName = 'C:\Program Files\bilogmg\Examples\CB2Key.KEY',
       OFName = 'C:\Program Files\bilogmg\Examples\CB2omit.OMT',
       DIF;
>ITEMS INAmes = (ITEM001(1)ITEM041);
>TEST1 TNAme = 'CB_LP', INUmber = (1(1)41);
>GROUP1 GNAme = 'MALES', LENgth = 41, INUmbers = (1(1)41);
>GROUP2 GNAme = 'FEMALES', LENgth = 41, INUmbers = (1(1)41);
(8A1, 3X, I1, 33X, 42A1)
>CALIB PLOt = 1.0000;
```

Figure 12.23
Sample syntax file for differential item functioning analysis by BILOG-MG.

level. These are maintained as constants across the population. It is important for persons working in this area to keep these points in mind when conducting DIF investigation.

Procedurally, then, in DIF analysis researchers are interested in determining whether the b parameter is estimated similarly for the two groups. In BILOG-MG, for instance, the a parameter is estimated but constrained to be equal across groups. This is necessary to locate the item on the scale. The program does not estimate the c parameter. Accordingly, DIF, as estimated by BILOG-MG, is a 1PL procedure. A sample syntax file for DIF calculation by BILOG-MG is shown in Figure 12.23. Commands for the syntax and the FORTRAN command line are provided in the BILOG-MG manual.

These values are generally also displayed in separate ICCs, one each for the focal and reference groups. Figure 12.24 shows the ICCs and associated item information curves for a reference and focal group (females [bottom panel] and males [top panel], respectively) for one item. Notice especially in Figure 12.24 that the b values (given at the top of each ICC and located by the arrow on the ability scale) are far apart between the groups. Significant differences in ICCs can be interpreted as evidence that DIF evidence exists (Lord, 1980).

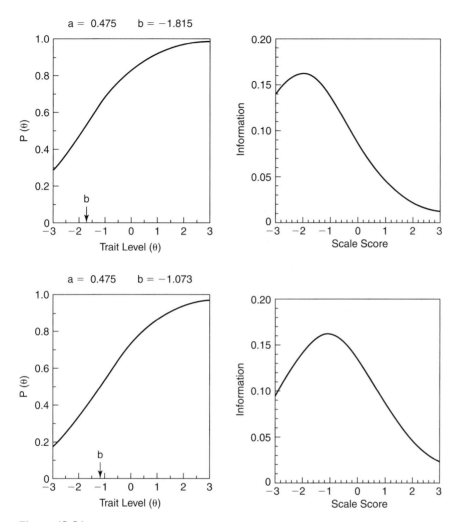

Figure 12.24
Differential item functioning shown in item characteristic curves and item information curves on one item for two groups: males (top panel) and females (bottom panel).

The mathematics of calculating these values are described by Thissen, Steinberg, and Wainer (1993), who also demonstrate its execution in several other programs, including MULTILOG, LISCOMP, SPSS LOGLINEAR, LOGIMO, and BIMAIN, although users should note that there are important differences among the estimating algorithms in each program.

An important concern in comparison of IRT-based trace lines is the question of how to determine whether a difference is significant. Sometimes, it can be determined by merely "eyeballing" the differences and making a reasonable judgment; however, a more precise method is desired that uses some test statistics. One popularly used method was developed by Raju (1988), who shows how to estimate the area between two ICCs. Raju's method is technical but recommended for the advanced user.

Other methods also compute statistics between the groups, first separately for each group and then together. By marginal maximum likelihood estimation, BILOG-MG can be employed. Such calibrated values are shown in Figures 12.25 and 12.26. In Figure 12.25, traditional item indices are calculated, first for each group and then for the total sample. These are followed by the IRT-based item parameter estimates (see Figure 12.26).

To make meaningful comparisons, the IRT-based threshold values in the reference group are linearly transformed, by an adjustment, to the scale for the focal group. This is important because it puts the parameter estimates for both groups in the same (and, consequently, comparable) scale. This adjustment factor is shown in Figure 12.27.

```
ITEM STATISTICS FOR GROUP: 1    MALES

                                              ITEM*TEST CORRELATION
  ITEM    NAME     #TRIED    #RIGHT    PCT    LOGIT/1.7   PEARSON   BISERIAL
  ----------------------------------------------------------------------------
    1    ITEM01    953.0     748.0    0.785     -0.76      0.181     0.254
    2    ITEM02    953.0     792.0    0.831     -0.94      0.187     0.278
    3    ITEM03    953.0     818.0    0.858     -1.06      0.152     0.236


ITEM STATISTICS FOR GROUP: 2    FEMALES

                                              ITEM*TEST CORRELATION
  ITEM    NAME     #TRIED    #RIGHT    PCT    LOGIT/1.7   PEARSON   BISERIAL
  ----------------------------------------------------------------------------
    1    ITEM01   3933.0    2690.0    0.684     -0.45      0.236     0.309
    2    ITEM02   3933.0    3272.0    0.832     -0.94      0.204     0.304
    3    ITEM03   3933.0    3511.0    0.893     -1.25      0.190     0.319


ITEM STATISTICS FOR MULTIPLE GROUPS    CB_LP

                                              ITEM*TEST CORRELATION
  ITEM    NAME     #TRIED    #RIGHT    PCT    LOGIT/1.7   PEARSON   BISERIAL
  ----------------------------------------------------------------------------
    1    ITEM01   4886.0    3438.0    0.704     -0.51      0.228     0.301
    2    ITEM02   4886.0    4064.0    0.832     -0.94      0.200     0.298
    3    ITEM03   4886.0    4329.0    0.886     -1.21      0.180     0.296
```

Figure 12.25
Traditional item statistics for differential item functioning for males, females, and multiple groups.

GROUP 1   MALES   ;   ITEM PARAMETERS AFTER CYCLE   3

| ITEM | INTERCEPT | SLOPE | THRESHOLD | LOADING | ASYMPTOTE | CHISQ | DF |
	S. E.	S. E.	S. E.	S. E.	S. E.	(PROB)	
ITEM01	0.862	0.475	−1.815	0.429	0.000	5.4	9.0
	0.048*	0.004*	0.101*	0.004*	0.000*	(0.7983)	
ITEM02	1.054	0.475	−2.220	0.429	0.000	2.5	9.0
	0.052*	0.004*	0.110*	0.004*	0.000*	(0.9810)	
ITEM03	1.186	0.475	−2.498	0.429	0.000	4.4	9.0
	0.056*	0.004*	0.118*	0.004*	0.000*	(0.8803)	

GROUP 2   FEMALES ;   ITEM PARAMETERS AFTER CYCLE   3

| ITEM | INTERCEPT | SLOPE | THRESHOLD | LOADING | ASYMPTOTE | CHISQ | DF |
	S. E.	S. E.	S. E.	S. E.	S. E.	(PROB)	
ITEM01	0.509	0.475	−1.073	0.429	0.000	4.7	9.0
	0.021*	0.004*	0.045*	0.004*	0.000*	(0.8578)	
ITEM02	1.040	0.475	−2.191	0.429	0.000	1.0	9.0
	0.026*	0.004*	0.055*	0.004*	0.000*	(0.9994)	
ITEM03	1.364	0.475	−2.873	0.429	0.000	6.7	9.0
	0.031*	0.004*	0.066*	0.004*	0.000*	(0.6719)	

Figure 12.26
Item response theory-based item statistics for differential item functioning for males and females.

PARAMETER		MEAN	STN	DEV
GROUP: 1	NUMBER OF ITEMS:			41
THRESHOLD		−1.002	0.928	
GROUP: 2	NUMBER OF ITEMS:			41
THRESHOLD		−0.877	0.944	

THRESHOLD MEANS

GROUP	ADJUSTMENT
1	0.000
2	0.125

Figure 12.27
Group parameter estimates and adjustment to threshold to reference group in differential item functioning analysis.

MODEL FOR GROUP DIFFERENTIAL ITEM FUNCTIONING:
ADJUSTED THRESHOLD VALUES

ITEM	GROUP		ITEM	GROUP	
	1	2		1	2
ITEM01	−1.815	−1.198	ITEM22	−2.112	−2.005
	0.101*	0.045*		0.113*	0.052*
ITEM02	−2.220	−2.315	ITEM23	−0.376	−0.312
	0.110*	0.055*		0.088*	0.043*
ITEM03	−2.498	−2.998	ITEM24	−0.695	−0.731
	0.118*	0.066*		0.088*	0.043*

Figure 12.28
Adjusted threshold values for focal and reference groups.

Then, the adjusted threshold values for focal and reference groups are calculated, as displayed in Figure 12.28. Finally, differences between values for the focal and reference group are given in Figure 12.29. The difference values are viewed as a relative amount, with large differences indicating DIF.

One way to test these values is with a traditional student t-test. The numerator is the difference between the groups on a given item, and the denominator is the

MODEL FOR GROUP DIFFERENTIAL ITEM FUNCTIONING:
GROUP THRESHOLD DIFFERENCES

ITEM	GROUP 2 − 1	ITEM	GROUP 2 − 1	ITEM	GROUP 2 − 1
ITEM01	0.618	ITEM15	−0.405	ITEM29	0.079
	0.110*		0.095*		0.101*
ITEM02	−0.096	ITEM16	0.007	ITEM30	−0.059
	0.123*		0.096*		0.113*
ITEM03	−0.500	ITEM17	−0.182	ITEM31	0.354
	0.135*		0.095*		0.123*

Figure 12.29
Difference in adjusted threshold values for focal and reference groups.

square root of the sum of the two standard errors, which is demonstrated in Equation 12.14 (S. E. Embretson, personal communication, April 2003):

$$t_{DIF} = \frac{b_F - b_R}{\sqrt{SE_F + SE_R}},$$ (12.14)

where b_F =   difficulty parameter for the focal group, and

b_R =   adjusted difficulty parameter for the reference group.

Another way to calculate significance of the DIF is to subtract the focal group's adjusted b from the reference group's, and if its absolute value is more than two (or three for a more liberal criterion) standard errors (which are given for each item in the BILOG-MG output), then it is significant. The criterion of a difference between groups of two standard errors may result in overidentifying items as DIF; hence, some researchers use the more conservative criterion of a difference greater than three standard errors. In either case, the standard error approach is reasonable as the metric for difference scores by BILOG-MG is a z-score, standardized unit.

where p =   item facility, and

Φ^{-1} =   inverse normal transformation, which has an effective range (1, 25), with a mean of 13 and SD of 4.

The IRT approach to DIF detection is quickly gaining popularity as more researchers incorporate IRT methods in their work. The procedures are both conceptually appealing and computationally approachable via any number of IRT-based programs or even by hand with a simple pocket calculator, although tedious (see chapter 10).

As shown in Figure 12.22 (but for a different point there), when studying DIF the ICCs for compared groups can be plotted together, making comparison direct and easy. Figure 12.30 presents such plots.

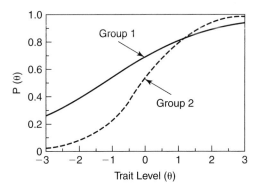

Figure 12.30
Item characteristic curves for two groups.

Summary

In this chapter, I identify the purpose of analyzing individual items, regardless of their format (e.g., multiple choice, Likert-type, PA). A variety of types of item analyses, including how they can be used during item development and revision, are also mentioned. Several procedures based on CTT are discussed and illustrated. This is followed by more item analyzing techniques, but ones using IRT. A number of examples of common computer output useful to such analyses are shown and then explained. A significant amount of the discussion is devoted to DIF (or item bias), explaining what it is and how the careful researcher may go about investigating the phenomenon with both CTT and IRT strategies.

Chapter 13

Examining Whole Tests

Introduction

Deciphering an Enigma

One of the most famous spy incidents of all time occurred during World War I, an occurrence now known by a notorious war artifact: the Zimmerman telegram. On January 16, 1917, the German foreign minister, Arthur Zimmerman, sent a telegram to the German ambassador to the United States, who was instructed to deliver it "in most secret" to the Imperial Minister of Mexico. The message: Mexico would receive the lands of Texas, New Mexico, and Arizona if the country's forces would help Germany conquer first Europe and then the United States.

Britain, France, and Germany had been engaged in a 3-year war, with no end in sight. The Brits had fought bravely in this bloody and terrible war. At Verdun alone, there were more than 60,000 casualties in a single day. More than 1 million people (mostly men) had been killed up to that point, with the count certain to rise. Said one historian about World War I, "It was a gigantic slaughtering machine." At first, the United States had remained neutral in World War I, despite France's plea for America to save them. Then, the Zimmerman telegram was intercepted. It was delivered in routine fashion to a low-level cryptographer. The message was a string of number groups, following a German code book. To decipher these secret messages, code breakers had to painstakingly work by trial and error. Mechanical encryption machines, such as ENIGMA, had not yet been invented. To the kismet of the allied effort, this public servant immediately realized that it was an out-of-the-ordinary secret message and that it contained time-sensitive material, but he could not decipher it beyond that. He notified his superiors and a team of cryptographers was assigned the task of revealing the telegram's meaning. They worked night and day, sleeping on cots and eating little, realizing only that the message contained something significant that could change the war's outcome. They knew lives were at stake—probably many thousands of them, civilians and soldiers. Finally, before it was too late, they made sense of Zimmerman's telegram. Upon learning of its content, the American government immediately made it public. With lightning speed, Congress declared war on Germany, which brought American aid and forces to England and the continent. America's effort was the decisive force in defeating Germany and in rescuing Britain and France from domination. No other secret message, past or present, has so dramatically and decidedly changed history as has the Zimmerman telegram.

Although measurement professionals do not have an ENIGMA-like machine to decipher a hidden meaning in the words printed on the sheets of paper constituting a test, they do possess other tools to examine what information wrought therein. Their tools are the theory and methods of psychometrics. By proper application, the trained measurement professional can use them to uncover a great deal of information about a test and thereby its interpretability.

Contents

In this chapter, I examine tools useful for investigating a composite test or performance activity. First, I look at the purpose for such whole test analyses and identify the tasks involved. From there, discussion turns to unidimensionality and local independence. With this precursory information in place, the remainder (and largest portion) of the chapter is devoted to explaining strategies useful to examining a test's internal structure. One primary route to whole test investigation is factor analysis in its various forms. I describe several of these forms, most particularly, factor analysis by principle axis and maximum likelihood methods, and principle components analysis. After this, I explain an IRT-based factor procedure called *full information factor analysis,* or full information FA. Then I examine several indices of unidimensionality, following with a discussion of structural equation modeling (SEM). The chapter ends with an explanation of whole test bias and its relation to DIF. Necessarily, some information in this chapter is for advanced students.

Examining a Test's Structure

Purpose

At the beginning of philosophy (and by extension, psychology) stands Socrates' precept: "Know thyself." This look inward to discover an essence is, in parallel fashion to a person's self-examination, precisely the point of investigating a test's structure. Examining a test's structure is to explore its internal, essential meaning. Such structural appraisal is done to determine whether evidence is uniformly and sufficiently focused to suggest a coherent, defensible interpretation of an intentional construct. The effort involved in this examination is called *looking at a test's structure.*

The probing is a tendentious argument for validity. When varying bits of data in a test each meet their specific technical criteria for merit, they can be assimilated into a body of evidence regarding the internal nature of a whole test. When such data are internally consistent, the interpretation is of a unitary structure for the test, and it reveals reliable interpretations about an examinee's cognitive functioning or true proficiency. In this way, examining a whole test gives meaning to use of the yielded scores, useful to decision making—that is, validity.

Tasks Involved

A test is like a complex machine with many parts, and no single piece of information can represent it fully. When examining a test, no single statistic or test evaluating method is sufficient to draw a complete picture of how it functions. For that, multiple pieces of information from various sources are needed. It would be wholly inadequate to factor analyze a set of test items and then maintain that a test's structure had been thoroughly examined. Hence, a number of tasks are needed to do the job.

Principally, in structural examination two superordinate tasks are involved, including (1) reviewing already-produced information, especially as such may relate to dimensionality interpretations; and (2) producing original information about how the test functions in a particular assessment context.

Unearthing and reviewing previously compiled information about a test is a straightforward activity, but not always easily accomplished. The pertinent information must be ferreted out from many different sources, and then it must be evaluated for its veracity. This is a kind of detective-cum-lawyer undertaking; namely, one that involves seeking out evidence and then building a case.

One obvious place to begin the detective hunt is with the test's author(s), who can generally supply a wealth of information and data, beginning with a rationale for building the test in the first place. The available information may be in a report or in a technical manual or other test-supporting publication. However, commonly, the needed information is not so conveniently sourced; as a result, it is then appropriate to contact the test's author(s) and ask a lot of questions. Sometimes, the author may be able to provide data for analysis.

Other sources also need to be tapped—for instance, a review of pertinent literature to identity existing research and investigate other contexts in which the test may have been used. There are many places to explore. For tests that are commercially published, one should check the common test catalogues and critiques, such as *Mental Measurements Yearbooks* and the companion *Tests in Print* series, produced at the Buros Institute of Mental Measurements, University of Nebraska (see *http://www.unl.edu/buros/indexbimm.html*. Retrieved March 6, 2005), and the ETS test collection (see *http://www.ets.org/testcoll/index.html*. Retrieved March 6, 2005).

After pertinent information is identified and collected, it must be evaluated. Initially, such an evaluation determines whether it is apropos to the context at hand. A helpful check here is to see whether the test has complied with industry-standard codes and canons for professional practice. Many publications and standards give direction and cite issues to consider when evaluating test-related information. I list a number of such guides in chapter 1.

Once it is determined that unearthed information is relevant to a current assessment situation, it should then be investigated for veracity. For example, clearly we know by now that it is insufficient to accept without question a test manual reporting that an instrument is "reliable and valid." One must dig further to learn how such conclusions were reached—by which methods and in what context?

In addition to investigating extant sources, producing original information about the test is often necessary. Here, the heavy lifting begins because such work is not easy; however, it can be engaging for the competent measurement professional or measurement specialist. This chapter is devoted to explaining numerous methods of mining data to the goal of test evaluation. Remember, too, that original information is often specific to the particular assessment context and population employed for the analyses, and that generalization is not axiomatic to test analyzing methods. For instance, revealing the principal factor structure of a test from data of just one test administration is useful, but it cannot be automatically considered the final word on a test's factorial composition in other testing contexts.

Role of Summary Statistics

One obvious early step in examining a whole test is simply to gather a variety of summary statistics. These indices reveal important information about a test's functioning with a group or with psychological interpretation, as a generalized expression of a latent variable. Likely statistics would include indices of centrality (e.g., mean, median, mode), dispersion (e.g., standard deviation, variance, range, standard error of the mean), and distribution (e.g., skewness, kurtosis). One cannot imagine a whole test analysis without such basic information at hand.

When analyzing summary statistics for whole test evaluation, often a primary consideration is examining the distribution of available scores. We study normal distributions, particularly the standardized normal distribution, in chapter 7. In most structural examination contexts, the scores are mainly useful when the distribution is normal in shape and other characteristics. (Skewed, bimodal, and other abnormal distributions may be important in research or in other specialized contexts.) There are many simple methods to garner an early indication of normality, linearity, and heteroscedasticity in a set of scores. For instance, one may review the skew and kurtosis indexes, determining whether they are within the range (3, −3) as a general guide for acceptance. Also, looking at a normal probability plot of scores, of quartiles, or of standard deviations is helpful. Then, too, many graphics are informative, such as histograms, stem-and-leaf displays, box plots, and others. Nonparametric tests can also provide clues about distributions. Figures 13.1 to 13.4 are illustrative.

However, in whole test evaluation one does not always anticipate symmetric dispersion in scores. For instance, in some licensing and certification programs, candidates have received extensive and focused training prior to assessment; thus, a negatively skewed distribution should be anticipated. Hence, it is also important to keep in mind the purpose of the appraisal.

In addition to simple descriptive statistics, clearly necessary, too, is information about reliability. As readers of this text realize, such indicators of a test's functioning are so important that I devote two complete chapters to reliability: chapter 5 to traditional reliability analyses and chapter 11 to G theory. Any whole test analyses would include evaluative information about reliability.

```
 Frequency     Stem &   Leaf

      30.00 Extremes      (=<124)
       1.00         12 .  &
       6.00         13 .  &
      16.00         14 .  &
      42.00         17 .  &&
      67.00         16 .  7&&
     111.00         17 .  137789&
     170.00         18 .  1347689&
     277.00         19 .  012347667889
     387.00         20 .  00112334776677889
     486.00         21 .  00111233334476677788899
     631.00         22 .  001122333447777666778888999
     698.00         23 .  0011112333344477666778888899
     811.00         24 .  00011112223333444777666677888889999
     876.00         27 .  0001111222333334444777766667778888889999
     907.00         26 .  000011112223333334444777666677788888888999
     872.00         27 .  000111122233333344477766667777888888999
     823.00         28 .  001112223333344477766677788888999
     812.00         29 .  0001112222333333444777666677888888999
     727.00         30 .  000112222333334447777666777788888999
     740.00         31 .  0001112223333444777666777788888999
     636.00         32 .  000112222333344477667788889
     729.00         33 .  0011223334447766778888999
     470.00         34 .  0011233344767788899
     407.00         37 .  0123334477678899
     323.00         36 .  00123347678899
     277.00         37 .  012347789&
     200.00         38 .  0123476789
     139.00         39 .  0124689&
      96.00         40 .  0479&&
      68.00         41 .  9&&
      37.00         42 .  &&
       7.00         43 .  &
       9.00 Extremes      (>=437)


 Stem width:  10
 Each leaf:         23 case(s)
 & denotes fractional leaves.
```

Figure 13.1
Stem-and-leaf display for large data set.

Figure 13.2
Box plots for the genders on
an English subject test.

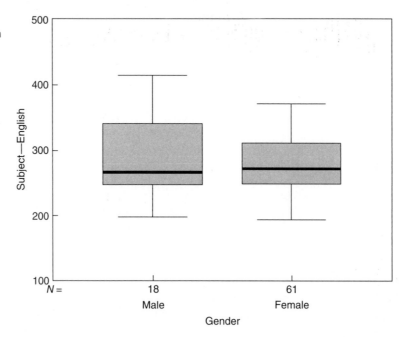

Figure 13.3
Normal probability plot of
nonstandardized values.

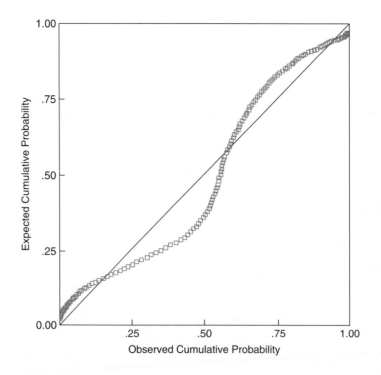

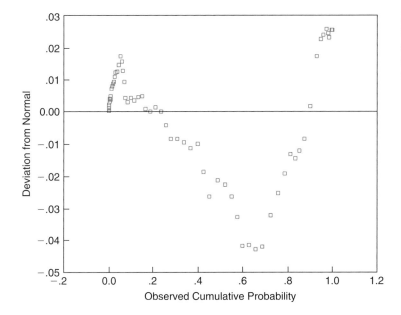

Figure 13.4
Detrended probability plot of standardized values showing deviations from normal expected values.

Unidimensionality and Local Independence

Necessary Background to Understand Unidimensionality

Examining the internal structure of a mental appraisal instrument is largely grounded in determining its dimensionality. Dimensionality was discussed extensively as a conceptual notion in chapter 7, and it has been mentioned at other times throughout the text. In chapter 10, I discussed it as an elemental assumption in IRT. For some readers, it may be useful to review these earlier explanations so the ensuing discussion is meaningful. Here, our purpose centers on how to use the idea for analysis of a whole test.

Most of the methods presented in this chapter pertain to evaluating unidimensionality in a set of items. However, note that the procedures for unidimensionality appraisal do not preclude the fact that some tests are composed of more than a single set of items and hence can yield scores with a multidimensional interpretation. Also, realize that unidimensionality in tests is not limited to just those with multiple-choice formatted items or dichotomously scored ones. Tests composed of Likert-type and other polytomous items should also be appraised for their dimensionality.

Difficulty in Determining Dimensionality

Most experts acknowledge that it is not easy to garner information needed for dimensionality investigation. Many of the processes are difficult to effect, requiring expertise in probability theory, higher-level statistics, and a firm grounding in psychology, particularly cognitive psychology. As often as not, findings are obtuse and hard to interpret. Further, such difficulty is compounded by the fact that many unidimensionality procedures are not fully developed. Hattie (1985) empirically reviewed more than 30 indices of unidimensionality and associated procedure. He concluded that most lack a coherent rationale and that many are mere adjustments to previous procedures. He found that methods that adjust the fit size of the residual are the most empirically satisfying. Hattie further suggested that unidimensionality be assessed within the framework of *local independence,* the circumstance in which all items are independent of one another for examinees of the same proficiency (i.e., ability) on the latent trait. (Recall that this assumption was described in chapter 10.) Indeed, most methods of assessing unidimensionality are described in terms of satisfying local independence.

A Beginning Place

A logical but often overlooked place to begin dimensionality investigation is with documentation accompanying a test, specifically with a test author's description of the measure's intended target and the test specifications. For dimensionality investigation, it is useful to learn the test author's intent and how the measure is grounded in theory. If an underlying test theory and the author's stated intention is for, say, a single dimension to be appraised, then this is useful information in whole test analysis. When multidimensional assessment is the goal, the researcher investigating dimensionality would also need that information.

Factor Analysis and Principal Components Analysis

Scope of FA and PCA Coverage

In this section, I briefly describe two related classical factoring procedures often used in whole test analysis: principal axis factoring and PCA. Later in the chapter, I discuss another Bayesian-based factoring method, full information FA, which is consistent with IRT, as well as SEM as a confirmatory factoring approach. Each procedure relies on different assumptions and is distinct in its focus. Hence, varying interpretations about a test's dimensionality are produced.

My focus in this discussion is more on how the methods may be used by measurement professional for investigating dimensionality and less on explaining the procedures themselves, beyond some obvious overlap. Readers will find a plethora of readily available books and sources describing methods of factoring (e.g., Gorsuch, 1983; Osterlind, 2001; Stevens, 1992; Tabachnick & Fidell, 2000). In addition to these sources, Harman (1967) wrote a classic work on FA. He greatly advanced the procedure, and his writing, although dated, still conveys valuable information. Also worth noting is a more recent book by Thissen and Wainer (2001) called *Test Scoring.* Aimed at an advanced audience, this fine work emphasizes modern factoring approaches, many with IRT and others using FA with polytomous items, most beyond the scope of our study. For trained readers, however, the work is an excellent resource. Other highly technical descriptions of FA procedures are proffered by Cooley and Lohnes (1971) and Wherry (1984), who also explain the interpretation of secondary factors in hierarchical FA as an alternative to traditional oblique rotational strategies. Of course, journal articles in the professional literature are another resource for information on factoring data, as are dozens of Web sites (e.g., *http://www2.chass.ncsu.edu/garson/pa765/statnote.htm*. Retrieved March 6, 2005).

A Focus on Psychology When Factoring

When factoring a test, researchers and test developers should keep in mind that the instruments under consideration are measures of mental attributes, and therefore, that psychological interpretations should predominate. This implies that interpretations from test data are neither transparent nor self-evident. As a reflection of psychology, a deep explanation is needed of a test's factors, components, or dimensions—more than mere labels. Important, too, when offering such information, the interpretation should be grounded in a particular educational or psychological theory, whether that be behavioral or cognitive. I mention this point because it is overlooked by many novices, as well as in some current test investigations, but it has been long recognized by experienced measurement professional. As far back as 1948, L. L. Thurstone argued that, "Factorial methods will be fruitful in the advancement of psychology only in so far as we use these methods in close relations to psychological ideas" (p. 408).

In addition, even though factoring is a useful strategy in structural examination, caution is advised to (a) not attribute more interpretation to the findings than the procedure properly allows, and (b) to limit generalizing FA or PCA findings only to circumstances for which there is accompanying justification. These cautions are given because they point out misinterpretations and unfounded extensions of data inferences commonly committed by novice test constructors. A neophyte test constructor may develop a set of test items, collect the data from a field test of those items, and then factor them, only to imagine the findings reveal once and for all the test's underlying structure. A common factor structure is not automatically permanent, nor can it be readily generalized to other assessment contexts. Providing contextual information that supports how the results may be properly applied to the test and to future populations is just as important as the procedure. Remember, factoring is part of building an evaluative argument for test validity.

Exploratory Versus Confirmatory FA and PCA

Before beginning FA and PCA in test analysis, however, the researcher or measurement professional should be clear on the purposes of factoring because this can help direct the methodology employed and almost certainly will influence the interpretation of results. Generally (but with important departures in specialized circumstances), factoring is for one of two purposes, namely, to reduce a large number of variables to a smaller and related set or to seek evidence for a particular theory in a data set. The first of these purposes is *exploratory analysis;* the second is *confirmatory analysis.* Readers are most likely familiar with these goals. As a general guide, exploratory factoring is done to investigate data by synthesizing communalities from an assortment of variables, and confirmatory analysis seeks to demonstrate a hypothesized latency in the data. For whole test analysis, the latency is presumed to be of a construct or trait.

Both exploratory and confirmatory factoring are useful in examining composite test scores, and researchers will likely conduct studies of each type at varying times. However, the choice of which factoring goal to use and when should be deliberate and carefully considered. The implications derived from each type of factoring are distinct, and different interpretations follow. It is easy to skip this consideration of factoring goals because sometimes nearly identical procedures may be used with either goal. A few briefly stated test scenarios will help one to appreciate the differences in factoring goals.

When developing a test, for instance, the test's author is often interested in extensively exploring the data to learn as much as possible about how a set of items or exercises is functioning in the real world. The author is exploring the data to see what communalities may arise. Another of the author's interests during development is to identify items that do not function in a manner consistent with other items. Identifying aberrant items is useful during development so they may be modified to be more consistent with the main body of items on the test or so they can be eliminated altogether. Both of these circumstances for FA lead to data reduction as the appropriate route for factoring. Hence, the author would choose the exploratory goal for factoring.

There are also circumstances during test development when confirmatory factoring approaches are wanted. When examining a test's structure, for instance, the concern shifts toward learning about latencies in the measure. Usually, a theory of learning of education is implied. Hence, dimensionality investigation calls for a confirmatory approach to factoring.

There are many classic studies where the confirmatory approach has proven useful. For instance, Spearman's look at a two-factor theory of intelligence, Thurstone's high scholarly look into differentiated mental abilities, and Guildford's "structure of intellect" model, all relied on confirmatory FA. In contemporary times, Sternberg's triarchic theory of love and Gardner's speculations into "multiple intelligences" also use confirmatory factoring.

Procedurally, when the factoring goal is confirmatory analysis, a number of factoring options for extraction of the initial set are available to the researcher. Usually, FA by principal axis factoring is recommended because this approach focuses on correlations; hence, just common variance contributes to the solution. Alternatively, alpha factoring can be employed because this route seeks to maximize reliability among the items, again, by looking at interitem correlations. More recently, however, attention is being directed toward employing SEM as a model-building approach to confirmatory factoring. SEM is intended for confirming a hypothesized, underlying dimension of a test and is consistent with measurement theory's attachment to cognitive psychology.

Initial Extraction of Logical Clusters

Factoring data, whether done for exploration or confirmation, seeks to discover groupings of variables from among a large set of them. In test development work individual items are considered as variables, despite this idea having both conceptual and practical problems. Like stars forming constellations in a clear night sky, items that have obvious, strong associations group together. Weaker associations are also successively formed until just single items remain. Even these, by definition, compose a "group", albeit of just one. That is, in factoring, during initial iterations of the procedure, every item conforms to a cluster, factor, component, or dimension. (The label of such groupings is given by what kind of analysis is done.) This step in the process is called *initial extraction*.

The clusters are initially deduced from an **R** matrix that holds the interitem correlations. Figure 13.5 presents a matrix of this type. In Figure 13.5 and other matrices like it, one notices immediately that the interitem correlations are low. In chapter 12, I discussed why this situation is typical when such matrices are composed of items that are dichotomously scored. When polytomous items (e.g., Likert-type) compose a test and are treated as individual variables in the analysis, the correlations are generally much higher and more variance is available for sleuthing out communality.

In a simple data set, identifying logical groups of interitem correlations can almost be done by eyeballing the **R** matrix; although to do so in practice would be specious. However, in nearly every data set (even in the simplest ones), one cannot consistently identify clusters among the correlations because there is no set criterion for making such judgments. Also, by sheer volume in the matrix, one simply loses one's way in the data. After all, for most tests there will be many interitem correlations in a matrix. A 50-item test, for instance, will have 1,225 of them! The exact number of correlations can be calculated by applying Equation 13.1.

$$\frac{k(k-1)}{2} \qquad\qquad (13.1)$$

		Q1	Q2	Q3	Q4	Q5	Q6
Correlation	Q1	1.000	−.116	−.158	−.490	.005	.024
	Q2	−.116	1.000	−.004	.074	.048	−.069
	Q3	−.158	−.004	1.000	.139	−.030	.089
	Q4	−.490	.074	.139	1.000	−.034	−.027
	Q5	.005	.048	−.030	−.034	1.000	−.143
	Q6	.024	−.069	.089	−.027	−.143	1.000

Figure 13.5
Portion of a correlation matrix, evidencing typical low interitem relationships.

Fortunately, the problem of identifying clusters consistently by a coherent method can be solved with matrix algebra, regardless of size or complexity in the data. The matrix-algebra operation of *diagonalization* yields sets of common item-by-item correlations that emerge as clusters or related groupings. The interitem relating is accomplished by examining either the items' variance (in PCA) or by using just the correlational values to reproduce the original matrix as closely as possible (the method of FA). The clusters are then interpreted.

During initial extraction, the amount of contribution of every item in the data set is shown by the initial *eigenvalues*. Eigenvalues are a special set of scalars associated with a linear system of equations in matrix algebra. They are interpreted as variance estimates, both the amount of variance in the observed variables accounted for by each factor (the total variance) and the percent of variance accounted for by each specific factor relative to the total variance in all the variables. Figure 13.6 shows these initial eigenvalues and associated percents.

Examination of the column in Figure 13.6, labeled "Total," reveals the obvious circumstance that not all factors (here labeled "components") represent meaningful

Component	Initial Eigenvalues			Extraction Sums of Squared Loadings		
	Total	Percent of Variance	Cumulative Percent	Total	Percent of Variance	Cumulative Percent
1	3.540	16.092	16.092	3.540	16.092	16.092
2	1.134	5.153	21.245	1.134	5.153	21.245
3	1.064	4.836	26.081	1.064	4.836	26.081
4	.998	4.537	30.618			
5	.972	4.418	35.036			
6	.964	4.382	39.418			
7	.950	4.319	43.737			
8	.917	4.169	47.905			
9	.905	4.115	52.021			
10	.900	4.090	56.111			
11	.882	4.007	60.118			
12	.880	4.001	64.119			
13	.859	3.906	68.024			
14	.851	3.869	71.893			
15	.824	3.744	75.637			

Figure 13.6
Initial eigenvalues revealing that the first factor accounts for much more in the total variance than do any other factors.

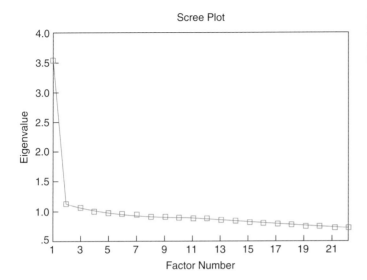

Figure 13.7
Scree plot showing a strong first factor relative to other factors.

groupings, just as not all stars can be grouped into constellations. Thus, the problem in factoring becomes one of deciding which factors (components) to retain in the analysis. The idea is to keep those that are meaningful descriptions of the data and discard inconsequential ones. There are two popular methods for making this decision. The first method is by visual inspection of the data. The brilliant German psychologist, James Cattell (a student of Wundt and influential upon E. L. Thorndike), realized early on that the eigenvalues could be plotted, making a visual criterion for selection possible. He called his plot a *scree plot,* an example of which is shown in Figure 13.7.

To interpret a scree plot, it is useful to know the definition of *scree.* This term derives from a Scandinavian noun meaning landslide. It is used to denote the accumulation of loose stones and rocks lying at the base of a hill or mountain. When used by geologists, scree is not included in determination of a mountain's height. In parallel fashion, Cattell looked at his scree plot and suggested that one use logical judgment to determine where the meaningful data ends and the rubble of insignificant eigenvalues begins. In Figure 13.7, it is apparent that one eigenvalue is much stronger than the others. Loosely, this is interpreted as indicating a single strong, overarching factor in the data relative to all other factors. It is evident that all other factors are—by comparison—insignificant.

However, *Cattell's scree criterion* is criticized as arbitrary because judgments about "insignificance" may differ. Henry Kaiser, another statistician, suggested a criterion of retaining eigenvalues that index one and above because this represents a reasonable percent of variance in most data sets. From Figure 13.6, we see that by Kaiser's criterion we would retain three factors. Researchers may apply either criterion, depending on purpose, especially fit to the data.

Also, at this stage in the analysis, an *initial factor loading matrix* is calculated. This matrix reveals the correlation between each item and the factors. It can be used for further refining the choice of how many factors to retain by reviewing what items load on which factor at this early stage. These initial factor loadings are not interpreted in the final solution, however, because the focus at this stage is on determining how many factors to retain.

Working from a Correlation Matrix

Although calculating the correlations is an early step in factoring problems, sometimes only the **R** matrix (rather than raw data) is available to the researcher, as may be the case in secondary data analysis. Most major software programs can accommodate this circumstance by calculating reliable factors using the **R** matrix (or the covariance matrix for PCA) itself. Figure 13.8 shows a portion of such a matrix with necessary accompanying information (i.e., *n*, mean, and standard deviations) in the top two lines as used in SPSS. One may copy this format for use in that program. SAS has a parallel procedure for factoring a matrix, as does Systat.

Figure 13.8
Portion of the SPSS data file formatted to process factor analysis directly from the **R** matrix.

| File | Edit | View | Data | Transform | Analyze | Graphs | Utilities | Window | Help |

1 : rowtype_   N

	rowtype_	varname_	q42	q43	q44
1	N		2000.00	2000.00	2000.00
2	MEAN		.63	.83	.66
3	STDDEV		.48	.38	.47
4	CORR	Q42	1.00	.12	.15
5	CORR	Q43	.12	1.00	.08
6	CORR	Q44	.15	.08	1.00
7	CORR	Q45	.17	.10	.17
8	CORR	Q46	.16	.14	.37
9	CORR	Q47	.54	.11	.16
10	CORR	Q48	.17	.21	.16
11	CORR	Q49	.16	.22	.17
12	CORR	Q50	.12	.15	.13
13	CORR	Q51	.12	.09	.07
14	CORR	Q52	.16	.15	.10
15	CORR	Q53	.11	.09	.07

Rotational Procedures in Factoring

After using FA procedures for awhile, however, one begins to realize that diagonal-izing an **R** matrix produces only gross groupings and many individual interitem cor-relations may be only moderately associated with a factor. This results in diminished communalities among the items and thereby yields consistently distorted sets, to one degree or another. In addition, when items are extreme (i.e., all examinees re-sponded correctly or incorrectly), interitem correlations can be 1s or 0s, producing an even more unauthentic result.

These problems with initial factors were recognized by statisticians as far back as Spearman, but few of them had real solutions. Then, about 40 years ago, Henry Kaiser, a renowned educational psychologist working at the University of California, Berkeley, produced a rotational solution to the vectoring process in diagonalization, thereby enhancing the likelihood of locating more complete communalities among items. In other words, more internally consistent factor loadings could be derived with matrix algebra. To do so, the unrotated factor loadings are multiplied by the transformation matrix to produce the *rotated factor matrix*. Kaiser's solution is called *rotation* and is now practiced as standard procedure in nearly all factoring problems. Figure 13.9 shows dramatically contrasting results for initial and rotated solutions (with principal axis factoring). As shown, the rotated solution conveys more coher-ence in the data.

The transformation matrix shows the exact amount of rotation applied to the ini-tial extractions to produce the rotated solution. Figure 13.10 displays this matrix for the factoring problem given in Figure 13.9. To interpret Figure 13.10, examine the off-diagonal elements for their relative size. When the value is relatively small, such as the value used in factor 1 to 2 (i.e., 0.289), there is little rotation applied; how-ever, when the value is big (i.e., generally, greater than 0.5), a large rotation is used. The latter circumstance is seen in factors 1 to 4 (i.e., 0.665). Consistent with this large rotation, the fourth factor loses all significance after the large rotation (see the right pane of Figure 13.9). As an example, if the fourth factor was not eliminated in the earlier stages, it can be discounted here with certainty.

Rotated solutions may also be displayed graphically. Such a graphical look at the solution is particularly useful for many purposes in assessment. It provides an initial identification of aberrant items, and it gives the researcher a glimpse into the di-mensional structure of the test. An example of a factor plot in rotated factor space is given in Figure 13.11. Notice that item Q73 appears apart from the others. Also, item Q76 is slightly divergent, and items Q75 and Q79 appear to trail upward modestly. These items should be examined, possibly for their wording and especially for their intended construct. Still, it is apparent that the great majority of items do locate close to one another, and a corresponding axis, indicating a degree of cohesion in the interitem correlation matrix—a preliminary indicator of unidimensionality in assess-ment of the targeted construct.

Over time, Kaiser refined his first rotational method (later termed *varimax*) into a number of optional rotational procedures (e.g., *promax, quartimax*), each useful for a different purpose. Since Kaiser's groundbreaking work, others have offered still

Initial Extraction

	1	2	3	4
Q6	461			
Q23	.426			-.210
Q22	.414			-.231
Q14	.377			
Q19	.373			
Q16	.361			
Q28	.360			
Q29	.333		.210	
Q11	.332	-.292		
Q40	.323			
Q31	.318			
Q20	.315			
Q30	.305			
Q21	.287			
Q35	.287			
Q32	.281			
Q34	.277		.224	
Q10	.275			
Q27	.274			
Q26	.269			
Q24	.263			
Q12	.261			
Q37	.260			
Q1	.255	.249		

Varimax Rotated Extraction

	1	2	3	4
Q23	.440			
Q22	.439			
Q19	.335			
Q20	.280			
Q21	.236			
Q18	.213			
Q24	.206			
Q16	.206			
Q27				
Q25				
Q26				
Q15		.632		
Q4		.546		
Q11		.395		
Q17	.205	.230		
Q10			.339	
Q1			.326	
Q9			.319	
Q14			.282	
Q6	.210		.281	
Q31			.218	
Q13				

Figure 13.9
Comparison of initial (unrotated) extraction with PCA, contrasted with varimax rotated solution.

more options, and today there are five or six commonly used rotational schemes in these analyses. Each rotation method is designed for a different circumstance, but all augment identification of common factors in a data set. The main point of Kaiser's work (and that of his followers) is that rotation produces a more complete and consistent reduction in the data than can usually be seen in initial extractions.

Also, depending on the interitem correlation matrix and the test maker's anticipated outcome, either *orthogonal* or *oblique rotations* may be tried. Orthogonal

Factor Transformation Matrix

Factor	1	2	3	4
1	.580	.583	.506	.261
2	.289	.047	.105	−.950
3	−.372	−.357	.856	−.036
4	.665	−.728	−.008	.165

Extraction Method: Principal Axis Factoring.

Rotation Method: Varimax with Kaiser Nomalization.

Figure 13.10
Factor transformation matrix showing the rotation applied to the initial data to produce the rotated solution.

relationships reflect independent pieces of information and thus are correlated only randomly. In contrast, oblique rotations are useful when the researcher hypothesizes that the components are not independent, such as in multidimensional appraisals. The choice between these rotational perspectives is important because it reflects different perspectives on the theory underlying the constructs being considered.

Family of Factoring Approaches

Students and researchers should be aware that FA is not a single, invariant method; rather, it is a family of extraction strategies, each intended for a specified purpose. Some of these extraction methods are maximum likelihood, generalized least squares, alpha, and more. Most commonly, however, when using FA in test development or analysis, the approach employed is principal axis factoring, although some specialists favor the maximum likelihood approach because it incorporates Bayesian estimation for a likelihood of factors.

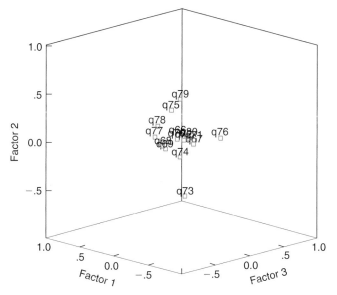

Figure 13.11
Factor plot in rotated factor space.

With principal axis factoring, the data in the **R** matrix is diagonalized in a manner that seeks to reproduce in the identified factors the original intercorrelations among the items (variables). The PCA approach to factoring is thereby focused on the correlational relationship among the items and less on assimilating their variance, making it a logical choice in test analysis. Because correlations are derived as cross-products of variables, only shared variance is put in the equation. Hence, with principal axis factoring, common variance is condensed into factors and unique variance is not included in the analysis. Unique variance is treated as error. Imaginably, then, the covariance matrix is unsuited to principal axis factoring. This contrasts with PCA, which does analyze the covariance matrix.

PCA in Test Analysis

PCA can be extremely useful to whole test analysis; however, understanding why is complicated. When building a test and its dimensionality is initially unknown, it is sometimes advantageous to presume that the full variance of each item contributes to the test's structure. Such presumption applies to individual items only and does not extend to the entire test. In other words, when examining a whole test, one can use PCA to investigate the contribution of individual items to a dimensional structure, but from this technique alone one cannot infer that dimensionally based items compose a unidimensional test. This is an instance in which the whole is not completely the sum of its individual parts because, most likely, some items are not well suited to the model. The interest for whole test analysis is in exploring generally whether the full variance of items (i.e., the *communalities*) can compose components. If only a single component is observed in the data, unidimensionality is indicated, if only preliminarily. The initial extraction of factors by PCA in this purpose should be followed by varimax as the rotational method because this strategy further forces the maximum amount of variance on the first component.

As a full variance approach, PCA begins by replacing ones in the positive diagonal of the **R** matrix before factor extraction. The effect of this process is to engage in the analysis only the variance that a variable shares with a component. The unique error variance of each variable is thereby removed. Final estimates of communality are interpreted as the proportion of variance in a variable that can be predicted from its underlying factors.

This focus for PCA makes it useful for reducing a set of test items into a smaller and more targeted group (i.e., component), a good test-building technique when used at an early stage. The test developer, initially, is interested in synthesizing variance, regardless of whether it is shared among the items or contributed uniquely by separate ones. Items that cluster to a second, third, or successive component are believed to be orthogonally distinct from the first one, and therefore, do not contribute to appraisal of the first construct. Because of this variance approach, a covariance matrix may be analyzed.

As a result of this route to variance explanation, test developers wanting to confirm a unitary structure to their work, often begin exploration by using principal components extraction and varimax rotation. This allows the test maker to easily interpret the factorability of their matrix.

However, because PCA does not separate common variance from unique variance in items analyzed, it is not suited to other specific test analyses goals. First, realize that this feature makes PCA generally unsuited to investigation of unidimensionality. This is logical because PCA is less precise than other factoring methods for identifying aberrant items, another important concern in test development and revision. Hence, PCA is not recommended for selecting items that contribute just to the first component.

To illustrate the complexity but concomitant utility of FA by principal components, examine the output of data from a real test shown in Figure 13.12. This test of mathematics achievement comprises three subtests (i.e., General Math, Algebra, and Geometry), each of which is made up of either two or three skills. The factor loadings provide an indication of the dimensional structure of the test. As shown, the General Math subtest loads most heavily on a single skill (Properties and notations) for its first factor and shares variance among the remaining skills (Practical application and Using statistics) for a second factor. The third factor is insignificant. Along with the General Math skill, both skills (Evaluating expressions and Equations and inequalities) from Algebra load on the first factor. The Geometry skills constitute a third factor, as indicated by their relatively heavy loadings. This information would lead a test developer or researcher to consider combining aspects of the first factor skills for General Math and Algebra) into a more coherent subtest. The Geometry subtest appears unitary as it is.

Differences Between FA and PCA

Both FA and PCA have a place in analyzing assessments of mental abilities. They can be used in test development as well as in whole-test analysis. Thus, the able measurement professional must be thoroughly versed in both procedures and have a good sense of which one could be used to advantage in what circumstance.

Cluster	Skill	Factor 1	Factor 2	Factor 3
General Math	Practical application	0.24	0.83	0.21
	Properties and notations	0.77	0.38	0.08
	Using statistics	0.26	0.76	0.30
Algebra	Evaluating expressions	0.74	0.17	0.38
	Equations and inequalities	0.72	0.18	0.41
Geometry	Two- and three-dimensional figures	0.30	0.22	0.83
	Geometric calculations	0.27	0.44	0.70

Figure 13.12
Factor loadings from a rotated factor matrix of a test composed of subtests and underlying skills.

Rotated Component Matrix[a]					Rotated Factor Matrix[a]			

	Component					Factor		
	1	2	3			1	2	3
Q16	.539				Q40	.404		
Q6	.462	.233			Q31	.363		
Q20	.449				Q29	.362		
Q23	.434				Q10	.310		
Q22	.395	.292			Q14	.300	.248	
Q19	.374				Q32	.285		
Q13	.371				Q26	.270		
Q14	.366	.253			Q35	.234		
Q12	.365				Q36	.232		
Q28	.348				Q9	.230		
Q1	.336		−.321		Q37	.215		
Q17	.312		.308		Q25	.204		
Q9	.283	.212			Q30	.200		
Q8	.282				Q39			
Q7	.230				Q41			
Q27	.222				Q27			
Q2	.207				Q5			
Q5					Q33			
Q29		.483			Q34			
Q40		.480			Q38			
Q31		.432			Q16		.492	
Q32		.403			Q20		.391	
Q36		.391			Q6	.280	.356	
Q10		.346	−.264		Q22	.270	.352	
Q26		.335			Q23		.336	
Q25		.312			Q28		.292	
Q41		.311			Q19		.288	
Q37		.302			Q17		.241	
Q35		.296			Q21		.228	
Q30		.277			Q1		.226	−.212
Q38		.258			Q24		.221	
Q39		.250			Q12		.212	
Q34		.249			Q13		.203	
Q21	.207	.220			Q2			
Q33		.205			Q8			
Q15			.724		Q7			
Q4			.645		Q15			.697
Q11		.205	.483		Q4			.535
Q3			−.382		Q11			.361
Q18	.263		−.293		Q3			−.244
Q24	.240		.271		Q18			

Extraction Method: Principal Component Analysis.
Rotation Method: Varimax with Kaiser Normalization.
[a]Rotation converged in 6 iterations.

Extraction Method: Principal Axis Factoring.
Rotation Method: Varimax with Kaiser Normalization.
[a]Rotation converged in 5 iterations.

Figure 13.13
Typical rotated matrices: one by PCA (left pane) and the other by FA (right pane).

Figure 13.13 shows some differences between PCA and FA that may affect various test development activities or whole test examination. In Figure 13.13, the identical set of 41 items is analyzed by both techniques using the same interitem correlation matrix. Also, varimax rotation was used with both analyses. The left pane shows extraction by PCA and the right by FA, principal axis factoring.

Notice especially that the same set of items do not compose the same factors. Item 16, for instance, is most highly associated with the first component but does not even register significance on this first grouping when the extraction is by FA (on the output, it is far down the list). In fact, many of the items constituting the first component group (by PCA) associate on the second factor (FA), and vice versa. This is a result of the differences in variance extracted by each technique. Also, notice that there is a tighter association of items (fewer cross-loadings) in the FA procedures than with PCA, indicating that the dimensionality is more associated with the noted items.

So, the logical question arises: Which procedure is right? Of course, as it stands—as readers will readily recognize—this question is not well framed because it ignores differences in purposes for the procedures. Nor is the context for using either procedure considered by the question. For a more reasonable appraisal of the techniques, one must look at understanding what purpose is best served by which extraction method, as well as the specific assessment context.

Computer Programs Useful for Data Reduction Procedures

Most full-featured statistical programs perform the calculations of FA and PCA, although there are noteworthy differences among many of them and peculiarities within each. Users are cautioned to be aware of them. The best known programs are probably SPSS, SAS, and Systat, but there are also other fine programs. Specialized FA and PCA programs include MicroFACT, which does analysis for large data sets and can accommodate both dichotomous and polytomous data. SCA performs a unique simultaneous principal component analysis to determine which components from one group describe the observations in another group, and VARCL calculates variance component analysis by maximum likelihood method. These last three programs are available from Assessment Systems Corporation at *http://www.assess.com/index.htm*. Retrieved March 6, 2005). Sometimes, a researcher may write computer code to perform these calculations because they are not too difficult with matrix algebra. Although some of these efforts are excellent, users that may be considering them are cautioned to become well informed about an author's assumptions and matrix procedures so the output can be properly interpreted.

Technical Problems with FA and PCA

FA and PCA, although exceedingly useful in whole test analysis, are not without shortcomings. Factoring an **R** matrix can be problematic in both test development and subsequent analysis. Description of factoring problems is technical but that need not slow our understanding; we only follow it conceptually and do not delve into the more involved mathematics, which are beyond our scope.

One reason for problems in factoring is that the correlational matrix must be of a specified form to allow for interpretable factors. Specifically, the matrix must be *Gramian,* meaning that all pairs of correlations and covariances are *positive definite.* No diagonal values can exceed 1. A more complete definition of a Gramian matrix is complex, involving the transpose of a second-order matrix. For our use, however, it means that the values placed in the diagonal of the **R** must be appropriate for the data set and purpose of the analysis. A non-Gramian matrix, or one that is not positive definite, can produce negative, and therefore nonsensical, eigenvalues. Principal axis factoring of such a matrix is faulty and not recommended (Roznowski, Tucker, & Humphries, 1991).

Another way to state the situation is to realize that when the eigenvalues for sets of associations are estimated from the data by methods of maximum likelihood, they can overstate interitem relationships, leading to larger-appearing communalities than exist in reality. Thus, the factored matrix is faulty in describing the interitem relationships. However, when the diagonal values are defined by the researcher as unity (the 1s, by definition in the PCA case), they may simply be reflecting a hypothesized relationship, rather than a true relationship. Again, a faulty matrix may be factored, and researchers are cautioned to be aware of the circumstance so as to not improperly apply a factoring solution to a data set.

A related problem also arises from the correlational matrix and may be unique to binary data. This is termed the *Heywood condition.* It exists for items that measure extreme values of ability or proficiency. Such extreme values exist when items are too easy or too difficult for the group of examinees, and they are shown when all examinees endorse a given item in the same way, typically as all correct or all incorrect. When two such extreme response items are correlated, the resultant coefficient is either 1 or 0, by definition, creating the condition where diagonal values can become greater than 1, or Heywood, again making the matrix non-Gramian. Under these conditions, relationships in the matrix of correlations cannot be meaningfully known, and correspondingly, cannot be meaningfully interpreted.

The situation here may be minimized, however, by presuming that the items represent variables that are not restricted to the range of the test but are true ability latencies with infinite range, only a portion of which is being examined. This psychological approach is consistent with IRT. Under the theory, the full range may be estimated by maximum likelihood methods, even though just a fraction of it is measured by the particular set of items on a given test. This leads to the specialized full information FA, described in the next section.

IRT-Based Full Information FA and MINRES FA

Full Information Item FA

To obviate some of the problems with FA and PCA described, matrices can be analyzed by a specialized factoring methodology based on IRT that considers the full range of the latent distribution of the measured construct, rather than tying results to just the observed data points. One such IRT-based method is *full information FA*

(Bock & Aitkin, 1981; Bock, Gibbons, & Muraki, 1988; McLeod, Swygert, & Thissen, 2001). Full information FA accomplishes data reduction by incorporating a Bayesian likelihood function into the solution. It provides probability estimates of factors for differing abilities along the measured range, regardless of the particular items used in the assessment, as long as they conform to IRT assumptions. With these assumptions, then, it is a more generalizable procedure than ordinary FA or PCA.

As an IRT-based approach, full information FA integrates a psychological interpretation into the findings. Factors are considered dimensions along latent variables, rather than merely a synthesis of commonalities, the interpretation of ordinary FA and PCA. This is not to suggest that findings by full information FA are different in kind from findings yielded by ordinary FA or PCA; instead, they differ in emphasis. With full information FA, the findings are of latent constructs and can be estimated at varying points along the measured range of ability or proficiency. For examining a test's internal structure, this can be a useful perspective because dimensionality is itself a concept deeply rooted in cognition that has (at least theoretically) an infinite range.

Because of the latent trait perspective, ordinary Pearson correlations are not suited to full information FA. Instead, tetrachoric correlations comprise the matrix to be factored; hence, the entire procedure is consistent in the assumption of latency in the variable. I described tetrachoric correlations in the next section.

Because of this perspective, a definition of unidimensionality that more firmly embraces cognitive psychology is needed. Hattie (1985) offers such a rationale for unidimensionality appropriate to full information FA when he says, "A set of items can be said to be unidimensional when it is possible to find a vector of values $\phi = (\phi_i)$ such that the probability of correctly answering an item g is $\pi_{ig} = f_g(\phi)$ and local independence holds for each value of ϕ" (p. 140).

This definition of unidimensionality does not conflict or alter the description of unidimensionality given earlier. It does, however, incorporate the notion of Bayesian probability theory because it suggests that dimensionality is wholly dependent on local independence. Both of these features further imbue the notion into cognitive psychology.

Another aspect of full information FA that contrasts with ordinary FA and PCA is that it is computationally intensive, whereas ordinary FA and PCA can be accomplished relatively simply with the application of ordinary rules of matrix algebra. Full information FA solves likelihood equations by integrating over the latent distribution of abilities for the examinee population. This type of integration is called *marginalization,* and it involves marginal maximum likelihood procedures. Details of the integration are beyond our scope but can be found in writings by Bock and his colleagues (Bock & Aitkin, 1981; Bock et al., 1988). Bock's algorithms for full information FA are implemented in the computer program TESTFACT (Wood et al., 2002).

TESTFACT requires syntax with FORTRAN statements as initial input. A syntax file for TESTFACT, which produces the output discussed as follows, is shown in Figure 13.14. This particular syntax has the item responses reduced to 1s and 0s, with the correct key as all 1s (see the fourth command statement "KEY"). Syntax files and analogous procedures to this section for the LISERAL and SAS programs can be accessed at *http://ourworld.compuserve.com/homepages/jsuebersax/irt.htm* (Retrieved March 7, 2005).

```
>TITLE
   ITEM FACTOR ANALYSIS OF CB- Math only (Form LP)
      with Tetrachoric option
>PROBLEM  NITEM=56,RESPONSE=3;
>RESPONSE ' ','0','1';
>KEY 11111111111111111111111111111111111111111111111111111111;
>TETRACHORIC RECODE,NDEC=3,LIST;
>FACTOR NFAC=2,NROOT=6,NIT=(5,0.02),ROTATE=PROMAX;
>FULL ITER=(20,3,0.01),OMIT=RECODE;
>SCORE LIST=100;
>SAVE CORRELAT,FSCORES;
>INPUT NIDW=4,SCORES,FILE= 'CB2000_Data.dat';
  (4A1,10X,56A1)
>STOP
```

Figure 13.14
Syntax file for TESTFACT for unidimensionality investigation.

Factors in the TESTFACT implementation of full information FA are first identi-fied as latent roots, again emphasizing their basis in deep psychology. Figure 13.15 shows the *N* largest roots for a data set from a test of mathematics achievement.

A specialized type of FA is shown in Figure 13.16. This type is called MINRES (for "minimized residuals") FA and was first developed by Harman (1967). MINRES is a factor analytic procedure that uses ordinary least squares by minimizing the residual sum of squares. MINRES can provide data useful to understanding the struc-ture of a test because it allows liberal violations of the normality assumption on the original distribution. Also, it accommodates small data sets.

In Figure 13.16 (only the first 10 items are shown), notice the distinct loadings on the first factor (the column labeled "1") in contrast to the second, indicating di-mensionality for this data set. The finding is useful because MINRES is an exploratory procedure and the number of factors is not originally hypothesized. With MINRES implementation in TESTFACT, the MINRES correlations are a starting point for full in-formation item FA. It is performed on the smoothed correlation matrix of tetrachoric correlations as a part of the IRT approach. Still, it is a specialized approach, useful in the conditions noted. Additional details on MINRES are given by Jöreskog (2003),

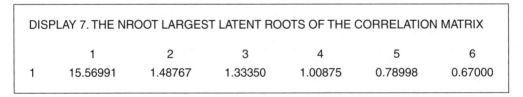

	1	2	3	4	5	6
DISPLAY 7. THE NROOT LARGEST LATENT ROOTS OF THE CORRELATION MATRIX						
1	15.56991	1.48767	1.33350	1.00875	0.78998	0.67000

Figure 13.15
Latent roots for full information item factor analysis.

```
DISPLAY  8.  MINRES PRINCIPAL FACTOR LOADINGS

                              1         2

      1    ITEM    1      0.499     0.016
      2    ITEM    2      0.472    -0.076
      3    ITEM    3      0.466    -0.104
      4    ITEM    4      0.435    -0.108
      5    ITEM    5      0.477    -0.108
      6    ITEM    6      0.503    -0.062
      7    ITEM    7      0.525     0.224
      8    ITEM    8      0.612    -0.185
      9    ITEM    9      0.467     0.039
     10    ITEM   10      0.378     0.067
```

Figure 13.16
Loadings for full information item factor analysis.

and an example of its implementation in TESTFACT is given by du Toit (2003). In addition, a form of MINRES is implemented in the LISREL program (Jöreskog & Sörbom, 2002).

Continuing the full information FA, the output is augmented by three additional figures, each providing slightly different information about the full information FActor structure (noted with first two initial caps as in a command statement). These are the standardized difficulty, communality, and principle factors (Figure 13.17); after rotation, the standardized difficulty, communality, and varimax factors (Figure 13.18), as

			DIFF.	COMM.	FACTORS	
					1	2
1	ITEM	1	−0.337	0.262	0.511	−0.015
2	ITEM	2	−0.946	0.234	0.480	−0.065
3	ITEM	3	−0.413	0.258	0.482	−0.161
4	ITEM	4	−0.413	0.213	0.441	−0.136
5	ITEM	5	0.206	0.251	0.474	−0.161
6	ITEM	6	−0.461	0.276	0.517	−0.091
7	ITEM	7	−0.007	0.294	0.539	0.057
8	ITEM	8	−1.101	0.412	0.628	−0.130
9	ITEM	9	−0.443	0.220	0.468	0.033
10	ITEM	10	−0.090	0.152	0.387	0.053

DISPLAY 14.   STANDARDIZED DIFFICULTY, COMMUNALITY, AND PRINCIPAL FACTORS

Figure 13.17
Standardized difficulty, communality, and principle factors.

Figure 13.18
Standardized difficulty,
communality, and varimax
factors.

DISPLAY 16. STANDARDIZED DIFFICULTY, COMMUNALITY, AND
VARIMAX FACTORS

			DIFF.	COMM.	FACTORS 1	2
1	ITEM	1	−0.337	0.262	0.381	0.341
2	ITEM	2	−0.946	0.234	0.392	0.284
3	ITEM	3	−0.413	0.258	0.460	0.216
4	ITEM	4	−0.413	0.213	0.413	0.205
5	ITEM	5	0.206	0.251	0.454	0.210
6	ITEM	6	−0.461	0.276	0.438	0.291
7	ITEM	7	−0.007	0.294	0.351	0.413
8	ITEM	8	−1.101	0.412	0.545	0.339
9	ITEM	9	−0.443	0.220	0.316	0.347
10	ITEM	10	−0.090	0.152	0.244	0.305

well as the promax rotated factor loadings, can be used for final interpretation (Figure 13.19).

Finally, the correlations between factors are given in Figure 13.20.

Examination of the output yielded by full information item FA shows familiar tables to traditional FA and PCA (Figures 13.9 and 13.13), and one may therefore be tempted to imagine that the results are similar with what would be found when

Figure 13.19
Promax rotated factor
loadings.

DISPLAY 19.   PROMAX ROTATED FACTOR
LOADINGS

			1	2
1	ITEM	1	0.306	0.236
2	ITEM	2	0.362	0.146
3	ITEM	3	0.507	0.002
4	ITEM	4	0.447	0.018
5	ITEM	5	0.503	−0.003
6	ITEM	6	0.422	0.125
7	ITEM	7	0.213	0.359
8	ITEM	8	0.542	0.122
9	ITEM	9	0.210	0.287
10	ITEM	10	0.136	0.275

```
┌─────────────────────────────────────────────────────┐
│                                                       │
│   DISPLAY   20.    PROMAX FACTOR CORRELATIONS         │
│                                                       │
│             1        2                                │
│                                                       │
│   1      1.000                                        │
│   2      0.777      1.000                             │
│                                                       │
└─────────────────────────────────────────────────────┘
```

Figure 13.20
Interfactor correlations.

analysis is done by ordinary FA and PCA. However, these results are very different, both numerically and theoretically, as discussed previously. Ensure an appropriate and latent-based interpretation is applied to the results from the procedure.

Tetrachoric Correlations

The full information item FA is best performed on a matrix consisting of a specialized kind of correlation called *tetrachoric correlation* (r_{tet}), not on the conventional **R** matrix of Pearson correlations. Tetrachoric correlations are used when it is theorized that two dichotomous items are actually estimates of two continuous latent variables (Drasgow, 1998). The emphasis here is on their latency. The r_{tet} is actually the Pearson correlation one would obtain if the two constructs were truly measured continuously. The primary advantage of tetrachoric correlation is that it is a Bayesian-based procedure that presumes a latent distribution for an item rather than a mere dichotomized value. Consequently, the IRT condition is addressed, making the data set more amenable to examining unidimensionality as a notion in deep psychology.

Tetrachoric correlations are calculated on dichotomized data that do not carry information about within-group variance; rather, the correlation is simply—but importantly—a symmetric measure of 1s and 0s for the two items in any correlation. This is like a cross-tabs between correct and not correct for two items. A matrix of such correlations is noted as $\mathbf{R_{tet}}$ to distinguish it from the matrix of Pearson correlations (so common it is merely noted as **R**). As mentioned, because integration is involved, calculating values for $\mathbf{R_{tet}}$ is difficult, so computer programs that implement the algorithm are suggested. The SAS, TESTFACT, and Systat (but not SPSS) statistical programs each calculate tetrachoric correlations and the resulting $\mathbf{R_{tet}}$ matrix.

Indexes of Unidimensionality

Procedurally, one of the strongest routes for determining unidimensionality is to develop an index indicating a degree of unidimensionality. Three such indices are as follows:

1. *Local independence index*—is based on the property of local independence
2. *Pattern index*—uses patterns of second-factor loadings derived from simplex theory
3. *Ratio of differences index*—uses shape of the curve of successive eigenvalues

These dimensionality indices can be explored with tests developed and scaled by either CTT or IRT methods; hence, one can use observed data as estimated scores of true scores, or the researcher may hypothesize latency for the data. Less technically, these indices can be used with FA, PCA, and full information FA. For tests scaled with CTT, either the raw or scaled scores may be used as input data. For IRT-based measures, the difficulty parameter (b) can be used. Because each index relies on a variant of FA, it may be useful for persons who are developing an index by one of these procedures to review the next section before calculating a unidimensionality index.

To illustrate methodologies, it may be clearest to simply list steps in preparing each index.

Local Independence Index

This unidimensionality index is based on the property of local independence and should be interpreted in this context. In producing the independence index, the researcher should restrict analysis to persons who have reasonably the same total score (or an estimate of the score on the latent trait), which may require the researcher to develop samples by ability strata. Follow these steps:

STEP 1: Build an aggregate variance–covariance matrix from samples of examinees with the same total score (three groups is customary).

STEP 2: Use a sign change procedure of centroid FA (see Harman, 1967).

STEP 3: Form a ratio of the sum of the covariances (following the sign change) to the absolute sum of covariances. Disregard the diagonal values.

STEP 4: Build a ratio by redoing step 3, but use the total group. To show unidimensionality, this ratio should equal 1 among items.

STEP 5: Compute a local independence index as the difference between the ratios of steps 3 and 4. The presence of multiple factors is indicated by small differences.

Pattern Index

The pattern index is developed on patterns of second-factor loadings derived from simplex theory. Development of the index follows these steps.

STEP 1: Prepare an **R** matrix and replace diagonals with the squared multiple correlations.

STEP 2: Rank items by difficulty and divide into two halves: easy and difficult.

STEP 3: Obtain four sums of second-factor loadings: one for each sign in each half.

STEP 4: Compute the absolute sums of opposite-sign sums for both halves (easy and difficult).

STEP 5: The smaller of the sums in step 4 is the pattern index. It should approach zero in a unidimensional test.

Ratio of Differences Index

Here, the shape of the curve of successive eigenvalues is used to determine unidimensionality. It can be used with matrices of phi coefficients, tetrachoric correlations, and variances–covariances (although the first two are preferred over the third), in addition to the customary Pearson first-order correlations. Steps for this procedure are the following:

STEP 1: Compute $\mathbf{R_{tet}}$ matrix.
STEP 2: Obtain phi coefficients.
STEP 3: Prepare a variance–covariance matrix.
STEP 4: Perform FA with principal axis factoring (rather than with PCA) with varimax rotation and obtain the scree test plot.
STEP 5: Examine the scree values and the eigenvalues to determine unidimensionality. A strong first factor should be evidenced.

For a more complete explanation of differences among these strategies, refer to *Heuristic Inquiry of Dimensionality in Binary Test Items* (Osterlind, 2003).

SEM and Hierarchical Linear Modeling

The notion of modeling psychological constructs in mental test data has been long admired as an approach that melds observed test data with their cognitive base. However, until the past couple of decades or so, the mathematics of this marriage were not well developed, and the programs used to implement theoretical ideas were difficult to use. More recently, however, with the advancement of powerful computers into everyday use, there has been a tremendous resurgence of interest in this type of statistical modeling. Not only has modeling as a methodology advanced, but also the development of newer versions of LISERL, and particularly the introduction of the graphically based AMOS computer program, has made the work much more available to researchers and test specialists.

Exploring unidimensionality in cognitive appraisal through statistical modeling is powerful primarily because it gives coherence to the confirmation of a cognitive base in a set of observed test data. As may be expected, this application of statistical modeling is confirmatory factoring. Although there are many types of reliability models, those that fall under the SEM family seem to be most beneficial to appraisal of the dimensional structure of a mental test. Here, we see whether a theory can be put into action.

The Basic Idea of SEM

SEM is a generalized, multivariate method for analyzing latent dimensions in psychological data. It can also be used to examine a test's structure and for more generalized theory building. Specifically, SEM assesses whether a set of variances and covariances from the test fit a hypothesized underlying arrangement of cognitive processes. That is to say, with SEM, researchers hypothesize that cognitive processes cause the behavior of observed variables and that this relationship can be modeled statistically. Further—and an important part of the process—the statistical models can be graphically portrayed (usually as path diagrams), thereby revealing a clearer picture of the conceptualization.

Mathematically parallel to FA, SEM figures a series of regression equations, each of which is held to represent a latent dimension that collectively builds a structure for the test. Because educational and psychological tests intentionally have some underlying dimensional aspect to them, SEM confirms whether it can be modeled, both as an equation and as a graphic. The more robust the underlying structure, the more its hypothesized existence is confirmed. For this reason, SEM is usually classified with confirmatory factor analyses when used to analyze whole tests. That is, in this kind of an examination, it confirms an extent of unidimensionality in a set of items.

One should appreciate, however, that SEM as an overall statistical procedure is very general and difficult to characterize. Accordingly, it may be applied in many circumstances beyond confirmatory factoring of whole tests. For instance, it can be used to classify second-order factors and other causal modeling relationships that define relationships between psychological phenomena. Realize, too, that as a model of the general linear approach to regression, it can give information about covariances and other types of correlational relationships. A classic example of this application for SEM is the hypothesis that the correlation matrix has the structure of a *circumplex,* the structural scenario conceived of by Guttman (1954), wherein having more items correct is a direct indication of greater ability or proficiency.

When employing SEM to examine the structure of whole tests, all the items may be considered as a group to model a single underlying dimension, or more commonly, groups of items can be analyzed to reveal multiple dimensions in complex instruments. From this it follows that SEM diagrams may be viewed as an isomorphic representation of a linear equations system, where SEM path diagrams are viewed as representing a causal flow from the latent structure to the observed variables.

Specialized SEM Terms

Not surprisingly, beyond technical description in and of itself, SEM employs a number of specialized terms. Two of them are especially tied to the procedure. These terms are *exogenous* and *endogenous;* they describe kinds of variables. These terms emphasize the psychological perspective of SEM as confirming the existence of latent structures. (Readers may recall that I introduced these terms in chapter 2, during the explanation of specialized measurement vocabulary.)

Exogenous variables imply that the originating cause for variability is external to the variable itself or to the model in which the variable is being considered. By SEM, presumably, the latent dimension is what causes the observed event, as measured by the variable. Graphical representations of exogenous variables have an away-pointing arrow to illustrate that its variance is going away to another more generalized variable or to error. They do not receive any arrows in the modeled relationship.

Endogenous variables are the analog of exogenous variables. These variables stem from inside the structure of the model itself and indicate a relationship opposite to exogenous variables. They are synonymous with a dependent variable. The arrows indicating influence from the exogenous variables point, generally, to endogenous variables.

How SEM Works

Working from the correlations with a test, SEM develops path coefficients for regression of observed variables onto the latent structure. Because the regression is of variance dimension, error is associated with the built models. Figures 13.21 and 13.22 show this relationship for one test and its component subtests. Figure 13.21 shows the omnibus structure of the CBASE English test as having two major factors: reading and writing. Following the content design of the test into increasingly more specific subgroups, Figure 13.22 shows a second-order model. Here, reading is hypothesized as having three parts (reading critically, reading analytically, and literature) and writing as having two parts (writing as a process and conventions of writing). Notice especially the direction of the arrows, indicating exogenous variables that point to endogenous ones. The numbers outside the represented circles are correlations between groups.

Further, notice in the path diagram that some variables are placed in square or rectangular boxes and some are placed in circles or ovals. *Manifest variables* are

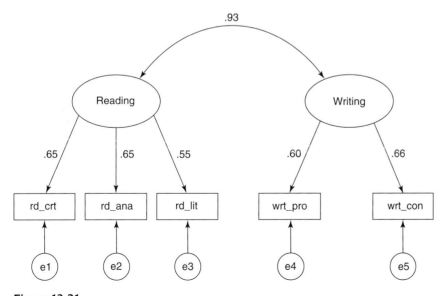

Figure 13.21
First-order factor model with two factors.

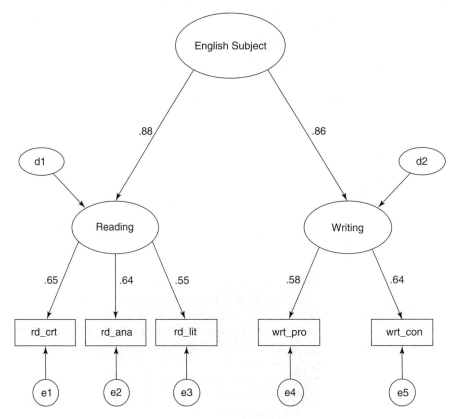

Figure 13.22
Second-order model for English.

shown in boxes, whereas *latent variables* are situated in ovals. This convention is particularly useful in developing and drawing the model.

Another important feature of SEM is to assess the fit of the model. Both LISERL and AMOS provide various fit statistics that should be heeded when conducting SEM research. When working with the AMOS program, refer to Byrne (2001) for a particularly helpful book on fit indices and the validation of assumptions.

Sources for SEM

Much to our benefit, there is a tremendous variety of books and other publications that explain SEM in detail. One fine text is *Basics of Structural Equation Modeling* (Maruyama, 1997). Jason T. Newsome, a professor at Portland State University, has compiled a list of more than 100 SEM books. His list can be accessed at *http://www.upa.pdx.edu/IOA/newsom/sembooks.htm* (Retrieved March 8, 2005). AERA (*http://www.aera.net/*. Retrieved March 8, 2005) offers a SEM special interest group. Additional, special interest groups can be found at *http://www.smallwaters.com/weblinks/* (Retrieved March 8, 2005). *Structural Equation Modeling—A Multidisciplinary Journal,* a specialized SEM journal, is another helpful source.

Whole Test Bias

In chapter 3, I introduce test bias and DIF, and in chapter 12, I explore DIF in individual items. Those explanations are integral to the present discussion of whole test bias, and readers who do not already have in their minds a clear understanding of the information given earlier should review it before proceeding. Examining a whole test for evidence of bias is useful in whole test analysis.

As a generality, with possible exceptions for specific assessment contexts, it is useful to apply *DIF* to the evaluation of individual items and *test bias* to a conclusion about an entire instrument, following the definitions I gave earlier.

Need for Competent Psychometric Analysis

Identifying test bias as a measurement phenomenon calls for both competent psychometric analysis and expert judgment about the particular testing scenario. I describe strategies for both types of inquiry. Realize, especially, that such work is usually fraught with complexity and difficulty, and seldom does it conclude with a clear "yes" or "no" declaration. Regardless of difficulty, measurement professional and other measurement professionals have a responsibility to forthrightly address the issue of test bias and DIF when it is appropriate to do so.

Especially when examining test bias, keep in mind that lacking substantive and empirical evidence for bias in a test—based on proper psychometric DIF analysis—one cannot state that bias is present. In other words, mere anecdotes or sentiments about a test should not be bandied about by a responsible test user, policy maker, or other person because confusion and inaccuracies may result. Also, without competent investigation, the presumption cannot be made that a test is free from bias. If the phenomenon has not been investigated, or if the inquiry does not reach conclusion, is only cursory or not competently done, the proper description is that no conclusion about bias (or DIF) can be made.

As measurement professionals and other social scientists know, this area of mental appraisal is so charged with emotion that only the highest ethics and the most rigorous methods of measurement research should be employed when studying test bias or DIF. The stakes here are too high for "junk" science.

Whole Test Bias as Systematic Error

Whereas DIF focuses attention on the performance between groups on individual test items, whole test bias addresses issues concerned with differences between groups on the complete test instrument as used in a particular testing circumstance. Whole test bias is presumed when a specific source of systematic error in the items or exercises—and thus unrelated to the construct being assessed—is present for one group but not the other. *Systematic,* it is recalled, denotes that the error occurs consistently for all members of a subgroup, and hence is not *random,* which is haphazard for the entire population. The main criterion for bias is that it emanates from group-based systematic error.

There is a useful distinction between bias that is internal to the test instrument and external bias. Both are a consequence of systematic error. However, *internal bias* is direct measurement error as expressed by invalid item covariances, whereas *external bias* results in different predictive validity. When item covariances are dissimilar for groups of examinees who are truly equal in their ability or proficiency, measurement error is systematically dissimilar. This is an unwanted artifact internal to the test. External bias can exist when a testing-related situation exists that influences groups differently.

Identifying Sources for Systematic Error

Albeit whole test bias is caused by error in the measuring process, it is generally not possible to precisely pinpoint a specific source for the error, although informed evaluation may give some noteworthy clues. Some sources for error could lie within the test's items or exercises. The vocabulary, composition, or phraseology of the items and exercises may elicit reactions unrelated to the construct that are different for each group. Recall the discussion about cultural treatment of dogs in questions on a reading test cited in chapter 3 as an example of a circumstance that could elicit test bias. Such bias is internal to the test instrument and would evidence multidimensional appraisal when unidimensional assessment is desired.

The sources of systematic error could also just as likely be something like an aberrant test administrator or environmental effects, resulting in external bias. For example, suppose a test is administered to two groups from the same population, and each administration was performed by a different individual. One test administrator was wholly professional in presentation and demeanor, whereas the second test administrator was closer to the character in the novel *Silas Marner,* whom author George Eliot described as a "crass bonehead capable of sneering at the progress of the human race." Probably, each group would have a reaction to the test administrator (presumably one being positive and the other negative), and this reaction might influence the groups' scores. This is an example of systematic error in the testing situation that is unrelated to the construct on the test instrument. The point is that the source for test bias does not directly emanate from the items or exercises. Hence, bias can be concluded from the testing context and have nothing to do with the items and exercises themselves. Remember, validity is an issue of meaningful interpretation and use of the scores in a context, not the instrument per se.

Regardless, knowing where the systematic error originates neither confirms nor obviates test bias by itself. This is not the criterion for correct identification of whether the phenomenon is extant. In fact, identifying possible sources of systematic error for a particular subgroup is follow-up research work, after there is sufficient evidence to suspect whole test bias in a particular testing context.

Some persons suggest that a procedural step in reducing the chances for test bias may be to conduct a *sensitivity review;* that is, to examine the vocabulary, usage, and phraseology in the test (e.g., Bond, Moss, & Carr, 1996). Although this step can have value, imprecise or evocative wording should actually be taken care of initially with competent editing. Often, a sensitivity review can degrade the item's meaning by injecting the vanity of political correctness with the banning of certain vocabulary words based only on one's feeling, or other idiosyncratic criteria. I discuss this topic more in chapter 16.

Identifying the Presence of Systematic Error

In nearly all situations, the conclusion of bias is only made from multiple pieces of evidence, both convergent and divergent. A bias declaration from evidence of just a single source would require extraordinary justification.

One logical starting point for bias investigation is to examine DIF for each item. In chapter 12, I explain DIF and describe several strategies appropriate to its investigation. The conclusion of DIF for a large percentage of a test's items or exercises is strong evidence for whole test bias. Still, despite its primacy, it is just one source for evidence, and bias should not be concluded on DIF analysis alone.

Examining differences in the standard errors for groups is another useful piece of information. For meaningful comparisons of standard errors, the groups' distributions must be matched by ability or proficiency. To accomplish this by CTT methods, the overall test distribution may be partitioned into fractile groups for approximate matching, usually quintiles. This strategy is also used with other group comparison techniques, such as with item analysis. Far better, however, when using standard error comparisons based on CTT, is to employ an external criterion for matching abilities or proficiency.

When error contrasts are based on IRT methods, the entire latent distributions may be compared. One way to ensure the distribution of each group is similar is to compute separate parameter estimates with 0 and 1 as the mean and standard deviation of the reference group. Figure 13.23 shows these values for two groups, males and females (note in the figure only the different mean and standard deviations; the quadrature points and posterior weights are to directly relevant.)

The test information functions between the groups can also be compared. Especially useful is comparison of the standard error. These plots are given in Figure 13.24 for the two groups. By now, readers are probably familiar with these plots and can easily identify that the test information function is represented by a solid

```
GROUP:  1    MALES     QUADRATURE POINTS, POSTERIOR WEIGHTS, MEAN AND S.D.:
                 1          2          3          4          5
POINT         -0.3203E+01 -0.2972E+01 -0.2740E+01 -0.2509E+01 -0.2277E+01
POSTERIOR      0.2572E-04  0.1639E-03  0.7030E-03  0.2190E-02  0.5269E-02
  . . . . . . . . . . . . . . . . . . . . . . . . . . . . . . . . . . . .
                 26         27         28         29         30
POINT          0.2583E+01  0.2814E+01  0.3046E+01  0.3277E+01  0.3509E+01
POSTERIOR      0.4783E-02  0.2391E-02  0.1047E-02  0.4014E-03  0.1347E-03

MEAN           0.00000
S.E.           0.00000

S.D.           1.00000
S.E.           0.00000


GROUP:  2    FEMALES   QUADRATURE POINTS, POSTERIOR WEIGHTS, MEAN AND S.D.:

                 1          2          3          4          5
POINT         -0.3328E+01 -0.3096E+01 -0.2865E+01 -0.2634E+01 -0.2402E+01
POSTERIOR      0.1454E-03  0.2903E-03  0.5565E-03  0.1089E-02  0.2216E-02
  . . . . . . . . . . . . . . . . . . . . . . . . . . . . . . . . . . . .
                 6          7          8          9
                 26         27         28         29         30
POINT          0.2458E+01  0.2690E+01  0.2921E+01  0.3152E+01  0.3384E+01
POSTERIOR      0.3267E-02  0.1696E-02  0.8527E-03  0.4141E-03  0.1919E-03

MEAN          -0.11411
S.E.           0.01667

S.D.           0.94189
S.E.           0.01230
```

Figure 13.23
Latent distribution score by item response theory for two groups to be compared: males and females.

line and a specific scale score is read from the left vertical axis. The dotted line represents the standard error curve and a specific score is read from the right vertical axis.

Following these comparisons, it is useful to examine the likelihood functions for each group. In fact, contrasting the log of the likelihood functions between the DIF and non-DIF models provides a most useful analysis of whole test bias. The procedures for this analysis are relatively straightforward. The likelihood estimate is computed twice, once for the reference and focal group, and again without group identification. These two estimates are then compared. By convention, the likelihood

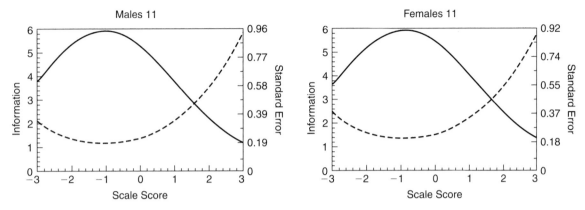

Figure 13.24
Test information functions and standard error plots of two groups: males and females.

function (which is normally impressed in log metric as a Bayesian estimator) is doubled and the negative is taken.

Figure 13.25 gives the −2 log likelihood values for the preset example.

As seen in Figure 13.25, the estimates appear relatively close and they yield a difference of about 59 (viz., 230309.7865 − 230368.5627 = 58.7762). To evaluate the difference, the −2 log likelihood values are related to the chi-square distribution with degrees of freedom equal to the number of parameters estimated. In this example, $df = 41$ because only a single item parameter is estimated for each of the 41 items on the test. Distributed as χ^2 on 41 degrees of freedom, evidencing no whole test bias ($\alpha = 0.05$, critical value $= 65.7585$).

Even though BILOG-MG is particularly well suited to this kind of whole test investigation, such a finding should not end all investigation. It is only of one feature, item difficulty across the range of items in this assessment. It does not address item discrimination, for example, or the presence of external bias. More important,

```
            Estimates for DIF model

 -2 LOG LIKELIHOOD:        230309.7865
 CYCLE     3;   LARGEST CHANGE=    0.00114




        Estimates for non-DIF model

 -2 LOG LIKELIHOOD:        230368.5627
 CYCLE     3;   LARGEST CHANGE=    0.04249
```

Figure 13.25
Estimated differences between DIF and non-DIF models.

absence of whole test bias cannot be taken as evidence that there is no DIF in individual items. This investigation must be done separately, as described in chapter 12.

Not Reached and Omitted Items

Finally, there is another aspect of examining whole tests that impacts test interpretation. This concern is of *not reached items* and *omitted items*. Not reached items are stimuli that the examinee did not respond to because of time. In timed, power tests (e.g., SAT, ACT), not reached items are those at the end of the test still remaining when the "stop" command is given. There is no possibility of learning whether an examinee would have responded correctly to the stimulus. Usually, an examinee's score is given on just the set of items completed; hence, for a particular examinee who did not reach some items, those stimuli are ignored in calculating ability estimates. However, if enough examinees from the population did respond to a late-appearing item, then the item statistics are used in item parameter estimates.

Omitted items are distinct from not reached items and are considered in nearly all IRT models. Omitted items are those stimuli that the examinee elects not to answer and can usually be identified by the fact that at least one item after the omitted item was attempted. Omitted items have the potential for responses, but (presumably) because of uncertainty about the correct answers (i.e., examinee ability or proficiency), he or she skipped them. Such items are calibrated along with all other items and can provide valuable information about both the measurement instrument itself and especially about the examinee.

Summary

This chapter explores appraisal activity for a testing instrument as a whole, with particular emphasis on its internal structure. I look at the notion of unidimensionality and then note a number of procedures useful to its determination, including FA, PCA and full information FA. Then, I present a number of indices useful to dimensionality investigation. A lengthy discussion of whole test bias and related reviews is also included.

Chapter 14

Establishing Standards

Introduction

A Time to Set Standards

Certainly one of the most remarkable scientific discoveries of all time is penicillin. It revolutionized medicine, transforming it from a medieval practice lacking a basis for how or why things worked or failed, to one characterized by an understanding that bacteria causes infection. A scientist named Alexander Fleming, working at St. Mary's Medical School in London in 1928, was apparently a messy person, for his lab was often in disarray with dirty flasks and unwashed jars. Even some toxic chemicals were not kept in safe, labeled bottles. He never seemed to get around to cleaning up the place. One day, while looking at a sink filled with grimy Petri dishes, he noticed that one of the dishes had a blue-colored mold growing on it. He looked closer at the mold through his primitive microscope and saw that some dangerous bacteria he had left growing in the dish had died. He wondered immediately whether something in the mold had killed the bacteria. He performed a series of experiments that seemed to confirm his suspicion. Unwittingly, through his discovery of the power of penicillin for controlling some bacteria, he had uncovered the cause for many diseases (i.e., bacteria), as well as a way to control their growth. Regrettably, scientists showed little interest in Fleming's discovery until 10 years later, when a group of researchers at Oxford University in England picked up on Fleming's work and began using penicillin to kill bacteria in humans. Almost immediately, the number of deaths from infections at that hospital declined dramatically. Bacterial diseases that had plagued humanity since the beginning of time could finally be effectively fought. Fleming and the Oxford researchers were eventually recognized for their remarkable discovery when, in 1945, they were jointly awarded the Nobel Prize for Medicine.

In measurement, setting standards is also messy work. Like Fleming's experiments, it is effort with a purpose, namely, to employ test information to reliably make classificatory decisions. In this chapter, I explain the meaning and implications of standard setting, as well as describe several schemes for setting a standard.

Contents

This chapter focuses on practical aspects of setting standards. I begin by examining the meaning of *standard setting* in educational and psychological measurement, and move quickly to defining the many relevant terms (e.g., *cutscore*, *performance standards*, *internal* vs. *external standard setting*). Then, I describe some statistical decision theory as it applies to standard setting. A discussion of selecting and training judges is given next. After that, I describe a number of standard-setting methods. Finally, attention is directed to features of standard setting that are pertinent to performance assessments.

Understanding and Defining a Standard

Understanding Standard Setting

Standard setting, when used in the context of cognitive skills appraisal or for proficiency assessment, is the process of defining test performance levels that have implication for interpretation and use of the scores. The most common use of setting performance levels is to make classifying decisions, such as "pass" versus "not pass," or to label proficiency levels like "high," "medium," and "low," but it can also be used in other ways.

Three recondite points pervade serious thinking about standard setting. First, it is a *process* encompassing numerous considerations and requiring many steps; second, it is contextual, meaning that the methodology appropriate for one testing program or assessment scenario may be very different from what is useful in another context; and, third, human judgment is involved in every standard-setting enterprise. I explain each concern.

As to the first point, setting a standard is a process rather than an assignment requiring only a single step. Affecting the process often requires significant scholarly effort. Many important issues require careful consideration, usually needing deliberation by numerous persons. Further, these deliberations should not be mere casual conversations; rather, they should be carried out with a methodology, as in a research study with customary scientific protocols. This chapter highlights many such issues and explains a number of standard-setting approaches, each requiring deliberation and inquiry by methods of science.

In practical application, standard setting tasks include

- Determining a rationale for using a test to make classificatory decisions,
- Investigating the authenticity of a particular test for the intended purpose,
- Establishing criteria for the standard of proficiency, skill, or ability that is to be evaluated,
- Deciding on points along the test's score scale that reliably reflect that standard, and
- Considering consequences of implementing the cutscore in the particular assessment context.

Even completing all these responsibilities is not the end of standard setting. To ensure its enduring relevance, the process should also incorporate an ongoing validation effort, covering the entire assessment program.

Novices to standard setting often imagine that it is as simple as designating a particular point on a score scale as the *cutscore,* the place where a classifying decision is

Illustrative parts of standard setting

Setting a cutscore as one step in the process

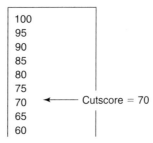

Develop rationale for employing a test score in this context

Validate evidence that the scores yielded by the measure are appropriate for this purpose

Define the standard (e.g., "minimal competence")

Articulate the meaning of "minimal competence" in this context

Consider consequences of applying the cutscore to individuals

Evaluate validity to monitor relation of test performance to relevant criteria (ongoing)

The one step of deciding on the cutscore does not constitute the complete process.

Figure 14.1
Illustrative depiction of multistep process in standard setting.

made. Regrettably, in some testing programs, this is all that is done. Likely, we each know of an instance where a testing program adopts 70% as the cutscore because that is remembered as the stereotypical "C" passing grade in school. This approach can lead to poorly conceived decisions—decisions that may have serious consequences for examinees. Of course, invalidity results in these cases. As we learn in this chapter, however, purposefully and meaningfully setting a standard is a much more involved process. Figure 14.1 inexactly shows that actually selecting a cutscore is only one step among many, and that it properly fits into a more involved process.

An example of a standard-setting scenario will illustrate the point that it is both a process requiring many steps and that the tasks are particular to a testing program. Consider an appraisal scenario that is common to many educators. Suppose a group of educators are focused on setting a standard for satisfactory completion of a high school curriculum. The involved parties must first identify *why* it is important to have a capstone exit criterion—after all, for the most part, American schools have operated seemingly satisfactorily for more than 200 years without one. Only after a rationale and a purpose are established should the educators determine *why* a test is the appropriate genus for the capstone experience. After these considerations, they could then select or develop an appraisal instrument, and just as important, provide validating evidence that this particular instrument could be thus employed. Then, they would engage a methodology to determine which score point(s) on the test's scale represents the ideas for "standards" that they have in mind. As a part of a methodology, they should calculate probable outcomes using sample data, and they should discuss some reasonable outcome scenarios and "what ifs." Finally, the educators must develop a plan for ongoing validation studies, including gathering information related to the consequences of their decisions and to the continued relevance of the test. Through this scenario, one sees that standard setting can be involved work, indeed.

The second point regarding standard setting is to realize that the methods will vary with each new testing situation. The previous scenario illustrates this point. However, another consideration that premises different methods in varying assessment situations is that, most often, standard setting resides within a politically based context where decisions often have implication for policy and rules. Obviously, these considerations will vary with each new scenario, again making standard setting a situation-specific enterprise.

One should not interpret political concerns in an assessment program as necessarily maleficent. Political contexts cannot be avoided, and measurement professionals should not ignore them. In fact, often the attention to standard setting engendered by politics presents an opportunity to measurement professionals to educate stakeholders about relevant issues.

The final point about standard setting is that, although the methods of science must be followed, the tasks will involve deliberation and judgment by people. Currently, there is no wholly numerical method to set a standard devoid of human judgment. The statistics that are used throughout a standard-setting endeavor are applied to numbers that originate in human judgment. At many points throughout this chapter, I explain methods to make such judgment informed and consistent; however, the point to realize is that standard setting is a judgmental activity.

Defining a Standard

For assessment, a "standard" represents something that is established by authority as a criterion for the measure of quantity. This notion is implemented by specifying levels of proficiency or defining attributes of a latent trait. Significantly, the standard is not the cutscore per se; rather, it is the reason for making a cutscore. The standard addresses the question, "How much is enough?" In some contexts, this is determined to be minimal competence on specified skills, abilities, or proficiencies, or even latent traits. In other circumstances, it could be mastery of the skills. At still other times, it is held as one's performance relative to peers. Each criterion cited is a standard.

A few examples serve to illustrate standards. The first example involves sports teams, which establish standards routinely. Many National Baseball League teams have a standard for each regular player, such as, "the player shall observably contribute to winning games." This standard usually has criteria of something like a minimum .250 batting average, 1 RBIs (runs batted in) per 10 "at bats," and no more than 1 fielding error for each 90 innings played (exceptions are made for large-draw players). The standard for the baseball team corresponds to the educator's standard of "satisfactory completion of a high school curriculum." The criterion for determining whether the standard is being met (e.g., batting average, RBIs, fielding numbers) is analogous to a cutscore on a high school proficiency test.

Another example is when a law firm may set a standard of being a "fully contributing partner." Commonly, this is gauged by the number of billable hours the lawyer contributes to the firm each month—its criterion or "cutscore." Of course, in business, boards of directors regularly set standards for a CEO of "increasing stockholders' equity," which is often translated into stock valuation or possibly quarterly sales quotas for each sales representative or sales territory.

The point to garner from these illustrations is that the standard is the goal for measuring quantity, but it is not the score or amount itself. The batting average, billable hours, or sales quota is not the standard. These are quantifications against which the standard is judged and is parallel to our cutscore in educational and psychological testing. Similarly, in assessment, the standard is minimal competence (or the other citations shown previously) in a discipline. On a test, the cutscore is the gauge of whether the standard has been met, but it is not the standard itself.

A real world example of standards in educational assessment is given in the three levels of proficiency adopted by the National Assessment of Educational Progress (NAEP), illustrated in Figure 14.2. Notice, particularly, that the "standard" is defined by the achievement level and its accompanying definition. The cutscore is not mentioned at this point.

By now, we realize that each standard is unique to a particular testing context; they are also not universal. Hambleton (2001) offers this useful comment on finding "the" performance standard: "It is now widely recognized by workers in the educational testing field that there are no true performance standards waiting to be discovered" (p. 114). In other words, no committee of experts or other overarching authority can define a standard to which all, or even most, assessment programs would adhere to without due consideration of their unique circumstances. That work must be done anew, prompting a standard-setting study each time.

Achievement Level Policy Definitions	
Basic	This level denotes partial mastery of prerequisite knowledge and skills that are fundamental for proficient work at each grade.
Proficient	This level represents solid academic performance for each grade assessed. Students reaching this level have demonstrated competency over challenging subject matter, including subject-matter knowledge, application of such knowledge to real world situations, and analytical skills appropriate to the subject matter.
Advanced	This level signifies superior performance.

Figure 14.2
NAEP achievement level descriptors.
Source: From *How NAGB Guides the Assessment,* by National Center for Education Statistics, 2004, from *http://nces.ed.gov/nationsreportcard/about/nagb/nagb_naep.asp#nal* (Retrieved March 9, 2005.). Copyright 2004 by the National Center for Education Statistics. Reprinted with permission.

Purpose of Standard Setting

The purpose of setting a standard is to make classification decisions. That is, having a cutscore allows the decision maker to group examinees or candidates into categories that are interpretable in some meaningful context. The categories circuit information appropriate to a particular decision. For example, if a test were used for entry into a training program, the classification may be into groups of "admit" and "not admit." If the decision involves a licensing and certification program for an occupational field, the two categories could be "proficient" and "not proficient." Often in licensing and certification programs, the sufficiency of quantity is judged in relation to its consequence on public safety, as for instance in practicing medicine or law or for driving a car or flying an airplane.

Significantly, cutscore information is not limited to show just two categories. The information may be intended to indicate degrees of proficiency, such as in open-ended essays where an examinee may achieve a score in any of several categories. The NAEP program, for instance, uses the categories illustrated previously and includes a fourth but undefined category called "Below Basic."

Making classifying decisions has more use than immediate practical application. Such decision can also be employed in research settings. For instance, research studies with simulated data from Monte Carlo procedures, or a small data set that is expanded by bootstrapping or another sampling technique, may also require standard setting. Often one goal of such research studies is to determine outcomes from hypothetical circumstances, thus paving the way for sound decision making in real world testing programs.

Standard Setting and Validity

Experts in standard setting agree that the activity is a concern of score interpretation and use, and thus an important part of validity (Glass, 1978; Jaeger, 1989; Kane, 2001). This point is easy to realize given the fact that setting standards for the purpose of making classificatory decisions is the application of test scores for a particular use, a very core concern of validity. It follows, then, that determining the usefulness and effectiveness of standard setting in a given testing context is validity evaluation.

As we learned earlier (see chapter 4 and elsewhere), validity evaluation requires one to amass empirical information about a particular interpretation. In fact, the *Standards for Educational and Psychological Testing* (American Educational Research Association, American Psychological Association, & National Council on Measurement in Education, 1999) stipulate that standard setting should be data based, stating that "cutscores with distinct interpretations should be established on the basis of sound empirical data concerning the relation of test performance to relevant criteria" (p. 60).

A careful reading of this requirement reveals that validity evaluation with standard setting is not an empirical examination of the cutscore per se but of whether the standard itself is supported by the proposed use of the cutscore. Focusing attention on the standard, rather than on the cutscore, will keep a right perspective because the cutscore should flow from the standard and not the other way around.

Determining whether the cutscore manifests decisions that support the standard is proper validity evaluation.

In addition, other precepts of the *Standards* draw attention to standard-setting issues in a validity context. Some relevant standards are cited in Figure 14.3. Chapter 4

Some Standards that Explicitly Address Cutscores and Standard Setting with Tests

Standard 4.19
When proposed score interpretation involves one or more cutscores, the rationale and procedures used for establishing cutscores should be clearly documented.

Standard 4.20
When feasible, cutscores with distinct interpretations should be established on the basis of sound empirical data concerning the relation of test performance to relevant criteria.

Standard 4.21
When cutscores defining pass–fail or proficient categories are based on direct judgments about the adequacy of item or test performances or performance levels, the judgmental process should be designed so that judges can bring their knowledge and experience to bear in a reasonable way.

Standard 13.9
When test scores are intended to be used as part of the process for making decisions for educational placement, promotion, or implementation of prescribed educational plans, empirical evidence documenting the relationship among particular test scores, the instructional programs, and desired students' outcomes should be provided. When adequate empirical evidence is not available, users should be cautioned to weigh the test results accordingly in light of other relevant information about the student.

Standard 14.4
When empirical evidence of predictor–criterion relationships is part of the patterns of evidence used to support test use, the criterion measure(s) used should reflect the criterion construct domain of interest to the organization. All criteria used should represent important work behaviors or work outputs, on the job or in job-relevant training as indicated by an appropriate review of information about the job.

Standard 14.7
If tests are to be used to make job classification decisions (e.g., the pattern of predictor scores will be used to make differential job assignments), evidence that scores are linked to different levels or likelihoods of success among jobs or job groups is needed.

Standard 14.15
Estimates of the reliability of test-based credentialing decisions should be provided.

Figure 14.3
Standards from the *Standards for Educational and Psychological Testing* that explicitly address cutscores and the use of standard setting with tests.
Source: From *Standards for Educational and Psychological Testing* (pp. 59-60, 149, 159-160, 162), by American Educational Research Association, American Psychological Association, & National Council on Measurement in Education, 1999, Washington, DC: American Educational Research Association. Copyright 1999 by American Educational Research Association.

of the *Standards* sets forth an overview of cutscore topics as they may relate to validity evaluation.

Although there are many routes to developing information useful for validity evaluation of standards (some are discussed in the following sections), Kane (2001) suggests that it could be presented in the form of an *interpretive argument*. He says,

> To validate a performance standard and the corresponding cutscore is to validate the interpretive argument in which the standard and cutscore are embedded. . . . The aim of the validation effort is to provide convincing evidence that the cutscore does represent the intended performance standard and that this performance standard is appropriate, given the goals of the decision process. (p. 57)

Through interpretive argument, the test user can build a case for employing a standard in whatever the assessment context is at hand. The discussion of building an interpretive argument for validity evidence was proffered in chapter 4.

Establishing Serious Scholarship in Standard Setting

Over the years, standard setting has evolved from mere authoritative statement to serious scientific inquiry. Here, we look at a few important steps in this evolution. More than 50 years ago, when educational and psychological testing was often simply accepted at face value, a seminal contribution to standard setting was made. Nedelsky (1954) developed a remarkably sophisticated and far-sighted method for making classifying decisions, which he labeled *borderline groups*. Borderline groups are examinees or candidates that are not clearly above or below a criterion but just on the cusp—the regions where the decision must be made. I explain procedures for determining borderline groups later in the chapter. However, more important than his method was the fact that Nedelsky traduced the notion that standard setting was a simple matter. Through his empirical approach to the idea of setting a standard and establishing a considered criterion, he brought to the fore the idea that standard setting is both complex and evidentiary. Most important, he helped measurement professionals and others realize that standard setting should be based on sound science. This precept has guided serious work in standard setting ever since.

Another major advance in standard setting is documented in the second edition of the influential publication *Educational Measurement* (Thorndike, 1971), now in its fourth edition. In that early work, Angoff (1971) contributed a chapter titled "Scales, Norms, and Equivalent Scores," which described contemporary methods in terms of their psychometric qualities. This provided further impetus to the study of standard setting as serious scientific inquiry. Importantly, to one of the described procedures, Angoff added a footnote that offered a slight variation. Little did he realize that his modified process—now called *Angoff's Modified Procedure*—would become the most popular standard-setting procedure of the next several decades. Even today, it is widely employed in many assessment programs, especially those used with licensing and certification requirements. Angoff's *Educational Measurement* book is now classic reading for measurement professional.

Livingston and Zieky (1982), building on earlier work disseminated in a special issue of *Journal of Educational Measurement,* published *Passing Scores: A Manual for Setting Standards of Performance on Educational and Occupational Tests.* Indisputably, more than any other work in the field, this short pamphlet cemented a methodological perspective to the task of setting standards and has provided guidance to numerous serious testing programs for more than 20 years. Livingston and Zieky's article was later expanded into a pamphlet that remains hugely influential as a how-to manual.

Statistical Decision Theory as Theoretical Underpinnings

The theoretical underpinnings for setting standards reside within the notion of statistical decision theory, wherein reliability questions are explored in four broad areas, including (1) descriptive models of decision making; (2) general probabilistic models of choice and ranking, including test theory and probabilistic measurement; (3) various process-oriented models; and (4) general categorizations. Among these domains, the second area is of primary interest to measurement professional because this is where *Luce's choice model* (Luce, 1959) applies to standard setting. This model sets out a theoretical, mathematical approach to defining the likelihood of particular *events* in terms of their reliability over time, or likely reproducibility. An "event," in this context, is classifying a candidate on the basis of the test score, where the classification may be any category used in a standard, such as "pass" or "not pass."

Statistical decision theory is complex and arcane, involving theoretical mathematics, and the details of these underpinnings are beyond the scope of this text. Yet, it is important for our study to realize that standard setting has mathematical groundings. This theoretical work stems from probability theory generally and choice theory more particularly, as articulated by R. Duncan Luce, a renown theoretical statistician. Interested readers may refer to *Choice, Decision, and Measurement* (Marley, 1997), a Festschrift to Luce, for details and references to Luce's many works on the topic, as well as the contributions of many others.

Some Practical Aspects of Standard Setting

Standard Setting and Judgment

As we realize by now, setting a standard involves human judgment. In fact, the reliance on judgment is an integral part of virtually all the methods. Hambleton (2001) says, "all standard setting methods involve judgement" (p. 92). Thus, when studying standard setting, the term *judgment* is itself another important concept to understand.

Ideally, judgment is perspicacious, but in the real world we know that wisdom is sometimes fleeting in many people's sphere of thought. More practically, we must recognize that human judgment is imperfect but still useful. The utility to standard setting is that human judgment can be reliable. In fact, as we learned earlier—recall from chapter 6 the concept of *threshold* in relation to Thorndike's *just noticeable difference,* and later, Thurstone's fully articulated *law of comparative judgment—* reliable judgments are eminently plausible, and in fact, occur all the time.

To understand the role of judgment in standard setting, we must recognize the distinction between two other words: *arbitrary* and *capricious.* Arbitrariness is an unavoidable part of decision making in standard setting and elsewhere. It means that choices are made between alternatives. Judgments that are arbitrary are not necessarily poor choices, but they are discretionary. Here, we could just as readily select one alternative over another. We look for some coherent reason, a rationale or criterion to select a particular alternative. We make arbitrary judgments every day. I decide to wear a yellow shirt, rather than a green one. A test maker decides to scale an instrument with a mean location of 50, rather than 500. There is nothing wrong with making arbitrary choices, but in standard setting, arbitrary judgment must be based on a coherent rationale. I chose the yellow shirt because it coordinates with my pants. The test maker scaled the test with 50 as mean so it would not be confused with the 500-point scale of the SAT. The choice of shirt or scale is arbitrary, but it is made coherently, with logic and reason. Likewise, for standard setting, the arbitrary judgments should be coherently supported. Several scholars have commented on the arbitrariness of setting standards (e.g., Block, 1978; Kane, 2001).

Now, move from the reasonable nature of making arbitrary judgments to the extreme of "capricious" judgments. We realize that although standard-setting decisions are unavoidably arbitrary, they should never be capricious. Capricious decisions are wholly whimsical and often irrational. Here is where I chose the yellow shirt over the green one for no reason: One may simply say, "I felt like it." Although picking a shirt is only a trivial matter, in standard setting the import of the consequences means that we should take special care to avoid judgments that are capricious. An example of capricious behavior is seen in Queen Marie Antoinette of France, who in the 14th century was informed that her subjects were so poor and so low on basic food supplies that they had no bread to eat. The French Queen capriciously said, "Well, then, let them eat cake." Her comment—which illustrates how far removed the French aristocracy was from the lives of ordinary people and is often cited as a prime impetus for the French Revolution—was irrational and not based on coherent thought processes. In other words, Marie Antoinette was capricious. When setting a standard, capricious decisions can be harmful and are an obvious threat to valid score interpretations. To sum, then, judgments in standard setting are arbitrary (and presumably based on a rationale), but should never be capricious.

Difficulty in Setting Performance Standards

As is readily imagined, setting performance standards is a task fraught with difficulty. Some of the reasons for the difficulty are obvious, whereas others may be more subtle, lying in the details of a particular standard-setting enterprise. Nearly 30 years ago, Gene Glass (1978), a noted authority on standard setting, called attention to the fact that setting a defensible standard is easier said than done. More recently, Kane (2001) reiterated Glass's concern by stating that "it is arguable that the main thing that we have learned over the last 20 years is how difficult it can be to set a defensible standard on a test" (p. 54).

One of the most obvious reasons for the great trouble in setting a standard is that it typically leads to decisions about policy, an arbitrary (but, it is hoped, not capricious) form of expression. Arbitrary decisions such as public policy—even when wise and beneficial—cannot be easily evaluated as right or wrong. More logically, judging policy is a matter of anticipating likely outcomes. Similarly, measurement professionals have a duty to educate and inform policy makers of anticipated consequences and adverse impacts of a particular decision (Kane, 2001). In fact, this can be one of their most important roles in standard setting.

Of course, policy results from a political process, and clearly, the role of politics in standard setting is both palpable and evident, as mentioned earlier in the chapter. Measurement professionals involved in standard setting should neither ignore politics nor deride the fact that such considerations exist. Instead, they should use their expertise to ensure standard setting is conducted using a coherent method so policy makers may have full and accurate information. Then, too, as is often the case with political decisions, there may be legal implications. For a discussion of the legal implications of setting standards in varying contexts, see Carson (2001).

However, public policy, political, and legal considerations are not the only reasons for difficulty in setting performance standards. Another reason for difficulty is that setting standards is more than just the application of objective methods. It is as much an art form as a science. Cizek (2001) captures this aspect of standard setting most effectively for measurement professional when he says, "Standard setting is perhaps the branch of psychometrics that blends more artistic, political, and cultural ingredients into the mix of its products than any other" (p. 5).

This means that measurement professionals are more than mere technicians, applying the latest methodology. They must be sensitive to the environment in which an assessment enterprise operates, as well as to the interests of the stakeholders. Further, as we have already seen, standard setting can be largely idiosyncratic and particular to each testing context. Thus, no single methodology can be relied on as appropriate for all contexts. As often as not, even known methods must be modified to suit a given circumstance. All these reasons contribute to making it a difficult enterprise.

Content Standards and Performance Standards

In standard setting there are two types of standards, including (1) content standards and (2) performance standards. Content standards specify things to be known and things to do. For instance, the major 15 precepts (and 123 subdivisions) we use in test development and test score use given in the *Standards for Educational and Psychological Testing* (American Educational Research Association et al., 1999) are content standards. In parallel fashion, in psychology and many other fields, there are articulated standards of ethical behavior. In chapter 1 in the Suggested Readings section, I list some of these that apply to measurement professionals. These documents set content standards.

In K–12 education, in particular, there are many examples of content standards. For illustration, the National Education Standards and Improvement Council (1993) defined content standards for our nation's schools. Also, content standards in education gained national prominence when the National Council of Teachers of Mathematics (1989) published its seminal set of standards for the teaching of mathematical sciences. Soon, educators from other disciplines (e.g., English and language arts, science, social studies, art) developed parallel standards. The Mid-Continent Regional Educational Laboratory has published a useful compendium of such standards and benchmarks from many school-based subjects (Kendall & Marzano, 1996). These standards can be an invaluable resource for measurement professional and other professionals working on standard setting.

The second type of standard is performance standards. Performance standards are specifications for determining a level of performance that includes both the nature of the requisite evidence and the quality of an examinee's performance. For example, in educational assessment, the evidence of a performance standard may be the completion of a given task, such as writing an essay, performing a musical recital, or demonstrating a scientific experiment. The quality of the performance is articulated in the rubric required to satisfy an established criterion level.

Performance standards are not wholly distinct from content standards, but they are different in type. One way to view the two types is to realize that performance standards are the life force of content standards in that they articulate ideas implicit in content standards. According to the *Malcolm Report,* "performance standards are essential to gauging whether content standards are met" (National Education Standards and Improvement Council, 1993, p. iii). A content standard may be the articulation of an ideal (e.g., candidates will have the skills necessary to successfully carry out a certain task), whereas performance standards set out particular details of evidence and quality (e.g., on the XYZ test, a cutscore of 724 is required for licensure.)

Internal Versus External Evidence for Standard Setting

The evidence for standard-setting decisions may come from sources either *internal* to the particular instrument and processes used or *external* to it. Internal methods of data collection for setting standards rely on whole test analysis (see chapter 13) and item-level data (see chapter 12). Often in these procedures, experts are used to make judgments about the difficulty or the discrimination of the tests or the items. Such decisions are viewed as having the weight of expert authority, an important resource in test analysis.

Evidence external to the test itself is often correlational in nature. Correlational relationships, however, are not limited to just those described by Pearson r. Analysis of variance, generalizability techniques, and other kinds of direct correlations (e.g., phi, tetrachoric) can also provide important descriptions of the relationships between variables. Hence, external evidence can contribute to validation in standard setting. Remember, however, that although this approach has the advantage of reducing systematic error by setting a standard that relies on evidence external to the instrument, it also has the disadvantage of the mixed criterion problem discussed earlier in validity evaluation. Generally, it is best to employ standard-setting methods that rely on both internal and external evidence.

Proposed Steps of Standard Setting

Against this backdrop, then, many questions about standard setting become practical, such as, "How does one set standards for a given appraisal?" and "How many experts will I need?" In a no-nonsense article, Hambleton (2001) explains an 11-step method for setting performance standards:

1. Choose a panel (large and representative of the stakeholders).
2. Choose one of the standard-setting methods, prepare training materials, and finalize the meeting agenda.
3. Prepare descriptions of the performance categories (e.g., basic, proficient, or advanced).
4. Train panelists to use the method (including practice in providing ratings).
5. Compile item ratings and/or other rating data from the panelists (e.g., panelists specify expected performance of examinees at the borderlines of the performance categories).
6. Conduct a panel discussion; consider actual performance data (e.g., item difficulty values, item characteristic curves, item discrimination values, distractor analysis) and descriptive statistics of the panelist's ratings. Provide feedback on interpanelist and intrapanelist consistency.
7. Compile item ratings a second time that can be followed by more discussion, feedback, and so on.
8. Compile panelist ratings and obtain the performance standards.
9. Present consequences data to the panel (e.g., passing rate).
10. Revise and finalize the performance standards, and conduct a panelist evaluation of the process itself and their level of confidence in the resulting standards.
11. Compile validity evidence and technical documentation.

Citing these recommended steps for standard setting serves our purpose of gaining an understanding of the process, but practitioners wanting to follow them in a live standard-setting enterprise are referred to the original source for a fuller explanation.

Attention to the Judges

Because standard setting relies on judgment by people, selecting and training judges is a paramount concern. Given the great number of standard-setting methods and the variety of appraisal contexts, it will scarcely be surprising to appreciate that no single set of rules can guide either the selection of judges or their training. Still, particular considerations are relevant to most standard-setting plans, and I describe them in this section. An extended discussion of selecting and training judges in many testing situations can be found in Raymond and Reid (2001).

Selecting Judges for Setting Standards

Three deliberations are required to properly select judges who are suited to the tasks involved in standard setting. First, in a given assessment context, there should be thought about who may be appropriate to judge. This concern is captured in the question, "What is the role of judges in this standard setting project?" Different assessment programs seek to satisfy various goals, and certainly, qualifications needed for one program will not necessarily satisfy another. For example, if a high school proficiency test is used for certifying completion of an academic curriculum, the role of judges may be to represent various stakeholder groups, such as teachers, school administrators, businesspeople, school board members, college admissions officers, and parents. Persons from these stakeholder groups are likely to have a lot of contact with high school students.

In another standard-setting context, however, the concern about who is well matched to the task may be entirely different. Suppose an assessment program has public safety as its principal concern, as is the case with paramedics or emergency room nurses. Obviously, in this context, it would not make sense to include persons for the reason that they may represent a group likely to have contact with the injured or ill individual (e.g., insurance carriers). Presumably, judges are included because of technical and content expertise, as well as field experience. Through these examples, we see that determining the role of judges is a necessary early deliberation to successful standard setting.

A second consideration for selecting individuals who compose a standard-setting group—one made after the role of the judges has been determined—is to set qualifications for judges. The requirements may be as simple as being a member of a certain group. If, for instance, the perspective of parents is needed, then a parent it should be! At other times, qualifications should be based on technical or content expertise in the particular discipline, as well as field experience.

In standard setting, persons with special expertise are called *subject-matter experts* (SMEs). The *Standards for Educational and Psychological Testing* (American Educational Research Association et al., 1999) stipulates in Standard 4.21 that SMEs be included in appropriate circumstances, particularly in contexts where judgment is based on the adequacy of item or test performance. (We review some of these methods in later sections of this chapter.) With SMEs, "the judgmental process should be designed so that judges can bring their knowledge and experience to bear in a reasonable way" (p. 60). SMEs are usually identified for their expertise, experience, and reputation among peers. Candidates for SMEs should possess all three qualifications and caution is advised against exaggerated reliance on any one SME. Technical expertise is usually judged by education or training, and experience is generally thought of as active time in the field. Reputation, as a criterion, however, is a more difficult quality to evaluate. When considering reputation, remember that casual comments and anecdotes about a person may be based on the individual having a pleasing personality, hardly a substitute for a fact-based look into a person's verifiable qualifications.

An additional consideration in selecting judges is the practical issue of deciding on the optimal number. There is no single recommendation on this point, but due deliberation should be given to it, depending on circumstance. Occasionally, even research into the question may be worth the effort for the empirical information it can yield. One expert on standard setting suggests that when research is called for, the "How many judges?" question can be addressed by considering the ability to generalize the results garnered from a single standard-setting session to many more. Says Jaeger (1991),

> Participants [in a standard-setting panel] should be selected through procedures
> that permit generalization of their collective recommendation to well-defined
> populations. . . . The number of participants selected should be sufficient to provide
> precise estimation of the standard that would be recommended by an entire
> population of participants. (p. 10)

This design could call for a generalizability study. In the generalizability study, primary attention would center on the reliability of the cutscore, wherein one would estimate its standard error. Logically, the study would include a facet describing the number of judges. Kane (2001) and Raymond and Reid (2001) also recommend this technical approach.

Consistency Among Judges' Ratings

Two primary considerations are necessary when training individuals to become competent judges. First, the persons must be clearly informed of the conditions or criteria for making the judgments. If, for example, a group of school teachers is directed to score essays, but given no further instruction, their ratings would likely be spurious and of little use for decision making. However, when criteria for scoring are clearly articulated and communicated to the judges, their rating will be useful. For an example of clearly specified scoring criteria, refer to chapter 9 and the discussion of preparing scoring rubrics for determining categories of writing proficiency (in particular, review Figure 9.11).

The other consideration in training judges is *interrater agreement*. High interrater agreement occurs when there is a scale for rating and judges assign the same score points to the same observation from an examinee. In many PAs, and especially in writing assessment, anchoring is the process of training judges so the individual determinations about an essay are consistent among all judges. Consistency of rating among judges is checked by interrater reliability indices. Some methods to gauge this include the following:

- Raw agreement indices
- Odds ratio and Yule's Q

- Tests of marginal homogeneity
- Tetrachoric and polychoric correlation
- Latent trait models
- Latent class models
- Log linear, association, and quasisymmetry models
- Kappa coefficients
- Methods for Likert-type or interval-level data
- Intraclass correlation and variance components methods

Information about these indices, as well as a fine discussion of issues to be considered in interrater reliability, can be accessed at *http://ourworld.compuserve.com/homepages/jsuebersax/agree.htm* (Retrieved March 8, 2005). Persons interested in this topic are encouraged to review this information.

Regardless of the quality of the training, instances inevitably arise when judges disagree or assign inconsistent ratings. Many assessment programs devise decision rules about these scoring inconsistencies. For example, a rule may be made where the final score is the average of two judge's ratings, or their sum. Typically, if the scale is fairly limited in range—say, on the order of 0 to 6 or 7—the common practice is to average them or, in some cases, to sum them (where summed ratings are used). When larger differences occur, however, a third judge may be brought in to provide yet another rating. The three judgments could then be averaged.

Interrater agreement is important because it leads to consistency of decisions for the pool of candidates by the judges. Here, a special application of reliability is invoked, called *decision consistency*. Decision consistency is a reliability not ascribed to the instrument (as one might typically use reliability) but to the rating process itself. Decision consistency is the act of making replicable decisions by other judges applying the same standards. G theory is an appropriate route to studying decision consistency, particularly as it applies to D studies (G theory and D studies are described in chapter 11).

Selecting Judges for NAEP Standard Setting

The NAEP program is perhaps the most widely recognized standard-setting panel; therefore, a brief look at it is useful for learning about standard-setting panels. The NAEP standard-setting panel is large and deliberately constructed. Initially, it was determined that representation of many groups was the prime consideration. The groups were as diverse as persons from business and industry, parents, representatives of higher education institutions, persons who were not employed in education, and so on. From this decision, a sample plan was devised to ensure individuals within each group were represented. Nominees were selected, and criteria for making a recommendation were developed. Finally, the participants were chosen based on training, experience, and reputation. Figure 14.4 shows the NAEP panel groups. This was indeed an involved process, and the NAEP experience demonstrates the effort required in some programs to build a proper standard-setting panel.

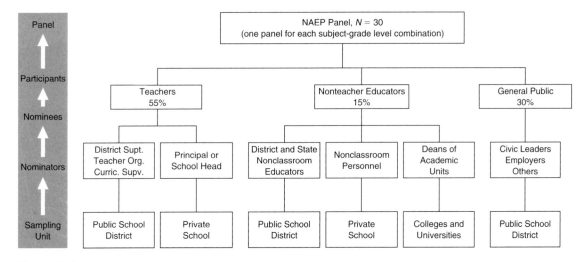

Figure 14.4
Participant selection for NAEP standard setting.
Source: From *Setting Performance Standards: Concepts, Methods, and Perspectives* (p. 131), by G. J. Cizek, 2001, Mahwah, NJ: Lawrence Erlbaum Associates. Copyright 2001 by Lawrence Erlbaum Associates. Adapted with permission.

Some Standard-Setting Processes

In addition to selecting and training judges, measurement professionals responsible for technical aspects of a standard-setting project must select or devise a method to set criteria for a standard. The choice is not always easy because there are more than 30 recognized methodologies and many more variations. As emphasized, no one method is uniformly superior to the others, nor can any be applied generally; rather, the professional must consider the exigencies of a particular effort and develop a plan suited to it.

A number of methods are described in this section, with an emphasis on those that either are popularly used or present promising direction. Particularly, for modern methods, information beyond what is presented here can be found in Cizek's (2001) *Setting Performance Standards: Concepts, Methods, and Perspectives.* Many classical means, some still popular, can be found in original sources, including works by Angoff (1971), Linn (1989), and Livingston and Zieky (1982).

Until more recently, three classical methods seemed dominant among standard-setting enterprises. Each requires judges to rate test items, and each is named after its inventor: Angoff, Nedelsky, and Ebel. The Angoff method (with a customary modification described momentarily) is still in widespread use, particularly in licensing and certification programs and in many other small-scale testing programs. Use of the Nedelsky and Ebel methods, however, seems to be rapidly declining; thus, they are not presented in this text. Regardless, details about these methods can be found in many sources, including Angoff (1971) and Livingston and Zieky (1982). I describe Angoff's modified method first and then move to explain more modern methods.

Imaginably, there is tremendous attention to standard setting by researchers, and some promising results have come from their efforts. One modern approach to scoring PAs is the modern *bookmarking procedure*. Other recent work by Hambleton (2001), Hansche (1998), Jaeger (1995), Mills (1998), and Plake (2001) suggests that most promising standard-setting approaches for PA appraisal focus on actual examinee papers (responses to the PAs) and classification scales. These methods emphasize either (a) analytic judgment or (b) integrated holistic judgment. An application of each method is also briefly introduced in this section.

Modified Angoff Method

The *modified Angoff method* for standard setting is especially popular with tests comprising items in the multiple-choice format, although after adjustment it can also be used with PAs. However, it is not commonly employed with PAs and is poorly suited to tests that have items with polytomous formats.

In the Angoff process, a panel of expert judges is assembled and asked to consider the test items. The judges must be expert in the content and have a good sense of the abilities of likely examinees. Further, this method requires rigorous training for anchoring of judges before use. Their task is to imagine a group of borderline examinees, say 100 individuals, who are on the cusp of ability to show mastery. It is important to appreciate that the imaginary examinees from this group are presumed to show mastery—but at just a bare minimum. Hence, they are "minimally competent." It is important that judges have a uniform understanding of minimal competence at the requisite ability level in the context. After this is ensured, the judges consider the test items themselves. They begin by examining the first item on the test and estimating how many individuals in the minimally competent group would correctly endorse the item. Because the imaginary group is 100 persons, the judges' guesses are expressed as a percentage passing, from 0% to 100%, or in terms of probability, from .00 to 1.00. An easy item may achieve a rating of .80 or higher, whereas a more difficult one may be marked at .4. Each judge offers a rating independent of the other judges.

When a particular judge designates a percentage that deviates from the others' ratings by a large amount, the judge may be asked to defend the rating. Usually, however, judges' ratings remain secret to avoid the sway of a strong personality. A simple rating form can be developed for recording responses.

When all judges have submitted their ratings, they are summed and averaged for that item. This value is the *item passing score*. The process continues for each item on the test. Sometimes, when item data from previous administrations of the test are available, the ratings are compared with the observed item *p*-values. Armed with the additional information, the judges are asked to reconsider their original percentages and submit modified percentages. This practice should be employed only when the data are garnered from a group of examinees similar in sample characteristics to the anticipated future groups and under similar test administration conditions.

When the process is complete for all test items, the separate item passing scores are then summed and averaged, yielding a whole *passing percent*. To obtain the actual cutscore, multiply the percentage times the number of items in the test. Of course, the process must be repeated when new items are added to the test.

Despite its popularity, the modified Angoff method is not without considerable shortcomings. Most notably, it can be viewed as insubstantial because of its reliance on summed item values, which are notorious for having low item intercorrelations (Linn & Shepard, 1997). Because of this failing, some researchers recommend a variant procedure called the *bookmark standard setting,* a method that allows judges to focus their attention on the expected performance of minimally proficient examinees without the additional task of estimating absolute item difficulty.

Bookmark Standard Setting

Bookmarking is a relatively recent development in standard-setting procedures that is rapidly gaining acceptance in assessment and psychometric communities. It is often viewed as an alternative to the Angoff method because its features address some weakness in that method (Buckendahl, Smith, Impara, & Plake, 2002). For instance, it can appropriately accommodate PAs, something Angoff cannot do without significant adjustment. Also, it is conceptually appealing because it takes advantage of latent trait methods by requiring items and exercises to be hierarchically ordered, a feature made manifest by IRT scaling. Although scaling a test or PA with IRT is not a requirement for bookmarking, item difficulty and discrimination ratings are needed. Because these characteristics are most reliably estimated by IRT parameters, nearly all applications of bookmarking employ IRT-scaled tests.

Another strength of the procedure is that it combines a statistical estimate of item parameters with the judges' ratings, adding the strength of statistics to judgment. Further, judges are asked to make estimates of students' performances only on whole tests (or significant parts of them), rather than on individual items, as required by the Angoff method. Such global ratings are generally closer to a student's observed achievement than ratings done at the item level. In addition, some researchers investigating bookmarking suggest that it more clearly relates the selected standards to classroom instruction.

Bookmarking is used in several important large-scale programs that incorporate PAs. It was adopted by NAEP for its anchoring procedure and by several state education programs (e.g., Maryland, Colorado, Hawaii, Missouri).

The steps in the process vary with application and may be relatively straightforward or more involved, requiring rounds of review. In any instance, however, the method requires considerable thought for execution. I describe a simple version as introduction. However, a more involved, step-by-step approach is described by Lewis, Mitzel, Green, and Patz (1999).

The procedure requires a number of rounds of review by judges and stakeholders. First, a committee of stakeholders is organized and levels for standards are determined and described. These can be just two levels, as in "pass" versus "not pass," but it is more common that three, four, or five levels are stipulated. For example, the Colorado Student Assessment Program articulates four levels, including Advanced, Proficient, Partially Proficient, and Unsatisfactory. In another testing program of students with learning disabilities, and an interesting application of bookmarking, five categories were used: (a) Independent, (b) Functional Independent, (c) Supported Independent, (d) Emergent, and (e) Not Evident (Olson, Mead, & Payne, 2002). In addition, for validity in interpretation, it is important for a description of each standard to be thoughtfully considered, rather than designated by a quickly assigned label.

Next, a panel of judges with content expertise is selected. Depending on program context, the judges may be composed of the same individuals that constitute the committee defining the standards. The judges make rounds of review, each intended to bring their individual decisions closer to consensus about where to place a particular standard on the test's scale. Often there are three rounds of review.

Prior to the review rounds, test items and exercises are placed in booklets. A booklet may contain a PA prompt and the accompanying items. When there are several such exercises, there will be many such booklets. The booklets (hence, the items and exercises constituting them) are hierarchically ordered according to a stipulated criteria, as illustrated in Figure 14.5.

Most commonly, item parameters specified in the latent trait scaling are used as criteria, such as item difficulty, item discrimination, pseudochance, or some combination of these. These characteristics are, of course, the 1PL, 2PL, or 3PL of IRT. In the bookmarking procedure, this is referred to as *item mapping*. One must pay careful attention to properly map items, which can take the form of a validity evaluation of IRT model fit (see chapter 11 for a discussion of model fit). If the IRT model is ill

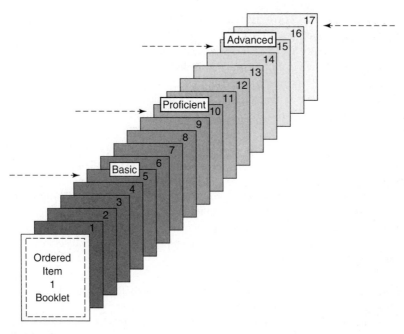

Figure 14.5
Illustration of ordered item booklets for implementing bookmarking procedure.

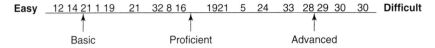

Figure 14.6
Bookmark standards along item mapping scale.

suited to the data available for the population of examinees, the mapping will be poor and the bookmarking process compromised.

A judge's task is to consider the items and exercises on the test or assessment and then refer to the item map, placing bookmarks at the minimal point along the item map for a given standard. Figure 14.6 illustrates the procedure for a program with three standards: "B" for "Basic," "P" for "Proficient," and "A" for "Advanced." In the figure, items are identified by their number.

Analytic Judgment Method

The *analytic judgment* method was developed by Hambleton and others on a National Science Foundation research team that sought to identify new standard-setting approaches. Details about the approach can be found in the original work (Plake & Hambleton, 2001). Simply, however, the analytic judgment method is similar to holistic approaches, such as the *body of work* method and the *integrated holistic judgment* method presented in the next section. It examines sets of writings and other performance tasks, and aims to classify a student's performance across the assessments into categories. The categories are the performance standards, and they may be indicative of a broad scale such as "Below Basic," "Basic," "Proficient," and "Advanced." These categories of performance can be divided further into levels, such as "low," medium," and "high."

Interestingly, the goal of the analytic judgment method is not to homogenize opinions by forcing consensus among the judges; rather, the goal is to exploit separate insights and perspectives that individual judges may have about a student's work. Each judge is encouraged to share his or her reasons for making particular assignments. Along the way, standard-setting administrators have a record of what scores, grades, and marks a student received on their work. This information is not shared with judges because they are to have no prior knowledge of a student, including previous grades earned. Quantifying the judges' opinions can be done by different methods, but the purpose is to calculate a performance standard that captures the meaning of the relationship between the original scores on individual papers and the judges' holistic categorization.

This method has been employed successfully in several state assessment programs, including those of Pennsylvania, Georgia, and Michigan. It is especially useful for standard setting with complex performance assessments.

Integrated Holistic Judgment

Cutscore specialist Richard Jaeger (Jaeger & Mills, 2001) suggests a modern method that combines aspects of holistic judgment with empirical criteria. In this approach, called "integrated holistic judgment," the judges are required to classify a student's responses to an entire set of items (Jaeger used NAEP items in his study). A principal advantage of the integrated holistic judgment method is that it does not require judges to conceptualize the abilities or traits of the borderline student, a shortcoming of the Angoff procedure. Also, as an iterative procedure, judgments can be refined with successive ratings.

Initially for the method, judges place each student's work in 1 of 12 categories, ranging from "far below basic" to "highly advanced." After this, students' scores are revealed to the judges who refined their estimation into lower bounds for the NAEP classifications of Basic, Proficient, and Advanced. Next, the panel members are asked to make two judgments: whether a student's performance was clearly within a NAEP standard or just barely within it. This again helps establish a lower bound for classifying responses.

With a lower bound for each standard set by collective holistic judgment, a cutscore can then be calculated. These calculations are simple and direct, and in Jaeger's application, merely "averaged the test scores assigned to students whose work was placed by any judge in one of the categories immediately surrounding a desired performance standard" (Jaeger & Mills, 2001, p. 323). This was termed the *boundary*. To overcome bias in estimation procedures, a regression (both linear and quadratic) was fit to the data in a series of models defining the functional relation between judges' ratings and students' obtained total scores.

Classic Methods Based on Judgments of Individual Examinees

The next two methods—called the *borderline group* method and the *contrasting groups* method—do not rely on direct judgments about test items; rather, each necessitates a judgment about individual test takers. They require two bits of prior information about the examinees, including (1) the total test score (usually a raw score) for each examinee, and (2) information about the adequacy of the examinee's knowledge and skills in the field. Such information is useful to judges who must place examinees into categories of competence, such as "qualified" or "not qualified." To avoid the possibility that knowledge of an examinee's test score could influence that decision, it is recommended that the test score information not be available to the judges until after the placement decision is made.

Judges make their placement decisions based on many factors that may include external criterion, such as a job evaluation or prior grades in a similar course. Regardless, the decision-making process must be credible and meaningful. Livingston and Zieky (1982) suggest that the information is not overly difficult to assemble because it derives from judgments that many professionals in society are well practiced at making. For instance, a teacher routinely gauges the adequacy of students in a particular discipline, and employers and line supervisors often judge the skills of their subordinates and colleagues. Sometimes, however, judges have neither an external criterion nor other meaningful and useful information, making the task—and these methods—inappropriate.

Persons considering these methods are advised that making a judgment is fraught with danger if not done with care and skill. One is cautioned from too quickly adopting the Livingston and Zieky naiveté and simplistic optimism that such decisions will automatically be consistently made.

Nonetheless, they recommend that the judgments be based on four criteria:

1. The judges themselves must be qualified to make the specific judgments.
2. The judgments are focused on the skills and cognitive processes covered by the test.
3. Because tests are a "snapshot-in-time," the judgments about examinees' abilities should reflect their skills at the time the test is taken.
4. The judgment should reflect the judges' true opinion, eschewing all prejudices and preconceptions.

Borderline Groups Method

The *borderline groups method* presumes the examinees can be reliably divided into three groups, including "qualified," "unqualified," and "borderline." This initial grouping is based on the judges' pronouncement of an examinee's skill or ability level. In practice, it is usually not too difficult to place examinees into one group or the other. The difficulty, of course, is in identifying placements for students who should be located in the borderline category. A consensus among judges is often used to facilitate this placement, for any individual judge may be in error. In addition, it is vital to reliable judgment that the judges possess a common understanding of knowledge, skills, abilities, or characteristics of hypothetical individuals in each group. The cutscore is simply the median score achieved by the group constituting the borderline category. Sometimes, particularly when there are few examinees (e.g., less than 100) and the score scale is long (e.g., 0 to 100), a smoothing technique in which disparate points are regressed to the center must be applied to the data to achieve a functional progression of scores.

The borderline group method is not recommended unless there is empirical evidence that the judges can make their placements reliably (or have a meaningful and useful external criterion for doing so) and unless the group of examinees is sufficiently large that a distribution of scores is available within each category. For these reasons, this method is seldom used. It is important to be aware of the technique, though, because it shows the basic idea behind most cutscore methods.

Contrasting Groups Method

The *contrasting groups method* also begins by making placement decisions about examinees, only this time there are just two groups: "qualified" and "not qualified." Again, the criteria for making such placement decisions apply, as do the same cautions and admonitions. With the population (or an appropriate sample) divided into two groups, the test scores come into play.

The scores are separated into the placement groups and a frequency distribution is prepared for each group. The groups are then compared to determine the cutscore that divides them. There are three comparisons to be considered: (a) the difference dividing the groups where distributions overlap, (b) the upper bound of the "not qualified" group, and (c) the lower bound of the "qualified" group. Figure 14.7 has three illustrations of the two distributions, each displaying one of the considerations.

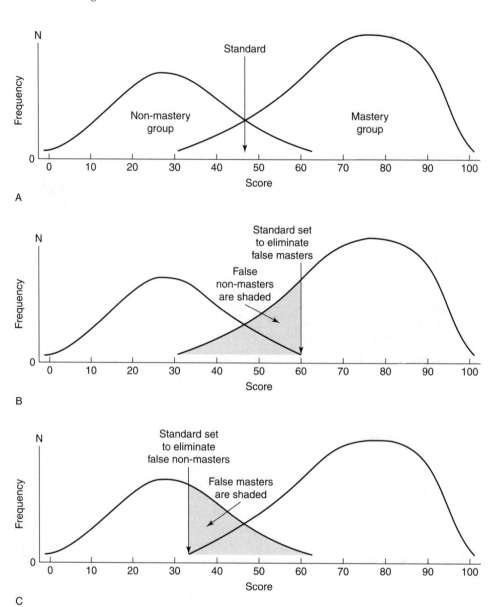

Figure 14.7

Procedures showing groups in contrasting groups methods.

Source: Adapted from Roeber, E. (2002). *Setting Standards on Alternate Assessments* (Synthesis Report 42). Minneapolis, MN: University of Minnesota, National Center on Educational Outcomes. Retrieved January 2, 2005, from the World Wide Web: *http://education.umn.edu/NCEO/OnlinePubs/Synthesis42.html.*

Figure 14.7A shows the absolute difference between the groups, splitting at the point where the distributions overlap. This method allows that there are some persons with qualifications who are placed in the nonmastery group (by measurement error or otherwise) and vice versa for the mastery group. This method seems to split the difference attempting to minimize original misclassifications.

The second choice for a cutscore in the contrasting groups method is shown in Figure 14.7B. Here, the cutscore is set at the upper extreme of the nonmastery group. This eliminates all nonmasters. It is a more severe method than the one shown in Figure 14.7A. If, however, the criterion for original placement is appropriate and examinees are reliably categorized into their respective mastery groups, it is a useful procedure, especially when public health or safety is a goal of the assessment program. For example, this plan may be appropriate for determining mastery of medical specialties, where mistakes in certification or licensing are most unwelcome.

The complement to placing the cutscore at the upper end of the nonmastery group range is to place it at the lower end of the mastery group range, as shown in Figure 14.7C. This method is generous to examinees because they receive the benefit of the doubt for measurement error, which is likely larger in the lower tail of a distribution of scores.

Obviously, caution is needed when using the contrasting groups method, regardless of which place is selected as appropriate to set the cutscore. Each cutscore point has both advantages and disadvantages. Deciding on the cutscore point is probably best judged in the context of a particular assessment program or situation. It is also advised that when using this method, one should conduct external validity studies to investigate the phenomenon of classification error.

The Body of Work Method

First devised in the 1990s, the *body of work* method is a comparatively recent development. Originally, it was proposed for the public school assessment program in Maine; it has since been employed in six other state assessment programs. This method has laid the foundation for other work in setting standards on PAs, specifically modification by Cohen, Kane, and Crooks (1998), and development of a more sophisticated version, the *analytical judgment* method, seen earlier in this section.

The body of work method takes advantage of an educator's expertise and experience in dealing with a large number of students. The method is a holistic approach to standard setting; judges read and study students' writing across a variety of samples, as well as review students' answers to multiple-choice test questions. With this broader perspective, the judges then match each student's response set to performance-level categories. The fact that it can be applied to mixed-format samples of work makes it especially attractive for assessment programs that have such multiple formats.

Kingston, Kahl, Sweeney, and Bay (2001) describe two events in the process, one that occurs before the standard-setting panel meeting and a second that occurs during the meeting. According to Kingston, in the first event, the tasks are to (a) create names for performance levels and general performance-level definitions,

Technique	Description
Reasoned Judgment	A score scale (e.g., 32 points) is divided into a desired number of categories (e.g., 4) in some way (e.g., equally, larger in the middle, etc.); the categories are determined by a group of experts, policy makers, or others.
Contrasting Groups	Teachers separate students into groups based on their observations of the students in the classroom; the scores of the students are then calculated to determine where scores will be categorized in the future.
Modified Angoff	Raters estimate the percentage of students at the bottom score range who are expected to "pass" each test item; these individual estimates are summed to produce an overall percentage of items correct that correspond to the minimum passing score for that level.
Bookmarking or Item Mapping	Standard setters mark the spot in a specially constructed test booklet (arranged in order of item difficulty) where a desired percentage of minimally proficient (or advanced) students would pass the item, or standard setters mark where the difference in performance of the proficient and advanced student on an exercise is a desired minimum percentage of students.
Body of Work	Reviewers examine all data for a student and use this information to place the student in one of the overall performance levels. Standard setters are given a set of papers that demonstrates the complete range of possible scores from low to high.
Judgmental Policy Capturing	Reviewers determine which of the various components of an overall assessment are more important than others so components or types of evidence are weighted.

Figure 14.8

Standard-setting techniques applicable to alternate assessments.

Source: Adapted from Roeber, E. (2002). *Setting Standards on Alternate Assessments* (Synthesis Report 42). Minneapolis, MN: University of Minnesota, National Center on Educational Outcomes. Retrieved January 2, 2005, from the World Wide Web: *http://education.umn.edu/NCEO/OnlinePubs/Synthesis42.html.*

(b) create subject-specific performance definitions, (c) create folders of student work, (d) select and invite standard-setting panel participants, and (e) complete a panelist test review.

Tasks during the standard-setting meeting include (a) presenting an overview of the process, (b) training panelists, (c) performing range finding, (d) selecting additional folders of student work, (e) performing pinpointing, (f) analyzing data, and (g) evaluating the process. An explanation of these tasks is provided in the original source.

Obviously, this method requires a lot of effort from many people. The practical aspect of gathering many samples of work from a large number of students is also labor intensive. Therefore, before beginning a standard-setting project that employs this method, it is worthwhile to secure informed commitment from judges and investigate the availability of relevant data. If the commitment is made, however, this method can produce useful results for holistic evaluation of a student.

Other Statistically Based Methods

Roeber (2002) developed a chart that organizes some of the methods discussed into categories. This chart is reproduced in Figure 14.8.

Of course, to measurement professional it is inviting to explore statistical approaches to standard setting. There have been several such attempts, including those using IRT and cluster analysis (see, for example, Sireci, 2001). For the most part, these methods are exploratory and should be used with caution. Still, such research holds promise for the future of standard setting. Because these methods are currently evolving at a rapid pace, their current versions are not described in this text. Readers may refer to Sireci's work, as well as to current journals, to find these exploratory advancements.

Summary

This chapter is about standard setting. I begin by explaining what a standard is in the context of mental assessment and develop the notion as to its purpose. From there, I explore a number of relevant topics, such as validity in standard setting. Practicalities are also addressed, such as the difficulties one is likely to encounter in conducting such a study and issues related to selecting and training judges. The second half of the chapter describes eight standard-setting methods, with particular attention given to procedures that are modern or show promise for future work. A number of illustrations are also given.

Chapter 15

Equivalence: Linking and Equating

Introduction

The Great Ode

Ludwig van Beethoven's Ninth Symphony, op. 125 (commonly referred to by its lyric "Ode to Joy"), is held by many musicologists to be the most perfect music ever written. This judgment is due in part to its considerable technical merit, and even more to the sense of wonder and awe the notes inspire. The late conductor Leonard Bernstein once said that when he starts to lead an orchestra in the Ninth, he feels the heavens open up and pour out onto the earth. Several nations, as well as the European Union, have adopted the symphony as their national anthems, and one country even has a measure of the music printed on its national currency. Thousands of songs are takeoffs of the Ninth Symphony; doubtless, many more have been inspired by it. The words, too, are well known, belonging originally to Schiller's poem *An die Freude,* or *Ode to Joy.* Many of the world's major religions have adopted the symphony as doxology, adding words to reflect their own theology, but keeping the music as originally written by the great German composer. Some computer historians even maintain that our contemporary compact disk was intended to play for 74 minutes because that is the symphony's exact length. From the first performance of Beethoven's Ninth at the Imperial Court Theatre in Vienna on May 7, 1824, until today, people across the globe love this glorious piece. Hearing this symphony brings our humanity to the surface; it swells us with pride just to be alive and makes us feel capable of great things.

We realize that it was not only inspiration that created the soaring effect of Beethoven's music, but also effort and technical expertise. Hard work and technical skill will serve us, too, in addressing many important and practical testing problems. One particularly important area for exploration in measurement is finding similarities, or even equivalence, between tests. Technically, this idea is held in the measurement conditions of linking tests, equating test scores, and determining test equivalence. It is to these ideas that we now turn.

Contents

Chapter 15 begins by explaining several important terms, including *test equivalence, test equating,* and *linking.* From there, I offer some comments about working with test equivalence, particularly stressing the role of measurement professionals in fostering proper interpretations. Next, several equating designs are described, both through classical means, such as linear equating and equipercentile equating, and many more modern procedures. The newer approaches culminate in IRT methods for equating. Throughout the chapter, I stress the importance of properly interpreting the results of a particular test equivalence method.

Understanding Terminology

In the area of test equivalence, three terms dominate: (1) test equivalence, (2) test equating, and (3) linking tests. Although it may appear that these terms can be clearly defined, unfortunately varying and inconsistent definitions appear in the technical literature, and their usage by measurement professionals is conflicted and unpredictable. I hope not to add to the hodgepodge of opinions; however, it is necessary to find a common understanding in order to proceed. Thus I provide definitions of the terms as I use them in this text. Readers will find these definitions to be consistent with those of most experts. The varying meanings and uses for these terms by both laypersons and measurement professionals emphasize the need for careful interpretation of results of any equivalence investigation. Clearly, too, the lack of consistency in usage is a clarion call to measurement professionals to bring a uniform meaning to these important terms—such common understanding will advance measurement science. Let us begin by defining "test equivalence," the term having least disagreement among measurement specialists.

Test Equivalence

Two tests are equivalent when the interpretation of results is such that it does not matter which test the examinee took. In other words, both tests assess the same construct, have identical reliability, and yield information that has an indistinguishable interpretation. Gullicksen (1950) proffered this definition more than 50 years ago. In terms discussed in chapter 3 (see the Meaning of Parallel Test Terms section), such tests are at least congeneric and may be parallel or even strictly parallel, although this final degree of rigor is unlikely in real world settings. Lord and Novick (1963), along with other experts, have long endorsed this description for test equivalence.

The most important criterion for test equivalence (rather than focus exclusively on variance terms as applicable in the discussion in chapter 3) is that an identical (or reasonable facsimile) interpretation of the underlying trait or assessed proficiency results from both tests. Of course, the strictness of the standard must be relaxed in practical testing situations so "indistinguishable interpretation" is not taken so literally that it can never be met in real world tests. Although the idea of common ground must be taken very seriously, as long as two tests convey essentially similar information appropriate to a given situation, we may regard their interpretations as functionally indistinguishable. Note particularly that the description of equivalent (or congeneric) tests makes no mention of need for the two instruments to share all, or even a portion of, their stimuli. In effect, then, they may or may not comprise the same items or exercises. In fact, neither the items nor their format is relevant to whether tests are equivalent. Many testing programs have *alternative forms* of their tests, some of which may be equivalent.

Further, the scales or metrics for measurement or the scoring schemes do not need to be identical for there to be equivalency between tests. Each test can be expressed on its own scale and have unique scoring. However, as a condition of test equivalence, when scores are differently expressed, the scores on one test must be able to be moved to the other's scale by a simple linear transformation. This is an important notion to heed when considering test equivalence.

Test Equating

The second term to explain is test equating. Test *equating* is a statistical process for expressing the scores of one test on the scale of another test with maximum precision. The fact that equating is a statistical process means that an algorithm expressing probability (i.e., a function of the probabilistic model discussed in chapter 6) is employed, and hence, imprecision is a part of test equating. Only for *strictly parallel* tests can equating produce results that are exact, and even this may be only a theoretical condition. Most logically, too, equating is strictly linear, as a part of the GLM.

It should be unmistakably understood that statistical equating applies to scores but not to the content appraised by tests. This means that although scores of a source test can be expressed on the scale of another target test, one cannot infer an interpretation of the target test's construct from an equated score. An illustration may make this crucial point clearer. Suppose an examinee took Test A and an equating process has been properly applied to express the examinee's score on the scale of Test B. The equated score does not imply that the examinee was measured on the construct appraised by Test B. It only means that the score achieved on Test A can be transformed to appear on the same scale used by Test B. Kolen and Brennan (2004) state, "Equating adjusts for differences in difficulty, not for differences in content" (p. 3). This is a limitation of test equating, and one that test users should heed.

Test equating has many practical applications useful in a wide array of assessment contexts. One of the most common circumstances for equating tests occurs when an assessment program comprises several tests that are intended to be functionally equivalent, within practical limits. The tests may share many items, but each may also have unique items. The instruments derive from the same test content specifications and may even be composed of items developed for the same item pool, using identical procedures for their development. Often, such tests are considered *alternate forms* and sometimes a test author maintains that the tests can be used interchangeably. Such claims should be viewed cautiously, and regardless of these strengths to equating, one should never indiscriminately report test scores without referencing that score to what form the examinee took. This admonition is not only in the interest of accuracy, but also a condition of full disclosure.

Linking Tests

The third and final term in the equivalence triumvirate is linking. *Linking tests* refers to procedures by which two or more tests may be reported on the same scale. Some authors call this *common-scale equating*. The argot "linking," however, is consistent with the *Standards for Educational and Psychological Testing* (American Educational Research Association, American Psychological Association, and National Council on Measurement in Education, 1999), as well as in accordance with Linn (1989) and Mislevy (1992), both renowned experts in the field.

Linking does not imply that the tests are equivalent, nor does it suggest that the scores of one are equated to the other's scale. Instead, linking may be thought of as reporting scores on a long scale, one portion of which is covered by one test and another portion by the next test, and so on for as many tests as are linked. Linking tests is a common practice among developers of test batteries for schools, allowing the reported scores for each successive grade to be shown in a manner that suggests higher achievement or more development. Grade-equivalent scores—although fraught with technical difficulties—suggest this hierarchal arrangement in their scales. This kind of linking, from one level to the next level to the next, is called *vertical linking*. Sometimes, linking is also referred to as *vertical equating* (Kolen & Brennan, 2004).

Some authors use the term *horizontal linking* to convey the idea of equated scores across level tests. Although rare, there are times when this term is well suited to describe a testing program. Almost exclusively, such circumstances arise when the equating is by IRT estimates of item and examinee parameters, and the scale is theorized as a continuum of a latent ability along the range $(-\infty, +\infty)$. Horizontally linked tests are designed such that each one covers a portion of the full range in the latent trait. In some standard-setting contexts, the bookmarking procedure (see chapter 14) takes advantage of the same idea as do tests that are horizontally linked.

Each equivalence term is depicted in Figure 15.1, conveying a sense of their relationships.

Working with Equivalence

Fostering Proper Interpretations

Measurement professionals should recognize that the very notion of test equivalence or equating has intuitive appeal to many groups that use test-related data. Teachers, school administrators, and many parents would like to scale tests so a continuous grade-related growth model may be realized for children and adolescents throughout their schooling experience. It is perfectly logical to imagine that a fourth grader should read at the fourth grade level, which should be one grade ahead of third graders and one grade below fifth graders. Test scales should (or so the layperson's reasoning may go) unerringly reflect this intuitive logic. Psychologists, human resource specialists,

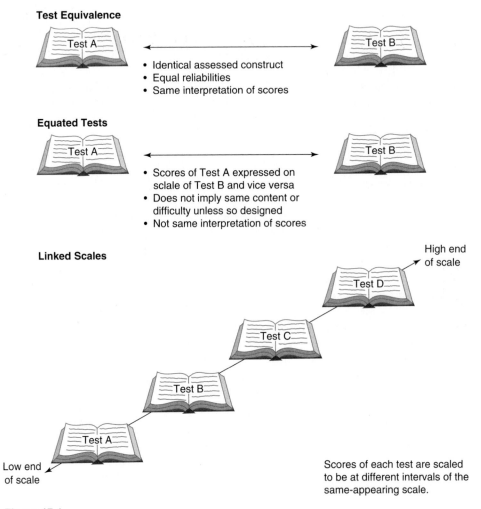

Test Equivalence

Test A ⟷ Test B

- Identical assessed construct
- Equal reliabilities
- Same interpretation of scores

Equated Tests

Test A ⟷ Test B

- Scores of Test A expressed on sclale of Test B and vice versa
- Does not imply same content or difficulty unless so designed
- Not same interpretation of scores

Linked Scales

High end of scale

Test D

Test C

Test B

Test A

Low end of scale

Scores of each test are scaled to be at different intervals of the same-appearing scale.

Figure 15.1
Graphic depiction of some test equivalence terms.

and admissions officers, as well as persons from many other groups, also express a desire for reliably equated scores or equivalent tests.

Possibly the loudest call for equating tests, however, comes from educators and policy makers who seek evaluation results of the Elementary and Secondary Education Act, Title I. The results of this program, as is widely known, rest largely on scores of standardized achievement tests. Each participating school district can select a test that they believe best reflects their own goals and curriculum. The challenge for the program evaluators is to find a way to compare the results from the many diverse test scales. For years, legislators, in particular, held out hope that the program's evaluation could be uniformly done across the variety of tests. The scale of NCEs was originally developed to suit this need. (Although the NCE scale has many features to recommend its use in some circumstances, it is not a uniform measure for equating tests, nor do its developers make such a claim.) However, the goal of exactly linking these many tests is not easily realized.

Both conceptual and technical issues abound, making the task a difficult one indeed. In fact, the technical obstacles are so great that the goal may not ever be fully realized. The prestigious Board on Testing and Assessment of the National Research Council (1999)—a group that included many of the nation's foremost measurement professional—thoroughly studied the difficulty of establishing equivalence between tests and concluded that the development of a single scale to which all (or just many) widely used educational and psychological tests could be linked is simply an impossibility. Their report stated grimly that "comparing the full array of currently administered commercial achievement tests to one another, through the development of a single equivalency or linking scale, is not feasible" (p. 4). In other words, by current means, no "metascale" that would link many widely used educational tests can be devised. The board's somber conclusion is also a requisition to measurement professionals that they interpret test equivalence with extreme accuracy and clarity.

Still, one should not misapply the board's conclusion—they did not suggest that any and all test equivalency and linking of scales or tests are impossible or even undesirable. We know, of course, that in many smaller projects, test equating is done with regularity and often successfully.

Regardless, because equating or linking work is technical, with results frequently circumscribed by arcane language, and because the results are often placed in the hands of untrained persons, there is a high likelihood of misinterpretation of findings. Of course, misstatements about test results are only very rarely made with intent. Nonetheless, this casualness in discussion of technical content by untrained individuals is not healthy. Such danger has long been recognized by professionals within the measurement community. Accordingly, the *Standards* (American Educational Research Association et al., 1999) make a number of stipulations dealing with comparability and equating. Their intent, of course, is to promote appropriate and meaningful use of test scores. Several of the relevant standards are listed in Figure 15.2.

This circumstance reinforces the important role measurement professionals play in the process of test interpretation and use. Measurement professionals working on test equivalence projects must do more than present information, however accurate. They have an ethical responsibility to become involved in appropriate ways with users of the information to ensure the data are properly and meaningfully applied in decision making. Working in the area of test equivalence is tricky business, and any measurement professional or measurement professional should take deliberate care to adhere to high standards of workmanship.

Current Research and Directions

In earlier chapters, I mentioned several important psychometric contributions to establishing test equivalence. Often, research into these areas overlaps with work in scaling and norming. Recall Angoff's (1971) significant chapter in the second edition of the

---

Standards Addressing Linking and Score Comparability

Standard 4.10   A clear rationale and supporting evidence should be provided for any claim that scores earned on different forms of a test may be used interchangeably. In some cases, direct evidence of score equivalence may be provided. In other cases, evidence may come from a demonstration that the theoretical assumptions underlying procedures for establishing score comparability have been sufficiently satisfied. The specific rationale and the evidence required will depend in part on the intended uses for which score equivalence is claimed.

Standard 4.11   When claims of form-to-form score equivalence are based on equating procedures, detailed technical information should be provided on the method by which equating functions or other linkages were established and on the accuracy of equating functions.

Standard 4.12   In equating studies that rely on the statistical equivalence of examinee groups receiving different forms, methods of assuring such equivalence should be described in detail.

Standard 4.13   In equating studies that employ an anchor test design, the characteristics of the anchor test and its similarity to the forms being equated should be presented, including both content specifications and empirically determined relationships among test scores. If anchor items are used, as in some IRT-based and classical equating studies, the representativeness and psychometric characteristics of anchor items should be presented.

Standard 4.14   When score conversions or comparisons procedures are used to relate scores on tests or test forms that are not closely parallel, the construction, intended interpretation, and limitations of those conversions or comparisons should be clearly described.

Standard 4.15   When additional test forms are created by taking a subset of the items in an existing test form or by rearranging its items and there is sound reason to believe that scores on these forms may be influenced by item context effects, evidence should be provided that there is no undue distortion of norms for the different versions or of score linkage between them.

Figure 15.2
Standards relevant to linking and equating scores.
Source: From *Standards for Educational and Psychological Testing* (pp. 160–162), by American Educational Research Association, American Psychological Association, & National Council on Measurement in Education, 1999, Washington, DC: American Educational Research Association. Copyright 1999 by American Educational Research Association.

important *Educational Measurement,* and later, the work by Peterson, Kolen, and Hoover (1989) in the third edition. Both sections provide essential background to persons working with test equivalence. More recently, Kolen and Brennan (2004) authored *Test Equating, Scaling, and Linking: Methods and Practices,* an invaluable resource that covers numerous important issues and gives detailed descriptions of the major techniques, including useful examples. These works are remarkable contributions to the literature and "must-haves" for the library of a serious measurement professional.

Equating Designs

Introduction to Designs

The first point to realize about research designs appropriate to test equating is that the design is itself part of equating. Just as ANOVA as a statistical technique cannot exist apart from a particular research design (e.g., between groups, with fixed or random effects, repeated measures), equivalence procedures cannot occur separately from a research design. More particularly, the design is mainly a matter of logistical aspects of test administration and data collection. Consequently, before a measurement professional or measurement professional may decide on a methodology for equating, much information about the testing program (and especially its administration) must be known. Some questions to ask include: "Are the tests administered simultaneously to the same group of examinees, or will more than one group be involved?" "If two groups are used, how much alike are they?" "What are the individual reliabilities of the tests?" "How many items are common between the tests?"

Obviously, when test administration circumstances can be arranged in advance so a particular research design may be affected, the findings can usually be directed to a desired question or problem needing attention. Just as obviously, it is difficult to fit an equating or linking design post hoc to a testing context.

In this section, the single group equating design and the random groups equating design, as well as three common equating designs, are explained, including the common-item nonequivalent groups equating design. Figure 15.3 previews each

	Random Groups	
	Group 1 (random)	Group 2 (random)
Administered Form	X	Y
	Single Group Counterbalancing Design	
	Group 1 (random)	Group 2 (random)
First Form Administered	X	Y
Second Form Administered	Y	X
	Nonequivalent Groups (Common) Design	
	Group 1	Group 2
Administered Form	X with subset X_1	
Administered Form		Y with subset X_1

Figure 15.3
Schematics showing various research designs useful for equating.

design. Of course, there are more than these three common equating designs but most apply to particular circumstances. Some of these additional designs can be found in varying sources (e.g., Kolen & Brennan, 2004; Petersen et al., 1989).

Even among the three designs to be discussed, none are appropriate to all equating or linking strategies. They are each contextual; which is to say, it matters where they are used. Any of them can fit somewhere but not just anywhere. Knowing which design to use with what method is part of using them properly.

In the following descriptions, assume a conversion for Test Form A, raw scores to scaled scores, has been established, and that Form B is a new form to be equated to Form A. Now, with this introduction, we are ready to turn to the designs themselves.

Single Group Design

The *single group equating design* is simple on its face, although a number of technical and practical considerations require attention for its successful implementation. In the single group equating design, both tests to be equated are administered to all subjects in a group. In other words, both Form A and Form B are administered to the same examinees. In addition, the forms are administered one after another, presumably even on the same day, to minimize the intervening effects of learning, fatigue, or forgetting on performance. This is advantageous because examinees have scores on both forms, and differences in difficulty can be estimated directly from the summary statistics for the two forms without having to address the confounding effect of differences in the groups' ability levels.

For instance, suppose the developer plans to use Form A and Form B as alternate forms, assuming they assess the same construct (an important point in this example), but initially does not know whether they are equally difficult. Both tests are administered to one group of individuals. The tests are administered, scored, and summary statistics are calculated. The test developer discovers that the group obtained a mean score on the first test (Form A) of 48 and a mean of 50 on the second test (Form B). In this elementary illustration, Form A is concluded to be, on average, 2 points more difficult than Form B.

In using this design, and in reaching the conclusion that Form A is more difficult than Form B, it is necessary to assume that an examinee's score on the second form (Form B) is not affected by the fact that he or she had previously taken the first form (Form A). This stipulation is difficult to satisfy in practice. In real world research and production situations, the measurement professional would consider likely sources of error (e.g., nuisance variables, randomization) and attempt to control them to the extent possible. Two common sources of error in this design are fatigue and practice, the former tending to depress scores on the second-administered test form and the latter perhaps inflating them a bit if there is transference between the forms.

To reduce error effects such as fatigue and practice, a *counterbalancing design* is recommended. There are several techniques to achieve counterbalancing. One method is to prepare two test booklets, one each of Form A and Form B, and to simply distribute them during administration by alternating Form A and Form B to every other person. Reverse the process during the second administration so, in the end, half the group took Form A first and B second, and vice versa. This method is called *spiraling,* particularly when there are more than two forms to be administered, as in matrix sampling designs. Variations of this design may be devised, but it is not recommended that the items from both tests be randomly printed on each test booklet because this would not replicate the final tests and the equating relationship would not be preserved.

The single group equating design has the obvious advantage of reducing group heterogeneity because the group comprises the same individuals. Thus, sampling errors—the greatest threat to equating designs—are diminished. Only measurement error remains to be considered.

The standard error in this equating design is calculated as follows:

$$\sigma_{T_{y^*}} = SD_y \sqrt{(1 - \sigma_{XX}) \left[\frac{z_x^2 (1 + \sigma_{XX}) + 2}{N_i} \right]}, \qquad (15.1)$$

where $\sigma_{T_{y^*}}$ = true standard error (by CTT),

   $z_x = x - \bar{X}/s_x$, and

   N_i = total of all groups.

The true standard error of Y is defined when the deviation from the mean of X equals z.

Random Groups Design

Often, practical and logistical exigencies prohibit using the single group equating design. Enter the *random groups equating design,* an important alternative to the single group approach. In this devising, rather than varying items for order of administration, the examinees are randomly divided into two groups (or more if more than two tests are linked). Then, each test form is randomly assigned to a group. In researcher parlance, this is *randomization of subjects* (the examinees) and *random assignment of treatments* (the test forms). A spiraling process is usually used for this design, where alternate examinees in the group are administered either Form A or Form B. This process leads to two comparable, randomly equivalent groups taking Form A and Form B, similar to the single group with counterbalancing design. If large representative groups of examinees are used, then the differences between means on the forms can be a simple, direct indication of the average difference in difficulty between the forms. In using this design, it is important that the groups be as similar as possible with respect to the levels of ability being measured in the test.

Practically speaking, the random groups design is often preferred over the single group design because it shortens testing time and helps adjust for the effects of fatigue and practice on testing scores. This means it is now possible to equate more than one new form at a single administration by including the new forms in the spiraling process. Nonetheless, all forms must be available and administered at the same time, which could be difficult in some situations. Also, because the spiraling process is used for random assignment, any systematic seating of the examinees would defeat the randomness, resulting in less comparable groups. Moreover, in the random groups design, a much larger number of examinees is needed than in the single group design, so each subgroup, although randomly selected, could be presumed to represent the entire population of future examinees. Because the design replaces intersubject variability with intrasubject homogeneity, the counterbalancing is purposeful.

Caution is advised with this design because research demonstrates that randomization is a relatively inefficient way of controlling systematic error, or bias. The standard error of linear equating for this model is given in Equation 15.2:

$$\sigma_{T_{y^*}} = \sqrt{\frac{2S_x^2(z_x^2 + 2)}{N_i}},$$ (15.2)

where $\sigma_{T_{y^*}}$ = true standard error (by CTT),

$z_x = x - \bar{X}/s_x$, and

N_i = total of all groups.

As before, the true standard error of Y is defined when the deviation from the mean of X equals z.

Common-Item Nonequivalent Groups Design

The *common-item nonequivalent groups equating design* is more complex than the previous two and presents additional logistical difficulties, but it is considered superior to single group equating designs because a number of counterbalancing issues are simultaneously addressed. In this model, the procedures of the random group equating design are followed initially (i.e., random selection of individuals for each group and then random assignment of a given test form to each group), with the addition that a subset of items common to both Form A and Form B are administered to both groups. Neither group completes the test forms in their entirety, reducing the effects of lengthened testing time, as well as practice and fatigue. The common-item nonequivalent design is widely used.

Two variations exist for this design, depending on whether the common items will or will not be included in the final score or on the final test instruments. If these common items are included (i.e., they are a subset of items contained on both test forms to be equated or their scores contribute to the examinee's final score on the test), they are said to be *internal*. The internal common items should be interspersed among other items on each test form. However, when the common items constitute a separately administered test (in addition to Form A and Form B), or the score of common items does not contribute to the final score of the test, these common items are referred to as *external*.

However, there are serious threats to this design. First and possibly most problematic is given the fact that the group of examinees taking Test Form A is not equivalent (or more likely, of unknown comparability) to the group of examinees taking Form B, a difference in ability levels between the groups may seriously confound supposed differences in difficulty levels of test forms. Sometimes the difference is so great that no statistical procedure can possibly separate group difference from test difference.

Because of this issue, the items selected to be commonly administered are very important to the success of the design. First, they must be representative of all items and content on the original test form. This may be accomplished by selecting items that cut across the test content specifications. In other words, if 12 items are directed at a specific aspect of the construct, then three or four could be randomly chosen as some of the common items. Second, there must be a sufficient number of common items so reliability among them is not compromised. In addition, the internal common items should be exactly the same and occupy similar positions on both Form A and Form B.

When data are gathered for equating with the common-item nonequivalent groups equating design, the most important consideration is the relationship of the common items to each test form. A correlation coefficient, as one way to asses this relationship, would be a logical first step. This also means that the length and variance of each test form and the common items must be roughly comparable so reliability between each form and the set of common items can be compared. Generally, here, anticipated reliabilities are in the range of 0.8 for each test and a Pearson r of not less than 0.7. Weaker associations may be a marker for not using such a design.

Traditional Equating Methods

When following the precepts of CTT, the two most common methods of equating are *linear equating* and *equipercentile equating*. Although both procedures may be applied to all three equating designs, considerations among the designs differ. In Figures 15.4 to 15.5, we can study the relationship of these methods for two test forms.

These figures show a relationship between two methods that is close and seemingly direct. However, the two methods may not always produce such close correspondence. Close results may only be anticipated when both tests are produced from the same test specifications (giving roughly similar item difficulties between the test forms), both test forms are on the same scale, both are comparatively long tests (e.g., number of items exceeds 30), and the groups from which data are collected are sufficiently large to have scores appearing at most points along the range (roughly, more than 100). Meeting these criteria helps reduce two kinds of error that can influence equating statistics: measurement error and sampling error. With little error, the methods produce similar outcomes.

For these traditional equating methods, the relationship between scores for different forms is established through setting characteristics of the score distributions equal for a particular group of examinees. For instance, in linear equating, the mean

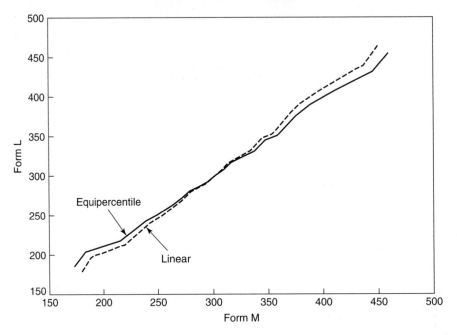

Figure 15.4
Illustration of the closeness of two equating methods with close test forms.

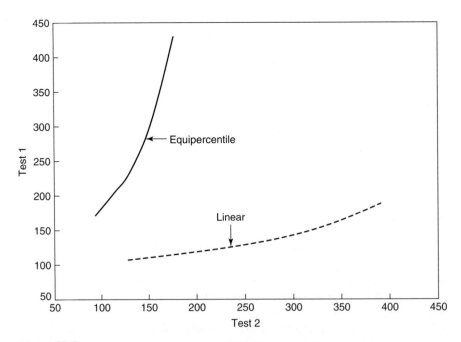

Figure 15.5
Illustration of the dissimilarities of two equating methods with vastly different tests.

and standard deviation on different test forms are set as equal. In equipercentile equating, the score distributions of different test forms are set as equal so they have similar means, standard deviations, and distributional shapes. This further implies that if the test distributions are also close—that is, they have nearly identical skewness and kurtosis indices—the results of linear and equipercentile equating will be practically the same, as shown in Figure 15.4. However, this is far from the result when the tests are different in distributional characteristics and content, the circumstance in Figure 15.5.

Linear Equating

Linear equating is very similar to mere scale transformation, as introduced in chapter 7. As such, it is more suited to the single group equating design. When scores on two test forms are equated, the equated scores are often interpreted as though they have the same standard deviation about the mean. The equating transformation between scores on different tests is always of the form shown in Equation 15.3:

$$l_y(x) = Ax + B, \tag{15.3}$$

where l_y is the linear transformation equation from test score x onto the scale of y, and A and B are parameters estimated from the data, with A slope and B intercept.

When expressing the equating in setting standard scores on two test forms as equal, the transformation is given in Equation 15.4. Note that symbols for a sample (rather than population), mean, and standard deviation are given (e.g., $\overline{X}$, SD_A):

$$\frac{x - \overline{X}}{SD_X} = \frac{y - \overline{Y}}{SD_Y}. \tag{15.4}$$

As is readily recognized in the formula, this relationship is a straight line throughout the scale's range, and differences are expressed in standard deviation units. The difference between any score on the first test (Form A) and its mean is an equal number of standard deviation units from the mean of Form B. The relationship expressed in Equation 15.3 is put into practice with the more convenient form for converting scores given in Equation 15.5 (after rearranging Equation 15.4):

$$l_y(x) = \frac{SD_Y}{SD_X}x + \left(\overline{Y} - \frac{SD_Y}{SD_X}\overline{X}\right), \tag{15.5}$$

which is in the form of Equation 15.3, with $A = \dfrac{SD_Y}{SD_X}$ and $B = \overline{Y} - \dfrac{SD_Y}{SD_X}\overline{X}$. Do not confuse this with a regression model, where the regression equation using x predicting y is different from the regression equation when regressing x on y. On the contrary, in the equating situation, the relationship between x and y is stable regardless of which test score is to be converted.

Consider the example previously described for the single group design, in which the mean on Form A was 48 ($\overline{X}_X = 48$) and the mean on Form B was 50 ($\overline{X}_Y = 50$).

Suppose, too, the standard deviations for the two test forms are $SD_x = 5$ and $SD_y = 6$. The linear transformation equation is then

$$y = \frac{6}{5}x + \left[50 - \frac{6}{5}(48)\right] = 1.2x - 7.6.$$

Once the linear one-to-one relationship between two test forms has been established, it is a straightforward matter to convert any raw score on Form A to be on the same scale on Form B. If x is 60, then $y = (1.2 \times 60) - 7.6 = 64.4$. Likewise, if x is 35, then $y = (1.2 \times 35) - 7.6 = 34.4$. Consequently, it could be easily seen that the difference in difficulty levels between the two forms changes along the possible score range. In this example, the difference for scores around 60 (e.g., $64.4 - 60 = 4.4$) is greater than the difference for scores around the mean (e.g., $50 - 48 = 2$) and around 35 (e.g., $35 - 34.4 = 0.6$).

Linear equating can be directly carried out for simple (i.e., fixed) groups design and random groups design. As this equating does not account for sample effects, administration conditions, and other common sources of error (e.g., fatigue, practice), it is prudent for researchers to employ the method only within the context of a coherent design. Further, linear equating is not recommended with test forms that vary greatly in the difficulty of their items, or when the groups taking each form are heterogeneous in either the construct under appraisal or in some other consideration that may introduce error.

Having established the suitability of the common items for the equating process, it is time to put their yielded information to work, namely, to provide data so the means and standard deviations of Test Forms A and B may be appropriately adjusted. Remember, the overall goal of linear equating with the design is to adjust the means and standard deviations to comparability between Forms A and B. This is accomplished by regression of each test form on the common items.

Linear equating can be applied to the common-item nonequivalent design, where the scores on the common items are used to estimate the means and standard deviations for both Form A and Form B, assuming each examinee had taken both test forms. The design involves two populations. Therefore, it is essential to combine them to have a synthetic population for equating; this is done by adopting certain weights. Because only one form is administered to each group of examinees, the means and standard deviations for those who do not take one form cannot be estimated directly from the given data. Suppose group 1 examinees take Form A and group 2 take Form B; the synthetic population means and variance for Forms A and B would be estimated as shown in Equations 15.6 through 15.9. C represents the common items, as a subtest:

$$\hat{\bar{X}}_T = \bar{X}_A + r_{XC}\frac{SD_X}{SD_C}(\bar{C}_T - \bar{C}_A) \tag{15.6}$$

$$\hat{\bar{Y}}_T = \bar{Y}_A + r_{YC}\frac{SD_Y}{SD_C}(\bar{C}_T - \bar{C}_B) \tag{15.7}$$

$$\hat{\sigma}_X^2 = SD_{X_A}^2 + r_{XC}\frac{SD_X^2}{SD_C^2}(SD_{U_T}^2 - SD_{U_A}^2) \tag{15.8}$$

$$\hat{\sigma}_Y^2 = SD_{Y_B}^2 + r_{YC}\frac{SD_Y^2}{SD_C^2}(SD_{U_T}^2 - SD_{U_B}^2). \qquad (15.9)$$

With these values known, the standard equation can be solved:

$$l_y(x) = \frac{SD_Y}{SD_X}x + \left(\overline{Y} - \frac{SD_Y}{SD_X}\overline{X}\right). \qquad (15.5)$$

Many models have been developed to estimate the means and standard deviations that cannot be directly estimated from the data, each with different statistical assumptions. Tucker and Levine methods are commonly used for this purpose. More detailed illustration can be found in Kolen and Brennan (2004).

Then, too, equating, like other statistical procedures, is not free from random error. One cannot merely assume a particular score on one form will unerringly estimate its equated score on the other form. Thus it is essential and necessary to introduce standard error of equating, an index expressing equating error due to sampling. In addition, standard error of equating helps estimate the sample size needed in equating design to obtain a certain degree of precision in equating and provides a criterion for comparing equating methods, as well as equating designs. For linear equating, the standard error comes from sampling fluctuation in the mean and standard deviation of scores on two test forms. The general formula is given in Equation 15.10:

$$SE[l_y(x)] = \left\{\left(\frac{SD_y^2}{2}\right)\left(2 + \frac{(x - \overline{X})^2}{SD_x^2}\right)\left(\frac{1}{N_y} + \frac{1}{N_x}\right)\right\}^{\frac{1}{2}}, \qquad (15.10)$$

where $l_y(x)$ = transformed scores on scale Y for a fixed value x of X,

N_y = sample size for Form B, and

N_x = sample size for Form A.

Equipercentile Equating

Equipercentile equating, as the name implies, is matching percentiles on two tests. Then, the raw or scaled scores associated with a particular percentile can be read for either test. This method of test equating is theoretically similar to linear equating but computationally more complex. Still, it is within the scope of most statistical programs, with possibly only straightforward syntax or a direct command statement. Assuming identical score distribution shapes for the two forms, the method of equipercentile forms the equating relationship by setting the scores for two forms with the same percentile rank to be equal. The median (the 50th percentile) of raw scores of the group taking Test Form A are related and equated to the median score of the group taking Test Form B. Similarly, the raw scores of each percentile point (or other fractile) are equated so the proportions of scores below the equated raw scores for Forms A and B are the same. The generalized procedure means that the method can work successfully in a broader array of testing situations than can linear equating, particularly when the distributions are not similar.

The definition of equipercentile equating suggests that the cumulative distribution function of scores on Form A converted to the Form B scale is the same as the distribution function of scores on Form B. The theory assumes the distributions of scores are continuous, but test scores are more often than not discrete. One example would be number right scores, which only take the integer values and hence are considered as categorical. Thus, one common approach is to view the discrete scores as continuous by adopting percentiles or percentile ranks.

Because the interest in equipercentile equating is to find a score on Form B that has the same percentile rank as a score on Form A, the general formula of the Form B equipercentile equivalent of score x on Form A is

$$e_y(x) = y = Q^{-1}[P(x)], \qquad -0.5 \leq x \leq n_x - 0.5, \qquad \textbf{(15.11)}$$

where $e_y(x)$ = symmetric distribution function for converting score x on
            Form A to the Form B scale,

   Q^{-1} = inverse of percentile rank function for Form B,

   $P(x)$ = percentile rank of x on Form A, and

   n_x = number of items on Form A.

Equation 15.11 suggests that two steps are involved in finding the equipercentile equivalent of score x on the scale of Form B: First, the percentile rank of x on Form A is calculated according to its own distribution, and then the corresponding Form B score that has the same percentile rank is found in the Form B distribution. Equation 15.11 is symmetric in that it can also be used for finding the Form A equipercentile equivalent of score y on Form B, only in its inverse form, $e_x(y) = P^{-1}[Q(y)]$.

In practice, usually just a small number of the 99 percentiles are used, say 6 to 10 fractiles (e.g., the 2nd, 16th, 25th, 50th, 75th, 84th, and 98th). The more fractiles employed for direct comparison, the more accurate the estimation between scales. There are also obvious practical considerations. First, the scale must be relatively long to allow meaningful discrimination between percentiles. If, for instance, the scale has only 30 points, there will inevitably be a large gap when raw scores are converted to percentiles. Usually, one way to avoid the limit range and discreteness is to make the groups sufficiently large to accommodate a spread of scores. Those observed scores should not be overly skewed but should range within ±3 skewness and ±3 kurtosis (as a rough guide). This latter consideration will produce overestimation at highly represented raw score values and underestimation at all other raw score values.

Curve-smoothing strategies can be employed to partially accommodate gaps and anomalies in the scores to reduce random error. A wide variety of smoothing techniques, such as rolling weighted average, kernel estimates, and moving medians can be found in readily available sources (Angoff & Schrader, 1984; Fairbank, 1985; Tapia & Thompson, 1978; Tukey, 1977). Smoothing techniques are conceptually appealing, but many require methods beyond the scope of this text.

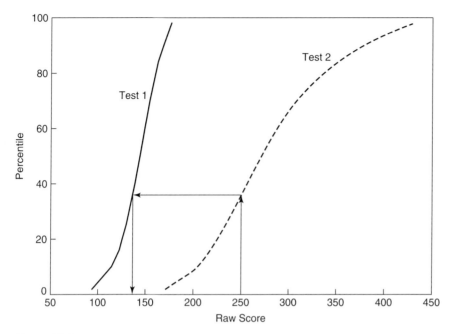

Figure 15.6
Graphic illustration of equipercentile equating process.

An example of equipercentile equating for two different tests is given in Table 15.1. Notice that the score ranges (including minimum and maximum observed scores) are far apart for the tests, although their distributions (see skew and standard error) are not. The correspondence between scores on the tests is simply read from the equivalent percentiles. At the median, for instance, a score of approximately 144 on Test 1 is equated to a score of about 270 on Test 2. It is important to remember that this equating does not imply equivalence in content between the two instruments, unless they have been developed from identical test specifications.

Based on the data in Table 15.1, percentile ranks for the two tests are plotted and shown in Figure 15.6, where the two lines represent the discrete frequency distributions of scores on Test 1 and Test 2. To find the equipercentile equivalent of a score on one test, just find the other test score with the same percentile rank. The arrows in Figure 15.6 illustrate this procedure. They show that a score of 250 on Test 2 has the same percentile rank as a score of about 135 on Test 1. Thus, 250 on one test scale is the equipercentile equivalent of 135 on the other.

The equivalents of the scores for the two tests can also be plotted, using the same information in Table 15.1. Similarly, Figure 15.7 illustrates that a score of 140 on Test 1 can be converted to 260 on the Test 2 scale.

A close examination of Figure 15.7 reveals a problem with the method of equipercentile equating. The equivalents of the scores do not cover the entire range

Table 15.1
Descriptive Statistics and Selected Percentiles for Equipercentile Equating

		Test 1	Test 2
N	Valid	1066	1239
	Missing	0	305
Mean		141.8949	281.4173
Standard error of mean		0.625921	1.855223
Median		143.6818	270.35
Mode		148	213
Standard deviation		20.4361	65.30279
Variance		417.634	4264.455
Skewness		−0.54169	0.528001
Standard error of skewness		0.074918	0.069505
Kurtosis		0.126405	−0.34248
Standard error of kurtosis		0.149697	0.138898
Range		117	315
Minimum		66	148
Maximum		183	463
Sum		151260	348676
Percentiles	2	94	172
	10	114	205
	16	123	217
	20	126	223
	25	130	233
	30	133	241
	40	138	256
	50	144	270
	60	149	289
	70	154	310
	75	157	324
	80	160	338
	84	162	352
	90	168	379
	98	176	430

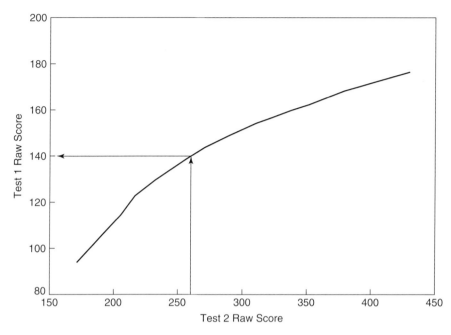

Figure 15.7
Equivalent raw scores on the two tests.

of raw scores on both tests. The reason is simply that the maximum and minimum observed scores on Test A and Test B are converted to each other because they have the same percentile rank. Thus, when the observed scores do not cover the possible raw score range, the equivalents will, in turn, never cover the possible raw score range. This leads to an extrapolation, with the danger of introducing large errors. To avoid this, the two tests should be parallel forms, and the two groups of examinees should be kept as homogeneous as possible. And, the smoothing discussed above will help here, too.

Equipercentile equating can be applied to all three designs mentioned previously. Similar to linear equating, applying it to the single group design assumes that factors such as fatigue or practice do not affect the second test scores; applying it to the random groups design assumes that the differences between the two groups are small enough to be ignored. The application of the equipercentile equating method to common-item nonequivalent design is more complicated because there are differences in the abilities of the examinees and in the difficulties of the test forms. Therefore, to implement the method requires frequency distributions to be estimated for the forms that would have been obtained if every examinee had taken both forms. Thus, the common items are used to adjust the difference between groups: The scores from both groups are combined and used to simulate the frequency distributions for both test forms that would have been obtained if the two groups had taken each of them. A more detailed procedure of simulating distributions can be found in Kolen and Brennan (2004). When the correlations between scores on the common-items subtest and each form's total scores are relatively small, it would be advised to ignore the common-item information to reduce equating error. In this situation, equating can take place by applying the equipercentile method to the data in the same manner as with the random groups design.

Standard errors of equipercentile equating quantify the amount of random errors that are due to random fluctuations in the cumulative frequency distributions of scores on Forms A and B. The standard errors can be estimated either asymptotically or through a bootstrap procedure. Equation 15.12 shows one form's asymptotic derivation:

$$SE[e_y(x)] = \left\{ \sigma_y^2 (pq/\phi^2) \left(\frac{1}{N_y} + \frac{1}{N_x} \right) \right\}^{\frac{1}{2}}, \qquad (15.12)$$

where p = proportion of scores below x on Test Form A,

$q = 1 - p$, and

ϕ = value of the standard normal score below which p of the cases fall.

The equating error is the standard deviation of the transformed scores $e_y(x)$ on the scale of Test Form B for a fixed value of x on Form A.

IRT-Based Methods

Linear Equating IRT

The precision of equating by traditional methods depends on the test forms used and the characteristics of the particular groups of examinees tested. This means that only observed scores are used in the conversion, and no inference can be made to scores beyond those at hand. More specifically, as we know, with CTT-based equating methods the examinees should be random samples of one population and the test forms must be reasonably parallel (i.e., they measure the same ability and have equal content, difficulty, and reliability). In many testing contexts, the presumption of strictly parallel test forms is not easy to satisfy because most often two tests will exhibit varying difficulties and likely will have unequal reliabilities. Under such circumstances, observed scores cannot be reliably equated. IRT methods for equating and linking are based on likelihood functions, and therefore present an alternative to the traditional methods. Fortunately, under rules of likelihood expressions, these difficulties may be overcome.

One of the advantages of IRT models over the classical testing models is that the item parameter estimates are relatively invariant across populations, a point we study in chapter 10. The conversion using IRT methods should be independent of the groups used in equating. This presents us with an opportunity for employing IRT in test equivalence models. The general idea behind IRT equating is to place parameter estimations on a common scale so the ability or proficiency estimates for an individual will be the same, regardless of what test form is taken. This obviates the need for equipercentile equating and demonstrates that simple linear transformations are often adequate.

There are generally two common procedures for putting the item parameters for two tests on the same scale. One process calibrates the parameters for examinees and for items on both forms simultaneously. It is important to realize that when using this procedure, common examinees or common items are needed to tie the data for the two tests together to ensure both item and ability parameter estimates are on a common scale.

The other IRT-based procedure is to estimate all the parameters from separate calibrations, and then the two sets of estimated parameters for a set of common items are used to construct a transformation. Note that with this approach, the parameter estimates should not differ in the single group or random groups design. Because of the indeterminacy property of IRT parameter scales, normal distributions are more likely and the transformation between parameter estimates for the common items is a simple linear one. This is solved by definition, by setting the means and standard deviations of the distributions to 1 and 0, respectively.

As an example, suppose a three-parameter logistic IRT model has been chosen for the given data with the form (the 3PL model described in chapter 10):

$$P_i(\theta) = c_i + (1 - c_i)\frac{1}{1 + e^{Da_i(\theta - b_i)}}.$$

Clearly, $P_i(\theta)$ is a function of $a_i(\theta - b_i)$. If the parameters θ, b_i, and a_i are transformed to give θ^*, b_i^*, and a_i^* as the following equations show:

$$\theta^* = A\theta + B, \tag{15.13}$$
$$b_i^* = Ab_i + B, \text{ and} \tag{15.14}$$
$$a_i^* = \frac{1}{A}a_i. \tag{15.15}$$

where A and B are arbitrary constants. Then, after several simple steps of calculations, we see that $a_i^*(\theta^* - b_i^*)$ is equal to $a_i(\theta - b_i)$ and so the item response function $P_i(\theta)$ is unchanged. This also applies to other logistic and ogive models for $P_i(\theta)$. Therefore, the metric of the ability scale is arbitrary. Any scale can be chosen for θ as long as the same scale is used for b_i. This further suggests that if a_is and b_is of a set of items are estimated separately using two different groups of examinees, the two sets of estimated parameters will not be identical and the ability estimates will not be on the same scale. However, a linear relationship between ability estimates can be established using Equation 15.13. Various methods have been developed to estimate A (the slope) and B (the intercept) for this linear transformation. Momentarily, we see a program where this is put into practice in one context. For a detailed discussion of such procedures, see Stocking and Lord (1983).

If the ability estimates can be used for reporting, the equating is completed once the parameter estimates are put on the same scale. However, often the reporting of ability estimates is not feasible in that the interpretation is not that obvious and simple. Thus, true score can be used for equating by translating the ability estimates into the corresponding estimated true scores for test forms. If two test forms measure the same ability θ, then the relation between estimated true score and the ability are shown in Equations 15.16 and 15.17:

$$T_x = \sum_{i=1}^{n_x} P_i(\theta) \tag{15.16}$$

$$T_y = \sum_{j=1}^{n_y} P_j(\theta). \tag{15.17}$$

BILOG-MG Equating Procedures

Because BILOG-MG is probably the most popular IRT program employed for large-scale programs, it may be worthwhile to demonstrate some equating with it. This example uses equivalent groups equating design. Figure 15.8 shows a BILOG syntax file with the needed statements. Note particularly in the SCO (score) command that the rescaling is type 3 and that the location and scale values are given so examinee scores are reported similarly, regardless of test form taken. Rescaling constants are shown in Figure 15.9.

In this procedure, it is evident that linear transformation is all that is needed to reported examinees on the same scale, regardless of test form. This is an important result that should be studied closely.

```
TEST FORMS
>COMMENTS
College BASE data for equivalent groups equating design.

>GLOBAL   DFNAME='CB_items.DAT', NPARM=2, SAVE;
>SAVE     SCORE=''CB_items.SCO', PARM=''CB_items.PAR';
>LENGTH   NITEMS=50;
>INPUT    NTOT=50, NFORM=2, KFNAME=''CB_items.DAT', NALT=5,NIDCH=5;
>ITEMS    INUM=(1(1)50), INAME=(T01(1)T50);
>TEST     TNAME=CB;
>FORM1    LENGTH=25, INUM=(1(1)25);
>FORM2    LENGTH=25, INUM=(21(1)50);
(9A1,T1,I1,T7,25A1)
>CALIB    FIXED, FLOAT, NQPT=31, TPRIOR, PLOT=.05;
>SCORE    METHOD=1, RSCTYPE=3, LOCATION=300, SCALE=65, NOPRINT, INFO=1;
```

Figure 15.8
Illustrative BILOG-MG syntax for equivalent groups equating.

```
┌────────────────────────────────────────────────────────┐
│                                                        │
│    RESCALING WITH RESPECT TO SAMPLE DISTRIBUTION       │
│    ------------------------------------------------    │
│                                                        │
│              RESCALING       CONSTANTS                 │
│     TEST       SCALE         LOCATION                  │
│     SIM        43.762        249.749                   │
│                                                        │
└────────────────────────────────────────────────────────┘
```

Figure 15.9
Scaling constants for equating in BILOG.

Observed Score IRT Equating

Observed scores can also be equated under the IRT framework. If the item response functions $P_i(\theta)$ for n items in one test are identical, then the frequency of number right score x for person A would be

$$f(x \mid \theta_a) = \binom{n}{x} P^x Q^{n-x}, \qquad (15.18)$$

where $P = P(\theta_a)$ and $Q = 1 - P$. The marginal distribution of number right scores x for a group of N examinees on each test can be calculated using Equation 15.19:

$$f(x) = \sum_{a=1}^{N} f(x \mid \theta_a). \qquad (15.19)$$

After the marginal distributions are obtained with all item parameters and all groups on a common scale, the raw scores on two tests can be equated with them using equipercentile equating methodology.

Summary

This chapter focuses on understanding test equivalence. I explain practical and accepted definitions for test equivalence, test equating, and linking tests. Because this area of measurement is fraught with misleading information and ill-founded interpretations, there are words of caution about fostering proper interpretations when working with test equivalence. I also discuss some equating designs, as well as examine common equating methods, both those based on CTT and more that follow IRT estimations.

Chapter 16

Test Administration: Modes and Special Considerations

Introduction

Finding Innovation

The electronic numerical integrator and computer ENIAC was the world's first digital computer. Its creators applied for a patent in 1947, but they had begun developing the computer much earlier, around 1935. This was a period in history between the United States' involvement in World Wars I and II, when most of the nations of Europe and Asia were heavily engaged in fighting among themselves. Although the war's many fronts were "over there," the issues were global, and, generally, people realized that it was only a matter of time before America would be pulled into the conflict. Some in the U.S. Army portentously believed our military was woefully unprepared for war, and a military preparedness effort was begun.

Part of the drive to get the services ready for war was to learn about contemporary ordnance, including their likely trajectories, ranges, and degrees of accuracy. Formulas were available for such calculations, but they were tedious (just a few calculations took the combined efforts of a host of trained military personnel) and many thousands were needed. ENIAC, as a numerical counting machine, was held out as the solution to getting the work done. This new device used a rudimentary form of binary logic, allowing it to perform the four algebraic functions, find square roots, and even discriminate the sign of a number. It was powered by 19,000 vacuum tubes and was huge, taking up an entire room and weighing more than 30 tons. By all measures, the machine was extraordinary.

Even today, it is awe inspiring to realize that such a monster spawned many of the elements that compose today's advanced computers: electrical gates, buffers, and a modified Eccles-Jordan flip-flop as a logical, high-speed storage-and-control device. More remarkable is the fact that, aside from a few military planners, no one seemed particularly interested in ENIAC. It would be more than 20 years after it was declassified before the potential for mass computing power would begin to catch the eye of imaginative engineers at IBM and a few upstart entrepreneurs like Bill Gates, Steve Jobs, and Steve Wozniak. Finally, years after silently paving the way for the electronic revolution that changed the world, the power to ENIAC was turned off at 11:45 p.m. on October 2, 1955. By then it had been overtaken by more modern machines. We owe much to engineers from the U.S. Army and IBM who developed ENIAC.

In measurement science, we are well past the ENIAC stage of crude development, but there is still a long way to go. Some of our contemporary advances are taking us mightily down the developmental path, as we see in this chapter.

Contents

In this chapter, numerous specialized issues pertinent to tests, many of which revolve around test administration and the use of computers in testing, are addressed. It is here that two seemingly disparate areas come together for measurement professionals and others concerned with testing: technology and social outlook. Both areas—advances in technology and changes in social perspective—give impetus for special concerns about how tests can and should be administered.

New Issues, New Concerns

To proclaim that measurement science has evolved significantly over the past century or that technological changes are making assessment more convenient and purposeful than ever is scarcely a remarkable insight. The use of computers in mental measurement is possibly the most evident example. Their ever-advancing sophistication has created many possibilities for better assessment. We have already seen how IRT, a theory developed before the age of computers but advanced only after their use became widespread, owes much to technology. Then, too, technological advances have brought us a more convenient test administration, with assessment becoming more suited to capturing individual differences.

Less apparent but just as significant is the fact that our fast-evolving times have brought to the fore other assessment concerns that were long overdue. For instance, the measurement community now takes seriously concerns about protecting examinee rights and of being responsive when testing individuals with special needs. Other issues are just now being appreciated for their importance to proper and purposeful mental measurement. The following list illustrates some of these issues but is far from a comprehensive recitation. Some new measurement concerns include:

- Altering administration procedures to accommodate individuals with disabilities
- Providing valid tests in a language other than English
- Increasing our awareness of cultural implications during assessment
- Upholding examinee rights to privacy and confidentiality of assessment data
- Promoting the concept that test results contribute to proper decision making only when viewed as part of a particular context (and it should not be the sole basis on which a decision is based)
- Devising appraisals that more directly represent the construct (rather than using the proximal stimulus of item formats)
- Administering tests and reporting results via the Internet
- Incorporating technological advances, such as computer-adaptive testing and interactive, touch-screen technology and even voice recognition

- Introducing computer-driven scoring schemes, such as character- and handwriting recognition so examinees may conveniently construct an original answer on a computer screen or on a scannable answer document
- Increasing the integration of learning into the appraisal activity

This chapter focuses on these issues, but some of them have been mentioned or discussed elsewhere in this book.

Computer and Test Administration

Computerized testing is one of the most remarkable inventions of the late 20th century and a topic worthy of study in itself. For our more limited purpose, however, we should realize that a computer is typically employed in test administration in one of two ways: either with a *computer-administered test (CAT)* or with *computer-adaptive testing* (often shortened to *adaptive testing*, or sometimes called *tailored testing* or *individual testing*). There are vast differences between these modes of administration, although in both cases an examinee sits in front of a terminal for test administration and responds to the on-screen commands. We examine each idea for its own merits. Also, the International Test Commission has prepared a set of guidelines on Internet-delivered testing (*http://www.intestcom.org/itc_projects.htm.* Retrieved March 10, 2005).

Computer-Administered Tests

CAT is a sort of catchall term meaning that an appraisal is presented on a computer to an examinee in various ways and for different purposes. It may mean simply that an electronic version of a paper-and-pencil instrument is posted on some Web site. The examinee can be at any computer and log on to that site. Then the examinee reads the test's items or exercises on the screen, and possibly clicks on an icon or radio button to select a response, or there may be a line or space for the examinee to supply the response by typing on the keyboard. An example of a CAT is displayed in Figure 16.1. Of course, ensuring that the individual sitting in front of the screen is as reported or that he or she is indeed working alone are two important issues of CAT that are discussed momentarily.

Regardless, the advantages of CAT are numerous, but perhaps the foremost is that the scoring can be immediate, so examinees receive their results almost immediately on completion of the appraisal. Sometimes this feedback is item by item, although at other times it is programmed to appear at the end of the assessment for a whole test score. Of course, much more information can also be provided, such as a corresponding grade or percentile rank. Most standardized CAT programs at least provide raw scoring.

Another advantage to CAT is that it can easily accommodate *on-demand testing,* the circumstance in which the test is given at the examinee's convenience. Depending on the assessment program's policies, the examinee may, often at his or her convenience, simply log on to a secure Web site or insert a supplied CD-ROM (or other media) into a computer's drive.

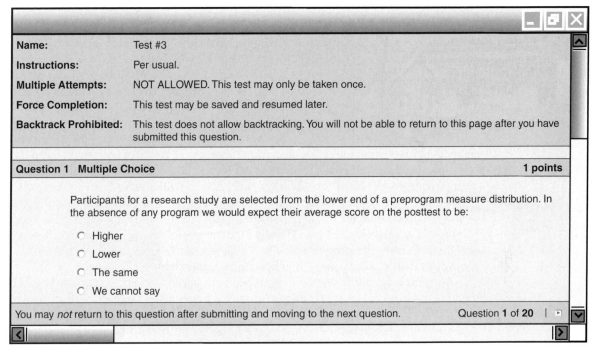

Figure 16.1
Screenshot as an example of a computer-administered test.

For test administrators, there are also advantages. For one, CAT is usually much cheaper because there is no printing of tests, securing of administration sites, or training of test administrators. Test developers can change questions easily, discarding poor ones or presenting alternate forms to other examinees or repeat test takers. The data are automatically collected in electronic format, obviating the need to scan answer sheets or hand-score tests. Accuracy is assured.

Of course, program needs and stipulations are the deciding factor when using CAT. For instance, in licensing and certification programs, examinees may be located across the country or even across the globe. CAT is a convenient way to reach them, as well as to keep the test updated with changes in content or other requirements.

Computers and Test Security

Employing a computer in test administration brings into focus special concerns for test security, as well as for examinees' rights to privacy. These issues are not new to testing, but with CAT they do require heightened attention and sensitivity. Obviously, when a test is remotely administered, there is concern that the examinee responding to the CAT is, in fact, the intended person. There are two ways in which this may be confirmed. In some circumstances, it may be acceptable to simply trust the person to accurately state his or her true identity (and perhaps require the test taker to digitally sign a code of ethical behavior). For some low-stakes appraisals, such as questionnaires and some surveys, this level of security may be adequate. However, when more security is warranted, it may be necessary to require examinees to come to a designated locale, present authentic identification, and take the test there. Most colleges and universities have a testing center designed for this purpose; a few private companies also offer this service. In either case, the cost is very high, and often there are logistical problems, such as the driving distance and the number of computers available.

CAT also has other security concerns because computer hackers can write malicious code to intrude into a secure testing site. Regrettably, hackers seem happy to keep pace (or often even a little ahead) with honest programmers who write software designed to protect Web site security. Each side is working furiously to keep one step ahead of the other. In 1994, the *Washington Post* lead with a story headlined, "Computerized Graduate Exam Called Easy Mark," and printed another article titled, "Computer Admissions Test Found to be Ripe for Abuse" (as cited in Davey & Nering, 2002). Since then, the problems have only increased. This is an area of concern that cannot be treated lightly. It even impacts each nation's homeland security.

With hacking, items that are developed and field-tested on a computer are vulnerable to copying by unscrupulous or ignorant persons. A large pool of items that requires continued updating by administration to large numbers of persons is also susceptible to corruption. Accomplished hackers can break into sets of electronic data. Even a simple screen snapshot can compromise test security.

Fortunately, the field is beginning to shift attention to this area. The American Psychological Association (APA; 1999) has initiated a discussion of test security concerns, and much of the discussion centers on computer security. Still, there is much work to be done. These are important issues for CAT.

Computer-Adaptive Testing

Description of Adaptive Testing

Computer-adaptive testing—also known as adaptive testing, tailored testing, or individual testing—is a variant of CAT. It is a special application of IRT, wherein each examinee's proficiency or ability parameter is estimated *while* the examinee takes the test. In other words, the ability or proficiency estimation does not commence only when the full complement of items has been presented to the individual, but it is done iteratively—and interactively—as the examinee is presented with each subsequent item. In the procedure, only items optimally matched to the ability or proficiency parameter as estimated during each iteration are presented to the examinee. In this manner, an examinee's proficiency or ability estimate is from a unique set of items. Because the pool of items is calibrated beforehand, the item parameters are known, and hence, the examinee's ability parameter estimate can be numerically transformed to the same scale as the items, thereby allowing individuals' scores to be compared.

The features of computer-adaptive testing make it both intuitively and technically appealing. First, and principally, because only items optimally suited (or within practical limits) to a particular examinee are presented, each person takes a test appropriate to his or her proficiency or ability in the domain. Items too easy or too difficult for the estimated ability are not presented. This is where the alternate names of "tailored testing" or "individual testing" derive. In addition, because only a suitable set of items is presented to an examinee, the standard error at that particular ability level is minimized. Some psychometricians have described this feature of computer-adaptive testing as its main rationale (e.g., Folk & Smith, 2002).

Second, computer-adaptive testing allows for many domains to be tested, and item pools can be changed and updated regularly to accommodate new information. This is a boon to test developers. Third, as with other computer-assisted testing schemes, the scoring is immediate, so examinees receive feedback without delay.

To be sure, there are difficulties and disadvantages to computer-adaptive testing. Among these is the fact that it is theoretically and mathematically demanding, making it unapproachable except by highly trained specialists. Hence, a classroom teacher could not implement computer-adaptive testing. There are no off-the-shelf computer programs available; each implementation is customized for a particular testing application.

In addition, computer-adaptive testing requires a very large pool of previously calibrated test items, something else not easily obtained. As is readily imagined, the expense of preparing and implementing a computer-adaptive testing assessment program is enormous, sometimes costing millions of dollars. Few organizations and almost no individuals have this amount of money to invest in an assessment program. Computer-adaptive testing is implemented only by large organizations with deep pockets and a staff of highly trained specialists. Nonetheless, some exceptional assessment programs do implement computer-adaptive testing. Likely, the best known example is the Graduate Records Examination (GRE). Computer-adaptive testing is also used in the Department of Defense's Computer Adaptive Test—Armed Services Vocational Aptitude Battery (Computer Adaptive Test-ASVAB), as well as in some licensing and certification programs like the Law School Admission Test (LSAT).

Despite practical exigencies against computer-adaptive testing, it is theoretically appealing, and current research work is advancing the schema dramatically (e.g., Drasgow, 2002). For measurement professionals, it is interesting to study computer-adaptive testing, and as more is learned about it, additional ways will be invented to use it more broadly. Computer-adaptive testing indeed has a bright future.

Computer-Adaptive Testing: A Scenario

The following scenario will help one to understand computer-adaptive testing in a practical application. Suppose one has developed a coherent rationale for computer-adaptive testing in a particular assessment program and has also defined the content domain sufficiently to develop a test. A further step in the process may be to construct a large pool of test items and to field-test them on a population with known characteristics. Then, the test developer would carefully scrutinize the items by both classical and IRT-based analyses so item characteristics may be identified and catalogued. For a computer-adaptive testing pool, there must be many items covering different aspects of the domain at different levels of difficulty and discrimination. It follows, then, that parameter estimates (at whatever number the test developer decides is appropriate) are calculated prior to implementing computer-adaptive testing.

Next, the test developer could detail who may be eligible to take the exam because potential examinees must possess characteristics similar to those exhibited in the calibration sample for the scores to be meaningfully interpreted.

At this point, the test developer has a number of technical questions to address, including:

1. What is an appropriate starting point for the computer-adaptive testing estimation of a given examinee?
2. What criteria should be used to select items to present to the examinee at any particular iteration of the ability/proficiency estimation?
3. At what point should the estimation iteration stop?

Most computer-adaptive testing programs address the first question by presenting all examinees with a beginning set of items of varying parameter estimates. These are called *anchor items*. Typically, a computer-adaptive testing will have 8 to 16 anchor items. The anchor items provide an initial response set from which the pattern of correct-to-incorrect responses can be used to make the IRT-based proficiency or ability estimates.

From the initial estimate of the examinee's proficiency, the test developer's answer to question 2 churns into the program to determine which item from among a pool of items is presented next to the examinee. Once the examinee response to this item is entered, the next iteration can begin. With this additional item, the response pattern is now more informative, and the parameter estimation can be done again. The process is iterative and interactive, and presumably becomes more accurate as the response pattern reveals more information.

The computer-adaptive testing program keeps track of the change in ability parameter estimation at each cycle. As more items are presented, the response patterns become more informative, the estimation is more exact, and a smaller change in the ability parameter estimate is evidenced. The test developer has previously answered question 3, and here this decision comes into play. When the ability parameter estimate change is sufficiently small, the program stops and the final estimate (usually in a log metric of typical IRT calibration estimates) is transformed to the common scale for reporting. This is the examinee's final score, ready for interpretation.

From what we previously learned about IRT estimation procedures, we know that the more consistent the pattern of responses by an examinee, the quicker the change in estimate between cycles diminishes, until further precision in estimation is deemed unnecessary. Because examinees will evidence different response patterns, the number of test items needed in a computer-adaptive testing program to reach satisfactory ability estimation will differ. Hence, examinees are presented with varying numbers of test items.

Although technically justified, the fact that examinees have tests of varying lengths that are reported on the same scale is difficult for many laypersons to comprehend. Often, they ask psychometricians for a simple explanation. Their question presents psychometricians with a challenge because test users must have confidence in the scores they use to make informed decisions. Although it is not necessary for laypersons and policy makers to understand technical features of computer-adaptive testing, it is important that relevant parties accept and have confidence that computer-adaptive testing is appropriate for their program. Here, too, measurement professionals play a vital role.

Learning More About Computer-Adaptive Testing

There are many sources from which to learn about computer-adaptive testing. Probably, the most authoritative book on the subject is still Wainer, Dorans, Flaughter, Green, Steinberg, and Thissen (2000) *Computerized Adaptive Testing: A Primer*, although much research published in technical journals is now surpassing the information in some of its chapters. A more current book on the subject, edited by Mills, Potenza, Fremer, and Ward (2002), contains a number of insightful essays on technical issues, as well as policy and procedural concerns. Further, Weiss (2004) compiled an extensive bibliography of research related to computer-adaptive testing, comprising more than 200 entries, and he maintains an instructive CAT Web site (see *http://www.psych.umn.edu/psylabs/CATCentral/*).

International Test Use and Computer Use

As the use of computers in testing becomes more widespread, it is apparent that issues in international test use will also grow in importance. The International Test Commission (ITC) is an organization devoted to addressing relevant concerns. The council for this group has prepared a set of guidelines entitled *ITC Guidelines on Test Use* for measurement professionals working in this area (see *http://www. intestcom.org*. Retrieved March 10, 2005). These guidelines present relevant information clearly and succinctly, and are a welcome addition to the professional literature.

Modern Scoring via Computers

The computer, of course, also has much to offer for innovative scoring, beyond the scanning of Mark Reflex or Transoptic scannable, bubble answer sheets. Pearson NCS, the largest builder and marketer of scanning equipment, is developing machines for both letter and handwriting recognition, although the latter is still not accurate enough for use in high-stakes testing programs.

One scheme that has current usefulness is one in which the examinee responds by writing in a designated box on a scannable answer sheet. When the answer sheet is scanned, a boxed-in area is converted to a graphic, which can then be displayed on a terminal. Trained personnel can see the graphic and make a judgment according to some predetermined scoring rubric. In practice, this technique has been successfully employed in many testing programs that require a written response by the examinee. A leader in this area is Ellis Page of Duke University, who has researched computer scoring of student essays and maintains that it can be reliably done to at least 87% accuracy (Page, 1994). A Web site describes his Project Essay Grader (PEG; see *http://134.68.49.185/pegdemo/MODEL.ASP*. Retrieved March 10, 2005). Others have also developed computer-based scoring methods. For instance, the ETS has developed a system that processes natural language (see *http://www.ets.org/research/erater.html*. Retrieved March 10, 2005).

Finally, there are software programs available that facilitate computer administration of exams and provide automatic scoring. These vary in quality, but one popular one is MICROTEST, offered by Pearson Education (see *http://www.chariot.com/microtest/index.asp*. Retrieved March 10, 2005). Knowledge Analysis Technologies, a private company, offers Intelligent Essay Assessor, which is described as "a proprietary web-based service . . . that automatically evaluates a student's writing skills and knowledge, and provides scoring and diagnostic feedback to both the instructor and student" (see *http://www.knowledge-technologies.com/*. Retrieved March 10, 2005). Such innovative thinking will certainly advance automated grading of essays.

Test Security and Copyright

The security of testing is an issue of great importance, both in terms of keeping instruments secure for future administration and in terms of protecting an author's copyright for intellectual property. It is obvious that paper-and-pencil tests should be kept in locked, secure storage until they are to be used. Even then, a "chain-of-custody" arrangement may need to be established to reduce the possibility of miscommunication as to who is responsible for them at any given time. The *Standards* (American Educational Research Association, American Psychological Association, & National Council on Measurement in Education, 1999) stipulates that persons who hold tests have a responsibility to keep them secure. Standard 5.7 stipulates that "test users have the responsibility of protecting the security of the test materials at all times" (p. 64). Test proctors—who in Britain, Ireland, and some other European countries are called *Invigilators*—can play an important role here, too.

The other issue of test security—protecting intellectual property—is just as important. Sometimes, students, researchers, teachers, or others may come across a test and be tempted to peremptorily use it for some purpose, such as appraisal or research without consideration of ownership. This is a breach of ethics. One should always contact the test's author and seek permission first. Says, the APA (1999) on test security:

> It is safest for authors to assume that all tests are protected by copyright, even if the work does not contain a copyright notice. Copyright vests in a work from the moment it is created, and neither a formal copyright notice nor registration at the U.S. Copyright Office in Washington, DC, is required. (p. 1078)

Measurement professionals have an obligation to attend to both aspects of test security.

The Americans with Disabilities Act and Testing

The American with Disabilities Act of 1990 (Public Law 101-336), commonly called the ADA (see *http://www.usdoj.gov/crt/ada/pubs/ada.txt*. Retrieved March 10, 2005), was passed by the 101st Congress and signed into law by President George H. Bush on July 26, 1990. The law is designed to heighten sensitivity to persons who have a disability, and protect their federal rights in employment and in other public circumstances. The ADA prohibits discrimination and ensures persons with disabilities have equal opportunities for employment, state and local government services, public accommodations, commercial facilities, and transportation.

Information about the ADA is plentiful and easily available from many sources, including agencies and the media. The U.S. Department of Justice administers the law and makes a Herculean effort to educate the public about ADA requirements. One source of information is the U.S. government home page on the ADA legislation, located at *http://www.usdoj.gov/crt/ada/adahom1.htm* (Retrieved March 10, 2005). Because the law is lengthy, complex, and technical, I do not describe its provisions—even the portions relating to testing—beyond noting its relevance to circumstances in which mental appraisals are made.

Administration of a test for a public purpose (e.g., employment, education, certification, licensing) must conform to ADA stipulations. Although individual testing circumstances may have legal implications, the law, as it applies to mental tests, is that the test's administration can in no way discriminate against any person who has a bona fide disability. A few examples illustrate the law's intent. Suppose a person has limited sight and cannot read a test's printed page, or imagine an individual with a physical disability that precludes marking an answer sheet. In both circumstances, the examinee's disability must be accommodated in such a way that the individual is able to take the test, with no reflection of the disability in the results. An accommodation, with regard to these examples, may be to provide a sighted person to read the test's questions or to have someone mark the answer sheet for the examinee with a disability.

Test administration often incorporates the following provisions, although my description of them should not be taken as an interpretation of the law:

1. The test administration agency must inform exam candidates that relevant provisions of the ADA apply, and the agency must do so in a manner that allows the following logistical steps to occur in a reasonable time period and manner.
2. An individual who believes he or she has a covered disability must respond to the test administration agency in a timely fashion. The person must provide the test administration agency with documentation of the veracity of the claim for disability status, written by an appropriately licensed professional (e.g., doctor, state licensed psychologist).
3. Together, the test administration agency and the eligible person then design a reasonable accommodation that will appropriately address the disability so no

discrimination based on the disability is evidenced during the test's administration.

4. The test administration agency must administer the exam to the individual according to the agreed-upon accommodation.
5. The person with a disability must make a good faith effort to follow all conditions of the prescribed accommodation.
6. The testing agency should provide information to test users about appropriate interpretation of the results so valid inferences may be made. This information may not discuss the disability itself but only interpretation of scores for valid inferences. In particular, the individual should not be singled out as different in any way.
7. The test administration agency cannot assess any separate cost to the individual with a disability, although the expense of making accommodations may be considered by the test administration agency when it sets a uniform exam fee for all candidates.

An example of a form used by a testing agency for this process is given in Figure 16.2.

Because there are many complex provisions to the law, even as it applies to test administration, one is advised to seek assistance through any of the many resources available from the Department of Justice or elsewhere for information pertinent to a given testing context.

Sensitivity Review

An important procedural step in examining a test during development is to conduct a sensitivity review of the items to ensure no language used in the item or exercise evokes unintended responses. Many test developers recommend this review (e.g., Bond, Moss, & Carr, 1996), and persons of each gender and from various ethnic heritages should be included in such a review. Criteria for the review should be established in advance of the actual reviewing sessions, and a training process should be conducted to ensure consistency among reviewers. Lacking this, there is a danger of idiosyncratic notions and personal prejudices overruling otherwise good items.

Sometimes, however, these reviews can be carried to the extreme, even beyond common sense, in a misplaced and uninformed conformity to "political correctness." For instance, many test development organizations institute quotas for the number of male- and female-sounding names, and even have quotas for ethnic-sounding names. Some even ban controversial subjects from writing passages, leaving only bland content admissible. Some researchers suggest that such number counting is a thinly veiled excuse to suppress points of view disapproved of by pressure groups (e.g., Ravitch, 2003). These kinds of sensitivity reviews, kept in proper perspective, are appropriate for public policy discussion.

Figure 16.2
Sample of a form used for
the Americans with
Disabilities Act protections.

OHIO
PUBLIC
SAFETY

- Administration
- Bureau of Motor Vehicles
- Emergency Management Agency
- Emergency Medical Services
- Investigative Unit
- Ohio State Highway Patrol

Title: Alternative Fire Testing For ADA Candidates   Policy Number: FP - 001

Date: October 19, 2001

Rational: To give accommodations to eligible candidates with a disability.

A student in a chartered fire training program who is eligible to take the state final written examination may file a request with the Division of Emergency Medical Services (EMS) for reasonable accommodations. Any student in a chartered training program with a documented disability, as that term is used in the American with Disabilities ACT (ADA), may qualify for reasonable accommodations.

The chartered institution is required to advise all students that they may request reasonable accommodations for the final written examination. Once a request has been made, the chartered training program must abide by the following guidelines in documenting their disability.

1. The Division of Emergency Medical Services shall examine all request for reasonable accommodations and may approve a request if the following documentation is provided:

    A. A statement from the Program Director of the chartered training program documenting the following details:
        1. The type of accommodations granted to the student while in the training program.
        2. Justification for the accommodations granted while in the training program.
        3. Verification that the student has successfully completed all of the program requirements for successful completion up to the date of request.
        4. Details of the disability and the type of accommodations being requested.
        5. Individual that will be administering the examination. Such individual must be associated with an educational institution with experience giving exam accommodation.

    B. A statement by the student requesting the type of accommodations needed.

    C. A detailed letter from the student's physician or a licensed professional healthcare provider who has diagnosed or treated the student, or a certified vocational evaluator who has evaluated the student. The letter must contain the following:
        1. The nature and extent of disability.
        2. Proposed accommodation.
        3. Rationale behind the proposed accommodations.
        4. Type of accommodations made to the student during training.

2. Request for accommodations shall be granted based upon the following:

    A. The student is a qualified individual with a disability who otherwise is eligible to take the state final examination.
    B. Accommodations are necessary to give the student and unbiased opportunity to take the examination.

3. The Division of EMS shall determine whether requested accommodations are deemed reasonable.

4. A representative of a local educational institution shall administer the examination through a chartered institution based on the accommodations granted by the Division of EMS. Such representative must have experience in the administration of exams and accommodations and shall be approved by the Division of EMS prior to administering special accommodations. The chartered training program must make arrangements to ensure the security of the examination and the integrity of the testing process.

5. The student is responsible for arranging and bearing the cost for appropriate evaluation.

_____   _____
          Program Director   Date

_____   _____
   Administrator of Chartered Program   Date

Summary

This chapter presents information about numerous important issues in testing, particularly as they are impacted by computers. I examine the issues in computer-assisted testing and the important, more recent development of computer-adaptive testing. I also cite important guides for international testing. Then, I briefly review international concerns and the ADA as it relates to testing, and close the chapter with a discussion of sensitivity reviews.

References

Alf, E. F., Jr., & Graf, R. G. (2002). A new maximum likelihood estimator for the population squared multiple correlation. *Journal of Educational and Behavioral Statistics, 27*, 223–235. (Accompanying workbook available at *http://www.sci.sdsu.edu/alfagrafics/*)

American Educational Research Association, American Psychological Association, & National Council on Measurement in Education. (1999). *Standards for educational and psychological testing.* Washington, DC: American Educational Research Association.

American Psychological Association (APA). (1999). Test security: Protecting the integrity of tests. *American Psychologist, 54*(12), 1078–1078.

American Psychological Association (APA). (2001). *Publication manual of the American Psychological Association* (5th ed.). Washington, DC: Author.

Amis, K. (1986). Introduction. In G. K. Chesterton (Ed.), *The man who was Thursday* (p. 13). London: Penguin.

Anderson, L. W. (2003). Classroom assessment: Enhancing the quality of teacher decision making. Mahwah, NJ: Erlbaum.

Andrich, D. (1988). *Rasch models for measurement.* New York: Sage.

Angoff, W. A. (1971). Scales, norms, and equivalent scores. In R. L. Thorndike (Ed.), *Educational measurement* (2nd ed., pp. 508–600). Washington, DC: American Council on Education.

Angoff, W. A. (1972). *A technique for the investigation of cultural differences.* Honolulu, HI: American Psychological Association. (ERIC Document Reproduction Service No. ED069686)

Angoff, W. A. (1982). Using difficulty and discrimination indices for detecting item bias. In R. A.

Berk (Ed.), *Handbook for methods of detecting test bias* (pp. 96–116). Baltimore: Johns Hopkins University.

Angoff, W. H. (1988). Validity: An evolving concept. In H. Wainer & H. I. Braun (Eds.), *Test validity* (pp. 19–32). Hillsdale, NJ: Erlbaum.

Angoff, W. H., & Schrader, W. B. (1984). A study of hypotheses basic to the use of rights and formula scores. *Journal of Educational Measurement, 21*(1), 1–17.

Arter, J. A., & McTighe, J. (2000). Scoring rubrics in the classroom: Using performance criteria for assessing and improving student performance. Thousand Oaks, CA: Corwin.

Ashbacker, P. R. (1991). Performance assessment: State activity, interests, and concerns. *Applied Psychological Measurement, 4*(4), 275–288.

Assessment Systems Corporation. (1995). *ITEMAN conventional item analysis program.* St. Paul, MN: Author.

Atkinson, R. C., Krantz, D. H., Luce, R. D., & Suppes, P. (Eds.). (1996). *Contemporary developments in mathematical psychology* (Vols. 1–2) New York: Freeman.

Auden, W. H. (1966). Under which lyre. In *Collected shorter poems: 1927–1957* (pp. 221–225). New York: Random House.

Baker, E. L., O'Neil, H. F., Jr., & Linn, R. L. (1993). Policy and validity prospects for performance-based assessment. *American Psychologist, 48*(12), 1210–1218.

Baker, F. B. (2001). *The basics of item response theory.* ERIC Clearinghouse on Assessment and Evaluation. College Park: University of Maryland. Retrieved December 6, 2004, from *http://edres.org/irt/baker/*

Bayes, T. (1763). An essay toward solving a problem in the doctrine of chances. *Philosophical transactions of the Royal Society of London, essay LII* (Vol. 53, pp. 370–418). London: Royal Society.

Bejar, I. I. (1986). Analysis and generation of hidden figure items: A cognitive approach to psychometric modeling. Princeton, NJ: Educational Testing Service.

Bejar, I. I., & Yocom, P. (1991). A generative approach to the modeling of isomorphic hidden-figure items. *Applied Psychological Measurement, 15*(2), 129–137.

Berliner, D. C., & Calfee, R. C. (Eds.). (1996). *Handbook of educational psychology.* New York: Simon & Schuster.

Bernoulli, D. (1954). Specimen theoriae novae de Mensura Sortis [Exposition of a new theory of measurement of risk] (L. Sommer, Trans.). *Econometrica, 22*, 23–36. (Original work published 1738)

Bernstein, P. L. (1998). Against the gods: The remarkable story of risk. New York: Wiley.

Best, J. B. (1999). *Cognitive psychology.* Belmont, CA: Wadsworth.

Birnbaum, A. (1958). *On the estimation of mental abilities.* Randolph Air Force Base, TX: USAF School of Aviation Medicine.

Birnbaum, A. (1968). Some latent trait models and their use in inferring an examinee's ability. In F. M. Lord & M. R. Novick (Eds.), *Statistical theories of mental test scores* (pp. 395–479). Reading, MA: Addison-Wesley.

Block, J. H. (1978). Standards and criteria: A response. *Journal of Educational Measurement, 15*, 291–295.

Bloom, B. S. (1956). *Taxonomy of educational objectives.* New York: David McKay.

Bock, D. R. (1972). Estimating item parameters and latent ability when responses are scored in two or more nominal categories. *Psychometrika, 37*, 29–51.

Bock, R. D. (1997a). A brief history of item response theory. *Educational Measurement: Issues and Practices, 16*(4), 21–32.

Bock, R. D. (1997b). The nominal categories model. In R. K. Hambleton (Ed.), *Handbook of modern item response theory* (pp. 33–51). New York: Springer.

Bock, R. D., & Aitkin, M. (1981). Marginal maximum likelihood estimation of item parameters: Application of an EM algorithm. *Psychometrika, 46*, 443–445.

Bock, R. D., Gibbons, R. D., & Muraki, E. (1988). Full information item factor analysis. *Applied Psychological Measurement, 12*, 261–280.

Bock, R. D., Zimowski, M., Muraki, E., Mislevy, R., Thissen, D., & Wood, R. (2002). *IRT from SSI: BILOG-MG, MULTILOG, PARSCALE, TESTFACT.* Chicago: Scientific Software International.

Bond, L., Moss, P., & Carr, P. (1996). Fairness in large-scale performance assessments. In G. W. Phillips (Ed.), *Technical issues in large-scale performance assessment* (pp. 117–134). Washington, DC: U.S. Department of Education, Office of Educational Research and Improvement.

Bond, T. G., & Fox, C. M. (2001). *Applying the Rasch model.* Mahwah, NJ: Erlbaum.

Borg, I., & Groenen, P. (1997). *Modern multidimensional scaling.* New York: Springer.

Boring, E. G. (1923). Intelligence as the tests test it. *The New Republic, 35*, 35–37.

Bormuth, J. R. (1970). *On the theory of achievement test items.* Chicago: University of Chicago.

Borsboom, D., Mellenbergh, G. J., & van Heerden, J. (2003). The theoretical status of latent variables. *Psychological Review, 110*(2), 203–219.

Bransford, J. D., Brown, A. L., & Cocking, R. R. (1999). *How people learn: Brain, mind, experience, and school.* Washington, DC: National Academy.

Brennan, R. L. (2001a). (Mis)Conceptions about generalizability theory. *Educational Measurement: Issues and Practice, 19*(1), 5–10.

Brennan, R. L. (2001b). An essay on the history and future of reliability from the perspective of replications. *Journal of Educational Measurement, 38*(4), 295–318.

Brennan, R. L. (2001c). *Generalizability theory.* New York: Springer.

Brody, N. (1985). The validity of intelligence tests. In B. B. Wolman (Ed.), *Handbook of intelligence* (pp. 353–389). New York: Wiley.

Brogden, H. (1946). Variation in test validity with variation in the distribution of item difficulties, number of items, and degree of their intercorrelations. *Psychometrika, 35*, 179–197.

Brookhart, S. M. (1999). The art and science of classroom assessment: The missing part of pedagogy. *ASHE-ERIC Higher Education Report, 27*(1).

Brown, C. W., & Ghiselli, E. E. (1953). Percent increase in proficiency resulting from use of selective devices. *Journal of Applied Psychology, 37,* 341–345.

Bruner, J. S. (1956). Freud and the image of man. *American Psychologist, 11,* 463–466.

Buckendahl, C. W., Smith, R. W., Impara, J. C., & Plake, B. S. (2002). A comparison of Angoff and bookmark standard setting methods. *Journal of Educational Measurement, 39*(3), 253–264.

Bulwer-Lytton, E. G. (1830). *Paul Clifford.* Retrieved December 6, 2004, from *http://www.bulwer-lytton.com*

Buros, O. K. (Ed.). (1972). *The seventh mental measurement yearbook.* Highland Park, NJ: Gryphon.

Burstein, L., Koretz, D., Linn, R., Sugrue, B., Novak, J., & Baker, E. L. (1996). Describing performance standards: Validity of the 1992 National Assessment of Educational Progress achievement level descriptors as characterizations of mathematics performance. *Educational Assessment, 3*(1), 9–51.

Byrne, B. M. (2001). Structural equation modeling with AMOS: Basic concepts, applications, and programming. Mahwah, NJ: Erlbaum.

Campbell, D. T., & Fisk, D. W. (1959). Convergent and discriminant validation by the multitrait-multimethod matrix. *Psychological Bulletin, 56,* 81–105.

Campbell, S. K., Wright, B. D., & Linacre, J. M. (2002). Development of a functional movement scale for children. *Journal of Applied Measurement, 3*(2), 190–204.

Carlin, B. P., & Louis, T. A. (1996). *Bayes and empirical Bayes methods for data analysis.* New York: Chapman & Hall/CRC.

Carroll, J. B. (1950). Problems in the factor analysis of tests with varying difficulty [Abstract]. *American Psychologist, 5,* 369.

Carroll, J. B. (1993). *Human cognitive abilities.* Cambridge, UK: Cambridge University.

Carson, J. D. (2001). Legal issues in standard setting for licensure and certification. In G. J. Cizek (Ed.), *Setting performance standards* (pp. 427–444). New York: Erlbaum.

Cattell, R. B. (1944). Psychological measurement: Ipsative, normative, and interactive. *Psychological Review, 51,* 292–303.

Charland, B. M. (1995). *Sigma Plot for scientists.* Dubuque, IA: Brown Communications.

Chomsky, N. (1957). *Syntactic structures.* Cambridge, MA: Mouton.

Cizek, G. J. (Ed.). (2001). Setting performance standards: Concepts, methods, and perspectives. Mahwah, NJ: Erlbaum.

Cohen, A. S., Kane, M. T., & Crooks, T. J. (1998). A generalized examinee-centered method for setting standards on achievement tests. *Applied Psychological Measurement, 12,* 343–366.

The College Board. (2005). *Scholastic aptitude test.* Princeton, NJ: Author.

Commission on Instructionally Supportive Assessment. (2001a). *Building tests to support instruction and accountability: A guide for policymakers.* Washington, DC: American Association of School Administrators.

Commission on Instructionally Supportive Assessment. (2001b). *Illustrative language for an RFP to build tests to support instruction and accountability.* Washington, DC: American Association of School Administrators.

Cooley, W. W., & Lohnes, P. R. (1971). *Multivariate data analysis.* New York: Wiley.

Coombs, C. H. (1950). Psychological scaling without a unit of measurement. *Psychological Review, 57,* 145–158.

Coombs, C. H. (1953). Theory and methods of social measurement. In L. Festinger & D. Katz (Eds.), *Research methods in the behavioral sciences* (pp. 471–535). New York: Dryden.

Cortina, J. (1993). What is coefficient alpha: An examination of theory and application. *Journal of Applied Psychology, 78*(1), 98–104.

Crick, J. E., & Brennan, R. L. (1983). *Manual for GENOVA: A generalized analysis of variance system.* Iowa City, IA: American College Testing.

Crocker, L. (2002). Stakeholders in comprehensive validation of standards-based assessments: A commentary. *Educational Measurement: Issues and Practices, 21*(1), 5–7.

Cronbach, L. J. (1951). Coefficient alpha and the internal structure of tests. *Psychometrika, 16,* 297–334.

Cronbach, L. J. (1957). The two disciplines of scientific psychology. *American Psychologist, 12,* 671–684.

Cronbach, L. J. (1975). Five decades of public controversy over mental testing. *American Psychologist, 30*(1), 1–14.

Cronbach, L. J. (1988). Five perspectives on validity argument. In H. Wainer & H. I. Braun (Eds.), *Test validity* (pp. 3–17). Hillsdale, NJ: Erlbaum.

Cronbach, L. J., Gleser, G. C., Nanda, H., & Rajaratnam, N. (1972). The dependability of behavioral measurement: Theory of generalizability for scores and profiles. New York: Wiley.

Cronbach, L. J., & Meehl, P. E. (1955). Construct validity in psychological tests. *Psychological Bulletin, 52*, 281–303.

Cronbach, L. J., & Shavelson, R. J. (2004). My current thoughts on coefficient alpha and successor procedures. *Educational and Psychological Measurement, 64*(3), 391–418.

Cronbach, L. J., & Warrington, W. G. (1952). Efficiency of multiple-choice tests as a function of spread of item difficulties. *Psychometrika, 17*, 127–147.

Cureton, E. E. (1950). Validity. In E. F. Lindquist (Ed.), *Educational measurement* (pp. 621–694). Washington, DC: American Council on Education.

Cureton, E. E., Cook, J. A., Fischer, R. T., Laser, S. A., Rockwell, N. J., & Simmons, J. W. (1973). Length of test and standard error of measurement. *Educational and Psychological Measurement, 33*, 63–68.

Davey, T., & Nering, M. (2002). Controlling item exposure and maintain item security. In C. N. Mills, J. J. Fremer, & W. C. Ward (Eds.), *Computer-based testing: Building the foundation for future assessments* (pp. 165–191). Mahwah, NJ: Erlbaum.

Debra P. v. Turlington. (1981). 644 F.2d 397 (5th Cir. Unit B).

Di Vesta, F. J. (1987). The cognitive movement in education. In J. A. Glover & R. R. Ronning (Eds.), *Historical foundations of educational psychology* (pp. 203–233). New York: Plenum.

Divgi, D. R. (1986). Does the Rasch model really work for multiple choice items? *Journal of Educational Measurement, 23*, 283–298.

Dorans, N. J. (2002). *The recentering of SAT scales and its effects on score distributions and score interpretations* (No. 2002-11, ETS RR-02-04). New York: College Entrance Examination Board.

Drasgow, F. (1998). Polychoric and polyserial correlations. In L. Kotz & N. L. Johnson (Eds.), *Encyclopedia of statistical sciences* (Vol. 7, pp. 69–74). New York: Wiley.

Drasgow, F. (2002). The work ahead: A psychometric infrastructure for computerized adaptive testing. In C. N. Mills, J. J. Fremer, & W. C. Ward (Eds.), *Computer-based testing* (pp. 1–10). Mahwah, NJ: Erlbaum.

du Toit, M. (Ed.). (2003). *IRT from SSI: BILOG-MG, MULTILOG, PARSCALE, TESTFACT.* Lincolnwood, IL: Scientific Software International. Retrieved December 5, 2004, from *http://www.ssicentral.com*

Duncan, O. D. (1984). *Notes on social measurement: Historical and critical.* New York: Russell Sage Foundation.

Dupont, P. (1977/1978). Laplace and the indifference principle in the 'Essai philosophique des probabilitiés'. Torino, Italy: Rend. Sem. Mat. Univ. Politec, 36, 125–137.

Ebel, R. L. (1951). Writing the test item. In E. F. Lindquist (Ed.), *Educational measurement* (pp. 185–249). Washington, DC: American Council on Education.

Eisner, E. W. (1999a). The uses and limits of performance assessment, pp. 658–661. *Phi Delta Kappan, 80*(9).

Eisner, E. W. (1999b). The uses and limits of performance assessment. *Phi Delta Kappan, 80*(9), 658–660.

Elliott, S. N. (1995). *Creating meaningful performance assessments.* Washington, DC: U.S. Department of Education, Office of Educational Research and Improvement.

Embretson, S. E. (1984). A general latent trait model for response processes. *Psychometrika, 49*, 175–186.

Embretson, S. E., & Reise, S. P. (2000). *Item response theory for psychologists.* Mahwah, NJ: Erlbaum.

Fagan, T. K., & VandenBos, G. R. (Eds.). (1993). *Exploring applied psychology: Origins and critical analyses.* Washington, DC: American Psychological Association.

Fairbank, B. A., Jr. (1985). Equipercentile test equating: The effects of presmoothing and postsmoothing on the magnitude of sample-dependent errors (Report AFHRL-TR-84-64). San Antonio, TX: Performance Metrics.

Fechner, G. T. (1966). *Elements of psychophysics.* New York: Holt, Reinhart, & Winston.

Feldt, L. S., & Brennan, R. L. (1989). Reliability. In R. L. Linn (Ed.), *Educational measurement* (3rd ed., pp. 105–146). New York: American Council on Education/Macmillan.

Ferguson, G. A. (1942). Item selection by constant process. *Psychometrika 7*, 19–29.

Fischer, G. H., & Formann, A. K. (1982). Some applications of logistic latent trait models with linear constraints on the parameters. *Applied Psychological Measurement, 6*, 397–416.

Fischer, G. H., & Molenaar, I. W. (Eds.). (2002). *Rasch models: Foundations, recent developments, and applications.* New York: Springer.

Fisher, R. A. (1912). On an absolute criterion for fitting frequency curves. *Messenger of Mathematics, 41*, 155–160.

Fisher, R. A. (1928). The general sampling distribution of the multiple correlation coefficient. *Proceedings of the Royal Society, A 121*, 654–673.

Flanagan, J. C. (1937). A proposed procedure for increasing the efficiency of objective tests. *Journal of Educational Psychology, 28*, 17–21.

Flanagan, J. C. (1948). *The aviation psychology program in the Army Air Force.* Washington, DC: U.S. Government Printing Office.

Folk, V. G., & Smith, R. L. (2002). Models for delivery of CBTs. In C. N. Mills, J. J. Fremer, & W. C. Ward (Eds.), *Computer-based testing* (pp. 41–66). Mahwah, NJ: Erlbaum.

Fox, R. E. (1994). Training professional psychologists for the twenty-first century. *American Psychologist, 49*(4), 207–210.

Frary, R. B. (1991). The none-of-the-above option: An empirical study. *Applied Measurement in Education, 4*(2), 115–124.

Frary, R. B., Cross, L. H., & Weber, L. J. (1993). Testing and grading practices and opinions of secondary teachers of academic subjects: Implications for instruction in measurement. *Educational Measurement: Issues and Practice, 12*(30), 23–30.

Frederick, B. N. (1999). Partitioning variance in the multivariate case: A step-by-step guide to canonical commonality analysis. In B. Thompson (Ed.), *Advances in social science methodology* (Vol. 5, pp. 305–318). Stamford, CT: JAI.

Galton, F. (1898). *Natural inheritance.* London: Macmillan.

Garrett, H. E. (1937). *Statistics in psychology and education.* New York: Longman, Green.

General Educational Development Testing Service. (2004). *Tests of General Educational Development.* Washington, DC: American Council on Education.

Glass, G. V. (1978). Standards and criteria. *Journal of Educational Measurement, 15*, 237–261.

Gorsuch, R. L. (1983). *Factor analysis.* Hillsdale, NJ: Erlbaum.

Gough, P. (Ed.). (1999). [Special Issue on Performance Assessment]. *Phi Delta Kappan, 80*(9).

Gould, S. J. (1981). *The mismeasure of man.* New York: W. W. Norton.

Guilford, J. P. (1946). New standards for test evaluation. *Educational and Psychological Measurement, 6*, 427–438.

Guion, R. M. (1977). Content validity—The source of my discontent. *Applied Psychological Measurement, 1*(1), 1–10.

Gulliksen, H. (1950). *Theory of mental tests.* New York: Wiley.

Guttman, L. (1941). The quantification of class attributes: A theory and method of scale construction. In P. Horst (Ed.), *The prediction of personal adjustment* (pp. 319–348). New York: Social Science Research Council.

Guttman, L. (1954). A new approach to factor analysis: The radex. In P. F. Lazarsfeld (Ed.), *Mathematical thinking in the social sciences* (pp. 258–348). New York: Columbia University.

Haladyna, T. M. (1999). Developing and validating multiple-choice test items. Mahwah, NJ: Erlbaum.

Haladyna, T. M., & Downing, S. M. (1988a). A taxonomy of multiple-choice item-writing rules. *Applied Measurement in Education, 1*, 37–50.

Haladyna, T. M., & Downing, S. M. (1988b). The validity of a taxonomy of multiple-choice item-writing rules. *Applied Measurement in Education, 1*, 51–78.

Hambleton, R. K. (1984). Validating the test scores. In R. A. Berk (Ed.), *A guide to criterion-referenced test construction* (pp. 199–230). Baltimore: Johns Hopkins University.

Hambleton, R. K. (1989). Principles and selected application of item response theory. In R. L. Linn (Ed.), *Educational measurement* (pp. 147–220). New York: American Council on Education.

Hambleton, R. K. (1994). The rise and fall of criterion-referenced measurement? *Educational Measurement: Issues and Practice, Winter,* 21–26.

Hambleton, R. K. (2001). Setting performance standards on educational assessments and criteria for evaluating the process. In G. J. Cizek (Ed.), *Setting performance standards: Concepts, methods, and perspectives* (pp. 89–116). Mahwah, NJ: Erlbaum.

Hambleton, R. K., & Murry, L. M. (1983). Some goodness of fit investigations for item response models. In R. K. Hambleton (Ed.), *Applications of item response theory* (pp. 71–94). Burnaby: Educational Research Institute of British Columbia.

Hambleton, R. K., & Rodgers, J. (1995). Item bias review. *Practical Assessment, Research & Evaluation, 4*(6). (ERIC Document Reproduction Service No. ED398241).

Hambleton, R. K., & Swaminathan, H. (1985). *Item response theory: Principles and applications.* Boston: Kluwer-Nijoff.

Hambleton, R. K., Swaminathan, H., & Rodgers, J. H. (1991). *Fundamentals of item response theory.* Newbury Park, CA: Sage.

Hambleton, R. K., & Zaal, J. N. (1991). *Advances in educational and psychological testing.* Boston: Kluwer.

Hannah, L. S., & Michaelis, J. U. (1977). A comprehensive framework for instructional objectives: A guide to systematic planning and evaluation. Reading, MA: Addison-Wesley.

Hansche, L. N. (Ed.). (1998). *Handbook for the development of performance standards.* Washington, DC: U.S. Department of Education and the Council of Chief State School Officers.

Harman, H. H. (1967). *Modern factor analysis.* Chicago: University of Chicago.

Harris, D. J. (1997). *Using reliabilities to make decisions.* Iowa City, IA: American College Testing.

Hattie, J. (1985). Assessing unidimensionality of tests and items. *Applied Psychological Measurement, 9,* 139–164.

Hays, W. I. (1988). *Statistics.* New York: Holt, Rinehart & Winston.

Herrnstein, R., & Murray, C. (1994). *The bell curve.* New York: The Free Press.

Heubert, J. P., & Hauser, R. M. (Eds.). (1999). *High stakes: Testing for tracking, promotion, and graduation.* Washington, DC: The National Academies Press.

Holland, P. W., & Thayer, D. T. (1988). Differential item functioning and the Mantel-Haenszel procedure. In H. Wainer & H. I. Braun (Eds.), *Test validity* (pp. 129–145). Hillsdale, NJ: Erlbaum.

Holland, P. W., & Wainer, H. (1993). *Differential item functioning.* Hillsdale, NJ: Erlbaum.

Hoover, H. D. (2004). *Iowa test of basic skills.* Chicago: Riverside.

House, E. R. (1980). *Evaluating with validity.* Beverly Hills, CA: Sage.

Howson, C., & Urbach, P. (1996). *Scientific reasoning: The Bayesian approach.* La Salle, IL: Open Court.

Huff, D. (1954). *How to lie with statistics.* New York: Norton.

Hughes, H. H., & Trimble, W. E. (1965). The use of complex alternatives in multiple-choice items. *Educational and Psychological Measurement, 25,* 117–126.

Irvine, S. H., & Kyllonen, P. C. (Eds.). (2002). *Item generation for test development.* Mahwah, NJ: Erlbaum.

Jaeger, R. M. (1989). Certification of student competence. In R. L. Linn (Ed.), *Educational measurement* (3rd ed., pp. 485–514). New York: American Council on Education/Macmillan.

Jaeger, R. M. (1991). Selection of judges for standard setting. *Educational Measurement: Issues and Practice, 10*(2), 3–14.

Jaeger, R. M. (1995). Setting performance standards through two-stage judgmental policy capturing. *Applied Measurement in Education, 8,* 15–40.

Jaeger, R. M., & Mills, C. N. (2001). An integrated judgment procedure for setting standards on complex, large-scale assessments. In G. J. Cizek (Ed.), *Setting performance standards: Concepts, methods, and perspectives* (pp. 313–338). Mahwah, NJ: Erlbaum.

Jensen, A. R. (1980). *Bias in mental testing.* New York: The Free Press.

Jensen, A. R. (1981). *Straight talk about mental tests.* New York: The Free Press.

Jöreskog, K. G. (1971). Statistical analysis of sets of congeneric tests. *Psychometrika, 36,* 109–133.

Jöreskog, K. G. (2003, March 13). *Factor analysis by MINRES*. Lincolnwood, IL: Scientific Software International. Retrieved September 3, 2004, from *http://www.ssicentral.com/lisrel/column13.htm*

Jöreskog, K. G., & Sörbom, D. (2002). *LISREL 8: A guide to the program and applications*. Lincolnwood, IL: Scientific Software International. Retrieved September 3, 2004, from *http://www.ssicentral.com/lisrel/mainlis.htm*.

Kane, M. B. (2002). Validating high-stakes testing programs. *Educational Measurement: Issues and Practices, 21*(1), 31–41.

Kane, M. B., & Mitchell, R. (Eds.). (1996). Implementing performance assessment: Promises, problems, and challenges. Mahwah, NJ: Erlbaum.

Kane, M. T. (2001a). Current concerns in validity theory. *Review of Educational Research, 38*(4), 319.

Kane, M. T. (2001b). So much remains the same: Conception and status of validation in setting standards. In G. J. Cizek (Ed.), *Setting performance standards* (pp. 53–88). New York: Erlbaum.

Kelley, T. L. (1921). The reliability of test scores. *Journal of Educational Research, 3*, 370–379.

Kelvin, W. T. (1889). *Popular lectures and addresses (1891–1894)* (3 Vols.). London: Macmillan. Retrieved January 4, 2005, from *http://zapatopi.net/kelvin/quotes.html*

Kendall, J. S., & Marzano, R. J. (1996). *Content knowledge: A compendium of standards and benchmarks for K–12 education*. Aurora, CO: Mid-continent Regional Educational Laboratory.

Khattri, N., Reeve, A. L., & Kane, M. B. (1998). *Principles and practices of performance assessment*. Mahwah, NJ: Erlbaum.

Kim, S.-H. (1995). Detection of differential item functioning in multiple groups. *Journal of Educational Measurement, 32*(3), 261–276.

Kingston, N. M., Kahl, S. R., Sweeney, K. P., & Bay, L. (2001). Setting performance standards using the body of work method. In G. J. Cizek (Ed.), *Setting performance standards: Concepts, methods, and perspectives* (pp. 219–248). Mahwah, NJ: Erlbaum.

Klein, S. P., & Kosecof, J. P. (1975). *Determining how well a test measures your objectives*. Los Angeles: Center for the Study of Evaluation, University of California, Los Angeles.

Kline, R. B. (2004). Beyond significance testing: Reforming data analysis methods in behavioral research. Washington, DC: American Psychological Association.

Kolen, M. J. (1988). Defining score scales in relation to measurement error. *Journal of Applied Measurement, 25*, 97–110.

Kolen, M. J., & Brennan, R. L. (2004). *Test equating, scaling and linking: Methods and practices* (2nd ed.). New York: Springer.

Kosslyn, S. M. (1994). *The elements of graphing data*. Monterey, CA: Wadsworth.

Kreisman, S., Knoll, M., & Melchior, T. (1995). Toward more authentic assessment. In A. A. Costa & B. Kallick (Eds.), *Assessment in the learning organization* (pp. 114–140). Alexandria, VA: Association for Supervision and Curriculum Development.

Kuder, G. F., & Richardson, M. W. (1937). The theory of the estimation of test reliability. *Psychometrika, 2*, 151–160.

Larry P. v. Wilson Riles. (1972). 343 F. Supp. 1306 (N.D. Cal.) (preliminary injunction). Aff'd 502 F. 2d963 (9th Cir. 1974); 495 F. Supp. 926 (ND Cal. 1979) (decision on merits). Aff'd (9th Cir., No. 80-427, 1984) (order modifying judgment, C-71-2270 RFP, 1986).

Lawley, D. N. (1943). On problems connected with item selection and test construction. *Recordings of the Royal Society of Edinburgh, 61*, 273–287.

Lazarsfeld, P. F., & Henry, N. W. (1968). *Latent structure analysis*. Boston: Houghton Mifflin.

Lewis, D. M., Mitzel, H. C., Green, B. F., & Patz, R. J. (1999). *The bookmark standard setting procedure*. Monterey, CA: McGraw-Hill.

Li, H. (2003). The resolution of some paradoxes related to reliability and validity. *Journal of Educational and Behavioral Statistics, 28*(2), 89–95.

Linn, R. L. (1980). Issues of validity for criterion-referenced measures. *Applied Psychological Measurement, 4*, 547–561.

Linn, R. L. (Ed.). (1989). *Educational measurement*. New York: Macmillan.

Linn, R. L. (1994). Performance assessment: Policy promises and technical measurement standards. *Educational Researcher, December*, 4–14.

Linn, R. L., Baker, E. L., & Dunbar, S. B. (n.d.). *Complex, performance-based assessment: Expectations and validation*. Los Angeles:

Center for the Study of Evaluation, University of California, Los Angeles.

Linn, R. L., & Shepard, L. A. (1997). *Item-by-item standard setting: Misinterpretations of judge's intentions due to less than perfect item inter-correlations.* Symposium presented at the Council of Chief State School Officers National Conference on Large Scale Assessment, Phoenix, AZ.

Lippman, W. (1922). The abuse of tests. *The New Republic, 32,* 9–330.

Lissitz, R., & Schafer, W. D. (Eds.). (2001). *Assessments in educational reform: Both means and ends.* New York: Allyn & Bacon.

Livingston, S. A., & Zieky, M. J. (1982). Passing scores: A manual for setting standards of performance on educational and occupational tests. Princeton, NJ: Educational Testing Service.

Logan, J. D. (1996). *Applied mathematics* (2nd ed.). New York: Wiley.

Longford, N. T. (1995). *Models for uncertainty in educational testing.* New York: Springer-Verlag.

Lord, F. M. (1952). A theory of test scores. *Psychometric Monograph No 7.*

Lord, F. M. (1959). Tests of the same length do have the same standard error of measurement. *Educational and Psychological Measurement, 19,* 233–239.

Lord, F. M. (1974). Estimation of latent ability and item parameters when there are omitted items. *Psychometrika, 39,* 247–264.

Lord, F. M. (1980). Applications of item response theory to practical testing problems. Hillsdale, NJ: Erlbaum.

Lord, F. M., & Novick, M. R. (1963). *Statistical theories of mental test scores.* Reading, MA: Addison-Wesley.

Luce, R. D. (1959). Individual choice behavior: A theoretical analysis. New York: Academic Press.

Luce, R. D., Krantz, D. H., Suppes, P., & Tversky, A. (1990). *Foundations of measurement* (Vol. III). San Diego, CA: Academic Press.

Madaus, G. F., & O'Dwyer, L. M. (1989). A short history on performance assessment. *Phi Delta Kappan, 80*(9), 688–695.

Mantel, N., & Haenszel, W. (1959). Statistical aspects of the analysis of data from retrospective studies of disease. *Journal of the National Cancer Institute, 22,* 719–748.

Marascuillo, L. A., & Levin, J. R. (1983). *Multivariate statistics in the social sciences: A researcher's guide.* Monterey, CA: Brooks/Cole.

Marley, A. A. J. (Ed.). (1997). Choice, decision, and measurement: Essays in honor of R. Duncan Luce. Mahwah, NJ: Erlbaum.

Marriott, H. F. C. (1991). *A dictionary of statistical terms.* New York: Wiley.

Maruyama, G. M. (1997). *Basics of structural equation modeling.* Thousand Oaks, CA: Sage.

McDonald, R. P. (1999). *Test theory: A unified treatment.* Mahwah, NJ: Erlbaum.

McLeod, L. D., Swygert, K. A., & Thissen, D. (2001). Factor analysis for items scored in two categories. In D. Thissen & H. Wainer (Eds.), *Test scoring* (pp. 187–250). Mahwah, NJ: Erlbaum.

McMullen, R. (1975). *Mona Lisa: The picture and the myth.* Boston: Houghton Mifflin.

McNemar, Q. (1946). Opinion-attitude methodology. *Psychological Bulletin, 12,* 82–99.

Messick, S. (1975). The standard problem: Meaning and values in measurement and evaluation. *American Psychologist, 30,* 955–966.

Messick, S. (1980). Test validity and the ethics of assessment. *American Psychologist, 35,* 1012–1027.

Messick, S. (1989). Validity. In R. L. Linn (Ed.), *Educational measurement* (pp. 13–105). New York: American Council on Education/Macmillan.

Messick, S. (1996). Validity of performance assessments. In G. W. Phillips (Ed.), *Technical issues in large-scale performance assessment* (pp. 1–18). Washington, DC: U.S. Department of Education, Office of Educational Research and Improvement.

Messick, S. (1997). History of modern psychometrics [Special issue]. *Educational Measurement: Issues and Practice, 16*(4).

Michell, J. (1990). An introduction to the logic of psychological measurement. Hillsdale, NJ: Erlbaum.

Michell, J. (1999). Measurement in psychology: Critical history of a methodological concept. Cambridge, UK: Cambridge University.

Miller, G. A. (1984). The test. *Science, 84*(5), 55–60.

Miller, M. D. (2002). *Generalizability of performance-based assessments.* Washington, DC: Council of Chief State School Officers. Retrieved December 5,

2004, from *http://www.ccsso.org/publications/details.cfm?PublicationID=148*

Miller, M. D., & Linn, R. L. (2000). Validation of performance-based assessments. *Applied Psychological Measurement, 24*(4), 367–378.

Mills, C. N., & Jaeger, R. J. (1998). Creating description of desired student achievement when setting performance standards. In L. N. Hansche (Ed.), *Handbook for the development of performance standards* (pp. 73–85). Washington, DC: U.S. Department of Education and the Council of Chief State School Officers.

Mills, C. N., Portenza, M. T., Fremer, J. J., & Ward, W. C. (2002). *Computer-based testing.* Mahwah, NJ: Erlbaum.

Minitab. (2003). Minitab release 14 statistical software for Windows. State College, PA: Author.

Minn, D. L. P. (2001). *Applied probability models.* New York: Duxbury.

Mislevy, R. J. (1992). *Linking educational assessments: Concepts, issues, methods, and prospects.* Princeton, NJ: Educational Testing Service, Policy Information Center.

Mislevy, R. J. (1996). Test theory reconceived. *Journal of Educational Measurement, 33*(4), 379–416.

Mislevy, R. J., Wilson, M. R., Erkican, K., & Chudowsky, N. (2002). *Psychometric principles in student assessment.* Los Angeles: National Center for Research on Evaluation, Standards, and Student Testing, University of California.

Moskal, B. M. (2000). Scoring rubrics: What, when and how? *Practical Assessment, Research and Evaluation, 7*(3). Retrieved January 4, 2005, from *http://pareonline.net/getvn.asp?v=7&n=3*

Moskal, B. M., & Leydens, J. A. (2000). Scoring rubric development: Validity and reliability. *Practical Assessment, Research and Evaluation, 7*(10). Retrieved January 4, 2005, from *http://pareonline.net/getvn.asp?v=7&n=10*

Muraki, E. (1992). *RESGEN.* Princeton, NJ: Educational Testing Service.

Muraki, E., & Bock, D. (2002). PARSCALE: IRT based test scoring and item analysis for graded response items and rating scales. Lincolnwood, IL: Scientific Software International.

Murray-Ward, A. (1999). *Assessment in the classroom.* New York: Wadsworth.

National Council of Teachers of Mathematics, Commission on Standards for School Mathematics. (1989). *Curriculum and evaluation standards for school mathematics.* Reston, VA: Author.

National Education Standards and Improvement Council. (1993). *Promises to keep: Creating high standards for American students.* Report on the review of education standards from the Goals 3 and 4 Technical Planning Group to the National Educational Goals Panel. Washington, DC: National Goals Panel.

National Research Council, Board on Testing and Assessment. (1999). *High stakes: Testing for tracking, promotion, and graduation.* Washington, DC: National Academy Press. Retrieved December 21, 2004, from *http://www.nap.edu/readingroom/books/highstakes*

Nedelsky, L. (1954). Absolute grading standards for objective tests. *Educational and Psychological Measurement, 14*, 3–19.

Neisser, U. (1967). *Cognitive psychology.* New York: Appleton-Century-Crofts.

Netermeyer, R. G., Bearden, W. O., & Sharma, S. (2003). *Scaling procedures.* Thousand Oaks, CA: Sage.

Newstead, S., Bradon, P., Handley, S., Evans, J., & Dennis, I. (2002). Using the psychology of reasoning to predict the difficulty of analytical reasoning problems. In S. H. K. Irvine & C. Patrick (Eds.), *Item generation for test development* (pp. 35–51). Mahwah, NJ: Erlbaum.

Nutter, J., Kutner, M. H., Nachtsheim, C. J., & Wasserman, W. (1996). *Applied linear statistics models.* Boston: WCB/McGraw-Hill.

O'Connor, J. J., & Robertson, E. F. (1996, December). *Johann Carl Friedrich Gauss.* Retrieved January 2004, from *http://www-gap.dcs.st-and.ac.uk/~history/Mathematicians/Gauss.html*

Olson, B., Mead, R., & Payne, D. (2002, October). *A report of a standard setting method for alternate assessments for students with significant disabilities* (Synthesis Report 47). Minneapolis: University of Minnesota, National Center on Educational Outcomes. Retrieved December 20, 2004, from *http://education.umn.edu/NCEO/OnlinePubs/Synthesis47.html*

Osterlind, S. J. (1983). *Test item bias.* Beverly Hills, CA: Sage.

Osterlind, S. J. (1990). Toward a uniform definition of a test item. *Educational Research Quarterly, 14*(4), 2–5.

Osterlind, S. J. (1998). Constructing test items: Multiple-choice, constructed-response, performance, and other formats (2nd ed.). Boston: Kluwer Academic.

Osterlind, S. J. (2001). SPSS for Windows workbook: Using multivariate statistics. Boston: Allyn & Bacon.

Osterlind, S. J. (2003). *Heuristic inquiry of dimensionality in binary test items.* Columbia, MO: Winemiller Conference on Statistical Inference.

Osterlind, S. J. (2004). *College basic academic subjects examination.* Columbia: University of Missouri.

Osterlind, S. J., & Merz, W. M. (1991). *Technical manual: College Basic Academic Subjects Examination.* Columbia: University of Missouri.

Osterlind, S. J., & Merz, W. M. (1994). Building a taxonomy for constructed response test items. *Educational Assessment, 2*(2), 133–147.

Osterlind, S. J., et al. (2004). *College Basic Academic Subjects Examination.* Columbia: University of Missouri.

Otis, A. S. (1922a). A method for inferring the change in a coefficient of correlation resulting from a change in the heterogeneity of the group. *Journal of Educational Psychology, 13,* 193–294.

Otis, A. S. (1922b). The method of finding the correspondence between scores in two tests. *Journal of Educational Psychology, 13,* 529–545.

Page, E. B. (1994). New computer grading of student prose: Using modern concepts and software. *Journal of Experimental Education, 62*(2), 127–142.

Paulos, J. A. (2001). Innumeracy: Mathematical illiteracy and its consequences. New York: Hill and Wang.

Payne, D. A. (2002). *Applied educational assessment.* New York: Wadsworth.

Pedhazur, E. J., & Schmelkin, L. (1991). *Measurement, design, and analysis: An integrated approach.* Hillsdale, NJ: Erlbaum.

Petersen, N. S., Kolen, M. J., & Hoover, H. D. (1989). Scaling, norming, and equating. In R. L. Linn (Ed.), *Educational measurement* (2nd ed., pp. 221–262). New York: American Council on Education.

Phi Delta Kappa. (1999). [Special Issue on Performance Assessment]. *80*(9).

Plake, B. S., & Hambleton, R. K. (1998). A standard setting method designed for complex performance assessments: Categorical assignment of student work. *Educational Assessment, 6,* 197–215.

Plake, B. S., & Hambleton, R. K. (2001). The analytic judgment method for setting standards. In G. J. Cizek (Ed.), *Setting performance standards: Concepts, methods, and perspectives* (pp. 283–312). Mahwah, NJ: Erlbaum.

Polin, L., & Baker, E. L. (1979). Qualitative analysis of test item attributes for domain references content validity judgments. Washington, DC: ERIC. ED211601.

Popham, W. J. (1997). Consequential validity: Right concern—wrong concept. *Educational Measurement: Issues and Practices, 16*(2), 9–15.

Popham, W. J. (1999). Assessment apathy. *Education Week, 18,* 32.

Popham, W. J. (2001). *The truth about testing: An educator's call to action.* Alexandria, VA: Association for Supervision and Curriculum Development.

The Psychological Corporation. (1977, January). *Test service bulletin #48: Methods of expressing test scores.* New York: Author.

The Psychological Corporation. (2003). *Stanford achievement test.* San Antonio, TX: Author.

Quetelet, A. J. (1969). *A treatise on man and the development of his faculties* (A facsimile reproduction of the English translation of 1842) Gainesville, FL: Scholars Facsimiles & Reprints. (Original work published 1835).

Raju, N. S. (1988). The area between two item characteristic curves. *Psychometrika, 53,* 495–502.

Ramsay, J. Q. (1998). *TestGraf98: A program for the graphical analysis of multiple-choice test and questionnaire data.* Montreal, Canada: McGill University. (Available at *ftp://ego.psych.mcgill.ca/pub/ramsay/testgraf/*)

Rasch, G. (1960). *Probabilistic models for some intelligence and attainment tests.* Copenhagen: Denmark Pedogogiske Institute. (Reprinted 1980 by University of Chicago).

Rasch, G. (1966). An item analysis which takes individual differences into account. *British Journal of Mathematical and Statistical Psychology, 19,* 49–57.

Ravitch, D. (2003). The language police: How pressure groups restrict what students learn. New York: Knopf.

Raykov, T. (2001). Bias of coefficient alpha for fixed congeneric measures with correlated errors. *Applied Psychological Measurement, 25*(1), 69–76.

Raymond, M. R., & Reid, J. B. (2001). Who made thee a judge? Selecting and training participants for standard setting. In G. J. Cizek (Ed.), *Setting performance standards: concepts, methods, and perspectives* (pp. 119–158). Mahwah, NJ: Erlbaum.

Resnick, L. B., & Resnick, D. P. (1992). Assessing the thinking curriculum: New tools for educational reform. In B. G. Gifford & M. C. O'Connor (Eds.), *Changing assessments: Alternative views of aptitude, achievement, and instruction* (pp. 37–75). Hillsdale, NJ: Erlbaum.

Rice, J. A. (1995). *Mathematical statistics and data analysis.* Belmont, CA: Wadsworth (Duxbury).

Roeber, E. (2002). *Setting standards on alternate assessments* (Synthesis Report 42). Minneapolis: University of Minnesota, National Center on Educational Outcomes. Retrieved December 20, 2004, from *http://education.umn.edu/NCEO/OnlinePubs/Synthesis42.html*

Rogers, W. T., & Bateson, D. J. (1991). The influence of test-wiseness on performance of high school seniors on school leaving exams. *Applied Measurement in Education, 4*(2), 159–183.

Rovinelli, R. J., & Hambleton, R. J. (1977). On the use of content specialists in the assessment of criterion-referenced test item validity. *Dutch Journal of Educational Research, 2,* 49–60.

Roznowski, M., Tucker, L. R., & Humphries, L. G. (1991). Three approaches to determining the dimensionality of binary items. *Applied Psychological Measurement, 15*(2), 109–127.

Rulon, P. J. (1939). A simplified procedure for determining the reliability of a test by split halves. *Harvard Educational Review, 9,* 99–103.

Samejima, F. (1969). Estimation of latent trait ability using a response pattern of graded scores. *Psychometrika* [Monograph Supplement No. 17].

Samejima, F. (1997). Graded response model. In W. van der Linden & R. K. Hambleton (Eds.), *Handbook of modern item response theory* (pp. 67–84). New York: Springer.

SAS Institute, Inc. (2002). *The SAS system for Windows.* Carey, NC: Author.

Schaff, W. L. (1964). *Carl Friedrich Gauss: Prince of mathematicians.* New York: Franklin Watts.

Seligman, D. (1992). A question of intelligence: The IQ debate in America. New York: Birch Lane.

Shavelson, R. J. (2004). Preface to Lee J. Cronbach's, My current thoughts on coefficient alpha and successor procedures. *Educational and Psychological Measurement, 64*(3), 389–390.

Shavelson, R. J., & Eisner, E. W. (2002). In memory of Lee J. Cronbach. *Educational Measurement: Issues and Practice, 21*(2), 5.

Shavelson, R. J., & Webb, N. M. (1991). *Generalizability theory: A primer.* Newbury Park, CA: Sage.

Shepard, L. A. (1997). The centrality of test use and consequences for test validity. *Educational Measurement: Issues and Practices, 16*(2), 5–8.

Sheridan, B. (2000). *RUMM2010.* Duncraig, Western Australia: RUMM Laboratory. Retrieved January 4, 2005, from *http://www.arach.net.au/~rummlab/*

Simpson, J. (1988). *Simpson's contemporary quotations.* Retrieved December 21, 2004, from *http://www.bartleby.com/63/30/6830.html*

Sireci, S. G. (2001). Standard setting using cluster analysis. In G. J. Cizek (Ed.), *Setting performance standards: Concepts, methods, and perspectives* (pp. 339–354). Mahwah, NJ: Erlbaum.

Sireci, S. G., Thissen, D., & Wainer, H. (1991). On the reliability of testlet-based tests. *Journal of Educational Measurement, 28,* 237–247.

Snow, R. E., & Lohman, D. F. (1989). Implications of cognitive psychology for educational measurement. In R. L. Linn (Ed.), *Educational measurement* (pp. 263–331). New York: Macmillan.

Snyderman, M., & Rothman, S. (1987). Survey of expert opinion on intelligence and aptitude testing. *American Psychologist, 42*(2), 137–144.

Spearman, C. (1904a). "General intelligence" objectively determined and measured. *American Journal of Psychology, 15,* 201–292.

Spearman, C. (1904b). The proof and measurement of association between two things. *American Journal of Psychology, 15,* 72–101.

Spearman, C. (1907). Demonstration of formulae for true measurement of correlation. *American Journal of Psychology, 18,* 161–169.

Spearman, C. (1910). Correlation calculated with faulty data. *British Journal of Psychology, 3*, 271–295.

Spearman, C. (1913). Correlations of sums and differences. *British Journal of Psychology, 5*, 417–426.

Spearman, C. (1927). *The abilities of man*. New York: Macmillan.

SPSS. (2002). *Sigma Plot 2002 for Windows*. Chicago: Author.

Sternberg, R. J. (1990). *Metaphors of mind: Conceptions of the nature of intelligence*. Cambridge, UK: Cambridge University.

Stevens, J. (1992). Applied multivariate statistics for the social sciences. Hillsdale, NJ: Erlbaum.

Stevens, S. S. (1946). On the theory of scales of measurement. *Science, 103*, 677–680.

Stevens, S. S. (1951). Mathematics, measurement, and psychophysics. In S. S. Stevens (Ed.), *Handbook of experimental psychology* (pp. 1–49). New York: Wiley.

Stiggins, R. J. (1994). *Student-centered classroom assessment*. New York: Macmillan.

Stigler, S. M. (1986). *The history of statistics: The measurement of uncertainty before 1900*. Cambridge, MA: The Belknap Press of Harvard University.

Stocking, M. L., & Lord, F. M. (1983). Developing a common metric in item response theory. *Applied Psychological Measurement, 7*, 201–210.

Stout, W. F. (1990). A new item response theory modeling approach with applications to unidimensionality assessment and ability estimation. *Psychometrika, 22*, 53–61.

Strunk, W., & White, E. B. (2000). *The elements of style*. Boston: Allyn & Bacon.

Suen, H. K. (1990). *Principles of test theories*. Hillsdale, NJ: Erlbaum.

Swanson, H. L., & Lussier, C. M. (2001). A selective synthesis of the experimental literature on dynamic assessment. *Review of Educational Research, 71*(2), 321–363.

Tabachnick, B. G., & Fidell, L. S. (2000). *Using multivariate statistics*. New York: Harper Collins.

Tapia, R. A., & Thompson, J. R. (1978). *Nonparametric probability density estimation*. Baltimore: Johns Hopkins University.

Tenopyr, M. L. (1977). Content–construct confusion. *Personnel Psychology, 30*, 47–54.

Terman, L. M. (1916). *The measurement of intelligence*. New York: Houghton Mifflin.

Thissen, D., Chen, W. H., & Bock, D. (2002). *MULTILOG: Multiple category item analysis and test scoring using item response theory*. Lincolnwood, IL: Scientific Software International.

Thissen, D., & Steinberg, L. (1986). A taxonomy of item response models. *Psychometrika, 51*, 566–577.

Thissen, D., & Steinberg, L. (1997). A response model for multiple-choice models. In W. van der Linden & R. K. Hambleton (Eds.), *Handbook of modern item response theory* (pp. 51–65). New York: Springer.

Thissen, D., Steinberg, L., & Wainer, H. (1993). Detection of differential item functioning using the parameters of item response models. In P. W. Holland & H. Wainer (Eds.), *Differential item functioning* (pp. 67–113). Hillsdale, NJ: Erlbaum.

Thissen, D., & Wainer, H. (Eds.). (2001). *Test scoring*. Mahwah, NJ: Erlbaum.

Thissen, D., Wainer, H., & Wang, X.-B. (1994). Are tests comprising both multiple-choice and free-response items less unidimensional than multiple-choice tests: An analysis of two tests. *Journal of Educational Measurement, 31*(2), 113–123.

Thompson, B. (2003a). Understanding reliability and coefficient alpha, really. In B. Thompson (Ed.), *Score reliability: Contemporary thinking on reliability issues* (pp. 3–30). Thousand Oaks, CA: Sage.

Thompson, B. (Ed.). (2003b). Score reliability: Contemporary thinking on reliability issues. Thousand Oaks, CA: Sage.

Thompson, B. (2003c). A brief introduction to generalizability theory. In B. Thompson (Ed.), *Score reliability: Contemporary thinking on reliability issues* (pp. 43–58). Thousand Oaks, CA: Sage.

Thorndike, E. L. (1904). *Introduction to the theory of mental and social measurements*. New York: Teachers College, Columbia University.

Thorndike, R. L. (1949). Personnel selection: Tests and measurement techniques. New York: Wiley.

Thorndike, R. L. (Ed.). (1971). *Educational measurement* (2nd ed.). Washington, DC: American Council on Education.

Thorndike, R. L., & Hagen, E. (1969). *Measurement and evaluation in psychology and education* (3rd ed.). New York: Wiley.

Thorndike, R. L., & Lohman, D. F. (1990). *A century of ability testing.* Chicago: Riverside.

Thorndike, R. L., & Thorndike, R. M. (1994). Reliability in educational and psychological measurement. In T. Husen & N. Postlewaite (Eds.), *International encyclopedia of education* (2nd ed., pp. 4981–4995). New York: Pergamon.

Thurstone, L. L. (1925). A method of scaling psychological and educational tests. *Journal of Educational Psychology, 16,* 433–451.

Thurstone, L. L. (1927). A law of comparative judgment. *Psychological Review, 34,* 273–386.

Thurstone, L. L. (1928). Attitudes can be measured. *American Journal of Sociology, 33,* 529–554. (Reprinted in Thurstone, L. L. [Ed]. [1959]. *The measurement of values.* Chicago: University of Chicago, pp. 1215–1933.)

Thurstone, L. L. (1931). *The reliability and validity of tests.* Ann Arbor, MI: Edwards Brothers.

Thurstone, L. L. (1948). Psychological implications of factor analysis. *American Psychologist, 3,* 402–408.

Tinsley, H. E. A., & Weiss, D. J. (1975). Interrater reliability and agreement of subjective judgments. *Journal of Counseling Psychology, 22,* 358–376.

Torgerson, W. (1958). *Theory and methods of scaling.* New York: Wiley.

Traub, R. E. (1983). A priori considerations in choosing an item response model. In R. K. Hambleton (Ed.), *Applications of item response theory* (pp. 57–70). Vancouver: Educational Research Institute of British Columbia.

Traub, R. E. (1994). *Reliability for the social sciences* (Vol. 3). Thousand Oaks, CA: Sage.

Tucker, L. R. (1946). Maximum validity of a test with equivalent items. *Psychometrika, 11*(1), 1–13.

Tufte, E. (1983). *The visual display of quantitative information.* Chesline, CT: Graphics Press. (Available from Science News Books, 1719 N. St., NW, Washington, DC 20036).

Tukey, J. W. (1977). *Exploratory data analysis.* Reading, MA: Addison-Wesley.

U.S. Congress, Office of Technology Assessment. (1992). *Testing in American schools: Asking the right questions.* Washington, DC: U.S. Government Printing Office.

van der Linden, W. J., & Hambleton, R. K. (Eds.). (1997). *Handbook of modern item response theory.* New York: Springer.

Vatow, J. D. F. (1948). Testing compound symmetry in a normal multivariate distribution. *Annals of Mathematical Statistics, 19,* 447–473.

Wainer, H. (1993). Measurement problems. *Journal of Educational Measurement, 30*(1), 1–21.

Wainer, H., Dorans, N. J., Flaughter, R., Green, B. F., Steinberg, L., & Thissen, D. (2000). *Computerized adaptive testing: A primer* (2nd ed.). Hillsdale, NJ: Erlbaum.

Wainer, H., & Lewis, C. (1990). Toward a psychometrics for testlets. *Journal of Educational Measurement, 27,* 1–14.

Wainer, H., Wadkins, J. R., & Rogers, A. (1983). *Was there one distractor too many?* Princeton, NJ: Educational Testing Service.

Walberg, W. J. (1984). Quantification reconsidered. In E. W. Gordon (Ed.), *Review of research in education* (Vol. 11, pp. 369–392). New York: American Educational Research Association.

Walz, G. W., & Bleuer, J. C. (Eds.). (2001). *Assessment: Issues and challenges for the millennium.* Washington, DC: ERICCASS.

Ward, A., Stoker, H., & Murray-Ward, M. (Eds.). (1996). *Educational measurement: Origins, theories, and explications.* Lanham, MD: University Press of America.

Wechsler, D. (1981). *Wechsler adult intelligence scale* (Revised). San Antonio, TX: The Psychological Corporation.

Wechsler, D. (1991). *Wechsler Intelligence Scale for Children* (3rd ed., Revised). San Antonio, TX: The Psychological Corporation.

Weiss, D. (Ed.). (1996). Special issue on multidimensional assessment [Special issue]. *Applied Psychological Measurement, 20*(3).

Weiss, D. J. (2003). *Bibliography on computerized adaptive testing (CAT).* Minneapolis: University of Minnesota. Retrieved December 27, 2004, from *www.psych.umn.edu/psylabs/CATCentral/*

Wherry, R. J. (1984). *Contributions to correlational analysis.* New York: Academic Press.

Wiggins, G. (1990). *The case for authentic assessment.* Washington, DC: Office of Educational Research and Improvement, U.S. Department of Education. (ERIC Document Reproduction Service No. ED328611)

Wiggins, G. (1998). Educative assessment: Designing assessments to inform and improve student performance. San Francisco: Jossey-Bass.

Wilkinson, L., & APA Task Force on Statistical Inference. (1999). Statistical methods in psychology journals: Guidelines and explanations. *American Psychologist, 54*(8), 594–604.

Will, G. F. (1990). *Men at work*. New York: Harper Perennial.

Williams, B. (1978). *A sampler on sampling*. New York: Wiley.

Wittrock, M. C., & Baker, E. L. (Eds.). (1991). *Testing and cognition*. New York: Prentice-Hall.

Wolstenholme, L. C. (1999). *Reliability modeling*. Boca Raton, FL: Chapman & Hall/CRC.

Wood, R., & Butterworth, A. (1997). Fair use of psychometrics in guidance. *Journal of Education and Work, 10*(3), 281–291.

Wood, R., Wilson, D., Gibbons, R., Schilling, S., Muraki, E., & Bock, D. (2002). *TESTFACT: Test scoring, item statistics, and item FA*. Lincolnwood, IL: Scientific Software International.

Woodcock, R. W., & Johnson, M. B. (1989). *The Woodcock-Johnson psycho-educational battery* (Revised). Chicago: Riverside.

Woolley, T. W. (2004). Classical versus Bayesian inference: A classroom illustration. *Teaching Statistics, 26*(2), 42–45.

Wright, B. D. (1968). Sample-free test calibration and person measurement. *Proceedings of the 1967 Invitational Conference on Testing Problems*. Princeton, NJ: Educational Testing Service.

Wright, B. D. (1997). A history of social science measurement. *Educational Measurement: Issues and Practice, 16*(4), 33–52.

Wright, B. D., & Stone, M. H. (1979). *Best test design*. Chicago: Mesa.

Yates, F. Y. (1981). *Sampling methods for censuses and surveys*. New York: Macmillan.

Yeh, S. S. (2001). Tests worth teaching to: Constructing state-mandated tests that emphasize critical thinking. *Educational Researcher, 30*(9), 12–17.

Young, F. W., & Hamer, R. M. (1987). Multidimensional scaling: History, theory and applications. New York: Erlbaum.

Zimowski, M., Muraki, E., Mislevy, R., & Bock, D. (2002). *BILOG-MG: Multiple group IRT analysis and test maintenance for binary items*. Lincolnwood, IL: Scientific Software International.

Name Index

Subject Index